ADVANCE PRAISE FOR CRITIC.
TESTING PROCESSES

Rex Black's book, *Critical Testing Processes*, is destined to become a classic. Rather than lecturing the reader, Rex makes key concepts come alive as we follow the adventures of Jamal, Kate, Jenny, and others of Software Cafeteria's "Sumatra" project. Rex's insight into understanding and improving the testing process will continue to guide all those who read this book.

Lee Copeland
Consultant and author of *A Practitioner's Guide to Software Test Design*
Software Quality Engineering

Rex uses examples, specifics, and a running case study to bring to life the ideas and suggestions in *Critical Testing Processes*. I recommend this book as a resource for current projects, a source of inspiration for future projects, and as an enlightening read for those looking to learn more about software testing and managing software testing.

Johanna Rothman
President and author of *Hiring the Best Knowledge Workers, Techies, & Nerds*
Rothman Consulting Group, Inc.

This book is a must-read successor to *Managing the Testing Process*. Rex's great insight in the testing field allows the book to drill down deep into the critical test processes and strike gold. And what's just as important as being a very good learning experience, the book is also very entertaining to read!

Tim Koomen
Co-author of *Test Process Improvement*
Sogeti (The Netherlands)

I plan on using Rex Black's new book, *Critical Testing Processes*, as a text for my Software Quality Assurance and Testing Management courses. *Critical Testing Processes* covers practical aspects of running a testing project from the early estimation phase through the entire development project. The book teaches how to deal with, and solve, many real-world problems related to people, processes, and technologies. The book includes a running example project with various characters—representing the different roles on a project—experiencing and applying the practical subject matter as presented.

This book is a winner! I highly recommend it. Bravo Rex!

Robert Sabourin
President, Principal Consultant, and author of *I Am a Bug*
AmiBug.Com, Inc.

Renowned author Rex Black has made a significant addition to the testing literature with his new book, *Critical Testing Processes*. Rex not only provides the test engineer and test manager with step-by-step instructions on how to set up a testing group and perform the testing task, but he takes the time to address the personal and interpersonal issues that can make or break a testing group. He also provides one of the best set of instructions I have seen on how to create a testing estimate.

Nicely done, Rex!

Rodger Drabick
Staff QA Engineer and author of an upcoming book on test processes
Lockheed Martin Mission Systems

Jamal Brown, the intrepid testing manager in *Critical Testing Processes,* is part of my professional existence now. In the process of reading the case study, I thoroughly identified with him, his issues, and his efforts, and I learned a lot about testing and test management.

Vipul Kocher
Testing Manager
Adobe Systems (India)

This book is a pearl! I have used its techniques and tools to make testing visible and manageable in my organization. It has helped us understand the testing craft.

Jakob Jensen
Project Manager
KMD (Denmark)

This is one of the best technical books I've ever read. It's comprehensive, yet easy to understand. Rex Black demystifies the technical jargon and gives you tools and information that you can put into practice immediately. Not only did I learn a lot, I thoroughly enjoyed myself in the process. How often have you actually smiled or laughed while reading a technical book? Rex has an ability to draw you into the material and make it come alive. Finally, as a woman I often find that technical books aren't very inclusive, so imagine my delight when I found that not only is *Critical Testing Processes* extremely well written, but that it is totally inclusive of many types of diversity.

Deb McCandless
Online and Software QA Manager
Nolo.com

This book takes the new or experienced test manager to the next step of not just testing, but the process of testing in order to succeed in his or her career. I would highly recommend this book to test managers who are looking to refine their process into tried and true examples as listed in this book. Rex has a unique way of creating a hypothetical case study with a typical test manager's day-to-day scenario and then discussing that scenario, which really helps, as it provides an example of how to apply what is getting discussed.

Chris DeNardis
Rockwell Automation
Supervisor Software Engineering

I found tons of useful, practical information in *Critical Testing Processes*. I've struggled with estimating and justifying testing efforts in the past, so when my next project starts, I will be referring to those particular chapters.

Becky Sowada
Test Manager
Macromedia

Many authors spent pages and pages on all different types of processes, but no one wrote how to adapt them to your needs. Critical testing processes is not just another process book, but provides practical help and first-hand information on how to bring a process model into the right context for your project. I am really pleased at how smoothly the new process works and how quickly management bought into the new ideas. I wish I had this book two years earlier. Thank you, Rex.

Markus Manleitner
Senior Software Integration Engineer
NexPress (Germany)

CRITICAL TESTING PROCESSES

Plan, Prepare, Perform, Perfect

REX BLACK

✦✦ Addison-Wesley

Boston ▪ San Francisco ▪ New York ▪ Toronto ▪ Montreal
London ▪ Munich ▪ Paris ▪ Madrid
Capetown ▪ Sydney ▪ Tokyo ▪ Singapore ▪ Mexico City

Many of the designations used by manufacturers and sellers to distinguish their products are claimed as trademarks. Where those designations appear in this book, and Addison-Wesley was aware of a trademark claim, the designations have been printed with initial capital letters or in all capitals.

The author and publisher have taken care in the preparation of this book, but make no expressed or implied warranty of any kind and assume no responsibility for errors or omissions. No liability is assumed for incidental or consequential damages in connection with or arising out of the use of the information or programs contained herein.

The publisher offers discounts on this book when ordered in quantity for bulk purchases and special sales. For more information, please contact:

U.S. Corporate and Government Sales
(800) 382-3419
corpsales@pearsontechgroup.com

For sales outside of the U.S., please contact:

International Sales
international@pearsoned.com

Visit Addison-Wesley on the Web: *www.awprofessional.com*

Library of Congress Cataloging-in-Publication Data

Black, Rex, 1964-
    Critical testing processes : plan, prepare, perform, perfect / Rex Black.
      p. cm.
    Includes bibliographical references and index.
    ISBN 0-201-74868-1 (alk. paper)
    1. Computer software—Testing. 2. Computers—Testing. I. Title.

QA76.76.T48B552 2003
005.1'4—dc21   2003052316

ISBN 0201748681
Text printed on recycled and acid-free paper.
4 5 6 7 8 9 DOC 09 08 07
4th Printing   July 2007

To my wife, Laurel; my daughters, Charlotte and Emma; and my two dogs, Max and Cosmo; for their love, support, and friendship.

CONTENTS

FOREWORD

Rex Black has done it again! Readers of his first book, *Managing the Testing Process,* undoubtedly have high expectations for future offerings from Rex, and they will not be disappointed in his latest offering, *Critical Testing Processes.* He has taken a complicated subject and described it in terms that are easily understood and contextually sensitive. Seemingly abstract testing processes are brought to life so that the readers can understand them and apply them in their own unique environments.

Rex and I have worked together on the consulting and lecturing circuit for some time now, and we often discuss, over a nice meal, how similar our philosophies are on how testing should be conducted and what is and is not important. When writing a book, you can easily get bogged down trying to spell out all the ideas that you think will be of value to the reader. Sometimes, in our quest to tell "all we know," the distinction of what is really most important gets lost in the shuffle. That's the beauty of this book. Rex has sifted through his considerable repertoire of testing experience and chosen 12 key processes.

Each of these 12 processes is explained in sufficient detail to allow the user to understand it, modify it if necessary, and implement it within their own organization. Rex has used an effective but unusual style in explaining these processes. First, he demonstrates their use through the eyes and actions of a fictitious (but believable) project team. Then each of these same processes is described in general terms with hints on using it in various cultures and contexts. Finally, each process is brought to life through Rex's actual experiences. Charts, tables, and examples are used frequently to help the reader visualize important concepts.

Readers of the recent book that I coauthored with Stefan Jaskiel, *Systematic Software Testing*, know that even though we recognize the value of tools, metrics, and technical processes, at the end of the day, building quality software depends on people. *Critical Testing Processes* is especially strong in its discussion of these often overlooked "human" factors of software engineering—including the interactions of testers with each other and with outside organizations. Rather than viewing testing as an isolated activity, Rex has described how the testing group and individual testers work within the context of the entire development effort.

I have been in the software testing business for more than 20 years and have found testing to be an exciting and rewarding career. Reading a book on the subject, however, is not always equally exciting. But Rex's informal, easy-to-read style makes learning about critical test processes easy, rewarding, and even fun! *Critical Testing Processes* is a book that all software testers will want to read from cover to cover and then retain for frequent reference. This is a book that is destined to be a software testing classic.

Rick Craig
Consultant and author of *Systematic Software Testing*
Software Quality Engineering
Tampa, Florida

ACKNOWLEDGMENTS

This book began when Magdy Hanna suggested a series of articles on the topic of test processes, to appear in the *Journal of Software Testing Professionals*. In addition to appearing in that magazine, portions of this book appeared as articles in *Professional Tester*, *Software Dioxide*, and *Software Testing and Quality Engineering*; on Stickyminds.com and Test and Measurement.com; and as a chapter in *The Testing Practitioner*, by Erik van Veenendaal. For their efforts with these early excerpts, I thank Robert Coutré, Esther Derby, Brian Hambling, Magdy Hanna, Linda Hayes, Brian Lawrence, Brian Marick, Denis Meredith, Jamie Mitchell, Caroline Quentin, Leslie Segal, Rebecca Traeger, Erik van Veenedaal, and Alyn Wambeke. I also thank readers of these excerpts and of my previous book, *Managing the Testing Process*, who took the time to send me comments and questions.

In addition, an international network of fine people were involved throughout the writing of this book. Some reviewed chapters as I wrote them. Some provided ideas, quotes, and case studies. Some provided complete sidebars. I thank Sue Bartlett, Randall Becker, Boris Beizer, Ross Collard, Lee Copeland, Rick Craig, Gary Dawson, Harvey Deutsch, Tim Dyes, Chris DeNardis, Rodger Drabick, Danny Faught, Larry Fellows, Peggy Fouts, Norman Hines, Kathy Iberle, Jakob Jensen, Cem Kaner, Vipul Kocher, Tim Koomen, Philippe Kruchten, Markus Mannleitner, Darcy Martin, José Mata, Deb McCandless, Dale Perry, Erik Peterson, Johanna Rothman, Barbara Ruf, Robert Sabourin, Greg Scala, Rebecca Sowada, Steve Splaine, Serban Teodorescu, Anne Tsou, Erik van Veenendaal, and Ed Weller.

In addition to my project and consulting work, I also teach a number of training courses. Many issues that I cover here have been topics of those courses. I encourage attendees to participate in these classes, and they usually do, sharing their personal experiences and anecdotes. If you've attended one of my training courses, I thank you for your help with this book, too.

Before I wrote my first book, I had no idea how much work happens behind the scenes in the publication process. Since this is my third book project, I have a much better idea, though I'm sure there are people who've helped put my ideas in your hands that I'll never meet. So, I thank everyone at Addison-Wesley, and especially Kim Arney Mulcahy, Marcy Barnes-Henrie, Bernard Gaffney, Peter Gordon, and Debbie Lafferty.

Finally and most significantly, I owe a tremendous debt of gratitude to my family. Writing a book is a time-consuming, stressful, and sometimes frustrating experience. My parents, relatives, and in-laws provided encouragement and support. My daughters, Emma and Charlotte, along with my dogs, Max and Cosmo, watched me write much of this book at various locations throughout our house with bemused good humor. I thank them for providing much-needed entertainment between keystrokes. Last but hardly least, my wife, Laurel, not only endures being an itinerant consultant's wife, but now has been put through the book-writing process three times. Laurel, you're the best.

I thank everyone who participated and helped me write a better book. Without the help of the people I've mentioned, this book would contain fewer good ideas and more bad ones. Of course, I am the author of this book, so I am the one ultimately accountable. There are mistakes, and those mistakes are mine. Please send comments, questions, and criticisms about this book to me at Rex_Black@RexBlackConsulting.com. Thanks for reading, and good luck with your critical testing processes.

PREFACE

I 've spent most of my 20 years in the software and hardware business in the arena of testing. For the first few years as a test practitioner, I struggled to keep my head above water. Ultimately, I mastered some basic tools and techniques.

As I learned more about testing, I started to notice certain common themes. Some of these themes had to do with events—good and bad—that happened over and over again on software, hardware, and system projects. For some of these events, I found that some teams could create order in their projects. These teams handled these common events better than the teams that bounced from one crisis to the next, reacting constantly, immersed in chaos. The successful teams had good processes.

Some of these successful project teams implemented written processes, while others accumulated "institutional knowledge" in their wise—and sometimes prematurely gray—heads. While I have nothing against a shared company culture, it's hard to pass along the processes you've learned unless you write them down—whether formally or informally, as checklists. This book takes the informal road. I describe 12 specific test processes, using checklists. Each process is critical to test-team success.

I describe these processes in chronological order. First we plan the test activities. Next we prepare to test. After that, we perform the tests. Finally, we perfect the system under test and the testing activities themselves.

Many other books have covered in great detail the topics of preparing and performing tests. So, instead of rehashing what we already know, I focus on opportunities for improvement. I devote 11 of the 17 chapters to the topics of planning and perfecting. By far, these are the areas where we as testers have the most difficulty. This is especially true for complex and critical projects.

Where will this book take you? During the early colonization of the American continent in the 1540s, Francisco Vasquez de Coronado searched the deserts of present-day Arizona and New Mexico for the Seven Cities of Cíbola, including El Dorado, a city whose streets were supposedly paved with gold. Juan Ponce de Leon searched for the Fountain of Youth. In 1911, one of the first management consultants, Frederick Winslow Taylor, wrote a book called *The Principles of Scientific Management*. Taylor espoused the idea of the one best way—the perfect process—for each activity on an assembly line or in any other industrial enterprise. But none of these three men found streets of gold, life without death, or perfect processes.

This book isn't about quixotic quests. There are no streets of gold that will make us effortlessly rich. We can't sidestep our human limitations. I don't have infallible processes. As Frederick Brooks wrote in *The Mythical Man-Month, Second Edition*, we don't have any silver bullets to kill our system project monsters, including the ones that live in quality and testing. That said, I have found many ways for testers to deliver valuable information and services to the project team, and each of these ways has its strong points and its weaknesses.

The processes in this book might differ from what you're doing now. In some cases, you'll decide, based on the success of your current processes, that you're doing a fine job already. In some cases, though, you may want to implement improvements. I'll discuss specific ways to do that, but two themes apply to process change throughout the book.

First, only change what's broken when changing it will help. Process change for its own sake, or process change to perfect an already good process, often doesn't help the test team or the organization. Indeed, such efforts can prove a dangerous distraction from what's truly important.

Second, change is often easiest when done in steps wherever possible. Change should be made as painless as possible. All the processes in the book were developed through incremental change as I realized that a better way of doing things would significantly increase the value my team could add, and fine-tuned my processes to achieve that.

The processes in this book aren't pie-in-the-sky theory, but rather grew out of my experiences on the ground as a practicing tester, test lead, and test manager. Your experiences and your challenges will differ from mine, so be sure to adapt my processes—

or completely reinvent your own—rather than trying to put a saddle on a cow. Following good processes can liberate you from the rote aspects of certain tasks, allowing you to focus on the fun, the fascinating, and the creative. When the processes you've adopted no longer solve the critical problems, when they need to evolve as your situations change, when they get in the way, then it's time to rethink how you do what you do. The processes I discuss here are lightweight checklists (things I want to remember to do), not bureaucratic regulations (things I have to do because someone told me to).

I hope that this book will start you thinking about the following questions: How do we do our testing jobs every day and on every test project as best as we possibly can? How do we deinstitutionalize our knowledge of how we do what we do? Even though we have varied experiences, is there a commonality of practices that we can share for critical testing processes that determine our success? This book gives you a compendium of proven testing processes to help jump-start the most critical testing process of all: the thinking process.

INTRODUCTION

I n the first sentence of *Anna Karenina*, Leo Tolstoy wrote, "All happy families are like one another; each unhappy family is unhappy in its own way." While Tolstoy certainly tells a great story in a moving and powerful way, this statement is wrong. The particulars for each family—happy or unhappy—may be unique, but some common causes of unhappiness exist. *Anna Karenina* is the story of a loveless spouse with a faithless mate, two common and connected curses for families around the world. Common causes of happiness exist for families as well: The blessings of healthy children, financial success, love and understanding, and shared interests are examples.

Organizations, like families, are social groupings, and also are happy and unhappy in common ways. People working in successful organizations enjoy pride in their work and a stable job with the prospect of career growth, among other things. People working in unsuccessful organizations become unhappy when they put in heroic and inadequately compensated efforts, especially when a lousy product is the final result. One of the causes of success for organizations engaged in system development and maintenance is the intelligent application of good processes, tailored for context, by happy, competent individual contributors and managers. In *Critical Testing Processes*, I'll walk you through 12 such processes for test teams.

BOOK SCOPE

What is a *critical testing process*? Well, a process is a set of actions, observations, and decisions taken to achieve some desired outcome. Some activities can happen in parallel, and some are sequential. The activities are related by the desired outcomes but do not necessarily have techniques or required skills in common. For example, one process we'll look at, the test release management process, includes selecting the content of the release, making the changes in the release, building the release, making installable media from that build, installing the new test release, and smoke testing it.

A process becomes critical when one or more of the following criteria apply.

- The test team repeats the process frequently as part of doing what it's there to do. Crisp handling of recurring processes leads to efficient and consistent execution of day-to-day testing duties. For example, the bug reporting process occurs again and again as a consequence of test execution.
- The process affects the ability of testers to work together, especially where a breakdown might damage a cohesive, cooperative team. To cite one instance, when the test team is running a set of test cases, the process should support a unique assignment of testing tasks that prevents accidental repetition of testers' efforts.
- The process involves peers or superiors. A test team that properly handles high-visibility processes builds a reputation for competence and reliability. For instance, when reporting test status, testers must present findings to peers and senior management in a way that effectively communicates the testing they have done, the problems they have found, and the value of the test operation.
- A process failure could lead to serious and possibly lasting negative outcomes. Consider the process of selecting what areas of the product should be tested. Missing a major class of customer-critical defects because of improper test focus will, at least, cause organizational embarrassment and incur increased costs, and may even physically endanger customers for certain types of systems.

In short, a critical process directly and significantly affects the test team's ability to provide valuable information and services within its organizational, operational, and technological context. Testers and test managers who master and continuously improve such processes can provide excellent information and services.

Imagine making a cake. You have your ingredients (the process inputs), your party (the project), your hungry guests (the project team and other project stakeholders), your kitchen (the testing context), your recipe (the testing process), and the cake you want to make (expected deliverables). Omit a couple of ingredients, decide one step's not important, be cavalier with the procedural order, disregard the kind of cake your guests like, and you'll end up bringing the wrong pastry to the party.

Not everything that happens on a development project involves a process. Consider debugging—the act of fixing a bug, often one described in a bug report. Once a programmer has reproduced the failure, there's no predefined process for debugging. There are common tools, like debuggers and syntax checkers. There are heuristics that programmers apply depending on the symptom of the failure and their past experiences. And there is technical knowledge about the kinds of errors that occur based on the source language, the target environment, the compiler, and so forth. But tools, heuristics, and skills are not processes. Debugging is more like grocery shopping than cooking: You only care about bringing your shopping cart (safely filled with every item on your supermarket list) to the cashier, checking out, and going on your way.

I picked these two examples consciously. The rap on processes is that they're boring. That only people without the requisite skills need them. That they're not creative. I disagree. What's more creative, cooking or grocery shopping? What's more difficult to master? What's more satisfying? Likewise, I find the process of bug reporting to be an interesting, challenging, and creative act that gets me back in touch with why I decided to be a tester in the first place. Conversely, when I write programs, debugging always reacquaints me with the tedium and frustration of coding that led me to leave programming and go into testing.

WHO SHOULD READ THIS BOOK?

This book is for everyone who is interested in improving their work as a test professional. It's for lead test engineers, test managers, development managers with testing responsibility, and anyone with some assigned duty, temporary or permanent, for making sure the testing portion of a system development or maintenance project goes well. It's for people who are guiding the improvement of testers or a whole test team. It's for test professionals, test teams, and organizations that have some basic test processes already in place—perhaps implemented using the ideas I presented in my previous book, *Managing the Testing Process*—and are now looking for ways to improve them. It's a book that, if applied at a senior manager or director level, can propel your testing team into the vanguard of the testing community, with significant return on investment.

Unlike most other books on software testing, which focus on nuts-and-bolts issues of performing specific tasks, this book will also help you understand the larger context in which and for which testing occurs. This book is not a sequel to my first book, *Managing the Testing Process*. In that book, I looked at the process as a whole, from the nuts-and-bolts perspective of key tasks and activities. *Managing the Testing Process* is different from other testing books because it has the test manager in mind, but is similar in that it is primarily tactical in focus. Such tactical books are important to mastering specific tasks but need to be complemented by a broader perspective, which is what you can gain from reading *Critical Testing Processes*. This book looks at the whole process and each constituent critical process. It is centered on processes—specific ways in which the tester delivers valuable information and services to projects—which tie together the individual tasks and activities we do from day to day. Whatever your role in testing, from test engineering to managing hundreds of test engineers, you will gain insights into what you do, why it's important, and how you can do it better.

DEMYSTIFYING PROCESSES

I've read some books on software engineering process improvement that, frankly, mystified me. I read and read, and when I was done reading, I had no idea how to apply the ideas I had just read. This book, unlike other books you might have read on processes, won't mystify you. When I introduce a process, I'll then give you a particular example of it in terms of a hypothetical case study that winds through the book. I'll then give you some tips on the behaviors and achievements of teams using good processes, how to handle process challenges, and ways to implement improvements. I'll season these general ideas with particular examples from my experiences as a test professional. In this way, I'll bring the processes to life for you.

To keep things simple, I present the processes as checklists. Checklists are a useful and lightweight way to implement process-oriented testing. They also allow you to gather metrics and improve your processes once you get matters under control. To tie the particular and general discussions back to specific elements of each process under discussion, I'll use a process checklist graphic like the one shown in Process 1.

Step #	Step	Done?
1.	Plan: Understand the testing effort	☐
1.A	Understand the operational (system, project, and process) context and the organizational context in which the testing will be performed.	☐
1.B	Define and prioritize the risks to system quality, and obtain stakeholder consensus on the extent of testing to mitigate these risks.	☐
1.C	Estimate and obtain management support for the time, resources, and budget required to perform the testing agreed upon in step 1.B.	☐
1.D	Develop a plan for the tasks, dependencies, and participants required to mitigate the risks to system quality, and obtain stakeholder support for this plan.	☐

PROCESS 1   STEP 1 OF A TESTING PROCESS

These process numbers are consistent throughout the book, not based on the chapter numbers in which they appear. Though you'll undoubtedly need to customize these checklists for your testing projects, you can find them included in the supporting documentation available for free download from www.rexblackconsulting.com. Download and adapt them as you see fit, subject to the license included with the download.[1]

Types and Relationships of Critical Testing Processes

Some critical testing processes are internal to the test team, carried out by and affecting testers only. Other processes are collaborative, involving other teams in the organization. I'm using the word "collaborative" rather than "external" because effective teams accept each other's work through proactive handoffs. In contrast, a hallmark of poor teamwork is seen when groups toss incomplete or poor-quality deliverables over organizational walls. A collaborative process might involve accepting or providing deliverables, or both. A collaborative process might entail a sequence of deliverables spanning multiple teams.

Each critical testing process is, to a greater or lesser extent, subject to the context in which it occurs. That is, the process must fit the people, the system, the project, and the organization involved. In context-sensitive situations, subtle factors can make a response appropriate in one case and inappropriate in another. For example, throwing food over your shoulder is generally inappropriate, but it might be appropriate if that food is spilled salt and you are among similarly superstitious people. Consider one example of test process context: Reporting test results to the management team requires good communication skills—and good communication is always sensitive to context—including knowing what to say to whom and when.

Testing, in the project context, is connected to a lot of different activities and groups. For example, see Figure I-1, which shows a simplified number of processes (arrows) and teams (circles) involved in the overall software development process during test execution. In this illustration, running tests is an internal process, as is tracking the results of the test cycle. Delivering bug reports is a collaborative process that delivers information to the development team from the test team through the process of running tests. Likewise, sending release notes for a given test release is a collaborative

---

1. Don't worry—you don't need to be an SEI CMM, ISO 9000, RUP, or other process guru to read this book. If you can use a numbered set of instructions to assemble a child's tricycle or cook tandoori chicken, the checklist-based approach in this book, brought to life in the case study, will be easy to follow, whether you have some exposure to these other approaches or not.

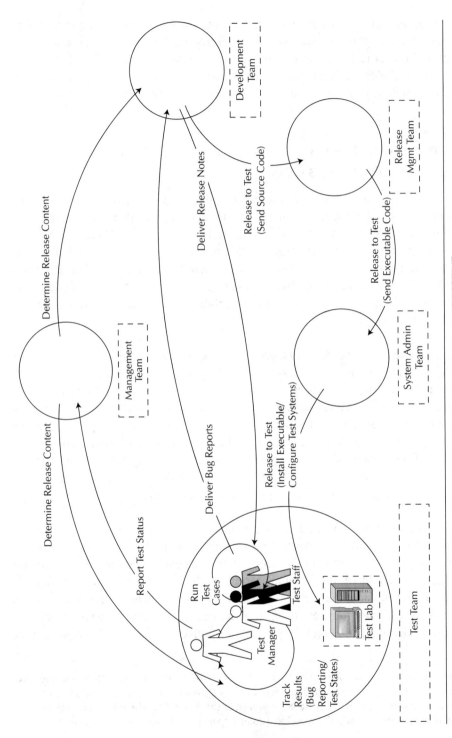

FIGURE I-1 FINDING BUGS AND GETTING THEM FIXED, A PROCESS PERSPECTIVE

process that delivers information from the development team to the test team into the process of running tests. Since reporting test status is a highly contextual process, the test manager communicates to the management team the progress of testing and the assessed quality of the product by using charts and metrics that the management team understands and that are appropriate to the development process. Finally, note the multistage collaborative process, releasing software to the test team, which I have broken down into collaborative subprocesses, shown in parentheses.

Many deliverables and dependencies must converge precisely—in time and fashion—on the test team so it can provide timely, accurate, thorough, and credible information and testing services. Such collaborative processes are especially critical. Similarly, contextual influences are often subtle and hard to discern. Testers must look closely at what really goes on—which may vary considerably from what others *say* or *think* is going on—before deciding on appropriate processes. The contextual and collaborative nature of many processes makes them harder to execute, because of the coordination, diplomacy, and negotiation that come into play when teams must adopt processes to support each other's needs or to adapt to the situational realities.

In addition, the tight coupling between the test processes themselves and between test processes and other project processes creates interdependence. Each process influences the course and outcome of all the others. This sets up feedback loops that smart testers can use to amplify their influence. Let me give you an example.

If you follow the interlinked processes in Figure I-1, the quality of the bug reporting process influences the quality of the test status reports delivered to management. The project team determines the quality of the test results reports, often based on whether these status reports provide the project team with useful information. Both the reality and the perception of the usefulness of this information matter. When the status reports *are useful* and *are perceived as useful*, that in turn builds a perception of testing as a good investment. That perception in turn bolsters the test team's credibility, which leads to more support for providing the test team with adequate resources. Such resources are a prerequisite for good test execution processes, including defect reporting.

CRITICAL TESTING PROCESSES IN CONTEXT

Critical testing processes arise within the context of a testing project, which in turn resides within a larger system development, maintenance, deployment, integration, or acceptance project. Identifying and studying these critical testing processes allows us to better execute our testing projects. As we examine the processes in the context of the testing subproject, keep in mind that we're looking at a set of activities that play out over time and deliver valuable testing services and information to the project team over the course of the project. So, I'll examine the critical testing processes in a chronological order: plan, prepare, perform, and perfect.

Part I, Plan, covers these processes.

1. Understand the operational (system, project, and process) and the organizational context of the testing to be performed.
2. Define and prioritize the risks to system quality, and obtain stakeholder consensus on the extent of testing to mitigate these risks.
3. Estimate and obtain management support for time, resources, and budget required to perform the testing agreed upon.
4. Develop a plan for the actions, participants, and dependencies required to perform the testing, and obtain stakeholder support for this plan.

Part II, Prepare, examines these processes.

5. Hire and grow a team of test professionals with the appropriate skills, attitudes, and motivation through staffing and training.
6. Design, develop, acquire, verify, and validate the test system (test cases, test data, test tools, test environment, test execution procedures, and so on) the test team uses to assess the quality of the system under test.

In Part III, Perform, you'll find these processes.

7. Acquire and install a test release, which includes some or all of the components in the system under test.
8. Assign, execute, track, and manage the set of tests to be run against each test release.

Part IV, Perfect, discusses the remaining processes.

9. Document the bugs found during test execution.
10. Communicate test results to key stakeholders.
11. Adjust to changes in the project context, and refine the testing process.

These 11 critical processes exist within the overall testing process. So, I'll discuss all 12 critical testing processes in this book.

SUMATRA, A HYPOTHETICAL PROJECT

Throughout this book, I use a fictitious project to illustrate the processes. This project is a new release of SpeedyWriter, a browser-hosted word processing application that runs on the major Web browsers supported on Windows, Linux, Solaris, and Mac workstations, implemented using Java, a Web server, an application server, and a file and database server. The company writing SpeedyWriter is Software Cafeteria, a medium-sized software development company based in Austin, Texas. Software Cafeteria is working on release 3.1 of this product, code-named *Sumatra*, with a scheduled release date in the United States of early next year, with major foreign-market releases to follow in the next three to six months.[2]

I tend to follow a structured, well-documented approach for testing on most projects. I'll illustrate the example project with various figures and tables taken from such documents. These documents are available for free download, along with the templates. So, the case study is both a narrative description and a set of test deliverables. You can read the case study, decide to adapt a process that I've suggested, and have on hand some tools for putting that process into action. I've gone to great lengths to ensure the usefulness and quality of these documents so that they can be a useful resource for you.[3]

TERMINOLOGY

When you read this book and look at the documents, you might come across terms that are strange to you. You might encounter terms that you've heard before but that I'm using to mean something different from what you've always understood the words to mean. This happens. There are lots of different dialects among test professionals. We don't have a commonly accepted body of knowledge or a glossary, which creates a challenge for us when we discuss our work. Accountants have generally accepted accounting practices. Doctors write diagnoses on patients' charts, and other doctors understand and use the same names for the same afflictions. As testers, we can't do that yet.

---

2. Regarding the characters in the case study, all the first names are real names, reflecting the cultural and gender diversity we find in the high-tech world. However, as the cliche goes, the characters, dialogs, and stories in the case study, while drawn from my professional experiences, are fictitious.

3. That said, the documents are from a fictitious case study. The data and metrics are reasonable, but you'll probably find that your metrics vary significantly from those in this book, perhaps by orders of magnitude. Also, I've populated the various examples with only the amount of data needed to make the points discussed in the book.

> **System, System under Test, System under Development, System Being Maintained**
>
> The entirety of the system (software, hardware, software and hardware, and so on) within the scope of the test effort. This often consists of more than the immediately obvious pieces. For office software, for example, in addition to the executable running on a user's desktop, there can be back-end (e.g., server) components that might have various third-party interfaces, documentation, the delivery and upgrade process, online databases or support facilities, hardware and firmware components, and even infrastructure like LANs, WANs, and the Internet. The word "product" is somewhat more generic, but could incorrectly imply that I'm discussing only mass-market, shrink-wrapped software.
>
> A system can also be a *system of systems*, where each system interoperates with and depends on one or more other systems, and where each system is essential to the operation of the system of systems. For example, a browser-based application, with the clients, the Web server, the application server, and the database server, is a system of systems.
>
> Finally, a system can also be a *family of systems*, where each system interoperates with one or more other systems, but where dependencies are limited and systems can be used in a standalone or integrated way. For example, Microsoft Office is a family of software systems.

So, whenever I use a term that I suspect might create confusion, I'll define what I mean. I'm not trying to create *the* definitions, but to let you know *my* definitions. I've included these definitions in specially formatted text boxes close to where I first use the term. To demonstrate the technique and to define a term I've already used loosely in this introduction, see the definition for "system." All the definitions are collected in one handy glossary at the back of the book.

ON USING THIS BOOK

Once you finish the book, you'll have read the processes I describe, looked at the case study and the examples, and cleared up any confusion that exists in the way I use certain terms. So, you'll be ready to jump in with both feet and initiate sweeping changes in your personal and team testing processes, right? Not quite yet, please. As I mentioned earlier, many testing processes—including most of the critical ones I'll examine—tend to be context-sensitive. To help you plot a course for process improvement, I'll conclude each process discussion with three major sections.

RECOGNIZE GOOD PROCESSES

How do we recognize good processes? We can look for test team behaviors and achievements that indicate the degree of success of the process. In other words, what does a test team do when executing a good process, and what benefits does the team receive? For example, if you start an exercise program, as you achieve success in your workout process, you'd see an increase in muscle mass, a decrease in body fat, and increased stamina. To promote the success of your exercise regime, you would probably exercise regularly, eat a healthy diet, and cut back on smoking. In the 12 processes we'll look at, these behaviors and achievements interact with and reinforce each other.

These behaviors and achievements exist on a spectrum. For example, I continued to smoke cigarettes during the first eight years or so of my exercise program, and I did experience success in my fitness goals. However, at some point, concerned about long-term effects to my health and a bit frustrated with my relatively poor stamina when running, I quit smoking cigarettes, which allowed me to drop a minute off my mile running time in the space of just a few months.

How do you know how your current processes are working? Perhaps you don't need to make a change. How would you know if the context would support the change you propose to make? These sections on recognizing good processes will help.

HANDLE CHALLENGES

In many cases, situations can create roadblocks and hazards for particular processes. A typical example is unrealistic management expectations. Some people think testers have, hidden in their clothing, a bag of magic quality pixie dust. This dust, sprinkled on a system, will drive out all the bugs. Some of these people will accept a realistic explanation of what testing can contribute to a project. Others are adamant that if testers do good work, they can make all the problems go away. Such expectations greatly complicate the process of getting managers to accept realistic estimates of the testing schedule and budget. Understanding these challenges and coming up with ways to handle them is essential if you intend to make changes in your organization and the way testing happens in it.

IMPLEMENT IMPROVEMENTS

Process improvement is often hard work. For example, implementing a good bug tracking process, including a well-chosen bug tracking tool, can take person-weeks of effort and longer than a month. It also involves not just effort, but persuasion. Sometimes getting approval to make a process change is harder than changing the process. There's often a larger constituency for the status quo than for any change you might propose, so change involves taking a risk, motivating change, and putting in a great effort to keep it going. Finally, process improvements involve a smart plan of attack. There's a process to achieving process change! I can't tell you what will work in every circumstance, but I'll try to give you some ideas to think about as you plan the changes.

Processes are not guarantors of success, but rather enablers of it—done right. Done wrong, processes can become cumbersome and consume a lot of resources and time on paperwork. For example, after a move, I tried to change my business address with my former URL domain registrar. I sent literally more than two dozen faxes and e-mails during six months of trying to make the change take place. Finally, I gave up and changed registrars. Their process got in the way of providing good customer service. We certainly do not want to create barriers to providing good testing services. The idea is to have just enough process, just enough structure, to provide the support and foundation for really excellent work.

In addition to using the right approach for process change, you'll need to pick your battles. If you decide to change every process discussed in this book the moment you put it down, you will fail. Worse yet, in the course of that failure, you will make a real hash of what you're currently doing well, which probably will cash in your political capital. So, at the end of the book, I'll talk about how to plan appropriate changes to the processes that need changes the most.

TO YOUR TESTING SUCCESS!

While the subject of this book is testing processes, the object of reading it is learning how to achieve greater success in your testing endeavors. Processes are simply a means to an end. For example, most people don't collect cookbooks to have them on shelves. People buy cookbooks to successfully prepare a good meal. If you go into my kitchen, you can spot my favorite cookbooks easily. They are scented with spices, anointed with cooking oil, and worn from repeated use. They'll pop open to the dog-eared pages containing my favorite recipes, the ones I cook over and over.

Chefs are not referred to as cooking process specialists. Their expertise is not measured in their recipe-following prowess. A chef is an expert when, again and again, the chef puts a fine-tasting meal in front of the guests at the time agreed on, having spent a reasonable price on quality ingredients.

Likewise, this book should help you succeed as a tester. I hope that, over the years, it too gets decorated with notes, dog-eared, and maybe even a bit torn from repeated referencing. I hope that the process checklists, templates, and examples I've provided become some of your favorite utensils for cooking up a successful test project. Ultimately, I've written a successful book if it helps you become a more confident, successful, and fulfilled test professional.

PART I

PLAN

In this first part of the book, we'll examine the processes related to understanding the test work to be done. This is the longest part of the book because this portion of the testing process is where we plant the seeds of success. We'll look first at how to situate a testing effort in the project. Then we'll examine the specific risks that testing can help us address. With that foundation in place, we'll look at two more processes, estimation and planning. After understanding the schedule and the costs, then the strategic and tactical details behind the test effort, we will move on to the next part of the book, ready to prepare for a successful test effort.

Step #	Step	Done?
1.	Plan: Understand the testing effort.	☐
1.A	Understand the operational (system, project, and process) context and the organizational context in which the testing will be performed.	☐
1.B	Define and prioritize the risks to system quality, and obtain stakeholder consensus on the extent of testing to mitigate these risks.	☐
1.C	Estimate and obtain management support for the time, resources, and budget required to perform the testing agreed upon in step 1.B.	☐
1.D	Develop a plan for the tasks, dependencies, and participants required to mitigate the risks to system quality, and obtain stakeholder support for this plan.	☐

1

START WITH THE BIG PICTURE: PUT THE TEST ROLE IN THE BROADER CONTEXT

W hy are we here? No, I don't mean why are human beings here on Earth; I mean why do organizations fund projects that need testing?

Organizations develop, maintain, or acquire systems to deliver some valuable product, service, or capability to some set of customers, users, and other stakeholders. The value delivered takes many different forms, ranging from entertainment (video games) to productivity (office applications), to national defense (weapons systems), to treating illness (medical devices). Customers, users, and other stakeholders have reasonable (and unreasonable) expectations of system quality. These expectations run the gamut from "just barely working" to "zero-defect." In general, customers, users, and other stakeholders expect systems to exhibit a preponderance of satisfying behaviors and the comparative absence of dissatisfying behaviors.

Even with sincere efforts to put quality in during system development, maintenance, or procurement, people make mistakes. These mistakes result in systems with lower-than-expected levels of quality. These gaps between expectations of quality and experiences of quality result in risks for the developing organization as well as the customers, users, and stakeholders.

These risks can motivate an organization to make quality-related investments, including investing in testing. Specifically, organizations might want to

- Decrease overall system costs associated with quality problems.
- Increase confidence in the reliable operation of the system.
- Reduce the likelihood of profit-, mission-, or even life-threatening incidents.

Customers, Sponsors

People who have paid, will pay, or might pay money to obtain the system. This payment can occur by funding the system directly, by supporting the funding of the system, by paying a vendor for the system, by purchasing a product or service that includes or uses the system, by paying taxes, or by some other direct or indirect means. A customer can be an organization procuring and/or deploying a system to employee-users or an individual buying a system for their own use.

Users

People who have operated, will operate, or might operate the system, or those who use the outputs or products of the system. Users are sometimes customers, but not always.

Stakeholders (in the system)

People inside or outside the organizations who are, will be, or might be affected by the project, the system, or the system's quality.

Quality

1. Fitness for use. The presence of features, attributes, and behaviors that satisfy customers and users, and the absence of features, attributes, and behaviors that dissatisfy customers and users. (This definition is appropriate for many contexts, especially market-driven systems.)
2. Conformance to requirements. The presence of features, attributes, and behaviors that satisfy all the stated requirements, and the absence of features, attributes, and behaviors that deviate from requirements. (This definition is appropriate in some contexts, especially contract-development projects.)[1]

- Improve their reputation in the area of quality for the system itself or the products or services the system supports.
- Obtain repeat and referral business from satisfied customers.
- Reduce legal exposure to defective-system lawsuits (for developing organizations) or customer lawsuits (for procuring organizations).
- Achieve schedule, budget, or regulatory goals for system release or deployment.

---

1. The first definition comes from J. M. Juran's book, *Juran on Planning for Quality*. The second definition comes from Philip Crosby's book *Quality Is Free*. In many situations, Crosby's definition is implicit in Juran's definition when the requirements gathering process works properly. To the extent that the requirements gathering process is flawed, this definition is less useful. However, in the case of contractual development projects, it might make more sense to think of quality as conformance to requirements and to link the contract, requirements, and testing together around that definition.

- Improve the accuracy of planning, schedules, and budgets for future projects.
- Obtain funding for current and future projects.
- Reduce the likelihood of accepting a system that can hurt the organization's ability to do business.

The motivations can depend on whether we are talking about testing by the development organization that is creating the system or testing by the procuring organization that is considering buying, integrating, and/or deploying the system.[2]

While historical data and models can help us make predictions about bugs (see Chapters 3 and 4), the exact number, extent, severity, and location of the quality problems are not known in advance. So, these potential problems are risks (possible negative outcomes or events). These risks endanger the quality of the system. A well-run test effort provides testing services and information that help the organization manage these risks to the quality of the system being developed, maintained, or acquired.

Expectation of Quality

The beliefs held by the customers and users about what level of quality the system should provide. Ideally, customers and users will hold reasonable expectations of quality.

When user or customer expectations are unreasonable, this often indicates a breakdown in the requirements gathering, business analysis, or change control activities. It is often not possible—and usually not desirable—to address unreasonable expectations of quality in the testing process.

Experience of Quality

The opinions about system quality, combined with the general levels of satisfaction or dissatisfaction, held by users and customers as they gain experience with a system. When the experience of quality matches the expectation of quality, the user or customer is usually satisfied; if the experience exceeds expectations, the user or customer is usually delighted; if the experience falls below expectations, the user or customer is usually dissatisfied.

---

2. Individual software purchasers seldom have the right under their contracts to perform acceptance tests of any sort. Indeed, at the time of writing, most shrink-wrapped software contracts explicitly exclude such tests. To learn more about this and other imbalances in the distribution of the cost of poor quality in the shrink-wrapped software market, I recommend checking out some of Cem Kaner's work, including *Bad Software* and his writings on UCITA at www.kaner.com.

System Lifecycle

The entire set of activities that occur in development, deployment, use, and obsolescence of the system, from initial specification and design through implementation and testing, to support and maintenance, and ultimately to cut-over and retirement of the system.

System Development Lifecycle

The subset of the system lifecycle associated with the initial development of a system; i.e., from specification and design through implementation, testing, and initial deployment.

To provide these services and this information to the organization, we carry out test processes within system development, maintenance, or acquisition projects. (In organizations with separate test groups, some of the activities occur as distinct subprojects carried out by those groups.) The test processes are sequences of actions, operations, and observations undertaken to achieve a goal. At the highest level, the testing process consists of four steps, which can overlap.

1. *Plan*—Understand the testing effort.
2. *Prepare*—Assemble the people and tests.
3. *Perform*—Do the testing and gather the results.
4. *Perfect*—Guide adaptation and improvement.

Ideally, the testing process begins the moment a system is conceived and continues until the end of the system's lifecycle (i.e., decommissioning, end of life, or termination of support).

This process is illustrated in Figure 1-1. If you've studied total quality management, you might recognize this cycle as a variation of the Plan-Do-Check-Act process for continuous quality improvement popularized by W. E. Deming.[3] Not only does the system improve continuously when testing is used intelligently throughout the system lifecycle, but, as a desirable side effect, the testing process provides information about other lifecycle processes. The project team can use this information to improve these processes.

---

3. See Mary Walton's *The Deming Management Method*.

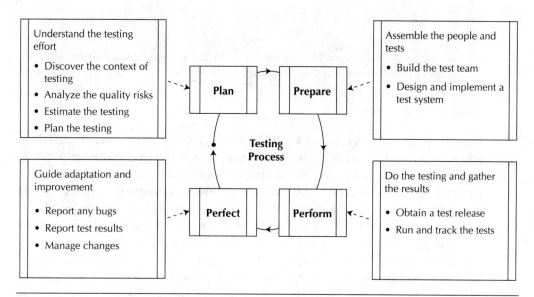

Understand the testing effort
- Discover the context of testing
- Analyze the quality risks
- Estimate the testing
- Plan the testing

Plan

Prepare

Assemble the people and tests
- Build the test team
- Design and implement a test system

Testing Process

Guide adaptation and improvement
- Report any bugs
- Report test results
- Manage changes

Perfect

Perform

Do the testing and gather the results
- Obtain a test release
- Run and track the tests

FIGURE 1-1 A TESTING PROCESS

Earlier, I listed a number of possible motivations for testing. How specifically does the testing process yield a return on investment? In many test projects, there are four major, distinct ways.

1. Find bugs that get fixed—or even prevent them.
2. Find bugs that don't get fixed—but are known.
3. Run tests that mitigate (potentially expensive) risks.
4. Guide the project with timely, accurate, credible information.

The test team delivers these benefits primarily in step 4 of the process, Perfect, through the communication of test results. The preceding steps in the process are essential to creating credible, accurate, timely, and thorough information for the key stakeholders, but by themselves these activities do not deliver value to the organization. The test team is unique in most organizations in that it serves primarily to create and communicate information for use within the organization itself; i.e., it provides feedback on the system and the project.[4]

---

4. This is true both when the test team exists within the system development or maintenance organization and when it exists as part of an organization accepting software from outside vendors or consultancies. However, in the latter situation, the value of testing depends almost entirely on items 3 and 4, risk mitigation and project guidance.

> **Bug, Defect**
> A problem that causes or would cause the system to fail to meet one or more user's or customer's reasonable expectations of quality.

Because the testing process occurs within a development, maintenance, or acquisition project, the testing process fits into the overall project context. But the situation is much more organic and fluid than, say, plugging an appliance into a wall socket. The presence of a testing process within the system lifecycle changes the system lifecycle process itself along with the projects that follow that lifecycle. The testing process influences and is influenced by the project and the system the project is developing or maintaining. The project team uses the information produced by testing to make specific adjustments to the project and the system. Individuals working within a larger organizational context carry out the project, and some of those individuals carry out the testing process. Management establishes an organizational context that influences the way these testers relate to the other people working on the project.

A Testing Process

Figure 1-1 showed a graphical view of the testing process, but I find checklists to be a more useful representation, as shown in Process 1. Many of the testing projects I've worked on allowed for considerable overlap and iteration in this process. Not all testing projects involved each step or substep. However, this generic process could be tailored to apply to most of the projects I've worked on. This process checklist should give you a good starting point if you intend to build a notebook of customizable processes.

If there are different phases of testing performed by different teams for a single project (which is typical of large projects), there can be multiple instances of the process underway at varying levels of formality within the project. For example, on one particular mass-market system development project my associates and I worked on, the development team did informal unit and component testing, the marketing team

> **Testing**
> Operationally, a process that assesses the quality of a system, providing services and information products that help the organization manage the risks to system quality. Organizationally, a team that provides these services and products for the projects they serve.

Step #	Step	Done?
1.	Plan: Understand the testing effort.	☐
1.A	Understand the operational (system, project, and process) context and the organizational context in which the testing will be performed.	☐
1.B	Define and prioritize the risks to system quality, and obtain stakeholder consensus on the extent of testing to mitigate these risks.	☐
1.C	Estimate and obtain management support for the time, resources, and budget required to perform the testing agreed upon in step 1.B.	☐
1.D	Develop a plan for the tasks, dependencies, and participants required to mitigate the risks to system quality, and obtain stakeholder support for this plan.	☐
2.	Prepare: Assemble the people and tests.	☐
2.A	Through staffing and training, build a team of test professionals with the appropriate skills, attitudes, and motivation.	☐
2.B	Design, develop, acquire, and verify the test system that the test team uses to assess the quality of the system under test.	☐
3.	Perform: Do the testing and gather the results.	☐
3.A	Acquire and install a test release consisting of some or all of the components in the system under test.	☐
3.B	Assign, track, and manage the set of test cases to be run against each test release.	☐
4.	Perfect: Guide adaptation and improvement.	☐
4.A	Document the bugs found during test execution.	☐
4.B	Communicate test results to key stakeholders.	☐
4.C	Adjust to changes and refine the testing process.	☐

PROCESS 1   A TESTING PROCESS

oversaw informal alpha and beta testing, and my test team performed formal integration and system testing. As another example, on an in-house IT project we worked on for a large financial institution, the developers did formal component testing, my test team ran the formal integration and system testing, business analysts and users did an informal user acceptance testing, and network operations ran the pilot testing.

Unit Testing

Testing of a small element or unit of the system.

Component Testing, Subsystem Testing

A testing phase focused on each component or subsystem of the system.

Alpha Testing, Beta Testing

Testing phases where the system is delivered to internal (alpha) or external (beta) customers and users for exposure to real-world workflows, data, and environments.

Integration Testing, Product Testing

A testing phase focused on the relationships and interfaces between pairs and groups of components or subsystems in the system.

System Testing

A testing phase focused on the overall and particular behaviors, functions, and responses of the system as a whole.

Acceptance Testing, User Acceptance Testing

A testing phase designed to demonstrate that the system under test meets requirements. The name "user acceptance testing" can imply that users run the testing.

Pilot Testing

A testing phase where the system is put into limited production under close supervision. Hardware pilot tests demonstrate the ability of the assembly line to mass-produce the system. Software pilot tests demonstrate the ability of the system to handle typical operations from live customers on live hardware.

In this chapter, I'll look at the first step in the process, the understanding of context. Understanding context is important, especially in a service-oriented, information-providing role like testing. Our work must fit into the broader contexts of the organization, the project, and the project's processes, right down to the finest details. If we want credibility and prospects for advancement in the organization, then we need to be competent testers that know how to deliver the utmost value to the organizations we serve.

To use a historical metaphor, the ultimate example of riding into a situation unaware of context is found in the final days of US Army General George Armstrong Custer. Custer's posthumous fame comes mostly from his role in the wars between the United States and Native Americans in the late 1800s. His last act in this sad period of US history began when he got himself into the Battle of Little Big Horn by believing he was hot on the trail of a small group of Sioux (one of the Native American nations). That trail actually led to a large force of Sioux warriors, under the command of Sitting Bull and Crazy Horse. Even less fortunate for Custer, the Sioux were gathered for a national conference on how to resist the ongoing, forcible US attempts to intern them in reservations. You could say the context of the meeting made them already ill disposed toward these uninvited guests. Custer and 264 of his men were killed in the ensuing battle, in which they were routed and then totally encircled on a hill. Wrong place, wrong time, wrong mission, wrong team. Unawareness of context leads to mistaken conclusions regarding what you are about, and those mistaken conclusions can be very dangerous.[5]

UNDERSTANDING OPERATIONAL AND ORGANIZATIONAL CONTEXT

Some testers and test managers are present when the host organization is started, and get to define the organizational and operational context of testing and testers from scratch. However, many test professionals join an existing company or department, either as part of setting up a new testing process or to work within an existing one. Beyond airy discussions about the best organizational and operational contexts, the more practical question for them is, How did the organizational and operational context for testing and testers come to be the way it is? The testing context generally persists in the short run, so the effective tester or test manager must understand and work within it.

Groups charged with performing testing activities come into being within a system development or maintenance organization for a variety of reasons. Sometimes, enlightened management understands right from the start the value of effective and efficient testing. In some cases, customer, market, legal, or regulatory requirements compel the company to adopt some standardized form of testing. In other cases, the company that has gone through life playing quality roulette, delivering systems to

---

5. Little Big Horn was not Custer's first episode of fearlessness. At the battle at Gettysburg he rode at the head of his cavalry troop into a squad of Confederate soldiers and had his horse shot out from under him. As he stood near the body of his unfortunate horse, he narrowly escaped death when, just in time, a Union private killed a Confederate counterpart who was about to shoot Custer. Bravery had worked for Custer, who was at the time of that incident already a general (the youngest to that date) in the US Army. Little Big Horn was the last and perhaps most ill-advised act in a life of risk taking. This offers another lesson for test professionals: Sooner or later, the habit of running big risks results in a big loss. For more on this fascinating character and his life, see Jeffrey Wert's biography, *Custer*.

customers after no or minimal testing by the programmers, finally has a near-death experience when a particularly bad release results in a lawsuit, the loss of a key customer, terrible publicity, or the resignation of essential staff members.

Understanding this history is an important part of making our testing process mesh smoothly with the project. To see why, let's contrast testers with other project contributors. Why are system architects, business analysts, programmers, and other engineers around? To build the system. The system can't happen without these folks. Even if a company chooses offshore development, the system must still be built somewhere by someone. Outsourcing doesn't change the way the builders of the system add value; it only complicates the process and in some cases results in cheaper, faster, or higher-quality systems . . . or the converse!

I mentioned four specific valuable types of information and services that testers provide. Smart project managers can use these services and this information to reduce the overall risk of project failure. However, in other organizations, managers might not see all these benefits or might believe, mistakenly, that testers can provide other benefits, like magically making bugs disappear.

You, like me, might have been frustrated from time to time by misconceptions about what testers can actually accomplish. Sometimes seasoned test professionals, having studied books and articles about "doing testing right," throw up their hands, saying, "I can't believe these people are doing all these stupid things!" Gerald Weinberg, on the topic of understanding apparently problematic existing situations, wrote perceptively in *The Secrets of Consulting* that "Things are the way they are because they got that way. . . . There were, at the time, good and sufficient reasons for decisions that seem idiotic today." Weinberg's advice applies to anyone coming into an existing operation with the intention of influencing, changing, or simply understanding the way it works.

So, if you have come into a situation that appears rational or otherwise, what can you do to point your efforts in the right direction? Process 2 is a context-discovery process that has worked for me.

I find that the steps in this process occur in parallel and that I usually need to repeat each step a few times. I also find that I need an open mind. I enjoy having the situation as seen by the participants become clear to me, which can happen in as few as two or three days. I try to keep my mouth closed and my opinions to myself as much as possible while I'm still soaking up new information about how things got to be the way they are and what people think I can do about it.

Step #	Step	Done?
1.	Understand the lifecycle process(es) used in your organization for system development, maintenance, or acquisition, including any planned or ongoing process improvement initiatives.	☐
2.	Study whatever testing, test-related, and quality-related documentation, data, and metrics exist, such as test plans, bug reporting databases, field failure data, test systems, and so forth. Understand who created these items, why they did so, why they did it the way they did it, and what was going on in the organization that led to all those decisions and forces that influenced the outcomes.	☐
3.	Discuss with other participants what testing activities they're doing—and what they'll continue to do now that you're on the scene.	☐
4.	Identify your peer-level stakeholders in the testing process. Talk with them to understand their current relationships with the people doing testing now, their expectations of how testing can add value, past disappointments or conflicts with the testing process or people involved in testing, and so forth.	☐
5.	Clarify with your managers and other senior managers what value they expect the test team to add and especially to what extent your role involves quality assurance as distinct from testing.	☐

PROCESS 2 A CONTEXT-DISCOVERY PROCESS

Quality Assurance (*contrasted with* Testing)

According to IEEE Standard 610.12-1990, "IEEE Standard Glossary of Software Engineering Terminology," quality assurance (QA) involves "all actions necessary to provide adequate confidence" in system quality and evaluating "the process by which [the system was] developed," whereas testing consists of activities "to detect differences between existing and required conditions (bugs) and to evaluate...features." In other words, QA focuses on end-to-end process correctness, while testing is an assessment of quality.[6]

Joining any existing group—a club, a religious organization, or a company—is ultimately a social act. Personality affects how people choose to socialize. Some people use boldness as a technique. Perhaps my process is too cautious and considered for

---

6. See *IEEE Software Engineering Standards Collection: 1997 Edition*, Standard 610, for a glossary defining these and other standard software engineering terms.

the bold. In the past I myself was bolder, but many of my experiences with such self-assured tactics have been negative. The more carefully I listen, the better I do. On that note, let's start with the first installment of our case study, the Sumatra project.

INTRODUCING THE SUMATRA PROJECT AND THE SPEEDYWRITER TEST TEAM

Jamal Brown manages the Integration and System Test team for Software Cafeteria. Software Cafeteria markets a Web-based integrated office application suite (OfficeArrow), containing a word processor (SpeedyWriter), a spreadsheet (JetCalc), a presentation tool (ZippyShow), and a relational database management system (LightningData). Jamal's organization provides testing services across the entire product line. He tests both new releases and maintenance releases; the latter occur both as monthly service packs and as emergency patches.

Jamal's Integration and System Test team works within a larger Engineering Services group. In addition to testing, this group provides various services to the System Engineering group, such as technical writing; release engineering; running the internal systems, infrastructure, and network; and customer support. The System Engineering group develops and maintains the OfficeArrow product line. Separate marketing, sales, and finance groups also exist. The Software Cafeteria organizational chart is shown in Figure 1-2.

On September 2, 2002, the Integration and System Test team attended a Software Cafeteria all-hands meeting. During a discussion of future product road maps, Kate Hernandez, the SpeedyWriter product manager, announced that a major new effort to deliver release 3.1, code-named Sumatra, would commence in a few weeks. Sumatra, she explained, would deliver some incremental improvements in table, file import, and header/footer functionality, but it would also include as its signature new feature an optional document management subsystem (DMS).

She then introduced Jenny Kaufman, a well-respected lead programmer from the 3.0 release effort, as the project manager for Sumatra. Jenny explained that because delivery in the first quarter of 2003 was critical, this project would follow an Incremental development model. Her team of programmers would first build the core function, the document management subsystem, in a sequence of increments and then would add the other functions. Each increment would be stable, tested, and ready to ship. This would require more extensive test execution than the previous, Waterfall model releases. However, she claimed an Incremental approach would give Software Cafeteria better control over both the quality and the release schedule for Sumatra. Past

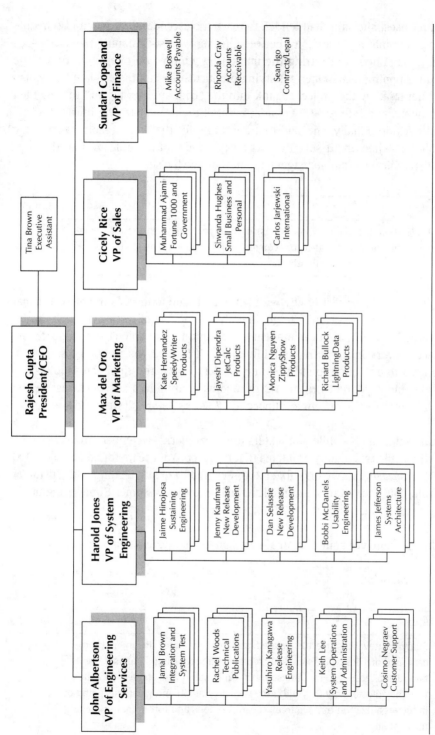

FIGURE 1-2 SOFTWARE CAFETERIA ORGANIZATIONAL CHART

Waterfall releases, she said, had tended to reach a crescendo of budget and schedule constraints culminating in a choice between, in her words, "shipping reputation-destroying garbage now and hitting the marketing window on one hand, or, on the other hand, shipping a customer-satisfying product three months too late." She also promised not to allow the project to sink into the "code-and-fix tar pit" that had led to the infamous and inferior 2.5 version, with all the accompanying burnout, cynicism, and attrition. Finally, she said that her target for the first incremental delivery was October 21—just about seven weeks away—and that it would contain the support for hierarchical storage management and not much else.

Step #	Step	Done?
1.	Understand the lifecycle process(es) used in your organization for system development, maintenance, or acquisition, including any planned or ongoing process improvement initiatives.	✔

After the meeting, Jamal met briefly with Jenny and Kate to discuss the project. Jamal was excited about an opportunity to get in early and do lots of testing throughout. He was concerned, though, about management commitment to deliver the resources he would need to work in the Incremental lifecycle. "If I heard you right," he said, "I'm going to need to get ready to start testing on October 21 and then continue testing through the end of March. On the 3.0 release, we only had a six-week test period planned initially—which, of course, slipped to 12 weeks before all was said and done."

"Yep," Kate said, "and—while you testers did great work—we ended up delivering a product with some real quality problems that time, too. Your team found almost 1,000 bugs in that release, but we only fixed 200. Cos and I are still dealing with customer fallout from that one," Kate continued, referring to the Customer Support manager, Cosimo Negraev. "Sure, it beat the 2.5 experience—"

"Mmm-hmm, I'm never doin' that again," seconded Jenny, as Jamal nodded.

"—but not by much."

Step #	Step	Done?
2.	Study whatever testing, test-related, and quality-related documentation, data, and metrics exist, such as test plans, bug reporting databases, field failure data, test systems, and so forth. Understand who created these items, why they did so, why they did it the way they did it, and what was going on in the organization that led to all those decisions and forces that influenced the outcomes.	✔

Jenny added, "Jamal, you've known me for a while, and you know I never really aspired to be a project manager. I've told the executive team that I would take this job, but with certain non-negotiable conditions. Getting beyond the old code-and-fix and Waterfall approaches was one of those conditions. If you run into trouble getting adequate resources—whatever you need—to start testing on October 21 and continue through March, just march into my office and sound off. I'll take it from there."

Kate, Jenny, and Jamal continued their discussion, moving on to the topic of unit and component testing and alpha and beta testing. Jenny explained that she planned to have each programmer write and run automated tests for their own objects as they created them, in a personal test environment, as a semiformal unit test. These tests, like the code itself, would be subject to peer review. Checking the code into the project repository was contingent on three criteria.

1. The unit tests passed.
2. The code review was completed and approved.
3. The test review was completed and approved.

The tests would become part of an automated component test that would run as part of the automated nightly build.[7]

Jamal was very glad to hear this, since it would help him solve a thorny technical challenge: integration testing. He suggested to Jenny that the test team work together with the development team to review the component tests, because his testers could then use those items as the foundation for integration testing. Jenny agreed that this would be an excellent idea. Both Jenny and Jamal discussed the resource issues related to this kind of testing, which is very effective and efficient but tends to prolong the development process and to require extensive testing involvement in the development testing phases.

Kate told Jamal that, as on previous efforts, her marketing group would plan and execute both an alpha and a beta test. The alpha test would occur when the first integrated build with the first full increment of functionality had passed all the component tests. It would consist of deploying the product in-house, including the Sumatra project team, as well as to some carefully chosen business partners.

---

7. This is simpler to implement than it might sound. For more information, see "Mission Made Possible," by Rex Black and Greg Kubaczkowski, originally published in Volume 4, Issue 4 (Jul/Aug 2002) of *Software Testing and Quality Engineering* magazine, now available online at www.stickyminds.com and www.rexblackconsulting.com.

The beta test would occur after the first cycle of system testing against the first functional increment was completed—given satisfactory testing results. Kate explained to Jamal that she would need to work with him closely to ensure that those features and behaviors most important for the beta test were covered thoroughly in the first cycle of system testing. Jamal replied that this was a good idea but that Jenny would also need to make sure that these features were among the first finished by the development team and that they received thorough component testing. Jenny agreed, commenting that she realized that Jamal couldn't "test quality into" a poor-quality product.

Step #	Step	Done?
3.	Discuss with other participants what testing activities they're doing—and what they'll continue to do now that you're on the scene.	✔

At this point, Jamal understood the context of his effort, at least as seen by Kate and Jenny. Since they were key stakeholders, it was extremely important that they saw how Jamal's team fit into the project. However, Jamal knew that understanding context is an ongoing effort. The best test professionals stay constantly alert for signs that people don't understand or agree with what they're doing. Pertinence is essential to credibility, and credibility, as any reporter or newspaper publisher can tell you, is essential to those who make a living providing information. Though Jamal had been at the company for over a year, he still planned to talk to his managers and peers to clarify their expectations, and to continue this process throughout the project.

Step #	Step	Done?
4.	Identify your peer-level stakeholders in the testing process. Talk with them to understand their current relationships with the people doing testing now, their expectations of how testing can add value, past disappointments or conflicts with the testing process or people involved in testing, and so forth.	✔
5.	Clarify with your managers and other senior managers what value they expect the test team to add and especially to what extent your role involves quality assurance as distinct from testing.	✔

TESTING WITHIN THE SYSTEM DEVELOPMENT LIFECYCLE

I've mentioned a couple of development methodologies or lifecycles: the Waterfall model (along with its V Model variant) and the Incremental model. In the case study, Jenny promotes the Incremental model as the best choice for the SpeedyWriter project.

Waterfall System Development Lifecycle

A development model where the development team performs a series of sequential phases to deliver a system. First the team defines the requirements, next they design the system, and then they implement it. Once the system is implemented, it goes through a sequence of test phases, starting with unit or component testing, followed by integration testing, and finally system testing. (In the case of contract or in-house system development, there is often an acceptance testing phase after system testing.) Some variations of this approach allow for overlap between the phases, rather than requiring completion of all of each phase's tasks before beginning the next phase.

V Model

A variation of the Waterfall model that shows the implementation tasks down the left side of the V and the testing tasks up the right side of the V. Across the V are lines showing how the outputs of each implementation phase drive the development of the test system needed for each testing phase. This is based on the observation that acceptance testing is driven primarily by requirements; system testing by requirements and design; integration testing by requirements, design, and code interfaces; and component testing by requirements, design, code interfaces, and code logic. Figure 1-3 shows a graphical representation of this development model, where the system can be purely software, hardware, a hardware/software system, or a family or system of systems.

How to select the best lifecycle model—or even a good one—for a given development project is well beyond the scope of this book. Each lifecycle model is designed to deal with certain kinds of project risks more effectively.[8] Lifecycle models also tend to be associated with certain kinds of system development, maintenance, or acquisition efforts. For example, on its Web site, Rational promotes the Rational Unified Process as superior for e-development projects using object-oriented technologies.

As the word "model" suggests, these lifecycles are abstractions and simplifications of how some people believe successful projects work. Similarly, I describe processes in this book that model how I think many successful testing subprojects work.

How many lifecycle models exist? A cursory Web search revealed links to dozens of different methodologies for object-oriented development. Some of these methodologies

---

8. A lifecycle model overview is found in Chapter 2 of Roger Pressman's *Software Engineering, Fourth Edition*, and in Chapter 2 of Stephen Kan's *Metrics and Models in Software Quality Engineering, Second Edition*.

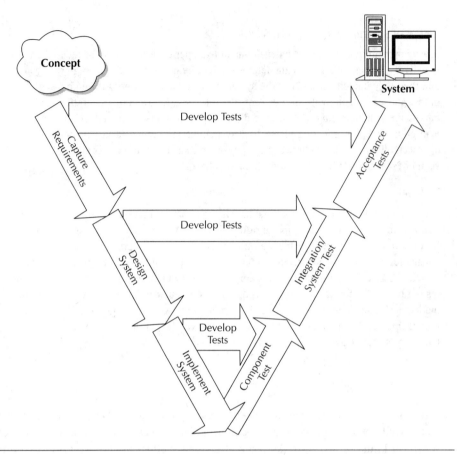

FIGURE 1-3 THE V MODEL OF THE WATERFALL SYSTEM DEVELOPMENT LIFECYCLE

talk about specific lifecycles, while others are more lightweight, imposing fewer constraints on order and phases, with more emphasis on people than process.[9]

How accurately do these models describe what should happen? As a quote attributed to both W. E. Deming and George Box puts it, "All models are wrong; some are useful." To some extent, the proliferation of models gives some indication of the dissent and controversy that exists over how systems should be created. The more widely used a lifecycle or methodology is, the more critics it attracts. For example, some have

---

9. See www.cetus-links.org for a collection of object-oriented-related links, including these methodology links. Various Web sites related to what proponents call agile methods like Extreme Programming also exist, describing the lightweight methodologies. For example, see www.martinfowler.com/articles/newMethodology.html.

Incremental System Development Lifecycle

A development model where a larger project is broken into a series of increments, each of which delivers a portion of the functionality in the overall project requirements. The requirements are prioritized and delivered in priority order in the appropriate increment. In some (but not all) versions of this model, each subproject follows a "mini-V" Model with its own design, coding, and testing phases. Whatever the process for each increment, test execution tends to start earlier, with the delivery of the first incremental test release, and continue at full strength right up to the moment of deployment or first customer delivery. Figure 1-4 shows a graphical representation of the model.

written about how terrible the V Model is.[10] Nevertheless, it remains a common approach. This is not simply a matter of inertia or intellectual laziness. The V Model also happens to be intuitive, widely known, and preferable to chaos. However, any given lifecycle or methodology can be appropriate and inappropriate, depending on the context. What should happen in one situation is usually not what should happen in another. Since each project is unique, managers and individual contributors should to tailor the chosen lifecycle to their specific needs.

Not only are these models approximations of what *should* happen, they are also approximations of what *actually* happens when people try to apply them to projects. Sometimes adaptations occur that are deliberate and intelligent, and sometimes adaptations are not so well conceived and smart. I've seen—and have had dozens of test professionals tell me stories about—projects that began using one lifecycle or another but then lurched into the code-and-fix ditch, often during the test execution period, when the project exceeded the original schedules or budgets.

Code and Fix

A development approach that eschews most planning, requirements gathering, and design activities, jumping directly into coding of the system and then fixing bugs that are found. Bugs may be found through formal testing by an independent test team, via ad hoc, informal testing, or by debugging alone. While sometimes suitable for small, low-risk, and low-complexity development or maintenance efforts, this model does not scale up well to large, complex, or high-risk projects.

---

10. For example, see Brian Marick's paper, "New Models for Test Development," originally presented at the Quality Week 99 conference and printed in the proceedings of that conference, now found at www.testing.com/writings.html.

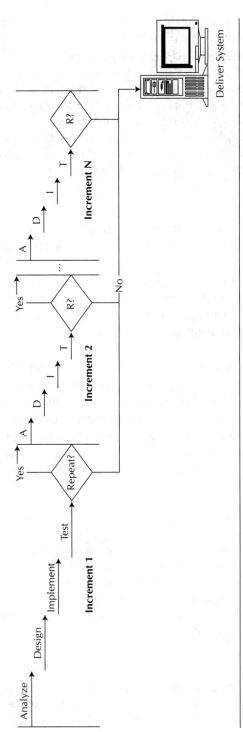

FIGURE 1-4 AN INCREMENTAL SYSTEM DEVELOPMENT LIFECYCLE

What does this proliferation of different and imperfect models mean for test professionals? The temptation can be strong to ignore this Tower of Babel of methodologies as a meaningless distraction. This is especially true because while some of the models provide specifically for testing (e.g., the V Model), some don't, or don't address the topic completely. Extreme Programming, for example, does a good job of stressing the importance of solid, automated unit and component testing by programmers but provides less guidance for integration and system testing. Because these different phases of testing tend to catch different kinds of bugs, testers must fill in the gaps when they work on projects that follow the Extreme Programming model.

There are three important considerations for testers on this topic. First, within the project context, we should stay flexible in fitting our testing within chosen lifecycles and methodologies. We should figure out how to adapt and provide valuable services and information, whatever is going on. We should also build flexibility into our plans so that if the chosen methodology degrades into a code-and-fix frenzy, we can continue to deliver valuable services and information even under conditions of chaos. Indeed, in this book I'll provide you with ideas that can help you succeed whether you are working within a rigorous, process-oriented project or a cyclone of code-spinning turmoil.

Second, fitting our testing process into the larger lifecycle implies a need to understand sequencing and dependencies. By sequencing, I mean how the specific parts of the testing process fit into the larger system lifecycle in terms of time. The V Model specifically calls for the design and implementation of the test system to start as early as possible. Testers following the V Model create test cases, test data, test scripts, test tools, test environments, and other test system components during the system development phases of requirements gathering, design, and implementation. The earlier test system design and implementation activities address acceptance and system testing, with the detailed design and implementation tasks driving the integration and component testing phases. Not all of the lifecycle models are as explicit about sequencing, but in each project we must pick the right time to begin each of the critical testing processes. That right time is influenced by the dependencies. For example, if we are writing requirements-based tests, we can't get started until we have requirements.

Third, within the broader context of the system development community, testers must increase their involvement in the ongoing discussion about lifecycles and methodologies. Process matters, too, and testing is an important piece of the system development process. Sequencing and dependency issues have a strong influence on the success of our testing subprojects. We should help those people who are talking about process understand the critical testing processes and how they relate to other development activities. Another major thrust of this book is to serve as part of that discussion.

ORGANIZING THE TESTERS AND THE TESTING

In addition to continuing controversy about methodologies and the operational context of testing within those lifecycle models, ongoing debate persists around the question of the proper organization of testers and testing. Testing can occur within the development team itself, inside the project, as an independent team providing services to the project, in some capacity in the organization acquiring the system, or as some mix of these approaches. A test organization, when it exists as a separate entity, can report to the development manager, the project manager, some other line manager, an executive manager, or one of the chief officers.

I prefer to manage or work within a distinct test team. I prefer independent test teams that do not report to managers with incentives counter to the finding of bugs and the accurate assessment of quality. However, I also prefer test teams that are integrated into the overall project team in terms of early involvement and the flow of information. I like to see this independent but integrated test team focus on handling the higher-level phases of testing—integration and system test—in a way that complements unit and component testing, which remain the purview of the development team. I also like to see a formal or informal test done by users or user surrogates, such as alpha and beta tests in the mass-market world and acceptance testing in the management information systems/information technology world. If multiple projects require testing services at the same time, I like to have a single test team provide services across all the projects.[11] Why do I recommend this approach?

For optimal bug detection and removal, a project needs structural, behavioral, and live testing. These three styles of testing tend to locate different bugs and produce different kinds of debugging information. For example, uninitialized-pointer bugs can affect behavioral tests in a variety of ways, often confusing tester and programmer alike. However, there are simple structural testing techniques (e.g., *lint* in the UNIX/C world) that can locate variables that might be used before they are set.

> **Independent Test Team**
>
> A group of people, distinct from those charged with building the system under test, whose responsibility is to effectively and efficiently assess and report on the quality of the system under test. I have most often seen this team acting as a service organization to the project team.

---

11. See Chapter 9 of my book *Managing the Testing Process, Second Edition*, for a further discussion of this topic.

Behavioral Tests, Black-Box Tests

Tests based on what externally observable things a system should do, often spelled out in requirements and high-level design specifications.

Now, structural testing tends to rely for the most part on programming and other technical skills, but behavioral testing often requires specialized testing and application domain skills as well (see Chapters 8 and 9). Two examples of testing skills are security and performance testing, in which the typical programmer is not versed. As an example of application domain skills, one of my clients writes geological modeling software for oil exploration. To test the functionality and workflows, one must be a geologist, geophysicist, or similarly skilled professional, not a programmer.

I find the projects I work on usually go more smoothly when programmers do some unit and component testing of their own code. Through the ascendance of approaches like Extreme Programming, such a position is becoming less controversial. Doing such testing requires both structural testing skills and programming skills. It makes sense for people charged with these tasks to live within the programming team. However, many programmers (I'm one) have trouble testing their own code. So, a good practice is to adopt a development process that provides for unit testing, where programmers finds bugs in their own software, and for component testing, where programmers test each other's software. (This is sometimes called "code swapping.") Variations on this approach use concepts like pair programming and peer reviews of automated component test stubs or harnesses.[12]

However, because of the special skills required for behavioral testing, grouping the people charged with these activities together in an independent test team makes sense for at least three reasons. First, having two or more similarly skilled people working on similar tasks provides for group synergy. For example, testers can review each other's test cases, test results, and bug reports. Second, a test team can foster

Structural Tests, White-Box Tests

Tests based on the internal details of how a system should work, often spelled out in detailed design, logic, and data.

---

12. For more on structural testing, see Brian Marick's *Craft of Software Testing*, Robert Binder's *Testing Object-Oriented Software*, and Boris Beizer's *Software Testing Techniques*.

morale, which is important for good testing because many tasks involve delivering bad news. Third, having a test team provides opportunities for specialization, skills growth, and career paths beyond just moving up into a programming position. All these factors interact to bolster test team performance and credibility.

A test team that provides services to multiple projects at once offers even more opportunities for specialization and growth. I have worked with one test team that provides testing services to a variety of PC system development projects. Within that team there are separate groups that specialize in network testing, Windows client testing, Windows server testing, UNIX testing, applications testing, and so forth. These groups assign highly skilled test professionals as needed to specific projects.

I like a test team with a test manager who is a competent, seasoned test professional as well as a capable manager. In this way, the test manager serves as a technical leader of the team as well as a manager, just as the best development managers I've known have been good programmers *and* good managers. Yes, at some level of management, you don't need to know how your direct reports do what they do. However, when a manager provides direct supervision of individual contributors, combining technical and managerial leadership in one person works very well.

Management of a test team is important because behavioral testing is a complex subproject within the overall project when handled by an independent test team. Many dependencies and interfaces exist between the project and the testing subproject. In addition, constant change in the project has both obvious and subtle test repercussions. The test manager identifies these dependencies and manages changes in them. The test manager must also bring significant people management skills to bear, especially in hiring and growing the test team. Finally, the test manager must be an effective advocate and communicator of the team's potential contributions and findings.

An independent test team must secure an adequate share of the project's resources. An independent test team must be able to report findings, both good and bad, in an unbiased fashion. So, the management structure should not create perverse incentives for the testers. For example, suppose the development manager receives a bonus for delivering a system with a particular feature set on time and within budget—not an uncommon situation. Now, what happens when the test manager reports to the development manager that within those feature, budget, and schedule parameters, the system will be very buggy? This situation—again, not uncommon—creates strains between the test manager and the development manager. What happens when this development manager's manager asks this test manager for an assessment of system quality and a prediction of when quality will be sufficient to ship? The test manager is then faced with an undesirable conflict of interests. The test manager can either tell the truth and expose the boss's failure, or sugarcoat the situation and undermine the test team's value to the organization.

I have heard from various colleagues and attendees of my test management seminar that organizations can resolve these political problems by aligning the organizational structure and everyone's interests with shipping a product that balances the elements of features, budget, schedule, and quality. For those organizations that prefer to reward project or development managers based strictly on schedule and budget, having the test manager report into an organizational structure that exists at a peer level with these project or development managers can restore the balance between quality, schedule, budget, and features.

OK, you've heard what I prefer, but there's plenty of latitude in those preferences. The case study shows one effective variant. Jamal Brown, the test manager, handles all behavioral testing of the various OfficeArrow products, which occurs during integration and system test phases. Jamal reports to an Engineering Services group manager, John Albertson, who is a peer executive with Harold Jones, the System Engineering manager. Both report to Rajesh Gupta, the CEO. Jamal has exactly the same standing, organizationally, as Jenny, his counterpart development manager.

Another variation involves having a service-based test team in which one dedicated senior tester follows each system from start to finish, playing the role of a subject matter expert (SME) or consulting test professional for all testing tasks associated with that system. Other members of the test team focus on providing test services across multiple projects at once. The consulting test professional, competent at both structural and behavioral testing, serves as the technical test expert for all testing on a system development project on the first day of the project. The consulting test professional works with the programmers to ensure good unit, component, and integration testing, reporting on a technical level to the development manager about these activities while remaining organizationally part of the test team. The test manager works with the consulting test professional and other test professionals, meanwhile, to plan, create tests, and set up a test environment for a separate, distinct system test phase. When the system test execution starts, the consulting test professional for the

Test Phase, Test Level

A distinct set of testing activities that address a particular group of quality risks, such as component test, integration test, system test, and acceptance test. (I tend to use the word "phase," while others use the word "level.")

system comes back into the test team. In this period of the project, the test professional serves as a valuable resource to the lead test professional and the test manager for the system testing. The consulting test professional has accumulated significant operational expertise with the system and has deep insight into its strengths and weaknesses, and can now consult with the test team. In Figure 1-5 you can see the team structure, including the two consulting test professionals (one on project A, one on project B) being temporarily assigned to their respective project team. (I have simplified this figure by leaving out the other possible contributors to each development project besides the test team and the development team.)

Figures 1-2 and 1-5 illustrate only two possibilities within a broad range of workable, effective organizational contexts in which testing can get done. I encourage you to explore the various project and organizational realities that affect the test team's organization before deciding which is right for you. I have talked to a lot of satisfied test professionals who worked in very different models from the two I've presented.[13]

Before we leave this topic, though, I'll spend a few paragraphs discussing one way of organizing testers that I find troubling. Some people advocate no test team whatsoever, just testers working alongside programmers within development teams. The arguments I have heard for this type of organization seem to center around the positive effects such integration has in terms of aligning testing with the actual developed system, finding more bugs, and supporting the debugging process.

As I mentioned earlier, I believe some testing should happen this way. I like structural testing as part of organized unit and component testing activities within the development group right at the start of coding. However, I reject the implicit proposition that testers who report to development managers will inevitably outperform testers reporting to independent test managers when measured on test effectiveness and efficiency, bug reporting, bug fix rates, and bug turnaround time. I'll explain why in subsequent chapters.

At this point, though, let me point out that test positions within development and maintenance teams are often considered junior programmer roles. Junior members of the staff tend to have less credibility than more seasoned members of the staff. Earlier I wrote that testing provides value primarily through the delivery of information.

---

13. See Ed Kit's book, *Software Testing in the Real World*, Chapter 13, for an extensive discussion of test organizational structures and the various advantages and disadvantages of each. Brian Marick also discusses test organizational structures and other contextual issues in his paper "Classic Testing Mistakes," found on his Web site at www.testing.com/writings.html.

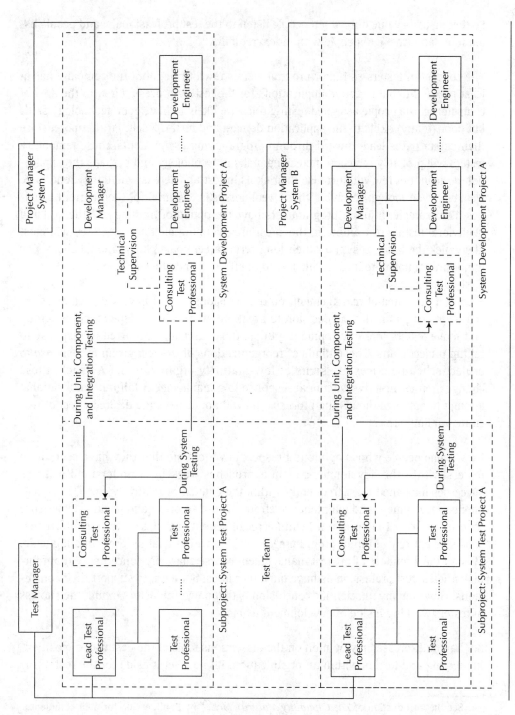

FIGURE 1-5 A VARIATION OF THE MULTIPROJECT TEST SERVICES TEAM ORGANIZATION

So testing adds value only when people listen to the test professionals, and people listen more attentively to people with more credibility.

The concept of testers as junior programmers strewn throughout the company has at least two additional negative implications for the testing process. First, in the area of competence, the people assigned testing roles are likely to have good technology skills but poor (if any) skills in the application domain and testing itself. Furthermore, since their career paths lead upward through programming assignments, these temporary testers will probably focus on increasing skills in technology and perhaps the application domain, but few will increase their skills in testing. Here is where they tend to be weakest, even though resolving these weaknesses is essential for their current activities. For example, if junior programmers have the option of training in structural and behavioral testing or training in the latest programming methodology, they will most likely pick the latter to support their long-term career goals. Such rational choices by junior programmers reduce the likelihood of effective and efficient testing.

Second, in the area of management, on the occasions when I have seen senior or executive managers make the decision to break up an existing independent test group and move testers into development groups, those decisions occurred in response to failing project plans. These kinds of reorganizations of the test group in response to project schedule crises are signs of low-maturity organizations. As such, these changes represent a dysfunctional response to a management failure, not a rational attempt to optimize the testing process, and will not achieve the desired effect of rescuing a failing project.[14]

Now, some people whose opinions I respect have told me that they have seen these testers-within-the-development-team approaches work. As I understand it, these successes happened most frequently within the context of relatively small, low-complexity development and maintenance efforts. These second-hand positive experience reports are true, I'm sure, but I cannot recall seeing any successful test effort that consisted entirely of junior programmers working within a larger programming team. Most of the attendees of my test management course share my concerns. Without formal studies, test professionals have only anecdotes, not data, to support their conclusions. However, my unscientific conclusion is that powerful factors inhibit the success of testers working inside of development teams.

So, having expressed my opinion on the dissentious topic of the best way of positioning testing and testers within an organization, I'll now set it aside for the rest of the

---

14. See the Introduction of *The Capability Maturity Model,* by Paulk et. al., for their comments on organizations that toss out testing at the first sign of a schedule or budget crunch.

book. Organizational structure will affect how some of these processes play out—especially highly contextual ones like results reporting—but won't make any of them vanish. Even test professionals who work alone as the sole testing resource on a project will likely find that most if not all the critical processes discussed in this book apply within their testing context.

MANAGEMENT DIMENSIONS

Part of being on a management or technical leadership career path is that, at some point, you hold your first position where you work regularly with peer and senior managers. Individual contributors for the most part work daily directly with their managers, who provide the individual contributors with daily direction. In such cases, management has one dimension for the individual contributor: interaction with the direct manager. For a senior tester or a test manager reporting bugs and test results to the project team as a primary job duty, that situation will change. When that change happens, it helps to be aware of the dimensions of management and how those affect the reporting of test results.

Earlier, I mentioned four valuable contributions of many test teams.

1. Find bugs that get fixed—or even prevent them.
2. Find bugs that don't get fixed—but are known.
3. Run tests that mitigate (potentially expensive) risks.
4. Guide the project with timely, accurate, credible information.

While the specific contributions your organization wants will vary, one key difference between these contributions is the difficulty required to structure the testing operation to generate the information and to communicate that information effectively to the project team. This is why, in my opinion, many test teams seldom get beyond the first half of the first item, finding defects in the system as currently constituted. In the right organizational, technological, and project contexts, if you can implement good processes for the 12 critical processes outlined in this book, you should be able to create the information that will allow you to achieve maximum return on the testing investment.

The creation of information primarily involves managing inward. By managing inward, I mean carrying out activities within the test team. In terms of critical testing process, these involve what I referred to in the Introduction as primarily internal processes.

But creating the information is not all that's required. The actual realization of the return on the investment happens through the effective communication of that information, and the information created must be linked to the project, organizational, and technological context.

The effective communication of information linked to the appropriate contexts involves primarily upward and outward management. Upward management includes how you communicate with your managers, other senior managers, and executive staff. Outward management includes communication with technical leaders and management peers in development, configuration management and release engineering management, sales, marketing, finance, operations, technical support, business analysis, and so on. See Figure 1-6 for a simplified example, but keep in mind that real projects are much more complicated. Your context might include a different set of specific upward and outward links.

If you are a lead test professional or test manager, your effectiveness in upward and outward management has a lot to do with both your real and perceived effectiveness in your position. To put it another way, your management superiors and peers measure your competence not only by how you create your information, but also—as much, if not more so—by how wisely you pick the information to create and how you communicate that information to them.

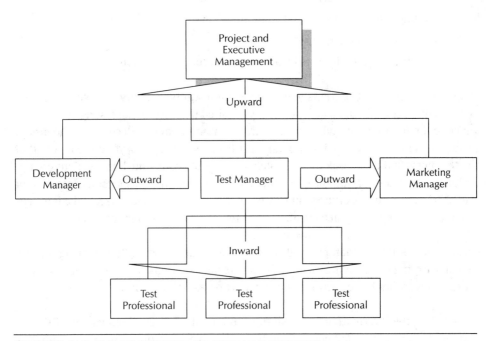

FIGURE 1-6 THE DIMENSIONS OF TEST MANAGEMENT

Upward and outward management presents the lead test professional or test manager with different challenges. Even seasoned software managers may not understand the role and value of testing. The field of software testing now includes a body of knowledge not even experienced test professionals can know completely. That makes the test professional's communication tasks even more difficult. Perhaps most important, when testing is done properly, reporting test results often means relating bad news to your peers and superiors. Competent testers seldom find themselves in the position of saying to the project management team, "All tests were run overnight; no significant bugs were found; ship it."

Upward and outward management challenges, unlike technical problems, don't often have hard-and-fast solutions. There are, however, techniques that can help. As I discuss critical testing processes that involve upward and outward management issues, I'll give you some ideas on how to address those issues.[15]

BEYOND TESTING PROCESS CONTEXT

In the first few pages of this chapter, I introduced the testing process at the highest level and then spent the rest of the chapter defining the contextual issues that affect that process. I'm going to move on to other topics now, but understanding and establishing context is not a one-time activity. Expectations change, new stakeholders join the project team, executives sometimes take a sudden interest in projects, and reorganizations can occur in midstream. Wise test professionals remain vigilant about context to remain effective.

Looking back on this chapter, you can see that we've already covered a lot of ground just in setting context. Establishing the context of testing requires a thorough discussion because the testing process exists in such diverse forms and settings. Understanding the context in which we operate—and sometimes fixing what's dysfunctional in that context—is an essential first step for testers, because it allows us to move from the nearly infinite set of testing tasks we *could* conceivably tackle to a more reasonable set of test tasks within our operational and organizational purview, those testing tasks we *might* perform to add value. The next few chapters will focus on developing a realistic, achievable plan with solid organizational support within the context you've established. I do this by first understanding what I *should* test and, then, what I actually *can* test. Each of those constituent planning processes, and all the subsequent processes that come later in the testing process, must mesh smoothly within the testing context to succeed.

---

15. Portions of this section appeared originally in "Effective Test Status Reporting," in *Software Testing and Quality Engineering* magazine, Volume 2, Issue 2 (Mar/Apr 2000), now available at www.stickyminds.com and www.rexblackconsulting.com.

2

Focus the Effort:
Analyze Quality Risks

W ithin the operational and organizational context established for our testing process, there are many tests we *might* run. In any real-world, complex system, the number of tests we could conceivably run would take person-years—if not person-centuries—to develop and execute. Somehow, we must focus on the vital test conditions we *should* assess, removing from consideration the enormous set of relatively unimportant conditions we *might* assess. What separates what we *might* test from what we *should* test? Quality.

In the previous chapter, I said that the testing process adds value by delivering testing services and information about the risks to system quality. For these services and this information to be valuable, I focus testing on behaviors that matter to customers and users, those behaviors that influence their experiences of quality with the system. Testing unimportant areas of the system gives false confidence where the tests pass and wastes development and testing time on trivial issues where bugs are found. Meanwhile, fundamental defects lurk in untested areas, confronting the users after release. To perform testing that is focused on the most critical risks to system quality, I lay a foundation with quality risk analysis.

Analogously, consider our programmer counterparts. Many development methodologies prescribe requirements gathering before the design and implementation of the system. Requirements gathering allows business analysts, system architects, and programmers to create systems that satisfy users and customers. Omitting requirements gathering can lead to building a system based on the project team's good ideas and best efforts that nonetheless falls short of real customer and user needs. Similarly, quality risk analysis allows us to understand what it would mean for the system under test to have quality—and how we might recognize when it doesn't.

Failure Mode

A particular manner or type of failure in the system; i.e., a category of bugs or failures with some distinctive similarity or similarities. Zero, one, or more specific bugs or failures can fall into a single failure mode (see Chapter 14). In any quality risk analysis where failure modes are considered, the granularity of the failure mode categories—i.e., broad categories that could include many bugs or narrow categories that could include only a few bugs—must be tailored appropriately.

Quality Risk

A potential failure mode, a way in which the system might not meet reasonable user and customer expectations of quality. Note that a quality risk is a potential, not guaranteed, undesirable outcome with a probability greater than zero and less than one.

Categories of quality risks exist. Because failure modes are also categories, categories of quality risks are thus categories of categories of potential bugs.

A QUALITY RISK ANALYSIS PROCESS

Quality risk analysis can follow a straightforward process, as shown in Process 3. You might find that you need to revise and update the risk analysis occasionally during the project. Good times for these revisions are at major milestones such as requirements freeze, design freeze, and code freeze.

JAMAL INTRODUCES THE TEAM TO QUALITY RISK ANALYSIS

After Jamal Brown, the Integration and System Test manager, had his discussion with Kate Hernandez, the product manager, and Jenny Kaufman, the development manager, he spent a little time gathering information about Sumatra and the document management subsystem. The document management subsystem would allow people to create, update, search, and share large collections of documents. Attorneys were a primary target market for this feature. They created, referenced, and retained huge sets of large case-related documents as part of their work. The document manage-

Key Quality and Testing Stakeholders, Key Stakeholders

Those staff members who have immediate contact with customers, users, or the testing process, as well as those who have insight into the technical details of the system.

Step #	Step	Done?
1.	Identify the key testing and quality stakeholders. Obtain stakeholder commitment to participate in a quality risk analysis.	☐
2.	Survey the key stakeholders about the techniques and methods for quality risk analysis. If appropriate, propose a technique. Obtain consensus on the technique and the method selected.	☐
3.	Gather ideas from the key stakeholders about the quality risks, the failure modes associated with those risks, the quality impact of such failures, and the priority of the risks. Identify the recommended action to mitigate each risk.	☐
4.	Report any incipient bugs identified in other project documents during the analysis, such as bad or missing requirements, design problems, and so forth.	☐
5.	Document the quality risks as appropriate for the technique used. Circulate the document to the stakeholders for approval. Iterate steps 3, 4, and 5 as necessary to finalize the quality risks, their priorities, and the recommended actions.	☐
6.	Check the quality risk analysis document(s) into the project library or configuration management system. Place the document under change control.	☐

PROCESS 3   A QUALITY RISK ANALYSIS PROCESS

ment subsystem needed to interact with hierarchical storage management systems with online (disk), near online (optical jukebox), and offline (tape) storage modes.

Jamal then talked to John Albertson, vice president of the Engineering Services group, into which Jamal's test team fit. Jamal explained to John that he'd been reading about a technique for quality risk analysis, Failure Mode and Effect Analysis (FMEA). He'd also spent some time talking with some people who'd had luck applying the technique to software. Given all the trouble Jamal had had over the last couple of releases with getting consensus on the right areas to test, he suggested to John that this tool could help him solve those problems. John encouraged him to give it a try.

Jamal then sent an e-mail to Kate and Jenny as well as Bobbi McDaniels, the Usability Engineering manager, Max del Oro, the vice president of Marketing, and Cosimo Negraev, the Customer Support manager. He let them know that he was going to perform a quality risk analysis to identify what areas needed testing, and he'd like to apply the Failure Mode and Effect Analysis technique. He suggested a full-day off-site meeting to identify and prioritize the quality risks as soon as the first draft of the requirements specifications was complete. Within a few days, Jamal received positive responses from all the participants, so Kate's administrative assistant set up a workshop at a local hotel's conference facility to take place in a week.

Step #	Step	Done?
1.	Identify the key testing and quality stakeholders. Obtain stakeholder commitment to participate in a quality risk analysis.	☑
2.	Survey the key stakeholders about the techniques and methods for quality risk analysis. If appropriate, propose a technique. Obtain consensus on the technique and the method selected.	☑

By the time the Failure Mode and Effect Analysis workshop rolled around, Kate and Max had released the first draft of the requirements specification, and a review of that document had occurred. All the attendees of the Failure Mode and Effect Analysis workshop were at the requirements review meeting, so Jamal saw no need to schedule time at the beginning of the workshop to review the product requirements.

At the workshop, Jamal familiarized the attendees with the Failure Mode and Effect Analysis technique and the concepts of brainstorming.[1] He mentioned that the scope of the Failure Mode and Effect Analysis effort in this case was limited to Sumatra-specific failures, rather than addressing problems that might exist in the current (3.0) release of SpeedyWriter. To start the event, he laid out some broad categories of quality risks into which specific failure modes would fit. Table 2-1 shows the list Jamal presented to the attendees.

Using this list as a launching point, Jamal began to brainstorm with the team on specific failures that fit into each category, and to ask what categories might be missing. Max came up with usability as a missing category, while Cosimo added competitive inferiority. Together, the group conceived about 80 specific failures, after some effort was taken at the end of the brainstorming session to eliminate redundancies and combine overlapping or similar items.

With the list of failure modes identified, it was now time to prioritize their risks to the system and to assign action items to mitigate the critical risks. Jamal explained the adapted Failure Mode and Effect Analysis technique he was using for quantifying risk. He asked the group to consider, for each failure mode identified, three factors—severity, priority, and likelihood—ranking them numerically from 1 (most risky) to 5 (least risky).

---

1. For more details on the Failure Mode and Effect Analysis technique, see Stamatis's book, *Failure Mode and Effect Analysis.* For a more concise treatment, you can also consult the short handbook *The Basics of FMEA,* by McDermott et al.

Quality Risk Category	What Kinds of Problems Fit into This Category?
Functionality	Failures that cause specific functions not to work
Load, capacity, and volume	Failures to handle expected peak concurrent usage levels
Reliability/stability	Failures that take down the system too frequently or keep it down too long
Stress, error handling, and recovery	Failures due to beyond-peak or illegal conditions (e.g., the side effects of deliberately inflicted errors)
Date and time handling	Failures in date or time math, formatting, scheduled events, and other time-dependent operations
Operations and maintenance	Failures that endanger continuing operation, including backup/restore processes, patches and upgrades, and so on
Data quality	Failures in processing, storing, or retrieving data
Performance	Failures to complete tasks on a timely basis under expected loads
Localization	Failures in specific locales, including character set handling, language support, grammar, dictionary, and thesaurus features, and error and help messages
Compatibility	Failures with certain supported browsers, networks, operating systems, and other environment elements
Security/privacy	Failures to protect the system and secured data from fraudulent or malicious misuse
Installation/migration	Failures that prevent or impede deploying the system
Documentation	Failures in installation and operating instructions for users or system administrators
Interfaces	Failures in interfaces between components

TABLE 2-1 GENERAL CATEGORIES OF QUALITY RISKS FOR SPEEDYWRITER

Severity—The seriousness of the effects of bugs in this failure mode, should any exist, from 1 (most damaging) to 5 (least damaging), on the following scale.

1. *Loss of data*—Bugs included in this failure mode could cause loss of user (end user, operator, and so on) or system data.
2. *Loss of functionality*—Bugs included in this failure mode could block use of a major functional area (can include nonfunctional problems like performance that impose unacceptable delays in functionality).

3. *Loss of functionality with a workaround*—Bugs included in this failure mode could block use of a major functional area, but a reasonable affected-user workaround exists.

4. *Partial loss of functionality*—Bugs included in this failure mode could block some unessential portion of a functional area.

5. *Cosmetic error*—Bugs included in this failure mode could allow normal functionality but with significant blemishes (especially in the user interface or system responsiveness).

Priority—The importance of fixing bugs in this failure mode, should any exist, based primarily on the ability of the delivered system to meet customer needs, though also on logistical project issues, regulatory or standards compliance, or other business considerations, from 1 (most important to fix) to 5 (least important to fix).

1. *Urgent*—Bugs included in this failure mode could require immediate resolution.

2. *Essential*—Bugs included in this failure mode could be must-fix for release.

3. *Valuable*—Bugs included in this failure mode could significantly reduce the value of the system to one or more customers or users.

4. *Desirable*—Bugs included in this failure mode could be fixed in this release if possible within feature, budget, and schedule constraints; otherwise, in the next scheduled release.

5. *Discretionary*—Bugs included in this failure mode could be resolved whenever possible in some future release, allowing for other priorities.

Likelihood—The probability of—and extent of impact associated with—bugs included in this failure mode, from 1 (most probable) to 5 (least probable). This rating takes into account three factors. First, for all bugs included in this failure mode, how likely are they to exist in the system, based on technical risk factors like complexity and past defect history? Second, for all bugs included in this failure mode, how likely are they to be missed by the developers (not including testing)? And third, for all bugs included in this failure mode, how likely are they to result in problems in daily use, as part of ongoing operations, or in given installations? If the programmers will not create bugs that cause the failure, or the code review process will catch such bugs, or the users will not use the system in a way to encounter the bugs, then the risk is low. If the underlying bugs will exist, the code reviews will miss them, and users will run into them, then the risk is high.

1. *Very likely*—Will almost certainly affect all users, operations, or installations.

2. *Likely*—Will probably affect many users, operations, or installations.

3. *Possible*—Might very well affect some users, operations, or installations.

4. *Unlikely*—Will probably affect a limited number of users, operations, or installations.

5. *Very unlikely*—Will almost certainly affect few if any users, operations, or installations.

Multiplying these three numbers—severity, priority, and likelihood—yields the risk priority number (RPN), which ranges from 1 (critically dangerous) to 125 (trivially unimportant).

As the group assigned risk priority numbers, they also assigned recommended actions to mitigate the risks during testing. For the most part, these fell into one of four levels of testing.[2]

1. *Extensive testing*—Testers should attempt, within the project constraints, to cover the functions and behaviors in these quality risks both broadly and deeply. When testers observe bugs related to these risks, they should expend significant time to reproduce and isolate the problem as part of writing the bug report.

2. *Balanced testing*—Testers should balance considerations of budget and schedule constraints to create a broad, but not necessarily deep, cadre of tests for the functions and behaviors in these quality risks. When testers see bugs associated with these risks, they should limit the time they spend reproducing and isolating the problem based on their assessment of the bugs' severity and priority.

3. *Opportunity testing*—If in the course of designing, implementing, or executing another test, testers can leverage the setup, testing, or teardown activities, or the data created to support the tests, to perform lightweight testing of some or all of the test conditions related to this quality risk, then they should perform such a test. Testers should limit the time they spend reproducing and isolating any problems found in these risk areas based on their assessment of the bugs' severity and priority.

4. *Reporting observed bugs*—Testers should not design or implement any tests for these quality risks but should report bugs related to these if they observe such problems. Testers should limit the time they spend reproducing and isolating the problem based on their assessment of the bugs' severity and priority.

---

2. As one of this book's reviewers, Steve Splaine, pointed out to me, we can also consider the relative expense of testing compared with other measures we might take to mitigate a given risk. Perhaps we can redesign the system, buy insurance, use code reviews, or some other approach.

The Sumatra team assigned these degrees of testing based on risk priority number. Risks with risk priority numbers from 1 to 8 were assigned extensive testing. Those with risk priority numbers from 9 to 24 were assigned balanced testing. Those with risk priority numbers from 25 to 48 were assigned opportunity testing. No testing was recommended for those risks with risk priority numbers above 50, though bugs in these areas would be reported. Exceptions occurred for some risks right at the boundaries. For example, two risks in the area of data quality were assigned risk priority numbers of 8, but the team recommended balanced testing because it was felt that extensive testing would consume too much time for the level of risk posed.[3]

Step #	Step	Done?
3.	Gather ideas from the key stakeholders about the quality risks, the failure modes associated with those risks, the quality impact of such failures, and the priority of the risks. Identify the recommended action to mitigate each risk.	✔

During Failure Mode and Effect Analysis, the Sumatra team noticed two areas of concern that were missing from the requirements specification. First, the requirements did not describe how the system should handle access permissions, relying instead by default on network logins. They realized that the system should also allow users to change their account identity within the document management subsystem itself. Second, the requirements specification didn't mention what should happen when the librarian did not load a needed media item like a tape, CD, or optical disk. Both these omissions served as early defect detection for the requirements document.

Step #	Step	Done?
4.	Report any incipient bugs identified in other project documents during the analysis, such as bad or missing requirements, design problems, and so forth.	✔

Based on the meeting, Jamal prepared the Failure Mode and Effect Analysis document (see Figure 2-1). He sent this document to all the attendees of the meeting, as well as to Harold Jones, the vice president of System Engineering. The various recipients made a few comments adjusting severity, priority, and likelihood up or down, but

---

3. In some cases, I'll include *cursory testing* as a category between *balanced testing* and *opportunity testing*. Cursory testing involves sampling a small number of quality risks in a particular area. I might also include *no testing* as a category after *reporting observed bugs*. No testing means that I won't report a bug even if I find one that relates to the quality risk in question.

Failure Mode and Effect Analysis (Quality Risk Analysis) Form

System Name: SpeedyWriter (with Document Management System add-on) Model/Product: SpeedyWriter Release 3.1 (w/ DMS)
Product Manager: Kate Hernandez Target Release Date: 1Q2003
Project Manager: Jenny Kaufman Prepared By: Jamal Brown
Other Stakeholders: Bobbi McDaniels (Dev), Max del Oro (Mkt), Cosimo Negraev (Sprt) FMEA Date: September 11, 2002
Test Manager: Jamal Brown FMEA Rev Date: N/A

Risk ID Number	Quality Risk Category	Failure Mode/Quality Risk/Effect	Severity	Priority	Likelihood	Risk Priority Number	Recommended Action	Who/ Which Phase (Unit, Component, Integration, System)?
1.000	Functionality	Failures that cause specific features not to work						
1.001		Regression of existing SpeedyWriter features.	1	1	3	3	Rerun entire R3.0 test set.	Test/IS
1.002		Can't cancel incomplete actions using cancel or back.	2	3	4	24	Opportunity testing.	N/A
1.003		Can't get and select from list of managed files.	2	1	3	6	Extensive testing.	Dev/UC-Test/IS
1.004		Can't get and select from a list of non-managed files.	2	1	4	8	Balanced testing.	Dev/UC-Test/IS
1.005		Check-in of new document to DMS fails.	2	1	2	4	Extensive testing.	Dev/UC-Test/IS
1.006		Check-in of existing document to DMS fails.	1	1	2	2	Extensive testing.	Dev/UC-Test/IS
1.007		Check-out of DMS documents fails.	1	1	2	2	Extensive testing.	Dev/UC-Test/IS
1.008		Load of online DMS document fails.	1	1	3	3	Extensive testing.	Dev/UC-Test/IS
1.009		Load of near online DMS document fails..	1	2	3	6	Extensive testing.	Dev/UC-Test/IS
1.010		Load of offline DMS document fails.	1	2	3	6	Extensive testing.	Dev/UC-Test/IS
1.011		Can't display or modify doc properties in DMS before saving.	2	3	5	30	Opportunity testing.	N/A
	Quality Risk Category Priority					2		
2.000	Load, Capacity, and Volume	Failures in scaling of system to expected peak concurrent usage levels						
2.001		System fails at or before 25 concurrent users.	1	1	3	3	Extensive testing.	Test/S
2.002		System fails at or before 255 concurrent users.	1	3	2	6	Extensive testing.	Test/S
2.003		System disallows 255 or fewer user accounts.	1	1	3	3	Extensive testing.	Test/S
2.004		System disallows 32,767 or fewer user accounts.	1	3	3	9	Balanced testing.	Test/S
2.005		System fails on documents larger than 100KB.	1	1	1	1	Extensive testing.	Test/S

FIGURE 2-1 THE TOP PORTION OF THE INITIAL FAILURE MODE AND EFFECT ANALYSIS REPORT

other than that, they deemed the document acceptable. Jamal finalized the changes and then checked the document into the project repository.

Step #	Step	Done?
5.	Document the quality risks as appropriate for the technique used. Circulate the document to the stakeholders for approval. Iterate steps 3, 4, and 5 as necessary to finalize the quality risks, their priorities, and the recommended actions.	✔
6.	Check the quality risk analysis document(s) into the project library or configuration management system. Place the document under change control.	✔

With the quality risk analysis performed, Jamal now had consensus from the Sumatra project management team on what areas *should be* tested. *Could* Jamal and his intrepid band of testers address all those areas, though? To answer this question, Jamal moved on to developing an estimate and a plan, as we'll see in the next few chapters.

RECOGNIZE A GOOD QUALITY RISK ANALYSIS PROCESS

There's a significant investment of time and attention required to execute a risk analysis process such as the one Jamal and his colleagues went through, but it's a good investment. (A less formal risk analysis can be cheaper and easier than a formal approach like Failure Mode and Effect Analysis.) A good quality risk analysis involves the following behaviors and provides the following benefits.

INVOLVE THE RIGHT PARTICIPANTS

Anyone in an organization can have opinions about the risks to system quality and the users' and customers' expectation of quality. When I initiate and facilitate a quality risk analysis, though, I choose participants based not on their opinions, but on who has insight into what defines quality and what risks to system quality exist. The important perspectives include

- The purposes for which the customers acquire the system and the uses to which the users put it
- The valuable system behaviors
- The narrow mission of the system and the broader mission(s) of organization(s) in which the system will be used

- The strategic marketing and technical direction for the product line (sometimes referred to as the *product road map*) or system family and for the companies developing, maintaining, acquiring, and using the system
- The process and technology used to design, implement, and maintain the system
- The capabilities and limitations of the testing process, the test team, and the test system

Table 2-2 describes the roles played by potential participants, since it is these roles that give individuals insight into these areas, along with some typical titles for people in these roles. Note that organizations building products for a market or a contract customer tend to differ from those building products for in-house users, so not all these roles will exist in your organization.

Table 2-2 is only a partial listing of the players who might be involved. Do you need—or even want—to invite everyone? Probably not. A quality risk analysis that looks at the requirements demands one set of participants, one that looks at the design demands another, and one that looks at implementation demands a third. The test participants may remain the same, or the test manager may delegate expert test engineers to handle the lower-level areas while participating personally only in the requirements-level analysis.

Some of the stakeholders may exist but not be available for the quality risk analysis. The customers and users are the most important example of this. It is ideal, if possible, to involve them in a requirements-based quality risk analysis, and those doing in-house information systems projects can sometimes do so. However, for those projects producing contract customer or mass-market systems, current customers and users often can't participate, and future customers and users are often unknown. In these cases, those key stakeholders who are closest to the customers and users—sales, marketing, technical support, and so on—must represent the users' and customers' interests in these analyses, serving as proxy stakeholders for the missing participants.

While some number of proxy stakeholders may be acceptable, my best experiences with good quality risk analysis were cross-functional and involved as many of the stakeholders as possible. The more perspectives we can get across the entire organization, the more comprehensive our list of risks and the more meaningful our prioritization of those risks will be. While requirements or design specifications are indeed helpful inputs for quality risk analysis, active, engaged cross-functional participation is a more important factor in the success of the quality risk analysis process. Let me illustrate with two anecdotes.

Role	Typical Title(s)	Gives Insight Into . . .
Position the system in the market	Marketing manager	System's value to customer or user
Gather requirements for the system	Business analysts Systems analysts	The users' needs and the mission the system will serve
Plot strategic product-line direction	Marketing manager Product manager Chief architect Chief scientist	Product or system road map
Select and guide strategic technical direction	Chief architect Development manager VP of development Chief scientist Chief information officer	Technical focus for long-term growth
Design the system under test	Business analyst System analyst Product architect Development manager Lead programmer	Constraints and limitations of the system design
Build the system under test	Development manager Lead programmer Programmer Member of the technical staff System analyst	Constraints and limitations of the system implementation
Design the test system	Test manager Lead test engineer	Constraints and limitations of testing
Document system behavior	Technical writer Technical publications manager	What you tell the users the system will actually do
Test the system	Lead test engineer Test engineer Test technician	Defects found in previous systems Challenging test cases
Interact with the customers and users	Sales manager Sales representative Sales engineer Account representative Business analyst	What behaviors the customers care about

TABLE 2-2 POSSIBLE PARTICIPANTS IN THE QUALITY RISK ANALYSIS PROCESS

Role	Typical Title(s)	Gives Insight Into . . .
Work with subsystem vendor(s)	Supplier quality engineer	What the vendor(s) test Known defects in the vendors' subsystems
Deploy/deliver the system	Release engineer Release manager MIS or IT manager	Technical challenges associated with building the system
Support the deployed environment	Network operations manager System administrator Configuration manager MIS manager	Behaviors of the network, hardware, and cohabiting software Operating procedures Exceptional procedures (e.g., disaster recovery)
Support the user and customers	Customer support manager Technical support manager User support manager Customer care manager Help desk staffer MIS manager	Actual usage profiles Known defects
Repair defects in deployed systems	Customer support engineer Technical support programmer Member of the technical staff	Known defects The difficulty of changing deployed systems
Fund or support the funding of the development or maintenance of the system	Customer (internal or external)	The business problem they want the system to solve or the value they expect it to add
Employ the system, directly or indirectly	User (in various classes)	How they use the system to solve a real problem or add value What typical data sets and scenarios are What problems they've had in the past
Be responsible for quality assurance processes	Quality assurance engineer Software engineering process group manager Quality assurance manager	Ensuring consistency of process and quality across all development efforts
Take personal ownership of product quality	Director of quality Chief executive officer Chief operating officer President	What defines "good enough" to wear the company badge

TABLE 2-2 CONTINUED

In one case, my lead test engineers and I applied Failure Mode and Effect Analysis where the project team had good written project documents, including requirements and design specifications. However, the project team did not participate in the analysis. Instead, we e-mailed drafts of the documents to the project team. Many of the key stakeholders declined to spend the time to give us good input. We ended up canceling tests during test execution—tests for which we'd spent significant time and resources developing data, cases, the test environment, and so forth—because the assessed levels of risk were not aligned with project priorities. In other words, the benefit of focusing the test effort was not realized because of the lack of stakeholder participation. The project documentation was simply not an acceptable substitute for cross-functional input in the quality risk analysis.

In another case, I used Failure Mode and Effect Analysis where the project team had no written project documents whatsoever. The cross-functional team that participated in the quality risk analysis brought all the knowledge needed to the meeting in their heads. This analysis was a success. The prevention of bugs through programming process changes and the detection of bugs through properly focused testing contributed to an on-time, quality product release. Certainly, the lack of requirements and design documentation had a negative impact on the project, including the testing effort. However, it did not significantly retard the quality risk analysis.

EMPLOY THE RIGHT TECHNIQUE

There are a number of techniques now available to us as test professionals when we want to analyze quality risks. I'm familiar with four powerful techniques that are being applied regularly with success.

- *Informal*—Identify a list of potential problems for the system, and then work with the key stakeholders to prioritize that list. Sources for this list of potential problems can include books, standard lists of software quality problems, your field failure list, and institutional knowledge about the kinds of bugs that afflict the type of system you're building.[4]
- *ANSI/ISO 9126 standard*—Within six quality characteristics—functionality, reliability, usability, efficiency, maintainability, and portability (FRUEMP)—define quality subcharacteristics, metrics for measuring the system's quality based on

---

4. For four lists of typical system defects, see the taxonomy of bugs in Boris Beizer's *Software Testing Techniques*, the appendix of common bugs in Cem Kaner et al., *Testing Computer Software*, Peter Neumann's *Computer-Related Risks*, and my list of software and hardware quality risks in *Managing the Testing Process, Second Edition*.

each subcharacteristic, and finally a way of translating those metrics into an assessment of quality.[5]

- *Cost of exposure (COE)*—Identify the potential problems and their effects, and then assess the cost to the business of the problem should it occur and the likelihood of its occurrence.

- *Failure Mode and Effect Analysis*—Identify the potential problems, understanding their effects (on customers and users), and then classify them (with stakeholder advice) in terms of severity (system impact), priority (business impact), and likelihood (chance of failure).

These are listed in order of increasing structure and precision. My preference is to be precise and quantitative whenever that's practical, so I like to apply the Failure Mode and Effect Analysis technique. However, I've found that technique doesn't always work in informal or fast-paced project contexts. So, I pick whichever technique matches the overall level of structure and precision pervasive in the project I'm working on. A formal analysis such as Failure Mode and Effect Analysis or cost of exposure requires commitment from the project team to participate in an often-extensive cross-functional meeting. An informal approach may involve simply talking to the key stakeholders one-on-one and circulating a short document to everyone later to get concurrence. Thus, the informal approach results in a more lightweight process that you might find easier to implement.

The more structured and formal approaches result in a more carefully calibrated, precisely targeted testing effort. In the Sumatra case study, the assignment of levels of testing based on risk priority numbers is an example of that kind of precise targeting. However, applying such techniques requires more skill and knowledge than the informal methods. For example, it took me six or seven projects to get really comfortable and proficient at Failure Mode and Effect Analysis. If you don't have the time to study the more structured techniques, don't want to take such a big step all at once, or just would rather ease into quality risk analysis, you may want to start with the informal approach.

---

5. See the ANSI/ISO Standard 9126 guide, and for a discussion on applying this standard, see "Measuring Software Product Quality during Testing," by van Veenendaal et al. This is also discussed in Pol et al.'s book about T-MAP. In addition, Stephen Kan's *Metrics and Models in Software Quality Engineering, Second Edition,* references two other quality lists for software with memorable acronyms—functionality, usability, reliability, performance, and sustainability (FURPS), along with capability, usability, performance, reliability, installability, maintainability, and operability (CUPRIMO)—that you can add to your FRUEMP mnemonic as a way of thinking about system quality. Finally, Karl Wiegers has an interesting discussion about quality attributes for software—including trade-offs between such attributes—in Chapter 11 of *Software Requirements*.

You can migrate from an informal to a formal technique if you later find that you need that kind of precision. I often use the informal technique as the foundation for Failure Mode and Effect Analysis, just to get the initial set of quality risk categories identified.

Whichever technique you use, the desired output is a prioritized list of risks to the quality of the system. The priorities assigned to each risk determine, to a great extent, the testing effort required. Typically, significant risks require thorough testing, moderate risks deserve limited testing, and unimportant risks get no testing at all.

Risk levels can be assigned non-numeric (e.g., high, moderate, low, none) or numeric values. I've encountered various numeric scales. I prefer a 1-to-5 descending scale for each of the three variables in Failure Mode and Effect Analysis, but one of my test management seminar attendees told me that his employer uses a 0-to-9 ascending scale based on the Quality Functional Deployment (QFD) technique, where 9 means high, 3 means moderate, 1 means low, and 0 means none. D. H. Stamatis uses a 1-to-10 ascending scale in his book *Failure Mode and Effect Analysis*.

Cost of exposure and Failure Mode and Effect Analysis are different in terms of format and presentation, but I've found I can convert from one to the other. Figure 2-2 shows the result of translating Figure 2-1 from Failure Mode and Effect Analysis to COE, which took me about an hour, including changing the 1-to-5 scale to the 0-to-9 scale mentioned earlier for Quality Functional Deployment.

A final note here is to keep in mind that you needn't use the same technique every time or even the same technique across every phase of the project. In some cases, you might want to use a business risk–focused analysis for integration and system testing, and a design and implementation risk–focused analysis for unit and component testing. Perhaps an informal approach is sufficient for unit and component testing, while a more formal approach like COE or Failure Mode and Effect Analysis is needed for integration and system testing. You'll sacrifice a little in consistency and cross-functional and cross-project coordination, but the flexibility can pay off in a more lightweight process that consumes fewer resources and allows you to move forward when time is critical.

SEPARATE THE VITAL FEW FROM THE TRIVIAL MANY

Whichever technique you apply, the power of the quality risk analysis lies in how you can use it to differentiate between major risks that you must address extensively,

Cost of Exposure Analysis (Quality Risk Analysis) Form

System Name: SpeedyWriter (with Document Management System add-on)
Product Manager: Kate Hernandez
Project Manager: Jenny Kaufman
Other Stakeholders: B. McDaniels (Dev), M. del Oro (Mkt), C. Negraev (Support)
Test Manager: Jamal Brown

Model/Product: SpeedyWriter Release 3.1 (w/ DMS)
Target Release Date: 1Q2003
Prepared By: Jamal Brown
COE Analyzed On: September 11, 2002
COE Revised On: N/A

Risk ID Number	Quality Risk Category	Failure Mode/Quality Risk/Effect	Potential Cost	Likelihood	Risk Priority Number	Recommended Action	Who/Which Phase (Unit, Component, Integration, System)?
1.000	Functionality	Failures that cause specific features not to work					
1.001		Regression of existing SpeedyWriter features.	9	3	27	Rerun entire R3.0 test set.	Test/IS
1.002		Can't cancel incomplete actions using cancel or back.	3	1	3	Opportunity testing.	N/A
1.003		Can't get and select from list of managed files.	9	3	27	Extensive testing.	Dev/UC-Test/IS
1.004		Can't get and select from a list of non-managed files.	9	1	9	Balanced testing.	Dev/UC-Test/IS
1.005		Check-in of new document to DMS fails.	9	9	81	Extensive testing.	Dev/UC-Test/IS
1.006		Check-in of existing document to DMS fails.	9	9	81	Extensive testing.	Dev/UC-Test/IS
1.007		Check-out of DMS documents fails.	9	9	81	Extensive testing.	Dev/UC-Test/IS
1.008		Load of online DMS document fails.	9	3	27	Extensive testing.	Dev/UC-Test/IS
1.009		Load of near online DMS document fails.	9	3	27	Extensive testing.	Dev/UC-Test/IS
1.010		Load of offline DMS document fails.	9	3	27	Extensive testing.	Dev/UC-Test/IS
1.011		Can't display or modify doc properties in DMS before saving.	3	0	0	Report observed bugs.	N/A
	Quality Risk Category Priority				81		
2.000	Load, Capacity, and Volume	Failures in scaling of system to expected peak concurrent usage levels					
2.001		System fails at or before 25 concurrent users.	9	3	27	Extensive testing.	Test/S
2.002		System fails at or before 255 concurrent users.	9	3	27	Extensive testing.	Test/S
2.003		System disallows 255 or fewer user accounts.	9	3	27	Extensive testing.	Test/S
2.004		System disallows 32,767 or fewer user accounts.	9	3	27	Balanced testing.	Test/S
2.005		System fails on documents larger than 100KB.	9	9	81	Extensive testing.	Test/S

FIGURE 2-2 INITIAL QUALITY RISK ANALYSIS RECAST IN COST-OF-EXPOSURE FORMAT

tolerable risks that you will address to some extent, and minor risks that you will for the most part ignore. To use an analogy, the risk analysis techniques are grates that catch rocks while not becoming plugged with sand.

I have observed a natural tendency, though, for the coarse grates to become fine filters. Participants in the risk analysis process resist making the hard choices and doing the rigorous thinking required to differentiate the potential showstoppers from the merely irritating. When this happens, every risk gets classified as a high risk. That may be true when dealing with safety-critical systems, but for most systems there exist a whole host of bugs that no development management team would delay a release to resolve or that are connected to any realistic user scenario.

Good testing looks for the bugs that can affect the users' and customers' experiences of quality. These are typically the problems that marketing, sales, business, or technical support managers will delay a release to have fixed. Testing for other kinds of problems, while perhaps noble and frequently praised at the beginning of the test effort, often results in ignored bug reports and dropped test suites at the end of a project.

It helps to frame the quality risk analysis discussion properly. The key question is not, Would we *prefer that* the system not have this particular failure mode on release? This question is not connected to project realities. In isolation, everyone is *for* better quality. The key question is, rather, What would we *give up* to ensure that the system not have this particular failure mode on release? In other words, is a potential quality problem something the project management team will pay to find and fix in terms of extra money spent on testing, foregoing revenues or possibly even deleting features while the release or deployment slips? Framing the matter this way allows you to get a more accurate assessment of risk priority.

FIND POTENTIAL BUGS BEFORE TESTING

Often, the value from doing a quality risk analysis starts to accrue before the first test case is written. Consider the quality risk analysis process as a form of structured peer review. Like any review process, the lessons learned from the process can diffuse into and influence the entire effort. This happens in three major ways.

First, the analysis can find actual instances of ambiguous, untestable, or unachievable requirements, design weaknesses, and even, if done at a code level, potentially problematic data structures and control flows. In that sense, the quality risk analysis process brings about a review of these documents, seen through the unique and helpful prism of risks to system quality.[6]

Second, beyond finding problems, the quality risk analysis process can also point toward solutions. For example, I have done quality risk analysis where the recommended action to mitigate particular quality risks included enhancing the code review process, the use of assertions in the system, step-by-step tracing of program execution in critical areas, and other defensive programming and quality assurance techniques. While the Sumatra case study shows the use of Failure Mode and Effect Analysis to focus testing, it can be used for true quality assurance purposes.

Third, the prioritization process acts as an early notification to the programming team of what we will test. As Boris Beizer has pointed out, sometimes the "threat of a test" is all that's required to prevent bugs.[7]If the development team knows where the test effort will focus, they might spend extra effort making sure those parts work.

In these ways quality risk analysis reduces the number of bugs that show up during test execution. As discussed in Chapter 4, bugs that are caught in the requirements and design stages cost significantly less to fix than those detected during testing. Before adopting techniques that lead to defect prevention, though, organizations must set aside counterproductive practices. Examples of practices that impede bug detection are tester incentives or performance reviews based on the number of bugs found during testing. In such situations, astute testers will soon grasp that they are working against their own interests by helping to prevent bugs.

When the quality risk assessment is used for preventive activities—e.g., requirements clarification, design improvement, defensive programming, and other quality assurance measures—make sure that everyone understands the need to further mitigate important quality risks with the appropriate degree of testing. As a test professional, I believe in prevention. However, I also exercise professional pessimism. How do I *know* that we've prevented a bug unless I test for that bug and satisfy myself it's not there? As the Russian proverb goes, "Trust but verify."

---

6. Ideally, the project team will also employ other methods of reviewing requirements, design, and code, rather than relying solely on quality risk analysis. For example, see Karl Wiegers's book *Software Requirements* for ideas on requirements reviews and also Rodger Drabick's article "On-Track Requirements," in *Software Testing and Quality Engineering*, Volume 1, Issue 3 (May/June 1999).

7. See Boris Beizer's *Software Testing Techniques* for this and other observations on how testing works—and doesn't work.

START AT THE RIGHT TIME

In the Sumatra case study, Jamal and his colleagues started the quality risk analysis as soon as a first draft of the requirements document was reviewed. Is this the right time? The Sumatra team didn't have the design specification, especially the network and software architecture, which can suggest a variety of design-specific failure modes, such as race conditions in databases and single points of failure with nonredundant servers. In addition to informing quality risk analysis teams about other possible problems, design information gives participants insight into the technical risk. Such insight enables those performing the quality risk analysis to do a better job of assessing the likelihood of the failure mode existing in the system. So, should quality risk analysis wait until the design specification is complete?

To some extent, the answer to this question depends on the testing techniques I will apply. On one hand, if I intend to do a lot of structural testing, having insight into the design and implementation of the system may be necessary for the risk analysis. If, on the other hand, my testing will be behavioral, I don't care too much how the system is built. While the structural details can improve the accuracy of the risk assessment in terms of technical likelihood, most of the other factors that one would consider in the quality risk analysis—and indeed the factors the Sumatra project team considered in their Failure Mode and Effect Analysis—have to do with impact on the user.

You can also do the quality risk analysis of the requirements and then have a shorter follow-up session once the design specification is completed. You could even repeat the follow-up a third time as more information becomes available in detailed or component-level design documents. I'm not recommending a quality risk review once a week, but certainly spending a little time at major project milestones revising the quality risk assessments is a smart idea. As the factors influencing the risk assessments become more technical, the list of appropriate attendees may tilt toward system architects and senior programmers and away from marketing and sales people.

ADAPT TO CHANGE

Sources of information that influence risk assessments do not arise solely at project milestones. It's also true that business priorities change over time, even during well-managed, stable projects. The likelihood of particular kinds of failures will become clearer once you have some experience testing the real system. I can count on learning more about the quality risks to the system as design, system development, and test development proceed. Sometimes it turns out that we have underestimated the resources and time required for the degree of testing agreed upon during the quality risk analysis. This means that fine-tuning and adjustment is required throughout the testing project. The quality risk analysis process needs to support, not stifle, continuous learning about risk and how best to manage it.

The usual approach to change management is to check the quality risk analysis document into the project repository and place it under a change control discipline, typically a change control board (CCB), which I'll discuss in Chapter 16. As the project team learns, and as project milestones drive the quality risk analysis update activities, the test manager—or whoever owns the risk analysis process—checks the quality risk analysis document out, updates the document as part of the review process, and then brings the updated document to the change control board for approval. While it's possible that the risk analysis found reductions in some risks—e.g., by discovering that the network or server architecture used to implement some piece of the system is resistant to some particular failure—the new risk analysis will typically result in some incremental increase in the scope of the overall test effort. If good planning is done up front (see Chapters 6 and 7), then this should not surprise people.

In some cases, though, you will discover large new areas of risk that imply significant changes to test project scope. Suppose the design specification for SpeedyWriter reveals that we want to have this system work not only on company intranets, but also across the Internet as an Application Service Provider system. Though this is not a product requirement for the current release, the system architect has decided that now is the time to position the system technically for such a challenge. This implies a number of new areas of testing, including slow (dial-up) connections as well as refinements to some existing areas, like browser compatibility and security.

Risk can change not only when we discover new risks, but also because of increases in risk in areas that everyone thought were handled. To give an example, on one project I managed, we discovered fairly late in the game that the performance test activities agreed to by one subsystem vendor in a large project had not been done. I discovered this omission when tracing test coverage back to the quality risk analysis (see Chapters 10 and 11). This discovery gave the project team a chance to increase the amount of testing needed to address the performance-related risks to system quality during integration and system testing. Of course, it would have been better had the omission not occurred, but the quality risk analysis gave us a tool to adapt to this change.

Ultimately, any change requires a reconsideration of the feature, quality, schedule, and budget trade-offs inherent in any system development effort. Effective project management teams know how to use such opportunities to revisit a decision with new learning in hand. Acting on better knowledge leads to better decisions. I work to set up processes that support this continual improvement and refinement of understanding.

Change control boards are often part of how that happens, providing a forum for open discussion and consensus building about the trade-offs involved.

In some organizations, people aren't this organized. In that case, you can use regular updates to the quality risk analysis document, along with a review of changes with the stakeholders. If you have the support of your stakeholders, you can schedule meetings at major project milestones, even without the benefit of the change control board. It'll mean more work for the test team, coordinating these trade-off decisions in the absence of a structure to guide the discussion, but testers can still gain significant value from the quality risk analysis process and continual updates of the analysis itself.

I find that I must remain watchful for changes in organizational, operational, technological, and project context and increases in knowledge that affect the quality risk analysis. I also have to be prepared to respond to those changes proactively. Rather than viewing this as a dreaded circumstance, I recognize that responding to changes means doing a more effective job of helping the project team manage quality risks.

HANDLE CHALLENGES

Before you start implementing quality risk analysis in your organization, you'll need to make a few decisions and develop some tricks to cope with some hurdles you'll likely encounter.

GETTING PEOPLE TO GET REAL ABOUT RISK

Risk is a concept that many people find familiar but seldom deal with rationally. Some people who drive cars every day without a second thought obsess about the possibility of being killed in a plane crash, even though people are a hundred times more likely to die in a car. Attempts to legislate risk out of existence go on in government bodies the world over, imposing tremendous inefficiencies in the name of marginal reductions in risk. People tend not to learn much about probability, statistics, and risk in schools or colleges, unless they are pursuing careers in mathematics, business, investment, or insurance. Very few reporters do an effective job of explaining risk to people in news stories that involve the topic. I only became aware of the levels of risk in my life and effective at managing them by studying risk and statistics.[8]

---

8. For two excellent, practical, nontechnical discussions about risk, see Peter Bernstein's *Against the Gods* and James Walsh's *True Odds*. These books don't address system testing, but they helped me understand risk and therefore my job. Most basic undergraduate-level textbooks on statistics are useful resources, too.

An inability to deal rationally with risk can cause problems on system development, maintenance, and acquisition projects. One test manager once told me that she had difficulty explaining risks to system quality to her managers. During two development efforts, she had warned them about serious gaps in their test coverage and advised them about the potential negative effects bugs in those areas could have on their customers. After each release, when those bugs failed to materialize, these managers would tell her, "See, the risk wasn't that high after all." She told me she was confused and had started to wonder if perhaps they were right.[9]

Undoubtedly, sometimes project managers are right when they make such proclamations. But sometimes they're just lucky. Sometimes very lucky. And luck never holds forever.

A misleading aspect of risk is that when we look toward the future, there is some statistical probability that an undesirable outcome will occur. The exact value of this probability, somewhere between zero and one, is usually unknown. When we look back to the past, though, the undesirable outcome either has or has not occurred. Probabilities of past events are either zero or one. To draw conclusions about risk levels based on a small number of fortunate outcomes indicates wishful thinking about how risk actually works. Our industry is replete with defunct companies—sometimes formerly major players like Ashton-Tate, the once-dominant player in the PC database sector—that took dangerous risks with quality once too often.

It's helpful to understand that expecting rational decision making about risk all the time from everyone in a project is expecting too much. A number of irrational factors will enter into every risk decision that people make. When people find a particular risk frightening, when the consequences are immediate and extremely dangerous in the short run, or when people have seen others take the same risk and pay a high price, they will tend to avoid such a risk, often more than the true likelihood and probable impact would rationally require. Conversely, when people imagine that they have control over the risk, when it's a risk they have chosen (and rationalized), when the consequences lie out in the distant future, or when similar risks have been run in the past with no negative outcome, people will accept such risks to a greater extent than logic would dictate.[10]

---

9. An interesting article on this political dimension, "The Risk in Risk Management" by Peter de Jaeger, appeared in *Software Testing and Quality Engineering* magazine, Volume 3, Issue 4 (Jul/Aug 2001).
10. For a further discussion of this topic, see Erik Simmons's excellent presentation "The Human Side of Risk," first published in *The Proceedings of the Fifteenth International Internet and Software Quality Week 2002* and now available at www.rexblackconsulting.com.

As test professionals, we tend to have lots of shared horror stories about how taking on certain quality risks led to a disaster. Therefore, for both rational and irrational reasons, I find that we tend to err on the side of excessive risk aversion. I've seen testers warn about certain pet quality risks over and over, on project after project. On each project, project managers ignored these warnings over and over, too. Not spending time on these risks turned out to be the right decision. Over a dozen or so releases, problems related to these quality risks didn't appear in the field. The testers were probably overestimating the likelihood of those quality risks.

However, a company that operates an e-commerce business, for example, and chooses not to load test or security test their Web site will eventually suffer a loss because of unmitigated risks in these areas. Competent system development, maintenance, and acquisition managers have learned to manage risk effectively, which is essential to avoiding significant financial damage to—and sometimes the complete demise of—the organization. As a test manager, I consider myself responsible for bringing realistic assessments of quality risks, including potential losses, to the project management team.

QUALITY RISKS FROM VARIOUS SOURCES

In the case study, all the quality risks Jamal and the cross-functional team identify relate to the nature of the system being developed. They start with various categories of failures to which systems are subject and then identify specific failure modes within those categories. In other words, they examine the quality risks that arise from the system context, because they're implementing functionality in some particular digital computer hardware and software architecture and technology rather than in, say, wire and beads, a set of gears, or plastic and wood.[11]

However, along with the quality risks associated with the system itself, there are quality risks associated with the project, the process, and even the organizational context within which the system is developed. For example, suppose the requirements continue to change until perilously close to the release date. Personally, I handle these kinds of risks during the test planning process (see Chapters 6 and 7). However, you can apply Failure Mode and Effect Analysis or other risk analysis techniques to iden-

---

11. The Museé des Arts et Métiers (Museum of Arts and Sciences) in Paris, France, includes an interesting collection of mechanical computers, including an abacus, an example of Charles Babbage's analytical engine, and a slide rule. When I saw those computers, I wondered how I would test them. I then wondered how upcoming leaps forward in computer technology— for example, the quantum-based computers scientists are working on now—will change the way we test systems.

tify and mitigate these risks, too. D. H. Stamatis, in his book *Failure Mode and Effect Analysis*, discusses the use of this technique for process-related quality risks.

WHO DRIVES THE QUALITY RISK ANALYSIS BUS?

The quality risk analysis process I describe in this chapter is a powerful technique. As I mentioned earlier, that power derives to a great extent from cross-functional participation. In fact, many quality assurance techniques create structured conversations that transcend organizational boundaries, focusing key stakeholders on a specific issue. However, the very cross-functional nature of such processes, and the wide nets they cast, can make people wonder who should initiate and facilitate the processes. This is a context-sensitive question. You might work in a company with a formal development process and a quality assurance group tasked with overall process and system quality. In such a setting, quality risk analysis might belong to some member of that quality organization.

In his book *Software Project Survival Guide*, Steve McConnell discusses risk management in the broadest sense, identifying and mitigating the significant risks that endanger our system development and maintenance efforts. McConnell recommends that each project have a risk officer who is in charge of making sure risks are identified, prioritized, and appropriately mitigated.[12] In such cases, this risk officer would be the natural owner of the quality risk analysis process.

Based on what I've seen and heard, though, the test team often inherits this process. Because this process is at its most powerful when it is cross-functional, that has some serious technical, personal, and political implications for the test professional who initiates and facilitates quality risk analysis.

On a technical level, the person must have the appropriate skill in the technique chosen. Informal methods are easiest and perhaps the best approach for the first-time practitioner, especially when the overall development process is not very organized. If you feel you need to try the more advanced techniques like Failure Mode and Effect Analysis, T-MAP, or ISO 9126, I recommend reading the reference materials mentioned in the Employ the Right Technique section earlier in this chapter. You might also want to prepare a summary of the technique for the other participants.

In the personal realm, the person running a quality risk analysis needs skills in the softer team management techniques of brainstorming, resolving conflicts and disagreements,

---

12. See *Software Project Survival Guide*, pages 93–101.

keeping a meeting on agenda and schedule, and so forth. Most seasoned managers acquire these skills over time, but if you haven't had a chance to pick them up, at least study the ideas first. Long, complex discussions such as those that arise during quality risk analyses take real personal skill to facilitate.

In addition, a test professional who runs a quality risk analysis meeting must have credibility and political support. If you feel, for either reason, that you don't have the clout to lead a meeting that includes the high-powered stakeholders identified earlier, try to enlist your manager or engage an experienced consultant to either facilitate for you or coach you and the team through the meeting. If you go into this process and make a hash of it, wasting people's time and allowing the meeting to get out of hand with no useful result, you can do immense damage to your credibility and political clout.

ELIMINATING THE APPEARANCE OF MAGIC IN THE QUANTIFICATION OF RISK

Lord Kelvin, the British scientist, once wrote that without quantification there is no real knowledge. It's a logical error, though, to turn that statement around and claim that anytime I can stick any kind of metric on an attribute, I have gained a profound insight into its inner workings. Numbers and metrics, by themselves, do not create magical powers in their users beyond the precision of the model.

In techniques like Failure Mode and Effect Analysis and COE, I derive risk priority numbers and then use those numbers to make decisions about testing. These numbers are useful in that they establish an ordering in the overall set of risks identified; i.e., I gain an understanding of the relative importance of risks. If you refer to Figure 2-2, for example, you can see that the following risk identifiers, 1.002, 1.004, 1.003, and 1.005, are ordered by descending risk priority number—3, 9, 27, and 81, respectively.

However, when risk priority numbers are close, it becomes difficult to draw any meaningful conclusion. The constituent parts of the risk priority numbers—especially assessments of business priority and likelihood—are based mostly on experience, intuition, and professional judgment. Even likelihood, which could be subjected to actuarial analysis, is seldom based on statistically valid data gathered across many, many projects. Even if we have such data, because each system project is a new thing, the extent to which we can extrapolate is limited. Insurance companies extrapolate risks associated with cigarette smoking to other forms of tobacco consumption, like cigar smoking. However, we can't really extrapolate from the failure modes observed on a client-server implementation of a system to the risk levels for a Web-based implementation of the same system.

The bottom line is that these quantifications of risk, while useful models of risk ordering, are imprecise approximations. A wise test professional must ensure that the other stakeholders, especially those new to the technique, understand the limitations of meaning in the numbers. Should you hear people making precise claims about the benefits of these risk management techniques—e.g., "If we mitigate all the risks with associated risk priority numbers of 30 or less by testing in multiple phases, we'll see a 37.5% reduction in costs of poor quality on this release"—then you can be sure that you need to spend some time scaling back the degree of magic people have attached to quantification.

Finally, be sure that *you* don't sacrifice your own judgment to the god of the numbers, either. In these examples I have shown the level of testing being driven by the risk priority numbers. In real life, I often need to test more thoroughly for some risks that, by the risk priority numbers alone, appear to be less dangerous than others, just because my professional judgment tells me that doing so is prudent. These quantifiable techniques are useful models of risk when applied with good judgment and flexibility.

DEALING WITH VARIATION IN RATINGS

To some extent, risk assessments are dependent on subjective assessments, on judgment calls. In a Failure Mode and Effect Analysis, the severity of a potential problem is usually clear, but priority and likelihood are often less so. The degree to which subjectivity and individual judgment are problems is reduced when the stakeholders agree on the assessment. If consensus forms around a particular risk being low priority and unlikely, then, assuming you have informed stakeholders involved in the process, that prediction will tend to be accurate.

However, suppose the stakeholders disagree on the subjective ratings. Wide variation in the assessments that the raters come up with indicates a lack of accuracy in the rating. In other words, the average across ten ratings from 1 to 5 doesn't mean much if the standard deviation across these ratings is high.

For example, assume that ten people participating in a risk assessment rate priority on a scale of 1 to 5. Two stakeholders rate a particular risk as 1, two others pick 2, two pick 3, two pick 4, and two pick 5. The average is 3, but the standard deviation is 1.5. From the data set, you can see that no agreement exists on the priority. The average is misleading. Even if you have a set of ratings closer to the statistical ideal of the normal distribution, like {1,2, 2, 3, 3, 3, 3, 4, 4, 5}, you still have six stakeholders who disagree with the average, 3, and a standard deviation of about 1.2.

In terms of priority, I often find that when disagreements arise, stakeholders are representing the interests of different classes of customers or users. For example, power users of an application may find the macro features important, while most users never see those features. Looking at the size and importance of the customer or user base that relies on a particular feature or is subject to a particular risk can enable some compromise to be worked out in the area of priority. Alternatively, perhaps some of the stakeholders are missing an important consideration. Open discussion about why people have selected the rating they have can drive people toward a consensus.

For likelihood, again, one consideration is user and customer segmentation and who uses what features or is exposed to what risk. The likelihood rating should apply across the entire user base. If something is likely only for a small user segment, but that user segment is very important to the company's long-term strategy, then priority should be adjusted upward, rather than fudging the likelihood number.

Another consideration for likelihood is technical risk. What is the likelihood of the underlying defect? Here, the stakeholders with a background in the technology should take the lead, provided they have relevant experience and knowledge. When people are building new systems with new technology to solve problems in new ways, the amount of insight based on experience is often low. People may come up with technical risk ratings based on their own personal levels of optimism and risk aversion. In such cases, I check to see if the likelihood is based primarily on conjecture rather than experience. If so, then you may want to note, in the risk assessment, the range of likelihood numbers recorded and the range of risk priority numbers those yield. You can then advise the project management team about the disparate risk assessments for particular risks, and let them make the call.

CONVINCING STAKEHOLDERS TO INVEST TIME AND ACCEPT REALITY

When you first implement quality risk analysis, you may find that people are enthusiastic, but that enthusiasm might dim once the extent of the investment becomes clear. A formal approach to quality risk analysis involves significant amounts of time and therefore money. Even informal approaches will require some amount of time from every stakeholder.

Perhaps just as significantly, it requires the willingness of every stakeholder to participate in decisions that don't always go their way. The participants must approach the task with an understanding that system development, maintenance, and acquisition realities constrain what can be achieved given particular budget, schedule, quality, and feature parameters. Zero-risk systems and 100% risk mitigation through testing are unrealistic expectations, but doing a better job of managing risks to the quality of the systems we develop, maintain, or acquire is possible for most organizations.

Dissatisfaction with the current state of affairs is one powerful tool at your disposal. Do your sales, marketing, and customer support people think everything is fine? If so, instituting this process may prove difficult. Often, though, people know that the organization can do better. However, the nontechnical participants must also understand that problems exist not because the technical team is lazy or malicious, but because the processes and the levels of skill in the team need improvement.[13] Quality risk analysis is one process improvement that can help.

IMPLEMENT IMPROVEMENTS

So, you're ready to try quality risk analysis, ready to use this as the foundation of your next test effort. Here are some ideas on how to get started.

1. Research the appropriate categories. Start by studying the categories of quality risk appropriate to your system. Earlier I mentioned four books that can serve as starting points. Various books on design and implementation of the specific type of system you're building—e.g., client-server, Web based, and so on—can provide ideas on technical risks as well.

2. Identify the key stakeholders. Who cares about quality and testing? Using your own understanding of the organization and Table 2-2, you should be able to find the people whose participation you need.

3. Sell the stakeholders on quality risk management. Armed with some ideas about how your system could fail and a list of people you expect will care, you can now approach these key stakeholders and tell them about your concerns. Help them understand how quality risk management can ensure that testing will focus on the right areas while avoiding wasting time on those areas that don't matter. Inform them about the process. Emphasize that this is a process for making intelligent trade-offs between different areas of risks—schedule, budget, features, and quality—and various categories of quality risks.

4. Institute a quality risk analysis process. With the backing of your stakeholders and a good idea of the risks that exist, start quality risk analysis. If you have no processes now, start with the informal technique. If you're using an informal technique, try to move to one of the formal approaches. Keep the process lightweight to maintain support.

---

13. See W. E. Deming's *Out of the Crisis* for more on management confusion of process capability limitations with staff indolence, especially his classic black-bead/red-bead exercise.

5. Use risk assessment to allocate resources. In the case study, Jamal and his colleagues assigned levels of testing based on risk priority numbers from their use of Failure Mode and Effect Analysis. You can also use less quantitative approaches if you feel that's more appropriate in your context. Coverage of a particular quality risk is not an all-or-nothing affair. The various levels of testing are points along a continuous spectrum. The basic idea is to use the level of risk as a guide for how much time and resources to devote to testing in any given area.

As you implement these changes, you can start to speak the language of risk in your testing. Talk about testing in terms of risk and risk management. You'll find discussing testing in this fashion is understood and well received. Risk management is a popular topic. Managers understand risk management intuitively, even if they have no formal introduction to the concept. I have found that even senior managers and executives who have limited understanding about testing understand what I mean when I talk to them about managing the risks to system quality. It doesn't just *sound* smart—managing quality risks *is* smart.

3

GAZE INTO THE CRYSTAL BALL: ESTIMATE THE WORK AHEAD

Once we've completed the quality risk analysis described in the previous chapter, we know what we *should* test. We understand the risks to system quality that threaten the success of the project and their relative importance. This is an invaluable insight, because without it our test efforts can easily become misaligned with quality, squandering time and money, wasting programmer effort, and giving management both false confidence and undue concern. To align the test subproject further, we must adequately cover these risks through well-engineered test cases. I'll return to this topic in Chapters 10 and 11 when I discuss designing and developing test cases, test data, test tools, and other parts of the test system.

I'd be skipping some important steps, though, if I started to design and develop my test system at this point. With a quality risk analysis done, I understand the risks that endanger the quality of the system. However, on successful projects, the project team balances quality against features, schedule, and budget. If I take my quality risk analysis as carved in stone, declaring that every recommended testing action and every high-priority quality risk must be covered, then I might unacceptably increase risks to features, schedule, and budget. For example, it might take too long to complete all the testing and thus the project, causing a schedule and budget overrun.

In this and the following two chapters, I describe the estimation process. The estimation process provides the mechanism by which I align my testing effort with the overall project's schedule and budget. During this process, I move from looking at what I *should* test to what I truly *can* test, within the project context. In the course of this process, I often have to drop certain activities, tasks, and resources from my test subproject's scope because of the cost. In doing so, I use the hierarchy of risk established in quality risk analysis as my net, catching the most important quality risks and de-emphasizing the less important.

Project

A temporary endeavor undertaken to create or provide some unique product, system, or service. The endeavor consists of some sequence of tasks, undertaken by a team of people under some set of resource and time constraints, to deliver the product, system, or service to some set of customers and users. The degree of change over the life of the project in the team, budget, schedule, requirements, and target customers and users can vary considerably.[1]

Subproject

A project within a host project that provides products or services to the host project. By this definition, the test efforts discussed in this book generally are subprojects. The accounting team's issuance of paychecks to project employees is not a subproject, since it's outside the project context. A quality assurance auditor ensuring documented process compliance is not a subproject either, since it serves the organization, not the project.

Test Subproject

The set of tasks required to provide test services and information to the quality and testing stakeholders on the project team to support the team's ability to manage quality risks.

Estimation

A prediction of the schedule and cost associated with a project. In the case of test estimation, it's a prediction of the schedule and cost associated with a test subproject.

Estimation is a formidable and challenging process. It is highly visible to the entire organization—especially when done poorly—and strongly affects the test team's ability to carry out its testing mission. It is also a process that many of us—myself included—find hard to do. It's easy enough to grind out a *reasonable-looking* Gantt chart using commercially available project management software. Looks aside, though, what we need are realistic, actionable, and truthful estimates. Let's examine how we can create such estimates.[2]

1. I have adapted this definition from the Introduction to *The Guide to the Project Management Body of Knowledge*, 2000 Edition, www.pmi.org.
2. Portions of this and the next two chapters originally appeared in an article, "Test Estimation," in *Software Testing and Quality Engineering*, Volume 4, Issue 6 (Nov/Dec 2002), along with a companion piece, "Factors That Influence Test Estimation," at www.stickyminds.com and www.rexblackconsulting.com. I thank Esther Dyson and Robert Coutre for their editorial help.

AN ESTIMATION PROCESS

The estimation process shown in Process 4 breaks down into five major steps, each with a number of minor substeps. Allow for lots of potential iteration within the major and minor substeps. Because this is such a complex and critical process, we'll look at the first step in this chapter, step 2 in Chapter 4, and steps 3 through 5 in Chapter 5.

From a purely mechanical viewpoint, the development of a work-breakdown-structure in this first step is made easiest through use of project management software. However, just because the project management tool generates nice-looking Gantt and network charts doesn't mean that I've gained insight into what's going to happen next. While I need to be able to use project management software, it's the insight into the future that I really want.

When you are creating a work-breakdown-structure, it's important to know when to stop decomposing the activities, tasks, and subtasks. In a well-formed work-breakdown-structure for a testing subproject, every task at the lowest level of decomposition has the following characteristics:

1. Measurable status

2. Clearly defined start and end criteria

3. One or more output—and possibly input—deliverables

4. An estimation of resource requirements, effort, duration, and other costs

5. A short duration

6. Independence (once the start criteria are satisfied) from other tasks inside or outside the test subproject

7. Clearly defined ownership, ideally one responsible person

8. A mapping to one or more of the recommended testing actions from the quality risk analysis (with all phases, activities, and tasks collectively covering all recommended testing actions)

9. An order of occurrence based on risk priorities, to the extent that dependencies and resource constraints allow[3]

---

3. This list of work-breakdown-structure criteria is adapted in part from Wysocki et al., *Effective Project Management*.

Step #	Step	Done?
1.	Working one-on-one or as a group with the assigned test team, develop the work-breakdown-structure and estimated schedule.	☐
1.A	Decompose the test project into phases.	☐
1.B	Decompose each phase into constituent activities.	☐
1.C	Decompose each activity into tasks and subtasks until each task or subtask at the lowest level of composition satisfies the criteria listed later in this section.	☐
1.D	Taking risk priority into account, set up dependencies, resource assignments, and dependent tasks internal to the test subproject. Document dependencies, resources, and tasks external to the test subproject (i.e., those that involve collaborative processes).	☐
1.E	Sanity check the durations and efforts at the subtask, task, activity, and phase levels. If possible, augment professional judgment and gut instinct with previous project data, industry metrics, and so forth. Identify and, if possible, resolve discrepancies between the test subproject schedule and the project schedule. Where discrepancies cannot be resolved, document the obstacles.	☐
1.F	Review the work-breakdown-structure and schedule with the individuals to whom you've assigned responsibility for each task, taking special care to surface any hidden assumptions or dependencies.	☐
1.G	Review the work-breakdown-structure and schedule with the entire test team along with any subject matter experts available within or outside your organization.	☐
2.	Use the work-breakdown-structure and schedule to develop a budget.	☐
2.A	Extract from your work-breakdown-structure a complete list of resources. For each resource, determine the first and last day of assignment to the project. If you have resources shared across multiple test projects within a given time period, understand the percentage allocation of each resource's assignment to each project during various time periods.	☐
2.B	Identify any incidental resources required to support these resources.	☐
2.C	Categorize the resources into staff, travel, tools, test environments, and, if applicable, outsourcing costs. Total by time periods and categories.	☐

PROCESS 4 AN ESTIMATION PROCESS

Step #	Step	Done?
2.D	Sanity check the budget details and totals. If possible, augment your professional judgment and gut instinct with previous project data, industry metrics, and so forth. Identify and, if possible, resolve discrepancies between the test subproject budget and the overall budget. Should resolution prove impossible, document the obstacles.	☐
2.E	Amortize budget items that are long-term investments, documenting the reuse opportunities and the period of time over which you expect to recoup the costs.	☐
2.F	If it is required or desirable, analyze the return on investment. If the return on investment is negative, review your assumptions about amortization in 2.E and repeat this step if necessary. If the return on investment remains negative, review those items on your estimated work-break-down-structure that consume the most money while contributing the least return, tracing back to the quality risks. Document the money losing activities.	☐
2.G	If permitted by your management, review the budget with your test team. Take special care to identify any missing resources, especially incidental ones. Iterate steps 2.D through 2.F if necessary.	☐
3.	Obtain management support for the estimated schedule and budget.	☐
3.A	Present the benefits of the test subproject.	☐
3.B	Outline the time and money commitment required to receive those specific benefits.	☐
3.C	Understand and attempt to resolve through iteration of steps 3.A and 3.B any objections to the estimate.	☐
3.D	If management commitment to the proposed budget and schedule cannot be gained, discuss specific areas of testing to be deleted, setting cost and/or schedule goals to be met to obtain management support.	☐
4.	Repeat steps 1 through 3 if necessary, fine-tuning the estimated schedule and budget, until resources and management commitment adequate to the (possibly adjusted) scope of the test effort are secured.	☐
5.	Check the approved budget and schedule documents into the project library or configuration management system. Place the document under change control.	☐

PROCESS 4 CONTINUED

> **Phase**
>
> A logically distinct stage of a project or subproject consisting of a collection of activities that all produce similar deliverables.
>
> **Activity**
>
> A logically distinct subset of a phase consisting of a collection of tasks that together produce a single major deliverable.
>
> **Task**
>
> The component work elements of an activity, being a coherent set of actions involving a related set of skills.

JAMAL PREDICTS THE FUTURE

Immediately after the Failure Mode and Effect Analysis workshop, Jamal sat down in front of his PC and started his project management application. He also started Speedy-Writer 3.0 on his system to begin capturing ideas for his test plan. Faced with two empty templates, he was momentarily daunted but then got down to work. OK, he thought, what phases will I have in this project? Let's see—I have to do my planning, we're going to have to write a bunch of new tests, I need to get Keith Lee and his System Operations and Administration (SOA) team to configure some new systems into our test lab, and then we'll run integration and system testing. He created those phases in his work-breakdown-structure.

Step #	Step	Done?
1.A	Decompose the test project into phases.	✔

The planning phase was easy enough to flesh out. He had already set the testing context with Jenny and Kate after the kick-off meeting and had begun the risk analysis. As he did the estimate, he was starting to write the test plan. He owned all of the tasks within the planning phase, so he allocated himself as the resource. The only dependencies were on the participation of the stakeholders—people external to the testing team—so he identified these for the draft test plan. Figure 3-1 shows the schedule for that phase.

Hmm, he thought, feeling a bit daunted again, where to start on the rest of the tasks? Jamal decided to work backward from the test execution phase. He was responsible

An Index-Card Approach to Building Work-Breakdown-Structures

While reviewing this chapter, Robert Sabourin, principal consultant of AmiBug, Inc. (www.amibug.com), mentioned an index-card technique he uses to develop work-breakdown-structures prior to or as an alternative to using a project management tool.

1. Start out with a stack of index cards. (Some people use large sticky notes.)
2. Write down one task per index card.
3. If you split a task, replace one card with two or more cards, one per task.
4. Outline the project by spreading the index cards across a conference table like a big PERT chart. Sort and shuffle the cards as needed, looking for patterns and gaps.
5. Once all the tasks are identified, one per card, and all the cards are in order, jot the dependencies on the back of each card.

Determining the priorities as discussed in step 5 may prove a bit daunting for larger projects. Instead of trying to accomplish step 5 in one fell swoop, you may want instead to use tape, a large whiteboard, and one or more whiteboard markers, according to the following three alternate final steps.

5. Go through the index cards and build a pile of those tasks with no predecessors. Tape them on the whiteboard at the leftmost side.
6. Go through the index cards again. Identify those tasks dependent only on previously identified tasks. As you do so, tape the index cards to the whiteboard to the right of the task(s) they depend on, and then draw a line connecting the successor task to the predecessor task.
7. Repeat step 6 until the dependencies are all identified and all index cards are taped to the whiteboard.

Once these steps are completed, you can enter the information into a project management system.

for system testing. Calling up Jenny's development schedule, he saw that the planned ship date was March 28, 2003, which, based on previous projects, told him that his team needed to complete the testing the week before to allow for delivery of the Golden Build for production. This gave him a target of March 21, 2003, for the system test exit meeting. The system would need to meet the exit criteria defined in his test plan on that date.

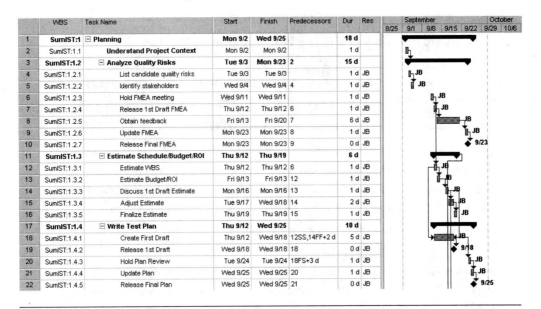

	WBS	Task Name	Start	Finish	Predecessors	Dur	Res
1	SumIST:1	⊟ Planning	Mon 9/2	Wed 9/25		18 d	
2	SumIST:1.1	**Understand Project Context**	Mon 9/2	Mon 9/2		1 d	
3	**SumIST:1.2**	⊟ **Analyze Quality Risks**	**Tue 9/3**	**Mon 9/23**	2	**15 d**	
4	SumIST:1.2.1	List candidate quality risks	Tue 9/3	Tue 9/3		1 d	JB
5	SumIST:1.2.2	Identify stakeholders	Wed 9/4	Wed 9/4	4	1 d	JB
6	SumIST:1.2.3	Hold FMEA meeting	Wed 9/11	Wed 9/11		1 d	JB
7	SumIST:1.2.4	Release 1st Draft FMEA	Thu 9/12	Thu 9/12	6	1 d	JB
8	SumIST:1.2.5	Obtain feedback	Fri 9/13	Fri 9/20	7	6 d	JB
9	SumIST:1.2.6	Update FMEA	Mon 9/23	Mon 9/23	8	1 d	JB
10	SumIST:1.2.7	Release Final FMEA	Mon 9/23	Mon 9/23	9	0 d	JB
11	**SumIST:1.3**	⊟ **Estimate Schedule/Budget/ROI**	**Thu 9/12**	**Thu 9/19**		**6 d**	
12	SumIST:1.3.1	Estimate WBS	Thu 9/12	Thu 9/12	6	1 d	JB
13	SumIST:1.3.2	Estimate Budget/ROI	Fri 9/13	Fri 9/13	12	1 d	JB
14	SumIST:1.3.3	Discuss 1st Draft Estimate	Mon 9/16	Mon 9/16	13	1 d	JB
15	SumIST:1.3.4	Adjust Estimate	Tue 9/17	Wed 9/18	14	2 d	JB
16	SumIST:1.3.5	Finalize Estimate	Thu 9/19	Thu 9/19	15	1 d	JB
17	**SumIST:1.4**	⊟ **Write Test Plan**	**Thu 9/12**	**Wed 9/25**		**10 d**	
18	SumIST:1.4.1	Create First Draft	Thu 9/12	Wed 9/18	12SS,14FF+2 d	5 d	JB
19	SumIST:1.4.2	Release 1st Draft	Wed 9/18	Wed 9/18	18	0 d	JB
20	SumIST:1.4.3	Hold Plan Review	Tue 9/24	Tue 9/24	18FS+3 d	1 d	JB
21	SumIST:1.4.4	Update Plan	Wed 9/25	Wed 9/25	20	1 d	JB
22	SumIST:1.4.5	Release Final Plan	Wed 9/25	Wed 9/25	21	0 d	JB

FIGURE 3-1 THE PLANNING PHASE SCHEDULE

Golden Build, Gold Master, GA Build

The build or release that is delivered to customers or installed for users. The test release into the test organization that precedes the Golden Build is often called the *Golden Candidate*. If the Golden Candidate is deemed to be sufficiently good, it becomes the Golden Build. (*GA* stands for *General Availability*, usually to all possible customers and users, as opposed to *Limited Availability*, such as a beta or early release to special customers.)

Golden Candidate

The planned final test release, which, if no must-fix bugs are found in it, will also be the version of the system released to the customers; i.e., the *Golden Build*.

Since the first increment would arrive on October 21, 2002, he knew that the system test entry meeting should occur on that date. The system would need to meet the entry criteria defined in his test plan at that time. He also knew that subsequent increments would arrive at four-week intervals. He entered these milestones and events into his scheduling software.

He was also responsible for integration testing. Integration would have to be completed by February 7, 2003, when increment 5, the last increment, was scheduled for

Test Pass

Execution of the tests defined for a given test execution phase (i.e., the entire test set).

Test Cycle

Execution of some subset of a test pass against a single, identifiable test release (see Chapter 12).

delivery. He planned for a week of testing beyond that date to fulfill the exit criteria and hold the integration test exit meeting. Integration was identified on Jenny's schedule as starting on September 30, 2002, so he assumed that they would have a working build ready for formal integration testing starting on October 7, 2002. He entered these milestones and events.

Within these boundaries, he would need to fit some number of test passes and, within each pass, cycles, for each test phase. He could use the scheduling software to figure that out, but that hadn't worked well for him before. Instead, since he liked to use a spreadsheet to track test case execution, he would put together the tracking spreadsheet now. Using the quality risks, he could come up with a rough list of the test cases his team would need, along with an estimate of how long each would take to run. Then he could use those numbers to calculate the duration of the passes, provided that he included some significant contingency for the test cases he was sure to miss in his rough list. He decided to assume a need to run 50% more test cases than he could anticipate now. He based this number on the last two projects, where his initial estimate of test case counts had been about 30% low and 60% low, respectively, of the final test case counts at system test exit.

He went through the quality risks one by one, mapping them to test cases and recording the coverage information. He also knew which test cases he had that would run currently, which ones would require updates, and which ones would need to be written. So, he started to accumulate this information in the test development phase of his scheduling software. He based the effort required for writing and updating test cases on previous experience, looking back at the schedules for the previous two projects.

Completing the first rough draft of his estimate, he looked over a summary of the test suites (see Figure 3-2). Jamal had added up the estimated effort for each test case in person-hours, along with the duration in clock hours. He needed both for his next estimate, where he derived the staffing levels and the number of test environments needed.

C	D	G	H	J	K
1	**SpeedyWriter Release 3.1 (w/ DMS) IST Test Case Tracking Spreadsheet**				
2					
3					
4 Test			Est.	Est.	
5 ID	Test Suite/Case	Phase	Effort	Duration	Comment
6					
7 1.000	*Functionality*				
22	Suite Summary	IS	62	72	
23					
24 2.000	*Performance, Load, Capacity, and Volume*				
30	Suite Summary	IS	10	40	
31					
32 3.000	*Reliability/Stability*				
35	Suite Summary	IS	4	336	
36					
37 4.000	*Error Handling and Recovery*				
41	Suite Summary	IS	14	14	
42					
43 5.000	*Installation, Maintenance, and Operations*				
48	Suite Summary	S	72	72	
49					
50 6.000	*Localization*				
59	Suite Summary	S	128	128	
60					
61 7.000	*Security and Privacy*				
66	Suite Summary	S	24	24	
67					
68 8.000	*Documentation*				
72	Suite Summary	S	28	28	
73					
74 9.000	*Integration*				
79	Suite Summary	I	48	96	

FIGURE 3-2 JAMAL'S ESTIMATE OF THE EFFORT AND DURATION FOR TEST SUITES

Jamal calculated his staffing needs and the pass durations for integration test, system test, and the overlapping period when both phases are active (see Figure 3-3). He excluded the localization testing from his staffing calculations, because he intended to retain a third-party lab to handle this, as he had done for previous releases. He planned for, at a peak, two automated test engineers (ATEs), one manual test engineer (MTE), and four test technicians (Tech). Since there would be one integration effort every four weeks, this would allow him one full pass through the test cases planned for integration testing against each increment; i.e., a four-week integration test pass.

For system test, he planned two full passes per increment, because he was concerned about regression while the builds were changing rapidly. (Note that Jamal is planning to receive bug-fix test releases as part of testing each increment, along with the initial build that includes the increment functionality.) Hmm, he thought, this Incremental approach sure creates a long period where both phases are underway. In a true Waterfall, I'd only need three technicians, and I'll bet I could get by with two. However, since two contract test technicians would only cost a little over $75,000, it was prob-

	D	E	F	G	H	J
83	**Integration Test Phase**				**Effort**	**Duration**
84	*Total Person Hours/Hours*				138	558
85	*Est. Person Weeks/Weeks*				7	7
86	*Proposed ATE Staffing*				1	
87	*Proposed MTE Staffing*				1	
88	*Proposed Tech Staffing*				0	
89	*Test Pass Duration (Weeks)*				4	
90	*Test Environments Required (w/ Some Sharing)*					2
91						
92	**System Test Phase (excl. Localization)**					
93	*Total Person Hours/Hours*				214	586
94	*Est. Person Weeks/Weeks*				11	7
95	*Proposed ATE Staffing*				2	
96	*Proposed MTE Staffing*				1	
97	*Proposed Tech Staffing*				3	
98	*Test Pass Duration (Weeks)*				2	
99	*Test Environments Required (w/ Some Sharing)*					4
100						
101	**Overlapping Phase Period (excl. Localization)**					
102	*Total Person Hours/Hours*				262	682
103	*Est. Person Weeks/Weeks*				13	9
104	*Proposed ATE Staffing*				2	
105	*Proposed MTE Staffing*				1	
106	*Proposed Tech Staffing*				4	
107	*Test Pass Duration (Weeks)*				2	
108	*Test Environments Required (w/ Some Sharing)*					5

FIGURE 3-3 CALCULATING THE STAFF NEEDED FOR OVERLAPPING TEST PHASES

ably worth that much to Software Cafeteria to gain the extra predictability of the Incremental approach.

Step #	Step	Done?
1.B	Decompose each phase into constituent activities.	☑
1.C	Decompose each activity into tasks and subtasks until each task or subtask at the lowest level of composition satisfies the criteria below.	☑

Incremental or otherwise, though, Jamal had noticed a bigger human resource problem. He'd originally thought he'd just reassign Emma Moorhouse and Lin-Tsu Wu, the automated test engineer and manual test engineer, respectively, who'd worked on SpeedyWriter 3.0, from their current duties on SpeedyWriter 3.0 maintenance releases to working on the new project. He would backfill them on that effort with two senior test technicians he thought were ready to become full-fledged test engineers. However, Emma and Lin-Tsu alone would not suffice. He needed another automated test engineer, because otherwise Lin-Tsu would be developing tests until November and Emma—worse yet—until January. This would interfere with test execution, since neither Lin-Tsu nor Emma would be available to supervise the work of the test technicians doing the test execution. He then reworked the test development portion of the schedule to reflect this additional engineer. He also added hiring tasks for the engineer and the four technicians, along with including a training and orientation period.

With the momentum of a solid first estimate building, he quickly checked his work-breakdown-structure against each of the nine criteria. The only issues he discovered were related to resource allocation, which he had estimated but still needed to finalize with Lin-Tsu and Emma. Working with the resource graphing capabilities of his project management tool—and adding some more tasks as he discovered them—he finalized his first cut of the estimate. To some extent, there was resource overallocation and underallocation, but these fluctuations occurred during the test execution efforts. During these periods, he knew he had discretion in assigning tests and reducing the planned number of test cases if need be.

Step #	Step	Done?
1.D	Taking risk priority into account, set up dependencies, resource assignments, and dependent tasks internal to the test subproject. Document dependencies, resources, and tasks external to the test subproject (i.e., those that involve collaborative processes).	✔

In addition, some of the overlap was really a matter of imprecision in the way he did the estimate. For example, Emma was overallocated during the initial weeks of system test execution because she was double-booked to both run and update the performance and load scripts. However, since those scripts wouldn't be ready to run, she couldn't do anything but work to update them. As long as he remembered that when he scheduled test execution, Jamal knew this wouldn't create an issue, provided that eventually all committed-to tests became ready to run and did so in the risk priority order.

To check those two conditions, he referred to the Failure Mode and Effect Analysis document again. Jamal revisited the estimate to verify complete coverage of each risk as committed in the Recommended Action field. He also checked that the tasks were tackled in risk priority order where such ordering might affect the ability to run tests in particular phases. He was somewhat hampered in this by not having a lot of visibility at this point into which specific features and bug fixes would drop into which increments, but he made some educated guesses, as all good managers must.

As Jamal went through this exercise, he recorded the quality risk coverage by test case in a special worksheet in the tracking spreadsheet. He decided to use a variation of the scale used for Quality Functional Deployment (as discussed in Chapter 2) based on the Recommended Action field of the Failure Mode and Effect Analysis chart, specifically as follows.

- 0—Test case does not cover this quality risk.
- 1—Test case provides opportunistic coverage of this quality risk.
- 3—Test case provides balanced coverage of this quality risk.
- 9—Test case provides extensive coverage of this quality risk.

In addition to making sure nothing was missed, this information would become invaluable for reporting results. Of course, since the test cases weren't actually written yet, Jamal was estimating again. This time he estimated what he thought the tests *would* cover. However, he was also designing the test cases at a high level in terms of what he thought the tests *should* cover. That estimate/design would need to be checked during test system development.

He discovered as he was tracking the risk coverage that the Failure Mode and Effect Analysis exercise had missed two particular interface risks. Not only did the client talk to the Web server and the Web server to the database server, but also the Web server talked to the application server and the application server talked to the hierarchical storage management server. Jamal added what he felt were appropriate risk entries in the Failure Mode and Effect Analysis chart, but he also sent an e-mail out to the various stakeholders to confirm his hunch.

To check his work, Jamal again reviewed a couple of schedules and other work-tracking documents from previous test efforts. His estimates seemed in line with what had actually happened on the previous projects, at least at the gross level of effort to develop automated and manual test suites and person-hours to run a test pass. Because of the long test phases and overlap inherent in the Incremental approach, though, his overall test project duration and staffing levels were considerably higher, almost double.

He also called up Jenny's development schedule and checked her resource assignments. She had two system architects, two user interface engineers from Bobbi's team, five Java programmers, one SQL/database guru, and one Web and application expert. This meant that the tester-to-programmer ratio was 7-to-11. Jamal knew that in the commercial software business, this number was well in line with industry averages, but he also knew that these numbers tended to be heavily context-sensitive.

Jamal was almost ready to move to the next stage, refining his estimate with his team and other testing experts at Software Cafeteria. First, though, he reviewed Jenny's and Kate's schedules and other details on their intranet sites one last time to see if he'd forgotten anything or if somehow he'd come up with a test subproject schedule that wouldn't serve the SpeedyWriter project's needs. Overall, the plan seemed fine, but he was still a bit unclear on how the marketing team's alpha and beta releases would affect his testing. Since no list of target features for these releases existed yet, he sent an e-mail to Jenny and Kate asking for a meeting to clarify the situation.

Step #	Step	Done?
1.E	Sanity check the durations and efforts at the subtask, task, activity, and phase level. If possible, augment professional judgment and gut instinct with previous project data, industry metrics, and so forth. Identify and, if possible, resolve discrepancies between the test subproject schedule and the project schedule. Where discrepancies cannot be resolved, document the obstacles.	✔

Next, Jamal asked Lin-Tsu and Emma to join him in his office to review their task assignments for the upcoming Sumatra project. He went through his schedule and the techniques he'd used to estimate the test execution phases. Then, he explained each task assignment and asked for corrections.

"Well," said Emma, "I think you're a bit optimistic believing we're going to find, hire, and have on board another automated test engineer in three weeks. That means that, assuming he has a job, our chosen candidate appears and accepts an offer within one week of you getting a hiring req, and then gives the standard two weeks' notice to his current employer. It's not as if there are a whole slew of people like that running around free."

"You're right," Jamal agreed, "it's probably more like four to six weeks with an aggressive plan. We could always go the temp-to-hire contractor option."[4]

"Given the road map for product releases this coming year," Emma replied, "we need another test automation person long-term. Temp-to-hire might be okay, but only if the contractor is serious about converting if he likes the work."

---

4. In the United States, Canada, and some parts of Europe, temporary staffing agencies and some third-party test organizations provide contract workers on short contracts (e.g., 60 or 90 days). At the end of the contract, the contractor may be converted to an employee. See Ruhl's *The Computer Consultant's Guide*.

"Or she," Jamal put in.

"What?" Emma asked.

"You said, 'If he likes the work.' Are you forgetting that two of the best test engineers on our team—the two of you—are women? Maybe our new automated test engineer will be another woman," Jamal replied with a smile. "But seriously, I see your point."

In addition, both Emma and Lin-Tsu expressed concern about the heavy workload during the initial couple of months of the project, when test system development, integration test execution, and even—once November rolled around—system test execution would be in full swing. "Look," Lin-Tsu pointed out in the resource chart, "I'm double-booked for almost three months!"

"Yeah, I know how it looks," Jamal admitted, "but you know how that works. You're writing tests, so you have to test the tests anyway. It'll impede our ability to run all the planned tests, but we shouldn't have any trouble finding plenty of bugs in the beginning. I just want to make sure we develop and run the tests in risk order, at least to the extent that the increment content lets us do that."

The discussion went back and forth for a while. Jamal agreed to transfer a test technician or two from each of the OfficeArrow suite maintenance release test efforts during lulls in the action on those maintenance releases to augment the Sumatra team. Jamal explained that while the test team was tight, with 14 people total, he felt they'd have enough capacity that he could shift people around for a day or two of test execution, shaving the maintenance testing a bit, without any ill effect on coverage there.

Step #	Step	Done?
1.F	Review the work-breakdown-structure and schedule with the individuals to whom you've assigned responsibility for each task, taking special care to surface any hidden assumptions or dependencies.	☑

Finally, Jamal printed enough copies of his planning documents—schedule, test tracking worksheet, and so on—for his own team, plus a couple for two people on Jenny's team who would be heavily involved in the unit and component test tool-smithing. As he handed these out, he asked each person not only to review his estimates, but also to come up with best-case, worst-case, and expected-case estimates for any task assigned to them or for tasks on which they had special experience or insight.

Gathering this information the next morning, Jamal checked his estimates. Most fell right into the "expected case" numbers each person had provided. As he reviewed the comments with each person, he asked for the reasoning behind their best and worst cases. One of the test experts on Jenny's team surprised him with his worst case on the integration test development.

"You know," Jack Nilson told him, "you could be right; it might take about seven weeks to put together and prove out an integration test harness. And the unit and component tests we programmers come up with might just fit into that harness hand-in-glove. I've seen it happen."

"But," he continued, "I've also seen whole integration test efforts blow up for a bunch of reasons, not the least of which is the incredible shrinking integration test window on the development team side. You know what I mean? The coding proper was under-estimated, so something has to give. Integration is one of those things that gives. So do unit and component testing. If that happens, you'll have a lot of extra work in your team, on account of all the bugs we don't find showing up hither and yon during system test. I'm not saying this is going to happen, and I'm not saying I've heard anyone suggest that time currently scheduled for integration activities is actually retained slack in our programming schedules under different names. I'm just saying that you may want to have a contingency plan for that kind of nonsense, 'cause it happens."

Jamal agreed. He made an appropriate note for his test plan, to include this as a potential risk.

Step #	Step	Done?
1.G	Review the work-breakdown-structure and schedule with the entire test team along with any subject matter experts available within or outside your organization.	✔

At this point, Jamal felt good about his schedule. But what would it cost to implement? More importantly, how could he show some value for that cost? Jamal decided to spend some time reading up on how testing could show a return on investment, before he launched into preparing an estimated budget.

Step #	Step	Done?
1.	Working one-on-one or as a group with the assigned test team, develop the work-breakdown-structure and estimated schedule.	✔

USING RULES OF THUMB FOR ROUGH ESTIMATION

In the case study, Jamal created a work-breakdown-structure based on the quality risk analysis. For development projects, development managers can create work-breakdown-structures based on requirements and designs. These are referred to as *bottom-up* estimation techniques. Such bottom-up estimates can be checked against *top-down* estimation rules. In more formal environments, metrics like function points and projected lines of code provide top-down estimates. However, in many environments, test managers must rely on simple rules of thumb that compare the relative sizes of various phases of the development project. Capers Jones, Martin Pol, and Tim Koomen have all published serviceable rules of thumb that can be useful. However, as Jones is careful to point out, such rules of thumb are inevitably imprecise and should be used in conjunction with a work-breakdown-structure if you need accurate project estimates.[5]

One of the most common rule-of-thumb techniques for test estimation is the tester-to-programmer ratio. In addition to the just mentioned works, I can recommend two articles that you can download from the Internet for such ratio-based estimates. One is Johanna Rothman's excellent paper "It Depends: Deciding on the Correct Ratio of Developers to Testers." In it, Rothman presents a risk-based approach for selecting the right ratio of testers to programmers, based on three contrasting case studies. She looks at risk areas related to the product, the project and its processes, and the team. Product risks include large size and high complexity. Project and process risks include tight dates; a lack of good development, testing, and project management practices; and a need for high quality. Team risks involve inexperienced testers, programmers, marketing staff, project managers, and other key players. Rothman's paper explains a way to analyze these risks to decide if increasing your tester-to-programmer ratio can help mitigate the risks to the quality of your systems. This approach fits in nicely with the techniques I've described in this book; since you're already thinking about quality risks, you can extend your thinking to include these broader categories.

---

5. Jones's rules of thumb for estimating development projects, including testing, can be found in *Estimating Software Costs*, especially Chapter 11. He recommends going beyond work-breakdown-structures to use automated software estimation tools, such as the tool sold by his company, but in my experience few software development and maintenance organizations use these tools. Therefore, a work-breakdown-structure prepared with the help of a project management tool is the most accurate manual technique available to the typical test engineer and test manager. Finally, Pol and Koomen include some estimation rules of thumb in Chapter 7 of *Test Process Improvement*.

In addition to Rothman's work, you can read Kathleen A. Iberle and Susan Bartlett's insightful paper "Estimating Tester to Developer Ratios (or Not)." They analyze the factors that influence the accuracy of tester-to-programmer ratio-based estimates. Iberle summarized the key points about using such ratios for me in an e-mail, where she provided the following rules.

1. A combination of inconsistent measurement systems and actual differences in ratios produces a margin of error in reported ratios on the order of 10x. Therefore, comparing your ratio with anybody else's ratio is useless. The effects of the measurement systems cannot be differentiated from the actual differences.

2. If a proposed ratio is more than an order of magnitude away from reported industry values, then some comparison may be useful. For instance, a proposal that the entire department should operate at 1-to-30 for all projects may be effectively countered by quoting industry ratios.

3. Using your own past ratios to predict future ratios on your own projects can be useful, under the following conditions.

   A. You are using a consistent measurement system.

   B. There's very little data on proposed functionality (otherwise a labor estimate [work-breakdown-structure] will be much more accurate).

   C. The predicted ratios are adjusted for whatever differences between projects are known.

   D. A margin of error of 25%–50% is acceptable.

If you need to deliver a tester-to-programmer ratio-based initial estimate, these two papers will provide you with the data you need to do it intelligently.[6] There's no reason to use just one approach, either. By mixing the rules of thumb that Jones, Pol, and Koomen provide with the risk-based techniques that Rothman gives and the ratio-influencing-factor model crafted by Iberle and Bartlett, you can refine your rough estimates. Doing multiple estimates using the different rules of thumb and then combining—such as by averaging—those estimates can improve the accuracy of such estimates. The variation between the models can give you best-case and worst-case estimates. Remember, though, that when accuracy matters, work-breakdown-structures are most likely your best bet.

---

6. Rothman's article is found at at www.jrothman.com, while Iberle and Barlett's paper appears in *Proceedings of the STAR West Conference 2001* and on Iberle's Web site, www.kiberle.com. I also enjoyed the chance to discuss this topic with Rothman, Iberle, and Bartlett while working on this book.

EFFORT, DURATION, AND DEPENDENCIES

So far, I've discussed the mechanics of a work-breakdown-structure and the decomposition of a project into constituent tasks. I've mentioned that there are rules of thumb that you can use for gross estimation or for checking the estimate you come up with through composition and work breakdown. So, assuming you use the decomposition process, what is a typical set of tasks within each phase and how long could you expect those to take? In the following subsections, I'll walk through each major phase in the case study Gantt chart to examine these topics.

PLANNING

As shown in Figure 3-1, Jamal broke the planning portion of his test project into four major activities. The first, understanding the project context, was the project kick-off meeting and subsequent discussions with Kate Hernandez, the product manager, and Jenny Kaufman, the development manager. This took a single day in his case, because Jamal had been working at Software Cafeteria for a while and the Sumatra product is an incremental enhancement of an existing system that Jamal and his team have tested before.

Some factors can make understanding project context more complex, as discussed in Chapter 1. For example, if you are new to the company, if the company has recently gone through a downsizing or reorganization, if the system is unique or new, if there are new technologies or processes involved, or if significant cross-functional support must be garnered for the project or the testing portion of the project, then understanding the project context may take a few days or even weeks.

The next activity in the planning phase is analyzing the quality risks. Jamal has decomposed this into seven constituent tasks. Listing the candidate quality risks involves looking through the various sources I referred to in Chapter 2 and picking the major categories of quality risks. It also includes studying the Failure Mode and Effect Analysis. It doesn't necessarily take Jamal's entire day, but the task would span a whole day. Identifying the stakeholders is Jamal's next task. Like understanding project context, this task is made easier by his tenure with the company. The same factors I mentioned earlier could make identifying all the stakeholders and getting them to commit to attending such a meeting more time-consuming than the single day Jamal had to spend.

The Failure Mode and Effect Analysis meeting itself can be an all-day off-site affair, as mentioned in Chapter 2. If you're using Failure Mode and Effect Analysis and doing a requirements-based analysis for a small to medium-sized system, a day is a reasonable estimate. A more complex system or an analysis that addressed design and implementation issues at a low level of detail could take longer. On one project, three of my test engineers each spent over two weeks performing a detailed-design-based Failure Mode and Effect Analysis on the half-dozen or so major constituent sub-systems. If you're applying the informal technique, the informal analysis could be done in a one-day meeting, if you can get everyone together. If you have to interview people one-on-one and then obtain concurrence on the list of risks, you might find you need more than one draft/feedback/update/finalize cycle, as Jamal has in his schedule.

This draft/feedback/update/finalize cycle consists, in Jamal's case, first of document-ing the results of the off-site analysis in a Failure Mode and Effect Analysis form. This can take anywhere from an hour or so to a full day, depending on the volume of the information gathered. Also, if you have used a one-on-one interview approach to gather the information, you're likely to find conflicting viewpoints, which you'll need to either resolve with the stakeholders or at least identify in the document. Jamal allo-cated a week for gathering feedback on the draft Failure Mode and Effect Analysis document, not because it takes five full days for each stakeholder to review the docu-ment, but because he had to wait for busy people to have an hour or so to study it. I've found in most organizations that giving people a week is reasonable. In your or-ganization it may not be, so think about your context. Do people read and respond to e-mail or requests for input quickly, or are there key stakeholders who are very busy and tend not to respond unless repeatedly prompted?

Jamal has allocated a single day to update the document once the feedback does come back, and then he plans to release a final version that same day. Again, if you use the interview approach rather than the group meeting, you may find that these updates take longer and that you have to release multiple drafts. This is why I prefer to have a stakeholders meeting to get agreement on the quality risks and their priorities. It's just too easy for the interview process to drag on and on. Since my test process is of-ten founded on the risk analysis, I'm impeded from getting any work done until I have a stable quality risk analysis.

Notice that Jamal has planned to begin his estimation and planning activities immedi-ately after the Failure Mode and Effect Analysis off-site meeting. The assumption he's making is that the meeting will end with general concurrence and only some minor adjustments to be made, so he's safe to start these processes right away. He's allo-cated a day each for doing the work-breakdown-structure and budgeting. This is a reasonable estimate for a seasoned manager tackling known tasks with a small team of skilled people. However, if you are taking on new tasks—say, it's your first project to include automation—then it will take longer. You'll need to give the people respon-sible for the tasks more than just a few hours to think about how long the new tasks will take. When I take on new tasks, I spend time talking to experienced peers, prototyping, and reading books, articles, and papers to learn the process. It might be entirely reasonable for the estimation process to take a couple of weeks in such circumstances. Also, if it is your first experience with preparing a work-breakdown-structure and a budget, you'll need to spend some extra time to learn both the techniques (e.g., how to use the project management software your company uses) and the underlying ideas of preparing a good schedule. My first project estimates, for projects with three or four people and lasting only a month or so, took me all day to prepare. Estimation has become second nature to me now, with 15 years of practice, but it's certainly not intuitive for the first-time manager, and it's easy to get lost in the complexities of the tools.

Jamal has planned a four-day period to get project management support and concurrence on a finalized estimate. He'll present the estimate to his manager, get ideas on what changes are needed, make those changes, and then finalize the estimate with his manager. The next couple of chapters will discuss this process, and you'll see how those tasks can play out. A four-day period may suffice if you feel comfortable that what you're proposing, for the most part, will be noncontroversial. However, if there's a large gap between what the risk analysis tells you *should* be tested and what budget and schedule realities say *can* be tested, then it may take a while to resolve those differences. As a test manager in such a situation, I need to help the project management team make informed decisions about the risks associated with pruning the test coverage. In such cases, I have had the negotiation and approval tasks in the estimation activity take weeks.

In addition to preparing an estimated schedule and budget, Jamal has a separate activity for planning. This activity and the test plan produced by it are discussed in Chapters 6 and 7. Jamal plans to spend a week writing the plan, which is a task that happens concurrently with estimation. Jamal's plan is going to explain the logistics behind the tasks identified in his work-breakdown-structure. Once Jamal has a draft plan, he will release it to the stakeholders for a week to review. Again, the reasonableness of such an estimate is a function of your stakeholders, just as it was for the Failure Mode and Effect Analysis document. The single cycle of review/update/release that Jamal plans over a course of two days is also dependent on the stakeholders and how they feel about the plan. If the plan is a complex one, it may take longer to get concurrence. If new and unfamiliar tasks are being planned, more care is called for.

Overall, Jamal has estimated a three-and-a-half-week period to complete all the planning tasks. Some of that is time spent waiting for reviews. Jamal will probably not spend anywhere near 140 person-hours of time, because of these waiting periods and because of the multitasking required of managers. I have found that I must take these built-in delays and distractions into account for most projects. In some cases, though, where I can focus on a single project, and planning is an internal matter, I have completed plans in a period of hours, sometimes less than a day. For more complex projects, I have seen planning take well over a month.

STAFFING

Figure 3-4 shows the estimated schedule for staffing. One thing to note is that one task, Obtain Hiring/Contract Reqs, is dependent on a task in the planning phase. In Jamal's schedule, he has to get initial approval for his budget and schedule before he can expect permission to begin hiring people. In your organization, that may not be the way staffing works. In some cases, final approval of the estimate is needed. I've also worked with clients where extensive contract negotiations of various sorts had to occur before hiring could commence. This can complicate and lengthen the staffing phase.

Jamal had planned on three weeks to find and hire an automation testing engineer, and five weeks to hire the test technicians. In the case study, Emma pointed out that this was probably overly optimistic, and Jamal agreed. During slow economic periods, a three-week hiring time frame might be entirely realistic. It also might be a realistic time estimate to bring a contractor on board. In the late '90s during the dot-com boom, though, planning three weeks to find a specialized, skilled test engineer to hire as an employee would have been unrealistic in most parts of the high-tech world. If you have a human resources department, they should be able to help you understand and estimate the staffing phase of your project more accurately.

Small companies and start-ups often don't have human resources departments. In such cases, you can rely on external resources to help you estimate staffing tasks. Given an accurate job description (a topic we'll cover in Chapter 8), local staffing and recruiting companies can tell how long it's taking them to fill positions like that. Staffing and recruiting companies do, however, expect to be paid to find an employee for you. They may provide you with a free estimate of how long it would take them to fill the position, but that doesn't mean that you can fill the position in the same amount of time. Online recruiting and staffing Web sites can give you some ideas on the time

	WBS	Task Name	Start	Finish	Predeces	Dur	Res	October 9/15	9/22	9/29	10/6	10/13	10/20	10/27	November 11/3	11/10	11/17	11/24	Dec 12/
24	SumIST:2	☐ Staffing	Mon 9/16	Tue 10/22		26 d													
25	SumIST:2.1	Obtain Hiring/Contract Reqs	Mon 9/16	Mon 9/16	14	0 d		9/16											
26	SumIST:2.2	Hire Additional ATE	Tue 9/17	Mon 10/7	25	3 w	JB[25	JB[25%]											
27	SumIST:2.3	Hire Technicians	Tue 9/17	Mon 10/21	25	5 w	JB[25			JB[25%]									
28	SumIST:2.4	Training/Orientation	Tue 10/8	Tue 10/8	26	1 d	JB[25			JB[25%],EM[25%],ATE									
29	SumIST:2.5	Training/Orientation	Tue 10/22	Tue 10/22	27	1 d	JB[25			JB[25%],EM[25%],LTW[25%],TT[400%]									

FIGURE 3-4 THE STAFFING PHASE OF THE SUMATRA TEST SUBPROJECT

required to fill a position, but it may not be tailored for your region, which can make a big difference. Your peer managers can also give you some ideas based on their own hiring experiences, but the time required to hire a programmer who knows C++ and XML is likely to be different from the time required to hire a test engineer skilled in a particular automation tool. If the success of the project is critically dependent on filling a particular position as quickly as possible, the recruiting firm's fee may be money well spent.

The last pair of tasks in this phase is training and orientation. Jamal and Software Cafeteria's human resources department have a one-day training session planned for new hires. This is consistent with some of the organizations I've worked with, though I've also heard of training periods as long as three months. In other companies, sink or swim is the training method of choice. (I'll revisit this topic in Chapters 8 and 9.)

For the staffing phase, Jamal has estimated a little more than five weeks. As with planning, this does not translate into 200 person-hours each for him, Emma, and Lin-Tsu. Interviewing can be a time-consuming activity, but careful screening of candidates as discussed in Chapter 8 can limit the number of interviews you need to conduct. My test teams and I typically spend about two person-days per interview and can usually interview fewer than five people to fill any given position.

TEST DEVELOPMENT

The longest phase of the Sumatra test subproject is test development. This is often the case when scripted manual and automated test techniques are being used, though time must be allocated up front for sufficient test development. Figure 3-5 shows the test development phase.

As with staffing, Jamal has established a dependency whereby test development does not start until he's gotten tentative approval—with some changes, perhaps—for his estimate. I prefer not to start test development until I'm sure I'm going to need the things—such as test data, test cases, test tools, test scripts, and test environments—that I intend to develop for later test execution.

The dependencies between the development activities indicate Jamal's preference in when these development activities tasks get done. Sometimes this preference is based on the priority of the risk covered by the tests to be developed. For example, document management functionality is seen as a higher risk than installation, operations, and maintenance, so Lin-Tsu is to finish writing the manual Document Management System Functionality test scripts before starting to update the Installation, Operations, and Maintenance test scripts.

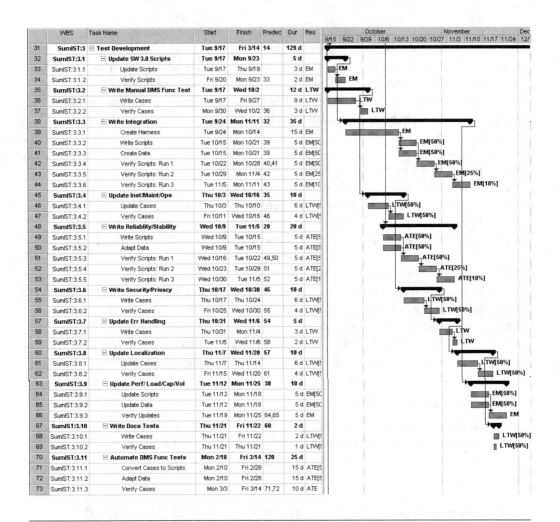

	WBS	Task Name	Start	Finish	Predec	Dur	Res
31	SumIST:3	⊟ Test Development	Tue 9/17	Fri 3/14	14	129 d	
32	SumIST:3.1	⊟ Update SW 3.0 Scripts	Tue 9/17	Mon 9/23		5 d	
33	SumIST:3.1.1	Update Scripts	Tue 9/17	Thu 9/19		3 d	EM
34	SumIST:3.1.2	Verify Scripts	Fri 9/20	Mon 9/23	33	2 d	EM
35	SumIST:3.2	⊟ Write Manual DMS Func Test	Tue 9/17	Wed 10/2		12 d	LTW
36	SumIST:3.2.1	Write Cases	Tue 9/17	Fri 9/27		9 d	LTW
37	SumIST:3.2.2	Verify Cases	Mon 9/30	Wed 10/2	36	3 d	LTW
38	SumIST:3.3	⊟ Write Integration	Tue 9/24	Mon 11/11	32	35 d	
39	SumIST:3.3.1	Create Harness	Tue 9/24	Mon 10/14		15 d	EM
40	SumIST:3.3.2	Write Scripts	Tue 10/15	Mon 10/21	39	5 d	EM[50
41	SumIST:3.3.3	Create Data	Tue 10/15	Mon 10/21	39	5 d	EM[50
42	SumIST:3.3.4	Verify Scripts: Run 1	Tue 10/22	Mon 10/28	40,41	5 d	EM[50
43	SumIST:3.3.5	Verify Scripts: Run 2	Tue 10/29	Mon 11/4	42	5 d	EM[25
44	SumIST:3.3.6	Verify Scripts: Run 3	Tue 11/5	Mon 11/11	43	5 d	EM[10
45	SumIST:3.4	⊟ Update Inst/Maint/Ops	Thu 10/3	Wed 10/16	35	10 d	
46	SumIST:3.4.1	Update Cases	Thu 10/3	Thu 10/10		6 d	LTW[
47	SumIST:3.4.2	Verify Cases	Fri 10/11	Wed 10/16	46	4 d	LTW[
48	SumIST:3.5	⊟ Write Reliablity/Stability	Wed 10/9	Tue 11/5	28	20 d	
49	SumIST:3.5.1	Write Scripts	Wed 10/9	Tue 10/15		5 d	ATE[
50	SumIST:3.5.2	Adapt Data	Wed 10/9	Tue 10/15		5 d	ATE[
51	SumIST:3.5.3	Verify Scripts: Run 1	Wed 10/16	Tue 10/22	49,50	5 d	ATE[
52	SumIST:3.5.4	Verify Scripts: Run 2	Wed 10/23	Tue 10/29	51	5 d	ATE[2
53	SumIST:3.5.5	Verify Scripts: Run 3	Wed 10/30	Tue 11/5	52	5 d	ATE[1
54	SumIST:3.6	⊟ Write Security/Privacy	Thu 10/17	Wed 10/30	45	10 d	
55	SumIST:3.6.1	Write Cases	Thu 10/17	Thu 10/24		6 d	LTW[
56	SumIST:3.6.2	Verify Cases	Fri 10/25	Wed 10/30	55	4 d	LTW[
57	SumIST:3.7	⊟ Update Err Handling	Thu 10/31	Wed 11/6	54	5 d	
58	SumIST:3.7.1	Write Cases	Thu 10/31	Mon 11/4		3 d	LTW
59	SumIST:3.7.2	Verify Cases	Tue 11/5	Wed 11/6	58	2 d	LTW
60	SumIST:3.8	⊟ Update Localization	Thu 11/7	Wed 11/20	57	10 d	
61	SumIST:3.8.1	Update Cases	Thu 11/7	Thu 11/14		6 d	LTW[
62	SumIST:3.8.2	Verify Cases	Fri 11/15	Wed 11/20	61	4 d	LTW[
63	SumIST:3.9	⊟ Update Perf/ Load/Cap/Vol	Tue 11/12	Mon 11/25	38	10 d	
64	SumIST:3.9.1	Update Scripts	Tue 11/12	Mon 11/18		5 d	EM[50
65	SumIST:3.9.2	Update Data	Tue 11/12	Mon 11/18		5 d	EM[50
66	SumIST:3.9.3	Verify Updates	Tue 11/19	Mon 11/25	64,65	5 d	EM
67	SumIST:3.10	⊟ Write Docs Tests	Thu 11/21	Fri 11/22	60	2 d	
68	SumIST:3.10.1	Write Cases	Thu 11/21	Fri 11/22		2 d	LTW[
69	SumIST:3.10.2	Verify Cases	Thu 11/21	Thu 11/21		1 d	LTW[
70	SumIST:3.11	⊟ Automate DMS Func Tests	Mon 2/10	Fri 3/14	120	25 d	
71	SumIST:3.11.1	Convert Cases to Scripts	Mon 2/10	Fri 2/28		15 d	ATE[
72	SumIST:3.11.2	Adapt Data	Mon 2/10	Fri 2/28		15 d	ATE[
73	SumIST:3.11.3	Verify Cases	Mon 3/3	Fri 3/14	71,72	10 d	ATE

FIGURE 3-5 THE TEST DEVELOPMENT PHASE OF THE SUMATRA TEST PROJECT

Sometimes the order in which I choose to develop tests depends on when portions or aspects of the system will be ready for testing. For example, the Performance, Load, Capacity, and Volume test suite is slightly more important (in terms of quality risk priority) than the Integration test suite, but the system will need to include the major document management system functions before Emma can test their performance. Integration can start as soon as the first pair of communicating components is ready in increment 1. So, Emma develops the integration test tools and scripts before updating the Performance, Load, Capacity, and Volume test suite.

Some of the test development work has to do with updating existing test scripts, both automated and manual. In these cases, larger complex test scripts will take longer to update than shorter ones. For example, Jamal and Lin-Tsu estimate ten days to update the Installation, Operation, and Maintenance tests, while they allow only five days for updating the Error Handling tests. These estimates are based on Lin-Tsu and Jamal's assessment that the document management system will introduce lots of operational overhead—such as changing offline media and maintaining the hierarchical storage management system—while the set of errors, while somewhat larger than for SpeedyWriter 3.0, still tends to focus on aspects like unavailable or corrupted files.

Updating the automated functionality regression tests (Update SW 3.0 Scripts) is estimated at five days, but updating the Performance, Load, Capacity, and Volume test suite is scheduled for ten days. This reflects Emma and Jamal's judgment that the changes to the existing functionality represent mostly some new dialogs that might arise through interaction with the document management system, along with the effect of some bug fixes on the existing functions. More significant performance implications are present in the document management system, and the set of possible states the system can be in is dramatically increased (see Chapter 10).

It takes longer to write new test scripts, manual or automated, than to update existing ones. Writing the new automated test scripts for document management system functionality is scheduled for 25 days, as opposed to the five-day update for the existing tests.

Test cases may need special data. For example, on a project where my test team and I were testing a home loan processing application, we had to have special data loaded on the application and some remote servers that provided credit-rating information to our system. On one project where a network of Interactive Voice Response (IVR) servers (e.g., telephone banking systems) was connected to a call center, we needed a shared customer database on the call center subsystem plus a subset of that customer data loaded on each Interactive Voice Response server. Creation of that set of data files involved purchasing a special test tool and expending three person-months of effort over a two-month period to generate the necessary data.

In the case of automated tests, you can sometimes use commercial or freeware testing tools. In that case, developing tests is a matter of programming or configuring the tool to do what you need. Emma is doing just that with the Performance, Load, Capacity, and Volume tests. However, you may also find that you need to build custom test tools. Emma is doing that with the Integration tests. Often, I've found that the stubs, drivers, and data used for good unit and component testing make excellent integration and system test tools.

The schedule should also include time for testing the tests, whether new or updated, automated or manual. To some extent, this time overlaps the first execution of the tests. However, I've found that including time and effort for verification tasks helps me keep the estimate accurate. Otherwise, the time to find and fix problems in the tests gets buried in the first time or two these tests are run, resulting in overruns in the test execution.

Throughout the scheduling of test development, Jamal, Lin-Tsu, and Emma call upon their previous experience on similar efforts to estimate the duration and effort involved in each task. Delphic Oracle, Three-Point, and Wideband techniques are participative approaches for tapping the wisdom of the team.[7]

There are also rules of thumb for test case development in Jones's *Estimating Software Costs*. However, I've seen far too much variation in test development to rely on these metrics to estimate specific test tasks. Looking back at four previous projects, I have the following metrics:

- Internet appliance—350 person-days to develop 170 test cases
- IVR network and call center—1,200 person-days to develop 1,157 test cases
- Home equity loan processing—20 person-days to write 37 test cases
- Marketing data analysis—45 person-days to write 86 test cases

This comes out to about eight person-hours on average to develop a test case, but the standard deviation is six person-hours. Each of these projects had a different mix of test case precision, number of conditions covered per test case, manual and automated testing, automation using commercial or custom-developed tools, test data development, and existing testware for reuse, among other factors. By comparison, applying Jones's rules of thumb for a 100,000 source lines of code (100 KSLOC) program yields about one person-hour per test case, an order of magnitude variation from my Internet appliance project and off by a factor of four for my marketing data analysis program project.

---

7. For an introduction to basic project estimation and other project management skills, I recommend Wysocki et al., *Effective Project Management*. This useful text, complete with hands-on exercises and a running case study, thoroughly explains estimation techniques. These techniques are team-based, iterative, best-case/worst-case/expected-case brainstorming. Also helpful is Rita Hadden's "Credible Estimation for Small Projects," published in *Software Quality Professional*, which explains a variation of the method, again drawing on project team expertise.

Jamal's Sumatra estimate shows about 75 person-days of effort to write between 40 (initial estimate) and 60 (including his 50% contingency) test cases. This is consistent with my data for the Internet appliance and Interactive Voice Response network and call center projects. I think it's probably safe to assume that similar projects with similar teams, technologies, and techniques will show similar metrics in terms of effort per test case, but again there are lots of factors to consider. Just assuming "Project B is like project A—on project A we spent two person-days per test case in test development; therefore, I can use that as an estimate and not look closely at the factors that influence test development time" would probably not yield very accurate estimates over time. Using someone else's rule of thumb will probably be even less accurate. As the example with Jones's rule of thumb and my data illustrates, order-of-magnitude differences can exist, and an estimate that is off by 1000% is not a very useful estimate.

Jamal and his team will be working on test development for most of the project, 26 weeks. However, the bulk of the test development work occurs over a period of 11 weeks from mid-September until the end of November. During this time, Emma, Lin-Tsu, and the new automation test engineer will be working almost full-time updating, writing, and verifying tests.

TEST ENVIRONMENT CONFIGURATION

In comparison with the extensive testware development phase, Jamal plans on a simple four-week effort to configure the test environment (see Figure 3-6). Clients and servers must be purchased first. The five-day and ten-day estimates, respectively, indicate a crisp, lightweight acquisitions process at Software Cafeteria. Also, the environment consists of common, commercially available, mass-market hardware and software only. No custom hardware or software development (except for SpeedyWriter

	WBS	Task Name	Start	Finish	Predec	Dur	Res	October / November
75	SumlST:4	⊟ Test Environment Configuration	Fri 9/20	Fri 10/18	11	21 d		
76	SumlST:4.1	⊟ Netscape Clients	Fri 9/20	Tue 10/1		8 d		
77	SumlST:4.1.1	Obtain Systems	Fri 9/20	Thu 9/26		5 d	NSC[5	NSC[500%]
78	SumlST:4.1.2	Set up/Configure	Fri 9/27	Tue 10/1	77	3 d	NSC[5	NSC[500%],SOA
79	SumlST:4.2	⊟ IE Clients	Fri 9/20	Tue 10/1		8 d		
80	SumlST:4.2.1	Obtain Systems	Fri 9/20	Thu 9/26		5 d	IEC[5(	IEC[500%]
81	SumlST:4.2.2	Set up/Configure	Fri 9/27	Tue 10/1	80	3 d	IEC[5(	IEC[500%],SOA
82	SumlST:4.3	⊟ Web/App/DB Servers	Fri 9/20	Tue 10/8		13 d		
83	SumlST:4.3.1	Obtain Systems	Fri 9/20	Thu 10/3		10 d	D1,A2	D1,A2,A1,W2,W1,D2
84	SumlST:4.3.2	Set up/Configure	Wed 9/25	Tue 10/8	83FS-7	10 d	D2,W	D2,W1,W2,A1,A2,D1,SOA
85	SumlST:4.4	Verify 2 IT Environments	Mon 9/23	Fri 10/4		10 d	EM[25	EM[25%],LTW[25%]
86	SumlST:4.5	Verify 3 Addl ST Environments	Mon 10/7	Fri 10/18		10 d	EM[25	EM[25%],LTW[25%]

FIGURE 3-6 THE TEST ENVIRONMENT CONFIGURATION PHASE

itself), special orders, or the like are contemplated for this project. I've worked on a few projects with custom hardware that involved lengthy periods to build the systems.

The setup and configuration effort is primarily borne by Keith Lee and his System Operations and Administration team. The three-day and ten-day turnaround times for clients and servers, respectively, indicate that Keith's team can respond quickly to Jamal's needs. I have worked on projects where this was not the case, especially where the network operations support teams were spread too thin. Sometimes there are security issues involved with setting up servers, especially if those servers will be attached to the corporate network. All these factors have to be taken into account.

A complex test environment can take a long time and involve a lot of effort to set up and configure. On one project I spent about two person-months planning and supervising the configuration of the test environment. The network operations team spent about 36 person-months doing the actual setup and configuration.[8]

Sometimes the effort to set up the test environment is trivial. On one project I had to buy a single PC workstation and upgrade the memory and processor on a server. I expended about a person-day of effort, including ordering, picking up, wiring into the network, installing the hardware, and checking the configurations. The duration was about three weeks, though, since my client and I had to come to an agreement on what environments they wanted the application tested in.

Jamal's estimate includes some effort on Emma and Lin-Tsu's part to verify the integration test and system test environments prior to the first passes of each test phase. This consists of running tests and looking for environment-specific failures. It's important to know that when you are reporting bugs in the system, those are due to actual system problems, not errors in the configuration of the test environment.

TEST EXECUTION

Jamal plans on doing 11 two-week test passes during system test. Three passes occur against the final increment. Jamal will accept a weekly test release—containing bug fixes for problems found in early test cycles—throughout system test, except for the last two-week pass, which he plans to run entirely against the Golden Candidate release. (See Figure 3-7 for a graphical view of this plan.) This plans rests on two assumptions.

---

8. See Chapters 6 and 7 of my book *Managing the Testing Process, Second Edition,* for some tools and techniques for managing such large test environment configuration efforts.

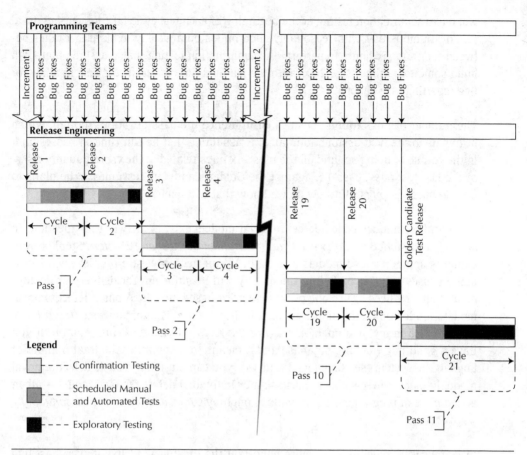

FIGURE 3-7 SYSTEM TEST EXECUTION PLAN DETAILS

The first assumption is that each pass can be run in two weeks. In the earlier discussion of the case study, Jamal used a spreadsheet to calculate how long each pass would take. He estimated how much human effort and environment resources each test case would require and then worked his staffing and test environment plans until he came up with two weeks. Of course, those are just estimates. Since he knew he'd discover additional tests to run, he adjusted his test case count up by an extra 50%, based on previous projects. There's also time built into the schedule for exploratory testing, which can increase or decrease as risk considerations relating to running the scheduled tests change.

One of the other factors he can't know for certain in advance is exactly how many bugs his testers will find each test cycle—which will make the test cases that find them take longer to run—and how many bug fixes will be delivered in each test release—which will make confirmation testing at the beginning of each test cycle take longer. My usual rule of thumb is that with reasonably good builds on a weekly test cycle, it takes between four and six hours to perform the confirmation testing. I also assume that I can build some extra time (say, 20%) into the planned time for each test case to allow for bug reporting (see Chapter 14).

The number of bugs found doesn't just influence the pass duration, though, which brings us to the next assumption. Jamal is assuming that he can run ten passes and, in the course of doing so, find all the must-fix bugs related to the critical quality risks. In the last test pass, pass 11, against the Golden Candidate test release, he plans to find no must-fix bugs. But how do we know that will happen?

Statistical techniques called defect removal models exist to answer this question. In *Metrics and Models in Software Quality Engineering, Second Edition*, Stephen Kan explains some of these models at length. If you need accurate predictions of how many passes you'll need before the quality will be sufficient for delivery or deployment, you may need to use one of these metrics-based models. A basic defect removal model founded on historical project data is discussed in Pankoj Jalote's *CMM in Practice* and also in my own book, *Managing the Testing Process, Second Edition*. If you have a good bug tracking database and a means for estimating the total number of bugs in the system (see Chapters 4 and 14), you can put Jalote's basic defect removal model in place. There's also a discussion of individual defect removal models—albeit aimed more at programmers—in Watts Humphrey's *Introduction to the Personal Software Process*.[9]

In many cases, schedules are more important than testing-and-fixing every last bug out of the product. This is one of the strengths of the Incremental development lifecycle. In the case study, should increment 5 prove to be unstable, the project team can back up to increment 4 and focus on getting that ready to ship in time for the announced date. Jamal is relying on this option when he plans the number of passes by simply working backward from the given ship date to the date on which he'll receive the first increment for system test.

Speaking of increments and delivery of particular pieces of functionality, I mentioned in the Test Development section that, to some extent, such considerations can drive when particular tests are developed. This is often a factor for test execution as well. If

---

9. It doesn't take a whole lot of data to build a projection of the total bugs to be found and fixed on a project, though it can be a challenge to make that projection accurate. One of the templates you'll find on the Web page for this book, "Estimated Bug Find-Fix Time.xls," demonstrates a very simple but often accurate model.

you happen to be running your project under a Waterfall system development lifecycle model and are responsible for system testing only, then one of the entry criteria for your test process may well be that you receive a feature-complete release before you start. In this case, all the functionality must be present before you start testing.

However, in an Incremental, Spiral, Extreme Programming, or other model where components and functionality arrive throughout the testing phase, estimation must take into account the arrival of certain components. This is always true for integration testing, which has to be driven by when the various communicating and interacting components are available. On one project, I worked with the project team to define a sequence of six integration testing *backbones*—starting with a few pieces of each subsystem and adding more pieces as they became available—the last of which was the entire system. These pieces were added in a risk-driven order, based on which problems would be most likely or most dangerous to the viability of the system's architecture. This has logistical and coverage implications beyond estimating effort and duration. I'll discuss these aspects more thoroughly in Chapters 7 and 11.[10]

Jamal has five planned integration test passes, all but the last pass four weeks long. Each pass corresponds to a single increment. This is analogous to the backbone technique I mentioned. Integration testing is about finding bugs in the communication and interaction of components, so Jamal is assuming that he can find all those kinds of bugs and confirm their repair in four weeks. Since this is Software Cafeteria's first experiment with the Incremental development lifecycle, that assumption may be incorrect. However, given the timing of the increments, this is a schedule that fits well with the overall project schedule.

Jamal's schedule includes 25 weeks of test execution, with extensive overlap between integration testing and system testing. The effort is 366 person-days, including the four test technicians, three test engineers, and some of Jamal's time.

MOVING ON TO DOLLARS AND CENTS

At this point, you should have a pretty good idea of how to develop a work-break-down-structure and an estimate of the schedule and resources required for a test sub-project. These estimates tend to be very detailed, accounting for time down to the day

---

10. As early as 1984, Boris Beizer had written a fine chapter on using risk to sequence system development and integration testing in *Software System Testing and Quality Assurance*. You can also find a thorough treatment of integration testing in *Systematic Software Testing*, by Rick Craig and Stefan Jaskiel.

and assigning resources to specific tasks. However, while a Gantt chart view of the schedule can give you the big picture in terms of time, most project management tools don't do such a good job summarizing the financial aspects. So, in the next chapter, I'll walk you through translating a work-breakdown-structure into a budget. In addition, we'll look at tying that budget back to what senior managers, executives, and stockholders really care about: return on investment.

4

IT'S NOT WHAT IT COSTS, IT'S WHAT IT SAVES: BUDGET AND RETURN ON INVESTMENT

A work-breakdown-structure and a schedule give us insight into the time and resources needed to perform our proposed test project, covering all the quality risks identified earlier to the extent proposed during the quality risk analysis. However, we're still missing one important perspective on the testing effort, the financial one. In this step of the estimation process, I'll discuss how we can create, from our work-breakdown-structure, a budget that aligns us with the financial constraints of the project. Armed with both the budget and the schedule, we'll have a complete estimate that can serve as our initial proposal to management.

During the discussion of the test project scope with management, I often must agree to reductions in the scope of testing. (That is, testing will cover fewer of the risks to system quality, will cover those risks I do test for less comprehensively, or a combination of both of these.) This reduction in scope continues until the project management team and I have moved from what we *should* test to what we actually *can* test, within the confines of the project context. A properly done quality risk analysis (as described in Chapter 2) can help the project management team guide intelligent, risk-driven reductions in the scope of testing.

Of course, we want to be careful when negotiating a workable schedule and budget that we don't fail to advocate adequate testing. Coming up with the *right* set of tests for a given project is not just a technical process, it's a political and business process as well. We must bring our credibility to bear on why we think certain tests are important to address the critical quality risks and why the resources we intend to expend on testing each quality risk are well spent. Fortunately, the budgeting process also provides test professionals with an important opportunity, that of estimating the

Return on Investment (ROI)

A measure of the value received from investing in some particular opportunity. The return on investment is the financial benefit of an investment less the initial cost of making the investment, all divided by the initial cost, as shown in the following equation:

$$ROI = \frac{(Benefit - Cost)}{Cost}$$

ROI is often multiplied by 100% to give a percentage.

return on investment in testing. There are a few techniques available to us for this purpose. Such return on investment calculations, while necessarily somewhat rough, help us advocate the most intelligent, thorough testing effort the project can support.

ANALYZING RETURN ON INVESTMENT FOR TESTING

The previous steps for creating a budget are mechanical, so I won't spend any time discussing those before demonstrating how Jamal handles the tasks. Instead, let's look at the return on investment for testing. How does testing add value for an organization?[1]

Let's start by facing the fact that some managers see testing as a big black hole at the end of the project. For these managers, the more money they throw at testing, the more it consumes. Other managers see testing as a value-adding activity that occurs throughout the project. They believe that smart test investments yield significant rewards.

As a test professional, you'll find that it's better to work for the later kind of manager, not the former. How can we convince managers that testing is a good investment, and

---

1. The following discussion provides a detailed treatment of various financial issues that might be more than you need or want to know. A simpler presentation of the same concepts can be found in my presentation "Four Ways Testing Adds Value," found at www.rexblackconsulting.com and accompanied by an audio recording of my keynote speech on that topic, given at EuroSTAR 2002 in Edinburgh, Scotland.

effectively communicate about those returns? To analyze return on investment for testing, let's revisit the following four ways I've said that testing adds value:

1. Finding bugs that get fixed—or even preventing them
2. Finding bugs that don't get fixed—but are known
3. Running tests that mitigate (potentially expensive) risks
4. Guiding the project to success through timely, accurate, credible information for project tracking

We can look at each of these ways to come up with a complete return on investment analysis. After introducing the underlying principles for each added value, I'll return to Jamal Brown, his SpeedyWriter budget, and his test subproject's return on investment.[2]

BUGS THAT GET FIXED—OR PREVENTED

Calculating the return on investment for bugs found (by testing) and fixed, or prevented by the work of the test team, prior to release involves a well-known approach called *cost of quality* analysis. The cost of quality—or cost of poor quality—technique breaks costs associated with quality into two categories, each with two subcategories, as follows:

1. Costs of conformance, which include all costs associated with ensuring and assessing quality in a system

   ▪ Prevention costs of conformance ($CC_{prevention}$) which include costs like training, peer reviews, and other true quality assurance techniques

   ▪ Detection (or appraisal) costs of conformance ($CC_{detection}$), which include the costs associated with preparing to test, running each test (once), and communicating the findings

---

2. Rick Craig, coauthor of *Systematic Software Testing* and fellow software testing consultant, pointed out to me that test cases become a valuable part of the documentation for the system. In an e-mail discussion on this chapter, he commented, "Another unheralded return on investment of testing is the fact that the test cases themselves can be considered part of the system documentation, especially on aging systems where the requirements and design specs are out of date. How often have you had a programmer come up and say, 'Rex, can I see your test cases so I can figure out how this is supposed to work?' In fact, that's a pretty good sign that as a tester, you have arrived."

2. Costs of nonconformance, which include all the costs associated with system quality problems; i.e., costs related to failure to achieve perfect quality on the first try

- Internal failure costs of nonconformance $(FC_{internal})$, which include costs associated with reporting bugs, repairing bugs, preparing a fixed build, confirming bug repair, regression testing, reworking tests and documentation, responding to changes in the system, delays in the release or deployment date, and the like

- External failure costs of nonconformance $(FC_{external})$, which typically include most of the internal failure costs plus the extra overhead of technical support, deploying maintenance releases and patches to the field, potential damage to organizational reputation and lost sales, dealing with angry customers, and other even more intangible costs

We can show the cost of quality mathematically, as follows:

$$C_{quality} = (CC_{prevention} + CC_{detection}) + (FC_{internal} + FC_{external})$$

You might ask, "So what? How do neat tricks for slicing and dicing accounting data help me?" Good question. This helps you, the underfunded test professional, because people who have researched this topic have found that, for most companies, regardless of industry, the costs of external failure tend to vastly outweigh the costs of prevention, detection, and internal failure. In Philip Crosby's book *Quality Is Free*, he explained that investments in quality can generate a quantifiable positive return on investment measured in terms of problems found and fixed before customers see them.[3]

The exact costs associated with internal and external failures tend to vary considerably for system development and maintenance. Industry-wide data is not easily found on the Internet or in publicly available studies. A well-worn rule of thumb, derived from Barry Boehm's *Software Engineering Economics*, says that a bug costs $1 if fixed during the requirements and design phase, $10 if found and fixed during programmer testing, $100 if found by an independent test team and fixed by the programmer prior to release, and $1,000 if found by a customer, fixed by a programmer,

---

3. An introduction to this topic is found in Crosby's book *Quality Is Free*. (As one reviewer, Rob Sabourin, pointed out, be careful that people don't misunderstand this title to mean that it costs nothing to achieve quality.) For more details, see Juran and Gryna's *Quality Control Handbook* or Campanella's *Principles of Quality Costs*. Finally, for application of this concept to software, see Slaughter et al., "Evaluating the Cost of Software Quality," in *Communications of the ACM,* Volume 41, Number 8 (Aug 1998).

tested internally, and then finally released as part of a maintenance release. These estimates may be either conservative or liberal for your context (see the sidebar, Calculating Defect Costs).[4]

These are average costs per bug—some bugs cost more to fix, some cost less, depending on the complexity of the fix, the amount of regression testing required, the effect of the fix on other parts of the system, and so forth. At any particular level of quality, the difference in the cost per specific bug doesn't matter. The payback that I'll demonstrate later assumes the test team will find bugs that would cost about $1,000 more to fix in the field than they would if they were fixed before release. In general, for you to achieve a positive return on investment, the total cost of detection and internal failure must be less than the total cost of external failure would be, had no testing occurred or no bugs been fixed. If the test team squanders its time and resources finding bugs that are not aligned with actual usage and the critical risks to system quality, then there is little payback, regardless of the number of bugs found.

The average cost per must-fix bug is probably not constant across different levels of system quality, though. This has some interesting implications that are worth mentioning here.

Let's say that you spent $1 million on your development project. Suppose you can measure customer satisfaction for your system on a percentage scale from 0 to 100. At 0% customer satisfaction, all your customers took advantage of a 30-day satisfaction-guaranteed warranty and returned your lousy system, so you realized no revenue at all on the project. If everyone returns your system, then your cost of nonconformance is at least $1 million, because the entire project was a waste of money because of poor quality. At 100% customer satisfaction, all customers were entirely satisfied with your system. If everyone was completely satisfied and no one returned the product, the cost of nonconformance would be only the cost associated with internal failure; i.e., fixing the bugs before release.

Let's say your development team introduces 1,000 defects into the system during development. Suppose that for defects detected internally, one-third are fixed in the requirements and design phases; one-third are fixed by programmers during coding,

---

4. Mark Fewster and Dorothy Graham quote slightly higher figures in *Software Test Automation*. Johanna Rothman reports field failures costing as much as $10,000 on average on her Web site (www.jrothman.com). Bob Bartlett, of the SIM Group, reported that one of his clients, a major bank, estimated that software failures in their production systems cost on average €150,000 (see "Power Testing," *Proceedings of the Fifth International Quality Week Europe* conference, page 191).

Calculating Defect Costs, by Ed Weller

In the absence of an accounting system designed to capture cost-of-quality information, how can you determine the cost of a defect? I have used the following approximations, in the absence of a defined process that is well executed by developers, testers, and support staff.

For system test, pick the date you started system test. This date will vary in definition from company to company but is quite often the event where all functionality is integrated into the product, and no new functionality is added (sometimes called the code freeze). From this point on, count (using your labor recording system) or estimate all effort by all people on the project until the date you ship the product. Subtract any effort in your end game that is exclusively spent on packaging the product for ship, but count any repackaging effort due to further defects discovered during the packaging process.

Now, subtract the time it takes to run one pass of the test suite error-free. While you'll have this figure if you follow the test execution process discussed in Chapter 13, this number can be difficult to estimate without test results tracking. If so, you might find that, as in many companies, this time can be ignored, since it introduces an error of less than 10%.

Finally, divide this effort number by the number of defects found and fixed during the test interval, where "fixed" means a change was logged in to the configuration management system. The kinds of bug reporting, tracking, and management processes discussed in Chapter 14 will support gathering this data.

The resulting number is your cost per defect. Note that the developers' time spent fixing defects, the release engineer's time rebuilding the release, the managers' time spent managing the work, and other project-related efforts are all counted, since none of this effort would be required if you were not finding defects. This same approach often works for integration test (or whatever phase comes before system test).

For unit test, getting this number from labor records and defect counts means that you have to be collecting effort by the activity of unit testing and counting defects discovered by unit testing. Few do this, but from experience, the cost per defect is a lot higher than developers, who hate to record both pieces of data, are willing to admit. In my consulting work, I have seen reports and data that indicate that approximating the unit test effort at about 50% of the total code and unit test effort will give you a good cost estimate.

For the number of defects, it's sad but true that this metric is not often available. For complex systems, I have seen this in the 8- to 32-hour range. For simple systems, developers will claim minutes per defect, but they often ignore the recompile, redesign, recode, and retest time. However, any time or money spent because of a bug represents a cost of nonconformance when in the test activity.

The hardest part of getting better numbers is that you must have a reasonably accurate effort-collection system. This means that when you find a problem in system test, all effort spent by testers and developers until the resolution of the problem as a defect in the product, or some other closure code, needs to be captured. The developer who enters "code" as the activity in the effort-logging system creates inaccuracies that make the cost per defect seem lower than it actually is.

I remember a test manager I worked with years ago who calculated the cost of the last defect in integration test for a large, complex flagship product. *It was 2.5 person-months*. He counted everything, did not believe the number, and recalculated it. The major part of the cost was the rerun of the entire test suite after the fix. The point of this is to be sure you capture all the costs, because the imprecise but fairly accurate numbers can be surprising.

The last comment leads to post-ship costs—costs of external failure, in cost-of-quality parlance—which include supplier and customer costs. As the supplier, you spend time finding, fixing, testing, rebuilding, and redistributing your software. In many companies, accounting rules force this effort to be calculated separately; other companies have a specialized maintenance group, and others subcontract defect repair. Don't forget the cost of your help desk function, either. The sum of these costs divided by the number of defects will give you another cost number to add to the test cost. The customer cost is often overlooked. How much lost productivity per day occurs because of blue-screen-of-death or other PC hangs or crashes? I remember a customer meeting where they stated that every hour of downtime caused by a system problem cost them about $1 million in lost manufacturing capacity. While this might not be reflected directly in your company's bottom line—unless you have service-level agreements with your customers—it leads to unhappy customers, who are often potentially *former* customers. Remember that Linux isn't popular because it is free; it is popular because it is free *and* reliable.

debugging, unit, and component testing; and one-third are fixed during the integration and system testing carried out by the test team. So, if we use Boehm's rule of thumb, for simplicity, a perfect system where all bugs were fixed before release would have the following cost of nonconformance:

$$\left(\frac{1,000}{3} \ bugs \times \frac{\$1}{bug}\right) + \left(\frac{1,000}{3} \ bugs \times \frac{\$10}{bug}\right) + \left(\frac{1,000}{3} \ bugs \times \frac{\$100}{bug}\right) = \$37,000$$

In terms of costs of conformance, let's assume that the more bugs there are in the system, the easier it is to detect them. If it takes less effort to find a bug, the cost of detection is lower. Conversely, the fewer bugs there are in the system, the harder it is to detect them. If it takes more effort to find a bug, the cost of detection is higher.

If you've ever tested a system that was full of bugs, you know that a competent test professional can find a bug at will in such systems. No planning, no tools, no test design, and no test development are required. Let's assume that in a system that would result in zero customer satisfaction, we could find the first bug for as little as $20.

As you continue to test, find bugs, and get new test releases in which those bugs are fixed, you have to work harder to find the next bug. Let's assume that a system with no bugs would result in 100% customer satisfaction, but the cost to detect the last bug through testing would be infinite.

In this model, testing and quality assurance will ultimately reach the point of diminishing returns, where the cost of quality hits a minimum as the cost of conformance equals the cost of nonconformance. [5]

Suppose that somehow we could predict customer satisfaction based on the defects remaining in the product. If so, then Figure 4-1 shows a graphical view of what our cost of quality might look like at various levels of customer satisfaction. The level of quality that minimizes the cost of quality occurs at 75% customer satisfaction. In terms of defects delivered to the customer, let's say this corresponds to about 100, meaning that 90% of the must-fix defects were removed. The investment in conformance—both quality assurance and testing—required to reach this level of satisfaction is about $125,000.[6]

Fortunately, you don't need to come up with an elaborate mathematical model and a fancy graph like this to use cost of quality. I'm going to demonstrate some simple

---

5. This idea that, at some point, the cost of conformance will exceed the cost of nonconformance is the standard cost of quality model advanced by Juran and Gryna in *Quality Control Handbook, Fourth Edition*. However, the latest thinking in the quality management movement is that, wisely done, the cost of conformance never exceeds the cost of nonconformance.
6. From the graph, you can see that the total cost of quality at this minimum is about $250,000, or 25% of the project budget. This may seem unrealistically low. However, in *Principles of Quality Costs*, Campanella et al. report that Raytheon Electronic Systems, as part of achieving a Capability Maturity Model certification of Level 4, reduced quality costs from around 80% of project costs to around 20%.

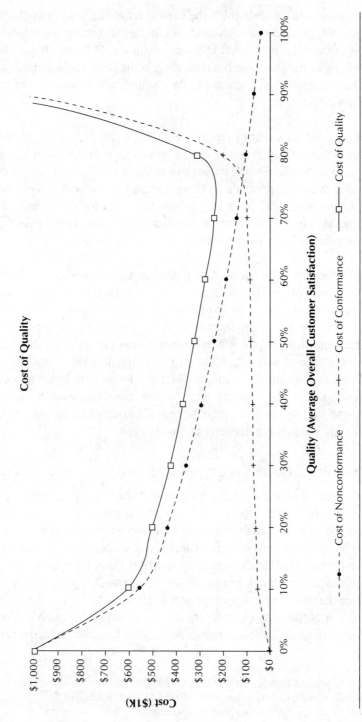

FIGURE 4-1 HYPOTHETICAL COST-OF-QUALITY GRAPH

ways to use cost of quality to discover the current return on investment in your testing operation, and, in some cases, to justify an increased investment. I'll show an example of this in the next installment of the case study later in the chapter. Jamal will only use Weller's technique for estimating costs of internal and external failure, an estimate of how many defects there are in the product, and an estimate of how many of those he can detect.

Finally, the early involvement of the test team often can prevent bugs, too. A test team that can review requirements or design specifications prior to the development, maintenance, or acquisition work proper can point out ambiguities, contradictions, missing details, and other problems in these documents. These problems would otherwise turn into at least one bug in the system, and often more than one. Testers, in my experience, are particularly effective as reviewers because they are good at asking "what if" questions and foreseeing particularly unusual situations.

The financial benefits that result from early test team involvement in this regard are the standard benefits offered by requirements and design reviews. These benefits are hard to quantify, because you'll have to track the problems found and fixed in documentation reviews to do so. Organizations that practice formal inspections or use careful defect removal models will have processes in place to track these problems, but most organizations will not. Whether these benefits are quantifiable or not, though, it's fair to say that given the considerably lower cost of fixing problems in documents compared with fixing bugs in code, the return per tester-hour invested in requirements and design reviews probably equals or exceeds the return that same hour of tester effort would provide later in the project.[7]

BUGS THAT DON'T GET FIXED—BUT ARE KNOWN

Even for bugs identified in the testing process that aren't fixed, the process has still added value. How is that? Let me use an analogy. Suppose you intend to take a long summer road trip in your automobile. Before leaving, you might stop at your neighborhood mechanic's garage to have her check out your car. She tells you everything looks fine under the hood, but you're driving on tires that have been known to fail under certain conditions of high heat, high speed, and low tire pressure. You can't afford to replace the tires, but you write a note to yourself to ensure that you operate the vehicle in a way that won't lead to tire failure, and to take additional precautions like checking your spare; keeping water, food, and a first-aid kit in the car; and so

---

7. In *Systematic Software Testing*, authors Craig and Jaskiel explain the idea of preventive testing and the ways to achieve it. Defect removal models are explained in Kan's *Metrics and Models in Software Quality Engineering, Second Edition.*

forth. This happens all the time with systems as well. Many of the bugs we find, rather than resulting in fixes, become known limitations and user precautions.

In some cases, we can actively prevent the user from entering a danger zone rather than eliminating it. For example, consider a SpeedyWriter flaw where the editor doesn't work with particular versions of Java in the browser. The installation routines could trigger an upgrade to a newer version upon user consent and prevent this particular condition from arising.

In other cases, we—and our customers—are stuck living with the bugs. In this situation, technical writers can document the known problems in release notes, user's guides, help screens, error messages, or other system documentation. Sales and marketing people can pass this information on to customers before the system is purchased or deployed. And the technical support team can load the open bug information into the support knowledge base, which is especially helpful if the bug report includes workaround information. I worked on a project where two of the junior test engineers spent a couple of weeks right before release working with the technical support manager, the technical support knowledge-base engineer, and some of the senior technical support staff to ensure that they understood the system as well as we did.

How much is it worth, all this knowledge about how the system's broken? Firm numbers are hard to come by. The extent to which workarounds and documented warnings defuse problems would be hard to calculate in any event, because a customer who solved his own problem with help messages or the user's guide doesn't call tech support to say he decided not to call tech support because of the excellent documentation. However, let's say that we can estimate the time saved by having a workaround for a problem when a customer calls in. If the system has been on the market for some time, we can look at the historical frequency of technical support calls per bug. (If it's a new system, we can, using our quality risk analysis, estimate the frequency of calls for particular bugs based on likelihood.) So, given some estimate of how many bugs we find that won't be fixed, we can estimate that savings in person-hours of technical support call center agent time.

TESTS THAT MITIGATE RISKS

So far, the only value identified for testing arises from finding bugs. We find a set of bugs and mitigate the damage through some mixture of repair, avoidance, workarounds, and warnings. This is managing the risks to quality in the sense that the post-release quality risks are reduced. We have found and dealt with specific conditions under which the quality of the system is threatened by a distinct, known hazard. We know of a failure mode that will affect some percentage of the system's users and customers some percentage of the time. We may not know those percentages with great precision, but we can look at averages. This allows us to measure return on investment as I mentioned earlier.

But is the only value of testing in the tests that fail? Or, to put it another way, does a test that passes waste the organization's money? In many cases, a primary objective of the organization is not so much to find bugs, as to reduce worry. This means that the value of testing derives not so much from the knowledge of what bugs we've found, as from the knowledge of what works and what doesn't work.

To quantify this value, we can use the economic concept of *substitution*. Substitution is the use of an alternative product or service that provides similar utility. In the case of relief from worry, the common solution is to buy insurance. (Insurance is just a statistically based mechanism for pooling risk across a large number of policy holders, so conceptually there's no reason why that pooled risk couldn't be quality risks to system projects.) What would it cost Kate, the Sumatra case study product manager, to insure her project against costs of nonconformance?[8]

Suppose that on an earlier project, before Software Cafeteria wisely hired Jamal to be its test manager, Kate had visited her neighborhood insurance agent. She said, "You know, Jimmy, I have this million-dollar system development project, and I have no idea what the level of quality is. None. It could be 0% customer satisfaction (everyone returns it) or it could be 100% customer satisfaction (everyone raves about it). I have no test team, just programmers testing their own code, so no one has the information I need to find out. I'd like you to sell me an insurance policy that will make me whole for all my costs of nonconformance."

Jimmy says, "Absolutely, Kate, I have the standard cost-of-nonconformance policy right here; sign on the dotted line, and that will be $427,000, including my 10% commission on top of XYZ Insurance Company's 25% markup." How did XYZ Insurance Company know to charge that amount?

If we strip away the markup (profit and operating costs) and commission, the actual cost of the insurance policy is $311,000. This is referred to as the expected payout, what the insurance company expects to pay on policies like this across its vast pool of policyholders. XYZ Insurance Company could come up with this number if it had a

---

8. Substitution is about similar utility, not identical replacement. Testing can tell us what parts of the system work and don't work, what risks to worry about and which risks not to worry about. However, testing won't repay the company's costs of nonconformance for bugs that do occur in the field, as an insurance policy would.

statistical model that bore out the cost-of-nonconformance curve shown in Figure 4-1, because the expected payout is the sum, across all the possible outcomes, of the product of the probability of an outcome and the cost of an outcome. If we assume, in the absence of any information about quality, that each of the 11 outcomes from 0% to 100% customer satisfaction is equally likely, then we can calculate the expected payout as follows:

$$\frac{1,000}{11}+\frac{553}{11}+\frac{437}{11}+\frac{355}{11}+\frac{290}{11}+\frac{236}{11}+\frac{188}{11}+\frac{145}{11}+\frac{106}{11}+\frac{70}{11}+\frac{37}{11} = \$1,000 \cong \$311,000$$

Where could we get a model for the costs and probability of various levels of quality? Would anyone actually buy such an insurance policy if it were offered at a fair price?

Insurance companies come up with models for expected payouts based on levels of risk. For life insurance, for example, risk is associated with certain physical exam results that measure health, certain behaviors that increase the likelihood of injury, and age. For car insurance, risk is calculated on the cost of the car you drive, your driving record, and, in some cases, your criminal history.

For system development, we could look at the likelihood and cost of certain kinds of outcomes ranging from total project failure to complete customer satisfaction across the industry in which we're doing the project, the technology with which we're working, the process maturity level in our organization, and the skills of our team.

Unfortunately, detailed data in those areas is not abundant, which explains why insurance policies for quality-related system project failures are not commonly available. Any model that we come up with is bound, in the absence of such data, to be rough. However, we do at least have a pretty good handle on the end points. We know the cost of total failure—the entire budget for the project or, in some cases, the entire value of the company. Assuming we can reliably estimate the number of defects in our product and the cost to fix the average defect before release, we can soundly approximate the cost of nonconformance at 100% customer satisfaction.

So, if we can come up with a model, even if only a straight line interpolation from project death by bug *tsunami* to total customer satisfaction through zero defects, that our management team will accept as close enough, does that mean they'd pay for insurance based on it? For some organizations, the answer would be yes. Some companies did buy—at very dear prices—insurance against computer failures related to year 2000 bugs. Even though that ended up being a relative nonevent, many of those who bought those insurance policies probably still consider purchasing those policies to be wise decisions. Had things turned out differently and the policies not been purchased, the failure of those management teams to manage that particular class of quality risks would certainly have landed many of them in court, perhaps even in jail.

For other organizations, especially small high-tech companies that develop systems as their line of business, part of how they make money is by performing high-risk ventures. As those who played the high-tech stock market in the 1990s know, big risks can lead to big rewards. (As those who held their high-tech stocks in the early 2000s know, it can also lead to big losses.) Some people choose not to have life insurance; other people consider it a prudent investment. Organizations are the same way. How much they'll pay to manage quality risks depends, in a large degree, on how risk-averse they are.

GUIDING THE PROJECT

If you dissect the phrase *quality risk management* carefully, you can see that this also implies an ability to make an informed decision. *Merriam-Webster's Collegiate Dictionary* defines "managing" as "handling or directing with a degree of skill," and "skill" as "the ability to use one's knowledge effectively and readily." In other words, to truly manage risks to quality, you must not only control the hazards you know about, but you must also gain knowledge about the system's overall quality and have some sense of what that means in terms of the future.

Look back at Figure 4-1 for a moment, focusing on the cost-of-nonconformance curve. Now, that curve is an approximation that will not apply precisely for any given organization, yours included, but the general shape—high on the low side of quality, low on the high side of quality—applies everywhere.

Most project managers I've worked with had a sense that the quality of the system affected the total costs of developing, maintaining, or acquiring that system over its lifecycle. Because part of management is always managing cost, such managers will want insight into quality. Project managers without accurate, credible, timely test results know very little about the level of quality in their systems at any moment. Further, they have even less insight into how the quality of those systems will evolve as the project moves toward a major milestone like an initial or maintenance release.

Testing can provide that insight. To do so, we must first understand the broad picture of quality risks, create a context for testing against those risks, run the tests to assess quality, and then deliver those findings in an effective, accurate, credible, and timely fashion. In this way, project managers can know what doesn't work, what works, and what remains unexplored. A well-run test project can also gather trend information that allows us to make meaningful predictions of future levels of quality and when the project will achieve a level of quality that is sufficient to release.[9]

Because we can communicate not just in terms of bugs and test cases, but also in terms of the customer's experience of quality, this assessment provides management with insight into the level of quality. How can we quantify what that insight is worth? Let's try by considering the alternative.

Let's start by observing that having accurate, timely, credible, and comprehensive assessments and predictions about system quality is a fundamental part of tracking project progress. In *Estimating Software Costs*, Capers Jones identifies four major root causes of failure, one of which is sloppy project status tracking.[10]

Jones reports that adopting better tracking practices can reduce project failure risk by approximately 50%. (He defines project failure as a schedule or budget overrun of 25% or more or outright project cancellation). Jones also reports that the risk of project failure in general is a function of project size, varying from about 2% for very small projects up to a whopping 85% for extremely large projects. Assuming something in the middle, let's say the risk of failure for a project was 40% with sloppy tracking. Good project tracking alone would bring the risk of project failure down to about 20%. If test results provide just half of the value of good status tracking, then the testing group is responsible for a 10% reduction in project failure risk through delivering good assessments and predictions to the management team.

What is a 10% reduction in risk worth? That depends on the project. If we're talking about a million-dollar project, say, then this is worth $100,000. (Notice that I'm again applying the expected payout calculation described earlier.) Such a number provides an admittedly rough estimate. Even Jones warns about the high variation in the figures he quotes. However, my take on the return on investment figures I've derived using Jones numbers is that, if anything, they tend to understate the value of test findings.

---

9. We'll look at the gathering, interpretation, and communication of test findings in more detail in Chapter 15. You can also refer to Chapters 4 and 5 of *Managing the Testing Process, Second Edition*.

10. This information originally appeared in *Patterns in Software System Failure and Success*, which is out of print, but Chapter 7 of *Estimating Software Costs* summarizes his findings. The other three causes are inaccurate estimation, poor planning, and insufficient testing. To the extent that testing affects these—especially the last one—we've already accounted for those returns in the first three subsections of this section.

Ultimately, the information that a test team can offer through an effectively communicated assessment of quality is immensely valuable to the organization. I suspect that value may even exceed the value provided in terms of bugs found and fixed before release, because it allows management to make informed decisions about quality risks with the same kind of insight that accounting departments provide for budget risks, marketing departments give for feature risks, and project management offices provide for schedule risks. While there remains a considerable amount of work to be done on the models that allow us to quantify the value of an accurate assessment of quality, it makes sense to include some estimate of this value as part of a return on investment analysis.

A FINAL NOTE ON RETURN ON INVESTMENT ESTIMATES

The point of any return on investment analysis you perform is to demonstrate the business case for the testing. In some cases, you may also want to demonstrate a business case for doing the testing that you currently do differently. For example, Fewster and Graham demonstrate the creation of a business case for test automation in *Software Test Automation*.

The business case for test automation brings up another useful fact. Some costs can be amortized across multiple projects. This applies not only to automated test scripts, but to the entire test system, including test environments, test environment configuration efforts, test data, reusable manual test cases, and other test objects. Be realistic, of course, but do keep this in mind when preparing your return on investment estimates.

On that note, it's important to keep return on investment estimates conservative. If you overstate your case to build spectacular numbers, and some manager catches you at it, you'll have done real damage to your credibility. It's also better to have sources rather than just plucking numbers out of the air. The best source for data is your own experience and past projects, because you'll understand that data better. Otherwise, you can use published data (like that in *Estimating Software Costs*) or information from other colleagues. However, for data from other people, you'll have to spend

---

Amortize

To distribute the costs and benefits of an investment across a series of time periods (e.g., monthly) or across a set of projects. This distribution represents the fair costs and benefits of the investment in each time period or to each project.

some time understanding the context in which the data came about and how the differences between that context and your context affect the data's validity for your purposes. Finally, sanity check your return on investment estimates and be ready to speak to the details. If you're going to claim that any single must-fix bug costs $1,500 if found in the field, be prepared to explain why.

JAMAL PREPARES THE BILL—AND THE JUSTIFICATION

Having studied return on investment for testing, Jamal returned to preparing his budget. Armed with his work-breakdown-structure, Jamal began with the human resources. He had decided to use a project-based assignment strategy for his test group, so Lin-Tsu, Emma, the new test engineer, and the test technicians would be assigned full-time to the project once they started.[11] Since he had other responsibilities, such as making sure that the maintenance release testing for the other products continued apace, he would assign himself half-time. He also included a travel allowance for himself, because he expected a need to visit the localization test lab, which was in another state.

While he was thinking about the localization lab, he also remembered that while he was analyzing coverage, he had sent an e-mail to a colleague he met at a testing conference asking her for a quote on usability testing. He included that quote in his budget. He wasn't really comfortable with the usability testing his team could do, since so much of the functional testing would be automated. (Automated functional testing, while efficient, often means that testers have less time to spend in hands-on interaction with each of the system's functional areas, which is key to observing usability problems.) Furthermore, no one on his team really had any insight into usability. Sure, he always urged his testers to "put their reasonable user hats on" when running tests, but that wasn't the same as having an expert look at it.

Looking at his test environment hardware, he needed two new server clusters (a Web, application, and database server) along with ten new workstations. On the software side, he would also need licenses for the servers, but he generally didn't need to include those in his budget, since Software Cafeteria had negotiated site licenses with the various vendors. Finally, for tools, he would need another license for the GUI automation and the load testing tools, so he added those amounts.

---

11. See Chapter 8 of *Managing the Testing Process, Second Edition,* for a discussion of project versus skills organization of test teams.

Step #	Step	Done?
2.A	Extract from your work-breakdown-structure a complete list of resources. For each resource, determine the first and last day of assignment to the project. If you have resources shared across multiple test projects within a given time period, understand the percentage allocation of each resource's assignment to each project during various time periods.	✔
2.B	Identify any incidental resources required to support these resources.	✔
2.C	Categorize the resources into staff, travel, tools, test environments, and, if applicable, outsourcing costs. Total by time periods and categories.	✔

Jamal looked over his first-draft budget, realizing he forgot to add a 20% contingency, which was his usual practice. With that contingency added in, the overall test budget was a little over $800,000 (see Figure 4-2). Compared with previous projects, this was high. However, then he looked at the average monthly cost of about $119,000. That figure was only a bit higher than previous projects. Just another manifestation of the early involvement and more intensive testing from the Incremental approach, he thought.

	A	B	C	D	E	F	G	H	I
1		SpeedyWriter Release 3.1 (w/DMS) IST Budget							
2		Sept	Oct	Nov	Dec	Jan	Feb	Mar	Total
5	Lin-Tsu Wu (MTE)	4,531	9,063	9,063	9,063	9,063	9,063	9,063	$58,909
6	Emma Moorhouse (ATE)	5,094	10,188	10,188	10,188	10,188	10,188	10,188	$66,222
7	TBH (ATE)	0	10,000	10,000	10,000	10,000	10,000	10,000	$60,000
8	Technicians	0	30,800	30,800	30,800	30,800	30,800	23,100	$177,100
10	Total Staff	$9,625	$67,550	$67,550	$67,550	$67,550	$67,550	$59,850	$410,975
12	Travel Allowance	$0	$0	$0	$0	$2,000	$2,000	$0	$4,000
14	Tools								
15	GUI Functional	$10,000	$0	$0	$0	$0	$0	$0	$10,000
16	Load Testing	10,000	0	0	0	0	0	0	$10,000
18	Total Tools	$ 0,000	$0	$0	$0	$0	$0	$0	$20,000
20	Test Systems								
21	Web Servers	$50,000	$0	$0	$0	$0	$0	$0	$50,000
22	App Servers	50,000	0	0	0	0	0	0	50,000
23	Database Servers	50,000	0	0	0	0	0	0	50,000
24	Clients	25,000	0	0	0	0	0	0	25,000
25	UPSes	6,000	0	0	0	0	0	0	6,000
26	Miscellaneous Supplies	1,000	0	0	0	0	0	0	1,000
28	Total Test Systems	$182,000	$0	$0	$0	$0	$0	$0	$182,000
30	External Labs								
31	Localization	$0	$0	$0	$0	$25,000	$25,000	$0	$50,000
32	Usability	0	0	0	0	0	25,000	0	25,000
34	Total External Labs	$0	$0	$0	$0	$25,000	$50,000	$0	$75,000
36	Contingency	$43,075	$13,510	$13,510	$13,510	$18,910	$23,910	$11,970	$138,395
38	Grand Total	$258,450	$81,060	$81,060	$81,060	$113,460	$143,460	$71,820	$830,370
40	Average Monthly Cost								$118,624

FIGURE 4-2 FIRST DRAFT OF THE TEST BUDGET

> **Fully Burdened Staff Rate**
>
> The cost for a single staff member, taking into account that person's salary, benefits, proportion of the infrastructure costs, and other associated costs of having employees.

Jamal hadn't seen a copy of Jenny's budget, but he knew that 11 engineers and two managers were assigned. At an average fully burdened technical staff rate of $120,000 per year, the development staff costs were about the same as his entire budget. Looking at some previous development budgets, he estimated that Kate would expect his budget to be between one-quarter and one-third of the overall project budget. I'm going to be a bit high, he thought, so I'll have to do a particularly good job selling this.

Step #	Step	Done?
2.D	Sanity check the budget details and totals. If possible, augment your professional judgment and gut instinct with previous project data, industry metrics, and so forth. Identify and, if possible, resolve discrepancies between the test subproject budget and the overall budget. Should resolution prove impossible, document the obstacles.	☑

The first step in his selling task would be to calculate the return on investment. Looking at his budget, he realized he could amortize the tools and test environments across the next 18 months, which, given their semiannual release schedules, meant three projects, including this one. Similarly, he expected to be able to amortize the test development work and configuration of the test equipment, which consumed approximately two person-months each of Emma, Lin-Tsu, and the new engineer's time. This came to about $60,000, so he would exclude all but $20,000 from this return on investment analysis.

Step #	Step	Done?
2.E	Amortize budget items that are long-term investments, documenting the reuse opportunities and the period of time over which you expect to recoup the costs.	☑

To analyze the return on investment for bugs found and bugs fixed, he needed an estimate of the number of bugs. He didn't have precise sizing data, such as lines of code or function points, since Software Cafeteria didn't use such statistics. However, with a little research into previous testing projects and the field-failure database, he found out that, on average, the systems had 35 bugs per programmer person-month that turned up either during testing or after release. There were about 75 person-months of programmer time scheduled for Sumatra. To keep his estimate conservative, he chose 2500 as the projected number of bugs. Since about 80% of those would end up getting fixed over the life of the project, he projected 2,000 as the number of must-fix bugs.

Based on previous projects, he knew that, on average, the test team managed to find about 80% of the must-fix bugs in the system. (Customers found the remaining 20%, typically, and reported them to technical support.) He hoped to do better under the new, less hurried regime, but he decided not to include such hopes in his return on investment analysis. So, he planned to detect 1,600 must-fix bugs. As a quick check, he multiplied this by his historical average test subproject cost per must-fix bug found, $500. He was happy to see that the figures matched. So, he started by assuming 1,600 must-fix bugs found.

This figure of $500 per must-fix bug counted the overall testing investment, both costs of detection and costs of internal failure associated with testing. Jamal next decided to calculate the average costs of internal and external failure for the defects.

To calculate the costs of internal failure for the test team, he first counted the retests. He had planned 11 total test passes. In six of those passes, new increments—new functionality—would arrive. So, five of the test passes were purely retests to confirm bug fixes and look for regression. The testing would go on for 22 weeks. Based on his budget calculations, the staff cost per test week was almost $17,000. This meant that the total test cost of internal failure was about $170,000, with a test cost per must-fix defect of $105 (see Figure 4-3).

On the development side, Jamal knew from Jenny that during the 22 weeks of testing, she planned for the development team to spend about half its time fixing bugs and about half its time working on new features for each increment. Using the fully burdened staff rate of $120,000 per year across the 13 people on the development team, Jamal calculated a figure of about $215 of development costs per must-fix defect. So, the total cost of internal failure per defect came to $320.

After release, the costs were associated with maintenance programmers who would fix bugs and enhance the program, and technical support staff who would field calls related to the bugs and to user error. From conversations with those managers, he knew that about 75% of the time in each group was spent dealing with bugs. Once a release went out, it was supported for a year. Based on the team sizes and the staff

	A	B	C	D	E
1	**Internal Failure**			**External Failure**	
2					
3	**Test Team Retest Costs**			**Maintenance Team Fix Costs**	
4	Retest Proportion	45%		Fix Effort Percentage	75%
5	Test Weeks	22		Maintenance Weeks	52
6	Test Staff Cost/Week (7.5 People)	$ 16,868		Developer Staff Cost/Week (2 People)	$ 4,800
7	Test Cost of Internal Failure	$ 168,679		Maintenance Cost of External Failure	$ 187,200
8	Test Cost per Bug	$ 105		Maintenance Cost per Bug	$ 468
9					
10	**Development Team Fix Costs**			**Technical Support Team Costs**	
11	Fix Effort Percentage	50%		Bug Effort Percentage	75%
12	Test Weeks	22		Support Weeks	52
13	Development Staff Cost/Week (13 People)	$ 31,200		Technical Support Staff Cost/Week (4 People)	$ 9,600
14	Development Cost of Internal Failure	$ 343,200		Technical Support Cost of External Failure	$ 374,400
15	Development Cost per Bug	$ 215		Technical Support Cost per Bug	$ 936
16					
17	**Cost of Internal Failure**	$ 320		**Cost of External Failure**	$ 1,404
18					
19	**Cost Savings Per Bug Found in Testing**				$ 1,084

FIGURE 4-3 CALCULATING SUMATRA INTERNAL AND EXTERNAL FAILURE COSTS

rates, this information enabled Jamal to estimate a cost of external failure of $1,404 per must-fix defect.

So, every must-fix bug found by the test team saved the company about $1,084. Tossed into the cost-of-quality equation, that yielded a benefit of about $1.7 million. Cool, he thought, already a positive return on investment and not even done counting.

Now, for the 500 or so bugs found and not fixed, usually about one-third of those turned out to be tester errors, mistakes in system configuration, and other nonbugs. This left about 300 bugs that were real problems that, for whatever reason, were deferred. Based on discussions he'd had with Cosimo Negraev, the Customer Support manager, having this information in the support knowledge base usually saved 15 minutes per related call. Further, Cosimo had mentioned to him that for each bug in the system, they usually received five calls. Again, using the fully burdened staff rate estimate of $120,000 per year, he came up with $60 per hour. So, the benefit of the found and not fixed bugs was about $25,000.

Next, Jamal looked at the value of risk mitigation. In the quality risk analysis process, the participants had rated the likelihood of problems in the following two quality risk categories as very high:

- Load, capacity, and volume
- Reliability and stability

From a conversation with Muhammad Ajami, the Fortune 1000 and government sales-person, he knew that problems in these areas would cost them at least $2 million in sales revenue. Large customers would encounter these problems most severely and would not tolerate them. Assuming that there was just a 50% likelihood of such failures, that meant that the risk mitigation benefit of testing in these areas alone was $1 million.

Finally, he looked at the benefit of the project tracking information. Having read Jones's book, he decided to use a 10%-of-the-project rule of thumb. Estimating his share—very roughly—of the project budget at 40% yielded an overall project cost of $2 million. The assessment and prediction information he would deliver to the project management team, then, by reducing the risk of project failure by 10%, would result in a $200,000 benefit.

Overall, Jamal came up with benefits from the testing plan he proposed of about $3 million, a 350% return on the testing investment (see Figure 4-4.) Though he was forbidden by Software Cafeteria policy to discuss budget numbers with his team, he was very comfortable with the conservative yet compelling return he was able to

	A	B	C
1	Sumatra Test ROI		
2			
3	**Testing**	**Costs**	**Benefits**
4	Staff (test development amortized)	$ 370,975	
5	External Labs	75,000	
6	Travel and Contingency	142,395	
7	Environments (amortized)	60,667	
8	Tools (amortized)	6,667	
9	**Total Investment**	**$ 655,703**	
10			
11	**Defect Estimates**		
12	Estimated Bugs Delivered to Test	2,500	
13	Estimated Must-Fix Bugs Delivered to Test	2,000	
14	Estimated Defect Detection Percentage	80%	
15	Estimated Found-Not-Fixed Bug Rate	20%	
16	Estimated Found-Not-Fixed Bugs	500	
17	Estimated Found-Not-Fixed Non-Bug Rate	67%	
18			
19	**Bugs Found and Fixed**		
20	Must-Fix Bugs Found	1,600	$ 1,734,400
21			
22	**Bugs Found and Not Fixed**		
23	Deferred Bugs Found	333	$ 25,000
24			
25	**Tests that Mitigate Risks**		
26	Sales Subject to LCV or Reliability Loss	$ 2,000,000	
27	Likelihood of Sales Loss w/o Testing	50%	$ 1,000,000
28			
29	**Guiding the Project**		
30	Project Cost at Risk for Bad Tracking	$ 2,000,000	
31	Reduction in Risk due to Testing	10%	$ 200,000
32			
33	**Total Benefits**		**$ 2,959,400**
34			
35	**Return on Investment**		**351%**

FIGURE 4-4 THE TESTING RETURN ON INVESTMENT FOR JAMAL'S FIRST DRAFT OF THE BUDGET

project. He looked forward to selling his budget to the project management team. After all, he was excited to get a green light to move forward.

Step #	Step	Done?
2.F	If it is required or desirable, analyze the return on investment. If the return on investment is negative, review your assumptions about amortization in 2.D and repeat this step if necessary. If the return on investment remains negative, review those items on your estimated work-breakdown-structure that consume the most money while contributing the least return, tracing back to the quality risks. Document the money losing activities.	✔
2.	Use the work-breakdown-structure and schedule to develop a budget.	✔

Do the Fast Always Eat the Slow?

Does time-to-market always trump quality? Until the dot-bomb phenomenon exploded in 2000, lots of people talked about *Internet time,* often in connection with throwing releases of unknown quality onto the Web with little if any testing. However, it's dangerous to take a dogmatic, inflexible position that schedule risks always outweigh quality risks in market-driven software and hardware. Let me illustrate with an anecdote.

The Personal Digital Assistant (PDA) market is already enormous and is expected to grow even larger. One of the first entries in that field was Apple Computer, which released the Newton years before the Palm Pilot came on the market. If it is a hard-and-fast rule that speed-to-market trumps quality, then Apple should own the PDA market. Why doesn't it?

When the Newton was first released, it suffered from serious bugs in its handwriting recognition abilities. One buyer of a Newton happened to be Garry Trudeau, the "Doonesbury" cartoonist syndicated widely in North America. He began to satirize the poor handwriting recognition in the Newton in an extensive series of cartoons over a period of weeks.

In this chapter, we've looked at a way to count the costs associated with this kind of damage to company reputation. These costs are primarily in the category of lost sales because of nonconformance to customer requirements. When companies make claims for their products that those products spectacularly or, perhaps worse, humorously don't fulfill, those companies set themselves up for a repeat of Apple's experience. It would be difficult to quantify the cost of nonconformance for the Newton's external failures, but a ballpark figure might come from imagining what it would mean to Apple financially every year if they were the leading seller of PDAs.

MOVING FORWARD, THEN LOOKING BACK

In this chapter, I outlined, and then demonstrated through Jamal's example, my approach for translating a work-breakdown-structure into a budget and analyzing the return on investment inherent in the proposed test effort. At this point, you have a solid estimate of the time and resources involved in addressing the critical quality risks, along with a justification for why doing so makes sense not only in terms of quality, but also financially. Nothing left to do but drop that package on a manager's desk and await praise of your business acumen and instant access to all your requested resources, right? Unfortunately, that's generally not the case.

In the next chapter, I'll wind down my discussion of estimation by starting out with the selling process. You have created a compelling proposal, but now you must sell it to management. You'll need to make them want the quality risks management products and services you can offer, and overcome the inevitable objections to the time and money involved in delivering them. After getting closure on selling a budget, I'll then engage in a retrospective on this challenging process of estimation. Before we move on to developing test plans, we should look at the indicators of good test estimation, the challenges to making good test estimates, and a road map you can use to move your test estimation process forward.

5

FROM ESTIMATE TO BASELINE: OBTAIN COMMITMENT TO REALISTIC, ACTIONABLE, TRUTHFUL ESTIMATES

In this chapter, I'll wind up my discussion on test project estimation. First, I'll look at what is perhaps the hardest step in the process, obtaining management commitment to the estimate we've prepared. Convincing managers to take the time and spend the money for good testing takes credibility and persuasiveness. A believable estimate and a compelling business case are key parts of this equation. The steps shown in the last two chapters give you some idea of how to develop them. However, ultimately your political capital and skills will be put to the test when you sell the estimate to management.

After I finish examining this tricky process, I'll look back at the entire estimation process. How do you know you've prepared a good estimate? What factors promote such estimates? What challenges exist? And how can you institute better estimation techniques? I'll answer those questions in the second half of this chapter.

SELLING THE ESTIMATE

Coming up with a good, solid estimate, including the return on investment, is hard enough, but getting management support is a challenge of a different kind. Even the best test subproject estimate with the most solid business case can run into obstacles. Some of these obstacles may cause you to scale back your original scope. Sometimes there is no alternative, since the organization truly can't afford to cover all the risks to system quality identified as important during the quality risk analysis. So, let's review some of the obstacles we encountered, and then I'll address ways we can surmount them.

Let me start off with the obstacles we create for ourselves as test professionals. Those of us in the field tend to see testing and quality as intrinsically important. Over years, certain truths about testing and quality become so obvious to us that it can affect our ability to communicate with those people who don't see the project through the same mental filters. Those people might include the managers we need to approve our budgets. So we often fail to communicate to our managers in terms those managers can understand. As James Bullock put it, "When we...try to justify testing, we often argue from a misconception...that testing is *the right thing to do*."[1]

Now, you and I might see testing as an important part of delivering a quality product. You and I probably agree that we are correct in that perception. However, the importance of testing is not necessarily obvious to a manager. This is especially true when that manager is looking at a proposed budget that eats up a substantial portion of the money needed for the overall project and a schedule that delays the ship date. Worse yet, some testers react to challenges to the need for testing by being self-righteous about quality. This kind of attitude sabotages their budgeting efforts.

To communicate effectively with project and senior managers, I try to see how testing fits into the bigger picture. Rather than see myself as the lone defender of quality, I picture my role as that of a testing professional. I help my project colleagues manage the risks to the quality of the system we're building, maintaining, or acquiring. What are those quality risk management services and information worth to them? Can I think of ways to communicate, in terms my managers will understand, why those products and services might be worth more than they think? Can I persuade people to test from a business perspective?

Once you start to see testing within a broader context, the business realities of testing will become clear, revealing the next set of obstacles. OK, a senior manager might say, testing is valuable, but look at the cost and schedule implications. Depending on the project, the human resources for testing often can compose 15% to 50% of the staff. Userlike test environments—essential for system testing—can be extensive, costly, and hard to maintain. Each test cycle after the first test cycle delays deployment. These delays are vexing to management because time is money for projects: Late ship dates mean contractual penalties, marketing windows missed, value not delivered to in-house users, and so on.

---

1. This and other thoughts are found in James Bullock's article "Calculating the Value of Testing," in *Software Testing and Quality Engineering*, Volume 2, Issue 3 (May/June 2000), and now available at www.stickyminds.com.

In some organizations, a senior manager may also see some political pain associated with proposing a slip in the schedule or a bump in the budget. The initial schedule and budget, even if it appears hasty and penurious to testers and other people doing the actual work, might have been secured only through great gumption on the part of the project management team. I am aware of a case where a project manager was fired in part for defending an intelligent investment in testing. I've found it pays for me to be sensitive to whether my test estimate, if approved, would force the project management team to reopen such a debate about the project schedule and budget. If so, then I'll include extra justification that will appeal to those most likely to resist such changes.

Most project managers are experienced professionals. They have usually been around a number of system projects and can recall a planned brief test execution phase that ballooned by one week, then two weeks, then four weeks, and so on, all the while the panic levels rising higher. So, an experienced project manager will see your budget and schedule for what it often is: a lower bound, a minimum investment in testing, a small opening bid.[2]

"Now wait," you might say, "didn't you just get through telling me in the last chapter that testing, intelligently done, produces a positive return on investment? That quality is free?" Yes, I did, and yes, that's true. However, that's only in the long run, over the entire system lifecycle. However, system development, maintenance, and acquisition efforts are often budgeted on a project basis, not a system lifecycle basis. For any given project, limited money is available. Therefore, on the one hand, the testing investment has a positive return on investment, but on the other hand, it also represents, like any investment, foregone expenditures elsewhere.

In some cases, we must convince managers who don't understand testing or have little experience with a well-run testing project. This creates additional obstacles to getting management buy-in. First, we have to make the managers aware of the value testing can offer the project. Second, we have a limited amount of time in which to do that, because most project managers are busy attending to all the other chain saws they're juggling. Third, some test managers find it hard to articulate the realities of testing to people who haven't been on the inside of a test project. As test professionals, we have

---

2. As Fred Brooks wrote in 1975 in *The Mythical Man-Month*, "Failure to allow enough time for system test, in particular, is peculiarly disastrous. Since the delay comes at the end of the schedule, no one is aware of the schedule trouble until almost the delivery date. Bad news, late and without warning, is unsettling . . . to managers [and] has unusually severe financial, as well as psychological, repercussions. The project is fully staffed, and cost-per-day is maximum. More seriously . . . the secondary [opportunity] costs of delaying . . . are very high. . . . It is therefore very important to allow enough system test time in the original schedule."

focused on a growing, changing, exciting specialty within the system development field. This means that many of our colleagues, including those who supervise us and approve our requests for resources, can't keep up with the pace of change in the theory and practice of testing. So they often can't understand the details of what we do, why we do it, or the dynamics of testing projects.

How can we surmount these obstacles? This is a contextual question, because ultimately this is a sales question. How do you sell something? That depends not just on the product and service, but on the buyer, and everyone is different. However, the overall process is simple: Make the product or service that you're selling desirable to the person you're trying to convince, and then deal with that person's objections to the sale. I generally use the following techniques.

For one thing, I try to sell my estimates based on risks. Given a solid quality risk analysis, I can make a strong case for what I'm proposing because I can tie in the issue of what failures in the field could mean to the business. Each task in the schedule, every dollar in the budget, traces back to some critical quality risk. What I try to do is make the value clear: "If we're worried about this risk, here's what it costs to mitigate it through testing." Spend some time sketching out catastrophic profit-, mission-, or even life-threatening incidents that you can detect before the release, especially for expensive budget items like servers and employees. Has a competitor or just another organization in a similar industry deploying a similar system become embroiled in a lawsuit because of a system quality debacle?

In addition, because I'm asking for a slice of a fixed pie—a portion of the overall project budget, which is often well defined at this point—I can't make this case in a vacuum. If I try to do so, then I'm playing a zero-sum game with my peer-level managers. So, part of my selling approach for a budget includes alliances. In Chapter 1, I talked about the challenge of building strong relationships with internal customers such as programmers, sales and marketing staff, customer support technicians, and network operations administrators. Now is a good time to leverage those relationships. Identify specific ways in which your budget supports providing the services and products these customers need. Identify which of those services and products you may not be able to offer should your budget be cut. Ask your peers for their support. Don't forget the human aspects of getting this support, too. Since testers perform a service role, testers must have a service-oriented outlook. I strive to build collegial, positive relationships with people on the project team, making sure that my test team and our work is seen as a supportive and positive factor for project success.

I also use my return on investment analysis. However, I'll go beyond just laying out the numbers. If I trot out a figure—"We're going to achieve a 375% return on investment in testing"—that's not very compelling except as the executive summary for a longer explanation of how I got that number and what it signifies.[3]

To explain return on investment, I go beyond the dry tactical categories—finding bugs, supporting bug fixing, mitigating risks, and guiding the project—to connect with why managers invest in testing to begin with. For example, how much will the test subproject we propose allow the organization to decrease overall system costs associated with quality problems? What level of confidence can we give management about the reliable operation of the system in the field? Don't be afraid of the intangibles, too. Just because you can't put a number on it, ask your managers what it would be worth to enjoy an improved reputation in system quality. What's it worth to reduce chaos, improve morale, and increase staff retention?

Reasonable project managers often respond to these points by saying to me, "Okay, I want the testing benefits, but why do they have to cost so much and take so long?" This is when I need to be able to effectively articulate a test project plan, the topic of the next two chapters. Our ability to explain the logistical realities and the dependencies between testing and the rest of the project helps managers see the challenges we face in testing. In addition, I need historical data, ideally from similar projects, to explain why it will take as long as I estimate for the project team collectively to find and fix the important bugs.

In some cases, there is excessive optimism about the quality of the system going into testing and overall project progress. In such cases, I point out that shortening the *approved* test schedule and trimming the *approved* test budget may make the published project release date and cost *look better* in the short run, but that reductions in adequate quality control actually increase the risk of schedule and budget overruns, often far beyond where those numbers would have ended up had a realistic schedule and budget been in place from the start. Bugs caught early through effective and efficient testing (including static testing like requirements, design, and code reviews) can be quickly and cheaply removed with little impact on the project. However, major bugs that appear in the last couple weeks can be fatal.

In the overall approach to selling my budget, I take care to advocate rather than pontificate. If I'm dealing with managers who don't understand testing and are skeptical about my budget and schedule, then my challenge is to rise to the task and put forward

---

3. In Douglas Adams's hilarious book *The Hitchhiker's Guide to the Galaxy*, a computer calculates the meaning of life to be 42. This result mystifies and chagrins the people who programmed the computer to figure out what life was all about. A free-floating ROI number might be equally unenlightening to your managers.

a positive, compelling case for the proposal. I may be passionate, but I avoid preaching. As part of selling an estimate, I consider the onus on me to be willing and able to educate peers, senior managers, and executives. If I properly motivate them—in other words, if I make what I'm selling desirable—then they'll want to understand what I'm proposing.[4]

JAMAL MAKES HIS CASE

On Friday afternoon, as he was winding down his estimate, Jamal called his boss, John Albertson, the VP of Engineering Services. "Hi, John," he said, "I'm going to be ready to discuss a proposed schedule and budget for testing Sumatra with you on Monday. Do you have some time in the morning?"

"Sure," John said, "I'll put you down for 10:00 AM."

Next, Jamal walked over to see Kate Hernandez, the SpeedyWriter product manager, with a copy of his schedule and budget in hand. "Hi, Kate, got a minute?"

"Sure, come on in. What's up?"

"Well," Jamal said, "I have a schedule and budget estimate that I intend to propose for this project and I thought I'd run it by you." He quickly laid out for Kate the various activities, the costs, and the ROI analysis. "Based on this budget and schedule, I think we can do a really thorough job of testing and give you very accurate assessments of where the project stands—and where it's going—at the weekly status meetings."

Kate scratched her head. "It is a bit higher than I expected. I looked at previous projects and came up with half a million for testing."

"Yes, but those test subprojects only lasted four or five months. Our per-month costs are only slightly higher than what we've seen on previous projects. I'm using mostly contract test technicians to keep the costs down."

After some further discussion, Kate agreed to see if she could trim some money from the marketing budget and from Jenny Kaufman's development budget to partially off-

---

4. You can find some other good ideas about selling testing to management in Jeff Payne's article "Quality Meets the CEO," which first appeared in *Software Testing and Quality Engineering* magazine, Volume 1, Issue 3 (May/June 1999), now at www.stickyminds.com.

set the $300,000 overage. The rest, she told Jamal, she'd work out with Rajesh and Max, the CEO and the vice president of Marketing, respectively.

On the way back to his office, Jamal stopped by Jenny's office to run his schedule and budget past her—at a high level—and to warn her about the possible budget trim she'd face. Jenny wasn't too happy about the cut, especially when she figured out it could result in the loss of a whole person. Jamal did a little horse trading at this point, though, offering to actually pitch in on the component test development. "Heck, we need those tests anyway, Jenny, so it won't hurt if we work with your team to develop a few of them."

"You know," Jenny said, "that would probably work out better that way, too. We could use some expert assistance on getting those tests and that test harness up and running."

After some further small talk, Jamal continued his trek back to his office, asking Jenny on the way out the door if she wouldn't mind letting Kate know this afternoon that, in general, she was in support of his estimated schedule and budget. Jenny agreed to send a quick e-mail documenting their discussion and that she was in agreement with a small adjustment to her budget, provided Jamal's team could provide extra support to her component test effort.

On Monday morning, Jamal went to see John. In addition to the solid estimate he had prepared, Jamal brought his reputation as an understated, reliable, and credible member of the management team. When he arrived, Harold, the vice president of System Engineering, was just winding down a discussion with John. "Good morning, Jamal," Harold said, "good to see you. Jenny mentioned that you two discussed an estimated schedule and budget for testing, and Kate told me that you had a pretty good plan together. Mind if I sit in for this discussion? I'd like to get educated."

Neither Jamal nor John had any objections, so the three of them spread out Jamal's Failure Mode and Effect Analysis worksheet, test coverage analysis, Gantt chart, budget, and return on investment worksheets on a long table in John's office and got down to work. Jamal started with the Failure Mode and Effect Analysis worksheet and the coverage analysis, saying, "Let's first look at how I came up with this estimate and what risks we're going to mitigate." He walked through the various risks—including why they mattered—and the test cases that covered them. This brought him to the work-breakdown-structure, where he showed the supporting tasks. Then he presented the budget and, finally, the return on investment worksheets. Throughout his discussion, John and Harold asked various clarifying questions, but made no comments. At the end, Jamal asked, "So, what do you think?"

Step #	Step	Done?
3.A	Present the benefits of the test subproject.	✔
3.B	Outline the time and money commitment required to receive those specific benefits.	✔

John nodded and said, "I think you've done a good job coming up with a very well-documented estimate, and I think you've done a good job of presenting it. But..."

"I was hoping there was no 'but' here," Jamal joked.

"I'm afraid there is. Harold, Kate, and I have kicked this around a bit, and I don't think we can come up with 800K for this. I'm guessing that 700K is more realistic."

Jamal replied, "I can cut the contingency out of the budget to get you that, but I don't think that's realistic. We'll end up needing that 20% somewhere—I just don't know where yet."

John nodded, but Harold put in, "You know, I'm guessing that that contingency is to cover unexpected schedule slips, right? If that's the case, you have two months' worth of test staff costs in there. Given this Incremental approach we're using, I think you could cut that in half. We won't slip more than a month, I'm sure."

"Sounds fair enough," Jamal said, "provided we all understand that if the schedule slips beyond a month, then I'm going to run over my budget." John and Harold nodded. "Now, we still need another 60,000 in savings to be within a $700,000 budget. We'll need to trim some testing for that."

"What if we don't hire this additional test engineer? That's almost exactly right."

"In that case, I'll have to push out the start of test execution by about a month, and I don't think I'll be able to fulfill my commitment to help Jenny with the component testing."

"Hmm," Harold replied, "that's no good. We're really counting on that."

"How about this?" Jamal suggested. "Instead of running the reliability tests and the stress tests in parallel on two distinct configurations every pass, what if we just buy one extra server configuration and alternate the reliability and stress tests every other pass? That will create something of a regression gap, because we have less information about which exact build affected the reliability or the stress handling, but it does save us $75,000 on the extra test environment."

Harold and John liked this idea—a lot. Jamal did, too. This actually would not only reduce the cost, it would also free up some of Emma's time, because she wouldn't have to worry about running both automated tests at once. John and Harold told Jamal to go ahead and run with that estimate. Jamal checked the schedule and budget documents into the project repository, and then got ready to start test planning.

Step #	Step	Done?
3.C	Understand and attempt to resolve through iteration of steps 3.A and 3.B any objections to the estimate.	☑
3.D	If management commitment to the proposed budget and schedule cannot be gained, discuss specific areas of testing to be deleted, setting cost and/or schedule goals to be met to obtain management support.	☑
3.	Obtain management support for the estimated schedule and budget.	☑
4.	Repeat steps 1 through 3 if necessary, fine-tuning the estimated schedule and budget, until resources and management commitment adequate to the (possibly adjusted) scope of the test effort are secured.	☑
5.	Check the approved budget and schedule documents into the project library or configuration management system. Place the document under change control.	☑

RECOGNIZE A GOOD ESTIMATION PROCESS

I've given you a lot of information about estimation in the last three chapters. You might think that all the complexity of the estimation process means it's really tough to spot good ones. However, with a little practice, you'll find it's not hard at all. We can recognize a good estimation process because it allows the team to do the following.

UNDERSTAND THE FACTORS THAT AFFECT THE ESTIMATE

System development, maintenance, and acquisition efforts—including the testing—are complex, high-risk human endeavors. Thus, it's important to combine good estimation techniques with an understanding of the factors that can influence effort, time, dependencies, and resources. Some of these factors can act to slow down or speed up the schedule, while others, when present, can only slow things down.

Some of these factors arise from the process by which work is done:

- The extent to which testing activities pervade the project or are tacked on at the end
- Clearly defined handoffs between testing and the rest of the organization
- The amount of change that occurs on the project, especially if you're using automated or precisely scripted manual tests
- A well-managed change control processes for project and test plans, product requirements, design, implementation, and testing
- The chosen system lifecycle, including the effectiveness, efficiency, and degree of organization of testing and project processes within that lifecycle
- Realistic and actionable project and testing schedules and budgets
- The timely arrival of high-quality test deliverables
- Timely and reliable fixes of the bugs that are found, especially when test phase entry criteria are violated
- Proper execution of early test phases (unit, component, and integration)

Some of these factors are material and arise from the nature of the project, the tools at hand, the resources available, and so forth:

- Existing, assimilated, high-quality test and process automation and tools
- The quality of the test system, by which I mean the test environment, test process, test cases, test tools, and so forth
- Reusable test systems and documentation from previous, similar projects
- An adequate, dedicated, and secure test environment
- A separate, adequate development debugging environment
- The availability of a reliable test oracle (so we can know a bug when we see one)
- Available, high-quality (clear, concise, accurate, and so on) project documentation, such as requirements, designs, plans, and so forth
- The similarity of the project and the testing to be performed to previous endeavors

Some factors arise from the people on the team, and these can be the most important of all:

- Proper skills, experience, and attitudes in the project team, especially in the managers and key players and in training and hiring new people
- Organizational changes, including wholesale midproject reorganizations

- Resentment and other relationship problems within the project team
- Overtime, weekend work, and off-hours shifts
- Burnout or morale problems, especially from previous projects
- Cultural norms and work habits
- The competence and experience of the project management team
- Inspired and inspiring managers and technical leaders, especially an enlightened management team who are committed to appropriate levels of quality and sufficient testing
- Project-wide appreciation of testing, release engineering, system administration, and other unglamorous but essential roles (i.e., not an "individual heroics" culture)
- Realistic expectations across all participants, including the individual contributors, the managers, and the project stakeholders
- The stability of the project team, especially the absence of turnover
- Established, positive project team relationships, again including the individual contributors, the managers, and the project stakeholders
- Competent, responsive test environment support
- The use of skilled contractors and consultants to fill gaps
- Honesty, commitment, transparency, and open, shared agendas among the individual contributors, the managers, and the project stakeholders

Finally, some complicating factors, when present, always increase schedule and effort:

- High complexity of the process, project, technology, organization, or test environment
- Many stakeholders in the testing, the quality of the system, or the project itself
- External dependencies, especially on nonstakeholders
- Location issues, in terms of geographically distributed project teams or office locations that make commuting or getting lunch time-consuming
- Many subteams, especially when those teams are geographically separated
- The need to ramp up, train, and orient a growing test or project team
- The need to assimilate or develop new tools, techniques, or technologies at the testing or project levels
- The presence of custom hardware
- Any requirement for new test systems, especially automated testware, as part of the testing effort

- Any requirement to develop highly detailed, unambiguous test cases, especially to an unfamiliar standard of documentation
- Tricky timing of component arrival, especially for integration testing and test development
- Fragile test data—for example, data that is time sensitive

On each project, specific aspects of the project in each category influence the resources and time required for various activities. When preparing a test estimate, the test manager and those on the test team who help with estimation must consider how each of these factors will affect the estimate.

Forgetting just one of these factors can turn a realistic estimate into an unrealistic one. Experience is often the ultimate teacher of these factors, but smart test managers can learn to ask smart questions—of themselves and the project team—about whether and how each factor will affect their project.

PAINT A REALISTIC PICTURE OF THE PROJECT'S FUTURE

The number one attribute of any good prediction of the future is, of course, whether it comes true. Did we predict the future accurately, with some reasonable degree of precision? Of course there will be some error, we'll be off by some percentage of time and money, but if we are good estimators, half our estimates should be high, half low. Also, the extent by which we'll be off should be measured in percentages like 10% and 20%, not whole numbers like factors of two, three, or four.

Sadly, many official project schedules and budgets are exceeded, often by significant amounts. Any given issue of a business newspaper or magazine will probably contain some postmortem story about an information technology or systems development project that went over budget and past schedule. I've seen this happen for a number of reasons.

- *New technologies*—In some cases, projects that apply new technologies are underestimated. No one really knows how long the work will take, since no one has done it before.
- *Team performance*—Some project teams do not achieve the necessary levels of effectiveness or efficiency because of turnaround, attrition of key personnel, lack of training, and so forth. (See Chapters 8 and 9 for some ideas on how to deal with this in the testing project.)

- *Lack of knowledge*—Some project management teams fail to apply good estimation techniques.

- *Lack of agreement*—On some projects, significant and ongoing disputes between key stakeholders prevent agreement on what exactly is to be built. Beyond the fact that we can't estimate the testing effort for an ever-changing target, a successful delivery can't occur.

- *Excessive external constraints*—Some project management teams build schedules and budgets around numbers dictated from marketing, users, accountants, and other people outside the process of system development, maintenance, or acquisition, which is a problem when the feature set and the level of system quality are also externally constrained.

- *Stretch goals*—Some project management teams proclaim targets they know will not be achieved in order to apply pressure to the individual contributors to work harder.

- *Funding*—In some cases, the sponsoring organization or company funders (e.g., venture capitalists) won't fund a project unless it costs less than a certain amount or delivers on a certain schedule, which unsurprisingly results in projects with exactly such budget amounts and schedule milestones.

With the exception of the first two factors, these are issues that we can—and I suggest should—deal with in the estimation process. I set as my goal preparing a realistic, actionable, truthful estimate and then negotiating appropriate changes in project scope and testing coverage as necessary to fit that schedule into the overall schedule.

Reality in estimation implies completeness. In other words, all the tasks necessary to create project success have been identified. I worked on a large development project that was distributed across six teams in three cities on two continents. In the initial schedule, the project team forgot to include integration and integration testing phases, activities, or even tasks. No effort was allocated to put together the constituent components from the disparate teams and make sure they meshed. That's unrealistic.

For an estimate to be real, it must include every phase, activity, and task required for success. Rigorously following the work-breakdown-structure decomposition rules discussed earlier is one way to promote completeness, as is getting the entire project team, especially the seasoned individual contributors, involved in the estimation effort.

Preparing a realistic schedule also implies obtaining and using realistic cost and effort estimates for each task. I worked on another large project where one key part of the project involved changing from flat-file data storage to a relational database. Only two weeks were allocated for developing the tools and a process for converting all the data from the old system architecture to the new. That's unrealistic, too.

For an estimate to be real, it must be based on rational task durations. Again, following good work-breakdown-structure practices helps, as do Delphi exercises and other techniques that draw on expertise within the team.

ASSIGN RESPONSIBILITY FOR ACTION

An actionable estimate is one where ownership of all the constituent tasks is clear to—and accepted by—all individual contributors and managers. I once saw a schedule where the decomposition had stopped at the activity level, each activity having half a dozen or so people assigned to it and lasting two or three weeks. How could anyone know what exactly was expected of them? To add to the confusion, the test team was called the "Quality Assurance Group." They thought—and were told—that their job was to implement process change. However, everyone else on the project team thought they were there to test the product.

I told the executive in charge of the project that I had no idea how he would judge where he was on the schedule or whether people were doing the right thing. With an actionable estimate, no one should be confused about what tasks fall within their realm of responsibility and how they can measure completion—in terms of key deliverables to the project—for every one of those tasks.

Actionable estimates take into account the limitations of the resources involved, too. For example, a classic mistake is to plan to use the same server cluster for both functional and performance testing at the same time. Another problem occurs when people plan on using test environments located in other offices, with no practical way to control the configuration and operation of the environments. Dependencies exist between testing tasks based on the resources that are used.

> **Critical Path, Critical Network**
>
> The set of tasks (in terms of task or activity duration) in the project work-breakdown-structure (honoring all the intertask dependencies) that must be completed on time for the project to complete on time. In other words, the set of tasks that, when laid end-to-end based on their dependencies, determine the earliest possible project completion date consists of those tasks on the project's critical path.

Actionable estimates must identify not just resource dependencies, but all dependencies, networks, and critical paths. We should recognize that our estimates will fall short of perfection. So, we should try to predict the repercussions when tasks finish late or go over budget. This is especially important for the test manager, who must understand when specific deliverables will be handed off to his team, by whom, and through what process.

Dependencies, networks, and critical paths are also an element in truthful schedules. The compounding of risk along the critical path is a startling but important fact for test professionals and managers to understand. Let's look at the math that explains how these risks compound.

Suppose you have a dozen tasks on the critical path for a project. Each has a 90% chance of completing within the allocated amount of time. Each has a 0% chance of completing in less than that time. Notice that the timely completion of each task is conditional on the timely completion of the preceding tasks. A statistical fact of life called Bayes Theorem, which deals with conditional probability, tells us that the last task on the critical path has less than a 30% chance of completing on time, which can be represented as follows:

$$.9 \times .9 \times .9 \times .9 \times .9 \times .9 \times .9 \times .9 \times .9 \times .9 \times .9 \times .9 = .9^{12} \cong .28$$

If the chance of each task completing on time falls to 75%, the overall odds of a timely completion fall to about 3%. Suppose, as is often the case, that the last task on the critical path is a milestone representing project completion? The compounding of risk along the critical path gives us an unemotional, logical, purely mathematical reason why using schedules as stretch goals, or a means to pressure people into working harder, is so counterproductive—and so frequently unsuccessful.

Contingency plans, slack, milestones, and phase entry criteria can help manage these dependency-related impacts to the schedule. Good estimates contain task failures within bounded periods of time. Good estimates allow us to react and reassess at regular intervals. Good estimates allow us to understand and manage the impact of critical-path and near-critical-path task time and effort overruns before a schedule crisis erupts at the end of a project.

PREDICT WITH HONESTY

Truthful estimates are also honest with and trusting of the team. When managers ask for estimates from their teams, they should accept those estimates as realistic, not as underhanded attempts by slackers to win an easy schedule. I remember a meeting where the project managers agreed that the current schedule was a fiction but decided to keep it anyway to set a stretch goal for the development team.

That kind of management style strikes me as dishonest and founded on an assumption that people are fundamentally lazy. As a matter of fact, most of the estimates I get from my team members are overly optimistic. I find that I have to discuss the underlying assumptions with people and often adjust their estimates upward. Sometimes the individual contributors don't see all the other "moving parts" that will affect their ability to be productive.

We need to be honest and trust our own judgment, too, especially when coming to grips with what we don't know yet. Plato, in *The Trial and Death of Socrates*, quotes that philosopher as suggesting that awareness of one's level of ignorance is the essence of human wisdom. I've seen early estimates that were off by as much as factor of two. I don't remember seeing any that were underestimates.

There are limits on how much we can know about how the project will turn out during the first few weeks. Again, slack, contingency plans, milestones, and phase entry and exit criteria allow us to mitigate this risk and respond early when we do see reality deviating from our estimates. Honesty requires the courage to speak up when we see this happening. In an honest estimating regime, all managers and individual contributors feel safe to point out these deviations to management when they appear.

Finally, preparing a realistic, actionable, truthful estimate also requires that we accept the context and constraints of the project. If I present to management a test subproject schedule and budget that slips the delivery date by 50% and overruns the budget by 200%, expecting management approval of that estimate is probably not realistic on my part. Now, it's true that testing is often slighted in project schedules. Often we do need to make a case for more testing, but that doesn't imply a stubborn refusal to accept rational limits.

I've spilled a lot of ink in these three chapters on this topic of estimation, so you probably have gotten the sense that this is something I care very much about. Why is this so important to me? I've worked on a number of projects where the estimation was done well, and those projects were such a joy. The project teams from top to bottom had a feeling of achievement and pride as milestones were met and the project succeeded. Key stakeholders outside the project team were happy when they got their systems on time and within budget. I've also worked on projects where, frankly, hard-working programmers, testers, and other individual contributors were exhorted, berated, and blamed for the results of bad estimation practices by management. On a couple of these projects, these bad estimates blew up right at the end, during test execution, leaving me scrambling to do something useful as other managers grumbled darkly about how long it was taking to finish testing. Bad estimation sets up the project and the project team to fail. Failure, whatever character-building attributes it may have, is a poor alternative to success.

So I think we, as software professionals, should start setting ourselves up for success. Project success relies on balancing features, schedule, budget, and quality. A realistic, actionable, truthful estimate right up front is an important part of how that balancing occurs. When we can have honest estimates in our project schedules, and be honest with our superiors, our peers, our teams, and ourselves in our discussions about estimates, that sets us up for success. When we know who is assigned to do what by what dates, and what dependencies and risks exist, that sets us up for success. Preparing a dependable estimate is not some dreary paper-pushing chore to be hacked out in Microsoft Project in an afternoon and then forgotten. Estimation is an essential management function for obtaining stakeholder commitment, setting realistic expectations, communicating honestly within the team about what is achievable, and guiding project success.

ESTIMATE QUICKLY

An estimate is useful because it's a prediction. An estimate allows us to forecast the future and plan accordingly. Your test project estimates—the schedule, the budget, and the return on investment—are predictions of the future in terms of time and money.

Like all estimates, your estimates will be imprecise and, to some extent, wrong. That's OK. You can predict tomorrow's weather perfectly if you're willing to wait until the day after tomorrow, but the value of a prediction is that you see into the future and gain an opportunity to take action in time to influence that future.

Just as with steering a boat, the earlier you start, the less strenuous and extreme your efforts must be. If you start too late, all the corrective action in the world won't help. (To continue my nautical metaphor, the effort to steer the *Titanic* away from the fateful iceberg started too late.) So, the value of an estimate is that it is in place in time for you to start taking action and that the implementation of the plan that springs from the estimate adds value in the ways I've discussed.

HANDLE CHALLENGES

In the case study, I presented an example of what happens when the estimation process works out well. Unfortunately, this process often does not go smoothly. Savvy test professionals gird themselves for estimation challenges.

WHAT KIND OF INVESTMENT IS TESTING, REALLY?

In the earlier discussion on return on investment, I simplified by calculating the costs and the returns as if they occurred in roughly the same time period. It's clearly true that the costs for testing are incurred across the project schedule. That's also true of the benefits for the information that guides the project, because the value of that information is realized during the project.

However, the value added by finding bugs, whether fixed or not, and by mitigating risks related to bugs that could happen, accrues over some period of time after the project. This introduces two qualifications to the return on investment approach that you should be aware of if you intend to apply the technique to justify your proposed budgets.

First, many projects have accounting and incentive practices that work against your return on investment analysis. In most cases, projects have a set budget that includes only the costs associated with the current release. Costs incurred by bad decisions made during the project that show up during maintenance don't get counted against the budget, just as benefits accrued that show up later don't get credited to it. So, the project management team, regrettably, has a built-in incentive only to find and fix the bugs absolutely necessary to get a working product out the door.

Let's revisit the hypothetical cost-of-quality model from the previous chapter, reproduced in Figure 5-1 for convenience. Suppose for a moment we're living inside a Dilbert cartoon, and assume that the project team only has to fix about half of the 1,000 bugs present in the system to get the product functioning well enough for deployment. That results in an average customer satisfaction rating of 10% based on the model.

Suppose further that we have a cynical project manager who decides that post-release bugs are the technical support manager's problems. Let's assume that half of the yet-to-be-discovered bugs surface each month, so the rate of bug discovery falls off to a negligible level roughly six months after release. While our model showed a cost of nonconformance of about $550,000 at 10% customer satisfaction, look at how Figure 5-2 shows the cost of nonconformance converging toward that number over the first six months. Furthermore, notice that prior to release, the return on investment for testing is actually negative, since the cost of conformance exceeds the cost of nonconformance.

OK, let's get out of the Dilbert cartoon—too depressing. Suppose we have a project manager who cares about customer satisfaction. She hires an independent tester to

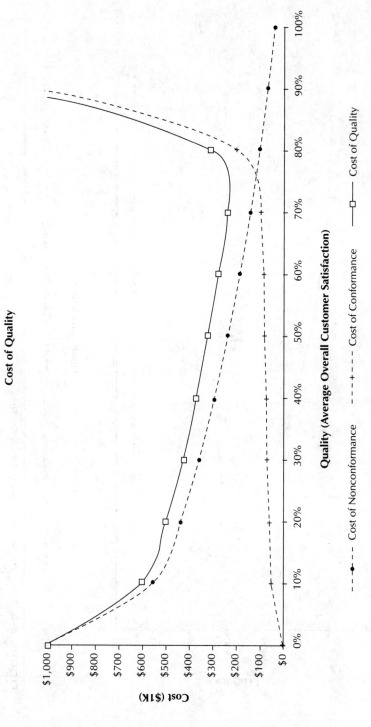

Cost of Quality

FIGURE 5-1 HYPOTHETICAL COST-OF-QUALITY GRAPH

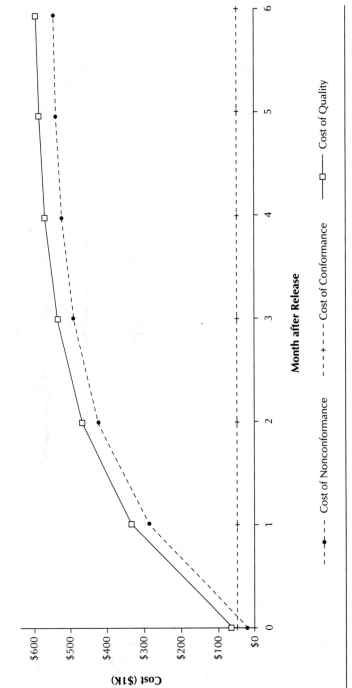

FIGURE 5-2 COST OF MINIMAL QUALITY OVER TIME

find most of the bugs before shipping. She also sets a development goal of fixing two-thirds of the bugs before release, about 150 more bugs than in the previous example. Figure 5-3 shows how her approach plays out over the initial release period. In the long run, the cost of quality has gone down by almost $200,000, a third of the previous example in Figure 5-2. This is a significant improvement.

However, in the short run, what the project accountants will see is a more expensive project. For project managers who are rewarded based on the profitability of the project, rather than on the long-term profitability of the system developed over its entire lifecycle, investing in testing will always be a leap of faith.[5]

Second, because some of the cost-of-nonconformance savings accrue over time, the length of that time period can reduce the return on investment. In accounting terms, this concept is referred to as the *net present value of money*. The net present value of money tells us that $1,000 in six months will be worth less than $1,000 today, because we could invest that $1,000 today and have more than $1,000 in six months. How much more depends on the rate of return of the alternative investment.

Let's revisit the case study to illustrate this point. For each bug that Jamal's team found that got fixed, his return on investment analysis assumed a return of about $1,100. However, that $1,100 savings is not realized upon release of the system. Instead, it occurs at some point in the future when some set of customers *would have* encountered that bug and demanded a fix for it. Because we can't know for any given previously resolved bug exactly when it would have surfaced—since it's no longer there to announce its nonexistence—the point of time at which the savings is realized is unknown and unknowable. However, we can look at aggregates.

In Chapter 4, I mentioned that support for the Sumatra release ends after the first year. Further, suppose that Cosimo Negraev, the support manager, tells Jamal that for each month in the first year, half of the bugs not yet identified in the release will be reported. If Jamal assumes an alternative rate of return of 18% per year, or 1.5% per month, he can analyze the second draft of his budget and calculate the return on investment using net present value, as shown in Figure 5-4. (Note that the amounts

---

5. Based on the hypothetical model, removing about 900 of the bugs would minimize the cost of quality. The model calculates this figure based on the underlying costs of conformance and nonconformance (at varying levels of customer satisfaction) and the relationship between shipped defects and customer satisfaction. In the real world, few, if any, project managers have this information at hand, making picking the optimal amount of testing and bug fixing difficult even for true believers in the cost-of-quality payoff.

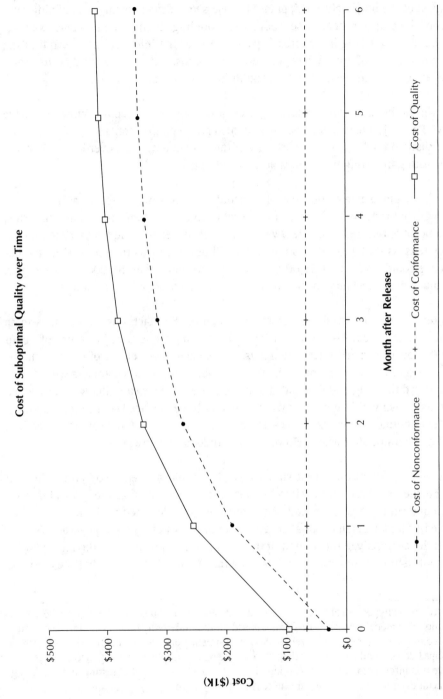

Cost of Suboptimal Quality over Time

Month after Release

Cost ($1K)

- - - ● - - - Cost of Nonconformance
- - - + - - - Cost of Conformance
————□———— Cost of Quality

FIGURE 5-3 COST OF IMPROVED (BUT NOT OPTIMAL) QUALITY OVER TIME

Sumatra Test ROI (Using NPV Analysis)

	Costs	Release (R)	R+1M	R+2M	R+3M	R+4M	R+5M	R+6M	R+7M	R+8M	R+9M	R+10M	R+11M	R+12M	Total Benefits NPV Dollars
							Benefits Received in Period								
Testing															
Staff (test development amortized)	$370,975														
External Labs	75,000														
Travel and Contingency	65,698														
Environments (amortized)	35,667														
Tools (amortized)	6,667														
Total Investment	**$554,007**														
Estimated Bugs Delivered to Test	2,500														
Estimated Must-Fix Bugs Delivered to T	2,000														
Estimated Defect Detection Percentage	80%														
Period	Total	0	1	2	3	4	5	6	7	8	9	10	11	12	
Estimated Field Bugs Avoided	1,600	0	800	400	200	100	50	25	13	6	3	2	1	0	
Estimated Found-Not-Fixed Bug Rate	20%														
Estimated Found-Not-Fixed Bugs	500														
Estimated Found-Not-Fixed Non-Bug Ra	67%														
Estimated Field Bugs Known	333	0	167	83	42	21	10	5	3	1	1	0	0	0	
Bugs Found and Fixed															
Must-Fix Bugs Found		$0	$867,200	$433,600	$216,800	$108,400	$54,200	$27,100	$13,550	$6,775	$3,388	$1,694	$847	$423	$1,683,540
Bugs Found and Not Fixed															
Deferred Bugs Found		$0	$12,500	$6,250	$3,125	$1,563	$781	$391	$195	$98	$49	$24	$12	$6	$24,267
Tests that Mitigate Risks															
Sales Subject to LCV or Reliability Loss	$ 2,000,000														
Likelihood of Sales Loss w/o Testing	50%	$0	$500,000	$250,000	$125,000	$62,500	$31,250	$15,625	$7,813	$3,906	$1,953	$977	$488	$244	$970,676
Guiding the Project															
Project Cost at Risk for Bad Tracking	$2,000,000	$200,000													
Reduction in Risk due to Testing	10%	$200,000													$200,000
Total Benefit (NPV)															**$2,878,482**
Return on Investment (NPV)															**420%**

FIGURE 5-4 TESTING RETURN ON INVESTMENT ADJUSTED FOR NET PRESENT VALUE

shown in this figure include the two cost savings agreed upon by Jamal, Harold, and John in the case study.)

Now, a return on investment of 420% doesn't really weaken Jamal's business case. But is an 18% annual yield a reasonable investment alternative?

More likely, some or all of the money Jamal is asking for could be invested in additional programming staff to add features or accelerate the schedule. What is the return on investment of those options? What are the rates of return of the various investment alternatives that exist between 0% of the budget spent on testing and 40% spent on testing, as Jamal is proposing?

I don't bring up these questions to discourage you from analyzing return on investment. It's important for test professionals, especially test managers, to attempt to understand the financial implications of what we do. However, when I calculate return on investment, I keep in mind the limitations inherent in such calculations. The models are intuitive from a high level of abstraction, but some details are problematic. These problems might lead people to disbelieve your numbers and could even create credibility and other political problems. In some cases, you might be better off without a calculation of return on investment.[6]

IT MIGHT LOOK LIKE MAGIC—BUT IT'S ONLY AN ESTIMATE

Just as the return on investment is an approximation, so is the entire estimate. (Of course, so is a weather forecast or any other prediction.) The estimation process that I laid out, for all its reliance on numbers and data, is not a precise science. I look at the past. I look at some numbers. I crunch those numbers in various ways. I talk to people about my assumptions. Out of that process pop a few documents that appear to prophesy the future. It's not miraculous that we can predict the sun will set each night. However, it is somewhat magical that we can predict the outcome of an undertaking as complex and unique as a system development, maintenance, or acquisition effort with any accuracy at all.

Nevertheless, it's important to keep in mind the imprecision of the result and the frequency with which we get it significantly wrong. I remember being quite enamored of

---

6. For example, Johanna Rothman, in an e-mail correspondence with me, pointed out that return on investment numbers can be easily manipulated. Further, such analyses can lead you to ignore important risks, as discussed in Cem Kaner's article "Quality Cost Analysis: Benefits and Risks," found at www.kaner.com.

my early project estimates. I'll admit that I sometimes went to great lengths to keep them accurate by tweaking the project around them, sometimes in ways that didn't make sense. If I assert in a schedule that a task will take five days and it doesn't, should I find a clever way to declare the task complete after five days? Wouldn't I learn more about estimation if I accepted that my estimate was wrong and rethought the matter?

Accepting and learning from our mistakes is always better for us in the long run, but it's not the essence of human nature to do so. It's often more natural to us to blame others. So, we might think the estimate was correct, but the team flubbed up the project and took longer than they should have done.

Good management requires that we revise our estimates rather continuing to blunder along, deluded or blaming others. If you had directions and a map that told you to drive *through* rather than *around* a tree, you would declare the directions and map wrong rather than insist on their accuracy and hit the tree, right?

There's a limit on the magic in your estimate. If you take care to create good estimates, you will have a substantially better chance of getting it right than if you pull numbers out of the air or conjure up Gantt charts and spreadsheets that have no connection to reality but happen to give senior managers the answers they want to hear. However, the process of estimating a system development, maintenance, or acquisition project is fraught with potential errors. Seemingly small mistakes in work-breakdown-structures can lead to wildly inaccurate estimates. Please don't misunderstand me: I do estimates and I do them carefully; because I'm not managing if I don't, I'm gambling. But I've learned not to see magical prescience where there is really only a very skillfully constructed and carefully cross-checked guess.

THE NINE-MONTH RULE

A well-known management aphorism says that no matter how many couples participate, it takes at least nine months—give or take a few weeks either way—to make a baby. In other words, there are certain tasks that, no matter how many people or other resources you allocate, have a certain inherent minimum duration. Failing to keep this aphorism in mind is one of the classic mistakes of estimation.

One trap is related to what Fred Brooks called the mythical man-month. Some people, when estimating system projects, calculate the total number of person-months required and then assume they could arbitrarily shorten the schedule by adding more people to the project. Brooks pointed out that this is a myth, because the very act of adding more people can increase the total number of person-months required. This is famously restated as Brooks's Law: "Adding more people to a late project makes it later." Fewer people can work more efficiently, and the communication overheads associated with coordinating the work across more people eventually outweigh the benefits.[7]

In some cases in testing, this tends to be less of an issue. For example, I have found that with scripted manual tests, I can often use test technicians with as little as one week of mentoring and on-the-job training, and can divide the work right down to the test case level. However, creating test data, configuring test environments, writing test cases, and developing automated testing scripts or tools is as problematic as programming and just as subject to Brooks's Law.

Another trap arises from unrealistic scheduling at the project level. This is often hard for test professionals without sufficient development experience to judge. However, you can look for some warning signs that the project is marching to the beat of a deluded drummer.

One such warning sign would be a published project work-breakdown-structure that didn't meet the criteria set out in Chapter 3. Unless someone has gone to the trouble of truly understanding the constituent tasks, the schedule is likely a creative writing project.

Another warning sign is when you hear that the scheduling process worked backward from an arbitrary ship date. This is made worse if people realized that significant gains in process performance were required to hit that date, so they simply assumed those gains would occur without putting in place any process changes to make them happen.

If you suspect that the project schedule is flawed, you need to be especially careful in terms of defining handoffs and test phase entry criteria. Otherwise, the schedule failures will leak silently into your test effort, and you might be held accountable. (We'll look at this in more detail in Chapters 6 and 7 when we discuss planning.) Furthermore, as important as contingency plans and retained slack are in any estimate, they are even more important when you are estimating a test subproject that will live within the context of a deficient schedule or budget for the overall system development project.

---

7. Brooks's book, *The Mythical Man-Month*, remains an excellent discussion on system project management details. He first published it in 1975 and published a revised edition in 1995. It is a measure of the commonality and endurance of the challenges facing systems development teams that this book remains timely, and the revised edition consists mostly of additions, not changes.

BE CAREFUL WITH NONSTAKEHOLDERS

Being honest with myself also means being honest about the test subproject context within the project and how others view the project to which I'm contributing. Testing subprojects tend to have strong connections outside of testing. Often these connections are to others on the project team. These people are direct stakeholders in the success of the project. So while you need to be careful to manage these dependencies in a logistical sense, you shouldn't have too much trouble motivating cooperation. As a wise manager once mentioned to me, "When everyone's in the same boat, throwing rocks into each other's end of the boat doesn't make much sense."

However, sometimes you will have dependencies on people outside the scope of the project—or even those who might be antagonistic to it. That is a powerful factor affecting the test estimate.

On one project, my test team had three such dependencies that proved very problematic. First, there was the system administration group that didn't make it a priority to set up the test lab. They were working on a number of other projects. They expected that the project we were working on would get canceled. They really didn't want to be bothered with setting up a dozen identically configured test workstations modeled on deployed-system configurations.

Second, there was the team responsible for administering the legacy system for which we were building a replacement. We needed access to this system as a *reference platform* or *test oracle* for determining the correctness of the results returned by the system under test. (I'll discuss test oracles in more detail in Chapters 10 and 11.) However, since the operators for this legacy system would, essentially, be out of a job should our project conclude successfully, they provided grudging support at best.

Finally, the overall information systems team, which managed deployment of software for which the (large) company had site licenses, didn't feel that we needed a dozen licenses for the bug tracking software. This problem became especially severe when we asked that two of the clients be set up remotely for a vendor that was developing most of the software.

None of the tasks we needed done by these nonstakeholders should have taken more than a day of one tester's time, explaining the need, helping ensure proper access, and verifying task completion before test execution. As it was, though, my test team lost at least three person-weeks dealing with the cumulative effects of foot-dragging and passive resistance. Calendar-wise, the entire period of time between planning and test execution became dominated by dealing with these issues. The issues would have been complete trivialities had the people in these other teams upon whom we depended carried out their responsibilities crisply. Since they weren't stakeholders in the project, though, they had no motivation to do so. This proved extremely damaging to the test subproject and the overall project as a whole.

This story points out a particularly acute example of what can happen when you have dependencies outside the project. One of the reasons that establishing context is so important is that it gives you insight into who supports the project—and your testing within it—and who does not. If I feel such foot-dragging will occur, I limit dependencies on those whose interests are not aligned with the success of the project to an absolute minimum, preferably zero. If I can't do so for whatever reason, I endeavor to keep those tasks with such dependencies off the critical path and warn management that I expect problems.

For whatever tasks that must have such dependencies, I build a lot of slack into them. I also expect to take a significant hit on efficiency in my portion of these tasks and any other dependent tasks. Finally, I obtain a solid, unambiguously worded, documented commitment from contributors and managers in these providing teams and define a rapid escalation path to management. In the next couple of chapters on test planning, I'll show you how I do that.

WHEN SELLING FAILS

Suppose I go through the entire process of estimating, including building a business case and a realistic estimate, only to be told, "We can't afford that and we don't have this long. Here's how much money you have, here's how long it can take; now go and test that system." Now what? At this point, what I can do is try to make intelligent trade-offs between depth and breadth of coverage. The quality risk analysis can be my guide for that.

When the project management team proposes to take risks I feel are unwise, then I do explain why I hold that opinion. While doing so, I keep in mind that entrepreneurs and technological visionaries *do* tend to be much less risk-averse than the average test professional. The response is sometimes along the lines of, "I hear you, Rex, and I understand your opinion, but I'm not going to spend more money and delay the schedule to mitigate those risks." If, for whatever reason, I end up testing less than I should, I'm careful to document the risks that go uncovered.

Being willing to compromise on the scope of testing and a sufficient budget and schedule to support that testing is not the same as abdicating. In other words, if I am advocating a realistic budget and estimate, management can either support that estimate, or they can reduce my testing scope and ask me to accept less time and money.

If, instead, they ask me to do what I initially said would take X dollars and Y months in for two-thirds the cost in half the time, then what are the implications? As Tim Koomen mentioned to me when he reviewed this chapter, "Never give away hours for free in [the estimate negotiation] meeting—[e.g.,] 'OK, we'll work a little harder and I think we can still meet your deadline'—as this makes you lose credibility." I agree wholeheartedly.

Finally, it can be particularly difficult to sell management on a realistic estimate when management has experience with bogus estimates from other managers or from predecessors in the test organization. If the previous test manager, say, simply pulled numbers out of the air and then failed to meet those schedule and budget targets, managers may have come to the opinion that no test manager actually knows how to estimate. I've joined organizations where the entire technical management team had been tarred with that brush. Whether that's fair or not, you will start with an estimate credibility deficit that you must overcome in such circumstances. As the old cliche goes, when you find yourself in a hole, the first thing to do is to stop digging. Be especially careful to produce only the best, most accurate estimates in these circumstances—but you always do that, right?

SAFETY- OR MISSION-CRITICAL SYSTEMS

Of course, positive return on investment is good, but there's more to life than money. In some cases, the systems we develop have implications in terms of human safety or business survival that go beyond any financial model's ability to quantify.

One of the strengths of formal quality risk analysis, such as the Failure Mode and Effect Analysis technique, is that it excels at identifying the truly critical quality risks and related specific failure modes for systems where people could die or the entire organization could go out of business. Should you be working in such an environment, be careful not to undo the power of your quality risk analysis during the estimation, scheduling, and budgeting process. Before you negotiate away an activity, task, or resource, make extra sure that the expense is not one required to address these critical, life-and-death, going-concern types of risks. If you honestly feel that shortcuts are being taken that will result in a risk to human life, then you may well have moral, legal, fiduciary, or professional responsibilities to act.

I would recommend making every effort to resolve any problems within the organizational management chain as a first start. You will be endangering all your political capital if you play this ham-handedly. It's important to keep in mind that you might be wrong. Indeed, all the players may be erring to some extent in their reading of the risks. You may be excessively risk-averse, while others may not be cautious enough.

Maintaining an open mind and compromising your principles are two different things. To communicate effectively, you'll need to listen and understand what others are saying as well as talk.

Further, if you feel the risks are compelling but others do not share your concern, perhaps you aren't communicating your concerns effectively. (We'll examine a tragic example of such failures to communicate in Chapter 15 in regard to the United States Space Shuttle Challenger mission in 1986.) People may understand and accept that you *are* concerned, but that doesn't mean that they will understand exactly *why* you are concerned. The onus is on you, if you feel life-threatening risks are being taken, to explain your concerns with data, in a compelling presentation, to people in the organization who can make a decision to do that right thing.

If you have exhausted all efforts to resolve the situation through normal channels, now what? You might have a legal responsibility to report certain actions that could endanger human life or public safety. Perhaps you'll feel compelled to act by your conscience. However, choosing to be a whistle-blower is not something to be done lightly. I recommend spending some quiet time reflecting on good advice from trusted friends, family, and legal counsel before making the decision.

IMPLEMENT IMPROVEMENTS

Learning to create and sell realistic, accurate, truthful estimates, together with managing subordinates and fellow managers, were probably the hardest lessons for me when I made the transition from individual contributor to test project manager. People have longed for prescience since the dawn of time, and mythology is full of tales of those who could foresee the future. I don't claim to have achieved the foresight of Pythia, the chief priestess of Delphi, but I can recommend the following steps to improving your estimating techniques.

1. Study the topic of estimation. It's important for those of us charged with estimating system testing efforts to have a basic grasp of the tools at hand. Therefore, learning how to construct a well-formed work-breakdown-structure is important. Understanding how to put together a budget and a business case is important. Since the testing business case rests to a great extent on the cost of quality, studying this topic is also important. You'll probably find that as you study these topics, you become not only more competent as a test professional, but also more credible. You are learning to speak the language of project managers. You are gaining the skills necessary to present and defend a test project

in the words they understand. You are also becoming able to debate proposals to trim testing budgets in terms other than by saying, "You wouldn't propose that if you cared about quality." Instead, you'll be able to talk specifically about risks, costs, and alternatives as well as make counterproposals that achieve mutual satisfaction and management support without rancorous exchanges.

2. Learn from the past, learn from the present, and learn from others. The basic test estimation techniques are an empty vessel that you can—and should—pour data into. Look back at past projects and replace the hypothetical data in the spreadsheets and work-breakdown-structures that accompany this book with data from your experience. Gather data from current and future projects that will help you with future estimates. Track your current projects against your estimates. Explore your blind spots. What tasks did you forget? Why? What activities don't you know how to estimate accurately? What would you need to learn or what additional data would you need to gather to be more accurate? Using the baselining features included in many project management tools is a good way to assess the accuracy of your estimation. Finally, share thoughts, ideas, and questions with others. Develop models for doing good estimation and send them to your peers. Present them at testing and project management conferences. Publish them as articles or books. This will not only help you get better, but you will also be doing a service to the testing community, because we all need to get better at estimating.

3. Understand the obstacles. In previous sections, I identified a number of possible obstacles to good estimating. Not all of those will apply to you. I recommend that you spend time understanding what obstacles exist within your context that can impede the adoption of good estimating practices. Develop some ideas about how to overcome those obstacles. When some of those ideas don't work out—as they won't—don't become angry or frustrated (for too long, anyway); just refine your approach and try again on your next project. If Fred Brooks's book, *The Mythical Man-Month*, is still topical 25 years after its first publication, that means that these problems are hard and you won't solve them in one fell swoop.

4. Practice, practice, practice. One you start to prepare work-breakdown-structures, create a corresponding budget, build a business case based on return on investment, negotiate committed time and resources from management to achieve that estimate, and manage a project according to that estimate, you'll find you get better at it each time. Keep at it, and after each project ends, ask yourself what you can learn about estimation.

5. Do what you can with what you get. If you want practice, you have to be *willing to* practice. If you're asked to run a test effort with what you feel are insufficient resources, don't feel compelled to walk away. There's almost always compromise

involved. Unless you're being asked to do something illegal or unethical, it might well be in your best interest to stick the project out. Keep your original estimate handy to see how things actually turn out. I've learned as much about estimation from the project train wrecks as I have from the ones that went perfectly.

With an approved estimate in hand, you're ready to move on to the next step. In the following two chapters, we'll look at planning a test effort. What are the myriad details that must all come together for us to succeed? If our estimate is a map, then the test plan is the driving directions. But in this case, the directions apply to an entire team of drivers, each of whom must end up in the same place without running into each other or anyone else. How can we make that happen?

6

Gain and Communicate Insights: Plan the Test Effort

S ome managers believe that their planning activities come to an end when they have prepared and received management approval for a work-breakdown-structure, schedule, and budget. While I would agree that a solid estimate with management support is essential to writing a good plan for any project, there are myriad details that remain hidden, unrecognized, and unannounced within such an estimate. When we prepare estimates, we make assumptions, we build in dependencies, we skip over contributions, and we take for granted that certain low-level processes will just...happen. It is dangerous when we assume a straightforward test subproject within the context of a project team that knows what we're doing, why we're doing it, and how we depend on each of them.

But how can we have such awareness in the project team unless we first create this awareness within ourselves and then enlighten our peers? Test subprojects consist of a web of complex, interdependent, volatile activities attached to many of the other activities in the larger project context. Even seasoned test managers have difficulty predicting the details of what will happen. To deal with this reality, we need to gain insight into the minutiae. Once we have this insight, we must communicate it to others and obtain their commitment and support.

In some cases, the test planning process has a distinct output, a written test plan. This plan may well be part of the information that the project team is counting on receiving from the test team. To promote understanding of such test plans, the project team may expect the test plan to follow a template, whether one of the organization's own creation or an industry standard. In other cases, the test plan may consist of little, if any, formal written output. In this chapter, I'll assume that you do intend to produce a written test plan. In either case, what's most important is that the test team understands what it is to do, and the project team agrees to support that effort and accept its results as sufficient.

A Test Planning Process

Process 5 is a process I use for test planning. The test plan template you use or the way you choose to document your test plans may influence the content and order of these steps quite a bit. For example, some test processes call for a master test plan for

Step #	Step	Done?
1.	Research, devise, collect, and document the strategy, tactics, and internal workings of the test subproject.	☐
2.	Negotiate and document the collaborative workings between the test sub-project and the overall project.	☐
3.	Finalize and document the remaining logistical and planning details, such as the risks to the test subproject itself and definitions of testing and project terms. Annotate any referenced documents. Write a one-page executive summary of the test subproject.	☐
4.	Circulate the plan for private (offline) review, often to the test team first and then to the wider collection of stakeholders and participants. Gather input and revise the plan, iterating steps 1 through 3 as needed. Assess any changes to the estimated schedule and budget (that exceed retained slack or contingency) resulting from the planning process, and obtain management support for such changes.	☐
5.	Circulate the plan for public review. Hold a review meeting with all the stakeholders. Gather any final adjustments needed, and obtain commitment that, with any modifications agreed upon in the review meeting, the plan shall be the plan of record for the test subproject.	☐
6.	Revise the estimated schedule and budget based on new knowledge gleaned from the planning process, including resource use. If this results in a slip in the schedule or an increase in the budget beyond any retained slack or contingency, escalate it to management for resolution. Negotiations about the new budget and schedule may cause iteration of the previous steps or reworking of the estimate.	☐
7.	Check the test plan(s) into the project library or configuration management system. Place the document under change control.	☐

PROCESS 5 A TEST PLANNING PROCESS

> **Test System**
>
> The test environment, testware, and test execution processes that the test team will use to assess the quality of the system under test.

the overall testing effort and separate detailed test plans for each test phase or level (e.g., integration test and system test). The kind of information that goes in each document affects how your test planning process works and might mean that you have, in effect, two or three test planning processes happening in parallel.

JAMAL HAS A PLAN

Jamal had begun to assemble the plan on September 12, but on the 17th, as he released an approved, revised, and final version of the estimate to management, he began to work on his plan in earnest. He started out by reviewing the quality risk analysis and documenting the scope in an IS/IS NOT table. Every risk for which the stakeholder team had recommended extensive or balanced testing went into the IS column, while lower risks went into the IS NOT column.

Jamal moved on to selecting the appropriate test strategies for each quality risk that was within scope. He had already decided on some of the strategies while he was preparing the work-breakdown-structure. For example, his team would use automated testing for most functionality and performance testing. However, some details remained open, and he now started to think those through. Error handling and recovery testing, he realized, should include a complete review of the error messages defined for the server and browser sides of the system, possibly by looking at the source files for the messages rather than attempting to exhaustively simulate every single kind of failure. Testing of load, capacity, and volume would probably require application program interface (API)-based tools to talk to the server-side APIs and force certain kinds of loads in addition to GUI-based, commercial off-the-shelf load testing tools.

As he resolved some of these issues, he started to grapple with the details of the test environment. His budget allowed him to purchase one additional server cluster, which he would add to the three already available from the previous testing project for the previous SpeedyWriter release, version 3.0. (He planned to leave one of the four clusters from the SpeedyWriter 3.0 project assigned specifically to SpeedyWriter 3.0 maintenance testing.) Because he would be doing a fair amount of manual and automated testing in parallel, he had planned to buy ten additional client systems beyond the five he could move from SpeedyWriter 3.0 testing. He had come up with these figures based on how much testing would be going on at any given moment and what testing could share server clusters or needed its own.

He revisited his initial estimates now, looking at which tests would run against which configurations in detail. Using the same analysis as he did during estimation, but now checking actual hours of server and workstation usage rather than just looking at gross durations, he confirmed that he needed four server clusters and eight additional workstations (see Figure 6-1). In the calculations in the bottom half of the worksheet, Jamal checked to be sure that the four server clusters were accounted for only once.

He was happy to see that his fine-grained calculations showed his initial rough hardware usage estimates to be either accurate or conservative. But how would the test environment—hardware, software, and networks—be configured? Jamal decided to create a diagram to help him visualize the test environment.

As Jamal worked on the test environment configuration diagram, he came to a disconcerting realization. The additional server cluster would fit into the lab, because the three systems could be stacked on a rack, but five of the ten additional workstations just would not fit. Additional space, at this point, was not in the cards, and he didn't want to split the test lab across multiple rooms anyway. If he tried to squeeze all the workstations in, that would leave insufficient room for people to actually work. Hmm, he thought, what now? There was no way to have one test manager, three test engineers, and four test technicians working simultaneously on ten workstations, because that would not allow for bug isolation, bug reporting, reading e-mail while tests

	D	E	F	G	H	J	K
100	**Overlapping Phase Period** (excl. Localization & Usability)				**Effort**	**Duration**	**Count**
101	Total Person Hours/Hours				255	494	
102	Est. Person Weeks/Weeks				13	6	
103	Proposed ATE Staffing				2		
104	Proposed MTE Staffing				1		
105	Proposed Tech Staffing				4		
106	Test Pass Duration (Weeks)				2		
107	Test Environments (Clusters, Wkstns, Nets) Required (w/ Some Sharing)						4
108	Server Cluster 1 (East) Usage (Taking Sharing into Account)						1
109	Server Cluster 2 (West) Usage (Taking Sharing into Account)						1
110	Server Cluster 3 (North) Usage (Taking Sharing into Account)						1
111	Server Cluster 4 (South) Usage (Taking Sharing into Account)						1
112	Workstation Usage						13

FIGURE 6-1 INITIAL DETAILED HARDWARE USAGE PLAN

were running, and so forth. In his experience, two workstations per test staff member was a good rule of thumb. How could he get closer to that ratio?

He remembered a test-management training course he'd attended where the instructor talked about using second shifts with contract technicians. "Offer to pay for an extra hour or two for working the undesirable shift," the instructor had said, "and you should have no trouble finding contractors happy to work the evening hours." Hmm, he thought, let's see what happens if I do that. He reworked the hardware usage plan based on 80 hours of workstation usage per week rather than 40 hours. (It's true that the average tester week consisted of 30 hours of test execution time, because of meetings, team discussions, and so forth, but the workstations themselves would need to be available for testing at all times during both shifts.) The result, as shown in Figure 6-2, was right on target, reducing the needed number of workstations to about ten. There would be at most five people testing in the test environment at any given time, which hit the 2-to-1 workstation-to-tester ratio perfectly. Revising his budget, he saw that the money he saved on the workstation purchase would just about cover the evening shift bonuses he would pay his contract test technicians, leading to a $4,000 increase in cost, well within the 10% contingency. He revised the test environment configuration diagram (see Figure 6-3).

Okay, I understand the environment, he thought, so who's running tests? At this point, he had identified two current staff members (Lin-Tsu and Emma), one new engineer to be hired, and four contract test technicians to be brought on for the duration of the testing effort. He now knew that the technicians would work two shifts. He captured this information, along with the various process implications of it, in his test plan.

	D	E	F	G	H	J	K
100	**Overlapping Phase Period** (excl. Localization & Usability)				**Effort**	**Duration**	**Count**
101	*Total Person Hours/Hours*				255	494	
102	*Est. Person Weeks/Weeks*				13	6	
103	*Proposed ATE Staffing*				2		
104	*Proposed MTE Staffing*				1		
105	*Proposed Tech Staffing*				4		
106	*Test Pass Duration (Weeks)*				2		
107	*Test Environments (Clusters, Wkstns, Nets) Required (w/ Some Sharing)*						4
108	*Server Cluster 1 (East) Usage (Taking Sharing into Account)*						1
109	*Server Cluster 2 (West) Usage (Taking Sharing into Account)*						1
110	*Server Cluster 3 (North) Usage (Taking Sharing into Account)*						1
111	*Server Cluster 4 (South) Usage (Taking Sharing into Account)*						1
112	*Workstation Usage*						9

FIGURE 6-2 REFIGURED DETAILED HARDWARE USAGE PLAN, WITH TWO SHIFTS

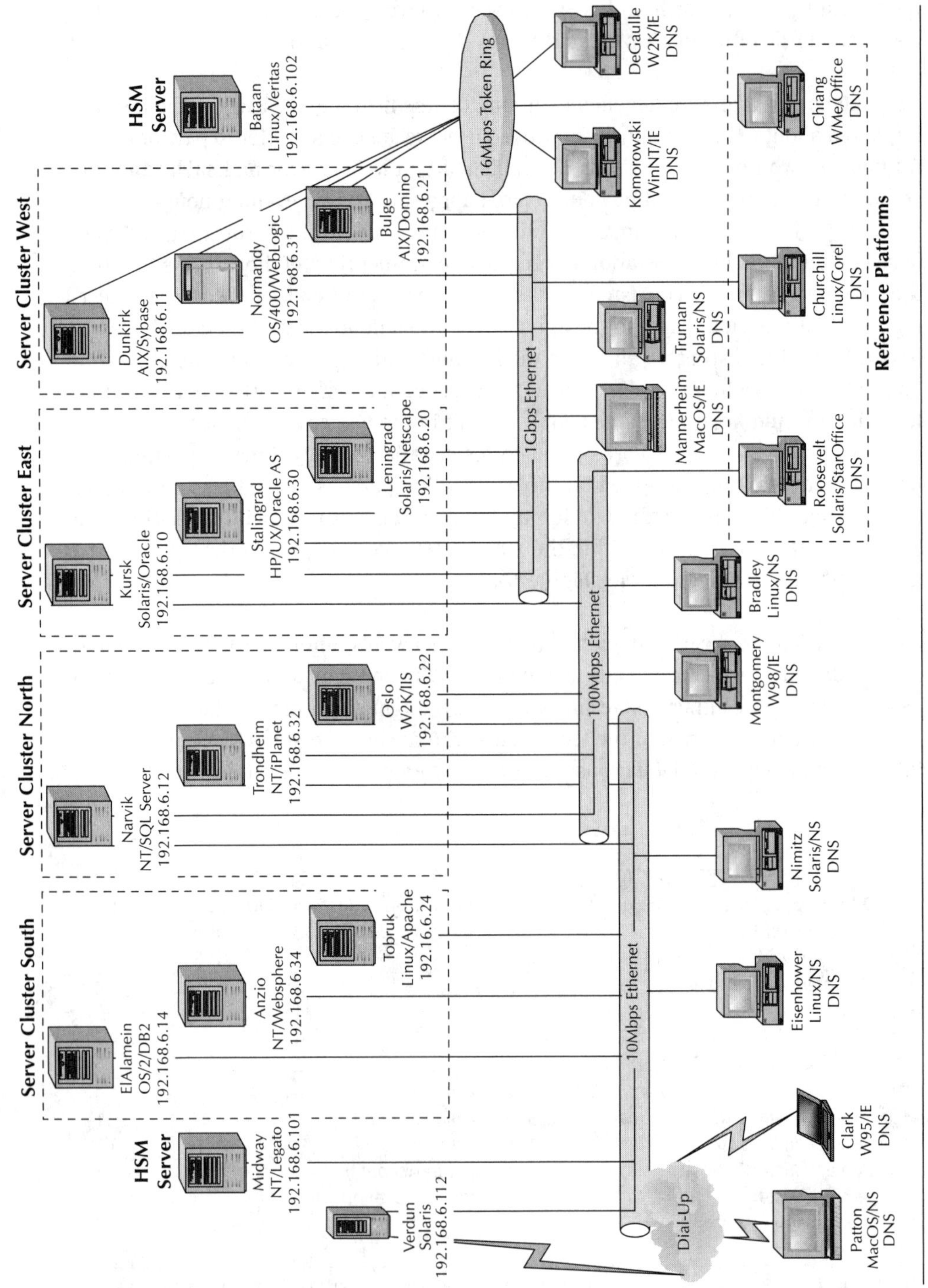

FIGURE 6-3 SUMATRA TEST ENVIRONMENT

Jamal looked at his work-breakdown-structure again. First, he extracted from the Gantt chart all the major milestones, especially the dependencies on other teams, like test releases, and documented them in the plan. In the process, he fixed an error in his original work-breakdown-structure having to do with some of the system test cycles lasting longer than one week. Initially, he was somewhat chagrined, but then he realized that even peer reviews and careful desk checking could not remove every error, whether from source code or project plans.

He began to particularize each of the tasks, activities, and processes he had outlined in the work-breakdown-structure. In the section on test development, he mentioned not only the specific areas to be covered by the new tests, but also details about how those tests should be built. For example, he identified a major test development work item, creating new privacy and security tests. These tests would be manual tests. Lin-Tsu would perform them using the graphical (browser) interfaces, various APIs, the UNIX and NT command-line interfaces, and the database interfaces. The tests would be both behavioral and structural. The testware she'd create included test data, test cases, macros, scripts, procedures, and so forth. He also expected Lin-Tsu to research known vulnerabilities for browser-based systems. This level of information, along with the information on test strategies he'd presented earlier, would, he hoped, give Emma, Lin-Tsu, and the new test engineer enough guidance on what kinds of tests he felt the team needed so that he could leave low-level design and implementation issues to them.

Finding the test plan from the previous SpeedyWriter 3.0 testing, he copied-and-pasted the sections on bug and test case tracking into his new plan. This section documented the fields in the tracking systems they used, but left out any detailed discussion of the processes of running tests or writing bug reports. To make sure the new test engineer and the test technicians understood how to perform these critical processes, he would provide them with a one-day training course shortly after they started, including take-away slides and class notes for later reference.

The test technicians, being junior and probably unskilled in testing, would each have an engineer assigned to mentor them. (He wrote himself a note to remember to give his test engineers his notes on how to be a good mentor, as well as to reread those himself, since he would be mentoring the new test engineer.) The mentor would review each technician's test results and bug reports. He had been happy with the way the SpeedyWriter 3.0 project worked in these areas. A few quick changes to bring it in line with this project and he was done with the first major step of test planning, documenting the internal aspects.

Step #	Step	Done?
1.	Research, devise, collect, and document the strategy, tactics, and internal workings of the test subproject.	☑

Now, on to the tough part: working out smooth handoffs and collaborative processes with the rest of the team. To start with, he found it useful in these situations to draw a picture of the context of the test effort (see Figure 6-4) as it interacted with the rest of the stakeholders, including the various flows of information products and services out of the test group and of test deliverables and services into the test group.

Okay, Jamal thought, now I just have to get agreement on how each of those inflows and outflows work. To start with, he called Keith Lee, the System Operations and Administration manager. He had an immediate request for Keith as well as a long-term one.

"Hey, Keith, how are you?" Jamal said as Keith answered the phone.

"Another day, another fire drill. The tech support guys need help configuring a weird customer environment, so I have my team swarmed all over that."

"Well, do you have a minute?"

"Sure, now's as bad a time as any," Keith laughed.

"I need your help in a couple of ways, one pretty immediate, one longer-term. You know, we need to start testing the first increment of Sumatra pretty soon—"

"Testing pretty soon? Wow, that project just started this month!"

"Yep, but we're on this Incremental lifecycle. More testing and earlier. I already have an approved budget and schedule. The budget includes some equipment purchases. If I get you the paperwork this week, can you have the hardware starting to trickle into the test lab and your team start working on configuring it by—" Jamal checked his schedule—"Wednesday?"

"Yeah, some of it. Servers take a little longer, but clients—definitely. When do you need everything configured?"

Jamal glanced at his Gantt chart again. "October 1. Starting next Monday, I'm going to have Emma and Lin-Tsu start testing out some integration tests in the test environment, so I'll need some support from your team then, too."

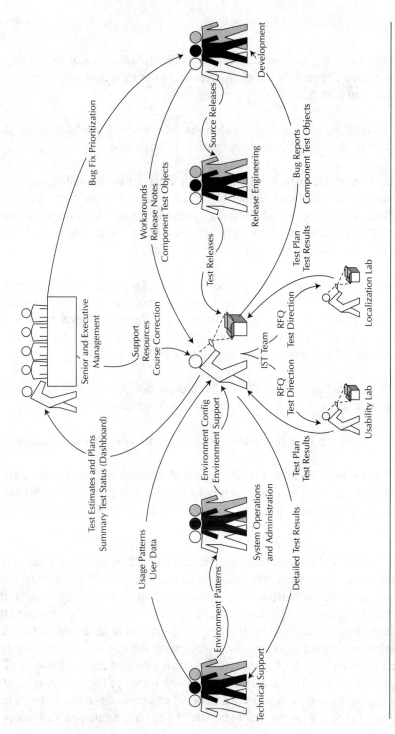

FIGURE 6-4 SUMATRA INTEGRATION AND SYSTEM TEST CONTEXT

"So far, so good."

"Which brings me to my next request. I'd like to identify a couple of people on your team as key contacts for resolution of environment problems. It helps to have a clear problem escalation path."

"Well, for servers, I'd say call Petra Fahimian. She's new, but she is good; don't worry. For clients, how about Inder Vaneshwatan?" Keith said.

"Hmm," Jamal said cautiously, "you know, Keith, I don't question Inder's dedication, but there was that incident on the SpeedyWriter 3.0 project where he misconfigured all those clients and we lost a whole week of testing. I gotta be frank with you up front, Keith. That incident and the way he responded to our concerns really filled his dance card with me and some of the folks on my team."

"Yeah, I hear you. I had a serious conversation with Inder about that whole situation and how he reacted. It won't happen again. Inder promised me that, and I'm promising you that. Of course, if anything *does* happen, I'm the second level of escalation. Please make sure your team knows that. If either Inder or Petra isn't on the case within a half hour of you paging them or calling them, call me."

"Okay, Keith, sounds fair enough. I'll lay that process out in the test plan. You should see the first draft later this week. Let me know if it doesn't look okay."

"You bet, bro'. Gotta get back to my crisis du jour," Keith chuckled sardonically.

"Have fun," Jamal said. He hung up the phone and thought, one down, two to go. He picked the phone up again and called Jenny Kaufmann first to discuss escalation for blocking bugs and bug report handoffs. Next, he called Yasuhiro Kanagawa to discuss the test release process.

After he had worked out the peer team interfaces, he moved on to the question of entry and exit criteria as well as status reporting. Jamal had worked for John Albertson for a little over a year, so he knew what John would expect and want for reporting. Harold Jones was new to the company, though, so Jamal wasn't sure what he'd be used to from a test manager. Rather than asking, though, Jamal decided to go ahead and draft his proposed criteria and then send those out, along with the test status reporting dashboard from SpeedyWriter 3.0. (The topic of test status reporting and dashboards will be addressed in Chapter 15.) The criteria he sent out are shown in Figure 6-5. He sent the e-mail message with the criteria and the dashboard to John and Harold, with CCs to Cicely Rice (the VP of Sales), Jenny Kaufman, Kate Hernandez, Keith, and Yasuhiro.

Integration Test Entry Criteria

Integration test shall begin when the following criteria are met.

1. The bug tracking system is in place and available for use by the Engineering Services and System Engineering teams.

2. The System Operations and Administration team has configured the integration test clients and servers for testing. The test team has been provided with appropriate access to these systems.

3. The Development team has placed at least two communicating components to be released to IST [Integration and System Test] for integration testing under formal, automated source code and configuration management control.

4. The Development team or the Release Engineering team has prepared a test release, containing at least two communicating components, both of which have completed component testing.

5. The Development team has prepared release notes that document the functionality in the test release.

Integration Test Continuation Criteria

Integration test shall continue provided the following criteria are met.

1. Each integration test release contains only components under formal, automated source code and configuration management control.

2. The Development team or the Release Engineering team prepares test releases from communicating components that have completed component testing.

3. The Development team accompanies each release with release notes that document the functionality in that release.

4. Some test release built from relatively up-to-date source code can be installed in the test environment in such a way that the release functions in a stable fashion. Furthermore, the test team can execute planned or exploratory tests against this test release in a reasonably efficient manner to obtain further meaningful test results.

Integration Test Exit Criteria

Integration test shall successfully conclude when the following criteria are met.

1. The test team has performed all planned tests against all planned integration builds.

2. The final integration test release contains all components that will be part of the customer-released (General Availability) version of Sumatra.

3. The Sumatra Project Management team agrees that sufficient Integration Testing has been performed and further Integration Testing is not likely to find more integration-related bugs.

4. The Sumatra Project Management team holds an integration test phase exit meeting and agrees that these integration test exit criteria are met.

System Test Entry Criteria

System test shall begin when the following criteria are met.

1. The bug tracking system is in place and available for all project participants.

2. The System Operations and Administration team has configured the system test clients and servers for testing. The test team has been provided with appropriate access to these systems.

3. The Development team has completed all features and bug fixes scheduled for increment 1 and placed all of the underlying source components under formal, automated source code and configuration management control.

4. The Development team has completed component testing for all features and bug fixes scheduled for the Increment.

5. Fewer than fifty (50) must-fix bugs (per the Project Management team) are open, including bugs found during component test and integration test.

6. The Sumatra Project Management team holds a system test phase entry meeting and agrees that increment 1 is ready to begin system test.

7. The Release Engineering team provides a revision-controlled, complete software release to the test team as described in the "Release Management" section.

FIGURE 6-5 INTEGRATION AND SYSTEM TEST PHASE ENTRY, CONTINUATION, AND EXIT CRITERIA (CONTINUED ON NEXT PAGE)

System Test Continuation Criteria

System test shall continue provided the following criteria are met.

1. All software released to the test team is accompanied by Release Notes. These Release Notes must specify the bug reports the Development team believes are resolved in each software release.

2. No change is made to the Sumatra system, whether in source code, configuration files, user documentation, or other setup instructions or processes, without an accompanying bug report or as part of the planned features or bug fixes for a subsequent increment.

3. The Release Engineering team provides a weekly, revision-controlled, complete software release to the test team as described in the "Release Management" section, built from relatively up-to-date source code. These releases can be installed in the test environment in such a way that the release functions in a stable fashion. Furthermore, the test team can execute planned or exploratory tests against this test release in a reasonably efficient manner to obtain further meaningful test results.

4. Fewer than fifty (50) must-fix bugs (per the Project Management team) are open, including bugs found during component test and integration test.

5. Twice-weekly bug review meetings occur until system test phase exit to manage the open bug backlog and bug closure times.

System Test Exit Criteria

System test shall successfully conclude when following criteria are met.

1. No panic, crash, halt, wedge, unexpected process termination, or other stoppage of processing has occurred on any server software or hardware for the previous four (4) weeks.

2. The GA-candidate increment (currently targeted to be increment 5) has been in system test for six (6) weeks.

3. The test team has executed all the planned tests against the GA-candidate system test release.

4. The Development team has resolved all "must-fix" bugs.

5. The test team has checked that all issues in the bug tracking system are either closed or deferred and, where appropriate, verified by regression and confirmation testing.

6. The Product Quality Dashboard Gauge indicates that Sumatra has achieved an acceptable level of quality, stability, and reliability.

7. The Quality Risk Coverage Dashboard Gauge indicates that all quality risks have been adequately covered.

8. The Project Management team agrees that the product, as defined during the final cycle of system test, will satisfy the customers' and users' reasonable expectations of quality.

9. The Project Management team holds a system test phase exit meeting and agrees that these system test exit criteria are met.

FIGURE 6-5 CONTINUED

Later that day, Jamal got a response from Harold, which included the original recipients as CC addressees.

```
Jamal:

Checked out the attachments. Dashboard's fine, but please stop by
sometime to explain difference between Fulfillment and Progress
charts.
```

Re: criteria, looks reasonable. Good that you recognize need for entry and exit decisions to be project-management-level. I worked with QA manager at last job who used some metrics that led to counterproductive debate about bug severities, meaning of word "is", etc., :-).

Two questions re: stopping testing.

Why 50 as magic number of open bugs for stopping?

How do you plan on measuring efficiency so we can recognize reasonable efficiency?

Good job,

H.

Jamal responded as follows, including all the recipients.

Hi, Harold—

Glad it looked good to you. I'll stop by re: dashboard tomorrow if that's okay?

As for PM-level decisions, yes, entry, continuation, and exit of test phases have to take into account not just quality issues, but features, budget, and schedule ramifications.

On that note, 50 isn't really a magic number, but it is around that point where the bug prioritization meetings tend to become unmanageable. In my experience, there's no point doing further testing if there's no way to manage the primary output of testing, bug reports. Does that make sense?

As for measuring efficiency, that's part of what the Progress chart will show us. If it's taking us three or four times as long to run tests as we'd planned—which we'll see on that chart—I'd suggest that we may want to consider other options. Again, this will be a business decision, where we balance quality, features, budget, and schedule. I'd rather not stop testing, but if no progress is being made, we should, I think, have a PM-level discussion about whether it makes sense to continue to expend the resources.

Hope that answers it.

Regards,

Jamal

Fifteen minutes later Jamal got a response to his message, CC'ing all, that read as follows:

```
Jamal:

That makes perfect sense. Pls consider the criteria officially
"fine by Harold".

Cheers,

H.
```

Step #	Step	Done?
2.	Negotiate and document the collaborative workings between the test sub-project and the overall project.	☑

All right, thought Jamal, I've pretty much got my plan now, but what could go wrong? What can I do to mitigate such risks, and, should the bad things happen, can I put a contingency plan in place to reduce the damage? He thought back on previous projects, looked at his change tracking database for the last few projects, and typed in a few risks along with contingency and mitigation plans. He stared at the wall for a while and then entered a few more. He checked some testing books on his desk and then typed a few more.[1] Table 6-1 shows what Jamal came up with.

Step #	Step	Done?
3.	Finalize and document the remaining logistical and planning details, such as the risks to the test subproject itself and definitions of testing and project terms. Annotate any referenced documents. Write a one-page executive summary of the test subproject.	☑

After coming up with his list of risks, Jamal set about creating tasks and reminders in his scheduling software so that he could check up on whether the risks were coming to pass. Figuring out the location of these land mines is one of the best parts of writing

---

1. For a discussion of a change tracking database, see Chapter 7 of my book *Managing the Testing Process, Second Edition*. In addition, Chapter 11 of *Managing the Testing Process, Second Edition,* contains a discussion of test project gas pedals and brake pedals; the latter are also risks to be mitigated.

Risk	Contingency/Mitigation
Breakdown in resolution and escalation process(es).	Attempt to work around blocking issue, accept inefficient progress and delays in plan fulfillment. OR Halt testing under continuation criteria, resolve process problem. OR Continue testing via workaround, meanwhile resolving process problem for next incident.
External lab(s) can't install Sumatra.	Prevent problem by thoroughly testing installation before sending a test release to an external lab. OR File bug report(s) against installation process. AND Send an experienced test engineer to install.
Last-minute, large-impact change in requirements, design, features, or other portions of development plan.	Accept increased quality risks due to incomplete testing of change. OR Accept increased budget risk by staffing up or outsource to do sufficient testing at last minute OR Accept increased schedule risk by delaying ship date.
Bad test release discovered after test cycle has begun.	Institute automated smoke testing in Release Engineering to detect bad releases. OR Stop testing during "blown" cycle, revert to the "last known good" test release, and continue testing, accepting the reduced fulfillment of planned tests and loss of efficient progress.
Test environment incomplete on integration test or system test phase entry date.	Start testing with those tests that can be run on the environment available, accepting limited test fulfillment, inefficient progress, and significant gaps in test coverage. OR Slip the planned test phase entry and exit dates day-for-day until the environment is available.

continued on next page

TABLE 6-1 RISKS, CONTINGENCIES, AND MITIGATIONS FOR SPEEDYWRITER

Risk	Contingency/Mitigation
Test environment incomplete for one or two whole phases.	Rework plan to lengthen phases as required, drop any tests that were dependent on the missing configuration(s), identify increased quality risks to project. OR Institute a third (graveyard) shift. (NB: This decision must be made before retaining technicians and may not provide total mitigation of the risks.)
Test environment system support unavailable or not proficient.	Accept inefficient progress and unfulfilled planned tests. OR Retain a contractor for the short term to provide support.
Buggy deliverables impede testing progress, reduce overall test coverage, or both.	Prevent problem via thorough component testing by Development team. OR Adhere to continuation criteria and stop testing if problem becomes too bad, accepting delay of schedule. OR Attempt to continue testing on current schedule and budget, accepting a poor-quality system release to customers.
Gaps in test coverage.	Exploratory (guerrilla) testing allows testing of areas not covered by planned tests. AND Possibly use structural coverage analysis techniques, field-failure analysis, and customer data to identify gaps to be filled. This should probably be decided on a resources-available basis during test design and development.
Unclear customer usage profiles/environments results in incomplete or incorrect testing.	Get information on actual customer usage from Customer Support as well as from Marketing's alpha and beta efforts and the Sales team, then create tests to cover those areas. OR Accept, due to schedule or resource limitations, the possibility of testing being misaligned with customer usage.
Slips in development schedule affect entry criteria readiness on scheduled dates.	Hold to entry criteria, reducing the number of features delivered by slipping the test and overall project schedules and letting the final increment(s) of functionality drop off. OR

continued on next page

TABLE 6-1 CONTINUED

Risk	Contingency/Mitigation
	Violate the entry criteria and accept the increased risk of poor quality due to insufficient time to find and fix bugs, which can include the risk of utter project failure.
Unanticipated resource needs for complete testing.	Acquire the resources and exceed the test budget. OR Delete some other testing and reallocate resources to the missing testing area. (NB: May not be possible for all situations.) OR Decide to skip the tests for which sufficient resources were not budgeted and accept the increased quality risks associated with that test coverage gap.
Test team attrition.	Accept temporary slowdown in planned test fulfillment. AND Backfill ASAP with contract tester having appropriate skills.
Key player (outside test team) attrition.	Identify alternate or backup people for each nontest key player. OR Backfill the role within the test team upon loss of the supporting person, resulting in inefficiency and slower planned test fulfillment.
Can't hire appropriate automated test engineer.	Use all available means to locate the ideal candidate, including recruiters. OR Increase [test] pass duration to allow for slower test fulfillment. OR Send a member of one of the test teams to "boot camp" training with the test tool vendor for quick ramp-up.[a]
Debugging in test environment.	Provide customer-like configurations for development as well as test, manage the configurations to ensure reproducibility of bugs in development environments. OR Accept the slowdown or stoppage of test plan fulfillment along with the reduction in efficiency caused by the need to restore the test environment after debugging.

TABLE 6-1 CONTINUED

a. I thank one of the reviewers, Deborah McCandless of Nolo.com, for contributing this item. She wrote, "[For this to work, you need] someone who has all the basic skills along with the drive needed to take the course and hit the ground running. This can be a great opportunity for someone to move forward on his or her desired career path. I did this with one of our junior programmers and it has worked out very well."

the plan, he thought. Now if I can just avoid stepping on them! Finally, Jamal wrapped up the plan by defining some of the terms, pointing the reader to referenced and supporting documents, and writing an executive summary. That evening, Wednesday the 18th, before leaving for the day, Jamal sent out his first draft of the test plan as an attachment to an e-mail to John Albertson, Harold Jones, Jenny Kaufmann, Kate Hernandez, Keith Lee, Yasuhiro Kanagawa, Cosimo Negraev, Rachel Woods, Max del Oro, Jaime Hinojosa, and Bobbi McDaniels. He sent a CC to Rajesh Gupta, Cicely Rice, and Tina Brown as well.

```
Hi, all—

Attached please find the first draft of my Integration and System
Test Plan for Sumatra. The supporting schedule, budget, and risk
analysis documents can be found on Jupiter in the Sumatra\Test
folder.

I realize that we're all busy, but please respond with feedback
by COB Friday. I will work that feedback into the plan over the
weekend and release a new version Monday. All of you will receive
an invitation to a meeting on Tuesday to review the revised ver-
sion of the plan for final approval. Lunch will be served. (Tina,
thanks for setting this meeting up!)

Regards,

Jamal
```

Satisfied that a good first draft of the test plan was out to the team, Jamal headed home. He knew, though, that while the hard work of writing was done, the challenging work of reviewing and obtaining commitment was just coming up.

Step #	Step	Done?
4.	Circulate the plan for private (offline) review, often to the test team first and then to the wider collection of stakeholders and participants. Gather input and revise the plan, iterating steps 1 through 3 as needed. Assess any changes to the estimated schedule and budget (that exceed retained slack or contingency) resulting from the planning process, and obtain management support for such changes.	✔

BEYOND THE PROCESS: KEY CONSIDERATIONS FOR THE TEST PLAN

For the most part, much of what goes into the plan either falls out of the quality risk analysis and estimate or is negotiated between the various key players. In the former

Test Strategy

The chosen approaches and decisions made that follow from the test project's and test team's goal or mission. The mission is typically effective and efficient testing, and the strategies are the general policies, rules, and principles that support this mission. Test tactics are the specific policies, techniques, processes, and the way testing is done.

case, what's important is that we accurately translate the information from our Failure Mode and Effect Analysis chart, schedule, and budget into a text narrative and illustrations. In the latter case, the key players are free to work out whatever roles and responsibilities make sense, at least within the constraints of the project. In both cases, to the extent the test plan addresses such topics, it simply captures, restates, and communicates existing information.

However, the test engineer or test manager writing the plan must carefully think through some topics. She must put forth the ideas, conclusions, and decisions on these topics so that those people reading the plan will understand, very clearly, what they are to do. Two such topics, test release management and test status reporting, will come up in later chapters as critical processes in their own right, so I'll defer discussion of them at this point. (It's important to remember that these issues, even though I'll discuss them later, should be addressed in the plans you write.) At this juncture, let's look at four nonprocess topics—test strategy, test resource planning, configuration management, and risk management—that are critical to address in your plans.

SELECTING STRATEGIES FOR TESTING

Let's start with test strategies. What's a test strategy? Different people use different words for the concept, but what I mean is explained in the previous definition. To get a sense of the context of test strategy and its relationships to the test team's mission and tactics—and the overall project—see Figure 6-6.

Figure 6-7 shows the test strategy from the Sumatra project. Such a strategy, while by no means universal, is quite common, at least as one instance of a specific family of test strategies. This family of test strategies advocates the following general approach.

- Develop a set of tests based on top-down test designs using a risk analysis, requirements, test objectives, and so on.
- Augment that set of tests with bottom-up test designs based on actual usage, use cases, customer data, and so on.

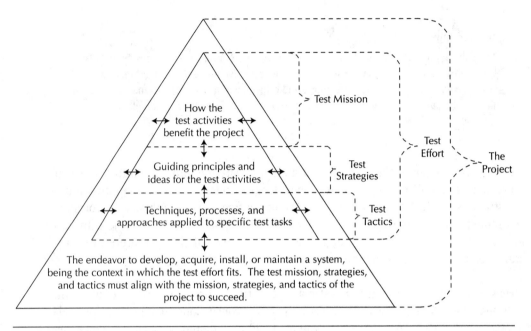

FIGURE 6-5 TEST TEAM MISSION, STRATEGIES, AND TACTICS

- Use exploratory testing to fill the obvious gaps.
- Apply structural analysis of some sort—dynamic (e.g., code coverage) or static (e.g., code complexity)—to identify hidden gaps in test coverage, and then fill those as well.

Test strategies along these lines are intimated in early works on testing like Myers's *Art of Software Testing* and Hetzel's *Complete Guide to Software Testing*. They remain popular today, though some variations leave off one or more of the later (i.e., post-top-down) steps.

However, there are other contenders. Kaner, Bach, and Pettichord, in *Lessons Learned in Software Testing*, advocate an approach that focuses on risk-driven exploratory testing. Some advocates of various so-called *agile methodologies* like Extreme Programming talk about the need for programmer-driven component "testing [of] everything that could break." To the extent such statements are directives, not statements of principles, they indicate the need for testing based on known technical weaknesses. I consider this a design-based testing strategy.

Another set of strategy decisions relates to whether, how, and to what specific tests a test team should apply test automation. Dustin, Raskha, and Paul, in *Automated Soft-*

Sumatra Test Strategy

• Develop automated and manual tests to cover all the quality risks identified as needing extensive or balanced testing, focusing on behavioral factors observable at some user interface or accessible API.

• Add test data or conditions within existing cases or new test cases to cover critical customer usage profiles, customer data, or known defects in our product or competitors' products.

• Use exploratory testing in areas that were not addressed previously and that appear, because of test results or intuition, to be at high risk of bugs. Update or define new test cases to cover found bugs.

• Run tests across a "customer-like" mix of server, network, and client configurations (the test environment).

• Repeat all integration test and system test cases, including SpeedyWriter 3.0 functional tests, multiple times across each phase to detect regression.

• Possibly, should time and resources allow or should concern about unidentified quality risks dictate, use structural coverage techniques to identify untested areas, and then add tests to cover critical test gaps.

FIGURE 6-6 HIGH-LEVEL SUMATRA TEST STRATEGY

ware Testing, have advanced a formalized approach to making this strategy decision, which they refer to as an Automated Test Life-Cycle Methodology. A less formalized approach to making the same decisions can be found in Fewster and Graham's *Software Test Automation*.

Yet another strategy consideration is the kind of test techniques to be used.

■ *Static*—Testing by examining system objects like requirements specifications, design documents, and source code. Code inspections and requirements reviews are two common examples. Weinberg in *The Psychology of Computer Programming*, McConnell in *Software Project Survival Guide* and Wiegers in *Software Requirements*, among many, many others, discuss this topic at length.

■ *Structural (a.k.a. white-box or glass-box)*—Testing by looking at the way in which the system was implemented. Data-flow testing, path testing, and transaction testing are three common examples. Beizer's *Software Testing Techniques* provides a large set of structural techniques.

■ *Behavioral (a.k.a. black-box)*—Testing by looking at the features and behaviors the system should exhibit. Equivalence partitioning and domain testing are common examples. Beizer's *Black-Box Testing* and *Software System Testing and Quality Assurance* discuss these topics at length, as does Kaner et al.'s *Testing Computer Software*.

- *Live*—Testing based on what users actually do with the system. Beta testing, usability studies, and, in some cases, user acceptance testing are examples. Kaner et al. discuss live testing to some extent in *Testing Computer Software*, while Nielsen addresses usability extensively in *Usability Engineering*.

These techniques are not rigid distinctions, like the taste qualities of sweet, sour, salty, and bitter, but rather a continuum, like cold, warm, and hot. For example, design-based tests, such as performance tests, are somewhat behavioral in that we know how quickly we want the system to respond to certain situations, but also somewhat structural in that we tend to test conditions that relate to known limitations in the technology. Because of this continuous nature, I prefer to think about these categories in terms of a spectrum of test granularity.[2]

It is generally, though not universally, true that the earliest testing on a project tends to be static, followed by structural, then behavioral, and finally live. To some extent, this is a happenstance of when certain kinds of test activities *can* start, though it is also true that each kind of testing tends to locate particular kinds of bugs that are harder to find subsequently with coarser-grained tests.

Conversely, the subsequent coarser-grained tests can often find bugs that earlier tests can't find. Two examples: Mistakes in conditions such as using "greater than" where "greater than or equal" was required are best found in unit testing; end-to-end performance problems can only be found in system testing.

Figure 6-8 shows the V Model, introduced in Chapter 1, annotated with the kinds of test granularity typically found at each level. When a project is following an Incremental model, all four granularities of testing may well be involved for most of the project.

> **Test Granularity**
> The fineness or coarseness of test focus. A fine-grained test allows the tester to check low-level details, especially of implementation; static and structural tests are finer-grained. A coarse-grained test provides the tester with information on general system operation and requirements; behavioral and live tests are coarser-grained.

---

2. Hung Nguyen talks about "gray-box" testing in his book *Testing Applications on the Web*, by which he means testing the behavior of the system while using some knowledge of key technical risks and design decisions to be more effective and efficient in looking for bugs.

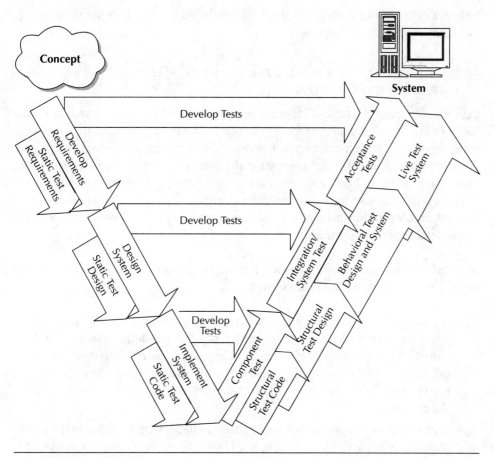

FIGURE 6-7 V MODEL ANNOTATED WITH TEST GRANULARITIES

Let me wind up this subsection with two observations. The first is that while many good sources are available to study the topic, selection of the right strategies for your test project will be as much an art as a science. Expect to become better at this over time. When you're new to test strategizing, seek out fellow practitioners, consultants, and colleagues with more experience who can help.

My reasoning for this advice follows from my second observation. Some seasoned test engineers and test managers run successful test efforts without writing down a single word in the form of a test plan. In some cases, these experienced pros have trouble even articulating why they test the way they do. Nevertheless, such practitioners, when working on projects that tolerate a lack of documentation, can do very well. A strong testing strategy, by itself, can make up for a lot of other weaknesses, including in the area of planning.

A SPECIAL CASE: REGRESSION RISK MANAGEMENT STRATEGIES

Before we set aside the topic of strategy for a while, let's return to that second-to-last bullet in Figure 6-7. Jamal is proposing to repeat previously run tests in an effort to catch regression. In general, regression risk exists anytime the system is changed, even down to one line of code.[3] Regression risk arises not just from code changes, but also from changes in hardware, firmware, configuration, databases, cohabiting software, networks, and so forth. On one Internet appliance project, a major source of regression risk lay in the uncontrolled and unannounced changes a vendor made to the firmware of the integrated modem.

Regression risk comes in a few flavors. One way of looking at regression risk has to do with when the regression is discovered.

▪ A programmer or engineer makes a change to the system resulting in a regression that is not detected by testing until other changes in the system have occurred. The larger the number of such changes that *have* occurred, the more difficult it will be to isolate the cause of the regression back to the offending change, especially when subsequent changes mask or influence the behavior of the regression.

▪ A programmer or engineer makes a change to the system resulting in a regression that is not detected by testing at all but is found by a customer or user. As just stated, the larger the number of changes that have occurred in the system before the user encounters the regression, the more difficult it will be to isolate the cause.

The first kind of regression introduces undesirable complications and delays into the debugging process, which can also delay testing. The second kind of regression negatively affects the customer's experience of quality. If either type of regression occurs in areas that are not being tested because of deliberate trade-offs between quality, schedule, budget, and feature risks, then such regressions, while unfortunate, are beyond the test team's control.

---

3. An extreme instance is a typo (a "6" instead of a "D") in SS-7 telephony software that resulted in massive (greater than 7 million) outages in various regions across the United States. See Neumann, *Computer-Related Risks*, page 16.

Regression

A system exhibits regression (or has regressed) when, as a result of a change, a new revision of the system, S_{n+1}, contains a bug not present in revisions S_1 though S_n that causes some previously correct operation to misbehave.

Regression Testing

Testing performed to catch bugs that cause regression.

However, if regressions occur in areas covered by testing, then they are due to a regression test gap. For the second kind of regression risk, assuming the regression occurs in a feature that you had tested before the offending change but not after, then the regression bug that hits your customer or user is also a test escape.

(As an aside, remember my discussion of testing economics in Chapter 4. The first kind of regression increases the cost of internal failure, which reduces the return on the testing investment. The second kind of regression represents an incurred cost of external failure. This failure belongs as much to the test team for not catching the regression as to the programmer who created the offending change.)

Another way of looking at regression risk involves the overall lifecycle—from initial concept to end of life or decommissioning—of the system. Suppose that we are working on release X.Y of a system and that we have previously released versions 1.0, 1.1, . . ., 2.0, 2.1, . . ., X.0, X.1, . . ., X.(Y-1). Two forms of regression could occur.

- A programmer or engineer makes a change to the system resulting in a regression to behaviors or features new to release X.Y.

- A programmer or engineer makes a change to the system resulting in a regression to behaviors or features introduced in some release previous to X.Y.

Regression Test Gap

For any given change or revision, the difference between the areas of test coverage provided by the entire test set and the test coverage provided by the tests that are actually rerun. For a customer release, the regression test gap can also be considered the extent to which the release was not exposed at some point during testing of that release to the entire test set.

The first risk is the least problematic. Since we're talking about a new feature, it's quite possibly something the product needs for some subset of the customer base, but perhaps not all customers care about it, which means the business risk is lower. Furthermore, since that feature or behavior has never been present in the product *from the customer's perspective*, the business risk is reduced because no customer workflows have grown up around the capability that must now be rethought. (The failure of previously announced features, though, could have an effect on *planned* workflows.) Finally, since development and testing of maintenance releases tend to focus on the new features and behaviors, the technical risk of such regressions and regression test gaps in the first place is lower.

Conversely, the business and technical risks are higher in all these three ways.

1. You often have limited information about what subset of your customer base is using what existing feature or behavior.
2. Any feature or behavior may very well have become an integral part of many of your users' workflows, greatly inconveniencing whatever subset of your customer base does use that feature or behavior.
3. Since both programmers and tests are focused elsewhere, you are more likely to miss the regression.

Table 6-2 summarizes these moment-of-detection and lifecycle factors and the associated risks.

Failure to implement effective and efficient regression testing strategies can lead to a vicious circle around and around the four foreseeable-outcome cells of that table. I

	Detected by Testing	Detected by the User
New Behavior or Feature	Increased cost and incurred delays to system release to achieve desired quality.	Failure to deliver promised release content. Cost of repairing the bug in the field. Possible damage to company image.
Existing Behavior or Feature	Significant costs to foresee and detect such regressions. Increased cost and incurred delays to release product of desired quality. Possible difficulty of repair because of staff turnover.	Breakage of existing aspects of the system, some of which may be integral to customer workflows. Cost of repairing the bug in the field, often in an expensive emergency-patch fashion. Serious damage to company image. Legal liability.

TABLE 6-2 Various Regression Scenarios and Foreseeable Outcomes

> **Test Escape**
> Any field-reported bug that could reasonably have been caught during testing but was not. The term can also refer to a bug that makes its way into a subsequent phase of testing, although it should have been caught in a previous phase.

once worked for a company where, for a time, we tried to get too much content out in each maintenance release with insufficient time for testing and debugging. During that period of thrashing around, before we got our maintenance release process under control, the president of the company received a letter from one of our customers that included the line, "I have never worked with a software company that cared less about quality." That is not a good situation to be in, especially as a tester. Rightly or wrongly, some of the blame for those regression test gaps that so upset your customers will end up sticking to the test team.

The best-known strategy for reducing regression risk is to repeat tests. Various approaches exist for picking the exact tests to repeat and the frequency with which to repeat those tests. Since this topic is beyond the scope of this book, I will again refer you to some other sources.

Since automated testing is all about setting up repeatable tests, any of the books on the topic should discuss ways to pick which tests to automate and which ones not to automate, along with optimizing the regression risk management capabilities of your automated tests. Both Fewster and Graham's *Software Test Automation* and Dustin et al.'s *Automated Software Testing* include such information.

Test repetition strategies for manual testing—along with some of the limitations on automated regression testing—are discussed in Chapter 3 of my book *Managing the Testing Process*. If you prefer to use partial rather than full regression testing strategies for your manual testing, you can use the quality risk analysis technique discussed in Chapter 2 of this book. You can also use bug trends, test case status, and overall test results, topics covered later in this book, to select your tests.

I'm aware of two other options that work to reduce these risks without full or partial retesting. The first is an analytical approach. One of my clients, whose complete set of integration and system test cases involves about 20 person-years of effort, does not have the time or budget to repeat more than 5% or so of its tests. (Those 5% are the ones that involve basic atomic functions, rather than the incredibly complex workflows the product implements.) Attempting to cover all these different workflows would be impractical.

So they used code coverage measurements to ensure that at least large sections of the underlying source code itself do not go untested. They achieved a rolling-four-week-average overall function-level coverage of about 75%, which, in their experience, effectively reduced the regression risks to a tolerable level. There are other analytical approaches that involve analyzing the changes that occurred and how those affect the system, but I have heard from people who tried to apply such approaches that they are impractical for all but the most trivial set of changes.

The second is an empirical approach: the use of extensive live testing. A large beta program, for example, will, if the right set of users is selected, give a good cross-section of the different workflows and types of data that are important to your customers. (The level of quality, though, must be suitable for beta testing first, or you risk alienating current or potential customers selected for the beta program.) For example, the regression problems associated with the modem firmware that I mentioned earlier were detected through beta testing.

Live testing doesn't eliminate the chance that some bugs will escape. On the one hand, unlike when using a repeated-test strategy with known coverage, you won't have a good idea of where those escaped bugs may be. On the other hand, if those bugs aren't important to any of your important users or customers, you probably shouldn't be wasting a lot of time testing them either. Certainly, under the risk-driven test approach I have outlined in this book, I would not build test cases to cover obscure, unimportant risks, and the importance of risks is, to a great extent, determined by whether customers care.

Finally, let me point out that some people have advanced object-oriented programming as a means for limiting regression risk and thus the need for regression testing. However, some work has been done on this topic that indicates that even with encapsulation and inheritance, if you use a component (object, method, and so on) in a way different from the way it was used before, regression risk exists. Since it's not possible to know with complete certainty that a change in one part of a program won't affect some other part of the program—however distant in terms of object instantiation or data flows—regression risk still exists.[4] For similar reasons, integration of commercial software or any software developed by a third party suffers from the same regression risks.

---

4. For more details, see Dewayne Perry and Gail Kaiser's paper "Object-Oriented Programs and Testing," found at citeseer.nj.nec.com/perry90objectoriented.html.

UNDERSTANDING TEST ENVIRONMENT EXECUTION RESOURCES

Along with the overall set of tests you run, the question of how many times to run each test is a powerful influence on your test resource needs. Allow me to leave aside the question of staffing, which is treated more completely in Chapter 8. For the moment, let me address just the question of the test environment resources we need to run our tests.

In the simple case of running manual tests on a standalone platform—say, a Macintosh-based office-automation program—you need as many systems as you intend to have test cases running at one time. Say you have 120 person-hours of testing planned for one week. Using a rule of thumb of 30 test hours per week per tester, you need at least four Macs in your test lab. My preference, though, is to have two user terminals—of whatever flavor—per tester, because of the need to isolate configuration or system-dependent problems.

Suppose, though, that four is the limit of platforms we can get. In that case, if we want two Macs per tester, then we can use a dual-shift approach, as Jamal did in the case study. When testing systems where the tests occur on rare hardware, such as engineering prototypes or massive corporate mainframes, a dual-shift approach is often necessary to fully employ precious hardware.

If you look at the "Basic Sumatra Test Tracking" spreadsheet that accompanies this book, specifically the "Test Case Summary Plan (1Shift)" and "Test Case Summary Plan (2Shift)" worksheets, you can see that I used a fairly simple calculation based on work hours and test duration to come up with the number of test server clusters needed.[5] Tests that were run off-site are not counted, of course. Tests that did not require nonexclusive use of a server cluster were not counted, once at least one server cluster was allocated for nonexclusive use by some other set of tests. In other words, two tests that do not require exclusive use of a server can share it, but one test that does not require exclusive use of a server still must have a server to test against, since any test that requires a server, exclusively or otherwise, will still need a server. (If this is still confusing, consider washing your hands. You can wash more than just your left hand with your right hand, but without your right hand, you'll have trouble washing your left hand.) The formulas in those worksheets are not 100% accurate but do provide a conservative yet not overblown estimate of hardware needs.

---

5. This and other supporting documents can be found on the "Library" page at www.rexblack-consulting.com.

Test Artifacts

Behaviors arising from the artificiality of the test environment or from a test process that diverges from the way the system will behave in the field; misleading behaviors or incorrect results reported by the test system.

The SpeedyWriter case study hardware environment is simple, but some test configurations can involve dozens of servers connected to hundreds of workstations in multiple locations across a variety of connections, both network and dial-up. For such configurations, see Chapters 6 and 7 of my book *Managing the Testing Process, Second Edition*, where I provided a database for planning and managing complex test configurations.

When you're testing networked systems, client-server systems, browser-based systems, mainframe systems, and the like, there is some sharing of certain hardware resources across multiple tests that can, and in some cases must, occur. For example, on one project we applied load generators to the server farm to simulate a customer base of 50,000 while doing manual testing through the appliances to ensure that the customer's experience of quality, especially in the areas of performance and reliability, didn't degrade.

However, you do have to be careful. For example, most performance testing requires dedicated use of an isolated test environment, to prevent test artifacts from creeping into the results. Error handling and recovery testing, load testing, and stress testing can produce environment-wide problems that ripple through to affect any other test running on the system. Even if such problems can be predicted, the effect of slow responses and system crashes on tester efficiency—and thus test project progress—must be weighed against the cost of additional hardware, using multiple shifts, running heavy-handed tests overnight, and other options.

Another complication that exists here arises when maintenance releases, emergency patches, and other product lines must also be tested by the same team in the same test lab. Either you will have to maintain enough environments to handle all these in separate configurations *or* you will have to force management to prioritize when two or more projects compete for the same set of test environment resources. The plan is a good place to lay out this trade-off.

Mainframes, servers, storage area networks, and the like are extremely expensive resources, and clever ways to share such resources are almost always required. However, for PCs, the saving-money argument almost never holds water in my opinion.

For example, testers have related using virtual machine software to run two operating systems on one PC at a time for testing purposes. Bugs identified on such configurations are suspect. (Such bugs would be not only suspect, but totally untrustworthy if they dealt with behaviors like performance, reliability, and other areas where resource usage is a major factor.) How do you know that some complex interaction between the OSes, the virtual machine software, the system under test, and other cohabiting software, drivers, and data didn't cause the failure? For this reason, bugs reported against such artificial test configurations are likely to meet with a jaundiced eye from the programmers who are asked to fix them.

For a better alternative, consider a dual-boot drive or multiple drives that can be selected at boot time. Sure, you have to reboot, but at least you don't have concurrently running tasks that can interact in your memory and on your CPU. However, since the average PC might cost less than a person-week of test engineer time—and a lost week of schedule time is usually more costly than a PC—how much inefficiency time should you be willing to tolerate just to avoid buying extra hardware or adding a second shift?

MANAGING TEST SYSTEMS AND ENVIRONMENT CONFIGURATIONS

Whatever resources you ultimately decide to deploy in your test environment, you will need some way to manage that environment. The policies and tools practically available to you depend quite a bit on the technology with which you're working. For platforms with IDE or SCSI hard drives, one part of your environment configuration management policy may include the creation and storage of master drive images— i.e., direct disk image copies, bit-by-bit, of known good configurations—that can be restored to the test environment as needed. For larger server farms and mainframes, commercial configuration management tools exist that can handle this for you.

The key here is that you know how to create customer-like configurations in your test environment and that you can restore those environments at will with minimal effort. Because you are testing, unexpected events will occur, and sometimes those events involve corruption of the test environment configuration. You do not want to get stuck rebuilding an undocumented configuration by hand in the middle of a test cycle, especially since Murphy's Law tells you that such an event will happen during the last test cycle three days before the scheduled release or deployment date!

No matter how easy it is to restore the configuration, though, you should take pains that it not get screwed up in the first place. Screwed-up test environments don't necessarily announce themselves, which means that you might submit a lot of spurious bug reports before you figure out what's going on. We need to make sure that testing itself doesn't screw up the test environment. In Chapter 10 I'll address the issue of proper test setup and teardown procedures, which are part of the puzzle.

We also need to make sure that programmers and other engineers don't screw up the test environment. For that reason, your test environment management policies should include effective password and access control. My policies also include two iron rules. First, no one should ever change the test environment in any way without the approval of the test manager or at least a senior test engineer. (This includes supporting organizations like network operations or IT. Regularly scheduled updates and maintenance must be suspended for the test environment for the duration of a test cycle, if not for the entire test project, because of the risk of meaningless test results.) Second, no one should ever engage in or allow debugging in the test environment except as part of a project management team–approved period of time during which any potentially affected testing is halted and after which the environment is restored to a known state.

People outside the test team, such as system administrators, network operations staff, and so forth, often manage complex test environments. This creates potential problems with test progress. You may end up waiting for a support person to come fix the environment so you can resume testing, but that support person may have two or three calls in ahead of yours. Put an escalation process in place to deal with this so that you're not the bad guy when testing is in the ditch for a whole day because external support didn't show up. Be especially careful, as I mentioned in Chapter 5, when you are relying on nonstakeholders in the success of the project for support.

Service-level agreements, along with the resolution and escalation processes, must be defined. These agreements must be more rigorous the more likely you think problems are. Furthermore, your escalation process must extend all the way up to some common manager or at least some management team that can force cooperation. In addition, people at the lowest level of the test team must feel completely comfortable and indeed compelled to escalate problems. I have seen cases where a perception of futility led individual contributors on the test team to decide just to handle the problem themselves or work around it. This is a hidden tax on the efficiency and progress of the test team. It must be clear to all that such under-the-radar changes in responsibility will not be tolerated or accepted.

I realize this sounds cynical, but it happens. Don't create hard feelings out of nowhere by telegraphing a distrustful attitude when negotiating these agreements, but don't set yourself up to be the punching bag of the project by ignoring the issue in a warm glow of wishful thinking about the solidarity of the working man and woman.

Finally, make sure you have a plan for managing the testware and other documents you and your test team will create during the effort. The simplest way to do this is to use the source code repository or configuration management system used by the overall project for the system source code. (Every project uses those now, don't they?) Once any document, script, report, chart, or other testware has been created and approved, check it into this repository. Assign it a version number, and increment the version number when you update any item.

Along with tracking the items, maintain a way of tracking what test items were used to test what versions of the system. For example, if you have set of test cases checked into the repository with version 6.1.2, you should be able to look at some cross-referencing document to know that you used that version of the test cases against test releases 3.1.007 through 3.1.021.

This kind of systematic cataloging and storing of test items may seem like a lot of work, especially if you're not familiar with configuration management principles. However, building up a repository of reusable testware, test results, test documents, and other test items is very useful for future efforts. Just as your system is not a throwaway set of source code, the tests are also valuable objects for future assessments of system quality.[6]

TEST SUBPROJECT RISKS

Not only do we need to use risk-based test strategies to provide superior quality risk management services and information products to our stakeholders and internal customers, but we also need to have a risk management strategy for the test subproject itself. An easy way to start thinking about this area of test subproject risk is to ask yourself, What elements must converge successfully for this testing project to succeed? No two test projects will be exactly the same, so count on the specific elements differing across your testing project. However, risks will tend to arise in one or more of the same areas I've mentioned for development projects.

- Features—What elements, factors, and activities enable us to deliver the right collection of quality risk management services and information products?
- Schedule—What elements, factors, and activities enable us to deliver these services and products in a timely fashion and on the dates committed to?

---

6. You can find an excellent introduction to configuration management, including the need to retain test objects, in Tim Kasse and Patricia McQuaid's article "Software Configuration Management for Project Leaders," which appeared in the September 2000 issue of *Software Quality Professional*.

- Budget—What elements, factors, and activities enable us to deliver within the overall project budget and in a way that results in a positive return on investment?
- Quality—What elements, factors, and activities enable us to deliver the test team's services and products in a way that generally satisfies the stakeholders and internal customers, and infrequently (if at all) dissatisfies the stakeholders and internal customers?

To the extent to that these enabling elements, factors, and activities are at risk, the success of your test effort is at risk.

You can often reduce the risks related only to features or budget through good up-front communication. What is the right scope of the testing effort, and how much are people willing to pay for it?

The problems with test project features and budgets arise when management dictates, "Here's a paltry, insufficient sum of money; now go make all the quality problems disappear." As discussed in Chapter 1, if you can clearly understand the context, understand the quality risks to be managed for the system, and help people understand the trade-offs, then you can make such unrealistic expectations go away. These risks now become a matter of project management competence, husbanding the budget and making sure it's spent effectively toward achieving the test project scope.

Quality risks to test projects are mostly about the ability to communicate findings. (I'll talk about this topic at length in Chapter 15.) This is an issue to consider during planning. In our case study, Jamal circulates his proposed reports and charts to management for approval. If you can't get approval for your proposed reports—or you think people don't understand them—then you stand a substantial risk in the perceived quality of your test project. Once again, correctly framing stakeholder expectations is key.

Schedule risks arise through the intricate interconnections between the test subproject and the overall development project. A prime example of a schedule risk to the test project arises from the late delivery of host systems. On one project, we had a quarter-million-dollar server get stuck in customs for two weeks because no one could figure out how to pay the duty, which, of course, delayed all the tests scheduled to run on that system for two weeks.

Many schedule risks are particularly nasty. You can get more money; you can drop features; you can relax quality requirements; but once a day is lost, it's lost for good. When testing suffers a schedule delay, the corresponding test phase exit date is often not allowed to move. This can lead to painful trade-offs at the project level on shipping an insufficiently tested and debugged product—i.e., one with poor and possibly even not fully assessed quality—or missing a marketing window. Careful identification and management of the risks attendant on the testing effort itself can help prevent these problems. Another thing that helps is working with the project management team to achieve a realistic overall project schedule.[7]

GETTING EVERYONE ON BOARD

Applying the processes and policies discussed in this chapter, I find I'm able to produce concise, effective documents that help me understand and communicate what the test effort is about, specifically. A good test plan is a fertile mixture of distilled planning data (from the Failure Mode and Effect Analysis, the schedule, and the budget) together with detailed processes, well-thought-out policies, clever strategies, and mutual agreements with stakeholders. Out of this plan will grow our test effort.

But I don't write good test plans by myself. I need the help of the rest of the project team. So before we move on, we need to make sure the plan is a high-quality plan, supported by all the stakeholders. In the next chapter, I'll close on the topic of test planning by examining Jamal's experience with getting everyone on board and then look back at test planning in terms of how we can create the best possible plans.

---

7. I mentioned Steve McConnell's discussion of project risk management in *Software Project Survival Guide*, pages 93–101, in an earlier footnote in Chapter 2. This is another context where you might find such techniques helpful.

7

FROM SUGGESTION TO COMMITMENT: ASSEMBLE STAKEHOLDER SUPPORT FOR GOOD TEST PLANS

Writing a test plan is all well and good, but a plan is just a document, a collection of words. These words come alive only when the project team puts the test plan into action. That is, a written plan is a suggestion that becomes meaningful only when people commit to carrying it out. The various key players—both inside and outside the test organization—must agree to do what they are called upon to do. The other key stakeholders in the test process and in system quality must agree that the test effort, as described in the plan, will meet their needs. In other words, will the test effort provide information and services to the stakeholders that will help them manage risks to system quality? Once these agreements are obtained, you have more than a document. You have a shared road map to a key piece of the project's future with a community of support.

In the course of getting from the first draft of the test plan to this shared road map and supportive community, we must build the commitment we need. In this chapter, I'll return to the test plan developed in the previous chapter and move through the rest of the planning process. Then, I'll look back at the entire process for test planning, discussing especially how we recognize good test planning and good test plans, some of the challenges that exist, and ways to implement improvement.

JAMAL MAKES HIS PITCH

On the morning of September 19, Jamal came into the office and was immediately confronted by a firestorm related to the "weird customer environment" Keith Lee had discussed the day before. Cosimo Negraev, the Customer Support manager, and Jayesh

Deprendra, the JetCalc product manager, were both waiting to see him. They speculated—in not necessarily gentle terms—that Lin-Tsu had missed a bug in the previous JetCalc release. When people used the words "test escape," Jamal's first thought was "environment-specific," so he spent the morning first smoothing feathers with them, then trying to re-create the bug in the test environment with Lin-Tsu, and finally demonstrating to Jayesh and Cosimo that while it was possible to make the failure occur without the specific customer configuration, it was pretty unusual.

"Sorry, fellas, that you went through this," Jamal said, "but I honestly don't think we can find every configuration-specific problem in our test environment with the resources we have. Jayesh, maybe I can work with you to design a thorough beta test program that covers more of the environments and data sets that we don't have?"

"Well, we have to come up with something!" Jayesh exclaimed. " 'Lousiest spreadsheet on the market today' is not a phrase I want to read in a product review again—unless it's about our competitor."

After a morning like that, Jamal was happy to immerse himself in e-mail. Sure enough, the feedback on his test plan had started to trickle in. Most of it was fine-tuning, but Kate Hernandez brought up a serious point. "You know, maybe I'm missing something," she wrote, "but where're the hierarchical storage management servers in the test environment?"

Holy crow, Jamal thought, we missed that in the Failure Mode and Effect Analysis session. Calling Keith, he confirmed that, at this time, no hierarchical storage management (HSM) devices were in the test lab. "Why would we have them?" Keith asked. "This is the first release to support HSM."

"Well, stand by for more requisitions from yours truly," Jamal said, "because we're going to need to buy some. We'll need at least one."

"Great catch," Jamal wrote back to Kate. "Working on fixing that right now."

Jamal then called a few of the people on the development team who were working on the hierarchical storage management support. They all said that they thought the technical risk was low—hierarchical storage management systems being proven technology that they weren't doing anything new with—but agreed that at least one should be in the mix. Next, he went out on the Internet and got some information about pricing for hierarchical storage management software and storage devices. Calling Kate, Jamal relayed his discussions and asked if she had any preference on which hierarchical storage management configuration they used. She told him that while she knew which software and devices some of their customers were using, she didn't really like the idea of spending the kind of money those systems cost to reproduce all those environments. She asked him to pick an affordable configuration that included the various features that interacted with their software and call that good enough.

"Tell you what," Jamal said, "please call Jayesh and ask him whether, after what happened this morning with JetCalc, he thinks that's a good plan."

"Why? What happened with JetCalc?"

Jamal related the whole story to her, finishing up with, "So, basically, the risk here is that the fewer HSM configurations we test, the more likely these kinds of field failures."

"Okay, I hear you, but if we're talking $7,500 and up for complete configured servers, it won't take too many different configurations to put a serious dent in our budget. How about we just pick two, one NT-based, one UNIX-based?"

"Fine with me," Jamal said. He then sent around the following e-mail to all the participants in the Failure Mode and Effect Analysis meeting and the participants in the test plan review. He also included Jayesh, to give him a chance to share his feelings about the problems that minimal test configurations could cause.

```
Hi, all—

Kate Hernandez noticed, in reviewing my test plan, that we had
not identified any hierarchical storage management servers to be
our test environment as part of the risk analysis. Conversations
with various developers and research on the Web have led me to
believe that the technical risk is low, though I am hardly an
expert. Since even entry-level HSM servers will cost about $7,500
per configuration, Kate and I are proposing that we purchase two
configurations, one NT-based, one UNIX-based.

If anyone has any opinions about this matter and pro or con sen-
timents about our proposal, please let us know.

Regards,

Jamal
```

Debate went back and forth on the topic, both as e-mails and drop-ins to Jamal's office. Finally, the debate ended with an e-mail from John Albertson, vice president of Engineering Services and Jamal's manager.

All—

After an informative debate benefiting all participants, please
note that Harold, Max, Rajesh, and I have discussed the matter of
HSM servers in the Sumatra test environment. While Jayesh and others have well-taken points about the need for diverse test configurations, the fact remains that we can't test everything—no one in
our product space can. We have to balance competing priorities
here. We think that Kate and Jamal's suggestion of testing two configurations does a good job of balancing budget and quality. When
we budgeted for testing, Jamal included a significant contingency
fund. Adding these two servers will consume 25% of that fund. In
exchange for that, Jamal's team will cover two popular HSM configurations. That strikes the senior management team as a wise balance. Therefore, we are instructing Jamal to proceed accordingly.

Again, we appreciate everyone's discussion and participation in
this discussion. At this point, please consider the matter
closed, and direct any further comments you might have to your
immediate manager.

/ja

Jamal smiled when he got that e-mail. Boy, I wish I'd had an e-mail like this one in
my message archives when I had the encounter with Jayesh earlier. This kind of stuff
really gets me out of the quality-whipping-boy role. He updated his test plan and
budget based on this change and then sent out new drafts on Friday the 20th.

Hi, all—

Attached please find the "review-ready" version of the test plan,
draft 2. We'll be discussing this draft on Tuesday at our review
meeting. I look forward to seeing all of you there.

Regards,

Jamal

Step #	Step	Done?
4.	Circulate the plan for private (offline) review, often to the test team first and then to the wider collection of stakeholders and participants. Gather input and revise the plan, iterating steps 1 through 3 as needed. Assess any changes to the estimated schedule and budget (that exceed retained slack or contingency) resulting from the planning process, and obtain management support for such changes.	☑

The review meeting itself was relatively uneventful. Jamal went through the plan page by page, introducing the key pieces of information found on each page. The attendees—John, Harold, Jenny, Kate, Yasuhiro, Cosimo, Rachel, Max, Jaime, Bobbi, Lin-Tsu, Emma, and two senior programmers—ate their sandwiches and asked occasional questions. A few people had helpful suggestions that led to some minor changes. For example, Jenny suggested that the release notes describe known limitations and bugs in the release in addition to the content of the release itself.

At the conclusion of the meeting, Jamal asked, "So, with the changes we've agreed to today, is everyone okay with this plan? Is there anything in there that doesn't make sense?" He looked around the room and saw only people shaking their heads.

"Any unreasonable requests of people? Unreasonable assumptions? Stupid assumptions?" Laughter and more shaking of heads.

John said, "Jamal, I think this plan is great. If we can execute according to this document, testing will go well. Max, Harold, do you agree?"

"Absolutely," said Harold. Max nodded assent.

"Good," John said. "Meeting adjourned."

Step #	Step	Done?
5.	Circulate the plan for public review. Hold a review meeting with all the stakeholders. Gather any final adjustments needed, and obtain commitment that, with any modifications agreed upon in the review meeting, the plan shall be the plan of record for the test subproject.	☑

Jamal, satisfied that he had a solid plan with solid stakeholder support, went back to his office. He made the minor changes discussed in the meeting and then checked the plan into the project document repository.

Step #	Step	Done?
6.	Revise the estimated schedule and budget based on new knowledge gleaned from the planning process, including resource use. If this results in a slip in the schedule or an increase in the budget beyond any retained slack or contingency, escalate it to management for resolution. Negotiations about the new budget and schedule may cause iteration of the previous steps or reworking of the estimate.	☑

Step #	Step	Done?
7.	Check the test plan(s) into the project library or configuration management system. Place the document under change control.	☑

RECOGNIZE A GOOD TEST PLANNING PROCESS

In the documents and templates that come with this book, you can take a look at the test plan for the Sumatra project.[1] Perhaps you agree with me that it is a good test plan. But a good planning process helps the test team do more than produce a pretty document.

ESTABLISH CLEAR CRITERIA FOR PHASES

I declared neutrality—or at least openness—on the question of software lifecycles in Chapter 1. The important consideration for testers, I believe, is fitting our testing process within the chosen lifecycles and methodologies. One of the ways we do this is by picking appropriate entry, continuation, and exit criteria for the test execution phases we are charged with running. If you look back at the criteria that appear in the Sumatra documents, these criteria establish quality and process checkpoints for the project. In other words, they set the standards by which we can answer yes or no to three questions.

- Can the project team deliver to the testing team what the testers need to start, continue, or conclude this test phase (project readiness)?
- Do the testers have or have they completed what they need to start, continue, or conclude this test phase (test subproject readiness)?
- Is the quality of the system under test sufficient to start, continue, or conclude this test phase (system quality readiness)?

The answers to the first two questions are generally clear-cut. Let me illustrate with some examples.

Suppose one system test entry criterion is that all of the features planned for release are completed. Suppose one integration test continuation criterion is that all test releases come from source components under configuration management. Suppose an

---

1. This and other supporting documents can be found on the "Library" page at www.rexblack-consulting.com.

integration test entry criterion is that we have a bug tracking system in place. Suppose a system test exit criterion is that all planned tests are run. All these criteria are either met or not met. These are examples that do not apply to all lifecycle models, but they do apply to some. A skilled and experienced test professional who understands the dynamics of the lifecycle context of the project can thoughtfully select appropriate and unambiguous criteria to address project and test subproject readiness.

Even with careful thought and substantial insight into the lifecycle model chosen, wrapping tight criteria around system quality readiness remains slippery. How do we know when the system is good enough for us to be able to start, continue, or pronounce complete some testing phase? These are hard decisions, subject to careful judgment and consideration. Well-written criteria can guide these thinking processes. In the case of starting and continuing, I usually express quality readiness (for test entry and continuation, not exit) in terms of the ability to effectively and efficiently run tests.

It's easy to pronounce a system unfit for testing under extreme conditions. I have seen systems so unstable as to crash every 15 minutes, requiring a lengthy reboot and reconfiguration process. Testing proceeded at a snail's pace, if at all, and told us very little about the system's quality other than "crashes a lot" over and over again. I have tested systems so full of large, functionality-killing bugs that most test cases were blocked from completion. Further testing revealed no useful new information, since we were blocked at every turn. I have worked on projects where release engineers could not build systems from the source code for days on end. The release engineering team could only deliver a system that was weeks (and many bug fixes) old. We could glean no meaningful quality information about the current system by testing such a stale release.

However, beyond such great obstacles, the question of sufficient quality becomes less clear. If we can test but only at half the planned progress rate, does that mean that we planned too aggressively or that the system is so lousy we should halt testing? How many bugs awaiting a fix (i.e., in the reported bug backlog) is so many that further testing will only increase confusion about the state of the system and lessen the ability of the project team to prioritize which bugs need to be fixed? In the case study, I picked 50 because, in my experience, more than 50 open bugs can't be covered in an hour-long bug triage meeting, and any standing meeting that lasts longer than an hour tends to lose participants as time goes on. However, differences in context could affect this number. For example, if your bug triage meetings discuss bugs in detail, perhaps 20 is the right number.

In terms of finishing a particular phase of testing, the question is even more difficult to answer. How do you know that you have found enough bugs in testing (and hopefully fixed them) along with having tested sufficiently? I have seen people try to quantify their way out of this bind. For example, I've read system test exit criteria like the following:

1. No open severity one bugs, fewer than 25 open severity 2 bugs, and fewer than 50 open severity 3 bugs

2. No more than 10% of test cases failed

3. Ninety percent branch and condition coverage for entire system test phase[2]

I find these criteria good in theory but weak in practice. I can recall numerous beside-the-point arguments with programmers and managers about whether some particular bug report is correctly classified as severity 1 or 2. By combining test cases, dividing test cases, and manipulating the counting of test cases, it's usually possible to make the test case pass and fail counts come out just about any way you want. And just because the tests exercised most of the decision branches, does that mean we checked the interesting conditions, verified the important data flows, and checked against correct expected results?

For this reason, I prefer to use the kinds of criteria shown in the Sumatra test plans. In my approach, the test manager or test lead gathers information and metrics on testing that allow him to report meaningfully on assessed system quality, the progress of the test project, and the response of the rest of the development team to the quality findings and testing effort. He then presents this information effectively to the project management team. (I'll discuss this process in Chapter 15.) The project management team must then balance the quality risks inherent in that information against budget, schedule, and possibly feature risks.

This balancing of risks applies not just to the quality-related criteria. Project management teams can and do waive project-readiness and test subproject–readiness criteria, sometimes for perfectly good business reasons. In some cases, though, balancing of risks is not appropriate, and quantifiable quality criteria are necessary. Examples include safety-related products and those products where a contractual obligation lays out the test criteria. In these cases, the test manager must adopt the appropriate criteria based on these constraints.

---

2. See Boris Beizer's *Software Testing Techniques* for a discussion of various structural coverage techniques, along with a discussion on entry and exit criteria.

ESTABLISH CONSENSUS, COMMON EXPECTATIONS, AND COMMITMENT

On most of my projects, the most important part of the test planning process has not been the document, but rather the consensus, expectations, and commitments embodied in it. I involve all the stakeholders in my approach to planning. They also have an opportunity to know, in advance, what specifically I intend to test—and not test. What kind of help I'm going to ask from them. How my team will interact with their team. How I think we should deal with unexpected events. Further, not only do they know what I'm proposing in advance, they can also debate and discuss these proposals.

The process I use to write test plans culminates the kind of participative, consensus-building approach that I use throughout the entire "Step 1: Plan" portion of the test process outlined in Chapter 1. Jamal built consensus around the test context in Chapter 1, around the critical quality risks in Chapter 2, around an estimate for tasks, time, and resources in Chapters 3 through 5, and now, in Chapters 6 and 7, he's built consensus around a specific plan. In other words, developing a written plan is the final step in making sure that every stakeholder in the testing subproject knows what you intend to do and that every key player knows their roles and responsibilities.

I once saw a clever saying on the side of a colleague's coffee mug: "I'm a manager. I keep exciting things from happening." We can say that the goal of planning is to do exactly that: Prevent unpleasant, exciting, panic-inducing surprises. Such surprises occur when we fail to foresee the intricate connections and assumptions in what we intend to do. Such surprises occur when we ask others to provide support they are not prepared to give. Such surprises occur when we report frivolous, inscrutable, or ill-timed test results. In the test plan, we reveal heretofore unknown or hidden details and build agreement around how we propose to handle them. The effective test engineer or test manager writing a test plan understands his audience, what they need to know and what they already know, and how to communicate with them in a written document.

Another aspect of understanding the audience is anticipating where the potential points of contention exist. The test plan should surface these areas of disagreement. If you can, propose a solution that you think will be acceptable to all parties. If you can't think of one—or have concerns about the attendant controversy—then you can use the test planning process to facilitate discussion. In the case study, Jamal gets the entire project team involved in working out the appropriate level of configuration coverage. Had Jamal simply written down that only two hierarchical storage management servers would be tested, then he would have been seen as the owner of that decision and the consequences of it. Instead, he provoked a discussion about balancing risks at the management level and then allowed his managers to make a decision.

[TBD: We need to decide how many HSM servers to include in the test environment. Kate and I are proposing two, one NT-based, one UNIX-based, because this balances the budget impact of additional hardware with the need to cover a variety of HSM configurations. Jayesh, John, Harold, Max, please advise on this point.]

Jamal handled the discussion and resolution of this issue through e-mail. I have also handled such debates within a draft of the test plan. For example, Jamal could have included the following paragraph in the test plan, right in the test environment section.

This approach is useful when you have the time to work out a final plan through multiple drafts. It does tend to take longer, and you will have to act as the focal point for any ensuing discussion. For simple, one-on-one questions, though, it can be an effective way to collect the open issues and distribute them in one swoop, rather than sending out dozens of e-mails to all the various players asking specific questions.[3]

One of the aspects inherent in the criteria handling approach I discussed earlier is that the project management team must commit to supporting that approach. We are entering into an agreement with the team, captured in the criteria, that we all will collectively make decisions about while moving through project phases provided that the test team can provide the information needed to assess the quality risks. In other words, testers agree to provide a particular set of services, and the project team collectively accepts ownership for a particular decision.

Another form of commitment exists at the peer level, with the owners of upstream processes. For example, on the Sumatra project, Yasuhiro and Jamal agree on how test

---

3. One reviewer of this book, Rebecca Sowada, test manager at Macromedia, mentioned a related technique you might consider. She wrote, "We do something similar [to using TBDs, except that] our test plans are in HTML format and published on the project's intranet site. Since we have change control happening for any document in the site, everyone has access to edit the document. I just create a 'Comments' section on the plan where people can ask questions as they review the plan. It's so easy, then, to adjust the plan, and link their comment to the relevant adjustment. Or to just add a response to their comment right in the 'Comments' section. Granted, I'm working with a small, intimate team of people, all of whom I trust to responsibly edit my test plan, so this approach works well. We still do a review meeting, but I find this approach to be more manageable than sorting through e-mail discussions. In addition, I avoid the issue of someone claiming they weren't on the e-mail list."

releases will get to the test team, Keith and Jamal agree on how test environment support will occur, and Jenny and Jamal agree on bug report handoffs. The agreement and commitment is obtained through the planning process and captured in the written test plan.

Formalization of agreement and commitment occurs in various ways. In some cases, just the fact that the conversations occurred and were captured on paper may suffice. In other cases, having the stakeholders and key players attend a review meeting does the trick.

On some projects, a more formal environment leads to document sign-offs, where the stakeholders and key players must sign the test plan, indicating that they have read, understand, and will participate in the execution of the plan. The decision of which approach to use is a contextual one. Pick whichever approach is most suitable given your organizational and project context.

COMPLETE AT A REASONABLE TIME

When is the right time for planning? To answer this question, let me first go back to the overall testing process. The planning step in that process includes creating a context, but the plan also specifies how the rest of the context creation will occur. The planning process is where I outline, at a high level, the test cases, data, and tools I'll need, and how we'll develop and employ those test objects. The planning process is also where I work out the test environments I need, and how those environments should be configured and supported. Some of these test objects and environments are expensive. Some take a long time to acquire or create. Some require additional staff members to develop or use. Some affect outside groups in ways that are expensive, protracted, or beyond their current capacity. For such activities, the project team needs as much advanced warning as possible, which means I should plan early.

However, there's another force at work here: the learning curve. The earlier I start planning, the less I know about how events will turn out, what strategies will be most effective for testing this particular system, what kinds of bugs the system will suffer from, and the exact design and intended functions of the system we're really building. This implies that I should plan late.

In an article posted on the Software Testing and Quality Engineering Web site, www.stickyminds.com, James Bach discusses planning and introduces an analogy of planning for a football game. Lee Copeland wrote a follow-up article where he expanded on that analogy. (For those of you not familiar with US football, baseball and cricket are somewhat similar in terms of play.) In football, coaches and quarterbacks call plays, often from scripted playbooks, but they also have to think on their feet, based on evolving conditions.[4]

However, to continue the analogy, there's more to a football game than 22 people running an inflated leather ellipsoid up and down a field. For example, tremendous effort goes into maintaining the grass on those fields. A sports stadium can take years to create. Even a baseball diamond laid out in an open field requires us to plan ahead by acquiring bases, a bat or two, some balls, some gloves, a tape measure, and so forth. Sports events require two teams, and if we intend to watch a well-executed game, the people on those teams must have the right skills. If we are to have spectators, we need seats.

A test project—or any project, really—is like that, too. Some activities of the project require thinking on your feet, but others require coordination, take time to put in place, cost money (which takes time to get), and involve people (who must be assembled and trained). Planning should address those long-lead items and be completed early enough to allow action in time for good testing.

PROMOTE REASONABLE FLEXIBILITY AND CREATIVITY

The need for early planning does not negate the point that Bach and Copeland make, though. Good plans and a good planning process should promote flexibility and creativity. In part, this means giving high-level strategic guidance to skilled test engineers and then allowing them to design and implement the right tests within those parameters. In our case study, Jamal tells his test engineers, Lin-Tsu, Emma, and the one who'll be hired, where he thinks they should use automation or manual testing, where they should use structural or behavioral approaches, and so forth. However, that's wide latitude, allowing considerable creativity in designing tests.

The test execution process that Jamal proposes is a bit more constrained. The test technicians will attend a training course where they'll be told the procedures for running various kinds of tests, how to report results, and how to write bug reports. Since the technicians are less skilled than the engineers, Jamal constrains their activities. If,

---

4. James Bach's article is called "Exploratory Testing and the Planning Myth," while Lee Copeland's article is called "Exploratory Planning." Both specifically address planning within the context of exploratory testing, but the same points apply if you intend to do scripted manual or automated testing. Lee Copeland also discusses exploratory testing and test planning in *A Practitioner's Guide to Software Test Design*.

however, you are working entirely with a team of skilled test engineers, you can leave much more open to interpretation and improvisation.

I also plan for flexibility. Good plans should bend under the pressure of the project, not break. Suppose you are planning a test against a scarce, shared hardware resource, like a corporate mainframe. If you plan only one cycle of testing and find bugs that must be fixed, then you have no plan for retesting the next test release with the bug fixes. Likewise, if you plan your team assignments too tightly, moving people from one project to another with no slack in between, what will happen when you need someone to spend an extra day on one project?

This kind of "what if" thinking is part of building a flexible plan. Building in contingencies for the what-ifs—at least, those I can think of—is how I create some of the flexibility in my plans. In the case study, Jamal has a three-page list of risks, contingencies, and mitigations. That may be extreme for your projects, but Jamal is planning an endeavor that exceeds three-quarter-million dollars and three-and-a-half person-years of effort. Due care must be exercised under such conditions.

Since I'm not omniscient, I also use retained slack (extra time and money) to create flexibility for those what-ifs I can't think of. In our case study, for example, Jamal has 10% slack in his budget and has planned for a 50% increase in his test execution activities. He's also planned for exploratory testing as part of the test effort because he knows that Lin-Tsu, Emma, and the other to-be-hired engineer won't be able to think of all the tests in advance. Further, Jamal reserves time and explicitly plans for expanding existing tests and creating new ones during test execution.

A good plan shouldn't just allow for flexibility, it should promote it. For example, I talked earlier about the need for the plan to establish clear criteria for entry into, continuation of, and exit from various test phases. However, I also mentioned that these criteria basically establish methods and points in time for examining quality risks to the project. The project team must weigh these quality risks against budget, schedule, and feature considerations, and may well decide to waive some of the criteria. When that happens, how will you proceed? Sure, you might not be as effective or efficient as before, but if you don't plan in advance for such situations, then you may have to make it up in the moment. While that might work, you won't have the same kind of flexibility as you would have had you planned earlier.

For example, on one project I had planned to do volume testing of some subsystem integration through automated tools. However, the tools weren't *quite* ready when the time came to run those tests. The project management team waived the entry criterion of "test tools ready." I was forced to improvise, which I did by testing parallel data flows across those interfaces with a large (about 50 people) team of test technicians. Since I had failed to plan for such an event, we had to use a relatively expensive temp agency for the techs, some of whom were not very professional. Worse yet, my team and I had no time to train them, so they made lots of mistakes that taxed the test engineers further. As an added inconvenience, because these were junior people with no test experience, we had to write detailed test scripts, which, given the time constraints, required the entire team of test engineers to be in the office all weekend working on those scripts 12 hours each day. And so, since the tests were written under duress, we made a lot of mistakes, including reporting spurious bugs and missing bugs. These problems could have been mitigated in advance with some planning on my part.

Of course, there are reasonable limits to flexibility and creativity. If you attempt to plan away every possible problem, you will discover, as Thomas Jefferson once wrote, "How much pain have caused us the evils which have never happened!"[5] Can you afford to have a complete parallel set of test environments in another location connected to a different Internet backbone just in case a meteor or a bomb strikes the test lab? In some cases, that might be reasonable, but I've never worked on a project that required that degree of flexibility.

Creativity, too, has its limits. Exploratory testing certainly can and does play a part in many well-run test efforts. However, it's important to set boundaries for testers so that we know what they've tested and we know that they've tested the right things. These boundaries vary considerably depending on the skills and experience of the test team, the need to precisely repeat the tests at a later date, the extent to which the results and tests must be documented, and so forth.

PRODUCE APPROPRIATE DOCUMENTATION

On most of my projects, the test plan is not an end in itself, but simply a means to promoting a successful test project. The written plan that comes forth from the planning process is a large part of how I communicate about the testing project to others and gain documented concurrence on a complex endeavor. Sometimes, though, the test plan is a product in its own right. When I've worked for and worked with independent test labs, the test plan was a deliverable to the client.

Whether the emphasis is on the test plan or the test planning process, some test professionals produce the resulting document according to a documentation standard. For example, your organization may have standardized on the Institute of Electrical

---

5. From Jefferson's "A Decalogue of Canons for Observation in Practical Life," which is among his collected papers at the Library of Congress Web site, www.loc.gov.

and Electronics Engineers (IEEE) format for its documents, in which case your test plan will need to comply with IEEE Standard 829. Certain development methodologies and the tools that automate them can influence or even determine how the test plan is documented. In certain regulated industries, law prescribes the documentation standards, often including the test plan. Examples include the nuclear and medical software industries.

The purposes the plan and the planning process serve also influence the appropriate level of detail and volume. Test plans written according to a particular standard must address all the topics specified in the template for that standard. Test plans that deal with complex situations—meaning complex in a business-domain, technical, project, or testing sense—generally require more care and often more verbiage than test plans for simple efforts. Test plans written for use by a team consisting entirely of trained testing professionals will probably be too vague for a test team that is composed to some significant extent of people with little if any experience in testing.

In our case study, Jamal is in the latter situation. In part he deals with some of the level of detailed explanation required through training and mentoring. However, he's also written a precise, detailed test plan.

Even when I must write precise and detailed plans, my bias is toward conciseness. I don't want to spend time and energy and paper describing aspects of the project that are obvious or already agreed upon. Jamal didn't have to explain the concept of Internet Protocol (IP) addresses in his test plan, because he can assume that everyone working on the project knows what they are. He didn't have to explain that the testers would use these IP addresses by pointing their browsers at the Web server to access Sumatra, because he can assume everyone reading the test plan will know that. (He may have to train some of the inexperienced test technicians.) The effective test engineer or test manager writing a test plan understands his audience and how to communicate with them in a written document.

I find that pictures are good substitutes for words in test plans. Describing the context of the test team within the project team and the architecture of the test environment are two obvious examples, which you can see in the sample test plan for Sumatra. You can capture complicated process flows in images, too. Even though it will take longer to draw a picture and, because of the size of a detailed image, it often increases the overall size of a document, I find that drawing pictures helps me visualize how things will work and helps make the test plan more readable.

On some projects, multiple test plans are needed. Test phases that are greatly separated in time may require separate plans, because you might not have all the information needed to write a single plan at one time. In some cases, the audience for various kinds of testing differs considerably, and this can lead to writing two plans. For example, an Internet appliance project I worked on had a separate hardware test plan and a software test plan. When you do write multiple test plans, it can help to keep all the plans brief by having common elements—e.g., the bug reporting process, perhaps—described in one plan and just referenced in the other documents.

Brevity of test plans does not imply a trivial effort in writing them. On the contrary, nothing is more trivial than grabbing a template and filling it with whatever comes to mind in the context of the headings in the template, and then chucking a 100-page document out for review. Such documents are not tools for effective and efficient test efforts; they are baroque ornaments or burnt offerings to the software gods. Brevity implies that use of the one correct word over the hundred almost-correct words. Gustave Flaubert, French author of *Madame Bovary*, is said to have spent hours agonizing over the perfect word. You needn't go to such lengths, but clarity of expression and a good writing style are important. As Mark Twain wrote, "The difference between the right word and the almost right word is the difference between lightning and the lightning bug."

PROVIDE OPPORTUNITIES TO CATCH ERRORS

In the planning process I use, the document goes through multiple reviews by the key stakeholders and players. These review processes serve two purposes, the first of which is building agreement and commitment. The second, though, is the usual purpose served by all review processes: to provide the opportunity to find problems. Both offline and face-to-face review processes allow omissions and bad assumptions to be found before they cause big problems during execution.

In our case study, Kate discovers that hierarchical storage management systems are missing from the test environment in the first draft test plan. This is an error that, had Jamal not circulated his plan for review at all, might well have not surfaced until testing was underway. If that problem had arisen then, it would have proved a distraction for Keith's team to set it up, along with distracting the test team in verifying the configuration and potentially introducing delays in the test effort. In addition, should the test team have discovered a bug late in testing that was related to the hierarchical storage management servers, the delay in locating that bug could have proved very detrimental to the project schedule and budget.

I also used the case study to illustrate the need to strike a balance in resolving any errors. As is the case during the quality risk analysis, there is a tendency toward scope creep during test planning when the plans go out for review. People have different risks they are concerned about, as Jayesh was in the case study. There is no cost to an external stakeholder for saying, "Hey, I want my pet test [or test environment or regression strategy or cycle length or...] included in your test effort." But if you are managing a test effort, there is an impact to your project. You must balance even legitimate requests from a key player or stakeholder to correct an error (reducing quality risk) against the other risks that increases in test subproject scope can create.

Testers should have the skills to handle review processes, whether their material is under review or they are reviewing someone else's. *Professional Tester* magazine published a series of articles on critical tester skills. They count reviewing as one of these skills and categorize it as a people skill.[6] I'll return to this topic of tester skills at more length in the next couple of chapters on hiring and staffing. In the meantime, for the test planning process, what's key here is that testers use reviews, inspections, walk-throughs, or some other static testing technique to catch errors in their test plans.

EXPLOIT SYNERGIES WITH THE PROJECT, DEVELOPMENT, BUILD, AND INTEGRATION PLANS

As a final indicator of a good process, the test plan and the test planning process need to be consistent and fit together with the development, build, and integration plans and planning processes. By this I mean that the process must address two concerns.

The first concern is the meshing of the planning processes happening above you and across from you in the organization. On an idealized project the following planning activities occur.

- The project manager or the project management team produces the project plan.
- The development manager or managers produce the development and integration plans.
- The release engineering or configuration management manager produces the build plan.

In our case study, Jamal had to know when the increments would be available for integration and system testing. He got that information from Jenny's plan. Information that the tester needs to write her test plan becomes available through other people's planning processes, so the tester must fit her planning process to these other planning processes.

---

6. See "People Skills, Including the Review as a Test Technique," *Professional Tester*, Volume 2, Issue 2 (June 2001).

Development Plan

The plan that specifies how the components that make up the system will be created, including sequencing of those components.

Build Plan, Release Engineering Plan

The plan that specifies how the various releases will be built for testing, ultimately, in the field.

Integration Plan

The plan that specifies how the various components will be assembled, hopefully in some logical, multistep sequence, until the entire system is ready to be built.

This leads to the second concern, the meshing of the plans produced. In our case study, Jamal plans to test complete systems as they will be delivered to customers during system test. What if Yasuhiro's build plan had specified creating the customer release process midway through system test? Testing, being on the receiving end of many upstream processes like this, can't ignore the realities so created.

Many projects do not develop all four of these plans. I worked as a test manager on a project with half a dozen subsystems where the managers of each subsystem programming team wrote development plans, but I had to write the integration plan as well as the integration testing plan. I often have to include considerable detail in the test release section of my test plans to cover for the lack of any build plan. In these cases, varying degrees of advice and decree exist, and the tester setting out other people's processes should take care not to overreach. In my experience, few people are as unwelcome on a project as a test manager who attempts to impose processes on other groups, whether for the good of the project or for his own convenience.

In some cases, plans *do* cover other parts of the development process that have interfaces with testing, but don't address all the important concerns for the testing process. For example, many project plans don't define the bug triage or prioritization process. That's a critical omission from the test process perspective. Release engineering, since it has interfaces with both the programming and the testing sides of the project, may have a plan addressing one set of needs but not the other. To the extent that these critical interfaces are not clearly defined in some plan, I usually define them in my plan, after reaching an agreement with the appropriate managers about how those processes should work. Drawing a context diagram, like the one in the Sumatra test plan, can help highlight these interfaces.

What about Cookie-Cutter Plans?

With a smoothly functioning testing process, it becomes possible to use canned test plans, especially for minor maintenance releases and patches. When I was test manager for maintenance releases of one application, we had a standard set of tests, which we augmented based on the release content, that we ran against each maintenance release. The plan and the process was the same each time.

These approaches can even work when the extent of testing must vary across releases. In a paper posted on my Web site, Bill Lind, a senior systems manager for Software Quality Assurance and Release Control at Freightliner, describes a six-level testing process that is used like a menu. (See "Freightliner Test Level Matrix" at www.rexblackconsulting.com.) The project team can specify a level 0 test effort, a level 6 test effort, or some level between, based on various project considerations. Some of these levels require a customized test plan, while others use a standard plan. The levels can be mixed, too, with selection of features of higher levels of testing added to a lower level, if need be. These kinds of approaches can turn test planning from a recurring chore into a one-time investment in process improvements that can be leveraged again and again.

HANDLE CHALLENGES

A number of challenges exist for the planning process and producing a good test plan. Let me take a moment, before we end our examination of this topic, to look at them.

TRANSCENDING THE TEMPLATE

In the documents that come with this book and on my Web site, I provide a test plan template.[7] I have already mentioned the test plan template in IEEE Standard 829. These templates are useful to make sure that you don't forget important topics. However, it's easy to fall into the trap of using a test plan template like a tax form or a multiple-choice exam. Templates are useful reminders, but they do not substitute for thinking, an essential part of good planning. Whatever template you choose to use,

---

7. See the "Library" page at www.rexblackconsulting.com.

make sure that the process does not degrade into "fill in all the blanks in the template with as little effort as possible," because this will seldom result in a useful plan.[8]

PLANNING FOR OUTSOURCING

In our case study, Jamal is going to use two independent test labs to accomplish two very specific test activities under some constrained conditions. It's popular lately, though, to consider outsourcing the entire testing effort. How does that affect your test plan? There are a number of issues that complicate test outsourcing. To handle this successfully, your test plan must deal with these challenges.

First, outsourced testing efforts can easily become misaligned with actual customer needs, get out of whack with the project as changes happen, fall behind schedule, or overrun the budget, often with little if any advance notice until recovery is impossible. Outsourced development and testing efforts based only on a fairy tale schedule, a tight budget, and ambiguous product requirements are very likely to fail. The test plan must include safeguards to keep the outsourced test team on track throughout the project.

Second, any risk management effort, including management of quality risks, is optimally a cross-functional effort. In Chapter 2, I discussed various techniques for such quality risk management. It is unusual for an outsource test lab to be in a position to do such cross-functional risk analyses. It is usually better that an in-house test manager, programming manager, or project manager drive the process through the planning stage, especially quality risk analysis, and then hand that plan off to an external facility for outsourced test execution.

Third, senior managers and executives, seeing their operations from on high, are sometimes beguiled by outsourcing organizations that tout cheap human resources and certified quality processes. These executives then make strategic decisions to outsource heavily, missing some critical details that come up at a tactical level when line managers try to execute.

For one thing, the logistical investments and inherent delays required to support geographically distributed projects of any kind are significant and, in some cases, unpredictable until you try. For another thing, just because the chosen outsourcing partner has *its* processes in order doesn't mean the company *retaining* the outsourcing part-

---

8. One of the reviewers, Deborah McCandless, test manager at Nolo.com, used the following analogy. "I think of [templates] like a wonderful, rich soup stock. They give me a good, strong base from which to create a wonderful mouthwatering dish." Given my soft spot for culinary metaphors, this one strikes me as perfect.

ner does. When the two companies try to work together, order meets chaos and major problems erupt. This is especially true when chaotic companies expect their outsourcing partners to be able to react gracefully from across great distances in space and time to often daily, major changes in the project plan.

Fourth, testing requires a variety of skills, as I'll discuss in the next couple of chapters. Some of these skills are related to testing—which a good outsource test organization will bring to the engagement—but others are related to the application domain and the underlying technology of implementation. You'll have to do a very careful job of selecting your outsource test partner if you need to find strong application domain and technological knowledge in their test teams.

That said, it's definitely possible and, in many cases, desirable to outsource to external test organizations as an adjunct to a small, efficient in-house test team that provides the appropriate leadership and the critical skills. The external groups can be used as extra hands to help execute testing when the time comes. (There are also ways to do that in-house, using cheaper test technician resources.) They can also be used as extra minds to help implement testing in areas where the specific in-house testing skills are not up to the tasks, notably areas like performance testing and security testing. Finally, the careful selection of outsource testing partners is important to ensure success.[9]

WHEN KEY PLAYERS DON'T SUPPORT THE TEST PLAN

In most of my test plans, there are key players outside of the test team. The case study has a fairly typical cast of characters: system support people, programmers, release engineers, and managers. The test team's dependencies on these external key players exist for two reasons, usually. First, those people may have a management mandate to provide the product or service the test team needs. Second, those people may be responsible, as part of the project itself, for predecessor tasks to testing tasks. In other words, the dependencies exist either for organizational reasons or for project reasons.

Most of the time—I'd say over 90% of the time in my experience—all the key players in the test plan either agree immediately to what I ask of them or agree to some mutually acceptable compromise. Sometimes, though, there are problems. When coming

---

9. The selection and use of outsource testing resources is a topic I cover in Chapter 10 of *Managing the Testing Process, Second Edition*. In the interests of full disclosure, I should mention that my consulting company performs outsource testing as well as other test-related consulting and training services.

into a situation where I think a support problem may exist, I use a gradually escalating approach.

I start off by considering the possibility that I may very well be off base in my request. Why am I assuming that the key player has a duty or role in playing the part I've assigned in the plan? Perhaps I'm just confused. I'll double-check my assumptions that influence my thinking before I start insisting that someone do something.

If it proves that the key player does indeed have a role to play, I try to convince him. I appeal to the person one-on-one. I explain the reason for my needs and why other people within the project context can't help. I then explain the impact of any delay or withholding of assistance on his part. If I get positive engagement from this discussion—an unambiguous acknowledgment from the person that he will support my request and agree to the role I have suggested—then I document that clearly in the test plan. When the test plan goes out for review, I include not just that person, but that person's manager.

It's important to be flexible in this discussion, to the extent you can. Compromise or horse-trading may be necessary to reach agreement. In Jamal's case, suppose that Keith had been unable to commit to having all the systems set up on the schedule they discussed. Perhaps Jamal could have offered to buy lunch and dinner for Inder and Petra if they would work over a weekend to get the systems up on time. Or Jamal could have agreed to accept some of the systems a few days later as long as some key systems were in place.

You may have to create or be open to unusual ways to have these conversations. I once had a meeting with a project team in Japan that was working with my client to create a new laptop computer system. I explained my proposed test plan to the entire team. During a break, the production line manager pulled me aside and invited me to dinner that night. At that meal, after he and I had shared some beer and sake, over an enormous sushi dinner, he confided to me that his production team would not be able to deliver all the engineering samples I had asked for in my test plan. As we finished off the beer and fish, we sketched out a new engineering prototype sample allocation plan that was both within his team's capabilities and provided my test team with enough units to fulfill our commitments, albeit more slowly than originally planned.

Should I fail to get the support I need in this fashion, I move to the next level, which is escalating the lack of commitment up the management chain, conceivably all the way to the common manager—who may be a vice president or even a CEO. You will need to exert all your political and communication skills in this endeavor. If you mishandle this escalation, it may damage your credibility and standing. I prefer to do this face-to-face, in one-on-one conversations, rather than in e-mails sent out broadly or in meetings.

The goal here is to convince some manager to prevail upon the holdout to support you. Beware the hollow promise, though. I have worked with a very few people who made commitments under pressure and then resorted to foot-dragging and malicious compliance to "even the score." If you think you can win this debate through management fiat—which is what you're doing—and that the person so prevailed upon will actually come through, then this level of resolution will work. Otherwise, you're better off proceeding to the next level of resolution.

The final level, for me, is to go to my manager and request the resources I need to handle the matter myself. This is a hassle, because no one is likely to be happy about this request and it's not as if you needed a new set of tasks to manage. If the task is redundant with someone else's team—which it almost certainly is, because there's the person you asked to do it in the first place—then you will need to be able to demonstrate that you have made every reasonable effort to enlist that person's aid. You will also need to be able to explain why the dependency exists, which can be difficult in some cases.

Some people find the process of escalation confrontational and damaging to team cohesion, so they absorb the extra work into their team silently. I have not seen this approach turn out well. I once helped a client set up a test plan, a test process, and a test system, and then handed the execution off to their test manager and her team. In the test plan, I had spelled out the release process, which the programming team owned. In the event, though, the programmers were unable to perform the test release duties. If she wanted a test release, it fell to the test manager to figure out how to do it.

Instead of working through the process I've outlined, she just assigned the release engineering work to someone on her team. This effectively downsized her test team and reduced her ability to run all the tests she had committed to perform in each test cycle. This created various management issues for her, including a perception of inefficiency and a lack of commitment in the test team.

In her position, I would have politely but firmly discussed the matter with the programmers' manager and the project manager (who was their mutual boss). I would express a willingness to take on the role if need be, but only given either a reduction in testing scope or an increase in staff. Training or consulting might also have been on the list if I accepted the additional role.

As I mentioned in Chapter 5, to the extent that you have key players on your test effort that are not stakeholders in the project, you have a special challenge here. If their interests are not merely neutral, but actually aligned against the success of the project, then you are really up against it. To the extent possible, avoid such dependencies. If it's not possible, give yourself plenty of time to resolve these issues by working through the escalation process I described earlier or using some other approach of your own creation.

Some support problems have to do with commitment, while others have to do with competence. In the case study, Jamal is careful to identify specific people as problem resolution resources to catch competence problems early. Inder was, in effect, put on probation with Keith in their discussion about support because of previous ability problems.

I once worked on a project where I failed to identify specifically in the test plan who the support personnel were. The network operations manager assigned a gentleman who, while perfectly *willing* to act as a UNIX system administrator, knew less about the topic than many on the test team. Half the time when he was called in to help, he proved unable to diagnose the problem. The other half of the time he usually implemented the wrong solution, resulting in wasted test efforts against misconfigured servers. Only competent, experienced professionals should support the test environment.

Whether with commitment or competence, these problems can come to light either during the planning phase—which is preferable—or later during execution. One of my goals for the planning effort is to ferret out and resolve (or at least mitigate) these issues before I start running tests.

In my experience, success at resolving external key player commitment problems hinges on two factors. First, I leverage the relationships that I have with other managers and peers. This is important not just in obtaining the support, but also for me to know how credible commitments of support are. Personally, I find that trust grows between professionals as we make promises to each other and keep them. When a person who has never let me down over six or seven projects says she'll do something, I believe her. A person I've never worked with before must come with good references.

Second, I strive to maintain throughout not just a reasonable position, but a carefully managed and broadly held perception of the reasonableness of my position. Should I become perceived as hysterical, exaggerating the situation, or extraneous to the process, I will have done irreparable damage to my credibility and relationships with my peers. A test professional can be effective only to the extent that people will listen to his findings and rely upon what he tells them.[10]

OBEYING THE LAW AND PLEASING REGULATORS

As a last challenge, let me point out that in some cases your test plan can set up an unpleasant encounter with law enforcement if you're not careful. On one project, we intended to test the end-to-end installation and maintenance release process for software that was written in the United States, installed onto a hardware platform in Taiwan, and then drop-shipped directly to customers in the United States again. There was just one wrinkle: The software contained encryption technology in the browser, which was classified as a weapon under United States law. Exporting this "weapon" without a Commerce Department permit was a serious crime, punishable at the time by five years in a federal penitentiary and the permanent penalties associated with such a conviction.

There are many such laws covering technology transfers across borders—or within them. For example, some European countries regulate encryption technology and may prohibit private possession of such software. What constitutes obscene material might even extend in some countries or jurisdictions to what you consider innocuous or artistic clip art included in your product. Current US law prohibits promulgation of technologies that can circumvent certain copy-prevention schemes such as those on DVDs.

There are ways that a test professional, merely trying to verify a product before delivery to customers, could unwittingly commit a serious crime with potential lifelong and even career-ending consequences. When in doubt, consult an attorney knowledgeable about what your product contains and the laws regulating its possession, transfer, and use.

Some test efforts are also subject to regulation by government officials. In the United States, the Food and Drug Administration regulates testing of software for medical devices. Department of Defense standards can apply to contracts with the United States military. Many other countries have similar regulatory mechanisms. These regulators must accept your test approach as valid, and that often extends to having to document that testing according to certain standards. In some cases, you have to receive regulatory approval for your documents. If so, keep in mind that these regulators are not stakeholders in your project. They are guardians of the public interest, health, and safety, and enforcers of laws. They will tend to be less concerned about your project's

---

10. On this general topic of key player support, you might also want to see Lee Copeland's presentation "When Helping Doesn't Help," found at www.stickyminds.com.

budgetary and schedule situations and more concerned about carrying out their duties to the taxpayers, the law, and the executive organs of the government.

IMPLEMENT IMPROVEMENTS

What you need to do specifically to implement a better planning process depends on the current state of your planning process. At a high level, the following approach may help.

1. Understand the objective of the planning process. Why do you need to plan? Is it to write a document? Is this document for internal or also external consumption? Is the planning process more informal? Is a written plan needed at all?

2. Understand the context of the testing effort, the plan, and the planning process. Who is the audience of the written plan? Who are the stakeholders in the planning process? Who are the key players in the testing effort?

3. If a written plan is to be prepared, decide how to create that document. What is the appropriate template or format? Must documentation standards be met? If not, what information do you need to capture?

4. Start simple. Don't worry about planning for every possible contingency and event. Work with the stakeholders to produce a good plan that will allow you to deal with the most likely situations. Don't be too verbose, but rather focus on writing down what you do write down clearly.

5. In your planning process, especially in your first experiences with it, use lots of consensus building, in person if possible. A test manager writing a test plan alone and sending that document out, decree-like, is unlikely to be effective. A test professional working closely with the key stakeholders and participants to craft a collaborative and contextually attuned test effort is very likely to plan an effective test subproject.

In applying this approach to improving your test planning process, you can refine technique and your documentation style gradually over a series of projects. I have developed my approach to test planning and my test plan documentation over my 15 years as a test project manager. You can build on what I've shared with you in these last two chapters, so you needn't go through a 15-year learning curve, but you should expect your planning process to improve iteratively and gradually. Project retrospectives are often a great opportunity for this, both at the project level and within the test team itself.[11]

---

11. I thank Chris DeNardis, one of the reviewers, for mentioning this to me in an e-mail.

The end of this chapter also marks the end of the first part of the book, the Plan part. In this first part, we've looked at four processes that chart a course for a successful test effort. Investing the time and attention in the planning portion of the testing process to set our test project off in the right direction often pays dividends later in the test project. On my past projects, much of what has gone right—the disasters averted, the teamwork enabled, the effective and efficient testing achieved—started during the planning portion of the testing process. As a test manager, I have long believed the old cliche that to fail to plan is to plan to fail.

We move now from figuring out what to do to actually doing it. The next step in the testing process finds us preparing the test system and the test team. Like having a good plan and good processes, having the properly prepared and appropriate people and tools available is critical to success when we ultimately perform the tests and work to perfect the system under test—and the testing itself.

Step #	Step	Done?
1.	Plan: Understand the testing effort.	✔
1.A	Understand the operational (system, project, and process) context and the organizational context in which the testing will be performed.	✔
1.B	Define and prioritize the risks to system quality, and obtain stakeholder consensus on the extent of testing to mitigate these risks.	✔
1.C	Estimate and obtain management support for the time, resources, and budget required to perform the testing agreed upon in step 1.B.	✔
1. D	Develop a plan for the tasks, dependencies, and participants required to mitigate the risks to system quality, and obtain stakeholder support for this plan.	✔

PART II

PREPARE

In this second part of the book, we'll examine the processes related to assembling an effective and efficient team of testers and an effective and efficient test system. We must have both, just as we must have two hands to clap. We'll start with the people, because the test engineers, test technicians, and other test professionals are the ones who will build the test system. Then we'll look at acquiring, building, and maintaining the test system itself. Once we've understood the intricacies of building a test team and a test system, we will move on to the third part of the book, where we perform the tests themselves.

Step #	Step	Done?
2.	Prepare: Assemble the people and tests.	☐
2.A	Through staffing and training, build a team of test professionals with the appropriate skills, attitudes, and motivation.	☐
2.D	Design, develop, acquire, and verify the test system that the test team uses to assess the quality of the system under test.	☐

BRING ON THE GREAT TESTERS: THE HOW AND THE WHO OF HIRING

We've now moved from planning to those interim processes that will prepare us to perform the tests. Before the test team can take on these processes, that team must be forged from carefully selected individuals. Excellent test teams achieve outstanding accomplishments, while mediocre ones sow discord within the development team and retard project success. Excellent test teams grow around good managers, and good managers nourish the careers of excellent test professionals within those teams.

Having the right test professionals on the team is essential for excellent testing. Indeed, low-maturity test teams with weak processes sometimes succeed just because the right team is in place. With good processes in place, selecting the right participants builds the foundation of a consistently successful test team. Only a team composed of qualified test professionals can succeed at the critical testing processes I discuss in this book.

The team building process consists of two major activities. First, we must hire the right people, those with the skills, knowledge, and attitudes that will enable them to do the work. Second, we must grow the skills of the team over time. This skills growth focuses on both getting better at doing things the team already does and getting ready to take on new challenges.

The team building process is highly collaborative and contextual. In some organizations, testers pass through the same hiring gauntlet as programmers. In some organizations, human resources departments define the specific steps for a candidate to become an employee. Training and other skills growth programs vary widely and are

> **Tester, Test Professional**
> Anyone working on test-related tasks such as those described in this book. More specifically, in this book, someone working in a test team, whether permanently or temporarily, as an employee, contractor, or consultant. I'm using this word or phrase as the analog to "developer" or "programmer" in the development team.

standardized in some companies. Rather than tackle the entire realm of human resource management, I'll focus on the attributes that affect testing.

In the area of hiring, we have to answer the question, Can this person help us assess the quality of the software? This is a different question from Can this person write code? or Does this person understand the business problem this system will solve? though qualified testers often need some amount of both technical knowledge and application domain expertise.

In the area of skills growth, we have to answer the question, Where does each employee's career path lead, what skills are necessary on that path, and how does that fit into the test team's collective skills needs? The same question applies for other teams, but the answer is unique, since the critical testing skills are unique.

A Team Building Process

Regardless of how the team building process is defined in your organization, it's a safe bet that the desired outcome is making practical arrangements for the most appropriate, competent person possible to hold each position within the company. That lofty and straightforward goal is often tempered by tactical necessities such as ensuring compliance with employment laws, promoting fairness in salaries and career paths, and responding to the local job market.

Being a process carried out by humans, the team building process must also bend to less rational but no less decisive influences. For example, people in the organization

> **Candidate**
> Someone who has applied to fill an open position and is somewhere along the hiring process but not yet officially hired.

who can affect or become involved in hiring decisions often have preconceived notions and past experiences. Another example includes management directives about various staffing topics that are often formed based on the management fad of the day or in reaction to some external fact or rumor. Ultimately, the choice of business associates is influenced by the same subtle psychological factors that influence the choice of friends, spouses, and clubs.

At the center of this maelstrom of influences, the team building process in most medium-sized to large companies is defined by the human resources department. That process might look like Process 6. In this chapter, we'll look at step 1; the next chapter will address step 2.

Step #	Step	Done?
1.	Hire appropriate test team members.	☐
1.A	Get permission to hire.	☐
1.B	Define and advertise the position.	☐
1.C	Gather and screen candidates, based on their resumes and phone interviews, eliminating unqualified or undesirable candidates.	☐
1.D	Interview qualified, desirable candidates in person.	☐
1.E	If appropriate, extend an offer to the most successful candidate, often via an offer letter.	☐
1.F	If the most successful candidate accepts, orient the new hire. If not, repeat steps 1.E and 1.F for the second-most-successful candidate, until either a successful candidate accepts or the process must restart at step 1.A. Notify rejected candidates that they should pursue other opportunities.	☐
2.	Foster team skills and career growth.	☐
2.A	Work with new hires to develop career paths.	☐
2.B	Regularly revisit the career paths for all employees and each employee's progress on their path.	☐
2.C	Actively manage the employee's skills growth necessary to reach employee and team goals.	☐
3.	Iterate step 1 as needed to add new people. Iterate step 2 continuously.	☐

PROCESS 6   A TEAM BUILDING PROCESS

Offer Letter

A letter from the hiring company to the successful candidate asking the candidate to accept the job for which they interviewed, usually including a detailed job description and quoting a specific salary and start date.

New Hire

Someone who has received an offer letter and responded, either verbally or in writing, agreeing to fill the offered position.

Human Resources Department, Personnel Department

A group that facilitates 1) the hiring of employees, contractors, and consultants; 2) defining personnel policies and procedures; and 3) planning and managing salaries and career tracks.

VARIATIONS ON THE TEAM BUILDING PROCESS

While the process just outlined is a typical, generic process for building a test team, many variations exist. These variations depend not only on organizational preferences and national employment laws, but also on the size of the company, the level of the employee, and the typical company career path.

For example, in some organizations, low-level employees get very little attention, especially if they initially come on board as contractors or casual employees. When I worked at a large university as a UNIX programmer, the hiring process for me consisted of talking to a couple of professors about a job description they had posted on the campus job board; after they conferred among themselves, they offered me the job. My orientation consisted of a half hour or so of conversation with some of the professors' graduate students about the project on which I was to work. Later, though, my employment status with the university became more serious. I then had to go through the formal process, including filling out a job application, in spite of the fact that I was already an employee!

Contrast this with the US armed forces, which expend tremendous thought and effort on the hiring, training, and career growth processes for enlistees and officers. Why the difference? At the university, there was no possibility that one day I would rise to dean, chancellor, or regent. Everyone expected me to spend a year or two working on C code and then to move on, which was what happened.

In professional military organizations, today's buck private may well one day be a noncommissioned officer upon whose judgment the lives and safety of dozens of people rely, and today's midshipman may one day be an admiral or command a Trident-equipped nuclear submarine, a position in which a person can truly influence the course of history. Military organizations promote exclusively from within, so excellent hiring decisions today at the lowest level, combined with continuous grooming of leadership and skills, lead to excellence in the senior ranks for tomorrow's keeping of the peace and fighting of the wars.

Nothing so momentous as the fate of the world turns on your team-building decisions for your test team, but the ability to surround yourself with talent will determine the success of the test effort, the perceived competence of the test team, and the career prospects of each tester. In all likelihood, your ability to affect the process per se, whether as outlined earlier or otherwise, is limited. Within the confines of any pre-defined team building process, though, you will need to make decisions and carry out actions with critical consequences for the test team. How you make those decisions and what you choose to do is more important than the process itself.[1]

THE SUMATRA TEST TEAM GROWS

Even while he was writing his test plan, Jamal Brown was recruiting his Sumatra test team. According to the budget approved by his boss, John Albertson, he could hire one test engineer and four contract test technicians. He most urgently wanted to hire the senior automated test engineer who would write and run regression tests for the new Sumatra functionality as well as reliability and stability tests. This person, he knew, would be tough to find.

Step #	Step	Done?
1.A	Get permission to hire.	☑

Jamal started out by working with the core of the Sumatra test team—Emma Moorhouse, the current automated test engineer; and Lin-Tsu Wu, the manual test engineer—to review the skills analysis for the team as it stood currently. Based on this

---

1. For more ideas on hiring, I recommend picking up a copy of *Hiring the Best Knowledge Workers, Techies, & Nerds: The Secrets & Science of Hiring Technical People,* a book by Johanna Rothman. Another good book is Patricia Ensworth's *The Accidental Project Manager.*

skills analysis, all three agreed that a job description such as the one shown in Figure 8-1 captured the position in broad strokes. Jamal posted this job description on various Internet newsgroups and in the job section of the classified ads in the local paper.

Step #	Step	Done?
1.B	Define and advertise the position.	✔

In response to this ad, Jamal received a number of resumes via e-mail and fax. As he received the resumes, he measured each candidate against the team's initial skills analysis, shown in Figure 8-2. To some extent, he took guesses, because the skills analysis is fine-grained and Jamal could only surmise what level of knowledge each candidate acquired or used based on the amount of time spent working on a project that required those skills. However, it did help him to filter out candidates who clearly didn't fit the minimum requirements.

Automated Test Engineer

Roles and Responsibilities

- Participate in a test automation tool selection process.
- Develop and execute automated tests using the selected tool.
- Integrate the test suites into the test management system and custom test harnesses.

Education

- B.S. in computer science, computer engineering, or electrical engineering, or two additional years of experience, or tester certification.

Experience

- Five or more years of experience in test automation.
- UNIX test experience required, ideally including development of custom automated test systems using scripting languages like ksh, csh, and tcl.
- Internet test experience highly desirable, including development of automated test tools.

Expertise Required

- A demonstrated career commitment to testing and/or quality assurance is preferred. The candidate should show a familiarity with state-of-the-art testing theory and practice, and be able to discuss how she applied the ideas in her previous positions.

Other

- Dress is business-casual and hours are flexible. Some weekends and evenings will be required.

FIGURE 8-1 AUTOMATED TEST ENGINEER JOB DESCRIPTION

Legend	0 = No Knowledge	1 = Some Knowledge	R = Required
	2 = Knowledgeable	3 = Expert Knowledge	D = Desirable
	TM = Test Manager	MTE = Manual Test Engineer	ATE = Automated Test Engr

Skills and Qualifications

	ATE Minimum Ratings	MTE Minimum Ratings	TM Jamal Brown	MTE Lin-Tsu Wu	ATE Emma Moorhouse	Team Minimum	Team Average
General Qualifications							
Education							
Bachelor of Science Degree (or +)	D	D	BS (CSE)	Ph.D. (CS)	BS (Bus.)		
Test Training or Certification	D	D	CSQE	ISEB			
Other					CPA		
Work Experience (Years)							
Test Roles	5R	5R	7	5	12		
Nontest, Computer	D	D	3	2	4		
Noncomputer, Domain	D	D					
Noncomputer, Nondomain					6		
Total/Any/Other	5R	5R	10	7	22		
Professionalism							
Oral Communication	2R	2R	3	1	2	1	2.0
Written Informal Communication	3R	3R	3	3	3	3	3.0
Written Formal Communication	D	D	3	0	1	0	1.3
Continuing Education	R	R	Yes	Yes	Yes	Yes	Yes
Test Team Building/Cross-training	2R	2R	3	2	2	2	2.3
Cross-functional Relationship Building	2R	2R	3	2	2	2	2.3
Reading (Retention, Reasoning, and Analysis)	2R	2R	3	2	2	2	2.3
Business/Technical Trends (Journal Reading)	1R	1R	3	1	1	1	1.7
Testing Skills							
General							
Testing Standards	2R	2R	3	3	3	3	3.0
Software Development Lifecycles	2R	2R	3	3	2	2	2.7
Testing/Development Processes/Maturity	1R	1R	2	2	1	1	1.7
Change Management	1R	1R	2	2	1	1	1.7
Relating Testing to Business/SDLC	1R	1R	3	3	1	1	2.3
Planning							
Estimation	D	D	3	1	1	1	1.7
Documentation	D	D	3	1	1	1	1.7
Cost of Quality	D	D	3	2	1	1	2.0
Quality Risk/Failure Mode and Effect Analysis	D	D	3	2	1	1	2.0
Quality Risk Analysis and Management	D	D	3	2	1	1	2.0
Design and Development							
Behavioral (Black-box)	2R	2R	2	3	2	2	2.3
Structural (White-box)	D	1R	1	3	2	1	2.0
Static (Requirements, Specifications, Documentation)	D	2R	2	3	2	2	2.3
Reliability (Statistics)	2R	D	1	1	2	1	1.3
Performance (Modeling/Simulation/Testing)	2R	D	1	2	3	1	2.0
Code/Dataflow Coverage	2R	2R	2	3	3	2	2.7
Quality Risk/Requirement Coverage (Traceability)	1R	2R	3	2	1	1	2.0
Automation (Development)							
COTS Execution (Silk, Validor, etc.)	3R	D	1	1	3	1	1.7

FIGURE 8-2 TEST TEAM SKILLS ANALYSIS (CONTINUED ON NEXT PAGE)

Software Cafeteria Test Team
Skills Assessment and Management Worksheet

Legend	0 = No Knowledge		1 = Some Knowledge		R = Required		
	2 = Knowledgeable		3 = Expert Knowledge		D = Desirable		
	TM = Test Manager		MTE = Manual Test Engineer		ATE = Automated Test Engr		

Skills and Qualifications	ATE Minimum Ratings	MTE Minimum Ratings	TM Jamal Brown	MTE Lin-Tsu Wu	ATE Emma Moorhouse	Team Minimum	Team Average
COTS Test Management	D	D	3	1	1	1	1.7
Custom Toolsmithing	3R	D	3	1	3	1	2.3
Configuration							
Test Data Generators	1R	D	1	1	2	1	1.3
Version Control	1R	1R	2	2	3	2	2.3
Configuration Management	D	1R	1	2	1	1	1.3
Integration Testing	D	1R	3	2	1	1	2.0
Execution							
Manual Scripted	D	3R	3	3	1	1	2.3
Manual Exploratory	D	3R	3	3	1	1	2.3
Automated	3R	D	1	1	3	1	1.7
Bug Isolation	3R	3R	3	3	3	3	3.0
Bug Reporting	3R	3R	3	3	3	3	3.0
Test Status Reporting	2R	2R	3	2	2	2	2.3
Test Metrics (Dashboard)	1R	1R	3	2	3	2	2.7
Average Testing Skills			2.4	2.1	1.9	1.4	2.1
Domain Knowledge							
Word Processing							
Windows Applications	1R	2R	3	3	3	3	3.0
UNIX Applications	D	D	1	1	2	1	1.3
Macintosh Applications	D	D	0	1	3	0	1.3
Graphics and Figures	1R	2R	2	2	1	1	1.7
Tables	D	1R	1	2	1	1	1.3
Mathematical/ Engineering	D	1R	1	3	0	0	1.3
Document Management							
Windows Applications	D	D	1	2	2	1	1.7
UNIX Applications	D	D	0	0	1	0	0.3
Macintosh Applications	D	D	0	0	1	0	0.3
Other	D	D	0	0	1	0	0.3
Hierarchical Storage Management	D	D	1	2	3	1	2.0
Document Interchange							
Windows Applications	D	D	1	2	3	1	2.0
UNIX Applications	D	D	1	0	3	0	1.3
Macintosh Applications	D	D	0	0	3	0	1.0
Printing							
Color	D	D	0	0	2	0	0.7
Laser	D	D	1	1	2	1	1.3
Inkjet	D	D	1	1	2	1	1.3
Publishing/ Binding	D	D	0	0	2	0	0.7
Web Publishing							
HTML	D	D	1	3	3	1	2.3
XML	D	D	1	3	2	1	2.0
Other	D	D	1	1	2	1	1.3
Application Domain Knowledge			0.8	1.3	2.0	0.7	1.4

FIGURE 8-2 CONTINUED

226

Software Cafeteria Test Team
Skills Assessment and Management Worksheet

Skills and Qualifications	ATE Minimum Ratings	MTE Minimum Ratings	TM Jamal Brown	MTE Lin-Tsu Wu	ATE Emma Moorhouse	Team Minimum	Team Average
Legend	0 = No Knowledge		1 = Some Knowledge		R = Required		
	2 = Knowledgeable		3 = Expert Knowledge		D = Desirable		
	TM = Test Manager		MTE = Manual Test Engineer		ATE = Automated Test Engr		
Technical Expertise							
Programming							
C/ VB (3GL)	1R	D	2	2	3	2	2.3
Java/ C++ (OO)	1R	D	0	1	2	0	1.0
Shell (Tcl/ Ksh) Scripting	2R	D	3	2	2	2	2.3
Code Complexity and Metrics	1R	D	2	0	2	0	1.3
Operating Systems							
Windows	1R	1R	2	3	2	2	2.3
Linux	1R	1R	2	2	2	2	2.0
Solaris	1R	1R	2	1	2	1	1.7
Mac OS	D	D	0	2	3	0	1.7
Other	D	D	1	1	3	1	1.7
Networking/ Internetworking							
TCP/ IP, FTP, RCP (Internet Architecture)	1R	1R	2	1	1	1	1.3
Browsers (NS, IE, etc.)	1R	1R	2	3	1	1	2.0
Network Application Architecture (Tiered)	1R	1R	2	3	1	1	2.0
Network Hardware	1R	1R	2	3	1	1	2.0
Systems and Servers							
Java-based Web Servers	1R	1R	1	3	3	1	2.3
Database Servers	1R	1R	2	3	3	2	2.7
Mainframe	1R	1R	1	2	3	1	2.0
Average Technical Expertise			1.6	2.0	2.1	1.1	1.9

FIGURE 8-2 CONTINUED

Step #	Step	Done?
1.C	Gather and screen candidates, based on their resumes and phone interviews, eliminating unqualified or undesirable candidates.	☑

For those candidates that did measure up, Jamal, Emma, and Lin-Tsu conducted phone interviews to refine their estimations of each candidate's skills. Jamal also made a point of discussing the salary range established for this position, along with the career path Software Cafeteria would offer the successful candidate.

This resulted in a further filtering, with three candidates proceeding to the next round of the hiring process. Jamal scheduled in-person interviews with each of these candidates.

Working with the human resources manager, he decided that candidates would spend their half-day interview period as follows:

1. Half-hour orientation on the company from Bob Frankel, the human resources manager
2. One-hour one-on-one interview with Jamal
3. One-hour group lunch interview with Jamal, Emma, and Lin-Tsu
4. One-hour audition interview
5. Half-hour comfort check with Jenny Kaufman, the development manager, and Kate Hernandez, the project manager
6. Short debriefing with Bob Frankel

Bob Frankel called each candidate to set dates and times.

Two of the interviews proceeded without any noticeable spark. The candidates seemed competent enough, but a ringing cell phone and some personal matter related to the grocery list distracted one candidate more than once during the interview. After that issue was disposed of, his questions focused primarily on his concerns that he not be required to work more than 45 or so hours per week. Some comment about "needing to have a life outside work" kept coming up. While Jamal felt that such concerns were fair—especially in the high-tech, start-up world—even after he explained his commitment to limited overtime during short periods of time only, the candidate continued to insinuate that a position at Software Cafeteria might involve lots of overtime and weekend work. The other candidate, while more attentive, mentioned twice that she was not excited by the salary offered and asked whether there was any "room for negotiation" in that figure.

However, the third interview, with the candidate whose resume is shown in Figure 8-3, went very well. Dinesh clearly had the skills required and also demonstrated a positive attitude toward the position. Dinesh told Jamal and Emma that with his growing family, he wanted to stop working as a contractor, with the short engagements, uncertainty, and unreliable health insurance. He expressed a desire to settle down into a long-term job at a stable company, which alleviated Jamal's concerns about the job-hopping he had done as a contractor.

Audition Interview

A portion of the interview process that involves demonstrating the skills required to fill the position; e.g., writing a test case or reporting a bug.

Dinesh Kumar

Professional experience	2000 - Present Denial180	Buffalo, New York

Senior Test Engineer, Consultant
- Developed testware for proprietary SDK. Developed a test system to dynamically generate test cases for a web-based app. Developed data driven GUI automation test tool using Segue SilkTest. Set up initial load tests using Segue SilkPerformer.

1999 - 2000   DefunctBank   Providence, Rhode Island
Senior Test Engineer, Consultant
- Evaluated and implemented testing tools, specifically test automation, incident tracking and SCM. Developed functional, load, and performance tests for a web-based financial application using Mercury Interactive LoadRunner.

1999   Rustbucket Motor Credit   Detroit, Michigan
Senior Test Engineer, Consultant
- Develop testing and quality assurance processes for client/server application development environment. Evaluated automated test tools, made recommendation for purchase and defined test automation infrastructure.

1998 - 1999   Star69   Calgary, Alberta
Senior Test Engineer, Consultant
- Develop test plans and automated and manual test procedures for client/server application used in a proprietary telephony system. Test environment is QA Partner on NT 4.0.

1998 - 1999   BFSP Software   Wimberdoodle, Pennsylvania
Quality Assurance Engineer
- Develop test plans and automated and manual test procedures for database migration, update, and conversion utilities. Test environment was QA Partner on NT 4.0 and Windows 98 clients.

1996 - 1998   DefenseGiant   Seattle, Washington
Quality Assurance Engineer
- Develop test plans and automated and manual test procedures for a military records system and supporting utilities. Evaluated defect tracking systems to select. Test environment was Windows NT 4.0/3.51 and Windows 9x clients with HPUX Oracle servers using QA Partner.

1994 - 1996   BigTestCompany   Orlando, Florida
Quality Assurance Engineer
- Develop test plans and automated and manual test procedures for various Intersolv PVCS products, including Version Manager and Tracker. Test environment was QA Partner on Windows NT 4.0 and 3.51 and Windows 95 and 3.1.

1989 - 1994   DenseByte   Albuquerque, New Mexico
Quality Assurance Engineer
- Develop, maintain, and perform test procedures on Density, a database retrieval and report generation system. Test environment was AutoTester, UNIX shell scripts, VMS DCL, and C on UNIX, VMS, DOS, and Windows.

FIGURE 8-3 RESUME FOR DINESH KUMAR, SUCCESSFUL CANDIDATE (CONTINUED ON NEXT PAGE)

Professional	1988 - 1989 DenseByte	Albuquerque, New Mexico
experience	**Programmer Analyst**	
(continued)		

• Developed software using proprietary pattern recognition utilities. Applications included database research system. All development was done using C on PCs.

1988 - 1988   Depends   Albuquerque, New Mexico
Programmer Analyst

• Developed enhancements and performed system maintenance on PCs for life insurance illustration application. Converted application from FORTRAN to C.

1986 - 1988   Big Massive Utility   Albuquerque, New Mexico
Programmer Analyst

• Developed interprocessor communication control software, using FORTRAN on VAX./VMS, for a SCADA gas and electrical operations system. Communications applications included graphic display, remote transmission unit, and user application support for system services.

1986 - 1986   Scorpion Tech   Albuquerque, New Mexico
Programmer Analyst

• Participated in development of a point of sale system controlled by a SWTPC 68010- based processor.

1985 - 1986   Labyrinth, Inc.   Albuquerque, New Mexico
Programmer Analyst

• Assisted in the design and coding of a fourth generation language and applications development system for PCs. Developed user documentation.

1984 - 1985   TelComSwitch   Albuquerque, New Mexico
Programmer Analyst

• Developed and maintained user interface software for the host computer of a telecommunications system. Designed and developed software to support the Distributed Architecture ACD86 1.3. Coordinated with technical writers to ensure completeness and accuracy of the user documentation.

1981 - 1984   DatumSphere   Albuquerque, New Mexico
Software Certification Specialist

• Certified software for telecommunication systems; established requirements and procedures for testing, reviewing and analyzing design and functional specifications; designed and coded test systems.

1979 - 1981   Chaos Computing   Phoenix, Arizona
Programmer Analyst

• Developed and maintained software for an interactive mapping graphics system. Designed and developed software to access the graphical and non-graphical databases and reformat information for reporting.

1979 - 1979   Forko   Albuquerque, New Mexico
Programmer Analyst

• Developed and maintained software for academic use, principally interactive programs for scientific and business applications. Consultant to faculty and students.

FIGURE 8-3 CONTINUED

| Professional experience (continued) | 1978 - 1979 | Brainiac Univ. | Wimberdoodle, Pennnsylvania |
| | **Programmer Analyst** | | |

• Developed a real-time data acquisition program for heart research. Developed data analysis software to support the acquisition program.

| Papers | November, 1996 | EuroConference | Paris, France |

"Integrated Test Automation" co-authored with Bob Jones, Jenna Brucker, and Hemamalini Chowdry.

| Education | 1975 – 1977 | Brainiac Univ. | Wimberdoodle, Pennnsylvania |
| | **BA Criminology** | | |

FIGURE 8-3 CONTINUED

For the audition interview, Jamal and Emma asked Dinesh to run one of the automated tests. He did so successfully, noticing not only a bug in the product but also a suspicious behavior in the automation scripts themselves. Lin-Tsu reviewed the bug report Dinesh wrote, finding it insightful, concise, and thorough.

Step #	Step	Done?
1.D	Interview qualified, desirable candidates in person.	☑

Since Jamal's postinterview discussions with Emma, Lin-Tsu, and Bob Frankel were very positive, Jamal decided to hire Dinesh. Bob and Jamal, using the job description and the skills assessment, wrote an offer letter. To facilitate orientation, Jamal scheduled an hour a day of Emma's time to mentor Dinesh once he started, and asked Bob to prepare the latest copy of the employee handbook for Dinesh. He also started to plan on presenting a one-day training session for Dinesh and the new technicians, sometime in the next three or four weeks.[2]

Step #	Step	Done?
1.E	If appropriate, extend an offer to the most successful candidate, often via an offer letter.	☑

2. Chris DeNardis, in his article "Perspectives from a Test Manager" in *Software Testing and Quality Engineering*, Volume 2, Issue 5 (Sep/Oct 2000), now available at www.stickyminds.com, recommends training in the software itself and the issuance of a "Tester's Guide" to each new tester as well.

| 1.F | If the most successful candidate accepts, orient the new hire. If not, repeat steps 1.E and 1.F for the second-most-successful candidate, until either a successful candidate accepts or the process must restart at step 1.A. Notify rejected candidates that they should pursue other opportunities. | ☑ |

IDENTIFYING AND MANAGING THE CRITICAL TEST TEAM SKILLS

One of the key tools in the case study just described was Jamal's critical test team skills spreadsheet. He used this document to generate the initial job advertisement, to screen resumes, and to create the job description. How can you create such a skills spreadsheet for your teams?

The first step is to figure out what the critical skills are for your test team. I like to use a top-down approach for doing this. If you look closely at Figure 8-2, you can see that I have identified four major categories of skills: general qualifications, testing skills, application domain knowledge, and technical expertise.[3]

The first category, general qualifications, is unremarkable. In most organizations, there is some basic level of skill and education required to hold a position. For test professionals, though—i.e., as producers of information products and services—effective verbal and written communication under both formal and informal conditions takes on additional importance. Also, the ability to read closely and with tremendous attention to detail is necessary for static testing activities like reviews, inspections, and walkthroughs.

More interesting, though, are the areas of testing skills, application domain knowledge, and technical expertise. I find it helps to visualize a three-dimensional skills continuum, as shown in Figure 8-4. We can place various test staff members in this space, based on their specific skills, and also we can generalize how the various positions map into this space.

Different projects and teams have different requirements in each of these three areas. In the Sumatra test team, application domain knowledge is the lowest level of compe-

---

3. In addition to this tool, which I originated on my own years ago, many other test professionals have created such tools. The critical skills spreadsheet shown in this chapter incorporates many ideas from a skills assessment spreadsheet created by Hung Nguyen. I thank Hung and LogiGear Corporation (www.LogiGear.com) for sharing his version. James Bach, Bernie Berger, and Elisabeth Hendrickson also provided ideas about the critical skills required for testers.

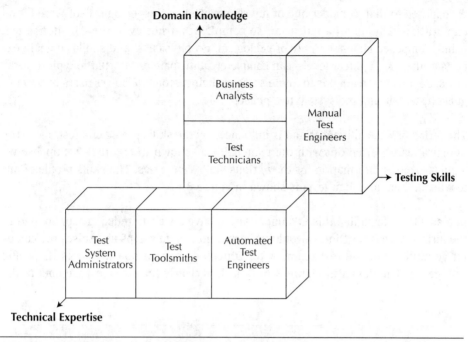

FIGURE 8-4 SKILLS CONTINUUM AND TEST STAFF POSITIONS

Testing Skills

Abilities relating to accomplishing test-specific tasks, like developing effective test cases and writing thorough bug reports.

Application Domain Skills, Subject Matter Expertise

Skill or understanding pertaining to whatever field or tasks we're dealing with in our software or hardware; in other words, understanding how our customers and users will employ our creation.

Technical Skills

Aptitudes addressing the particular techniques and tools we intend to use to create our system, such as programming languages server and network architecture.

tence for our test team. Is that OK? It depends on the product. A word processor is a straightforward application, familiar to most computer users. While word processing applications now contain a lot of fancy bells and whistles, most word processor users focus on a fairly narrow subset of features. Even given the number of test plans, articles, papers, and now books I have written, I suspect I only use about 20% of the facilities in my chosen word processor.

As opposed to that, consider one of my clients. They write geological software for oil exploration. This is an application so complex that not even their in-house test team—composed almost entirely of geologists, geophysicists, and similar domain experts at the test engineer level—can completely anticipate or test all the typical workflows. So, this test team has to invite some of their customers' power users to serve as guest testers during the system test phase.

The hiring process influences and is influenced by the skills profile of a test team. The Sumatra team started out with the team skills as shown in Figure 8-2. Suppose we summarize this information for the various skills categories. The skills profile of our test team, then, at a high level is shown in Figure 8-5.

In a small test team like this, it's important to have a well-rounded group. So, part of the hiring process for Dinesh would be seeing how he fills gaps and raises the cumulative abilities of the test team. After Dinesh comes on board, the skills profile changes to that shown in Figure 8-6. Dinesh is clearly the strongest member of the

	A	B TM Jamal Brown	C MTE Lin-Tsu Wu	D ATE Emma Moorhouse	E Team Minimum	F Team Average
1		Software Cafeteria Test Team				
2		Skills Assessment Minima and Averages				
4	Average Testing Skills	2.4	2.1	1.9	1.4	2.1
5	Average Domain Knowledge	0.8	1.3	2.0	0.7	1.4
6	Average Technical Expertise	1.6	2.0	2.1	1.1	1.9

FIGURE 8-5 SUMMARY SKILLS PROFILE

	A	B TM Jamal Brown	C MTE Lin-Tsu Wu	D ATE Emma Moorhouse	E ATE Dinesh Kumar	F Team Minimum	G Team Average
1		Software Cafeteria Test Team					
2		Skills Assessment Minima and Averages					
4	Average Testing Skills	2.4	2.1	1.9	2.6	1.4	2.2
5	Average Domain Knowledge	0.8	1.3	2.0	2.0	0.7	1.5
6	Average Technical Expertise	1.6	2.0	2.1	2.8	1.1	2.1

FIGURE 8-6 SUMMARY SKILLS PROFILE AFTER THE HIRING OF DINESH KUMAR

team (excluding management skills) and pulls up the team average in technical expertise and testing skills. The use of cross-training will enable Dinesh's abilities to be shared with the rest of the team, pulling these averages up even further, a topic to which I'll return in the next chapter.

REGARDING TEST TECHNICIANS

Not only does Jamal plan on hiring Dinesh, but he also needs to hire four contract test technicians. The concept of a test technician may be foreign to you, so let me explain what I'm talking about. I hire and employ test technicians—lesser-paid, lesser-skilled test team members—to execute manual and automated test cases, report test results and bugs, and do whatever else a test engineer needs them to do. When I talk to people about test technicians, there are often questions and concerns. What is a test technician and where does one find them? How can we make this relationship work for both employee and employer? Does using test technicians undermine the argument that testers need skill in the areas of technology, application domain, or testing?

In terms of skills required to do a job, there certainly are many test tasks that require skills or expertise in the underlying technology, the application domain or problem space addressed by the system, and, not least of all, testing. (By testing skills I mean all skills in the critical processes discussed in this book, among other testing skills such as design, documentation, and theory of automated and manual tests, not just test execution.) These tasks require test engineers, people who bring the skills, experience, and knowledge of a software engineer or programmer but with a testing focus to their work.

However, it is also true that many test tasks—especially scripted manual regression testing, installing software to test, or configuring test systems—can be rote, repetitive

---

Test Engineer

A test team member skilled, educated, and experienced in all areas of testing (planning, design, implementation, and execution) as well as possessing appropriate technical expertise and application domain knowledge. (In some states and countries, people with a title containing the word "engineer" must hold a professional license.)

Test Technician, Test Specialist

A test staff member less skilled, educated, and/or experienced than a test engineer in one, two, or all three of the critical skills areas (testing, application domain, and technology). Test technicians are usually qualified for scripted manual test execution and other straightforward technician-level tasks.

activities. In some cases, automation is not a practical solution. For example, when a test team is doing regression testing of a system with a nonstandard interface, sometimes automation tools won't support the interface and no one has time to develop an in-house automation tool. Rather than use an expensive, highly skilled test engineer, I prefer to hire test technicians to perform such roles.

Acknowledging that some areas are rote, repetitive, and within the capabilities of lesser-skilled staff members does not undermine testing itself as a unique skill. The presence of technicians within a test team should not undermine parity with and respect by other contributors in the organization. Further, because the test manager can assign appropriate tasks to test engineers and test technicians based on their skills, the presence of test technicians should improve morale, not harm it.

No one would suggest that the head chef of a restaurant is less skilled because he hires people to wash the customers' dishes, or that because there are interns in the White House, the presidency is a low-level job. We avail ourselves of the advantages offered by differentiation of skills and abilities all the time in life and in business. In fact, I would argue that failing to use technicians and forcing engineers to do work that does not require their level of skill and experience does damage to the image of testing as a profession—as well as wasting money.

Technicians come from many sources and have many backgrounds. An ad placed in the local paper and on the Internet usually brings in quite a few qualified candidates in many regions of the United States. I understand that in some areas of the United States, along with much of Europe and many places in Asia, test managers have difficulty finding qualified test technicians and employing such candidates productively when they do find them, because of differences in job markets, professional expectations, income disparity, and so forth. However, people trying test technicians for the first time are often surprised at how easy it is to create a place for such people on the team, how effective they are, and how channels through which one would not find test engineers nevertheless prove useful for recruiting test technicians.

I find on my projects that my best test technicians fall into the following three categories:

- Students or recent graduates, especially of technical institutes or certification programs
- Second-career professionals, especially retired military personnel looking to get started in the computer business
- Former technical support, help desk, and call-center staff, especially those who have worked with the technology or application domain

However, you want to cast the net widely. You can afford to set the skills bar low for technicians, because you're going to teach them what they need to know. What's really important for test technicians is a willingness to learn, a self-starting, hardworking approach to employment, and the right attitude.

You do need to plan on training technicians. For contractor test technicians, I have used both mentoring by their supervising test engineer and a one-day training course. For permanent employees on a career track in your company or for complex application domains, your specific context may require more training and mentoring. Incoming test technicians need to learn the basics of testing: managing quality risks through testing; structural and behavioral, manual and automated testing concepts; how to run a scripted manual test; how to write a good bug report; an introduction to the other documents they're likely to encounter (e.g., a test plan); how testing fits into the development lifecycle and software economics; and the challenges of test execution.

You also need to allow for more supervision and guidance for technicians, especially those without a solid track record, than you would for seasoned professionals. I have seen a real diversity here. I had two test technicians who conquered significant technical challenges in test tool development efforts in short order and came back asking for the next assignment long before I expected. I had one test technician who sat in a test lab doing nothing for hours waiting for a new test release to show up without bothering to call anyone or escalate the blocked condition. (All three technicians were recent recipients of computer science degrees at major, accredited universities.) It's often hard to assess exactly how someone will work out as a test technician, so be prepared to watch closely and provide course correction.

This may seem like a lot of hassle, but the payoff is definitely there. First, you avoid burning out your skilled testers on work they find stultifying, which improves overall team morale. Second, the company can save a lot of money with the intelligent use of technicians, which can make the prudent test manager who employs technicians wisely a hero, along with enabling that same test manager to have a much larger team and get more testing done than she otherwise would.

Third—and not least of all—the test manager who takes a chance or two on a seemingly underqualified test technician may be in for an enlightening surprise. I have hired a few—but very few—test technicians who let me down, but most have met my expectations in terms of what they could get done. At least three come to mind that, in my opinion, are among the best employees I have ever had. You have a chance to give people a break, a way into a different position, a different job, perhaps a whole different career. I encourage you not to get hung up on minor and ultimately unimportant distinctions about one year or two years of experience, B.S. or A.S. degree, but rather create a lower rung in your organization that allows you to let in people who may become your best employees.

TEST TEAM STAFFING VARIATIONS: TEMPORARY ASSIGNMENT, ROTATION, FARM TEAM, AND BACKWATER

So far, I've been discussing hiring and career paths with an implicit assumption that people will join the test team, work there for some portion of their career, and move up the organization to senior technical or managerial roles. This is certainly one way—and not an unusual way—for career paths to work, but it's hardly the only way. I'm aware of some common alternatives that are worth mentioning.

The first is the temporary assignment of people employed elsewhere in the organization into the test team. These people may augment the team during test execution or be the entire team throughout the test subproject. Often, the assignees are users or technical support staff for the system under development and bring considerable application domain expertise to their testing. If these people can be brought in early, during the planning and preparation stages discussed in the first two parts of this book, they can also help ensure that the testing reflects actual customer usage.

This can be effective, especially when the assignees augment an existing team of test engineers. In these cases, the influx of application domain expertise often fills a void in the test team's collective skills that would otherwise lead to serious test omissions. For example, remember that earlier I mentioned one of my clients, a maker of oil exploration software. The guest testers they invite from their biggest customers participate in system testing. They bring their own data sets and are encouraged to test the system as if they were using it. This allows them to test workflows and data scenarios that would otherwise go unexercised.

Problems can arise, though, when test teams consist entirely of temporary assignees. Such teams—whether composed of application domain experts or technology experts—tend to lack essential testing skills. I once saw an entire project—with a multiyear schedule and a multimillion-dollar budget—collapse in part because people not competent to perform testing were placed in entire charge of a critical testing effort for one subsystem.

Another alternative is rotation, an approach that is perhaps not nearly as common as it deserves to be. As one example, people might transfer from the programming team to the test team, from the test team to the technical support team, from the technical support team to the programming team, and so forth. In other words, these three teams are considered the system's technical team and change duties every few months. In the course of this rotation, people acquire a thoroughly well rounded set of skills, with the assistance of managers who keep track of these skills for each employee as well as for the teams they manage. The people who've told me they are using or have used this approach have uniformly expressed satisfaction with the results.

The use of rotation implies that all the managers through whose teams people will rotate agree to this approach. The human resources department, if it exists, will also need to support such staffing arrangements. Collectively, the managers will need to ensure that current employees who will be rotated understand the goals and agree to the assignments. Structure and careful skill management are required to ensure that the people rotating into a new position have appropriate job assignments for their skill sets (otherwise, rotation can negatively affect the effectiveness and efficiency of any or all the teams). Because testing and technical support are often seen as undesirable postings by programmers, considerable interpersonal skill will be required to implement such a plan. New hires, likewise, will need to know up front about the rotation plan.[4]

I have also heard from test managers in organizations where the test team is the place where new hires, particularly those destined for programming duties, spend some period of time to learn the product. I have heard from some test managers running such groups that the arrangement works well for their companies. I have three reservations about it, though.

First, it emphasizes application domain and technology knowledge as key to effective testing, but minimizes test-specific skills. Also, as I mentioned in Chapter 1, it's difficult to get testers in this role to grow those testing skills, since such skills growth is

---

4. Robert Sabourin, principal consultant of Amibug and a helpful reviewer of this book, reports great success with well-structured rotation programs, too. He wrote to tell me, "I have used many rotation variations. One of the best was to have members of the User Education (Training), Technical Support, Installation, and even Development teams be assigned for one day per month to the testing team, no exceptions, even managers! During their day, these folks would work on running and reviewing or even designing usage scenarios and related functional test procedures. We made it into a fun thing which brought in a lot of extra testing help, benefiting all teams and dramatically increasing the respect shown towards the test team overall! Trainers, writers, and support staff were able to get an early chance to see and play with new software, and they had a feel for what was coming down the pipe. In addition, all developers involved improved their unit testing skills and worked much harder on pre-release tests and smoke tests before throwing builds at the test team!"

not aligned with their career paths. Second, the continual turnover in the test team adds new difficulties to the test manager's position, which is already hard enough. It seems to me that to make this approach work, the test manager—indeed, the entire organization—will have to work together to resolve these problems.

The third problem with using test teams as training grounds arises when you find one or more test staff members you can't promote. Certain people turn out to be inappropriate for promotion into other areas, for whatever reason, and managers of those groups refuse to accept them. This problem is not unique to this approach but occurs anytime the test team becomes a backwater or a dumping ground for those rejected from or by other parts of the organization. This is, of course, the most challenging of team building situations for the test lead or test manager. When I have faced this situation, the implicit message was, "Here, you can have these people deemed undesirable for whatever reason; go make testing happen that way." Some of these folks did turn out to be bang-up testers, but others were endless sources of grief for me.

You might think that accepting people as a favor to other managers would be appreciated, but in my experience, it's not. I once worked with a marketing manager who decided that someone, while working as a programmer, had screwed up his pet feature. The reality was that the marketing manager had more than his share of blame in the outcome because of his failure to define the feature's requirements.

This programmer got placed in the test group as punishment, but whenever particularly important testing projects came up, this marketeer would micromanage the test effort by insisting that the erstwhile programmer in question "not work on anything important." By acquiescing to this arrangement to avoid making political waves, I only succeeded in painting myself into an ever-smaller box. My options became increasingly limited, and everything I assigned the poor ex-programmer to do got tarred with the brush of his perceived previous failure. I recommend avoiding this backwater role. Defining the skills, education, and experience needed to be a test engineer or test technician on your test team is part of setting the admissions bar high enough to prevent this problem.

However your test team is created, if it is anything other than a one-off collection of people to test a product that will require no ongoing maintenance, you will need to build a team around this collection of people. This team must possess the appropriate skills, experience, and knowledge for the testing effort to go well. The testers must have the correct attitudes to work effectively and interface smoothly with the rest of the project team. And to maintain motivation, the test work each tester does, if it continues for any length of time, must fit into his overall career path.

EDUCATION, TRAINING, CERTIFICATION, AND THE PROFESSIONALIZATION OF TESTING

Education appropriate for testers can be gained through a number of venues. First, we have college education. In the example job description in Figure 8-1, a bachelor's degree is a requirement for test engineers. I also noted continuing education as a requirement; some companies provide tuition assistance for employees to attain master's or even doctoral degrees.

But do testers need formal education? I usually prefer test engineers on my teams to have a college degree. It's dangerous to generalize too much, but I've found that getting a four-year or advanced degree indicates a level of perseverance, combined with an ability to master tough material, that stands people in good stead.

Some people have told me that they felt all testers should have a college degree if the same is true of all programmers and other technical people on the organizational staff. The argument usually goes as follows: If you intend to build the test team as a parallel technical team, having parity with the programmers and other technical peers, then the lack of a degree requirement if all other teams have such requirements will retard or defeat that objective. However, when we discuss this topic in my test management classes, one or more attendees almost always comes up with a perfectly reasonable argument for why degrees shouldn't matter or an example of a tester with a degree who had neither perseverance nor learning ability.

Suppose you decide, for whatever (legal and legitimate) reason, that testers do need a formal education to be on your team. OK, well, which degree? If you think that technological expertise is most important, then perhaps you'll want testers with computer science or software engineering degrees. If you think that application domain knowledge is key, then perhaps you'll want testers with degrees in business administration, accounting, or whatever specific problem your system helps its users solve. If you think that testing skills are the most important, then, unfortunately, your options are limited. A few software engineering and computer science curricula are starting to include testing courses—some even are creating specialized degrees in testing—but the number of graduates holding such degrees will likely, for the near future, remain small.

If a broad education in computer technology is necessary, there are possibilities beyond four-year college. Some high schools in the United States are now technical high schools offering courses in computers. The military, also, provides computer training for some enlistees and officer candidates. Community colleges in the United States grant two-year degrees, and there are technical or trade schools that can provide a solid grounding in computer technologies.

In some cultural contexts, a four-year (or more) college degree in a specific field is seen as essential. For example, when I discussed this topic with my test management peers in India, they told me that a college degree was a requirement simply to land an interview, not to mention a job. Likewise, Japan is a country where a formal college education is generally seen as an essential part of how you begin your career.

Whether one has a formal college education or not, specialized training and continuing education are often requirements. There are various training courses, seminars, and certification programs available. A wide variety of testing conferences, usually including tutorials, and publicly scheduled training events are held all over the world.[5]

The courses and papers presented at conferences and publicly scheduled training events are given by top-notch practitioners in the field. To be accepted for a conference, papers go through a peer review by a board of experts. The presenters of training courses are usually published authors, senior consultants, or practitioners with decades of experience in testing.

In addition to the professional conferences, there are also plenty of commercial ways to get training. Training is a big business around the world. Whether you're in Bangor, Maine, or Bangalore, India, you'll probably see advertisements to become a Microsoft System Certified Engineer through training and an exam. Some of the test tool companies now offer certification training, too. Finally, both nonprofit and for-profit companies offer training and certification in testing skills.

In *After the Gold Rush*, Steve McConnell describes a commonly accepted body of knowledge, along with certification programs aligned with that body of knowledge, as one hallmark of a profession. A variety of certification programs related to testing skills exist. If you're considering one of the many certification programs, I'd encourage you to ask the following questions.

- To what extent does the body of knowledge or syllabus relate to real-world testing activities, skills, and best practices?
- Who developed and maintains the body of knowledge or syllabus?

---

5. From personal experience, I have presented or licensed training courses on testing and test management throughout the United States as well as in Canada, Europe, the Middle East, Australia, South Asia, and East Asia. I have attended and spoken at testing conferences in the United States, in Europe, in the Middle East, in South Asia, and in Australia.

- What qualifications, experience, and credibility do the developers and maintainers of the body of knowledge or syllabus have as recognized test professionals?
- Is training required to take the certification exam(s)? If so, what qualifications, experience, and credibility do the developers and presenters of the training courses have as recognized test professionals?
- Can the certification exam(s) be taken over the Internet?
- Is there a minimum amount of real-world experience required along with passing one or more exams to obtain the certification?
- Does the certification program follow any industry standards, and are those standards applicable to you?
- Does the certification program focus on quality assurance or testing?
- How does the cost of the certification program compare with other programs that might offer a similar body of knowledge or syllabus?
- Is recertification or ongoing education required to maintain the certification, and if so, what are the costs associated with that?
- In what countries is the certification program offered and recognized?
- What do your peers and other testing professionals whose opinions you respect—and who have no hidden agendas—think of the certification program?
- Does the certification program advocate a "one true way to test," an overly prescriptive, context-insensitive approach?

There are good certification programs out there for those looking to obtain credentials as a test professional. There are also bad certification programs. The authority to grant a certification is typically not granted by any body or organization other than the certifying body itself. In other words, most certification programs are what could be described as *fiat certifications*, backed only by the credibility, experience, and credentials of the people involved in the program. Even the good programs vary widely, so I encourage you to do your homework before you select a certification program.

In addition to these programs, some of the testing tools vendors offer certification in the use of their tools and, in some cases, the specific development methodologies they recommend. However, such programs, given their provenance, will always be at least perceived as—if not actually—in service of the overall profit-making objectives of the tools vendors themselves.

Companies like Cisco and Microsoft offer certification in their specific technological skills, and certifications are available in specific application domains like finance and law. As helpful as these programs may be in technology and application domain skills, I believe that software testing is now a de facto specialized profession within the realm of system engineering, with its own unique skills. Competent testers must acquire and demonstrate mastery of these skills. It may be a while before the education options available for testing skills—whether through colleges, trade schools, or certification programs—catch up to the needs in this regard.

ATTITUDE MATTERS TOO

Hiring isn't just about abilities. Some critical tester attributes have less to do with skills than with outlooks. Of course, we all know what it means when we say someone has a good attitude. There are generally recognized professional outlooks. However, within testing, some additional proclivities are important.

First is what I call *professional pessimism*. This means approaching testing tasks with an operating assumption that the product has bugs and the test team will find them. However, it also means that test professionals keep this outlook bounded within an overall assumption that quality is just one of the general categories of risks that endanger the project. Testers must advocate quality and the customer's experience of it, but they must not do so in an adversarial, personal, or disruptive way. Rather, we must do so in a way that connects with the business realities of system development and maintenance.

Second, testers need to bring balanced curiosity to their role. To find bugs, testers must be curious, both when writing and when running test cases. A lack of curiosity leads to perfunctory test cases that don't explore the most promising nooks and crannies. A lack of curiosity leads to bug reports that don't connect the failure observed to the customer's experience of quality. However, balance is important because we have a large set of tests to write and run with limited resources and time. The test professional must consider the question, How much effort is enough effort on this particular task?

Third, and related to balance, is an ability to focus. By this I mean understanding the key priorities and focusing efforts on those. This is hard because those priorities tend to change rapidly. (Of course, the test manager must clearly communicate priorities— and the reasons those might change—to the test engineers and technicians.) I have known otherwise-excellent testers who, because of an inability to focus, had difficulty completing assigned tasks at consistent levels of quality in a timely fashion. Although they possessed considerable test expertise, this one flaw in their temperaments limited their potential.

Fourth, a tester must be willing to accept a generalist and supporting role, focusing on a steady, reliable process rather than achieving glory or glamour through individual heroics. Even in enlightened companies that provide a solid career path and peer-level treatment for testers, testing is sometimes seen as a job with many undesirable attributes. For example, the spotlight shines on the test team right at the end of the project, when any excessive optimism in the project plan becomes evident in schedule slips and budget overruns. As another example, testers must bring bad news to the development team. No matter how good testers become at diplomacy and communication, they will occasionally meet with resistance and defensiveness in that role. Both these realities create stress in the testers' lives. Good testers are willing to labor in an often underappreciated and poorly understood role.

Fifth, testers must be willing to work hard. Because the spotlight is on the test team at the end, as schedules slip, budgets evaporate, and tempers flare, the human tendency to throw more effort at the project will kick in, and kick particularly hard on the test team. This needn't make any rational sense. For example, on one project I had a development manager who made disparaging comments about the test team because we weren't working 16-hour days like the development team. I told my client contact that since there were hundreds of bugs queued up in the defect tracking system waiting for the developers to fix them, the test team was not the project bottleneck. Nevertheless, we ended up adding a night shift and running tests seven days a week to manage the perception that the test group somehow wasn't doing its part.

Sixth and finally, testers must be willing to stand up and advocate quality—reasonably and within a rational business context, but also firmly and with conviction. If a tester files a bug report that a programmer doesn't like, and is confronted by said distressed programmer, she shouldn't bow her head, stick her hands in her pockets, and meekly mumble, "Oh, okay, I guess I'll cancel that bug report."

Instead, she should square her back, listen to the programmer's argument, and then say something like, "Yes, but, if I were the customer and I saw this kind of behavior, I'd be unhappy. Perhaps I am making a big deal of nothing, though, so we can let the change control board (or bug triage committee) sort this out in their next meeting." An erect and supple backbone is a requirement for a good tester.

BEYOND THE OBVIOUS INTERVIEW QUESTIONS

One of the aspects of unique testing skills (which some people neglect) is that we can't interview testers as we interview everyone else on the development team. A lot has been written about interviewing for programmers. A recent search on Amazon.com reviewed a list of books recommended for those about to interview for a software engineering position.

However, programming skills are not a sufficient—or in some cases even a necessary—qualification for all test professionals. I recommend some questions that go beyond the typical "Write me a program that copies a file..." or "Describe a difficult time in your career and how you dealt with it."

- On your last project, did you expect tests to pass or to fail? Why? On this project, would you expect the converse? Why?

- Tell me about some test cases you've run recently where you were sure a failure occurred. How did you know? How did you verify your expected results?

- The last time you reported a bug, what manner and tone did you use to discuss that bug with other members of the development team? Were you happy with that outcome? Tell me about a time you reported a bug when you felt your manner and tone got in the way of effective communication.

- Tell me about a time when you felt strongly that a problem you'd found would negatively affect the customer's experience of quality, but not everyone agreed with you. How did you effectively advocate your controversial bug report, or was that even your job?

- Tell me about some projects you've worked on where testing work was particularly fun and interesting. What parts were fun and interesting? What parts weren't fun or interesting? Tell me about a test project you've worked on where nothing was fun or interesting. Why do you think that was?

- Tell me about a time when you managed to disagree without being disagreeable. How about a time when you didn't?

- In this job, you'll need to keep track of lots of test cases, test data, test environments, test releases, bug reports... (add whatever else is pertinent to your environment). The status of each of these items may change daily. Tell me about how you keep track of such large sets of ever-changing stuff.

- Sometimes, this position might entail working 60 hours per week/some weekends/evening shift (whatever is true in your organization). Are you able to do that? Give me an example from your past experience of working these kinds of hours, if you could. What happens when you get burned out from work? How do you handle it?

- Tell me about the last time you struggled with the question of the right amount of time to spend writing a test case. How about the right amount of time to spend isolating a bug? If you are assigned six tests to run in a day, and the second test finds a bug, how do you decide when it's OK to jeopardize completion of the four remaining tests to research that bug?

- Tell me about what kind of information your previous managers have given you and how they communicated that information so you could maintain proper focus. How about a time when that information didn't come through and you lost focus?

- How would you apply what you learned on (some previous) project to testing our product? What behaviors and activities have you engaged in on previous projects that you wouldn't repeat?

- Why do you like testing? What are you career plans? Do you see a career for yourself in testing? Where do you see yourself in the next five years? Where do you see testing as a specialty in the next five years?

Many others are possible, but you get the idea. Being a good tester is about more than just skills and education; it's about attitudes, temperament, and outlooks, too. You'll want to structure your interview process accordingly.[6]

Hiring in a Nutshell, by Deborah McCandless

Prehire planning is the most critical (though often missed) step in a hiring process. Determine the needs of your team at the very beginning of the hiring process, and you will save time and eliminate personnel problems down the road, even on a single testing project.

Start by reviewing a detailed job description or a list of general QA skills and knowledge appropriate to the level for which you're hiring. Next, inventory the skills and knowledge of your current team. A simple way to do this is to place a check mark next to the items on the general QA skills list or job description. Use this information to determine any gaps or weaknesses in the team overall or for a specific project. Then build your job posting, interview questions, and tests to address the needs of the team, the project and the company.

A helpful trick to use when developing tests is to have a few people take the tests and give you feedback. This helps you to determine a number of things, such as the following.

- Are the instructions clear and concise?
- Do the test results tell you what you need to know?
- Was it too easy (or too hard)?
- How long on average did it take people to complete the test?

---

6. For more ideas on recruiting, interviewing, and hiring testers, I can also recommend Johanna Rothman's book *Hiring the Best Knowledge Workers, Techies, & Nerds: The Secrets & Science of Hiring Technical People.*

Review and rank the resumes. (A good way to save time and money is to have a folder of "keeper resumes" for those people who weren't right for this position but were still top-notch. Call or e-mail those people when you have an opening.) Be sure to pay attention to skills or knowledge that is transferable from one profession to another. Follow up with phone interviews of the top candidates. This allows you to find out if they were truthful about their skill set and are likely to be a good fit. After the phone interviews, rank the applicants again and invite the top applicants for an interview. If you plan to test them, be sure to let them know that they will be tested.

Keep the interview environment as comfortable as possible to ensure more open and honest answers. You will want to ask all the usual questions (their strengths, what skills they'd need to build, past work experience, and so on). Using open-ended questions allows the applicant to do most of the talking. Encourage them to ask questions; people who ask questions are often good at testing. Build questions that help you evaluate their abilities or skills in prioritization, problem solving, time management, organization, analysis, teamwork, documentation, communication, follow-through, conceptualization, following directions, being detail oriented, flexibility, performance under pressure, and having goals and motivations. Develop targeted questions for use in each step of the interview process: the phone interview, the team or peer interview, and the manager's interview.

FROM ADDING PEOPLE TO GROWING SKILLS

So far, I've focused mostly on hiring and otherwise adding new testers to a test team. This is, of course, an important part of how the test team grows. Work requires workers, and we must find the appropriate people for the tasks at hand.

However, most professionals do not want to merely come in to a job and do the same thing over and over, learning nothing, applying existing skills. Professionals want a career path, which implies growth in skills. Additionally, the set of skills required for our test team is often dynamic. Expanded test team scope, new technologies, and new products require new skills in the team. In the next chapter, I'll look at how we handle this part of the team building process, fostering team skills and career growth. Once we've addressed that topic, we'll look back at the overall team building process to recognize a good one, handle the inevitable challenges, and implement improvements.

9

GROW EXCELLENT TEST TEAMS: SKILLS, ATTITUDES, AND CAREER PATHS

I n the previous chapter, I covered the first half of the team building process, those issues associated with hiring. Clearly, a large part of building a strong test team is assembling the right collection of people. However, there is the long-term, nurturing aspect of team building as well. To have a good, thorough process, we need to attend to this aspect. Let me spend a few pages on this second part of the team building process, and then I'll reexamine the entire process to close on this topic.

JAMAL AND LIN-TSU DISCUSS SKILLS GROWTH

September was a busy month for Jamal. Not only was he planning for the Sumatra project and handling maintenance release testing for a couple of other OfficeArrow products *and* hiring five new testers, but everyone on his current team was up for their quarterly skills growth review. Jamal took this responsibility seriously, since he knew that the long-term viability of his test team, along with the loyalty of his team members, depended considerably on providing a career path for each test team employee. So, he spent a whole afternoon in the office on Saturday, September 21, looking over his skills assessment worksheet and thinking about what needed to happen. He sent the assessment out to the entire test team with the following e-mail.

```
Hi, all—

Attached is the skills assessment spreadsheet. The worksheet
named "Skills Management (S02)" is the current skills summary.

Looking at this, I see we're weakest in the area of application
domain knowledge, especially in non-Windows word processors. I
think this could be an issue, especially for manual testing, dur-
ing the coming months.
```

Also, while we're strong in testing in general, there are some
weaknesses I'd like to see addressed in the automated testing
areas of reliability testing and in integration testing.

Please spend a few moments over the next couple of days thinking
about the areas you'd like to increase your skills in, keeping the
team needs mentioned above in mind. I'll schedule meetings with
each of you next week to put plans in place for skills growth.

Regards,

Jamal

Jamal decided to start with Emma and Lin-Tsu, since he wanted them to get started right away acquiring the skills they would need for Sumatra. So, on Tuesday the 24th, Lin-Tsu and Jamal met in his office for half an hour. After a few moments of small talk, Jamal got down to business.

"So, Lin-Tsu, what are your thoughts about skills improvement for the next quarter?"

"Well, you know that I want to get more experience outside of the Windows arena, but technology isn't really a weak spot for us. How about this, though? Based on your e-mail, I think I can work on improving my application domain skills—specifically word processing and document management—including the Mac and UNIX platforms."

"That sounds great. I was hoping you'd say something like that," Jamal said encouragingly. "Any thoughts on how to do that?"

"Yeah, actually, there's a conference coming up in a few weeks on the topic of document management," Lin-Tsu replied. "They're offering a couple of tutorials during that conference that also look useful." She handed Jamal the flyer for the conference.

Jamal studied it, making affirmative noises. Finally, he looked up and said, "Hey, this could be pretty good. You know, though, we're all limited to two conferences or training events per fiscal year now. Are you sure this is one of the two you want to attend?"

"Yes, for a couple of reasons," she responded. "First, it's going to get me the right training at the right time. Second, it's in San Diego, which is where my brother and sister-in-law live . . ."

"Ah!" Jamal smiled.

". . . so I'd planned on leaving the night of the Thursday before, taking a vacation day, then being out there the whole week."

"Hmm," Jamal said. "Any way we can hold off on the vacation day right before the conference? We've got a lot on our plates with this Sumatra project. I'm afraid that ten whole days will slip something on the schedule—something that might hurt."

"But I *am* saving the company lots of travel money. There's the weekend stay-over and the fact that I'll stay with my brother, which cuts out the hotel bill."

Jamal sat back and thought a minute. She does have a point, he admitted to himself, and it seems unfair to be picayune about a single day under the circumstances. Of course, it's really more than a single day, because she'll be leaving early for her flight on Thursday, most likely. But, it's probably the right thing to do for the company, saving all the money like that.

"Okay," Jamal said, "can we make a deal? You leave on Thursday night, and I'll skip counting Friday as a vacation day—I'll call it a comp day—if you come back on Friday from the conference and work Saturday that weekend to catch up. I'll be here with you."

"Sold," Lin-Tsu agreed, smiling.

"Now, how about some ways we can apply all that knowledge you're going to soak up?" Jamal asked.

Jamal and Lin-Tsu talked further about how she could use those skills in her testing. She discussed some specific tests she planned to create and run. Jamal mentioned that Dinesh Kumar, the new test engineer who would be starting in about two weeks, had talents in the areas she was discussing.

"If you don't mind," Jamal said, "I'll ask Dinesh to review the tests you come up with. That way, he can transfer some of his knowledge to you."

"That sounds great. Based on this plan," she concluded, "I should achieve skill levels between two or three on each of the four skills in the areas of word processing and document management across the Mac and UNIX systems."

"Great. Let's set the goal of boosting your skill level by one in these areas in the skills tracking spreadsheet. We can both be pleasantly surprised when you do better later—how's that?"

"Excellent!"

"That will put you ahead of schedule when we do your annual review in January. Start thinking about your annual review, too, please, Lin-Tsu, so we can set more good goals for you this year. I'm really pleased with the progress you're making on your career path, so I'd like to start positioning you for a promotion next year."

Step #	Step	Done?
2.	Foster team skills and career growth.	☑
2.A	Work with new hires to develop career paths.	☑
2.B	Regularly revisit the career paths for all employees and each employee's progress on their path.	☑
2.C	Actively manage the employee's skills growth necessary to reach employee and team goals.	☑

USING SKILLS ASSESSMENT AS A CAREER GROWTH AND TEAM MANAGEMENT TOOL

In the previous chapter, you saw how the skills assessment worksheet provided a useful hiring tool for any kind of test team, small or large, specialized or homogeneous, project-based or skills-based. You can use this spreadsheet to figure out where the weaknesses in your team exist and to hire people to strengthen those areas. Based on resumes, you can use the skills spreadsheet to select candidates and then use the skills list again to focus the interview on those particular areas of expertise you're trying to add to your team.

As you can see from Jamal and Lin-Tsu's conversation, the skills assessment worksheet is also a powerful tool for career growth and test team skills management. If you look ahead to the detailed job description shown in Figure 9-3, you'll see that one of the job requirements is that each employee "participate in a quarterly test team critical skills assessment and management session with the Test Manager, setting and achieving skills growth in at least three agreed-upon areas per quarter through internal (cross-training) and external (seminar/tutorial/conference) skills growth opportunities."

The test manager and each employee should sit down regularly and decide on areas where the employee can improve. It's likely that the test manager will have areas in which he wants to strengthen the team's skills, as Jamal did, and the employees will have areas where they would like their own skills to grow to advance on their career path. Through targeted assignments, mentoring, and external training, the test team can continually grow and improve.

The Critical Skills Spreadsheet: Open Record or Private Personnel Information?

When I use the critical skills spreadsheet as a hiring and skills growth management tool, I use it openly. In other words, everyone, to the extent they want to, can see what each person's self-assessed skills levels are and what their growth plan is. I'm trying to foster a team environment that way, where people are open and honest about what they're good at and what they need help with. People can know who to ask a particular question.

It also fosters honesty in the self-assessment. I've found that a tester might fool me about any given skill, since I mightn't have time to check out each claim in detail, but other members of the test team will notice. I sometimes mention this to people when I'm explaining the skills self-assessment process, especially if I feel they might be tempted to puff themselves up.

If you choose to share this information openly, I believe that two cautions must be observed.

1. Don't use this process and the information it generates as part of the yearly review process or to determine salary increases. On my teams, the only requirement is that people participate actively in the skills growth process. I don't tie the increases in skills ratings back to any objective in the yearly review. This means that the skills management information is not part of someone's annual review and thus not private personnel data. If, for whatever reason, you decide to use these numbers directly—e.g., including an objective in a yearly review, such as "Increase by five skills points in each of the three major areas"—then the skills assessment is private personnel data and must not be shared.[1]

2. Don't share the information with your managers or your management peers if you suspect it will be used as a tool for deciding who to promote, who to lay off, or who to cherry pick from the test team. I keep this information private within the test team unless it becomes a company-wide standard and every team's data is out in the open.

That's my approach, and some have told me that it's a radical approach. If you decide to implement this technique, I recommend that you speak to someone in your personnel or human resources department about any privacy policies your company may have that affect what kind of data you can gather and how that data must be handled.

---

1. Some organizations do skills reviews only as part of a yearly review. I think this is too infrequent, since skills growth must be a constant part of enhancing team capabilities. In addition, there's a risk of tying a skills growth process such as this too closely to the performance review, because it might become difficult to separate employee evaluations and bonuses from the numerical increase in skills that employees achieve. Any linkage, real or perceived, can lead to artificial inflation of the skills growth by employees, which will reduce the value of the process.

This is not only to the benefit of the test team. To provide a career path for the people on the test team, the test manager must help them acquire the skills and experience they'll need to meet the challenges of their next assignment. This may be within the test team—e.g., moving from test technician to test engineer—or it may be further in the organization—e.g., moving from senior test engineer to help desk manager. Therefore, the test manager and each member of the test team should work together to synchronize the skills growth process with each employee's career path.

RECOGNIZE A GOOD TEAM BUILDING PROCESS

At this point, I've covered the entire team building process, so let's look at what a good team building process allows the test team—and the candidate—to do.

OPERATE ON A WIN-WIN PHILOSOPHY

When you are hiring people, you'll want to select the best people from the pool of candidates, those most qualified to help you assess product quality, supporting the broader goal of managing product quality risks. If these people are career employees, you'll then want to move them along a career path that advances each tester's goals and enables ever-increasing levels of effectiveness and efficiency from the test team. When you are the person being hired, you'll want to find the perfect job for this stage of your career and know that the job will provide advancement along your intended career path.

The essence of a win-win hiring philosophy is that all parties, employees and employer, will benefit from each employee's relationship with the employer. These benefits are both long-term and short-term. Unfortunately, some hiring managers—especially in tight economic times—approach hiring and work as a zero-sum game like chess or poker, games with losers as well as winners. In zero-sum games, a party can benefit only through the losses of other parties. A healthy workplace, created by enlightened management, does not play zero-sum games. In a healthy workplace, wealth is created, knowledge is gained, and lives are enriched by a sense of accomplishment.

Through the team building process, one candidate chooses and is chosen to be the new hire for the previously open position, and other candidates reject or do not receive offers. Mutual satisfaction of all parties' objectives—including those not hired—can occur when

- We attract appropriate candidates.
- We reject unsuitable candidates.

- We make offers to one or more qualified candidates.
- Those suitor candidates receive the right information upon which to make a decision to accept or decline those offers.

See Figure 9-1 for an illustration of this process.

Different attributes and factors affect the goodness of this process depending on whether you look at it through the candidates' and employees' eyes or the employer's eyes. From the candidate's or employee's perspective, the overriding questions are, "Is this the right job for me? Will I find the encouragement, experience, and skills growth I need in this position to take the job I want next?" From the employer's perspective, the questions are, "Is this candidate the right tester for the job? Can this person grow in their skills to help us meet new challenges?"

When we set up the team building process, we want a high-quality process for all participants, because, unlike poker or chess, being part of a team is not a zero-sum

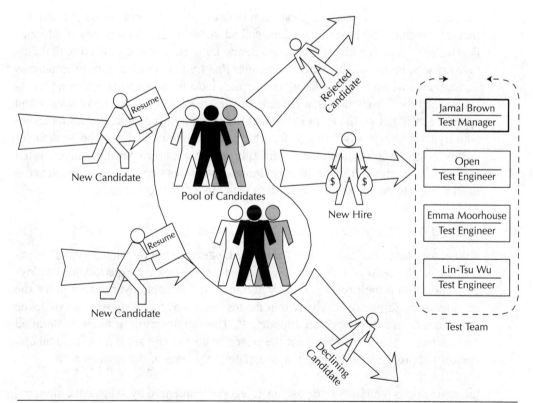

FIGURE 9-1 FROM CANDIDATE TO EMPLOYEE

game. Both sides need to make a fully informed decision based on the right criteria. A process that provides either side with less than all the necessary information can create one or both of two negative situations.

1. A candidate accepts a job he later regrets taking, leading to employee disgruntlement and probably counterproductive behavior.
2. The test manager extends an offer to a candidate she later regrets hiring, leading to remedial action by the manager. Such actions to rectify employee attitudes and behavior, even if they succeed, create a distraction for the test manager.

Should unresolved issues prevail, either the employee departs with all the difficulties inherent in turnover, or he continues to give a suboptimal performance, with possible attitude problems to boot. The best that can possibly happen with an opaque process is that each side by accident stumbles into the right match, which is far too haphazard an approach to take for something so critical.

Part of the win-win aspect of a good team building process occurs through providing that information. The next few sections will address the important pieces of information for new hires, the hiring organization, and both. However, it's also true that attitude matters. Philosophies matter. Companies that try to take advantage of employees through misleading or tricky hiring techniques, locking in low salaries during recessions, and other sleazy tactics, often reap the just reward of low employee loyalty and teams that will not go the extra mile when the company needs that effort. Employees who try to talk their way into jobs for which they're unqualified, who lie on their resumes, or who won't synchronize their skills growth with the company's needs, often end up fired or stuck in unfulfilling positions. Both sides—employer and employee—must come into the team building process ready to help the other side.

ACCURATELY DEFINE THE JOB

Mutual assistance can only happen when both parties agree on what services we expect the employee to provide. Lacking clearly defined employer expectations, employees cannot fulfill their roles except by accident, and the employer cannot judge the employees' performances fairly. Within the test team's overall purpose, we can define how each employee's position supports it. The job description must be detailed enough that it's clear what we want the person to do, yet still allow for individual discretion and professional judgment appropriate to the level of the employee.

Job descriptions tend to fit into position-categories influenced by skills, education, experience, and specialization. Typically, if I have positions open at a junior level that don't require college degrees or significant experience, I give such testers the title of test technician. Because the roles here don't involve lots of experience, there's very little opportunity for specialization. At more senior levels, I tend to have people with titles like manual test engineer, automated test engineer, test toolsmith, and test environment administrator. On test teams where extensive application domain knowledge is required, you may also want business analysts or subject matter experts. At any level, as people become more skilled, the word "lead" might become appended to their title, and technicians may advance into engineer, toolsmith, or environment administrator positions.

Based on the level of detail I'm advocating, the job description shown in Figure 9-2 isn't adequate. It's fine for soliciting resumes or job applicants, but a real job description, such as might appear in an offer letter, in an employee's personnel file, and as part of a person's yearly review, would look more like what's shown in Figure 9-3.

While it's important to make expectations clear, we need to remember that precise ways of quantifying jobs, skills, and responsibilities can create an illusion of control that exceeds the reality. One manager I discussed this issue with shared with me that she and her supervisor, after adopting a rigorous, metrics-based way of measuring performance and employee ability, decided to perform a test before using it. They would discuss in advance, without looking at their metrics, where they expected each employee to score. They then ran the metrics and, lo and behold, everyone scored close to the expected value. This told them one of two things was going on: 1) They had cooked the books to hit their preconceived numbers; or 2) these metrics are a fancy way of rationalizing what we already know. We can—and should—strive for as objective a process as possible, but we can't take subjectivity out of the process of evaluating candidates or employees. Temper any attempts to tightly regiment the tester's job description with fairness and an understanding that we are not programming a machine, but explaining our expectations for a human being.[2]

PROVIDE THE EMPLOYEE WITH A LONG-TERM CAREER PATH

Testing has a bad reputation. Many people have managed to build a successful career in the field, but too many people still see it as a career-killing dead end to be escaped as quickly as possible. This perception is a reality only in that some managers practice

---

2. For a more detailed discussion of people management issues like this, take a look at *Winning at Project Management,* by Robert Gilbreath, or *The Accidental Project Manager,* by Patricia Ensworth.

JOB TITLE:	Manual Test Engineer
FUNCTION:	Develop and execute manual test suites according to company and industry standards; Develop and maintain test status tracking tools; and, Perform other testing-related duties as required.

JOB TITLE:	Automated Test Engineer
FUNCTION:	Participate in the test automation tool selection process; Develop and execute automated test suites using COTS and custom tools; Integrate test suites into the test management system and custom test harnesses; and, Perform other testing-related duties as required.

JOB TITLE:	Test Toolsmith
FUNCTION:	Develop custom test automation tools for APIs and GUIs; Support and capture development unit test tool efforts; and, Perform other testing-related duties as required.

JOB TITLE:	Test Environment Administrator
FUNCTION:	Select, install, and configure the test network, test servers, test workstations, and test databases (i.e., the test environment); Install regular test releases onto the test environment as required to support the testing process; and, Perform other testing-related duties as required.

JOB TITLE:	Test Technician
FUNCTION:	Execute manual and automated tests; Report test status and bugs to engineer-level supervisor; and, Perform other testing-related duties as required.

FIGURE 9-2 TITLES AND ROLES FOR TEST STAFF MEMBERS

this tester pigeonholing. However, technical contributors who have seen colleagues get stuck in test roles against their wishes often become averse to holding such roles themselves, even if only temporarily.

For example, I once interviewed someone for a position as a test manager who didn't know that was the position he was interviewing for. He had once been a test manager, and he described it as an embittering experience. He said he wouldn't take a testing position under any circumstances. Apparently, no one had asked him what he wanted to do; they just saw testing on his resume and stuck him in that category. I find that sad, not for the least reason that it's unnecessary.

JOB TITLE: Automated Test Engineer

REPORTS TO: Test Manager

FUNCTION: Participate in the test automation tool selection process;
Develop and execute automated test suites using COTS and custom tools;
Integrate test suites into the test management system and custom test harnesses; and,
Perform other testing-related duties as required.

Duties And Responsibilities

A.   Technical

- Review requirements, specifications, user documentation, help files, and other project documentation to ensure quality of the products and tests to be developed; i.e., perform manual static testing.

- Select and develop appropriate test automation tools, applying the latest techniques in test automation; e.g., data-driven testing.

- Use risk-driven techniques to develop, maintain, and execute automated test suites for various Software Cafeteria products; i.e., perform automated dynamic testing.

- Work with the Development team to capture and reuse automated Unit Test Cases, Test Stubs and Drivers, and other Development test objects.

- Participate in the Change Control Board to identify the quality implications of known bugs and the impact of proposed changes to product definition on the testing process.

- Work with the Release Engineering team to create and maintain an automated nightly build verification ("smoke") test.

- Ensure proper version control and configuration management of all test objects developed and test environments used.

B.   Results Tracking and Reporting

- Research and document bug reports following agreed-upon processes immediately upon discovery of a quality problem.

- Update test execution status following agreed-upon processes as part of regularly scheduled test status updates.

- Trace test cases and results back to specific quality risks.

- Assist the Test Manager in the creation of test project status reports and metrics (e.g., Test Dashboard).

C.   Management and Supervisory

- Provide the Test Manager with accurate and precise estimates for assigned task duration, along with confidence levels and foreseeable dependencies.

- Assist the Test Manager in preparing test plans, budgets, and schedules.

- Participate in tester interviews, including administering "audition interviews" for Manual Test Engineer, Automated Test Engineer, and Test Technician candidates.

- Provide technical guidance to junior-level test engineers and/or test technicians assigned to assist the Automated Test Engineer.

- Provide the Test Manager with performance assessments for assigned junior personnel.

FIGURE 9-3 DETAILED JOB DESCRIPTION FOR OFFER LETTER AND PERFORMANCE REVIEW (CONTINUED ON NEXT PAGE)

D.   Skills, Education, and Career Growth

- If the Bachelor's Degree requirement has been waived, enroll in an approved course of study toward a Bachelor's Degree as described under the Employee Career Development Assistance Program.

- Once the Bachelor's Degree requirement is satisfied, enroll in an approved continuing education program as described under the Employee Career Development Assistance Program.

- Participate in a quarterly test team critical skills assessment and management session with the Test Manager, setting and achieving skills growth in at least three agreed-upon areas per quarter through internal (cross-training) and external (seminar/tutorial/conference) skills growth opportunities.

- Subscribe to and read one or more journals or trade magazines related to software testing and/or software quality as described under the Employee Career Development Assistance Program.

- Purchase, read, and present a Test Team Training Session on one or more books per quarter related to software testing and/or software quality as described under the Employee Career Development Assistance Program.

E.   Attitudes and Initiative

- Develop and maintain good professional working relationships, especially within the test team and with those who interact regularly with the test team.

- Focus on the important testing and project priorities as agreed-upon with the test manager.

- Effectively balance curiosity about tests, test results, and bugs with project constraints on budget and schedule.

- Exhibit a demeanor of professional pessimism; i.e., in a pleasant and non-confrontational fashion work with determination to find, document, and advocate the repair of bugs.

- Show initiative in setting and meeting goals within an environment of managed change.

- Understand the role of testing within the software development lifecycle and business-related project constraints, and effectively advocate for the best possible customer experience of product quality within those parameters.

Employee:

I have read and fully understand the job description outlined above. I also understand that failure to perform to expectations set above might result in disciplinary action and/or dismissal.

By: ....
(Signature)

....
(Typed or Printed Name)

Title: ..Automated Test Engineer..........................

Date: ....

Employer:

The employee accepting this position shall be reviewed and evaluated based on this job description and ordinary and customary standards of professionalism. No change to this job description shall occur without the employee's consent.

By: ....
(Signature)

....
(Typed or Printed Name)

Title: ..Test Manager..

Date: ....

FIGURE 9-3 CONTINUED

Based on what I have seen in my work and heard from my seminar attendees, most career path opportunities for testers fall into two categories: the rite of passage and the tester track. In the first category, testing is an initiation, a temporary obligation, or both. In the case of initiation, people are brought into testing as a starting point, to learn the product and the company. In the case of a temporary obligation, people spend time in the testing department for a given project before going back to whatever they did before, typically not to return to testing again.

I have two problems with such techniques. First, they undervalue the degree of skill required to be a good tester, especially the test-specific skills. No testing skills are required to attain the position, since the position is imposed, not attained. In addition, because of the temporary nature of the assignment, there is no incentive to improve the necessary skills other than fear of failure to escape from testing because of a bad performance review.

Second, such incessant and involuntary turnover in the team makes the test manager's existence difficult. If people have an assignment they don't want—or want to conclude so they can move on to what they really want to do—what kind of work can we expect from them? If people are perpetually coming into a group, how much inefficiency do lost expertise and the need for endless basic training impose? Is it even remotely possible to build a team and manage collective skill levels when everyone is a short-timer?

The tester track makes testing a separate technical track within the company. The track must reside at a peer level with programming, customer support, sales engineering, operations, and all other technical career ladders. It must also provide for transition between technical tracks and to a management career track in the same ways as these other technical paths. People should join the test team because they want to be there, stay as long as needed to fulfill career goals enunciated to and planned by the test manager, and go on to do other things in the company with fond memories of their time in testing.

The rotation approach discussed in the previous chapter is actually a variation of the tester track technique. (In small companies, this rotation can happen easily since there are fewer organizational barriers to instituting rotation.) In this situation, each technical member of the team is on a broad technical track, gaining knowledge, skills, and experience in all technical realms of the development and maintenance effort. Testing, programming, customer support, and other technical roles are seen as equal and complementary. People rotate between the roles, spending one project as a tester, the next as a programmer, the next as a customer support person, and so forth. As I mentioned in the previous chapter, the various managers must work together to ensure that each person gains all the necessary skills—in testing, technology, and application domain—to work effectively in all stages of their rotation.

I prefer the tester track and rotation approaches, but any clearly defined career path is better than nothing. If there is no career path defined, then the default is that the testing organization is a backwater and often a dumping ground for the barely competent and the malcontent. In the times I've seen this happen, the law of the jungle prevailed. Those who perceived themselves as stuck in a testing job fought tooth-and-nail to escape. These efforts severely damaged test team cohesion and distracted the test manager. If you find yourself in this rut, my advice—what I wish I'd done when I was stuck in it—is to fire the most disruptive of the malcontents and incompetents immediately. Then expend as much political capital and energy as possible working with the management team to implement some career path strategy that is fair and acceptable to all involved.

GIVE EMPLOYEES APPROPRIATE AND FAIR SALARIES

An old management cliche is that money is not a motivator, but it can be a demotivator. In other words, while you won't be able to inspire someone to keep a job they hate because the money exceeds their expectations, you can cause someone to hate a job they otherwise enjoy because the money's insufficient. Another important consideration is that pay scales be equitable and rational, both internally in the company and in terms of the local job market. I'm not sure this is true for everyone, but I can certainly say that my job satisfaction has rarely been a simple linear function of how much money I was making.

Money matters in a couple of ways. One is that the wage someone is paid should be commensurate with their skills, education, and experience, along with the value they are adding for the company. Companies speak volumes about how much respect they have for testing—as a functional area, for testers as individuals, and for the test team's contributions—when they set the pay scale for testers comparably to that of other technical career tracks.

Another way money matters is that these wage scales become a self-fulfilling prophecy. If wages are comparable and a clear career path is available from testing to other positions in the company and vice versa, then the only factor a candidate need consider is whether he'll enjoy and do a good job of testing. However, if test positions provide lower wages or no career path, then only people who can't do anything else at the company will accept test positions. This leads to a justification for lower wages to testers along with an even-greater justification for a dead-end career path for testing.

You may have some trouble selling the idea of a parallel pay scale for testers to your managers. This is especially true if, in combination with a lack of a career path, testing has become a pariah organization. It's hard to argue that your testers deserve a raise if half the team is composed of people who, having barely escaped firing, were relegated to a testing backwater. However, if you accept this status quo to avoid conflict, you will only bring on more conflict and difficulty later. If testing is an undesirable swamp in your organization, then take the situation in hand and resolve it. Fight this battle early in your tenure—before even coming on board if possible—and don't let it fester.

Salary surveys and trade magazines tell conflicting stories about pay parity between developers and testers. Of course, many salary surveys are self-selecting, and any article you read depends on current economic conditions, the local job market, the reporter's preconceived notions, and so forth. In some cases, recruiters and candidates report salaries 10% to 15% lower for test staff than for developers. However, some salary surveys for testers show testers no longer earning less than our technical peers, when factors like years of experience and educational background are equal.[3] You can use these salary surveys to build a case for the organization that a peer-level, professional test team is the wave of the future and that your company should be moving toward that future, too.

RETAIN EMPLOYEES WITH SUFFICIENT EDUCATION, EXPERIENCE, AND SKILL

In the previous chapter I discussed some of the tools available to the hiring manager to ensure that we hire the right people. In my own personal toolbox, key among these are the job description and the critical skills spreadsheet. My goal in applying these tools is to attract, hire, and build a test team around an appropriate group of people. While appropriateness certainly has a number of indicators that are difficult to quantify, I often find that measurable indicators like education, experience, and skill help me find good candidates.

In the previous chapter, I also looked at some of the training options available to the professional tester. I'm not prepared to suggest one single set of educational criteria for all testers. I would suggest, though, that you think about what level of education is appropriate within your test team, considering the overall organizational context,

---

3. *Quality Professional* magazine carries these annually. You can also use Web resources like www.salary.com.

each of your tester's long-term career path in the organization, and your specific skills needs.

I prefer to work not just with educated testers but also with experienced ones. Typically, I look for five or more years of experience in my engineers. Technicians I'm willing to hire with no experience, because such inexpensive testing resources allow my test teams to perform a lot of regression testing we might otherwise be unable to afford. However, it takes longer for inexperienced engineers to move up the ranks. Experience is especially important for testers because so much of a tester's job is telling people things they don't want to hear and handling a kaleidoscopically changing situation. While people learn to program in college when they get their computer science degrees, they don't necessarily learn how to cope with unhappy peers and managers.

Finally, in the area of skills, I find the critical skills spreadsheet a useful guide during hiring. You must use it with care, though. Rigid application of this approach can close the door to certain people who might prove to be great testers. For example, why state that every tester must know how to program if most of your team does strictly behavioral testing? Often I've found that very sharp people can pick up skills very rapidly. You may want to adjust your hiring process to allow such quick studies onto your teams. However, someone who is woefully underskilled in many of the critical skills you identify will take longer to become a fully contributing member of the team, and this ramp-up time will entail mentoring or other support from the rest of the team.

ALLOW APPROPRIATE SPECIALIZATION

In some cases, what might appear to be gaps across a large team in various team members' skills are, in fact, evidence of specialization. Our case study test team for Software Cafeteria shows a small team of expert test generalists, with the only differentiation in tasks being automated and manual testing. Also, note Jamal's high expectations for test engineers in terms of the skills required.

In a small team, specialization is dangerous, because it makes each player in some sense irreplaceable, at least in the short term. In terms of skills assessment, one key metric is minimum skill levels, because each member must be competent in many areas. Assuming that no one will get sick, pregnant, or have a death in their family during a project is a risky plan, but that's what we do when we have specialization in small test teams.

For larger teams, more specialization may make sense. On one project I managed, we tested an Internet appliance. We broke testing into two areas, server-side and client-side. The server-side testers focused on the large server farm that provided e-mail, software update, and other services. The client-side testers focused on the actual Internet access devices.

So I brought on two test engineers, one for the server testing, one for the client testing. The server test engineer had UNIX and test automation experience. The client test engineer had a strong background in e-mail, browsers, and Internet technology. I also retained a usability test engineer. Because we needed to simulate an installed user base of 50,000, I brought on two test toolsmiths. These two people ended up reusing a lot of unit test stubs and drivers to create load generators that allowed us to test the servers—and the response of the clients when connected to loaded servers—at the desired load levels. Because we were using a lot of manual test cases, the test engineers wrote scripted, precise test cases that they then assigned to a team of six test technicians for execution. This team, being a reflection of the project, worked very well.

Some test teams have to service multiple projects at once. For example, one of my clients has a single, very large test organization referred to as its Testing Center of Excellence. They recognize that testing is a specialty unto itself. In such large service organizations, the test management team can choose various ways of organization. One way is project-based, where testers are assigned to a single project for the duration. Another is skills-based, where testers move onto and off projects as their particular areas of expertise are required, perhaps with a single permanent lead test engineer or test project manager.[4] Yet another option is to be service-based, organized around the specific services your team provides.[5]

A candidate who is perfect for a skills-based organization might not succeed for a project-based one. Some testers really want to grow in specific technical areas. Only a skills-based test organization will allow that specialization. A perfect candidate for a project-based team might not succeed in a skills-based organization. For example, I once worked with a test engineer who lacked the ability to multitask very well. He found assignment to multiple projects at once disconcerting.

An excellent test team can become a poor one overnight if corporate dictates result in a reorganization from one model to another. I have also seen one mediocre test organization become an excellent one by going to a skills-based model and cultivating ex-

---

4. See Chapter 8 of *Managing the Testing Process, Second Edition,* for more on such test team management issues.

5. For a discussion of service-based test organizations, see Robert Sabourin's "At Your Service," originally published in *Software Testing and Quality Engineering*, Volume 3, Issue 3, and now available on www.stickyminds.com.

pertise and specialization. I believe either model can work if the management team understands specialization and how it affects your team when deciding upon a team building process.

HANDLE CHALLENGES

Even when you have all your hiring process issues worked out, several challenges will arise.

WHAT DO TESTERS NEED TO KNOW—AND WHAT CAN YOU GET?

One of the areas of ongoing debate in the testing world is what skills are critical for the tester. I've broken skills down into four categories: general, technical, application domain, and testing. I believe that the relative importance of each category depends considerably on the particular system under test, including the business and technical context of that system. However, some people have advocated advanced technical knowledge—at the same level as the development team—as a necessity for all testers. Others have expressed skepticism at testing groups composed of people not expert in the application domain. How do we decide what kind and level of skills make for a qualified tester?

There are three aspects to this challenge. First, there is the question of defining competence. What does a tester really need to know to be an effective and efficient tester? The requirements in terms of technical knowledge are often a function of how many structural (white-box) testing, quality assurance (code reviews), and test automation tasks the tester will perform. The application domain expertise needed depends on the complexity, obscurity, and risks related to the business problem the system addresses. A word processor is an obvious application, while oil exploration software is not. Only virtual casualties are incurred when a video game fails, while lives depend on wholly reliable weapons-control systems.

However, I have encountered situations when a tester will be—or could be—doing strictly behavioral (black-box) testing in a non-safety-critical environment, but when I proposed using test experts or test technicians—people with minimal application domain and technical skill—the reaction was negative. One prospective client wouldn't use nonprogrammers as testers for its video games because they wanted the test team to handle both structural and behavioral testing. When I suggested using cheaper test technicians for the behavioral testing and just hiring one or two (expensive) resources with technical and testing skill for structural testing, they declined. At one client, the loan call-center manager was skeptical of the testing done on a loan-processing application because I was using professional testers, not call-center bankers. This skepticism persisted even once testing started and we found serious bugs in the product.

These examples illustrate the second part of this challenge. Because testing is about generating information, credibility of the test team is a key factor to success. So, regardless of *actual* competence to test the product, if the perception of key players in the development effort is that the test team is not competent, the test team will not be credible. Should that happen, the test team stands a good chance of failure and dissolution, even if excellent testing work is being done.

So, once you accept that testers not only need *to be competent*, but also *to be perceived as competent* by key players in the development effort, you will hit the third part of the challenge: Finding testers who are strong in your particular application domain, experienced with the technology you're using to solve the problem, and possessed of strong testing skills and the right attitudes, is difficult indeed. You will have a better chance of doing so if you can hire consultants or contractors, because many people with this triad of capabilities are out in the free job market commanding top dollar for their skills.

However, it's difficult to convince management to fund a test team of expensive consultants. Also, since you want to build an ongoing organization, consultants and contractors might help you bootstrap it, but you shouldn't build in long-term dependence on such resources—unless you can convince them to convert to permanent employment. (The exception is that you can staff your permanent team to handle the day-in, day-out workload that's present all the time, and plan to use contractors and expert consultants to get you over high points in workloads and special skill requirements, especially those associated with overlapping projects, unique testing challenges, rush jobs, and so forth.) Hence, your conundrum: You must field an affordable, competent, credible test team.

Where you should strike the balance is very contextual. You'll need to work this out with your managers and other key players. As you work through the job definitions, keep in close contact with the key players and your managers. Understand the credibility and affordability issues associated with setting the bar lower or higher. Make sure that everyone buys into the trade-offs you have to make. Don't field a perfectly competent team that nonetheless fails for not measuring up to other's (sometimes unrealistic) expectations in terms of skills or return on investment.

WHITE ELEPHANTS

When I was growing up, I sometimes accompanied my mother and grandmother on various antiques-shop trips. Antiques were less glamorous then than now and often went under the name of "second-hand items," "hand-me-downs," or even "white elephants." The last phrase always mystified me—my mother explained it as being derived from the copious stock of plaster elephant statuettes one could always find in such shops—but it certainly proved memorable.

Sometimes, test managers are expected to stock their team at the white elephant store. One test team I managed was staffed almost exclusively with people who had failed to make the cut as programmers when I took it over. One of these individuals turned out to be an excellent test engineer. The other two people, though, showed no more skill at testing than they had at programming. I was given the option of firing them, but no guarantee I'd be able to backfill the positions.

Being older and wiser now, I have learned to resist the rush of the white elephant.[6] One development manager, faced with a person who had decided to quit his position as a release engineer, demanded that I accept that person into the test team. I refused. One business analyst brought in an unemployed relative for an interview because he heard that the test team was hiring. It was clear from this person's resume that he was unqualified. I made sure to ask pointed questions in the group interview—in front of the business analyst's peers—that gently but clearly highlighted this person's lack of skills and experience in the critical areas we needed filled.

Lest you think me paranoid or overly judgmental, let me point out that I'm not alone in these concerns. Boris Beizer wrote, "I've had my share and fill of the 'wretched, the poor,' the incompetent, the neurotics, the psychotics, [and] the alcoholics."[7] Cem Kaner, Jack Falk, and Hung Nguyen agree that test managers have to resist efforts to jam the test team full of failed programmers.[8] People should join the test team because they want to be there and because their skills, knowledge, and personality make them a good fit. You're better off understaffed by one person than having one bad apple on your test team.

---

6. Thanks to one of the reviewers, Rob Sabourin, and the Web site he referred me to, phrases.shu.ac.uk/meanings/410050.html, I now know the exact meaning and origin of the term "white elephant."
7. Boris Beizer, *Software System Testing and Quality Assurance*, page 317.
8. Cem Kaner, Jack Falk, and Hung Nguyen, *Testing Computer Software*, page 359.

That said, a failed programmer might have failed for any number of reasons, poor management not the least among them. If a person has the right skills, knowledge, and attitudes to be competent and be perceived as competent on my test team, then I wouldn't let the fact that he was the ugly duckling of another group keep me from bringing a swan on board my team.

USING CONTRACTORS AND CONSULTANTS

In some cases, the right person for the job isn't an employee, but rather a contractor or consultant. For transient needs—temporary staffing to meet peak project work-loads—using contractors makes a lot of sense. I do a fair number of bootstrapping projects where I come in with a team of contractors, get the test operation underway, and then manage a transition to a permanent team, often helping with recruiting and sometimes having part of the temporary staff convert to permanent employment with the client. This works out well for me and for my clients. You may want to have a con-sultant provide training services or occasional advice on thorny problems.

Before hiring a consultant or contractor, define what you're hiring that person to do. I get phone calls and e-mails frequently from people that translate into "I have some amount of vague organizational pain associated with testing and I want you to make it go away." In some cases, further digging reveals to me that the underlying prob-lems aren't testing problems, but management problems that show up during the test execution phase.

If you can specifically define what you want a consultant or contractor to do, both of you can enjoy a successful engagement; otherwise, beware. For example, suppose you say to a sales representative at a temporary staffing company, "My testing takes too long; I need some automation." Immediately your fax machine will explode with resumes from everyone who has ever seen, touched, or been in the same room as a test automation tool. If you hire someone from that pool of candidates just based on the number of years they've spent doing automation or because they know the tool you are considering buying, a negative outcome is likely.

Instead, suppose you call your friendly neighborhood recruiter and say, "Listen up. We have decided that we are having too many problems with regression in our main-tenance releases. Rather than hiring a dozen more manual testers, we'd like to invest in a decent automated suite of tests. So, I need someone to come in and work with us to select a tool. That person should have experience with multiple tools and no partic-ular ax to grind. Once the tool is selected and deployed, we want the person to help us develop that suite of tests and then train one of our senior test engineers in how to use the tests and the tool. After that, the contractor should go away or phase out over a period of a few weeks. One of the measures of the contractor's success is how well this person manages to make himself or herself obsolete without disrupting the test operation on his or her exit. We plan approximately six months for this effort, but we're open to being educated about the real size of the engagement by the candidate. Finally, every candidate you send for an interview should be able to provide us with three references from companies for which they've done projects like this before. Are our requirements clear, or do you have questions?"

When evaluating the qualifications of consultants and contractors, you'll need to answer a number of questions. You're quite often looking for a level of skills and experience well beyond your own. How do you know when you're listening to an expert, as opposed to a well-honed sales pitch? How do you know that the contractor or consultant who has achieved certification in some area of technology, the application domain, or testing can and has applied that knowledge to a real-world project? How do you know that the contractor touted by that recruiter on the other end of the phone as the ideal candidate won't turn into a headache a few days after the recruiter has cashed his commission check? Do you understand the problem you want this person to solve well enough to know who can solve it—and to recognize that they have solved it in the past?

Qualified consultants and contractors have a solid trail of enthusiastic references that speak positively of the work they did. Engagements do tend to differ in the specifics, but I focus on the skills, attitudes, and education that I've identified as important in my team. How did the contractor apply test automation skills to solve a real development or maintenance effort problem? How did she interact with others in the test team—and outside the test team? What kinds of problems did she have at the engagement? How did the various educational qualifications she has help her do a good job?

In addition to a reference, perhaps the candidate secured the right to use one or more items from a previous client as an example of his work. A wise consultant or contractor will have clauses in his contract that allow him, after removing identifying information, to use work samples.

Qualifications are also demonstrated by a trail of publications or speaking engagements related to testing. Known experts review most journals, magazines, and books published on the topics of testing and test management. While controversial and sometimes disputed articles are published, for the most part someone profoundly ignorant of testing, with no insights into the processes and pitfalls, will find it impossible to get published. Electronic forums like Internet newsgroups and discussion lists may also demonstrate testing knowledge, though the lack of peer review means that the guru and the blabbermouth may consume the same amount of bandwidth in some crowds.

If possible under local laws, another way to ensure a good fit between a consultant or contractor and your specific needs is a trial period or cancellation clause in the contract. I'm not recommending anything unfair, though some people do try to cancel contracts with consulting firms on flimsy grounds. Instead, I'm talking about putting measurable milestones in place for evaluation of the consultant's or contractor's work. These milestones should provide for the assessment of both progress and quality. Should matters not be working out, the contract should provide for a fair, no-fault, but prompt way for you, as the client, to end the contract and dismiss the consultant.

The policy of my own firm, as a consultancy, is that we only want to make money from satisfied clients—because of the kind of reference and word of mouth we get from happy customers—so we include such cancellation policies in our contracts. Another benefit of such clauses is that by firming up the specific work to be done and the schedule on which it's to occur, they prevent you from overreacting to a minor incident that does not affect the reason you retained the consultant or contractor in the first place. If termination for cause is triggered by specific concerns, spelled out in a contract, that should help keep people focused on what the contractor or consultant is there to do.

Finally, let me mention that the entire complex and sometimes painful process of hiring consultants or contractors can be simplified considerably by building, and then tapping, a network of relationships in the software testing community. If you read a posting on a newsgroup or an article in a testing magazine that strikes a chord with you, you might find that the author is a consultant specializing in just the area you need help with. Talk to peers you've met at training seminars and conferences to see who they've used. Check with other consultants to find out about a company's or an individual's professional reputation.

IMPLEMENT IMPROVEMENTS

As I mentioned at the beginning of the previous chapter when I first started discussing the team building process, this process is very contextual and subject to many external influences. Therefore, the specifics of improving this process will depend a lot on what you're doing now and what's possible within your organization. Neverthe-less, let me throw out a few ideas that I have found apply broadly.

1. Ensure compatibility between the testing context and the test team. Another value to the context setting process in Chapter 1 is that it allows you to under-stand whether you are building the right team. How can you best serve the or-ganization's needs?

2. Introduce skills assessment and management. If you know how to serve the or-ganization, then you can start to think through the critical skills required to carry out these tasks. You can build a skills assessment worksheet. If you have an existing test team, make sure to include them in the process of developing the critical skills list.

3. Develop a career path for employee testers. Define the means for career growth within your test team. Work with the human resources manager or your peer managers to create a true career path that runs upward from the entry position through other positions in the company.

4. When interviewing new candidates, use the skills assessment, the career path, behavioral interview questions, and audition interviews to select people with the right skills, experience, goals, attitudes, and abilities.

Hiring and growing a test team is hard work, but with great rewards. Being part of a solid team—whether as a manager or as an individual contributor—is one of the most fulfilling professional experiences possible. These last two chapters have focused on a management perspective for this process, since the lion's share of the responsibility falls to managers. However, individual contributors can and should participate, espe-cially in growing their skills and adjusting their attitudes and expectations.

With the right team in place, we can move on to the next preparatory step. It's time to build a test system. With the right team and the right test system, we will be ready to perform our tests.

10

ARCHIMEDES' BATHTUB: DESIGN AND IMPLEMENT TEST SYSTEMS

Legend has it that Greek King Hieron commanded the inventor and mathematician Archimedes to come up with a method for determining the quality of his crown. For the king, quality meant the presence of a single satisfying attribute, pure gold, and the absence of many dissatisfying attributes, baser metals. Archimedes was at a loss until one day, as he settled into his bathtub, he observed water spilling over the rim. Discovering the principle of buoyancy—which would allow him to determine the quality of the crown—he exclaimed, "Eureka!" As testers, perhaps we should step into Archimedes' bathtub, too, since we must design and implement an effective and efficient test system that will allow us to assess the quality of the systems we test.

Our objective of assessing quality implies a couple of goals for test system design and implementation efforts. First, we should aim our test system at those risks to system quality judged most critical, based on relative importance, as discussed in Chapter 2. Second, if we want to assess quality, we should test in a way that allows our testers to gain an accurate understanding of what the customers' and users' experiences of quality will be. Therefore, we must provide our testers with a high-fidelity test system that truthfully reproduces the customers' and users' experiences of quality.

My own mental model of a test system consists of three major elements, as shown in Figure 10-1. This figure might imply a formal, imposing system to you, but it need not be. Test system design and implementation sometimes begins years before the system under test is delivered to the test team, but sometimes it begins the same day. Sometimes the test system exists in a large test lab, on gigabytes of disk space, in thick three-ring binders, but sometimes it exists entirely in the testers' heads.

Test Environment

The hardware, software, infrastructure, materiel, and locations required to perform the test effort.

Testware

The test cases, test data, test scripts, test tools, test logs, test reports, and associated user's guides or documentation.

Test Execution Process

The methods by which the testers and other key test participants will use the testware in the test environment (see Chapter 13).

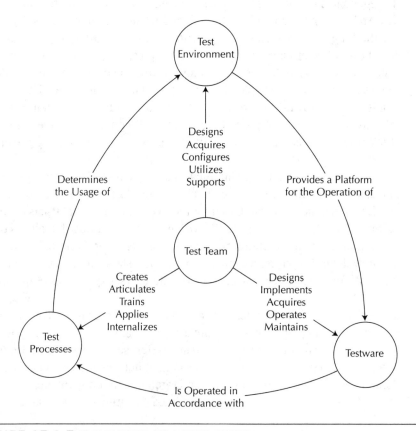

FIGURE 10-1 THE ELEMENTS OF A TEST SYSTEM

Test design occurs whenever and however testers spend time deciding how to test specific areas of the system and how to look for specific problems. Effective and efficient test design is asking the right questions about what *could be* broken.

Test implementation occurs whenever and however testers spend time implementing those design decisions. Effective and efficient test implementation is building a test system that answers the right questions about what *is* broken—and what *is not* broken—in the order of the priority of the risks to system quality and in a way that relates to the customers' and users' experiences of quality.

That combined design and implementation effort may result in anything from notes, sketches, and models on a whiteboard to a bookshelf of bound test cases and scripts, along with disks and tapes full of specially devised data. Effective and efficient test system design and implementation can take as little as a few minutes to as long as months. The kinds of context considerations discussed in Chapter 1 determine the kind of formality, permanence, and structure required.

A TEST SYSTEM DESIGN AND IMPLEMENTATION PROCESS

The specific details of the test system design and implementation process vary considerably based on the test strategies employed, the context of the test team, and the technologies underpinning the test system and the system under test. Process 7 is a generic process that you can tailor for your specific needs.

EMMA CREATES STRESS ON THE JOB

During the planning phase, Jamal had assigned Emma Moorhouse to update the performance, load, capacity, and volume tests for the new Sumatra features. On November 11—one day ahead of schedule—Emma began working on this activity.

The most critical quality risks involved the system's behavior at storage and usage limits, which would fit into the Performance, Load, Capacity, and Volume test suite. (Figure 10-2 shows the associated quality risks.) The system needed to support up to 255 users logged in at once and 32,767 user accounts total, managing documents up to 32MB in size. Once the online storage space filled, files needed to migrate to near-online, then offline storage. Files that had migrated to near-online and offline storage needed to return to online storage when accessed, replacing older files that then

Step #	Step	Done?
1.	Create or update an outline of test suites that can cover the risks to system quality for which testing has been identified as a recommended action.	☐
2.	Select an appropriate test suite and discover a new set of interesting test conditions within the most critical still-uncovered risk area; e.g., conditions that might provoke a particular set of failures or model actual usage. Define at a high level how to assess the correctness of results under those test conditions.	☐
3.	Select the appropriate test techniques, given the test conditions to be explored, the verification of expected results desired, the time and budget available, the testability features of the system under test, the test environment, and the skills present in the test team.	☐
4.	Design, develop, acquire, enhance, configure, and document the testware, the test environment, and the test execution process to produce those conditions and verify those behaviors using the selected test techniques. Augment theoretical test techniques with empirical techniques, especially customer/user data, field failure reports (previous and competitors' releases, similar products, and similar sets of risks to system quality), sales and marketing predictions on future usage, and other customer-centered inputs.	☐
5.	Should any testware, test environment, or test execution process elements prove unattainable during step 4 because of resource, schedule, or other limitations, repeat step 4 iteratively to accommodate any such limitations.	☐
6.	Test the test system, using static techniques (e.g., reviews) and dynamic techniques (e.g., running the test).	☐
7.	Check the testware, test execution process description, test environment configuration information, test system test documentation (from step 6), and any other documentation or files produced into the project library or configuration management system. Link the version of the test system to the version of the system under test. Place the item(s) under change control.	☐
8.	Update the quality risks list based on what was learned in developing this latest set of tests. Evaluate coverage of the quality risks with the new test system. Identify remaining uncovered quality risks for which testing action is recommended.	☐

PROCESS 7 A TEST SYSTEM DESIGN AND IMPLEMENTATION PROCESS (CONTINUED ON NEXT PAGE)

Step #	Step	Done?
9.	Repeat steps 2 through 8 until all quality risks are covered to the extent testing action was recommended. Ensure that the quality risk documentation in the project repository is updated. If schedule or budget restrictions curtail development without all critical quality risks covered, produce a report of uncovered quality risks and escalate that report to management.	☐
10.	If time and resources allow, iterate steps 2 through 8 using structural analysis (e.g., McCabe complexity or code coverage) to identify areas needing further testing.	☐

PROCESS 7 CONTINUED

Test Condition

A system state, output, result, or circumstance created by executing a test case, especially one that is interesting from the perspective of assessing system quality.

Test Case

A sequence of steps consisting of actions to be performed on the system under test. (These steps are sometimes called the *test procedure* or *test script*.) These actions are often associated with some set of data (preloaded or input during the test). The combination of actions taken and data provided to the system under test leads to the test condition. This condition tends to produce results that the test can compare with the expected results; i.e., assess quality under the given test condition. The actions can be performed serially, in parallel, or in some other combination of consecution.

Test Suite

A collection of logically related test cases, possibly with reuse of cases across multiple suites.

migrated to slower storage to free up the necessary disk space. Not only must the migrations work, but they needed to happen with maximum transparency to the users and quick escalation of blocking situations to the document librarian (e.g., the CD-ROM on which the data file resides is not loaded in the jukebox), with 99% system uptime, and with no loss of data.

Failure Mode and Effect Analysis (Quality Risk Analysis) Form

System Name: SpeedyWriter (with Document Management System add-on)		Model/Product SpeedyWriter Release 3.1 (w/DMS)
Product Manager: Kate Hernandez		Target Release Date: 1Q2003
Project Manager: Jenny Kaufman		Prepared By: Jamal Brown
Other Stakeholders: Bobbi McDaniels (Engr), Max del Oro (Mkt), Cosimo Negraev (Support)		FMEA Date: September 11, 2002
Test Manager: Jamal Brown		FMEA Revision Date: September 20, 2002

Risk ID Number	Quality Risk Category	Failure Mode/Quality Risk/Effect	Severity	Priority	Likelihood	Risk Priority Number	Recommended Action	Who/Which Phase (Unit, Component, Integration, System)?
2.000	Load, Capacity, and Volume	Failures in scaling of system to expected peak concurrent usage levels						
2.001		System fails at or before 25 concurrent users.	1	1	3	3	Extensive testing.	Test/S
2.002		System fails at or before 255 concurrent users.	1	3	2	6	Extensive testing.	Test/S
2.003		System disallows 255 or fewer user accounts.	1	1	3	3	Extensive testing.	Test/S
2.004		System disallows 32,767 or fewer user accounts.	1	3	3	9	Balanced testing.	Test/S
2.005		System fails on documents larger than 100KB.	1	1	1	1	Extensive testing.	Test/S
2.006		System fails on documents larger than 1MB.	1	2	2	4	Extensive testing.	Test/S
2.007		System fails on documents larger than 32MB.	1	3	3	9	Balanced testing.	Test/S
2.008		Insufficient offline migration is too-frequent.	4	4	4	64	Report observed bugs.	N/A
2.009		Excessive offline migration results in "thrashing".	4	4	4	64	Report observed bugs.	N/A
2.010		Migration to offline fails.	1	2	4	8	Balanced testing.	Test/S
2.011		Migration to online fails.	1	2	4	8	Balanced testing.	Test/S
2.012		Librarian not notified when media load is needed.	4	3	4	48	Opportunity testing	N/A
2.013		User not allowed to wait for media load.	2	3	5	30	Opportunity testing	N/A
2.014		User wait for media load timing/escalation count wrong.	5	4	5	100	Report observed bugs.	N/A
Quality Risk Category Priority						1		

FIGURE 10-2 LOAD, CAPACITY, AND VOLUME RISKS FROM THE SUMATRA QUALITY RISK ANALYSIS

Step #	Step	Done?
1.	Create or update an outline of test suites that can cover the risks to system quality for which testing has been identified as a recommended action.	✔
2.	Select an appropriate test suite and discover a new set of interesting test conditions within the most critical still-uncovered risk area; e.g., conditions that might provoke a particular set of failures or model actual usage. Define at a high level how to assess the correctness of results under those test conditions.	✔

Emma studied the requirements documents, stared at the ceiling a bit, walked around the office, and cracked open a couple of her testing books and conference proceedings for some ideas. Finally, she decided on three test techniques.

First, as a general framework for her testing, she would use Hans Buwalda's *soap opera* approach, constructing an extreme but supported scenario. Suppose, she thought, I had a huge collection of attorneys defending a group of large multinational corporations against a substantial class of plaintiffs. Specifically, let's assume a collection of law firms with 32,767 attorneys working on an extensive class-action lawsuit filed against their collective clients, which are spread all around the world. Seven days a week, 24 hours a day, 255 of these attorneys will be logged on to the system, all creating, referencing, and archiving documents in the document manager. Documents vary in size from zero to 32MB, so let's make the overly conservative assumption that the average document size is 16MB, with random sizes around that average and at least one at each extreme. This is not a realistic situation, perhaps, but it is within the requirements, and it forces the system to operate at the limits of its capability continuously.[1]

Second, during development of the functional test cases, Lin-Tsu had discussed with Emma how the edit engine interacted with the document management system by causing it to move through various states. For example, when SpeedyWriter starts, no file is open, but then the user can request that a file be retrieved through the document management system, which causes the document management system to present a list of known documents. From that point, the user can select a document or check a new document into the system. Each action takes the system into a different state.

---

1. See Hans Buwalda's paper "Soap Opera Testing," presented at STAR East 2000, published in the *Proceedings of the STAR East 2000 Conference* and now available at www.stickyminds.com.

Once the user is editing a document managed by the document management system, periodic saves can cause the available online space to be exhausted, resulting in migration of currently online and near-online documents to the next level of the storage hierarchy. Other actions result in other states being entered. Some of these states indicate successful storage or retrieval of a document from the system, others indicate a need to wait for an external action by a librarian, while still others indicate an error. Lin-Tsu had applied a control-flow-based testing technique, as described by Boris Beizer, to tackle the functional testing. Emma expected this technique to prove useful during load testing as well.[2]

Finally, Emma realized that she wouldn't have 255 testers available to her, especially not 24 hours a day, seven days a week. However, she could use their load testing tool to write some simple automated scripts that could cycle the system through various states and keep the system operating constantly. These scripts would act much like the *dumb monkeys* described by Noel Nyman. These scripts can only detect that the system is in an unexpected state, not check how the system came to be in that state. However, she would augment this automated testing with complete testing of the states and the various transitions that can occur between them by running manual functional tests during the load tests.[3]

Step #	Step	Done?
3.	Select the appropriate test techniques, given the test conditions to be explored, the verification of expected results desired, the time and budget available, the testability features of the system under test, the test environment, and the skills present in the test team.	☑

Having selected appropriate techniques, Emma began creating the supporting testware. For the soap opera scenario, she created all 32,767 accounts on the Web server, using a simple program to generate the account information in ASCII format and then the database file loading utilities to get those accounts into the account table on the database server. She used a TCL script to create the files to be edited. She planned to use these same scripts again to edit the files. These scripts created files that followed a simple, predictable pattern.

---

2. See Beizer's *Black-Box Testing* and Lee Copeland's *A Practitioner's Guide to Software Test Design* for this and other useful techniques.
3. See Noel Nyman's article "Using Monkey Test Tools," originally published in *Software Testing and Quality Engineering* magazine, Volume 2, Issue 1 (Jan/Feb 2000), and now available on www.stickyminds.com.

Lin-Tsu had developed a state graph that showed the states and how the system went from one to another. Emma reused that graph. For the dumb monkeys, she created simple scripts with her automated tools. These repeated basic actions of creating, loading, editing, saving, and reading documents to and from the document management system. The scripts knew an error state when they got into one, but otherwise paid no attention to how their actions affected the system under test. Because Emma's data files followed a pattern, she could create a simple script that checked the correctness of the files, and using the document management system's own directory export facility, she could check that there were no orphaned (unlisted) or missing (listed but not present) files in the document management system.

Step #	Step	Done?
4.	Design, develop, acquire, enhance, configure, and document the testware, the test environment, and the test execution process to produce those conditions and verify those behaviors using the selected test techniques. Augment theoretical test techniques with empirical techniques, especially customer/user data, field failure reports (previous and competitors' releases, similar products, and similar sets of risks to system quality), sales and marketing predictions on future usage, and other customer-centered inputs.	✔

As Emma created these objects, she realized two things were missing from the test environment that she needed. For one, she didn't have sufficient virtual-user licenses for her load testing tool. For another, she had only two limited hierarchical storage management systems. She wanted to test with some of the bigger and more feature-rich systems available.

She set out to discuss this with Jamal, who she found in the test lab. Jamal was in the midst of a fairly celebratory conversation with a test technician who was telling him about a bug she'd found.

"Great bug, Hemamalini. Keep finding those nasty ones," Jamal said with a smile. He then turned to Emma and asked, "I get the sense there's something I can do for you?"

"In looking at the test environment in terms of performance testing, I'm concerned that—er, well, wondering about—our hierarchical storage management situation." Jamal's smile faded as the topic came up. Emma hurriedly continued, "I mean, I remember that whole debate back in September about HSM servers, but I don't think we're going to be able to load the system in a few interesting ways with these base-model servers we have."

"Tell me more, specifically, about what you can't test."

Encouraged by this opening, Emma launched into an extensive description of some particular capacity and volume tests that would require more CPU, network, and disk drive performance and horsepower than the two servers in the lab. She described two specific types of performance problems she'd read about that they'd definitely not be able to catch.

"So," Jamal asked, "what are you suggesting? Purchasing one more server? Two more?"

"I was thinking about this one on top"—she handed Jamal a few printed Web pages— "and the one at the bottom there."

Jamal read the papers quickly. He whistled. "Healthy price tags."

"Yes," Emma admitted, "but bugs in this area could call the whole viability of the product into question."

Jamal thought for a minute. "Okay," Jamal said slowly, "I hear you. I'm a risk-averse kind of guy, you know, so I don't want to blow this off, even though we did address this issue before." He paused. "Here's what we'll do. Let's you and I have a meeting with Kate, Jenny, and whoever on the development team is in charge of this area. You lay out your case on the technical risks, we'll hear the system architect perspective, and then we can reevaluate the business issues."

The meeting happened later that afternoon. Both Kate and Jenny at first were a bit put out by the whole matter rising up again, vampire-like, at this point in the project. However, Emma and Bob Marshall, the lead programmer in the area of storage management, were soon discussing serious technical points, and the managers were lost in the details. The consensus emerged between the two, though, that while there were some risks, those risks were limited to situations near the maximum file size and with particular RAID disk array configurations.

"So," Kate said, "what about this? If I can find a potential customer or two with the right files and configurations who's willing to beta test Sumatra for us, would that suffice?"

Bob said, "Well, I think it would, yeah."

Emma hesitated, then retorted, "Functionally, maybe, but almost certainly not in terms of performance and load. That kind of testing requires special skill. Haphazard beta testing won't do for such tests."

This set off a sidebar discussion between Bob, Jenny, and Kate. Jamal, sitting next to Emma, scribbled quickly on his note pad, "You travel to sites—do test there?" She shrugged her shoulders in resigned assent and wrote underneath it, "OK—but less efficient and slower."

Jamal then broke in with, "You know, Kate, we might be able to make that idea work. Do you think you can convince our would-be customers to let Emma visit their sites and do the performance tests there?"

Kate looked out the window for a moment and then spoke. "Yeah, I guess we could do that. The travel is sure to be cheaper than the hardware." She looked directly at Emma and said, friendly and smiling but obviously serious, "I'm sure Emma's not going to scare the customers by telling them stories about Sumatra bugs, right?"

"No, no, I won't do that," Emma responded quickly, shaking her head.

"It's settled, then," Kate said. "There are two actions items. Jenny and I will work together to identify one or more appropriate beta test sites for this particular test. We'll get names and contact information to you, Jamal, by the end of this week. Jamal, you and Emma need to figure out how to run those tests at the customers' sites. Since we'll be using automated tools, I take it there are some logistics issues?"

"Yes, probably," Jamal replied. "We should probably also plan on meeting again in a couple of weeks to discuss when we think the system will be ready for these tests. I'd suggest that we finish the in-house performance tests first. Those are currently scheduled for"—he rustled around in his project notes for a minute—"when we receive increment 3 in December, around the 15th or so. That would give us a target somewhere in early January, but it'd be worth revisiting the issue on December 2 to see where we stand."

Step #	Step	Done?
4.	Design, develop, acquire, enhance, configure, and document the testware, the test environment, and the test execution process to produce those conditions and verify those behaviors using the selected test techniques. Augment theoretical test techniques with empirical techniques, especially customer/user data, field failure reports (previous and competitors' releases, similar products, and similar sets of risks to system quality), sales and marketing predictions on future usage, and other customer-centered inputs.	☑

Step #	Step	Done?
5.	Should any testware, test environment, or test execution process elements prove unattainable during step 4 because of resource, schedule, or other limitations, repeat step 4 iteratively to accommodate any such limitations.	✔

Since that was acceptable to all involved, Jamal made three notes for himself. One was to schedule the follow-up meeting. The next was to update the project work-break-down-structure and schedule to include two weeks of off-site work—and thus on-site unavailability—for Emma. He suspected this would reduce some of the testing that could be done while she was off-site. However, he hoped that, by then, Dinesh would be able to ensure that the automated testing continued, albeit at a reduced pace. The final note was to make sure that Emma had cross-trained Dinesh in the execution of the automated tests by the time she went off-site in January. Emma headed back to her office to complete the design and implementation of these tests, with the added challenge of needing to make them portable.

On November 18, with the tests written, Emma started to verify the scripts and data. First, she held a peer review of the testware with Lin-Tsu and Dinesh. This meeting, which lasted a couple of hours, found a few defects, especially in the scripts. Emma spent the afternoon following the meeting correcting those. Since the number of defects found in the review was small, she decided not to schedule another peer review of her corrections. This was one of the types of judgment calls that Jamal encouraged his own team to make within the various processes.

At this point, increment 2, which lacked some of the key features of the intended release, was installed in the test environment. Writing some test stubs, Emma found she could run her scripts and find any major problems that might exist. The trick was doing so without interfering with ongoing testing. She worked out a period overnight when the tests could run and set them up to initiate at that time. This revealed further bugs in the tests, so Emma spent the rest of the week fixing and retesting the scripts until she felt they were ready for use in increment 3. Finally, Emma checked all the associated files—test data, test cases, tools, and so forth—into the project repository. Figure 10-3 shows the test case development status for two test suites as of Wednesday, November 20, as Emma was winding down her work.

Step #	Step	Done?
6.	Test the test system, using static techniques (e.g., reviews) and dynamic techniques (e.g., running the test).	✔

Step #	Step	Done?
7.	Check the testware, test execution process description, test environment configuration information, test system test documentation (from step 6), and any other documentation or files produced into the project library or configuration management system. Link the version of the test system to the version of the system under test. Place the document(s) under change control.	☑

Stub

A (usually small) piece of software that fills in for or replaces a component of the system under test or the test system to approximate some of the functions being "stubbed out" to the extent necessary to perform certain desired tests.

In the course of developing the tests, Emma also discovered a previously unconsidered requirement, setting a limit to the number of files the document management system could display in a list. This was escalated to the change control board (see Chapter 16), which collectively decided that 1,024 would be a reasonable number that worked within the technical design and would satisfy the users.

	A	B	C	D	E	F	G	H	I	J	K
1			Sumatra Integration and System Test Case Tracking Spreadsheet								
4	Assigned	Test			Plan	Act	Plan	Actual	Exec	Exec	
5	To	ID	Test Suite/Case	Status	Ready	Ready	Effort	Effort	Effort	Duration	Comment
7		1.000	*Functionality*								
8	EM	1.001	File	Ready	9/23	9/20	8.0	8.5	2.0	4.0	
9	EM	1.002	Edit	Ready	9/23	9/20	8.0	9.0	0.5	4.0	
10	EM	1.003	Font	Ready	9/23	9/20	8.0	8.5	0.5	4.0	
11	EM	1.004	Tables	Ready	9/23	9/24	8.0	8.5	3.0	4.0	
12	EM	1.005	Printing	Ready	9/23	9/22	8.0	7.5	2.0	4.0	
13	LTW	1.006	Managed Files	Ready	10/2	10/3	6.0	6.5	2.5	2.5	
14	LTW	1.007	Non-Managed Files	Ready	10/2	9/30	6.0	6.0	4.0	4.0	
15	LTW	1.008	DMS Check-In New	Ready	10/2	10/3	6.0	5.0	2.5	2.5	
16	LTW	1.009	DMS Check-In Existing	Ready	10/2	10/3	6.0	7.5	3.0	3.0	
17	LTW	1.010	DMS Check-Out	Ready	10/2	9/29	6.0	5.5	3.5	3.5	
18	LTW	1.011	DMS Load/Migrate Online	Ready	10/2	10/1	6.0	5.5	3.5	3.5	
19	LTW	1.012	DMS Load/Migrate NOL	Ready	10/2	10/3	6.0	5.5	3.0	3.0	
20	LTW	1.013	DMS Load/Migrate Offline	Ready	10/2	10/5	6.0	7.5	3.5	3.5	
21	LTW	1.014	DMS File Information	Ready	10/2	10/6	6.0	4.5	2.5	2.5	
22			Suite Summary		10/2	10/6	94.0	95.5	36.0	48.0	
24		2.000	*Performance, Load, Capacity, and Volume*								
25	EM	2.001	Solaris Server	Ready	11/25	11/18	16.0	15.5	2.0	8.0	
26	EM	2.002	NT Server	Verify	11/25		16.0		1.5	8.0	
27	EM	2.003	Linux Server	Ready	11/25	11/17	16.0	9.5	1.5	8.0	
28	EM	2.004	AIX Server	Verify	11/25		16.0		1.0	8.0	
29	EM	2.005	Network	Ready	11/25	11/20	16.0	16.5	1.0	8.0	
30			Suite Summary		11/25	11/20	80.0	41.5	7.0	40.0	

FIGURE 10-3 AN EXCERPT FROM THE TEST DEVELOPMENT STATUS

Emma, upon hearing of this decision, checked the FMEA chart out of the document repository and added two risks associated with this limit. The first had to do with failure at normal-sized directory listings, like 100 files; the second with failure at the extreme boundary, 1,024 files.

Step #	Step	Done?
8.	Update the quality risks list based on what was learned in developing this latest set of tests. Evaluate coverage of the quality risks with the new test system. Identify remaining uncovered quality risks for which testing action is recommended.	✔

THREE CRUCIAL CONSIDERATIONS

In the next chapter, we'll look more closely at each area of the test design and implementation process. However, for the remainder of this chapter, let's look at three important design considerations. These considerations are the method of determining the correctness of test results, the kind of documentation required for a test system, and ways to deal with the combinatorial explosions that can occur in the number of possible test conditions. Senior test engineers, test system architects, and test managers should think carefully about each of these considerations before test design and implementation begins. Consistency in these areas is important for a high-quality test system in the long run, along with achieving effective and efficient testing for each test project.

TEST ORACLES

A test oracle is a system, method, or technique for predicting the correct behavior of the system under test under specific conditions. The challenge of defining a good test oracle is best illustrated through an example. Suppose you wanted to test a function that returns the sine of its argument, given in radians. You could hearken back to your old high school trigonometry course, remembering some of the notable values for sine functions, shown here.

$$\sin 0 = 0$$

$$\sin \frac{\Pi}{6} = \frac{1}{2}$$

$$\sin \frac{\Pi}{4} = \frac{\sqrt{2}}{2}$$

$$\sin \frac{\Pi}{2} = 1$$

> **Test Oracle**
>
> A system, method, or technique for predicting or assessing the correctness of behavior of the system under test under specific conditions.

From there, you can exploit the fact that for angles from $\Pi/2$ to Π radians, the sine function is a mirror image around a vertical axis at $x = \Pi/2$, while for angles from Π to 2Π radians, the sine function is a mirror image around the $y = 0$ axis. This gives you 13 known values on the curve, allowing you to check for gross errors. To be more precise, you'd need to approximate the sine function. (For example, a Taylor series offers ever more precise—and complex—ways to approximate a function through increasing the number of terms.) However, the more terms we add, the more complex—and therefore error-prone—the oracle itself.

A test oracle capable of predicting all the correct behaviors of the system under test could be as complex and hard to build as the system under test. (In some avionics systems, multiple versions of the software are written and results are compared to determine which of the multiple responses is correct.)

To simplify, we can restrict our oracles by ignoring certain inputs, outputs, or behaviors. In the example, I started out by ignoring all but gross errors and then applied a high-order Taylor series approximation to the problem, ignoring errors of minor precision. But what if precise correctness of the sine function is critical to the proper targeting of an intercontinental ballistic missile—or the anti-ICBM defense system that must calculate an intercepting course to knock down such a target traveling at hypersonic speeds?

If you have a competitive system, a legacy system, or any other system that can mimic some or all of the behaviors of the system under test, then you have an oracle. For example, I once worked on a testing project for a home equity loan processing system where the old client-server system provided the oracle for our new browser- and intranet-based system; each loan application was submitted to both systems, and the products offered were compared for approval, interest rate, maximum amount of loan, monthly payment, and term. Precision and trustworthiness can be issues with such an approach, though. If the monthly payment is off by a cent, will the bank's customers care? And who says the legacy system is correct? Perhaps a discrepancy between the system under test and the expected result indicates a bug in the oracle?

In some cases, you can bypass precise prediction and trust your testers. For example, in our SpeedyWriter case study, we can—and probably should—leave certain aspects

> **Reference System**
>
> A special type of *test oracle* where a system already in existence mimics or models some or all of the desired behaviors of the system under test.

of correctness to the tester's discretion in the area of *reasonable user expectations*. If a certain error message is supposed to pop up when the user tries to overwrite a read-only file, the tester can probably figure out that the entire pop-up message window should be on the screen and should have the focus. Further, you might trust the tester to decide whether the error message is correct.

While this kind of reasonableness oracle often applies to end-user software, the extent to which the tester must have application domain expertise to make such predictions varies. Most good exploratory testing techniques rely to some extent on tester-as-oracle approaches, though my experience with exploratory testing also includes using reference systems as oracles.

Even an accurate oracle may not tell you everything you need to know. In the sine wave example, my Taylor series calculation can tell me the returned value of my sine function, but it tells me nothing about how long that sine function can take. In the case of a missile defense system or in weather prediction systems, the speed of calculation is just as important as precision, because a result that arrives after the incoming missile or the tornado does the users no good!

The concept of an oracle comes from Greek history and mythology. Oracles foretold the future, often based on domesticated animal bones and entrails. While, to my knowledge, no sheep has yet been harmed in the design, implementation, and execution of test cases, that's only because we're not quite desperate enough to try such solutions in the area of test design. For systems where precise oracles are necessary, considerable effort may be required to create them.[4]

APPROPRIATE DOCUMENTATION

Some people fill whole shelves with binder after binder of test documentation. Some people write down almost nothing. Both kinds of testers have succeeded and both have failed. Between these two extremes lies a whole spectrum of documentation options,

---

4. For more on test oracles, see Doug Hoffman's paper "Using Oracles in Test Automation," at www.softwarequalitymethods.com.

with satisfied and dissatisfied practitioners. What are the considerations that drive the amount of documentation we should produce?

When we document the test system, we are typically trying to be precise about our testing. Test case precision exists on a spectrum from exploratory to scripted. Scripted test cases precisely specify the actions, data, and expected results, with little or no ambiguity. A precisely documented test system captures the configuration of the test environment precisely, too, with little or no ambiguity.

Ambiguity might seem at first blush to be a bad property in testware. It certainly is a bad property for a requirement or a quality risk definition. Unambiguous testware supports repeatable tests, important for regression testing. Unambiguous testware also allows test result interpretation to be less dependent on the person running the test. Unambiguous testware is auditable, in the sense that others can examine the testware and know exactly what was tested.

However, such precise test cases also have downsides. Writing a test case that is very precise also means writing a test case that is very verbose and complex. Complexity is not linear with size—as our programmer peers know—but is exponential. For example, writing this book, which is about 100 times longer than my typical test status reports, took well over 1,000 times longer to write. Sometimes I don't have the time or the resources I need to document the test system as precisely as I'd like.

The more precise the testware, too, the more precise one's foreknowledge must be. If, during test implementation, I try to document exactly how the user interface will work, I may find during test execution that I was wrong. This will lead to rework of the testware, hardly an efficient use of time. Finally, while precision does enable reuse for regression testing, reuse also implies maintainability. The more precise the testware, though, the more work required to change it when the system changes.

Some amount of ambiguity is unavoidable. Imagine a scripted manual test for Speedy-Writer. Would a test case like the following qualify as unambiguous?

1. Start SpeedyWriter. Application should open in browser.
2. Create a new document. Blank document should appear.
3. Type in four lines of text. Verify no text is lost.
4. Save the file. Verify that the *File Save As* window appears.

Notice that significant ambiguities remain. Which browser should we start Speedy-Writer in? How would we know that the application had opened properly? How should we create a new document—using the mouse to pull down command menus or using hot keys? When we expect to see a blank document, does that mean a blank screen, or should there be a toolbar at the top, a scroll bar on the side, and so forth? Can we use font effects on the text, or would that be adding too many test conditions? What should the *File Save As* window look like?

The only way I can have completely precise, truly unambiguous scripted manual or automated tests is if I can predict in advance the exact image on every screen on the network containing the system under test, every bit in storage (RAM, CPU cache, disk, disk cache, video memory, and so on, and so on) on every system on the network containing the system under test, and every network packet traversing the network containing the system under test. And I'd have to be able to predict this at every single moment in time while I was testing. And even then I'd probably be missing *something*.[5]

On the one hand, the following influences, considerations, and factors tend to be positively correlated with or create opportunities for increased levels of documentation.

- The need for regression testing and reproducibility. If I need to run the same tests again and again—especially if I must run *exactly* the same tests again and again—then I'll need to document precisely what I did, how I did it, the data I used, and what I expected to happen.

- The need for auditability. If I think I may have to defend the testing effort (e.g., in a lawsuit), then writing down exactly what was done is important. For example, in contractual development settings (such as defense work or custom programming) and regulated environments (such as medical device and nuclear control software in the United States), testing must conform to particular standards.

- The current or future use of automation. If I intend to automate some functional or other tests that we have previously run manually, having a stable, well-understood test execution process that uses well-defined test cases promotes successful test automation.

- The need to formalize and standardize the test process and documentation. Formalized processes tend to follow templates and documentation standards (see Chapter 17), which means that a minimum level of documentation is specified by the standard.

- The risk level of the system. Safety-critical and mission-critical systems must behave in very precise ways, every single time those systems are used. A

---

5. Some examples of test cases at various levels of precision and documented in different fashions can be found in Chapter 3 of my book *Managing the Testing Process, Second Edition*.

meticulous, cross-referenced, extensively documented approach to testing is generally required to achieve the necessary levels of confidence in the system.[6]

- Tight time windows for test execution. I once had to run a series of tests for potential date handling problems with a server farm. These tests involved setting the servers' clocks and loading certain data sets very precisely and then evaluating what happened when certain interesting time-related states occurred, such as the rollover from December 31, 1999, to January 1, 2000. If any test case was omitted or improperly executed as the states occurred, we had to at least repeat that interval of time. In some cases, we had to start at the beginning of the sequence. Precise documentation enabled crisp execution of the tests.

- The complexity of the test execution process, the test case, and the system under test. The human brain is able to juggle only so many pieces of information at once. A complex test, especially one in which order, timing, and data must happen precisely, requires sufficient documentation to ensure that the right things happen at the right time and that we look in the right places for failures. For example, a test case could include an expected result step saying, "Confirm that the e-mail attachment is displayed correctly," when testing an Internet appliance, but would "Confirm that the flight deck gauges have the proper readings" suffice if we were testing the avionics of the Concorde airliner?

- The need to capture knowledge. Tests that are specified imprecisely because it is common knowledge how to run them may not pose a problem, but test cases and procedures that reside in one person's head create an organizational and management risk to the test team.

- The need to guide inexperienced testers and share knowledge. Certain people who would be otherwise unqualified to participate in testing of a system can make positive contributions given proper guidance. Some of that guidance can be provided in the form of written test cases. Written test cases allow me to cast my net wider for testers and have better luck staffing my test projects. Written test cases can enable people to be positive contributors when they'd otherwise not be able to participate. Written test cases allow people to spread the collective skill of the test team around to others.

- The degree to which the test system is a product. If the test system is a deliverable to some other organization—or if it will or could be delivered after the testing is done, for whatever reason—then documentation can help transfer the knowledge of how the testing was done and any tools, data, scripts, and so forth work. Good documentation also enhances the professional image of the testing done and the test team that did it.

---

6. See especially Chapter 2 of *Computer-Related Risks,* by Peter Neumann.

On the other hand, the following influences, considerations, and factors tend to be positively correlated with or create opportunities for decreased levels of documentation.

- The time and resources available to design and implement the test cases. A shoestring budget or a tight schedule may compel me to document less than I'd like. Time I spend documenting one test case precisely is time I'm not spending writing another test case, so if I have to choose between leaving high-risk areas untested or leaving some details of the testing to the discretion of the tester, I'll take the latter.

- The skill levels of the testers, especially those who will execute the test cases. Less skilled testers may need more guidance.

- Motivational concerns. Over time, testers may find running the same set of precisely documented test cases over and over again tedious and demotivating. If the other factors, especially safety-critical ones, require precise documentation, then trading off assignments and creating time for exploratory testing in the mix of tasks can help.

In general, the following influences, considerations, and factors interact with the appropriate level of documentation in various and complex ways, increasing or decreasing it.

- Efficiency, reuse, and maintenance concerns. I sometimes find that some parts of the test process must be specified precisely to ensure efficient testing, such as how to ensure that two people don't accidentally run the same test at once. However, I might choose to be less precise about details related to the user interface if I think that it will be subject to frequent change. If precision is required, I can refer to other project-related documents rather than repeating that information in test system documentation. Likewise, if standard checklists are available for certain kinds of tests, I can refer to those checklists rather than reproducing them in my test system.[7]

- Test and project stakeholder expectation and requirements. Sometimes project managers expect to see particular types or formats of documentation. Sometimes, the test system is a deliverable. I worked with a client once that had a vendor selling them a large, complex subsystem to integrate into the system under test. I advised my client that they would be wise to make delivery of the vendor's test cases, test results, and test tools part of the contract so that we could effectively test their subsystem in the context of our system.

---

7. See, for example, the comprehensive set of checklists for Web testing available in Steve Splaine and Stefan Jaskiel's excellent resource, *The Web Testing Handbook*.

- Beliefs, rational and otherwise. Some testers, programmers, and managers think, "Hey, we don't have time for all that paperwork; we just need to focus on testing." Others think, "You know, documentation and standards represent the distillation of lots of careful thought and past experiences, and we should follow best practices to minimize project risk." To the extent that one position or the other represents a rational choice based on the factors in this list—or other rational factors I've omitted—then either position can be correct. I also find that I have certain biases based on my past experience that lead me to the second school of thought. You probably have your own biases that have worked for you, and there's nothing wrong with wanting to stick with approaches that have worked for you before. What is wrong, though, is to allow beliefs about documentation (or other practical issues) to become so rigid that you practice rituals rather than making rational decisions.

- Lack of knowledge and chaos. Finally, we have two unfortunate but not uncommon factors that influence documentation choices. Some people simply don't know how to document test systems or are unaware that there's more than one option available. In some contexts, change is so pervasive, so omnipresent, so continuous that any attempt to write anything down would result in the document being obsolete before it was finished.

As extensive as this list may appear to be, there are certainly other influences, factors, and considerations that could affect this issue of documentation. Committing to various levels and approaches to test documentation is a serious decision, calling for careful consideration of all the applicable forces at work.[8]

COMBINATORIAL EXPLOSIONS

Suppose you have a screen-oriented system, like a program that accepts and processes a loan application. It has 100 fields spread across four screens. There are some binary fields, such as "Have you declared bankruptcy in the last seven years?" There are some fields that accept integer ranges, such as "How many years have you lived at your current address?" There are some fields that accept free-form text, such as "Enter the name of your employer." There are more than a million trillion trillion (1×10^{30})—possibly more than a trillion trillion trillion trillion trillion (1×10^{60})—potentially interesting data combinations that could be entered into such a set of screens, though a large number of nonsensical and impossible combinations can be

---

8. I had the benefit of an interesting e-mail discussion with Gregory Daich, Ross Collard, Michael Bolton, and Robin Goldsmith that helped me clarify my thinking in this area. I thank them for their time and acknowledge their contributions to this section.

eliminated. For example, if the loan applicant responds, "No" to the question about whether he has any vehicle loans outstanding, then the subsequent fields having to do with the outstanding vehicle loans, such as monthly payment, amount owed, term, and lender, would necessarily be blank. Even if the nature of the application is such that many of these nonsense combinations can be eliminated—say, 99.999% of the potential data combinations—that still leaves over a trillion trillion data sets. While it's possible that you can find a way to generate all that data in some realistic time frame, what you won't have time to do is to verify the expected results.

Another example of this arises when you test a standalone PC application that runs on multiple versions of the host operating system and on multiple platforms. Each variation in operating system—including service packs and patches—combines with each support platform and each possible cohabitating program to create another enormous matrix of potential test environment configurations. The order of installation of the service packs and cohabitating programs can be a significant variable, too. The cohabitating-program bugs in Windows PCs are commonly referred to as *DLL hell*. A common shared library is overwritten by a new version of that library during installation of an additional program; this new library proves incompatible with the previously installed programs that use it, rendering those previously installed programs inoperable. If you have 100 programs and you want to exhaustively test the effect of the order of installation of these programs, then there are over a trillion trillion trillion trillion trillion trillion trillion trillion trillion trillion trillion trillion trillion (about 9×10^{157}) conditions to test.

These are two examples of a common problem in test design, the combinatorial explosion. A variety of techniques have been advanced to help prune these large and unruly test sets down to a manageable size. Since any detailed treatment of even one of these techniques would be well beyond the scope of this book, I intend to introduce the techniques briefly and then direct you to further readings, should you think any specific technique might prove helpful.

In terms of configuration combinations, the technique I've commonly used includes three steps. First, I identify important configurations. What makes a configuration important is the likelihood of bugs (technical risk) and the prevalence of the configuration in actual use (business risk). Second, I plan to distribute the various test cases I intend to run across the different configurations. Third, I plan to vary the configuration I run the test against each time I rerun the test in subsequent test cycles.[9]

---

9. This technique is described in more detail in Chapters 3 and 5 of my book *Managing the Testing Process, Second Edition*.

Another family of techniques applied to combinatorial explosions is referred to variously as design of experiments, Taguchi methods, all-pairs (less commonly, all-triples), and orthogonal arrays. These techniques usually look at interactions between pairs or triples of the various factors and pick a small subset of the enormous potential set that covers the interesting interacting pairs. The name "orthogonal array" derives from the fact that part of the technique involves constructing an array consisting of columns, each column representing one of the factors or variables—e.g., fields on a screen. Interacting pairs of these factors or variables are populated into the columns—excluding illegal, unreachable, or impossible combinations—until each interacting pair is covered by at least one row in the array.

A variety of books have been written about the Taguchi method, though they are not specific to software. I am aware of two papers on the topic that are specific to software. One is by Genichi Taguchi and Rajesh Jugulum, "Principles of Taguchi Methods for Software Testing." The other is by Elfriede Dustin, "Orthogonally Speaking." Perhaps some of the clearest descriptions of the concept as applied to software, though, can be found in Rick Craig and Stefan Jaskiel's book, *Systematic Software Testing*, and in Lee Copeland's book, *A Practitioner's Guide to Software Test Design*.[10]

Somewhat related to this is a technique called hazard analysis, or cause-and-effect analysis. This starts with specific types of problems (the undesirable effects)—for example, overwriting of a shared DLL with an incompatible one—and tries to discern all the possible ways in which that could occur (the root causes). That way, testing can focus on those combinations in the huge combinatorial space that are particularly likely to cause failures. You can find a specific example of this idea applied to software testing in Yasuharu Nishi's article "Resource Path Testing: A Framework for Design of System Testing."[11]

Similarly, various types of domain analysis or equivalence partitioning can be applied. These analyses divide the (enormous) combinatorial space into a small set of domains. Within each domain, we assume the system will handle all the various data combinations equivalently. Within these domains, there are a small number of interesting

---

10. Taguchi and Jugulum's paper appeared in the *Proceedings of the Second World Congress for Software Quality*, while Dustin's paper appeared in *Software Testing and Quality Engineering*, Volume 3, Issue 5 (Sep/Oct 2001). Craig and Jaskiel's discussion appears in Chapter 6 of their book. You can find tools for generating all-pairs or orthogonal array tests at www.phadkeassociates.com and www.lumsoft.com.
11. Nishi's article first appeared as a paper in the *Proceedings of the Second World Congress for Software Quality* and subsequently was published as an article in *Software Quality Professional*, Volume 3, Issue 3 (June 2001). A discussion of cause-and-effect diagrams can be found in Kaoru Ishikawa's *Guide to Quality Control*.

points; testing at those points tells us whether the system's handling of the entire domain those points represent is correct. The way in which the system under test defines or implements these domains can make this analysis—and the resulting set of tests—simpler or more difficult, which means that applying this approach up front during program design is likely to yield benefits in terms of simpler testing. Boris Beizer covers this topic extensively in his books *Software Testing Techniques* and *Black-Box Testing*, as does Lee Copeland in *A Practitioner's Guide to Software Test Design*.

Finally, another technique involves use cases—paradigmatic uses or workflows through a system—perhaps combined with boundary value analysis to select the specific data items used. This is an approach I've used with some success testing a screen- and field-oriented loan application processing system where the workflows were very linear. That is, most usage proceeded through the fields on the screens—and through the screens themselves—in a strictly defined sequence that allowed us to exclude a huge set of potential variations in input order that were highly unlikely or even impossible in the real world. Ross Collard provides an excellent discussion of this technique in his article "Test Design: Developing Test Cases from Use Cases."[12]

SHIFTING TO THE MANAGEMENT PICTURE

This chapter has taken a technical look at test design and implementation. We've looked at a single test suite in the case study, and we've seen how Emma applied best test design and implementation practices to build her piece of the test system. We've looked at some important practical consideration for those designing and implementing test cases. However, we still need to examine the whole process, the bigger picture, and the management angles. Given infinite time and money, we could write the perfect test system that would tell us everything about the quality of the system under test. But we have practical limits. In the next chapter, we'll look at these limits and then examine the test design and implementation process from a global perspective.

---

12. Collard's article was originally published in *Software Testing and Quality Engineering*, Volume 1, Issue 4 (Jul/Aug 1999), and can now be found at www.stickyminds.com.

11

FILL THE BATHTUB: TEST SYSTEM COVERAGE AND QUALITY

In this chapter, let's close our examination of the test system design and implementation process. First, let's look at a key consideration: knowing when enough tests have been created. Various ways in which we can measure the completeness of testing are often referred to as *test coverage*. It turns out that beneath this simple phrase runs a continuum of techniques. All these complementary techniques allow test professionals to measure the ways in which their tests do—and don't—address areas of interest.

Completeness of testing is certainly one important aspect of a good test system, but there are others. I'll wrap up this chapter by looking back at the entire test system design and implementation process. How do we know we have a good process? What challenges exist? How can we move from a current process that may not be working to a better process?

A BRIEF SURVEY OF TEST COVERAGE ANALYSIS TECHNIQUES

Before we return to our friend Jamal and his particular challenges with test coverage, let me briefly discuss some common test coverage techniques. In the few pages available, I cannot provide an exhaustive introduction to the complex and varied topic of test coverage. However, I'll introduce the ideas that I'm going to use in the case study.

I've provided references in case you want to research the topic more thoroughly. If you and your team focus primarily on behavioral testing, don't worry too much if you don't grasp every detail of the structural coverage portion of this section. Not coincidentally, these are the test coverage techniques that I have used—and have seen used most widely in the field.

Intuitively, when people talk about achieving good test coverage, what they mean is that the test system addresses most of the test conditions related to the system under test—or at least most of the important test conditions. If this definition sounds fuzzy, that's because it is. Fuzzy, imprecise usage of the phrase "test coverage" is common. Let me shave off some of that fuzz so you can see exactly what I'm talking about, because I'm using the phrase to mean distinct, quantifiable concepts.

To start with, the analysis of test coverage is the mapping of the tests back to some property of the system under test. These properties can be behavioral (associated with what the system is to do), structural (associated with how the system operates), or some mix of the two. The mechanism by which the mapping occurs can result in quantification of test coverage.

For behavioral (or black-box) coverage, imagine that for each quality risk you have identified, you have also identified at least one test case. Assuming that you have done a good job of quality risk analysis, and subsequently also done a good job of test design and implementation, then you have covered the quality risks.

You can measure this coverage by building a matrix with test cases on one axis and the quality risks on the other. (The case study will show an example of this technique.) For each test case–quality risk intersection—i.e., each cell in the body of the matrix—you can measure the coverage of the quality risk by that test case.[1]

In addition to tracing by quality risks, we can trace coverage of requirements, supported configurations, and use cases. If we derive the quality risks from requirements, configurations, and use cases, though, then quality risk coverage will be a superset of the coverage of these three areas.

Documents like quality risk analyses and requirements specifications are static models of how the system should behave. We can build other behavioral models, too. These models can capture the flow and kinds of data in the system, the sequencing of screens, the states the system can be in and the transitions between those states, the transactions supported by the system, and the sequence of processing that occurs. The models are graphical, with nodes and links between them, and these graphs can be translated into tables. You can assess coverage against these models, checking that each node and each link has an associated test case.[2]

---

1. Rick Craig and Stefan Jaskiel's *Systematic Software Testing* contains a good description of this technique, using the concept of test objective inventories.
2. This kind of technique is described extensively in Boris Beizer's *Black-Box Testing*.

Some people measure coverage as either present or absent, 0 or 1, check mark or no check mark. However, a more accurate assessment of coverage requires us to recognize that tests address areas of interest to some degree. We are limited in how precisely we can quantify this degree, but recognizing strong and weak relationships between tests and the area of interest (in this book, quality risks) is a good start.

Behavioral coverage assessments, such as those that look at requirements coverage, are related most closely—either directly or indirectly—with business risk. What is the extent to which certain failures would compromise the value of the system? We should test each area proportional to the impact of failure on the business value.

The other question we could ask is related to technical risk. What is the likelihood of certain failures occurring? We should test each area proportional to those risks, too.

To assess the coverage of technical risks, you can look at design elements. You can again build a model of the system and then check for coverage of that model. Simply identifying the major software and hardware subsystems in a larger system and the data and control flows between them provides a model for assessing technical test coverage. (Test coverage, design, and implementation based on this kind of information is sometimes called *gray-box testing*.) Going the extra step and analyzing the most likely failures for each subsystem and each interface between two or more subsystems, then tracing those items back to specific test cases, is even more complete (as discussed in the Test Execution subsection in Chapter 3).

Continuing down to the lowest level of the system, the individual lines of source code, we can look at technical risk in terms of complexity. Since the human mind can juggle only so many ideas at once, the more complex a given piece of code is, the more likely the programmer is to make a mistake. In the 1970s, Thomas McCabe came up with a way to quantify this idea, using what he called *cyclomatic complexity*. In cyclomatic complexity, each decision point—a place where the program can take two or more paths based on certain conditions—increases the complexity of the code. The more complex a piece of code—for example, a function or method—the more extensively it needs to be tested (if not reengineered).[3]

---

3. For more information on McCabe's cyclomatic complexity metrics, you can read the entry on cyclomatic complexity in the Software Engineering Institute's Software Technology Review, http://www.sei.cmu.edu/str/descriptions/cyclomatic_body.html. Alternatively, see the entry on measurement—complete with an extensive bibliography—in the *Encyclopedia of Software Engineering, Second Edition*.

McCabe refers this set of tests—which increases in size with cyclomatic complexity—as *basis tests*. This is a kind of test coverage where a least one test causes control to flow through every decision point and every statement between each decision point. The number of basis tests for a function is generally the same as the complexity of a function. Basis test coverage is one kind of code coverage, one measured statically by analysis of the code and the tests.[4]

More frequently, people measure code coverage dynamically, by keeping track of control flows during testing. Common test coverage tools measure the percentage of lines of code executed over the course of running the entire collection of tests. Coarser-grained tools such as profilers measure whether functions are executed.[5] By looking at what wasn't executed during testing, test engineers and managers can decide whether to augment the tests to mitigate particular technical risks.

Often, behavioral testers—especially in independent test teams—tend to focus on behavioral test coverage, while structural testers—especially programmers—tend to focus on structural test coverage. However, this approach can represent a missed opportunity to fill gaps in testing. If you use behavioral techniques to design and implement tests, then using behavioral coverage analysis can only tell you whether you forgot something. While that's an important thing to know, it would also be good to know whether your behavioral technique has left significant technical risks exposed. This means that applying structural test coverage analysis techniques to a set of tests developed through behavioral analysis—and vice versa—can be an effective technique for finding and eliminating coverage gaps.

Test Coverage

1. Structural: the extent to which the test system covers, or exercises, the structure—the code, subsystems, or components—in the system under test.
2. Behavioral: the extent to which the test system covers, or exercises, the behavior—risks to quality, operations, activities, functions, and other uses—of the system under test.

---

4. For more on basis tests and other kinds of code coverage testing, see Boris Beizer's *Software Testing Techniques,* Bill Hetzel's *Complete Guide to Software Testing*, and Lee Copeland's *A Practitioner's Guide to Software Test Design.*
5. As a service to the testing community, Danny Faught, principal consultant of Tejas Software Consulting, maintains an extensive list of test tools, including coverage analyzers, at www.tejasconsulting.com.

JAMAL ASSESSES COVERAGE

As November came to a close and test development ended—only slightly behind schedule, Jamal was pleased to note—he reviewed the quality risk coverage statistics. As Emma, Dinesh, and Lin-Tsu had created tests, he had asked them to assess the relevance of those tests to each of the quality risks identified during the Failure Mode and Effect Analysis. The relevance assessments fell into four categories, to which he had assigned numerical identifiers.

- 0: No coverage—The test case does not trigger any behaviors related to this quality risk and so is unlikely to reveal related failures.
- 1: Opportunistic coverage—The test case triggers a small sample of behaviors related to this quality risk, providing an opportunistic search for related failures.
- 3: Balanced coverage—The test case triggers a wide sample of behaviors related to this quality risk, providing a broad search for related failures.
- 9: Extensive coverage—The test case triggers a wide sample of behaviors related to this quality risk and explores those behaviors deeply, providing an extensive search for related failures.

As Jamal received this information, test case by test case, he traced this detailed view of coverage to a broader, test-system-wide view. He did this by creating a spreadsheet that listed down the left side all the test cases that his team had developed. Along the top of the worksheet he listed the major risk categories, the specific risk identifiers, and the risk priority numbers from the quality risk analysis worksheet, the Failure Mode and Effect Analysis. Next, for the intersection of each test case with a risk, he entered the relevance (coverage) assessment provided by the test engineer who wrote the test case. A portion of this worksheet is shown in Figure 11-1, with the quality risk identifiers listed across the top in the second row.

He noted that the only quality risk not covered at or beyond the level of testing specified in the Recommended Action column of the Failure Mode and Effect Analysis chart related to usability. Oh, he realized, I forgot to add a test suite for that, even though we have money budgeted for a usability study. As a matter of fact, he remembered, I need to follow up with accounting and see if the purchase order has been approved for that contract. He added the test suite to the test tracking worksheet and updated the risk coverage worksheet. Finally, he checked the updated document into the project repository.

	Test ID	Test Suite/Case	Functionality 1.000	1.001	1.002	1.003	1.004	1.005	1.006	1.007	1.008	1.009	1.010	1.011		Load, Capacity, and Volume 2.000	2.001	2.002	2.003	2.004	2.005	2.006	2.007	2.008
RPN			2	3	24	6	8	4	2	2	3	6	6	30		1	3	6	3	9	1	4	9	64
	1.000	Functionality																						
	1.001	File	9	1	0	3	1	1	1	1	1	1	1	0		0	0	0	0	1	1	1	0	0
	1.002	Edit	9	1	0	0	0	0	0	0	0	0	0	0		0	0	0	0	0	0	0	0	0
	1.003	Font	9	1	0	0	0	0	0	0	0	0	0	0		0	0	0	0	0	0	0	0	0
	1.004	Tables	9	1	0	0	0	0	0	0	0	0	0	0		0	0	0	0	0	0	0	0	0
	1.005	Printing	9	1	0	0	0	0	0	0	0	0	0	0		0	0	0	0	0	0	0	0	0
	1.006	Managed Files	1	1	9	1	1	3	1	1	0	0	1	1		0	0	0	0	1	1	1	0	0
	1.007	Non-Managed Files	1	1	0	9	3	3	0	1	0	0	1	1		0	0	0	0	1	1	1	0	0
	1.008	DMS Check-In New	1	1	0	0	9	1	1	1	0	0	1	1		0	0	0	0	1	1	1	0	0
	1.009	DMS Check-In Existing	1	1	0	0	0	9	1	1	0	0	1	1		0	0	0	0	1	1	1	0	0
	1.010	DMS Check-Out	1	1	0	0	1	1	9	1	0	0	1	1		0	0	0	0	1	1	1	0	0
	1.011	DMS Load/Migrate Online	1	1	0	0	1	1	1	9	1	1	1	1		0	0	0	0	1	1	1	1	1
	1.012	DMS Load/Migrate NOL	1	1	0	0	1	1	1	9	1	1	1	1		0	0	0	0	1	1	1	1	1
	1.013	DMS Load/Migrate Offline	1	1	0	0	1	1	1	9	1	1	1	1		0	0	0	0	1	1	1	1	1
	1.014	DMS File Information	0	0	0	0	1	1	1	1	1	1	1	1		0	0	0	0	0	0	0	0	0

FIGURE 11-1 A PORTION OF THE SUMATRA QUALITY RISK COVERAGE ANALYSIS

Step #	Step	Done?
8.	Update the quality risks list based on what was learned in developing this latest set of tests. Evaluate coverage of the quality risks with the new test system. Identify remaining uncovered quality risks for which testing action is recommended.	✔
9.	Repeat steps 2 through 8 until all quality risks are covered to the extent testing action was recommended. Ensure that the quality risk documentation in the project repository is updated. If schedule or budget restrictions curtail development without all critical quality risks covered, produce a report of uncovered quality risks and escalate that report to management.	✔

During planning for the integration testing, he, Lin-Tsu and Emma, along with Jenny Kaufman and her senior programmers, had done a technical risk analysis of the network and system architecture. This risk analysis had driven the order and extent of the integration tests that his test engineers had designed and implemented. To close the loop, Jamal had asked the Emma—who was the lead engineer for the integration tests—to trace each integration test case back to the specific technical risks that it covered. Therefore, Jamal felt comfortable that, from a high-level-design and architectural perspective, the integration testing would cover the technical risks.

Okay, Jamal thought, how about lower-level design and implementation issues? How about doing some structural coverage analysis against the next passes of integration and system test to see what's getting tested and what's not getting tested, code-wise? They had gone slightly over in terms of the scheduled end date for test design and implementation. However, in the budgeted hours they had done well, coming in 30 hours or so under. Jamal saw three options:

1. Buy a code complexity tool, get trained in how to use it, measure the complexity of the system, and increase test coverage against those particularly complex areas.

2. Buy a code coverage tool, get trained in how to use it, measure statement and branch coverage by instrumenting and testing the system, and then fill in the high-risk gaps.

3. Use the built-in profiling tools available in some of the development environments or freeware code coverage tools to try for an inexpensive measure of coverage at a gross level.

Jamal realized that he hadn't the time or money for options 1 or 2. If test development had come in well under budget and Emma, Lin-Tsu, and Dinesh had lots of spare time, he could have perhaps worked in one of those two options. However, he could ask Dinesh, who was turning out to be a very quick study and had some background in code coverage as well, to look into option 3. If nothing worked out, fine, but perhaps there were some low-cost, low-impact routes to making this happen. He headed to Dinesh's office to talk to him about the idea.

"Hey, Dinesh, do you have a minute?"

"Sure, Jamal, what's up?" Dinesh said, turning away from his computer.

"I know you've finished the reliability and stability scripts at this point and also won't be starting the document management system functional test scripts until February, so I was wondering if I could give you a side project to work on along with leading the test execution work?"

"You bet."

Jamal said, "I've just finished looking through our quality risk coverage analysis—you know, the relevance ratings I asked for as the tests were written—and the technical risk coverage analysis that Emma did as part of integration testing. We're looking real good in terms of black-box and gray-box coverage."

"That's good," Dinesh interjected, nodding.

"So," Jamal continued, "the one thing I don't know about, in the area of coverage, is structural, or white-box coverage. How much of the code have we tested? I know that Jenny's team, when they did their unit and component testing, had a standard of 90% or higher. However, that's a different kind of testing. We could find different bugs covering the same code with our tests. Therefore, what I want to ask you is the following. First, can you find a tool for quick, cheap code coverage analysis? Perhaps some freeware tool or something included in the development environment."

"Does it need to be sophisticated?" Dinesh asked. "I mean, do we need to be able to measure just statement coverage, or do we need to be able to go all the way down to condition and path coverage?"

"Well," Jamal replied, "I'd love to be able to get to condition and path coverage, but I suspect that we'll have to settle for statement coverage, or perhaps just function coverage. But I'm open to whatever you come up with. If you could do some research and lay out some options for me in the next three or four days, we could make that call."

"Okay," Dinesh replied, "that's sounds doable."

"The second part of the assignment, of course, is to actually do the code coverage analysis. You'd need to work with someone in Yasuhiro's release engineering team to produce instrumented test releases and then install those in the test environments. To know how much we cover, we'd need a complete pass of all our tests. If we can move quickly enough, maybe this can happen as part of pass 3 of integration testing and pass 4 of system testing. I'd rather not do this much later, because there's always a chance that the instrumented version of the program won't fail in the same ways as the noninstrumented version."

"Understood," Dinesh agreed.

"Finally, based on the gaps we identify—and I'm sure we'd find a few—I'd need you to work with Emma and Lin-Tsu to beef up the testing. I suspect any gains would be opportunistic, given how little time and budget will remain, but at least we can deal with the most risky elements. Maybe you could compare our coverage against the component and unit test coverage to see if there are chunks of code no one has tested."

"Got it," Dinesh replied. "Sounds like an interesting assignment. I'll get started this afternoon, right after I get through analyzing some of the test results that Hemamalini sent me this morning."

"Good. Let's touch base tomorrow to see where you are, okay?"

"Okay," Dinesh replied, turning back to his computer.

Step #	Step	Done?
10.	If time and resources allow, iterate steps 2 through 8 using structural analysis (e.g., McCabe complexity or code coverage) to identify areas needing further testing.	☑

RECOGNIZE A GOOD TEST SYSTEM DESIGN AND IMPLEMENTATION PROCESS

Completeness is surely one part of the puzzle, but there are other considerations in building test systems properly. Ultimately, designing and implementing tests is a creative engineering process, so the deliverables of that process are important, along with the attributes of the process itself. What does a test team do and achieve with a good process?

PROVIDES CAPABLE TOOLS FOR ASSESSMENT OF QUALITY

When I build a test system my aim is to build something useful in terms of my larger goal, which in this case is to assess the quality of the system under test. What would it mean for my test system to have such capability?

Foremost to me is that the test system cover the risks to system quality, as discussed earlier. That is, for those areas most likely to be problematic or most important to my customers and users, I need to explore the potential for failure. Risk is not a discrete attribute, but rather a continuous one. Risk is always present to some degree. So during the quality risk analysis process, I work with the project team to assess this degree of risk and assign a proportionate degree of testing. The test system, therefore, must allow me to perform the kind and extent of testing appropriate for the risks covered.

In testing, we always balance competing motives of depth of understanding and breadth of coverage, of certainty and progress. The desire for certainty inspires the tester to create extremely detailed, repeatable test cases that touch every nook and cranny of the feature, function, and behavior under consideration. However, while the tester is hard at work writing such test cases, she is not engaged in writing other test cases covering different conditions, other quality risks. So, there is always a balance of forces between the desire to cover one more condition and the need to cover all critical quality risks well enough within the allotted time and budget, leading to a trade-off of risks.

In the risk analysis process in the case study described in Chapter 2, the Sumatra project team assigned one of these four levels of recommended actions for most quality risks:

- Extensive testing
- Balanced testing
- Opportunity testing
- Reporting observed bugs

The various levels of testing are points along a continuous spectrum. Testing at the extensive end of the spectrum gives the highest level of confidence in our quality assessment. Testing that merely reports observed bugs only tells us that to the extent that normal usage profiles bring the tester through that risk area, any bugs that have been observed are noted.

My list gives only four of many possible points you could identify along the spectrum. You could choose to make this finer-grained, should you wish. These recommended actions serve as hints to the test engineer. I expect test engineers to use professional judgment to design and implement the right tests within the parameters of the recommendations.

Different spectrums of risk might apply to different systems. The Sumatra project is producing a word processing package for professional use. Thus, the risks are significant. The impact on productivity or even continuity of business is potentially high should failures occur. Safety-critical systems like medical devices, industrial controls, and battlefield computers have a spectrum of risk that pushes the test team toward more extensive testing. Entertainment systems like computer games or DVD players have a spectrum of risk that allows for a more easygoing approach. Regardless of the quality risk profile of the system under test, though, some quality risks are more important than others. Testers should expend a larger share of the test system design and implementation effort—along with the test execution effort—against those risks.

Covering the critical quality risks is important, but we can do so in such a way that the tests do not relate to the customers' and users' experiences of quality. I worked with a talented team of developers once who designed a performance test for a large UNIX server used in the system under test. Performance was indeed a key quality risk for the system. However, because of the way they designed and implemented their test tools, the performance test only assessed the performance at about 60% system load. At 100% load my test team and I later found that the system not only failed in terms of performance, but would actually crash. The test system we built as testers truthfully represented the actual usage profile, while the developers' test system did not.

An effective test system must be a high-fidelity test system, truthful to the customers' and users' experiences of quality. Test execution processes must provide for using the system under test in a user-like fashion. The test system should allow the testers to assess the correctness of system behavior in all the workflows and usage scenarios with all the important data sets. The test system must create all the test conditions necessary to align the testers' experiences of quality with those of the users and customers. This implies also that the test environment must be close enough to the deployed or customer environments to allow us to find environment, configuration, and compatibility issues, too.[6]

EFFICIENTLY IMPLEMENTS, USES, REUSES, AND MAINTAINS THE TEST SYSTEM

High-fidelity test systems focused on the critical quality risks will be effective, but I generally don't have all the time and money in the world. This means that my test system must be efficient as well as effective. *Merriam-Webster's Collegiate Dictionary* says that to be *efficient,* some thing or system or person must be "productive of desired effects...without waste." In other words, this definition tells us to spend the right amount of time and money on each necessary task to achieve the desired effect—in this case, a capable test system. This definition has many implications for test systems.

Avoiding waste implies, for one thing, using the minimal amount of time and money necessary to build a test system. For example, if I ignore the Recommended Action column in the Failure Mode and Effect Analysis chart and set out to build a test system

---

6. For projects where large, complex configurations will be deployed, or where many different customers and users will have many different configurations, the test manager may find herself faced with a significant "miniproject" in order to put such an environment in place in the test lab. See Chapters 6 and 7 of my book *Managing the Testing Process, Second Edition*, for some ideas on how to handle such endeavors.

that provided extensive coverage of all the identified risks, that would be wasteful. Covering risks to the extent required and no further is part of efficiency.

Not squandering money on useless elements of the test system is another part. Buying tools without doing a cost-benefit analysis first often results in the *shelfware* phenomenon. Some companies have literally millions of dollars' worth of computer-aided software testing tools sitting in disused corners of people's offices. Slavishly adhering to inappropriate documentation standards can also produce enormous binders of test cases and procedures that are written, referred to once or twice, and then never looked at again.

However, I find I must take care to balance efficiency of design and implementation with efficiency of use. To carry forward the earlier examples, I have seen too little documentation of the test effort—when combined with a general lack of testing skill in the test team—result in a lot of ad hoc testing that covered the same ground over and over while critical quality risks went unaddressed. I have seen automated testing tools, applied intelligently, result in enormous gains in efficiency over time.[7]

When thinking about spending money, I find it useful to differentiate carefully between waste and investment. Spending $1,000 on a bug tracking tool is certainly an investment. The first bug that doesn't escape to the field because of good bug tracking practices will likely pay for the tool. Spending $5,000 to put a test server in the same office as the people implementing and running tests on the server, rather than trying to use one 500 miles away, is an investment. I have seen lost time cost more than $5,000 in the space of a few weeks on test projects.

A knee-jerk, penurious "no" to buying the right tools and environment, to spending the time to write good test cases, to implementing procedures that take a little longer but result in doing the job right every time, will result in inefficiency of a painful sort. Insufficient, shoddy test systems impose a tax on every test task you and your team perform, a tax in the form of lost time. That might cost a few minutes here and there, but sometimes it'll be whole days of testing lost. "Penny-wise and pound foolish," as the saying goes, is just another form of waste, just like buying test tools that are never used.

Using the test system often involves setup and teardown activities to get ready to run a test case. For example, you may need to load a large database full of test customers

---

7. See Mark Fewster and Dorothy Graham's book *Software Test Automation* for a description of how to apply automated testing tools intelligently to receive a significant and demonstrable ROI based on improving testing efficiency.

to get ready for volume testing. Sometimes these activities can be leveraged across multiple test cases. This can make testing more efficient, since setup and teardown time is pure overhead with no payoff in terms of quality assessment.

While other considerations are important, in general I like to see test cases and other test activities run as quickly as possible. So, given equal coverage, a manual functional test that requires three hours to run is usually preferable to a manual functional test that takes four hours to run. Even for automated tests, speed of conclusion matters. I'd rather have an automated test suite that runs over the lunch break than one that takes all night to run, even if no additional effort is associated with the all-night run. (Of course, I do want to use that precious overnight test time if I can with automated tests, so an efficient test system would allow me to string together a whole sequence of automated suites, each an hour or two long, into a 16-hour supersuite.) I can turn the test around more quickly if it runs in an hour than if I must wait until the next day.

And I find I must further balance efficiency of initial implementation and use with efficiency of reuse, especially maintenance. It's often easy to slap together a simple testing tool or test data file. However, if I don't give it some careful thought, reusing that tool or data for other tests or subsequent projects is difficult. I find that a significant amount of housekeeping and documentation is necessary for those portions of my test system that I intend to reuse and maintain.

In the case study in the previous chapter, Lin-Tsu's state diagram for functional testing was one of the tools Emma used to design and implement her performance tests. Lin-Tsu might have been able to prepare her tests by understanding the state flows in her own head and not spending the additional time to create the diagram. However, the creation of the diagram—writing down what she knew so she could share it with her colleague Emma—provided an opportunity for reuse.

Closely related to efficiency is reliability. Running the same tests over and over to get believable results isn't efficient. Automated tests that can't run unattended are not reliable. Tests that are tightly coupled—i.e., one test case sets up the data and initial states for the next—often suffer from cascading failures. In this case, one test fails, causing the system to be in the wrong state for all the following test cases. These subsequent test cases also fail, not because the system under test is broken, but because the test system is fragile. All these situations result in lots of wasted testing and analysis time, and furthermore tend to result in many test result interpretation problems, which I'll cover when I talk about test execution in Chapter 13.

Two other potential sources of test inefficiency arise from dependencies between test cases and in data sets shared across test cases. In some situations, testers build test

Test Data

The set of inputs, whether from the user interface, from a stored file, or from another communicating system, that is used in a test case.

Testing Tools

Any system that helps someone perform a testing task, such as designing, implementing, verifying, executing, measuring, or interpreting test cases, test data, or test results. Tools can be spreadsheets, templates, databases, complex custom-developed in-house utilities, or commercially available systems. Tools can be composed and integrated. Some test tools, like capture/playback systems and code coverage utilities, were designed as test tools, while others, like debuggers and scripting languages, play the role accidentally.

Test Management Tools

Tools that manage the objects associated with and the results produced by test systems. Bug and test tracking systems are common examples, but more sophisticated systems provide end-to-end facilities for the test design, implementation, and execution processes. Such systems are often integrated with testing tools, though this sometimes limits the usefulness of the tool to those tests supported by the testing tool.

cases that set up the preconditions for subsequent test cases. This means that if, for whatever reason, a test case can't be run, all subsequent dependent test cases are blocked. This isn't a problem if the blockage is due to functionality that doesn't work. However, if it's simply an issue of test logistics, this results in unnecessary delay and constraints on the testing process. Ideally, I want to be able to pick any test case and assign it to any tester on any given day during test execution based strictly on priority, availability of the test environment, and the skills of the tester. Having to consider who is running other test cases on what dates complicates this process and often introduces needless impediments to completing planned tests. Given the time pressures that usually exist during test execution, this is a real problem.

Shared data sets create similar problems. If one test case creates or updates the data necessary for other test cases, that creates a test case dependency. If two tests share the same or related records from a set of tables or files, then those two tests can't be run at the same time. If they inadvertently are run at the same time, that will probably create the impression we've found a bug. This can result in a need to rerun the test at best—at worst, the misinterpretation of the situation as a bug. The former situation wastes the test team's time. The latter wastes not just the test team's time but also the development team's and conceivably the project team's time, in addition to damaging the credibility of the test team.

Finally, usability is an efficiency issue. A test system that my test team finds easy to use is one they're likely to use more effectively and more quickly. The more automation is involved, the more a test system becomes like a software system. Even manual test systems, though, should be designed and implemented in a way that makes the test system easy to use for the test team.

SELECTS THE RIGHT TECHNIQUES

Effectiveness, efficiency, reliability, and usability are more likely to occur if I use the right testing techniques. When Glenford Myers wrote *The Art of Software Testing* back in 1979, he identified a handful of techniques. Those techniques remain usable today. A number of books, papers, and articles have been written since then, refining Myers's techniques and identifying many new ones. The varied palette available to test professionals makes us more effective and efficient, but the wide array of choices has also brought confusion and, to some extent, schism. What is the best technique? That depends. Any one *can be*, and no single one *is*.

As a general principle, risks to system quality drive the test conditions that testers need to create. In turn, test conditions drive the selection of techniques. In addition to organizational and technological context, there are two major considerations. One consideration is the degree—if any—of test automation as opposed to manual techniques. The other consideration relates to whether tests are dynamic or static, structural or behavioral, code-, data-, or requirements-based.

Test automation refers typically to the ability of the test system carry out unattended or partially unattended activities. These activities can perform actions on the system under test, deliver data to it, and compare the actual with the expected results. This can be done using commercial tools or custom-built ones. Test automation would appear to allow—and some of the commercial test tool vendors claim it does allow—the tester to design and implement a complete set of test cases and then repeat them ad infinitum with little if any associated cost. As those who have tried it will attest, though, this is not always how it works out.

Some kinds of tests are well suited for test automation. For example, I have used automated test tools for most performance and reliability tests. Functional regression testing of a stable system is also a good fit for automation.

However, certain kinds of tests don't lend themselves to automation at all. For example, many times testing of error handling involves forcing conditions like network failures, disk drive failures, and power failures. It is effortless for a person to pull a cable, disk drive, or power plug, but difficult for a machine to do so.

One of my clients attempted to automate configuration testing and then found that most of the work consisted of changing the operating system and applications installed in the test environment. Automating 10% to 25% of the work that involved exercising the system after configuring it didn't make much sense, especially since that work was broken up into hour-long segments interspersed between hours of manual work in a week-long test suite.

When automation does make sense, it is still a large and risky undertaking. The effort required to automate a test is not the same as the effort required to write manual test scripts. In my experience, to produce maintainable automated tests, an entire infrastructure must be built that allows the tester to subsequently specify actions, data, and expected results in some nonprogrammatical format. Simply capturing actions, inputs, and outputs and then replaying them has not worked for me in the long term, except for certain special circumstances where the user interface was truly immutable and the only changes were to the business logic behind that interface.

In addition to the effort required to build the test harness, there is an often-substantial investment in the tools themselves, which can costs hundreds of thousands of dollars. Finally, test automation introduces changes in the testing process and the skills needed in the test team, all of which must be managed. Because there are many ways for this undertaking to go wrong, horror stories abound of failed automation projects. I have one client who will not even allow the phrase "test automation" to come up in conversation, having once squandered hundreds of thousands of dollars on an effort that led to no payoff. The tool sits unused on a shelf; the unmaintainable scripts were deleted.

Test efforts needn't be manual *or* automated, they can be manual *and* automated. Those tests that lend themselves to automation can and in many cases should be automated, while manual techniques can be applied for the other tests. In some cases, a single test case can be both manual and automated. Functional testing of an Internet appliance that I worked on included a load generator to simulate 50,000 customers running while we performed functional tests to see how the system would respond and behave under load.

Test Script

In manual testing, the instructions on how to perform one or more test cases, also often called a *test procedure*. In automated testing, it refers to the corresponding machine-executable instructions.

A wide diversity of opinion about appropriate uses and return on investment in test automation will be found in discussions with seasoned practitioners. Some people—especially tool vendors—tend to be very enthusiastic about the benefits of these tools. Others exhibit more pragmatic or even skeptical viewpoints.[8]

Tests, whether automated or manual, can be static or dynamic. A static test does not involve execution of the source code. For example, some classify code reviews as static manual tests, while code complexity analysis, style analysis programs like *lint* in the C and C++ world, and even a compiler can be seen as automated static tests. A dynamic test—which is what most people think of when they think of testing—actually executes some or all of the system under test and compares expected results with actual results.

Dynamic tests have a level of focus, often referred to as structural or behavioral, as discussed in Chapter 1. Structural tests look for bugs based on the way the program operates internally, while behavioral tests look for bugs based on the behaviors the system is supposed to exhibit externally. The earlier phases of testing tend to be more structural, while the latter ones are usually more behavioral.

However, structural techniques and tools have a rightful place in system testing. The load generators for the Internet appliance testing I referred to earlier were derived from structural test harnesses created by the programmers during unit testing to test key application program interfaces (APIs) in the server functionality. This is also another example of reusability, discussed earlier.

Usually, I don't focus on selecting any one test technique. I prefer to consider each condition I want to create in the system under test and pick the right technique for that condition. In the case study, Emma applied multiple techniques to load, capacity, and volume tests. To return to the earlier metaphor, an artist doesn't pick the best color with which to create her work of art; she picks a whole set of colors for her palette, and she feels free to mix and change those colors as she goes.

---

8. For a sampling of the perspectives out there, see Kaner, Bach, and Pettichord's *Lessons Learned in Software Testing*; Fewster and Graham's *Software Test Automation*; Dustin et al.'s *Automated Software Testing*; Kaner's "Architectures of Test Automation" on www.kaner.com; and Bach's "Test Automation Snake-oil" on www.satisfice.com. In an e-mail discussion with Cem Kaner regarding test automation and the tendency of some people to oversell automation tool capabilities, Kaner wrote me to say, "There are solid benefits available from many of the automation tools, but these products are so over-hyped and the advice from some boosters on how to use these products is so bad, that in practice these tools and their salespeople and consultants often do more harm than good."

PREVENTS BUGS

In Chapter 2, I pointed out that quality risk analysis not only helps us decide where to look for bugs. It can also create opportunities to avoid bugs. A good test system design and implementation process can do the same. In the case study, Emma discovers that the document open dialog box had no specified limit on how many files it could display. This could have resulted in a reliability bug had the programmer not implemented any check on too large a list, because an overflow could have caused a system crash. Or it could have resulted in a functionality bug had the programmer implemented a limit he thought was reasonable but that users found insufficiently low.

This is often the case. Designing and implementing tests in advance—before the programming is done—allows me to discuss with the project team how the system should work. This dialog involves the system designers and programmers, users and analysts, and all the other project stakeholders. As I create my test system, I can talk to these stakeholders about what I intend to test and what results I expect to see. This quite frequently results in responses like, "You know, we hadn't thought of that possibility." Each of those responses is at least one bug prevented.[9]

HANDLE CHALLENGES

There are a number of challenges to designing and implementing good test systems, many of which are technology- and technique-specific. Tests for Web-based systems differ from tests for mainframe systems. Automated and manual tests, structural and behavioral tests involve different approaches. However, there are a few generic challenges that bear mentioning.

HOW MANY CONDITIONS IN A TEST CASE?

The efficiency and performance considerations I mentioned earlier would seem to indicate that *bigger* test cases are better than *smaller* ones. (I mean "bigger" in the sense of creating and evaluating many test conditions.) If the test conditions flow from the quality risks, then once we've covered all the test conditions, we've provided

---

9. Hetzel's *Complete Guide to Software Testing* includes a discussion of static testing that prevents bugs. Boris Beizer wrote in *Software Testing Techniques*, regarding early test involvement in a project, that sometimes the "threat of a test" is sufficient to prevent bugs, because the programmer, knowing you will run such a test, writes the program in such a way as to not have bugs that such tests would catch. Others have written that anything that happens before compilation is quality assurance rather than testing. For example, see Watts Humphrey's *Introduction to the Personal Software Process*.

the risk management service we're hired to perform. Testers create those test conditions by executing test cases, the mechanics of which I'll discuss specifically in Chapter 13. Thus the basic unit of test execution work is a test case. So, efficiency would seem to imply that we would want to maximize the number of test conditions covered in each test case. However, combining too many conditions in a single test case can give rise to a number of bad outcomes.

First, you might run across multiple bugs in a single step (action) of a test case, confusing which change in system state leads to the failure. Second, you might have one of these multiple failures that is so extreme in impact that it obscures the other, less obvious (but perhaps just as important) failures, leading to a test escape to the next test cycle or to the field. Third, you might have a failure that stops the test dead in its tracks, preventing you from exercising the conditions that reveal subsequent failures, which are sometimes no less important. Fourth, a test case with many conditions is more likely to fail than one with fewer conditions, all else being equal, so a summary of test status in terms of passed and failed test cases is likely to paint an overly pessimistic picture, which can damage test team credibility.

Nevertheless, a number of exceptions exist. For example, tests often called *acceptance test suites* or *smoke test suites* are designed to demonstrate system stability and conformance to requirements, the former for delivery to a customer and the latter for delivery to the test group. The expectation is that these tests will pass. Any failures indicate a need to hand the system back to the transmitting organization for further work. The objective is to complete such tests as quickly as possible, so having a large number of conditions covered in a single test is a good idea.

Another example arises when you can't help creating a number of interesting test conditions in one test case because the set of actions required to achieve the target test condition involves traversing a control flow that passes you through a number of other test conditions. To go back to our case study, notice that testing for the quality risks relating to the efficiency of file migration (identified in the Failure Mode and Effect

---

Smoke Test, Sanity Test

A test run against a proposed test release to ensure that it is stable enough to enter testing in the currently active test phase. It is usually a subset of the overall set of tests, preferably automated, that touches every part of the system in at least a cursory way. A good smoke test also keeps the system running long enough that gross problems with reliability and availability will show up. The term derives from electrical engineering, where you power up a circuit and watch for smoking components as an initial test.

Analysis charts as 2.008 and 2.009) would necessarily also cover risks relating to whether file migration works at all (identified as 2.010 and 2.011).

This example also addresses another situation where multiple condition coverage is unavoidable, when one or more actions tied to interesting test conditions set up the data or internal state necessary to evaluate the target condition. A clearer example of this situation is where you might test a database for updating a record, because you would have to insert a record to update it. In some cases, like the database example, you may create test conditions that you don't directly evaluate, but you can infer their status. Suppose you insert a record, check that the record count went up by one, delete the record, check that the record count went down by one, and then confirm the inserted record is not there. You can infer that the insert worked to insert a record, though all you've really checked are cumulative totals and the delete condition.

RETESTING THIRD-PARTY COMPONENTS

Another challenge that is becoming more common for testers is the integration of third-party components into the systems they are testing. What I mean here is that one group is developing a system (the development team) for a second group (the users and customers) that includes pieces delivered to the development team by a third group (the vendor, supplier, or outsourcing partner).

The situation can be further complicated by the presence of more than one third party—i.e., when multiple outside groups are delivering portions of the system. These third-party components can be either custom-developed or part of a larger commercial package. The challenges here are both technical and political.

Technically, there are two fundamental testing challenges. First, the testing done by the third party may not align with your assessment and prioritization of the risks to system quality. Second, the testing done by the third party probably did not include testing the component integrated into your system, so the third party's test team, no matter how competent, does not have a good grasp on what your customers' and users' experience of quality will be. You can overcome these problems by reviewing your supplier's testing efforts and filling the gaps in your own testing. However, it's often a good idea to integrate the collective test efforts and teams.[10]

The political challenges associated with either approach are significant. The third-party supplier might not want to share their testing results and test system with you.

---

10. See Chapter 10 of *Managing the Testing Process, Second Edition,* for some ideas on how to do this.

Such test information may tell you unflattering things about the quality of the component they're selling you or the kind of chaos that passes for a development process at your supplier's site. Even if the test results are good and the process is solid, the supplier may legitimately distrust the uses to which the information will be put. For example, I have seen cases where project managers tried to use the test results to negotiate after-the-fact discounts and to cancel contracts.

I've seen the disingenuousness work from supplier to buyer, too. One of my clients was taken for a ride by a software vendor. The vendor sold them a large server-based program that they claimed they had thoroughly tested. I said, "Fine, give us the test results and your test tools." They refused to give us the results, claiming the results were confidential. Cynic that I am, I immediately suspected that those results revealed their software to be full of known bugs and probably inadequately tested, too.

They did promise to deliver the tool but then backpedaled. It turned out the tool was so lousy and so poorly documented that no one but one of their test engineers could run it. They then had the audacity to bill my client well over $2,000 per day plus expenses for this test engineer to spend two weeks showing us how to use the tool. My cynicism was rewarded when, as I suspected, testing revealed many problems in their software that we needed the vendor to fix.

Whatever approach you take, I advise you to get it nailed down before the contract is signed and the project plan is finalized. Your suppliers and other third-party participants will be much more inclined to be flexible and helpful in this potentially embarrassing and dangerous realm if it's worked out before the fact. In addition, your project managers should know in advance that third-party components will mean extra testing. Many project managers assume—erroneously—that just because a vendor tested their component—or claims to have tested it—that no further testing will be required upon integration into your system.

VAGUELY DEFINED REQUIREMENTS, USAGE PROFILES, AND ENVIRONMENTS

I've stressed the importance of a high-fidelity test system, one that truthfully reproduces the user and customer experiences of system quality. This assumes, though, that I can figure out how the system will be used and the environments in which it'll be used. Sometimes these pieces of information are not provided to the test team.

In some cases, this is simply a matter of the requirements process being poor or nonexistent. For example, on one project, my team and I received a requirements document for a complex system that was all of one page long and said things like "Clients will have e-mail capability," "Client e-mail will support attachments," and "Browser will provide access to popular Web sites." We started asking questions like "Okay, what kind of e-mail encoding is supported?" "What kind of attachments, specifically?" "How big can the attachments be?" "What if a 'popular' Web site includes ActiveX controls, cookies, and so forth?" By asking these questions, we forced the project team to confront some issues that if left unresolved, would have turned into bugs. But it did impose a 20% to 30% overhead on our test development efforts.[11]

Sometimes the requirements process isn't broken so much as it's hard to define exactly what is needed. My associates and I built a test tool for a client that was in the midst of reengineering their system. It was hard to predict in advance what functions that tool needed to provide in what specific environments. As a result, we used a Spiral lifecycle model of system development, building and delivering a prototype every three or four weeks and asking the users (in this case, the client's test team), "So, is this what you need?" The answers were usually along the lines of, "Yes, but we need the ability to do this and this as well."

I have a lot of experience working in situations where the requirements aren't well defined for various reasons. My testers and I found we could effectively deal with such situations by increasing the amount of interaction with the project team. We ask lots of questions about how the system should behave, what the users will do with it, and what environments it will work in. Prototypes, simulations, and models have helped, too. The technical support staff, help desk staff, business analysts, and current users could tell us what people currently did with the system in many cases. The sales, marketing, or business analysts told us about the expectations for the new system.

I also find that I need to have people with a higher level of application domain knowledge on my test teams when requirements, usage, and field environments are poorly defined or just plain hard to define. If the test team doesn't have a precise definition of how the users will expect the system to behave under specific test conditions, then I'll need to have that capability within my own team.

One of my rules of thumb for projects with vague requirements is, "If in doubt, file a bug report." That is, report a bug in any situation where a test result could be reasonably construed as either pass or fail. This results in the project team using the bug reporting and change management processes (see Chapters 14 and 16) to facilitate a discussion about questionable behavior. While this is a subject that comes up more

---

11. For a discussion about good requirements and requirements processes, I like Karl Wiegers's book *Software Requirements*.

during test execution than during test development, the test cases need to be documented with the appropriate degree of ambiguity.[12]

BALANCING COVERAGE, SCHEDULE, AND BUDGET

The process outlined in this and the previous chapter does suffer from an inherent scope risk. Following it literally, the test team develops tests strictly in priority order, which means that complete coverage is available for the high-priority items before any coverage whatsoever is available for the lower-priority items. This is fine if you have exactly enough or extra time to develop all the tests committed to during the planning process. But what if you run out of time?

No matter how carefully I do my job of estimation, sometimes I get it wrong. I find it's most frequently test development tasks that I undersize, especially developing tools and automated tests. So, I'm careful to track progress against my schedule at least once a week. If a task goes over, I must quickly assess the effect of that delay on my test execution. It's undesirable—and often politically untenable—to delay the start of testing a component, a build, or a complete system because the testware, test execution process, or test environment is not ready.

This is where the risk and contingency planning discussed in Chapter 6 comes into play. If those test development efforts that you identified as at-risk begin to get out of control, you may need to revisit or even activate the contingency plan. For tests you intended to automate, the contingency plan might be, "Try to do it manually." Since there's probably some effort required to get ready for that manual test effort, knowing when to trigger that effort is important.

I find I have to be very careful to be honest with myself in this situation. I would prefer not to execute the contingency plan. After all, if it were my first choice in how to handle something, it would be part of my main plan, not my contingency plan. However, my preferences don't dictate reality all the time, so I need to remain clear-eyed about what the reality is. If some element of a project is out of control, there comes a time when I must rethink the approach and adopt a new one.

Externally imposed changes in plan or resource availability can affect my ability to develop all the planned tests, too. I find I can minimize the impact of these situations

---

12. Johanna Rothman's article "Testing in the Dark," *Software Testing and Quality Engineering*, Volume 1, Issue 2 (Mar/Apr 1999), now found at www.jrothman.com and www.stickyminds.com, can provide some additional ideas in this regard.

if I develop tests in bite-sized pieces. In other words, test development efforts, rather than being an all-or-nothing affair, should deliver some level of testing capability early and additional increments of testing capability often. A Spiral or Incremental lifecycle is well suited for test system development for this reason, especially for test tools and automated tests.

In some cases, you may find that it's necessary to revisit the trade-off between extensive and broad coverage. Earlier in this chapter, I talked about the spectrum from extensive testing through balanced testing through opportunity testing to simply reporting observed bugs. The extensive testing end of the spectrum is going to tend to consume a disproportionately large amount of the overall testing effort, including test system development.

So, it can make sense to develop balanced tests for these risks to system quality first and then go back and enhance them once all the other test coverage is complete. If you focus on developing extensive tests of the most-critical quality risks first but ignore the lower-priority risks, you may run out of time before you get to the lower-priority risks at all. This will mean that you have quite a bit of testing covering a very small set of risks to system quality, with no testing in the other areas. This might not be a trade-off that makes sense. Honest discussions and course correction with your managers and the other test stakeholders should the test development fall behind is the best way to reevaluate the trade-off and emphasis decisions made earlier.

IMPLEMENT IMPROVEMENTS

How can we improve test system development? Many answers to that question involve adopting new techniques and technologies. These are certainly important, but, being domain specific, are beyond the scope of this book. However, there are some general thoughts I can offer on the process itself that are worth considering.

1. Assess the quality of your existing test system, if any. If you are starting from scratch, great—you can build the perfect test system from the ground up. However, if you have an existing test system, ask yourself if it's a good one. If the answer is no, can you change the process and institute improvements that will allow you to do a good job of testing whatever projects are underway right now? Of course, if you increase test coverage in the middle of a project, you can be seen as raising the quality bar unfairly. Getting stakeholder buy-in is important. But I would encourage you not to ignore the task because it might be politically unpleasant. I found during the times I have done so that people tend to nod in agreement to statements like, "We don't want to raise the quality bar in

the middle of this project," but they will not react sanguinely to the specific gaps in test coverage that are associated with that.

2. Study and apply advances in test techniques. Part of the process I suggested in this chapter involves selecting appropriate test techniques. With the growth in the testing tools available, the rapid evolution of the underlying technologies for system development, and the new ideas being advanced by test practitioners, the test techniques appropriate for a particular test system are changing all the time. These changes need not mean that old ways of testing become wrong, but rather that improved ways are possible. Medicine offers an apt analogy here. Doctors are required to undergo continuing education to retain their medical licenses so that they can apply the latest ideas in promoting health and curing disease to their patients. The field of software testing is moving no less rapidly, so we must continue to study the advances to make sure we do testing as effectively and efficiently as possible.

3. Adopt a long-range plan. All of these recommendations are likely to work better if implemented over a long time. Test systems, like the systems we test, tend to develop inertia. Looking at how the test development process could be done better—and specifically how weakness in the test system right now affects your ability to do good testing—and then responding with a long-range plan for improvement is the way to go. This long-range plan should also consider that as you are trying to fine-tune your test system, the testing context will evolve as well. Any long-range plan for test system improvement and test system development process improvement must consider the future. What features and behaviors will the system offer? What organizational changes are on the horizon? What opportunities for change—e.g., management perceptions of a need for improvement—exist that can be leveraged?

4. Adopt appropriate documentation. There are plenty of templates for documenting your test system. But simply filling in the blanks on these templates will not necessarily result in the right level of documentation. If you have an existing test system, then you may find that your previous style of documentation was insufficiently precise. In that case, translating it to the newly adopted style may be something you want to start now and do over time. In the case of excessively detailed documentation, you may want to simply let that documentation gradually slip into obsolescence and replace it with the new style then. Either way, it is unlikely that you would have the time or the budget to apply a major change in style retroactively to a large test system, so a gradual approach might work best.

5. Assess and harmonize tester skills. What I'm suggesting in this section may well amount to a very fundamental set of changes to how you perform your testing. This means that you'll need to have a test team in place that's up to the

322   PART II   PREPARE

job. As your long-range plan comes together, you should revisit the critical skills list that you put in place earlier. What new skills are implicit in the changes you intend to make in your test system and your test system development process? Where does your team stand on those skills? You'll need to have a plan in place for bringing your test team up to the level of the testing process you propose. After all, what good are the perfect plan and the perfect process if you don't have a team qualified to execute them?

I have found, on projects where we used existing test systems, that gradual improvement was the easiest approach. Starting from scratch makes for a different set of challenges.

We've now reached the end of the preparation portion of the test process. We're ready to run tests, to discover the quality of the system under test. Let's get to it.

Step #	Step	Done?
2.	Prepare: Assemble the people and tests.	✔
2.A	Through staffing and training, build a team of test professionals with the appropriate skills, attitudes, and motivation.	✔
2.B	Design, develop, acquire, and verify the test system that the test team uses to assess the quality of the system under test.	✔

PART III

PERFORM

W ith the end of Part II and the opening of Part III, we've reached a logical breaking point, a major transition in the testing process. Jamal and his team have
reached the end of a distinct portion of the overall testing process. Until this point,
Critical Testing Processes has been about *getting ready*. Now, let's turn our attention
to performing the testing.

Performing the testing is more visible than planning or preparing for testing, but it is
often misunderstood as well. Again, faulty mission statements, often along the lines
of "making sure the system works," can rear their heads. When this happens inside
the team, disappointment and schedule overruns can occur when bugs are found.
When this happens outside the test team, conflict and surprise can arise when results
are reported. Chaos can erupt when a project team that failed to anticipate the need
for change must accommodate test findings that are bad news.

Step #	Step	Done?
3.	Perform: Do the testing and gather the results.	☐
3.A	Acquire and install a test release consisting of some or all of the components in the system under test.	☐
3.D	Assign, track, and manage the set of test cases to be run against each test release.	☐

12

AN ESSENTIAL HANDOFF: MANAGE TEST RELEASES

Even when people are aware of the need to deliver a test release to the test team, few are aware of the complexity and challenges associated with this process. Test release management is the downstream end of the system configuration management, revision control, system build, and system library maintenance activities. Like testing, these activities can have a tremendous impact on the project, for good or ill.

For testing to yield an accurate, meaningful assessment of quality, test release management and all the upstream activities must be performed with precision and alacrity. Imagine a drug trial where all, some, or even a few of the drug samples given to patients were adulterated with toxins or weakened with inert materials. What would your confidence be in that trial's findings on the safety and efficacy of the drug? Similarly, if it is not possible to identify, down to each constituent unit, the composition of the system under test during each test cycle, what can we really say about the quality of the system under test?

So, for the test release management process to work, we must start with known components that differ from previous components in known ways. We must assemble those components into a testable release at some level of completeness (appropriate to the test phase). We must deliver, install, and configure that release in the test environment. Only then can we begin to assess quality.

Without software to test, there can be no software testing. As obvious as this statement is, many software development organizations do a poor job of managing test release processes. Often, the role of building a test release devolves to a test organization ill prepared to handle the tasks. In these cases, the processes are defined reactively.

Instead, let's look at ways to handle this process through careful planning, before the fact, intelligently.[1]

A TEST RELEASE PROCESS

Process 8 is a practical test release process. This process will suffice for a product such as a personal computer application, a browser-based system hosted on application server, or a simple client-server system. I'll discuss the complications that arise with shared databases, custom hardware, and the like at the end of this chapter.

Step #	Step	Done?
1.	Select the content (bug fixes, new features, and documentation) for a particular test release.	☐
2.	Implement the changes required for the bug fixes and new features, checking those changes into the source repository as they are completed and unit tested.	☐
3.	Fetch the source files from the repository; compile, link, and otherwise assemble the build; and mark the build (in the build and in the repository) with a version number.	☐
4.	Smoke test the build. If the tests pass, continue with the next step; if the tests fail, figure out what went wrong, fix the problem, and return to the previous step.	☐
5.	Create an installable media image of the build, package it appropriately, and deliver it to the person responsible for installing it in the test environment.	☐
6.	Install the build in the test environment.	☐
7.	Smoke test the build in the test environment. If the tests pass, begin the test cycle; if the tests fail, uninstall the build, resume the old test cycle, and return the build to the development team to start over at the first step.	☐

PROCESS 8   A TEST RELEASE PROCESS

---

1. A number of quotes from fellow test professionals appeared in the original version of this chapter, published as "Test Release Processes" in the *Journal of Software Testing Professionals*, Volume 1, Issue 2. While I have removed the quotes to fit the overall style of this book, their ideas remain. I'd like to thank the following people, in alphabetical order, for their insightful contributions: Randall Becker, Ross Collard, Gary Dawson, Harvey Deutsch, Tim Dyes, Danny Faught, Peggy Fouts, Darcy Martin, and Barbara Ruf.

Build, Release, Test Release

An installable software, hardware, or system item—or even a whole system—transmitted to the test group for testing.

THE BIG BUILD HITS THE TEST LAB

On December 6 at 2:01 PM, Jamal joined the Sumatra Project Management team for the weekly change control board meeting. One of the items on the agenda was finalizing the content for increment 3. This increment was scheduled to enter system test on December 13, with the test effort starting against the first test release of increment 3 on December 16. Since the Sumatra test team had been effective at finding bugs to date, Jamal wanted to be sure that some of the bugs that were slowing down test execution were high on the priority list for this first increment 3 build.

In addition, since the development plan showed increment 3 as containing the bulk of the remaining functionality, he wanted to make sure that plan hadn't changed. In fact, Emma Moorhouse and Dinesh Kumar, two of the team's test engineers, had named the first release of increment 3 "the Big Build." There were a number of tests currently blocked, awaiting functionality scheduled for the Big Build. Jamal wanted to have some time to confer with his team on priority and logistics for these tests should they become unblocked by this new increment.

"Well," Kate Hernandez, the project manager, said, "we're all here now"—Jamal nodded an apology for his minute of tardiness—"so let's get started. Jenny, how about filling us in on where we stand with increment 3."

"Pretty well, on the whole," Jenny Kaufman, the development manager, replied. "Much better than things were looking just a few days ago. Two of the team managed to fix that showstopping data quality bug that Jamal's team caught in increment 3 integration

Repository, Library, Source Code Control System

A software application, usually running on a widely accessible server, that stores the source code, online help, HTML documents, audio files, and other files that, upon compilation and assembly, make up the installable software item, along with storing associated documents like test plans, risk analyses, and requirements specifications.

testing on Monday. And John finally figured out how to resolve that timing problem that was causing the lockup."

Kate gave Jenny a quizzical look, so Jenny added, "You remember the one that Hemamalini found in increment 1 system testing, where the hierarchical storage manager wasn't responding? Well, it was a timing issue in the server code that talked to the HSM server."

Jenny turned to Jamal and said, "I know John already told Hemamalini this, but please pass on a 'thanks' from me, too, because that bug would have been nasty to track down if she hadn't written that little script that reproduced the failure."

Jamal nodded and responded, "Hemamalini's a keeper, that's for sure. We need to find a place for her in the permanent staff somewhere."

Kate replied, "I'm already on top of that, Jamal. I've been talking to Harold and John, and we should talk after this meeting about some of our ideas. We think Hemamalini could be a real help to the development team in terms of building unit and component test harnesses."[2]

Jamal smiled and thought, The service organization attitude pays off again.

"But that's not why we're here," Kate concluded, getting back on topic by saying, "Anyway, so what I hear you saying, Jenny, is that we're on target for increment 3 on schedule on December 13, next Friday. Is that right?"

"Yes," she replied, "I think so. The only items at risk now are some of the advanced administrative features. We might need to slip those to increment 4."

Before Jamal could even raise his hand to speak, Kate turned to him and asked, "Jamal, what does that do to testing?"

"I don't know for sure; I'd have to get the specific list of features that won't work. Some of the security and privacy tests are basically attempts to circumvent access, read, modify, and delete restrictions created by the admin accounts. Also, some of the

---

2. For a practical discussion of implementing such techniques on a real project, see "Mission Made Possible," by Rex Black and Greg Kubaczkowski, which first appeared in *Software Testing and Quality Engineering*, Volume 4, Issue 4 (July/Aug 2002), and is now available on www.stickyminds.com and www.rexblackconsulting.com.

feature and stress tests depend on some of the nonhierarchical security features having to do with workgroup administrators. There could be blocked tests," Jamal concluded with a concerned expression.

"Gotcha," Kate replied and then turned to Jenny. "Okay, so Jenny, please get the list of features at risk to Jamal this afternoon." Jenny nodded in agreement. "Jamal, can you please go through that list and report to me tomorrow on the impact of testing? Also, if there is an impact, please work out a couple of mitigation options for each blocked or impeded test with Jenny. Jenny, please carve out some time in the morning to be available to Jamal for that effort. " Both Jamal and Jenny nodded.

"Okay, so other than those features, Jenny, you've gone through the plan of record and made sure that everything that's scheduled for increment 3 is or will be wrapped this coming week?"

"Yes," Jenny concurred, "all the items outside of those features we've discussed are either done or are low-risk, low-complexity items that we're confident will be done no later than next Friday and probably earlier."

"Good. Next order of business is bug reports, right Jamal?" Kate asked.

"Absolutely right, a topic near to my heart," Jamal smiled.

"Jenny, can you please go down the list of bugs scheduled to be fixed and dropped into increment 3?"

Jenny walked through the list slowly, looking around for comments and questions as she did. "1792, the file lock bug. 1793, 1798, 1799, and 1800, the misspelled error messages. 1699, Hemamalini's lockup bug. 1787 and 1788 turned out to be duplicates; the root cause of that data quality bug is the same."

Jamal, who had been ticking bugs off his report as she read them, interrupted, "Are you sure about that? Those bugs involved very different test cases and data."

Jenny replied, "Yeah, I know, but there was some sort of screwy configuration setting in the database server that we'd overlooked. It turns out there's a whole cluster of bugs you could have reported against that, but most of the ways of getting at them are blocked by stuff in increment 3."

Jamal shrugged and said, "Well, you could be right. I don't want to be a pest or second-guess your team, but if you'd ask the guys working on it to double-check, I'd appreciate it. Those two bugs block a whole raft of integration test cases that I'd really like to get through."

"I'll check," Jenny agreed and then continued with her list. She ran through about a dozen additional bugs that would be fixed. She concluded by asking Jamal, "Do you have any showstoppers or blocking bugs on your list that I didn't mention?"

"Well, actually just one," Jamal replied, "1815. I realize that's a brand-new bug, so it's a bit much to ask that it get fixed in a week, but since that blocks most of the testing using legacy browsers, I'm a bit concerned that we're going to lose out on some important configuration coverage if we don't get a fix in soon."

"Hmm," Jenny said, "I'll need to talk to the team about that, but it seems like we should be able to get it turned around. Our average closure period is around ten days, including the natural process overheads, right?"

"That's right," Jamal agreed, checking his charts, "if this turns out to be a run-of-the-mill bug that gets fixed in the average amount of time, the historical data for this project says you can get it in."

Step #	Step	Done?
1.	Select the content (bug fixes, new features, and documentation) for a particular test release.	✔

The meeting moved on to other topics, including progress toward subsequent increments. Shortly after the meeting, Jenny's precise list of at-risk increment 3 functions appeared in Jamal's e-mail in-box. Jamal printed four copies of the e-mail and then asked Emma, Dinesh, and Lin-Tsu to join him in a small conference room for a minute.

"So," Jamal explained, as he handed out the e-mail, "these features are at risk for increment 3. What I need each of you to do is to spend some time looking at how the absence—or just significant bugginess—of these features would affect your tests scheduled for increment 3. If there is any effect, please try to come up with a mitigation or workaround plan. I'll need to get e-mails from each of you with your analysis of this by mid-morning tomorrow, okay?"

All nodded assent and the quick huddle came to an end. The next morning, Jamal received e-mails from Emma, Dinesh, and Lin-Tsu. All predicted minor if any effects from delays in the arrival of the listed features. Jamal grabbed everyone quickly and asked them to join him in his office. "So, let me just make sure we're in agreement: The message I should send to the project management team is that the development team is free to slip those features to increment 4."

Everyone nodded, but Lin-Tsu added, "Well, with the usual caveats, right?"

Jamal cocked his head and asked, "Usual caveats?"

"Sure. There are the risks we can predict and the risks we can't predict. We can predict—because we know from experience—that anytime there's a delay in getting some feature into testing that's not accompanied by a delay in the release date, that means less testing for the feature, and that means the feature is at a higher level of quality risk in the field."

Jamal nodded in assent and murmured, "Yeah, of course."

"In addition," Lin-Tsu continued, "there are the risks we can't predict. We don't know how the system is built—by organizational design to some extent, right?—so we can't know whether the absence of these features is going to mask or expose other behaviors."

A circle of raised eyebrows led Lin-Tsu to elaborate. "Whenever these features drop in, they could lead to other bugs. Some could be bugs in new code, some could be regression bugs. We don't have a lot of insight into the likelihood of that because we don't know the details of how the code that implements these features interacts with other parts of the system. When these features arrive, they might make problems that seem serious become less serious. Or vice versa. Software isn't like a car, where if I had a problem with tuning the radio, I could at least expect that problem not to cause a flat tire.[3] Sometimes there are subtle and hard-to-anticipate consequences and interactions. I guess the point I'm trying to make—and one I've been thinking about for a while in relation to this Incremental lifecycle—is that the shorter the period of time that the final system under test is complete and in system testing, the more likely it is that the final assessment of system quality—I mean, at the system test exit meeting—is not entirely accurate."

---

3. This neat metaphor is found in Boris Beizer's three-part series "Software Is Different," available on Software Research's Quality Techniques Newsletter archive at www.soft.com/News/QTN-Online/qtnapr01.html, www.soft.com/News/QTN-Online/qtnmay01.html, and www.soft.com/News/QTN-Online/qtnjun01.html.

A chorus of "ohs" and "hmms" went around the four testers.

"So," Lin-Tsu continued, "I think now would be a good time to explain to the project management team the risk implications of delays in delivery into system test and the Incremental lifecycle in general. I'm not saying this Incremental approach is bad," she hastened to add. "So far it's been lots better than some of the other projects. But risk is always a trade-off, right? To get some of the flexibility we want in final content, we're probably pushing up the quality risk a little. Worth a mention, since we're the 'quality risk management gang,' right?"

Jamal smiled slowly. "Very astute thinking, Lin-Tsu, especially that part about the risks we can't predict. I'll make sure to mention to Kate in my e-mail that you pointed this out."

Based on this conversation, Jamal drafted a quick e-mail to Kate with a CC to Jenny explaining that while the delay in delivery of administrative features wouldn't affect testing in terms of efficiency, there was a risk-mitigation compromise being made. He wrote in one part, "As Lin-Tsu pointed out to me, there are two kinds of risks: the predictable and the unpredictable. We can predict that less testing of these features leads to greater risk when they ship. We can't predict, though, the ways in which prolonged testing of a system that is less than feature complete distorts the accuracy of our assessment of quality. (Lin-Tsu, by the way, should be considered for promotion to management for this insight and her many other competencies.) My team and I agree that we can tolerate a slip on these features to increment 4. However, if any major feature such as these doesn't make increment 4, I recommend we consider, in the preceding change control board meetings, whether to push that feature off to a subsequent maintenance release."

Jenny and Kate were both in accord with this e-mail. Jamal was gratified to overhear Kate and Jenny thanking Lin-Tsu for her observation in the hallway later that day.

On Friday morning, Jenny sent an e-mail to the Project Management team letting them know that increment 3 had been checked in. She attached a set of release notes. Thankfully, only one of the six features at risk was not there. She asked Yasuhiro Kanagawa, the Release Engineering manager, to build a release and smoke test it ASAP so she could catch and resolve any problems that arose that afternoon—or, worst case, that weekend if need be.

A couple of hours later, Yasuhiro sent a terse e-mail. "Build is good. Smoke results attached. Keith, please coordinate install with Jamal."

Step #	Step	Done?
2.	Implement the changes required for the bug fixes and new features, checking those changes into the source repository as they are completed and unit tested.	☑
3.	Fetch the source files from the repository; compile, link, and otherwise assemble the build; and mark the build (in the build and in the repository) with a version number.	☑
4.	Smoke test the build. If the tests pass, continue with the next step; if the tests fail, figure out what went wrong, fix the problem, and return to the previous step.	☑

Keith and Jamal ran into each other on the way to each other's offices and then laughed. "Friday evening's looming, huh Keith?" Jamal joked.

"You don't seem anxious to hang around here after 5:00 either, dude," Keith replied.

"You're right, I'm not. I have family coming to town over the weekend and I have to entertain. This is Austin, after all, so there's plenty of entertaining that can be done on a Friday night."

"You bet. So," Keith said, getting down to business, "what's the plan?"

"My vote would be, 'Second verse, same as the first,' right? We have an established process for installing the builds, so let's stick with it. Unless you think there've been problems?"

"No, no, I think it works fine, Jamal," Keith replied. "You shut down testing at 4:00 PM, and I'll ask Petra to install the build then. As soon as she's done, which should be less than an hour, your test tech—what's his name again?"

"Dale."

"Dale, right. Dale can start the smoke test in the test environment on his way out the door."

"Good plan," Jamal said.

"Of course—I thought of it," Keith joked. "Actually, Petra and Dale came up with the details, so I guess we should give them credit."

"You know," Jamal said, "there's a management cliche that there's no end to what can be accomplished if you don't care who gets the credit, but maybe that should really be that there's no end to what can be accomplished when smart people share the credit."

"I'd buy that," Keith replied. "Anyway, I'll go get Petra queued up—though I'm sure she already is—and wait for your call. You planning on stopping by this weekend to check the smoke test results?"

"I'll probably just log in via the Internet and check them that way. No point in spending a weekend in the office on a project that's going this well."

And it continued to go well. Before Jamal left to pick up his family at Austin's Bergstrom Airport, he checked with Dale.

"How's the smoke test, Dale?"

"Already up and running. So far, no failures."

"You and Petra seem to have that process wired, huh?"

"She installs it, I smoke it, then we all test it. Simple as A-B-C," Dale replied with a grin.

"I think a good process is always simple, Dale. Getting too clever has killed more projects that I care to remember, but on this one we're being smart by being simple."

"Have a good weekend, boss," Dale said.

"Hey, you too, Dale." Jamal looked at his watch. It read 4:50 PM. Jamal smiled and joked, "You know, Dale, in light of all your hard work, why don't you take the rest of the day off?"

Step #	Step	Done?
5.	Create an installable media image of the build, package it appropriately, and deliver it to the person responsible for installing it in the test environment.	✔
6.	Install the build in the test environment.	✔
7.	Smoke test the build in the test environment. If the tests pass, begin the test cycle; if the tests fail, uninstall the build, resume the old test cycle, and return the build to the development team to start over at the first step.	✔

RECOGNIZE A GOOD TEST RELEASE PROCESS

A good process is simple, as our fictional friend Jamal points out, but that doesn't mean it's simple to design a good and simple process. Across a number of projects, I've noticed this is especially true of test release management. There is a universal temptation to hurl stuff into testing as if system engineering were a form of trench warfare. A great deal of care and thought is required to put a good test release process in place. Let's look at project team behaviors and achievements when using good test release processes.

PROVIDE INSTALLABLE, IMPROVED, AND STABLE TEST RELEASES

I once did business with a company that had an excellent process for interacting with their customers. They surveyed customer satisfaction. They sent pleasant e-mails about their commitment to customer quality and resolving my problems when I filed customer service requests through their fast, automated Web site. There was just one hitch: They couldn't deliver a working, quality service to me. They never fixed any of the problems I reported to their customer service. So, I am no longer one of their customers.

The same applies to a test release process. The key indicator of a well-run process is that it results in the delivery, every single time, of a build that is suitable for testing. All of the other signs of a good process can be present. But suppose every test release is a nightmare of wasted time getting the build installed, a tangle of regression, and a tar pit of blocked tests, mid-test crashes, and other indicators of instability. Wouldn't you conclude that your test release process is seriously broken?

A good test release process will deliver a build that can be installed. The installation process must at the very least deposit all the contents of the build in the right locations, with the right access permissions, and in the right order. It should not damage the test environment by, for example, overwriting files used by other programs. If there are preinstall or post-install operations required for the installation to succeed, those should either be automated or appropriately documented for the kind of operators who will actually perform the installation. Many system environments, including Windows and UNIX, have commercial tools that can be used to create installable releases or packages.

A good test release process should usually deliver a build that is better than the one before. This means that, for the most part, stuff that worked before still works. It also means that at least some of the stuff that was broken before works better than it did in the previous test releases. As I'll discuss when we get to results reporting in

Chapter 15, two indicators of a project converging toward a successful completion are the steady shrinking of the total number of open bugs and a gradual reduction in the number of bugs found in each release. Thus, the general trend must be for improvement from one release to the next.

This general trend for improvement in builds arises in part from careful development and bug fixing by the programmers. On one project, about 20% of bug reports were reopened at least once—i.e., a bug that a developer claimed was fixed either wasn't fixed in the test release or was fixed at one point but broken again later. The testers had to reopen one bug report ten times! The upstream processes, programming and debugging, must include support for adequate unit, component, and, if appropriate, integration testing.

The best approach I've seen for such testing involves developers creating test cases for code as they write it and then checking those test cases into an automated testing harness when they check in the code. This ever-growing set of tests runs against every build as part of the build process, ensuring that the individual pieces continue to work properly. (In general, good developer testing, especially at the unit and component levels, is one sign of a good testing process, as I'll discuss in Chapter 17.) This technique, which is a software engineering best practice well over a decade old, is now coming into its own with the advent of the various agile methodologies for software development, which stress the concepts of test-first development and automated test harnesses.[4]

The other requirement for improvement is careful revision control and software configuration management. Two people working on the same module at once, with no source code control library to check code into, multiple copies of the source tree in different locations, and other such chaotic treatment of the system's underlying components, consistently results in bad test releases. There is no end to the amount of grief that can be avoided through a simple, lightweight configuration management regimen. Like unit, component, and integration testing through automated harnesses, this is another best practice that has been around for decades.[5]

---

4. Both Glenford Myers and Fred Brooks discuss test harnesses in *The Art of Software Testing*, first published in 1979, and *The Mythical Man-Month*, first published in 1975, respectively. For a discussion of modern test harnesses, see "Mission Made Possible," mentioned earlier.
5. My first UNIX development project, in 1983, included rigorous software configuration management under the supervision of a librarian using the SCCS utility. This was a decades-old well-established best practice *even then*, since Fred Brooks describes a "program library and accounting" system used on the OS/360 project at IBM in the early 1960s, in his chapter "Sharp Tools" in *The Mythical Man-Month*.

Now, even with installable builds; good unit, component, and integration testing; and effective software configuration management, a bad build can still get released to the test team. Sometimes the pieces work alone, but once put together, have problems that only show up in certain areas or under certain conditions. Many of us have heard a confounded programmer say, "It worked fine on my system."

Of course, there's no way to guarantee that a system will pass all the tests before it's released to testing. If we could guarantee that, then we wouldn't need to test. However, the 80/20 rule can help us avoid wasted time.[6] Most of the large problems—the test blockers, the system crashers, the data corrupters—will show up in the first few hours of testing. This is especially true if you run a broad set of tests to start with. This rule is the driving force behind the idea of smoke testing. Again, this is not a new idea either, since I worked on a project in the late 1980s that had extensive automated smoke tests integrated into the build and release processes.

PRODUCE PREDICTABLE, TIMELY, AND REGULAR TEST RELEASES

Even if a new release is installable, improved, and stable, accepting it for testing has a number of implications for the test operation. The test manager must communicate to the test team what tests they should run against this build. Someone must install the release, load any necessary data files, maybe update some databases, or modify dependent system configurations. In the case of client-server and other multiplatform test settings, installing a new release may involve installation on many computers. Sometimes the order of installation matters. The test team must ensure that the test release is ready for testing. If it's not, they must make it ready—for example, by patching the software on the fly, fixing a previously undiscovered test environment configuration problem, and so on. If we can't ready the test release, then the test team must remove it from the test environment. Once we finally have a test release properly installed and the test environment ready, the test team often is mandated to proceed to confirmation testing, which is verifying that those bugs reportedly fixed in the release are indeed resolved. Finally, having gone through all these steps, the test team can resume planned test activities. In some cases, we'll first want to do a complete regression

---

6. The 80/20 rule exists in a number of variations. The one I'm using here is the management version that says that 80% of the benefit of any activity tends to come from the first 20% of the effort. The 80/20 rule is more formally called the Pareto Principle, and it was first described as such by J. M. Juran. For an interesting discussion on this rule and its application to testing, see Erik Petersen's paper "Smarter Testing Using the 80/20 Rule" in the *Proceedings of the STAR West 2002 Conference*, available at www.stickyminds.com.

test (rerunning all previously run tests or retesting all previously tested conditions). In situations where the organization has multiple test projects going on at once, the arrival of a build for an urgent project can trump testing of other projects, requiring some significant and risky context-switching on the part of all or some of the test team.

While not all test groups experience such extensive effects, many do. Under these circumstances, installing a new release is not a decision to take lightly. Since it interrupts and changes the planned test activities, I and many other test managers I've talked to find it undesirable to have releases show up at unpredictable times. Likewise, because of the overhead associated with installing a new build, having them arrive too frequently can seriously affect forward progress. The more frequently test releases arrive that are buggy, unstable, or uninstallable, the more important it is to slow the test release process. (Such a situation also calls for smoke testing test releases before they arrive.)

However, because testing against a stale (i.e., outdated) test release can result in the reporting of already-resolved bugs, it is also possible to have test releases show up too infrequently. If it takes a long time to run all your tests, you might want to accept a test release prior to running all the test cases.

This brings us back to the topic of test releases, test passes, and test cycles, discussed in Chapter 3. Since the arrival of a test release is a trigger for a subsequent test cycle, having predictable and regular test releases allows the test team to schedule work around those releases. Notice in Figure 12-1 how Jamal is able to plan on periods of confirmation testing, scheduled testing, and exploratory testing within each test cycle. This regularity also allows him to predict how long it will take to run a test pass, because he can factor a known amount of test release overhead into the plan. He can schedule less urgent but no less important activities like updating test cases and data, fine-tuning automated test scripts, and other test maintenance activities, since regular and predictable test releases allow the test manager to plan the workweek in advance and to set time aside for various activities.

Conversely, projects that lack predictability and regularity of test releases often pay a high price for what they perceive as flexibility. The price includes ineffective and inefficient testing done by a harried staff using broken testware on unreliable test environments, scrambling to accommodate last-minute changes in plan. A chaotic, unpredictable test release process is corrosive to every other process described in this book. What organizations often don't realize is that behaviors that decrease overall team efficiency and effectiveness do not increase flexibility, they decrease it by stealing energy, focus, and that most precious project resource, time.

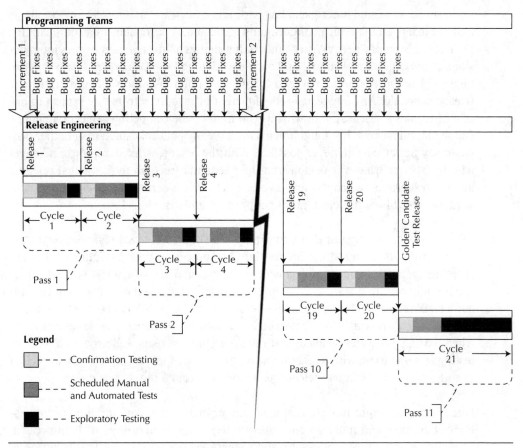

FIGURE 12-1 TEST PASSES, TEST CYCLES, AND TEST RELEASES

On one of the best-managed projects that I worked on, the development team started buttoning up their development activities for the agreed-upon release content on Friday, and by Saturday night the code was ready. The release manager would come in Sunday morning, and we received a test release every Sunday afternoon. By the time the weekend shift ended on Sunday evening, we had a new test release installed and sanity tested, ready for testing on Monday morning.

When multiple projects contend for a single set of test resources, this coordination becomes more critical—and more difficult. Just one chaotic project can, through unpredictable test releases, disrupt an entire test organization. One test manager memorably described this as "getting hit by the bad-project train."

Notice in the case study that Jamal has partitioned his team and his test environments into subteams and specific configurations dedicated to particular projects, including the new version of SpeedyWriter and testing maintenance releases of previous versions of the OfficeArrow suite. I find such partitioning based on projects helpful when I have one or more projects that tend to inflict a lot of last-minute changes on the test release schedule. Any suggested redeployment of resources from one project to another becomes a discussion in which I can involve the competing project managers. Call me Machiavellian, but I find it helps preserve my political capital to get other people to say no for me whenever possible. With the resources fixed, a project manager who insists, for whatever reason, that he needs the freedom to throw test releases into the test process whenever and as often as he wants can only create negative consequences for his own project, not other people's projects.

All of this is not to suggest that you can have a single, universal test release process for everything that comes into the test lab. The process shown in Figure 12-1 is appropriate for a development project with an Incremental lifecycle, a test set that can be comfortably run from start to finish in a couple of weeks, and a stable product without a lot of regression in each test release. In a Waterfall or V Model project, the increments are inappropriate. My best experience with maintenance release testing came when we had a feature-complete first release to the test team, followed by a week of testing and bug fixes, with a second release and week of testing, and finally a week of testing against the customer release as it worked through the release process.

Sometimes you might have to test emergency patches that contain one or two customer bug fixes and must go out within a week—or even a day—of being coded. These are very high risk endeavors, and a smart test release strategy that balances all the competing risks is key. Perhaps you provide the emergency patches only to those customers or users who are experiencing the problem and then include that patch in the next scheduled maintenance release, after thorough regression testing.

As you can see, different circumstances, including different places in the system lifecycle, can strongly influence your test release process. A customized set of standard processes, along the lines of what's in this book, can help. That way you can be smart once and reuse that wisdom over and over again, instead of making it up as you go along.

USE DEFINED, CUSTOMER-LIKE INSTALL AND UNINSTALL PROCESSES

I mentioned earlier that a release must at least be installable, but a good test release process includes an installation procedure that is well defined. In addition, at least during the system test phase and any subsequent test phases, I prefer the test release processes that use the same installation procedure that customers, operators, or users in the field will follow after the system is deployed or shipped. (This includes testing with the same kinds of privileges and accounts.) I also like to see—and test, of course—a process for uninstalling a test release, both because customers or the IS support team might need to do so and because it might be necessary to back out a bad test release.

The complexity of the install process is often a function of the system under test, as I'll discuss further later in the chapter. A Windows application typically has a straightforward installation process, while complex IT environments with multiple servers, sometimes distributed across a wide-area network, can take many person-hours of time to install. In all cases, though, the process should be made as simple as possible. Simpler processes are less prone to error and therefore more likely to result in a testable configuration sooner. Also, simpler processes can often involve fewer people. The possibilities for miscommunication, disagreements, and political issues increase with the number of people and groups involved, which increases the difficulty, duration, and likelihood of failure for any activity.

If the process is simple enough, the test team itself can do the work. This allows the test team to verify the install, uninstall, update, and patch processes themselves. In the case of shrink-wrapped software, this often involves testing the installation on a variety of system configurations. For IT software, the environment may not change, but variations like the order of executable installation or changes to the database; the use of patch, update, or fresh install processes; and the like create multiple test conditions. So, the installation process should cover all these tests, thereby sparing the test team an extensive and redundant installation test effort that must occur during the testing cycles themselves. After all, you have to install the releases at some point.

The uninstall process is, in the best case, a variation of the install process. For Windows applications, for example, the Control Panel allows access to both functions, and InstallShield-format packages support removal of files and registry changes as a menu selection. For Solaris, the package management utilities *pkgadd* and *pkgrm* provide like functions. In some situations, using a disk imaging utility like Ghost can allow the test team to preserve clean images of systems to which they may apply any level of release. However, in some very complex IT environments, backing out a change may be much more difficult than installing one, unless configuration management tools exist that can reliably undo any sequence of changes to a system. Nevertheless, I lobby hard for an uninstall facility. Without such capabilities, I have worked on projects where fatally flawed test releases destroyed the test environment, resulting in a week or more of downtime while the entire test environment was completely reinstalled, including the operating system, supporting software, and a previous version of the system under

> **Build ID, Release Name, Revision, Revision Number, Version, Version Number**
> Some sequence of numbers and/or characters that uniquely identifies the release.

test. I've heard similar stories from other test practitioners, so it's not just my bad luck. Do you have spare time for that in your test execution schedule?

On a UNIX network operating system project long ago, I saw the install and uninstall process done very well. The hardware environment was a heterogeneous mainframe/PS-2 network with Ethernet and token-ring infrastructure. An integrated program, launched from one server, could 1) install a fresh version of the operating system onto formatted hard disks on one or more servers or workstations, 2) update existing servers or workstations with updates or patches, or 3) back out updates and patches. During system test, we varied the process used every week to cover the possible combinations, providing both a clean release process into test for the subsequent week and, by the end of the system test phase, systematic testing of the install and uninstall facilities in the operating system.

GIVE THE TEST RELEASE A NAME THAT IT KNOWS

A test release that comes from a solid configuration management system will generally have an associated release identifier or revision number. Ideally, a simple command or action accessible to the tester will allow him to obtain that revision number from the system under test itself. For example, in most Windows applications, the menu selection Help/About will bring up a screen that includes a revision number.

This is important because, with the possible exception of acceptance tests, testers will runs tests against multiple releases and find bugs in each of those releases. They will log those bugs in a bug tracking system (see Chapter 14). In that bug report, the tester should identify the offending release. Without this information, it becomes difficult for developers to locate the root cause among the various changes in the code base, especially if the failure's symptom changes somewhat from one version to the next. In addition, managers may have trouble generating per-release bug-find-rate metrics.

For these reasons, a consistent naming convention is needed for any software released to test. The naming convention need not be meaningful. You could, conceivably, name releases Fred, Zedediah, and Hemamalini. However, I like to see sequence and simplicity in release naming schemes.

To start with sequence, we could use a naming pattern like A, B, C, and so on or 0001, 0002, 0003, and so on. The former approach is rather weak, though, since it will either roll over like an odometer or go to AA, AB, AC, and so on after reaching Z. In one successful release management regime I have seen, my client used the four-digit-number approach. Test releases occurred nightly, each with an incremented version number, and were smoke tested and used by the developers as a base for further development. Once a week, the release manager delivered the nightly test release to the test team. So, we received version IDs about seven numbers apart—e.g., 0103 for one test cycle, 0110 for the next test cycle, 0117 for the cycle after that, and so forth. Sometimes the version IDs were more than seven numbers apart, because sometimes developers broke the build, and more than one build occurred on a given day.

A wide variety of naming sequences can work, provided that any change triggers an increment in the version number. Anytime the contents of the underlying source code library change but the release ID does not, two test releases with identical release numbers are not the same and may exhibit different behaviors. Worse yet, sometimes the underlying source code in the repository doesn't change, but the test release does because someone didn't check the changed module into the library. These are paths to bug reporting chaos and irreproducible failures, which ultimately mean, again, inefficient and ineffective test execution.

In terms of simplicity, note that the tester need not know down to the individual file level what the release names mean in terms of a particular set of components. What's important is that the developers can figure that out, usually with the help of their source code control system. I prefer a single release ID number, which the repository tool can then break down into individual component release IDs and, if necessary, specific source file changes.

In addition to a logical naming schema, the tester must have a way to find out the release ID of the test release under test. I like techniques that allow me to interrogate the system—i.e., ask the system to tell me its own name. For example, I mentioned earlier the Windows standard for Help/About screens. As an example of a less user-friendly but still workable approach, in some UNIX applications, coding standards call for inclusion of a release ID string in the executable. Provided the symbol table is not stripped from the program, a tester can find that ID using the *strings* utility. For either approach to work, of course, the test release process must include either automated or manual processes for changing this identifier from one version to the next.

In some cases, one can't query the system itself, but rather the system that updates it. Let me illustrate this by example. I once tested a client-server system where the software that ran on the clients was pushed from a single server. This server had a database that included the client device identifier and the release ID for the test release last successfully updated to the device. By querying the server, testers knew which version of software any given client was running. To revisit the install and uninstall topic for just a minute, this system also provided a simple command-line interface that allowed us to change the release to be pushed to the client the next time it connected, both backward (uninstall) and forward (install). Voila—a nice, clean, consistent interface for install, uninstall, and interrogation activities. This example illustrates that with some careful forethought, a simple yet powerful utility can handle many of the issues related to release management, even in a complex environment.

BUILD FROM CAREFULLY SELECTED, COORDINATED, AND DOCUMENTED CONTENT

To illustrate the issues associated with test release content management and documentation, consider the following hypothetical situation. A system test cycle begins against a given release. During a week of testing against this release, the test team reports 30 problems, each as a distinct bug report. In addition, sales, marketing, or the business sponsors log six enhancement requests—i.e., new features to tune the product for the customer or user base. Collectively, these documents create opportunities for the project team to improve the quality of the product. However, the project team must manage the process carefully to ensure effectiveness and efficiency. Improving the quality of the product using these three dozen data items requires a process that deals with three questions in sequence.

1. How does the project management team select which of these 36 potential changes in behavior are candidates for inclusion in the next test release?
2. How does the development team notify the test team of which changes in behavior they believe were implemented through code changes?
3. How does the test team return a status on success or failure—change implemented without associated regression, change implemented but with an associated regression, or change not implemented properly—of these code changes to the development team?

Figure 12-2 shows a process to handle these questions that I have seen work. In this process, the bug reports and enhancement requests are considered at a cross-functional meeting. At this meeting, the project management team—including development, testing, sales and marketing or the business sponsors, technical or customer support, and perhaps operations—will evaluate the costs and benefits of each proposed bug fix and potential enhancement. This cross-functional team is often called a change management board or change control board. (We'll look at the change management process in Chapter 16.)

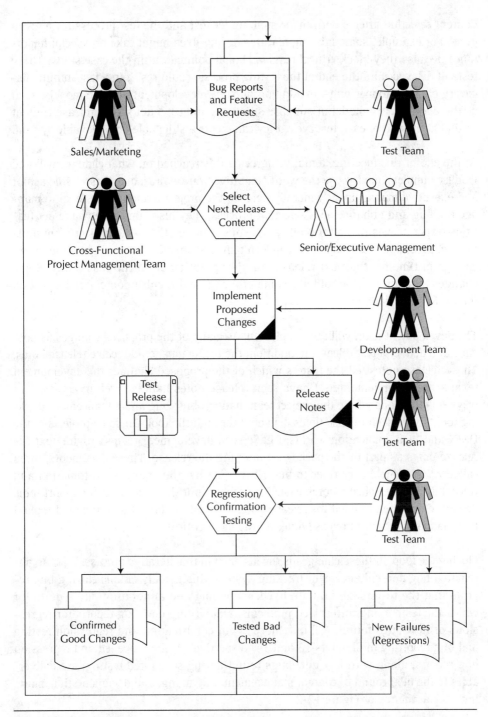

FIGURE 12-2 CHANGE MANAGEMENT AND THE TEST RELEASE PROCESS

Content selection affects both the system under test and the test process for a given cycle. For example, some missing features or bug fixes might take on special importance because they block critical tests, as Jamal pointed out in the case study. These tests, if delayed until the end of the testing process, could result in a last-minute discovery of showstopper bugs. In addition, in some development lifecycle models, such as the Evolutionary model in our case study, the project team stages release content so that at the end of each test cycle, they can create a shippable or deployable system.

At the end of this meeting, tentative agreement is reached on what changes will and won't be implemented. I use the word "tentative" for two reasons. First, while senior and executive management generally defer to the project management team to manage the bug and enhancement selection process, they also sometimes have pet features or pet peeves that—for political reasons if none other—the project team must handle. Second, the development team can't always complete implementation of every change in time for the next release, another point made in the case study. Some changes take longer than others. Some prove more difficult upon closer inspection than originally planned.

The development team will then implement as many of the proposed changes as possible and deliver a test release. In addition, the test team should receive release notes. These release notes tell the testers which of the proposed changes the development team actually implemented. I have seen release notes handled well in a variety of ways. In situations where the project team had a robust bug and enhancement tracking tool, I have seen release notes delivered through the tool. On some projects in the UNIX and Web application worlds, I have seen development teams provide text-file release notes as part of the package containing the release. These documents, often called *readme* files, may refer to bug IDs or just list the changes. Automation and traceability make release notes easier to prepare, but the lack of such support tools doesn't eliminate the need for release notes. Indeed, without the automated tools, I find manually produced release notes all the more critical.

Closing the loop on these changes is the last step in this iterative process. With an automated bug and enhancement tracking system, this usually entails closing bug reports that the testers confirm are fixed, reopening and annotating bug reports for which the testers find unresolved problems, and writing new bug reports for regressions or new bugs found. (I'll talk more about confirmation and regression testing and bug reporting in Chapters 13 and 14, respectively.) The reopened and regression bug reports, along with any new bugs found during scheduled testing, are deliverables to the next round of content management, bug fixing, and documentation, starting back at the top of Figure 12-2.

So far, this discussion has probably seemed a bit code-centric. Nevertheless, I'm talking about the whole system, everything in it. It's easy to overlook, but in situations where data and/or metadata have significant effects on system operation, the project team must manage and document these items as carefully as executable content. For example, I once worked on a project where one development team claimed that their component of the system was feature complete, but they kept changing the database schema for the master table that held the user information from one release to the next. This caused as much chaos in the testing effort as adding or removing features, since each field was associated with user interface changes and modifications to the workflows and transactions that affected the call-center agents.

HANDLE CHALLENGES

Good test release management processes rest on a solid foundation of established software-engineering best practices stretching back decades. Nevertheless, evolving technological and system complexity do create new challenges. In addition, there are managerial issues. Let's look at some of these challenges.

WHO OWNS THE TEST RELEASE PROCESSES?

In Table 12-1, I have condensed the seven-step test release process outlined earlier and added owners for each step. In some organizations, steps 3 through 6 live in a

Step	Tasks	Owner (Typical/Proposed)
1.	Select the content.	Cross-functional project management team
2.	Implement the changes.	Development team
3.	Make the test release.	Unclear/release engineer
4.	Smoke test the test release in the build/ configuration management environment.	Unclear/release engineer
5.	Package and deliver the test release.	Unclear/release engineer
6.	Install the test release in the test lab.	Unclear/system administration (complex systems) or test team (simple systems)
7.	Smoke test the test release in the test lab.	Test team

TABLE 12-1 TEST RELEASE PROCESS TASKS AND OWNERS

sort of no-man's-land. I've seen and heard of more than one project where key play-ers seemed to think that software magically migrated from the development team to the test team with no effort expended. Because the test team needs this migration to occur to begin testing, a frequent outcome is that the steps devolve upon the test team, which has neither the skilled people nor the spare time to take on this process without significant impacts on team efficiency and effectiveness.

When I have seen the test release process work smoothly, steps 3 through 6 have the owners I propose in Table 12-1.[7] The creation of the build, the initial smoke test of it, and the delivery of the test release belonged to a special project team member. This person goes by many names, but I'll use *release engineer*. To whom should she re-port? I'm not sure it matters. I have seen the testing team report to a development services group that also included release management (and user documentation). I have also seen the release manager as a separate member of the development team. Both approaches worked.

Barring the presence of a dedicated release engineer on your project team, the next-most-logical place for these roles to live is in the development team. After all, in each test release the development manager is proposing that the test team accept her team's work as ready for testing. Shouldn't she own the tasks associated with deliv-ering that test release, *demonstrably* ready for testing, to the test team?

COMPLEXITY OF THE SYSTEM UNDER TEST—AND BEYOND

As mentioned earlier, while it's desirable for the test team to test the install, uninstall, update, patch, and other such processes, the complexity of the system under test is a consideration. If you are testing a PC application, then installation should be an al-most trivially easy process. Even many UNIX OS variants now include user-friendly, even graphical, installation utilities.

However, suppose we start adding wrinkles like a database that may reside locally or on the network? How about three-tier architecture? Browser-based applications that talk to Web, application, and database servers? As the definition of the "system under test" expands to include multiple applications, sometimes running on multiple hard-

---

7. One of the reviewers, Markus Manleitner, mentioned that with the complex product his team tests, the smoke testing of the release in the build and configuration management environ-ment is done by a special integration testing team. He reports good results from this approach.

Release Engineer, Build Manager, Release Manager, Source Code Control Engineer

The person responsible for creating the test release from source code, data, metadata, help files, Web screens, and any other items needed to build the system.

ware platforms, and possibly communicating across various network architectures, the complexity inherent in "installing the system" will expand from something reasonably done by one test technician to a task that requires a team of specialists. Such a team would be far too specialized and valuable to spend most of their time testing, so they'd probably work in some other team, such as the network operations or system administration group.

In addition to challenging the test team's role in testing installation and other operational processes, such complexity makes the whole concept of what constitutes a "test release" very amorphous. I worked on one project where test releases consisted of specific collections of one or (usually) more applications as part of nine specific subsystems. A separate development team was building each of these nine subsystems, and each had a five-part version number—e.g., 101.252.17.19.2003. So, it would take a sequence of 45 numbers to identify a given test release.

Furthermore, in this project, there was no real way for any subsystem to interrogate any other subsystem about its version number or for any subsystem to communicate its version number if it were interrogated. This was a significant problem, because the subsystems were tightly coupled, with data and control flowing across subsystems in many of our test cases. A tester logged in to one subsystem could involve three or four other subsystems in a test, but only at best be able to interrogate the host subsystem for its release ID. Moreover, none of the subsystems knew how to respond to a version interrogation. In many cases, the subsystems consisted of multiple applications, utilities, database schemas, and other moving parts. The application visible to the tester might not know the versions of the other pieces.

OK, you say, I get it—sometimes really large, multisubsystem, multiteam test releases will be hard to manage. But surely, smaller, simpler projects won't have the same kinds of problems in this area.

That's not necessarily true. I worked on an Internet appliance project where the client had three separate software components. First, there was the client application, which provided the browser and e-mail functions. Second, there was the BIOS (firmware) on the Internet appliance. Third, there was also the firmware version on the modem. We had appliances in the test lab that, when we interrogated them, appeared to be running the same software, but that was because we couldn't interrogate the modems. It turned out that the modem firmware was changing under our feet because of external factors at the modem vendor's facility. These changes led to lots of connection problems in particular versions of the modem firmware. You can imagine how confusing it was to try to isolate intermittent dial-up networking reliability problems in ostensibly identical system configurations that weren't identical.

I'm not aware of technical solutions that can bridge disparate, arbitrary large and complex test systems. However, the problems mentioned earlier are not merely technical, but also a matter of change management discipline. Why did the modem vendor change the firmware without telling us? Because the project management team didn't tell them they shouldn't. Why didn't the programmers building the various subsystems create simple utilities for interrogating a central database to determine the system release ID, all 45 segments of it? Because management didn't tell them they should. In both cases, a properly working change control board, together with simple but sure methods for bundling and interrogating versions, would have solved these problems. As with release notes, just because off-the-shelf software engineering tools aren't available to solve the problem automatically, that doesn't remove from the project team the responsibility of solving the problem.

As with the complexity of the system under test, so too test release issues arise from the complexity of the test environment. Again, it's important to know what we're testing, and that includes the software and hardware on which the system under test runs. Unlike the system under test, though, the test environment should be changing little if at all during the test project. Rather than figuring out ways to provide for orderly, managed change as in the system under test, in the test environment we want to prevent change as much as possible. The only exceptions that I can think of are the need to change the definition of the deployed environment and the need to test multiple configurations when the system will run in lots of different deployed or customer environments.

The availability of tools for managing the configuration of the system under test and the test configuration will depend considerably on your target platform. Windows and UNIX platforms, including the Linux platforms, have a fairly broad assortment of such tools available, while less widely used platforms may not. Note also, though, that the right set of tools for this job depends not only on the target platform, but also on the intended distribution process. Again, at some point the project team will likely need to test the user or customer install, uninstall, update, and patch processes. Some simple approaches for test system configuration management can undermine the realism of the test environment and invalidate the results of such testing.

INCOMPLETE AND UNREALISTIC SYSTEM AND ACCEPTANCE TEST RELEASES

During early test phases (such as unit, component, and integration testing), testers—whether programmers, independent testers, or others—will naturally receive test releases that are incomplete, that include scaffolding, stubs, and drivers, or that otherwise vary from what will ultimately be delivered to a customer. Following Evolutionary and Incremental methodologies, early test releases to system test will likewise not contain all the features in the customer release. Even under a V Model or a Waterfall model lifecycle, formal and informal avenues exist for changing the definition of the system during system test. Formal avenues include change control boards, while informal avenues include wheedling or browbeating of programmers or managers to slip in pet features.

However, as Lin-Tsu pointed out during the case study, testing of incomplete or unrealistic test releases during late testing is inherently risky. It creates opportunities for undetected regression and hiding places for subtle bugs.

In addition, what is a bug fix but a small change in the definition of the system? Therefore, if we are fixing bugs, we are changing the system just as if we were adding new features. At some point the extent of change in the code base can become risky, whether we're adding new features or just fixing a large number of bugs. It is the change—the *code churn*—in the code that creates the risk as much as if not more so than the nature of the change.[8]

Unrealism is another issue. Unrealism can exist in the way the test release is delivered and installed, which undermines our ability to test the provisioning, release, delivery, and installation processes as they will occur in the real world. Unrealism can also exist in the system itself. For example, suppose we use a code coverage tool to instrument the source code, and then build and run the system test cases against that instrumented system. This can provide useful information in terms of the structural extent of testing, but what of the possibility of the instrumentation distorting the test results? This can happen when we use instrumented test systems for capacity, volume, stress, and performance testing, because the instrumentation increases the size

---

8. Some people use the percentage of new and changed code in the code repository as a metric for system test exit. This metric can give you some idea about the chances of regression or new bugs. Just as you want to see the daily bug find rate go to zero at the end of a project, you also want the weekly code change percentage to go to zero. Also, the less the code changes, then more meaningful the test results are over time. If 10% of your code is changing every week, then what do test results that are five or six weeks old tell you?

and decreases the performance of the system, albeit by some small percentage when we use good instrumentation tools.

The trick to handling these challenges is to balance the benefits against the risk. During early testing phases and even during early system test, you don't want the project team to clamp down on code changes or churn, because change is how features are being added and quality is being improved. In competitive markets, keeping up with the latest features and technology can be a strategic necessity, and it would be counterintuitive to allow our desire for a tranquil test environment to trump a business imperative. However, at some point the risk of change threatens another business imperative: delivering or deploying a quality system.

A smart test manager can help the project team balance these risks. Let me give an example. On an Internet appliance project following a V Model software development lifecycle, among our system test entry criteria was one that said that the system should be feature complete before we started the system test phase. At the system test phase entry meeting, we waived that criterion for two specific features: printing and audio support. The programmers were still working on these, and they were deemed important for the first release. It made sense to start system test anyway, though. For one thing, enough of the system was complete that we certainly had *a* system to test, if not *the final* system to test. For another thing, it was possible that technical obstacles would ultimately prevent us from finishing these features, so a delay in system test to try to get these features in would put our ship date at risk, based on features that might not make the initial ship anyway. What we did stick with, though, was the exit criteria of at least three weeks of testing without any changes other than low-risk bug fixes.

To some extent, you can reduce the risk of allowing unrealistic test releases during system test through your regression testing strategy. If you repeat tests as a regression testing strategy (see Chapter 13), then you can allow instrumented test releases and significant changes until the time you start the last complete run through all the tests. (Of course, there is a risk that you will detect a regression or hidden problem in this last pass, which can endanger the schedule, but that's a smaller risk than not finding the problem at all.) If you do not repeat tests at all, then any test run with an instrumented or stale test release is at increased risk for regression or hidden bugs in the final release.

IMPLEMENT IMPROVEMENTS

The test release process is one of the most context-sensitive processes. The generic process outlined earlier will work in many cases, but not all. The specific technology and tools underlying the process will greatly influence how you do it. They will also determine the leverage points that exist for you to get a return on investment for change here. However, I have found some general rules to consider.

1. Think about the potential test efficiency benefits of installable media, solid automated unit and component testing and regression testing of each test release, and smoke testing.

2. Likewise, consider the project efficiency benefit that might accrue from getting revision name and interrogation capabilities in place. Not being able to figure out where a bug exists is very frustrating to developers. It ends up being frustrating to testers, too, because bugs get marked as *irreproducible* when the real problem was that no one knew what was in the test lab during testing. At the test management level, a large loss of test team credibility can occur when developers frequently can't find problems reported by the test team. It's a shame when this arises simply because of a miscommunication, when the test team has no way of putting a name on what's being tested.

3. Look at the sources of inefficiency in your test execution and bug reporting processes. I have seen plenty of projects burn up two or more precious weeks at the beginning of a test phase because no one could figure out how to install a test release that worked. I've seen projects get stuck in endless loops of bugs, blocked testing, and incompatible components shoved together in the test lab.

Not only will your test process be more efficient with good test releases, but you'll be more effective. I prefer to phrase my lobbying for simple naming and interrogation processes in terms of providing better services to development. I sometimes say, "It's important for a professional test group to write good bug reports, so we want to tell you exactly what releases have particular failures. To do this in a reliable fashion, we need your help in creating good processes for naming and interrogation." Likewise, with confirmation testing, I like to say that we can do a better, quicker job of confirming bugs as closed if we know exactly what release they arrived in.

Good test releases indicate a level of process maturity and respect for the test team's time that bodes well for the project. As a matter of fact, of all the projects I've worked on, of the dozen or so that I thought were really excellently managed, every single one of them had good test release processes. The three projects that come to mind as the most troubled all had real difficulties getting their test release processes under control. You simply cannot do good testing without good test releases, and the failure to perform good testing is widely noted as a key failure factor for projects.

In addition to efficiency and project success, another factor in motivating good test release processes is inevitability. Sooner or later the project team must deliver an installable, stable release to customers or users. Sooner or later the project team must create robust install, uninstall, update, and patch processes for customer or user releases. Sooner or later the system will have a revision number, and the customers and users will need to be able to report that revision number should they find problems. Sooner or later people will need to coordinate all the components of the system and all the interacting components in the installed environment. Since solutions must exist for all the issues identified in this chapter sooner or later, why not start putting those solutions in place and testing them during the testing process?

Since the changes are inevitable, it's just a matter of timing. If you find that some people insist on putting off defining and creating good release processes until the end of the project, you can use your relationships with the customer service, technical support, help desk, and business analyst folks on the project team to help convince management of the need for change. Sales and marketing can help, too. If people who are close to the customers and users can be brought to understand the impact of poor—and poorly tested —release processes, then they can be convinced to support your calls for a test release process that surfaces potential issues earlier.

Once I've managed to motivate change, I generally let the development and release engineering people take the lead on defining the specifics of the test release process. After all, I don't really care about the particulars, as long as the process meets the criteria and resolves the challenges I've laid out in this chapter. I'm happy to work with people and assist in defining a good process, but I don't want to be perceived as dictating to others. This process is, after all, a handoff. In a relay race, the runners must work out together how the handoff occurs, since a failed handoff results in a baton in the dirt, a race lost. Keep your focus on the cooperative metaphor of the handoff, and you'll do a fine job when the time comes to implement changes to your test release processes.

13

ASSESS QUALITY: EXECUTE TEST CASES

F inally the time has come to do some testing. During the test execution process, the testers will use whatever test system we have put together to assess the quality of the test releases as we receive them. This is both a potentially exciting and a potentially scary point in the project because the quality of the system is unknown until the testers start pounding on it. Furthermore, the test team generally has a unique charter here, that of looking for ways to make the system under test get as far *out of control* and *away from the expected* as possible.

In addition, while all managers are expected to manage unexpected events within their areas of responsibility, the test manager is the only manager in the software development organization whose area of responsibility is *searching for* the unexpected. This search takes the form of running a set of tests. How does a test team take these tests, run them against an installed system, and capture information about the system under test, the test cases, and the test execution process itself?

A TEST EXECUTION PROCESS

Let's start with a generic test execution process, shown in Process 9. This process has a number of intersections with other processes. Step 3.D, reporting quality problems in the system under test, follows the process outlined in Chapter 14. Step 3.E, fixing test system problems, follows the process outlined in Chapters 10 and 11. Finally, step 7, reporting test cycle findings and status, follows the process discussed in Chapter 15.[1]

---

1. I thank Tim Koomen for reminding me of some of the test configuration management elements in the process.

Step #	Step	Done?
1.	Based on risk prioritization, project constraints, and any other pertinent considerations, select the test suites (from the test set) that should be run in this test cycle.	☐
2.	Assign the test cases in each test suite to testers for execution.	☐
3.	Execute the test cases, report bugs, and capture information about the tests continuously, taking into account previous test results for each subsequent test.	☐
3.A	Put the system under test and the test system into appropriate initial states. If these initial states are useful across multiple tests or multiple iterations of this test, save the initial states for subsequent reuse.	☐
3.B	Through data inputs and other stimuli, provoke the system under test into a desired test condition.	☐
3.C	Observe and evaluate the resulting outputs, behaviors, and states. Research any deviations from expected results.	☐
3.D	If appropriate, report problems in the system under test.	☐
3.E	If appropriate, report and/or resolve problems in the test system.	☐
3.F	Capture and report information about the test just executed.	☐
4.	Resolve blocking issues as they arise.	☐
5.	Report status, adjust assignments, and reconsider plans and priorities daily.	☐
6.	If appropriate, eliminate unrealizable or redundant tests in reverse-priority order (drop the lowest-priority tests first, the highest-priority tests last).	☐
7.	Periodically report test cycle findings and status.	☐
8.	Check any status documents, initial states, updated testware or other test system elements, or other useful permanent records produced into the project library or configuration management system. Place the item(s) under change control.	☐

PROCESS 9 A TEST EXECUTION PROCESS

Test Set

All the test suites that the test team plans to run during the current test phase (or level).

TEST TRACKING WORKSHEETS

In this chapter, I'll illustrate planning and tracking test execution through the use of what I call a test tracking spreadsheet.[2] The essential portions of such a spreadsheet are the test case summary worksheet and the test suite summary worksheet.

Figure 13-1 shows a test case summary worksheet as it would appear at the beginning of pass 5, once Jamal Brown, the test manager, has finished selecting the test suites and assigning each test case to a tester. The Assigned To column indicates the responsible tester. The Test ID column puts a unique four-digit number on each test. The Test Suite/Case column shows a short name for each test suite and, within each test suite, a short name for each test case. The Plan Date column shows the date by which Jamal wants the tester to have run the test case. The Plan Effort column indicates the number of person-hours Jamal estimates the tester will spend running each test case.

As the testers run each test case, they capture and report information about each test. One of the most essential bits of information is the state of the test.

- *Queue*—The test case is ready to run, assigned to a tester for execution in this test pass.
- *In Progress*—The test is currently running.

	A	B	C	E	F	G	H	I	J	K	M	N	O	P
1			Sumatra Test Case Summary											
2			Integration and System Test Pass 5 (12/16-12/27)											
3														
4	Assigned	Test			Test	Bug	Bug	Run	Plan	Act	Plan	Actual	Test	
5	To	ID	Test Suite/Case	Status	Environment	ID	RPN	By	Date	Date	Effort	Effort	Duration	Comment
6														
7		1.000	*Functionality*											
8	DLK	1.001	File						12/16		2.0			
9	JW	1.002	Edit						12/16		0.5			
10	BEZ	1.003	Font						12/16		0.5			
11	DLK	1.004	Tables						12/17		3.0			
12	BEZ	1.005	Printing						12/16		2.0			
13	LJ	1.006	Managed Files						12/16		2.5			
14	LJ	1.007	Non-Managed Files						12/17		4.0			
15	BEZ	1.008	DMS Check-In New						12/17		2.5			
16	BEZ	1.009	DMS Check-In Existing						12/17		3.0			
17	BEZ	1.010	DMS Check-Out						12/18		3.5			
18	LTW	1.011	DMS Load/Migrate Online						12/16		3.5			
19	HS	1.012	DMS Load/Migrate NOL						12/16		3.0			
20	HS	1.013	DMS Load/Migrate Offline						12/17		3.5			
21	HS	1.014	DMS File Information						12/17		2.5			
22			Suite Summary						12/18	1/0	36.0	0.0	0.0	

FIGURE 13-1 INITIAL TEST CASE SUMMARY FOR PASS 5

2. See my previous book, *Managing the Testing Process, Second Edition*, Chapter 5, for a detailed explanation of this tool.

- *Block*—Something prevented the tester from executing the test.

- *Skip*—For some reason, the tester decided not to execute the test.

- *Pass*—The tester ran the entire test and observed only expected results, states, and behaviors.

- *Fail*—The tester ran the entire test and observed one or more unexpected results, states, or behaviors seriously compromise the quality of the system with respect to the objective of the test.

- *Warn*—The tester ran the entire test and observed one or more unexpected results, states, or behaviors, but the underlying quality of the system with respect to the objective of the test was not seriously compromised.

- *Closed*—After being marked in a Fail or Warn status in the first cycle of a test pass, the next test release included a fix to the bug that resolved the problems with this test case.

In the course of running all the planned test cases in a test pass, testers move through the test lifecycle shown in Figure 13-2.[3]

In addition to the test case status, testers gather other important information. The Test Environment column (see Figure 13-1) is where they indicate what hardware,

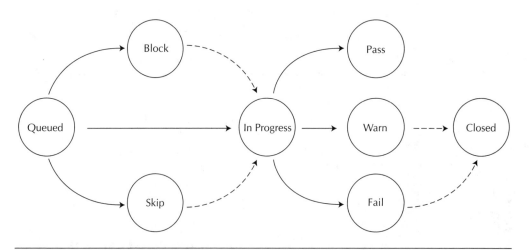

FIGURE 13-2 TEST CASE STATES AND LIFECYCLE

---

3. Some people use simpler sets of test states. Johanna Rothman, for example, mentioned to me that she does not use Block, Warn, or Closed, but instead uses Fail, In Progress, and Pass, respectively.

software, and other items they used to run the test. Bug ID and Bug RPN capture information about any bugs found (see Chapter 14). In the Run By column each tester enters his or her initials. Act Date is when the tester ran the test case, while Actual Effort is how many person-hours he or she expended, and Test Duration is the clock time required to run the test. (Test duration and effort can vary for automated tests or for manual tests that involve two testers.)

To get a better sense of what's going on across all the test suites—and to gather useful information for metrics (see Chapter 15)—I analyze the test status and test effort information in a test suite summary worksheet, as shown in Figure 13-3. This worksheet shows a summary for each test suite and for the entire test set. I classify as *fulfilled* those tests either run or skipped. (I count tests in a Warn or Closed state in the Pass column for simplicity.) I classify as *unfulfilled* those tests blocked or not yet completed. This allows me to analyze where I stand in terms of getting through all the tests.

The earned value section at the right analyzes whether we have gotten through the right number of tests in each test suite, given the actual effort expended. For example, if we have run seven out of 14 test cases, we have executed 50% of the tests (which would appear in the % Exec column). Suppose we have expended 40 person-hours out of a total of 50 planned person-hours? In that case, we've burned through 80% of the planned effort (which would appear in the % Effort column). This indicates that we are

	A	B	C	D	E	F	G	H	I	J	K	L	M	N	O
1				Sumatra Test Suite Summary											
2				Integration and System Test Pass 5 (12/16-12/27)											
3															
4		Total	Planned Tests Fulfilled				Weighted	Planned Tests Unfulfilled				Earned Value			
5	Suite	Cases	Count	Skip	Pass	Fail	Failure	Count	Queued	IP	Block	Pln Hrs	Act Hrs	% Effort	% Exec
6															
7	Functionality	14	0	0	0	0	0.00	14	14	0	0	36.00	0.00	0%	0%
8	Performance, Load, Capacity, and Volume	5	0	0	0	0	0.00	5	5	0	0	7.00	0.00	0%	0%
9	Reliability/Stability	2	2	2	0	0	0.00	0	0	0	0	0.00	0.00	0%	0%
10	Error Handling and Recovery	3	0	0	0	0	0.00	3	3	0	0	12.50	0.00	0%	0%
11	Installation, Maintenance, and Operations	4	0	0	0	0	0.00	4	4	0	0	72.00	0.00	0%	0%
12	Localization	8	0	0	0	0	0.00	8	8	0	0	128.00	0.00	0%	0%
13	Security and Privacy	4	0	0	0	0	0.00	4	4	0	0	17.00	0.00	0%	0%
14	Documentation	3	0	0	0	0	0.00	3	3	0	0	28.00	0.00	0%	0%
15	Integration	4	0	0	0	0	0.00	4	4	0	0	8.00	0.00	0%	0%
16	Usability Study	2	0	0	0	0	0.00	2	2	0	0	16.00	0.00	0%	0%
17	Exploratory	6	0	0	0	0	0.00	6	6	0	0	12.00	0.00	0%	0%
18															
19	Total	55	2	2	0	0	0.00	53	53	0	0	336.50	0.00	0%	0%
20	By Pct		4%	4%	0%	0%	N/A	96%	96%	0%	0%				

FIGURE 13-3 INITIAL TEST SUITE SUMMARY FOR PASS 5

unlikely to complete the remaining seven tests in the time scheduled (assuming that all the test cases are roughly the same size and disregarding priority issues). If the pattern holds across all the test suites, then we will run out of test execution time before we complete all the tests planned for the test pass. So, earned value gives the test lead or manager the opportunity to adjust the plan for the test pass before that happens.

THE ATTACK ON THE BIG BUILD

For their first activity every week, the Sumatra test team ran confirmation tests against the bug fixes in the new test release, as described in the Sumatra test plan. In the case of the Big Build, they had a lot of bugs to test. While the test team focused on confirmation testing, Jamal worked out the details of testing for the coming week.

Since this was increment 3, that meant that the first run of the localization and the usability test suites—both run by external test labs—would start this week. Jamal had asked Lin-Tsu to coordinate those activities with the test labs and had made a point to remind her of that last week. She had touched base with the labs on Tuesday and had scheduled delivery of the test release for Monday afternoon with both facilities. That would give her time to make sure the test release was ready before they started testing it.

The Big Build was going to be a big job, Jamal realized as he looked at the test case tracking worksheet. The only test suite he planned to skip during this test pass was the Reliability/Stability suite, but that meant that Emma Moorhouse, one of the automated test engineers, would run the Performance, Load, Capacity, and Volume suite, which was a larger effort.

The fact that the Christmas holiday fell right in the middle of the test pass also created a certain challenge. However, Jamal had leveraged his multicultural test team to avoid a completely dead week. He had already arranged for Lin-Tsu Wu, his manual test engineer, and John Woo, one of his test technicians, to take off the Chinese Lunar New Year holiday early next year instead of Christmas. Dinesh Kumar, one of the automated test engineers, and Hemamalini Shashidar, another test technician, would get an extra week on top of two weeks of vacation in April following the release to visit family in India and Bangladesh. Binyamin Zuckerman had visited his family in New York during Hanukkah. This way, each tester got to enjoy their own religious and cultural holidays, and he'd spread the effects of these holidays across many test passes. Now he'd reap the benefit, having a team of five over the Christmas week, down by just two people from the usual seven.

For the moment, though, Jamal focused on mapping out the test cases he needed the team to run during the coming test cycle this week. The first order of business, from a risk perspective, would be running tests that had previously been blocked, especially the functionality tests. Some of the changes dropping in meant that privacy, security, and error handling tests were also important.

Step #	Step	Done?
1.	Based on risk prioritization, project constraints, and any other pertinent considerations, select the test suites (from the test set) that should be run in this test cycle.	☑

Based on this prioritization, Jamal went through each test suite and assigned a planned completion date and a tester to each test case. Based on previous test passes, he also revised the planned hours for each test case. A partial snapshot of the test case tracking worksheet he came up with as part of this plan is shown in Figure 13-1.

Step #	Step	Done?
2.	Assign the test cases in each test suite to testers for execution.	☑

After completing the test assignments, Jamal printed seven copies of the test tracking worksheet for pass 5. Feeling that a group synchronization session was in order—and knowing that nothing makes for a well-received meeting like a good meal—he then sent an e-mail to the test team.

```
All—

The Big Build is here. The time has come for the most important
and challenging test pass of the project. To make sure we're all
in sync, please meet me in the test lab for a test pass kick-off
lunch at noon. I'll be handing out test case tracking worksheets
with the test case assignments, planned hours, and planned dates
for this test pass. To ensure promptness, I'll pick up lunch from
our favorite Indian restaurant, with the usual mild, vegetarian,
and kosher options available. Remember: those who live for the
nuclear hot chicken vindaloo and the aachar—like Emma and I do—
should show up on time or we WILL eat it all!

Regards,

Jamal
```

The meeting went swimmingly. There was a lot of work to do in a short period, but thanks to Jamal's up-front holiday planning, the workload was not overwhelming, even with Christmas. Perhaps more importantly, everyone on the team was eager to get their hands on the Big Build, a test release that was (almost) feature complete. As Luis Jacinto, one of the test technicians, put it, "Finally, a brimming mug of Sumatra, not one of those tiny little Italian espresso cups."

"Okay," Jamal said as the meeting—and the meal—wound down, "sally forth and find many bugs. I know they're hiding in the Big Build. I'll see you all at 4:00 PM for the shift handoff and afternoon status debriefing."

The testers went their separate ways to run their assigned tests. Luis Jacinto started his work with the managed file functionality test. The setup step of this test case involved starting a new instance of SpeedyWriter on a test client and then logging in to the document management system. The first step of the test involved creating a new file, entering and operating on some text in that file, and then checking the file into the document management system.

Step #	Step	Done?
3.A	Put the system under test and the test system into appropriate initial states.	✔
3.B	Through data inputs and other stimuli, provoke the system under test into a desired test condition.	✔

At this point, Luis discovered that the file-creation functionality was seriously broken, corrupting all new files when certain font operations were performed. He found that the only workaround was to check the file into the document management system immediately upon creation, before starting to edit it. In addition to running the planned test, Luis spent some time researching and writing the bug report. This took quite a bit longer than the scheduled two-and-a-half hours, but he wanted to spend the time necessary to isolate and document such a critical bug. Before moving on to the next test case, he used a pencil to write down the status information associated with running this test case in the test case tracking worksheet.

Step #	Step	Done?
3.C	Observe and evaluate the resulting outputs, behaviors, and states. Research any deviations from expected results.	✔
3.D	If appropriate, report problems in the quality of the system under test.	✔
3.F	Capture and report information about the test just executed.	✔

Luis then proceeded to the nonmanaged file test. However, before he could get too far into it, a system administrator inadvertently shut down Tobruk, the Linux Web server Luis was using. After some initial confusion, he got the server rebooted, but close to an hour evaporated as he tracked down this problem.

Step #	Step	Done?
4.	Resolve blocking issues as they arise.	✔

After the daily debriefing with the rest of the test team, Luis spent another couple of hours testing, then an hour reading and responding to various e-mails, before calling a ten-hour day to a close. He spent a few minutes talking to Binyamin Zuckerman, one of the evening shift test technicians, about the font-related bug he had found, since he had noticed from the test tracking worksheet that Binyamin was scheduled to run the font test that evening. They also talked a bit about Binyamin's recent trip to New York, especially his visit to the reconstruction site in Lower Manhattan. Finally, Luis headed out for a late dinner with some friends in downtown Austin.

Unfortunately, although Luis had closed the loop with Binyamin, he had not talked to Emma Moorhouse all day. That wouldn't have been a problem, except that when Luis sent his bug report out via e-mail for test-team-wide review, Emma was busy getting the automated Solaris performance tests running, so she didn't read it. And that wouldn't have been a problem either, except that the test scripts happened to depend on the correct behavior of exactly what Luis had carefully described as severely broken in his bug report.

So, when Emma left on Monday night, the Solaris performance tests were giving invalid results, but she didn't know it. (She hadn't implemented the features of the tool that would allow the scripts to send her a page if it was behaving incorrectly.) It wasn't until Tuesday morning that she discovered the oversight. Emma was frustrated and chagrined. First she vented to her coworkers and then she admitted to Jamal what had happened. Jamal responded with a worldly shrug and raised eyebrow, saying, "The joys of automated testing." Relieved but not surprised by Jamal's understanding outlook, Emma then reworked the test scripts in order to restart them for a run on Tuesday night.

Step #	Step	Done?
3.E	If appropriate, report and/or resolve problems in the quality of the test system.	✔

Based on the incident that occurred, Jamal realized that he needed to reinforce a process that had grown up informally over time. He sent out the following e-mail, marked urgent, to the test team.

All—

From the beginning of testing back in October, we've had an informal process of sending bug reports out via e-mail to the entire team for review and informational purposes. I think this process has been very helpful, both in fostering a high degree of professionalism in our bug reporting and in keeping us informed.

As a manager, part of my job is to institutionalize good ideas as part of our regular process. I've made an error in this regard, as I may have communicated the idea that reading those bug report e-mails is a low-priority activity, something that we can do once a day or even skip entirely if we're busy. However, keeping abreast of each other's test results—and considering how those results might affect our own testing work—is actually critical to effective and efficient testing.

To the extent that I led us to believe that reviewing each other's bug reports is a low-priority activity, I made a management mistake that I will now correct. Please consider reading each other's bug reports to be a central and recurring part of your daily work. Please make it a regular process, prior to starting the execution of any test case, to check your e-mail and read any e-mail from fellow testers related to bug reports. When sending out such e-mails, please make it a practice to have the first word of the subject line be "BUG:" followed by the bug ID and as much of the bug report summary as will fit in the e-mail subject line.

Some of you are already following the practices outlined in this e-mail. However, because of my failure to enunciate this policy at the start of test execution, some of you are probably not. In those cases, this new practice represents an increase in workload. If you believe that this change in the test execution process represents a significant increase in workload that will prevent you from completing previously assigned tasks by their agreed-upon dates, please feel free to come see me to discuss adjusting dates and/or assignments.

Finally, let me make clear that I am not sending out this e-mail to cast aspersions on anyone's work or to call into question anyone's judgment. I am extremely happy with the work everyone is doing on this challenging project. My objective is to correct a management oversight on my part, and to take this opportunity to improve the process. This incremental increase in workload will, in the long run, save us all time, promoting our efficiency and effectiveness.

Regards,

Jamal

Step #	Step	Done?
4.	Execute the test cases, report bugs, and capture information about the tests continuously, taking into account previous test results for each subsequent test.	☑

After the performance testing miscue was resolved, on Tuesday the testing continued at a quick, deliberate, yet careful pace. Luis continued his nonmanaged file tests in the morning, having a very productive testing session with that test case. He found six separate problems and filed six reports. Also, the simulated server crash the day before, while inadvertent, exposed a serious problem he otherwise would have missed. So, after discussing the matter with Lin-Tsu, he spent 30 minutes updating one of the error handling test cases to reflect the new condition. As it turned out, the nonmanaged file tests weren't totally completed until Wednesday morning.

On Wednesday afternoon at 4:00 PM, just as on every afternoon, Jamal sat down with the whole test team to debrief and transition from the day to the evening shift. One by one, he asked the testers to tell him which tests they'd run and how many person-hours each had taken, and to review for him all bugs found for each test. As each tester reported their status, Jamal updated the test case summary worksheet (see Figure 13-4). Once it was all over, Jamal updated the project metrics using the test suite summary worksheet (see Figure 13-5). This meeting usually took about 45 minutes, but with all the testing and excitement during the Big Build, they were lasting about an hour this week.

Following the team debriefing, Jamal looked at the updated test case summary and test suite summary. He realized that the security and privacy testing was now at risk for this test cycle. Binyamin was bogged down in a slew of important functionality bugs. John Woo, another evening test technician, had found a number of important problems in the documentation. Lin-Tsu was tied up with managing the localization and usability testing efforts. (These had become a larger than planned drain on her time because of regression bugs in the installation process.) This meant that everyone scheduled to run security and privacy test cases was tied up elsewhere.

Sumatra Test Case Summary

Integration and System Test Pass 5 (12/16-12/27)

Assigned To	Test ID	Test Suite/Case	Status	Test Environment	Bug ID	Bug RPN	Run By	Plan Date	Act Date	Test Effort	Plan Effort	Actual Effort	Test Duration	Comment
	1.000	*Functionality*												
DLK	1.001	File	Fail	SW/H2/B1	1832	1	DLK	12/16	12/16	2.0	2.0	3.0	4.0	
JW	1.002	Edit	Warn	SW/H2/B1			DLK	12/16	12/16	0.5	0.5	1.0	3.0	
BEZ	1.003	Font	Fail	SS/H2/B7	1832	1	BEZ	12/16	12/16	0.5	0.5	2.0	4.0	
DLK	1.004	Tables	Pass	SS/H2/B5			DLK	12/17	12/17	3.0	3.0	3.0	5.0	
BEZ	1.005	Printing	Pass	SW/H1/B6			BEZ	12/16	12/16	2.0	2.0	2.0	4.0	
LJ	1.006	Managed Files	Fail	SW/H1/B8	1832	1	LJ	12/16	12/16	2.5	2.5	3.0	3.0	
LJ	1.007	Non-Managed Files	Fail	SS/H2/B8	1832	1	LJ	12/17	12/18	4.0	4.0	6.0	6.0	
					1837	6								
					1838	25								
					1840	6								
					1845	3								
					1846	2								
					1847	8								
BEZ	1.008	DMS Check-In New	Fail	SS/H1/B6	1836	1	BEZ	12/17	12/17	2.5	2.5	6.5	5.0	
					1832	1								
					1841	5								
					1844	15								
BEZ	1.009	DMS Check-In Existing						12/17		3.0	3.0			
BEZ	1.010	DMS Check-Out							12/18	3.5	3.5			
LTW	1.011	DMS Load/Migrate Online	Fail	SS/H1/B2	1833	2	LTW	12/16	12/16	3.5	3.5	4.0	4.0	
HS	1.012	DMS Load/Migrate NOL	Fail	SS/H2/B3	1833	2	HS	12/16	12/16	3.0	3.0	3.0	3.0	
HS	1.013	DMS Load/Migrate Offline	Fail	SE/H2/B3	1833	2	HS	12/17	12/17	3.5	3.5	3.5	3.5	
HS	1.014	DMS File Information	Fail	SW/H1/B3	1833	2	HS	12/17	12/17	2.5	2.5	3.0	3.0	
		Suite Summary						12/18	12/18		36.0	40.0	47.5	

FIGURE 13-4 THIRD-DAY TEST CASE SUMMARY FOR PASS 5

Sumatra Test Suite Summary

Integration and System Test Pass 5 (12/16-12/27)

Suite	Total Cases	Planned Tests Fulfilled				Weighted Failure	Planned Tests Unfulfilled				Earned Value			
		Count	Skip	Pass	Fail		Count	Queued	IP	Block	Pln Hrs	Act Hrs	% Effort	% Exec
Functionality	14	12	0	3	9	9.60	2	2	0	0	36.00	40.00	111%	86%
Performance, Load, Capacity, and Volume	5	2	0	1	1	2.83	3	3	0	0	7.00	5.50	79%	40%
Reliability/Stability	2	2	2	0	0	0.00	0	0	0	0	0.00	0.00	0%	0%
Error Handling and Recovery	3	0	0	0	0	0.00	3	3	0	0	12.50	0.00	0%	0%
Installation, Maintenance, and Operations	4	0	0	0	0	0.00	4	4	0	0	72.00	0.00	0%	0%
Localization	8	1	0	0	1	0.50	7	0	7	0	128.00	22.00	17%	13%
Security and Privacy	4	1	0	1	0	1.00	3	3	0	0	17.00	4.50	26%	25%
Documentation	3	0	0	0	0	0.00	3	3	0	0	28.00	0.00	0%	0%
Integration	4	2	0	2	0	0.00	2	2	0	0	8.00	3.00	38%	50%
Usability Study	2	0	0	0	0	0.00	2	0	2	0	16.00	0.00	0%	0%
Exploratory	6	0	0	0	0	0.00	6	6	0	0	12.00	0.00	0%	0%
Total	55	20	2	7	11	13.93	35	26	9	0	336.50	75.00	22%	34%
By Pct		36%	4%	13%	20%	N/A	64%	47%	16%	0%				

FIGURE 13-5 THIRD-DAY TEST SUITE SUMMARY FOR PASS 5

That, Jamal realized, leaves me no choice but to call on the Reserve Tester: Jamal Brown. Try as he might, though, he knew he wouldn't get through 17 hours of tests in the next three days, not with the other fires burning in the test arena. He replanned the testing as shown in Figure 13-6.

Step #	Step	Done?
5.	Report status, adjust assignments, and reconsider plans and priorities daily.	✔
6.	If appropriate, eliminate unrealizable or redundant tests in reverse-priority order (drop the lowest-priority tests first, the highest-priority tests last).	✔

Thursday and Friday proceeded almost to plan, with only minor delays. Lin-Tsu and Emma, having a few tests to wind down on Saturday morning, agreed to meet Jamal in the test lab around 10:00 AM to put the cycle to bed. Dale, the test technician who ordinarily smoke tested the test releases, offered to come in as well to get the next cycle's release installed for a quick start on Monday morning.

Jamal consulted with his test engineers. Since the test technicians had been working long hours during the week, Lin-Tsu, Emma, Dinesh, and Jamal decided not to ask them to come in on Saturday to try to get ahead of the game. As Jamal said to his three test engineers over steaming cappuccinos, "No point in trying to sprint the marathon here. We have three months to go, and I'm guessing we'll need what's in those fellas' reserve tanks between now and then."

Jamal caught up with Dale shortly afterward. "Dale," he said, "I appreciate the offer, but I'd like to take a rain check and perhaps ask you to pull a weekend later in the project. Instead, why don't you just give me that magic checklist you have, and I'll smoke test the build myself?"

	A	B	C	E	F	G	H	I	J	K	L	M	N	O
1			Sumatra Test Case Summary											
2			Integration and System Test Pass 5 (12/16-12/27)											
3														
4	Assigned	Test			Test	Bug	Bug	Run	Plan	Act	Plan	Actual	Test	
5	To	ID	Test Suite/Case	Status	Environment	ID	RPN	By	Date	Date	Effort	Effort	Duration	Comment
70		7.000	*Security and Privacy*											
71	BEZ	7.001	Legal Actions Blocked						12/20		5.5			Replan: JHB 12/23
72	LTW	7.002	Illegal Actions Allowed						12/19		3.5			Replan: JHB 12/20
73	JW	7.003	Logins/Passwords						12/18		3.5			Replan: JHB 12/19
74	JW	7.004	Sharing						12/17		4.5			Replan: JHB 12/18
75			**Suite Summary**						12/20	1/0	17.0	0.0	0.0	

FIGURE 13-6 TEST CASE SUMMARY SHOWING THE SECURITY AND PRIVACY TEST SUITE REPLAN

Dale smiled, "Sure. I had other things in mind anyway, but I thought I'd offer."

Jamal then coordinated with Petra, the system administrator who usually performed the test release installation, to come in over the weekend. She agreed, perhaps more willing than she otherwise would have been, after hearing that Jamal would be there to work with her, smoke testing the build himself.

Finally, on Saturday afternoon, the testing cycle was done and the new release smoke tested. With the first cycle of pass 5 in, Jamal finalized the metrics and reports for the pass. (In Chapter 15, we'll see how Jamal presents these findings in the Monday Sumatra project status meeting.) He then checked the various documents he'd updated and created into the project repository.

Step #	Step	Done?
7.	Periodically report test cycle findings and status.	☑
8.	Check any status documents or other useful permanent records produced into the project library or configuration management system. Place the document under change control.	☑

RECOGNIZE A GOOD TEST EXECUTION PROCESS

Like the tip of an iceberg, the test execution process is the part that shows, but it floats on all the good work in the preceding eight processes. What are other test team behaviors and achievements that distinguish a good test execution process?

FIND THE SCARY STUFF FIRST

When thinking through the test execution process, I use various sources of information to make an educated guess about where the nastiest bugs live, and I test those areas first. When I'm first starting test execution, I use the quality risk analysis discussed in Chapter 2 to guide where I test first. Later, as I get some hands-on testing experience with the system, I have a better idea of the real risks from where I've found bugs—and where I haven't even tested yet. I can use this knowledge to fine-tune my judgment of where to test next. (However, I have to be careful not to let strictly technical considerations—e.g., where we've found bugs—blind me to the fact that customer usage and other business risks need to influence test prioritization, too.) In the case study, Jamal initially focused testing on previously blocked functionality tests, along with privacy, security, and error handling tests affected by features new to the latest release.

I'm also concerned about two special kinds of risks to quality: those related to bug fixes that don't actually resolve the problem and bug fixes that create new problems. Those risks are the domain of confirmation testing and regression testing, respectively. Because bug fixes that don't resolve problems are especially problematic, I like to run those tests first in each test cycle.

I extensively discussed strategies for dealing with regression risk in Chapter 6, but here let me point out that test execution is the time to put those strategies into action. One problem can arise for regression risk strategies that involve repeating tests, in that this approach can conflict with focusing on new tests and confirming bug fixes. I do not recommend throwing out your carefully considered regression strategy at the first sign of project trouble, but I allow myself to reconsider an approach that involves heavy repetition of tests if test results show regression to be a low risk, while other risks turn out to be much higher than originally believed.

Another example of scary stuff we want to find is the stuff we don't expect. A carefully planned, methodical set of test processes such as the one I've outlined in this book does help prevent classic testing blunders.[4] However, it can also create dangerous blind spots. A mistaken assumption during quality risk analysis can ripple through the entire test estimation, planning, and test system development processes, creating large, unseen holes in places that actually are important to test. Simply looking at the bugs you do find to figure out where more bugs exist won't solve this problem, because it tells you nothing about the bugs you aren't finding because you're not testing those areas at all. This is why I now augment many of my test plans to include exploratory testing as part of the overall strategy. In the case study, Jamal included exploratory testing in the estimate discussed in Chapter 3 and in his plan discussed in Chapter 6.[5]

Finally, testers should look for bugs beyond their immediate testing objectives. Especially with precisely scripted manual or automated testing, we can sometimes fall into the trap of ignoring bugs because they don't relate directly to what we're testing. For example, if I'm testing file-open functionality, and I notice a problem with

---

4. For another perspective on testing blunders, see Brian Marick's paper "Classic Testing Mistakes" at www.testing.com.

5. I recommend Kaner, Falk, and Nguyen's *Testing Computer Software, Second Edition*, and Kaner, Bach, and Pettichord's *Lessons Learned in Software Testing* for more information on exploratory testing techniques.

the file-import utility, even if that's the subject of another test, I should spend a little time tracking down and reporting the bug. This is especially true if the in-passing bug I notice *is not covered* by another test. This relates to the topic of opportunity testing, which I discussed in Chapter 2. In general, it's a good idea for testers to take the opportunity to find and report other bugs, provided it doesn't distract from the other testing goals. Part of a tester's job is to represent the quality expectations and experiences of a reasonable user. When I test software, I always look for behavior that if I were a reasonable user, I would find disturbing, confusing, incorrect, or otherwise troublesome. As a test manager, I continually remind my test team to do the same thing.

PRODUCE, GATHER, AND DISSEMINATE VALUABLE INFORMATION

Just as drug companies test drugs and engineers test engineering materials, we test software in order to learn something about it. The objective of the process is information. So, it makes sense to design our experiments—our tests—in such a way that we maximize the useful information gathered and get that information into the hands of people who can use it.

The primary kind of information dissemination is external. While we'll look at these topics more closely in Chapters 14 and 15, the main objective of testing is to produce information that the project team can use to make smart decisions about quality. The bug triage committee or change control board can prioritize bugs and decide which bugs to fix (see Chapter 16). The developers can decide how to fix those bugs. The management team can decide what course corrections to make in the project's direction. To enable these smart decisions, a good test execution process should provide for capture of test findings in clear reports and for circulation of these findings to the appropriate parties. In the case study, the testers entered bug reports immediately, and the test manager produced a weekly status report of the test cycle findings for management. As discussed in the case study in Chapter 12, Jamal also attends weekly change control board meetings that discuss and prioritize bug reports.

Another kind of information dissemination is internal. The results of all the previous tests can have some bearing on the subsequent tests. A positive example of this arose when Luis talked to Binyamin about the font bug he'd found. However, we also saw a negative example when Emma chose not to read Luis's bug report.

This process breakdown resulted in two negative outcomes. First was rework. Emma had to expend effort to rerun the Solaris performance test, and machine time was lost. Second, and perhaps more seriously, it introduced a one-day delay in finding four performance-related bugs. You might say, "Oh, well, what does a day matter?" But a project is nothing but a sequence of days, and days add up to weeks after a while.[6] Research on defect removal models has shown that finding and fixing bugs earlier reduces the total number of bugs found, resulting in savings in both money and time.[7] Using peer reviews of bug reports and test status reports can reduce these kinds of miscommunications, but the test manager needs to make sure that testers spend time on these tasks. Jamal's e-mail to his test team is an example of the kind of process that can work and the kind of management direction that can put it in place.[8]

As this example shows, this internal information is not just about the current project but can lead to improving the test system and the test process. You could say that while the test system tests the system under test through the test execution process, the system under test also tests the test system and the test execution process. This means that astute testers and test managers can glean information about the quality of the test system and the test execution process and find opportunities to improve them. In the case study, Luis and Lin-Tsu captured an improvement to one test case based on a serendipitous bug discovery. During initial test selection and assignment, Jamal adjusted the test execution times based on the previous test cycle.

As a final kind of useful internal information, in this case from a perspective of managing the work to be done, the test lead or test manager will want to make sure that the test team is completing all the planned testing activities. Here the earned value section of the test suite summary comes in. In the case study, Jamal looked at the earned value situation and saw that many of the test suites were taking longer than planned. This led him to analyze specific test suites remaining to be done. He realized that certain tests might not be completed soon enough or even at all without some remedial action. A good test process allows this kind of management perspective to see these situations as they develop, and take steps to mitigate the risks.

---

6. Fred Brooks discussed the danger of such small slips and the corrosive effects such attitudes about small slips have on a project over 25 years ago in *The Mythical Man-Month*. More recently, Tom DeMarco wrote in *The Deadline* that "there are an infinite number of ways to lose a day on a project, but not one single way to get a lost day back." Jealously guard your team's time and energy early in the project when there seems to be plenty of it, and you'll be glad you did later when time is tight and energy is flagging.
7. See, for example, Stephen Kan's book *Metrics and Models in Software Quality Engineering, Second Edition*.
8. Notice that Jamal recognized that the failure arose from a problem in the process, not a problem in the people. I mentioned Deming's red bead experiment earlier in this book as an example of why management needs to take responsibility for process deficiencies. This is another example. Rather than castigating Emma for the natural outcome of following the process as she understood it, Jamal accepted responsibility for the incident and fixed the process.

CORRECTLY INTERPRET TEST RESULTS

Of course, a characteristic that distinguishes valuable information from worthless noise is accuracy. In the great majority of cases, the test results we report should be correct. In the test execution process described earlier, substeps 3.C, 3.D, and 3.E ask the tester to check into discrepancies in test results carefully and distinguish between bugs in the system under test and bugs in the test system. Defining three distinct steps—as opposed to one step that says, "File a bug report if the expected and actual results don't match"—draws attention to the need to correctly interpret the test results.

Test execution is a human process. Since we are humans, our powers of observation and judgment are sometimes flawed. Our expectations of correct behavior are sometimes wrong. Inscrutable systems under test sometimes conceal evidence of correct and incorrect behavior. We might mistake a problem in the test environment, scripts, tools, or other parts of the test system for a problem in the system under test. For these and other reasons, we might report a failure when the program behaves correctly or, worse yet, vice versa (see Table 13-1).

These kinds of errors shouldn't surprise us. To see why, let's zoom in on a graphical view of step 3 of the test execution process. Figure 13-7 shows such a view. With all these different moving parts, misinterpretation is going to be an issue. Add to that the fact that other testers and project team members are likely to interact with the test system and the system under test while we're running tests, and such mistakes become all the more likely.[9]

To deal with tester observation and judgment problems, I have had senior testers review junior testers' results and assign the same test cases to different testers during

Behavior Is . . .	Tester Reports . . .	
	Pass	Fail
Correct	Increased confidence	Misplaced concern
Incorrect	False confidence	Useful diagnostic information

TABLE 13-1 THE OUTCOME OF VALID AND INVALID TEST RESULT INTERPRETATION

9. One of the reviewers, Steve Splaine, pointed out to me that this is especially true "if no effort has been made to partition [or] coordinate the use...of shared tests and data." This is certainly the case, and the potential problems become all the more acute the larger the team and the more complex the test environment.

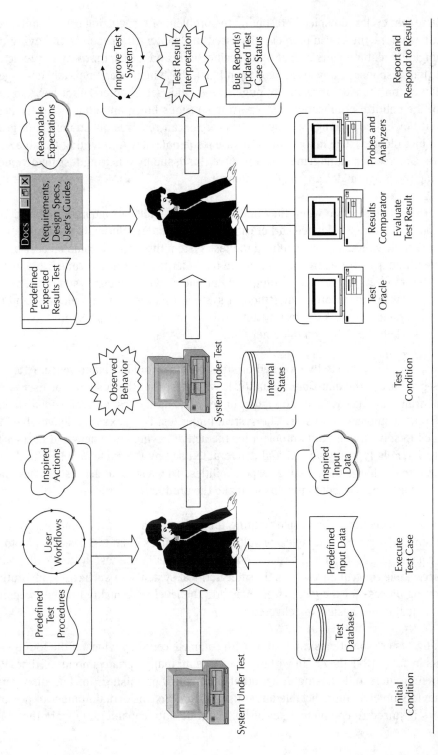

FIGURE 13-7 TEST CASE EXECUTION

subsequent cycles. Completely resolving the problem of recognizing correct and incorrect behavior—the oracle problem discussed in Chapter 10—depends on having unambiguous requirements and design specifications and a foolproof way of predicting the right response to any stimulus. When I lack these items—as I typically do—I generally err on the side of reporting bugs. (That said, see Chapter 14 for ways to deal with the political ramifications of reporting spurious bugs, and Chapter 16 for ideas about how a good change management process can resolves questions about gray-area bug reports.) The inscrutable software issue boils down to writing testable software. Only senior management can resolve this issue by ensuring test involvement during the program design and development.

What should testers do when they find a problem in the test system during test execution? The process I defined earlier calls for immediate resolution of the broken test. Some people would advocate putting the test system through the same process as the system under test: Report the bug in the tests, let the bug triage committee decide whether to fix it, gather metrics on quality problems with the test system—the whole nine yards. In other words, since the test system tests the system under test and the system under test tests the test system, this symmetry means we should follow the process when the shoe's on the other foot.

On most of the projects I've worked on, this process wouldn't make sense. After all, let's get back to the question of quality. If we accept that the customer or user is the final arbiter of quality, then the system under test and the test system have distinctly different customers and users. The system under test is an external deliverable, designed to solve a real-world problem for the actual paying customers and users. The test system is typically an internal deliverable used by the same people who developed it to discharge their testing responsibilities. The system under test is a product. The test system is a tool that helps us make the product.

That said, sometimes the people creating the test cases are not the same people who are running them. For example, consultancies sometimes build test systems and tools for companies. Also, in some cases, quality problems in the test system could have unacceptable consequences—e.g., in safety-critical systems. In such cases, instituting a testing process for the test system may add the level of formality needed to ensure that a quality test system is delivered.

Finally, testers sometimes can't know with complete certainty which of the four quadrants in Table 13-1 they're in without spending an inappropriate amount of time. Researching bugs and chasing down other unusual or promising (for bug discovery) behaviors involve unpredictable amounts of effort. So, the actual number of person-hours required to complete a set of tests can deviate considerably from the plan.

Testers need to remain cognizant of where their time is being spent. Test leads and managers must help their teams balance the need to make forward progress through the planned test cases against the need to know the meaning of their test findings with total certainty.

Not all bugs deserve the same level of research. An intermittent bug where an obscure error message appears in the wrong font once every ten or so times it appears can perhaps be safely ignored so as not to delay other tests for hours. However, an intermittent bug that sporadically corrupts a shared database may warrant postponing much of the test cycle until the failure has been isolated and the problem is reproducible.

EXHIBIT THE PROPER ATTITUDES

The topic of correct result interpretation brings us to attitudes. A good testing process should reinforce the proper attitudes of good testers, and the proper attitudes of the testers likewise enable a good testing process to produce useful results. As I mentioned in Chapter 8, the proper attitudes of a good tester include professional pessimism, balanced curiosity, and focus. Because testers need to remain skeptical and play the professional pessimist's role in the development project, I advocate an active bias toward reporting a bug when testing. This has the following implications.

- If in doubt, the testers assume that the observed behavior is incorrect until they satisfy themselves otherwise.
- The testers report as a bug any situation where the on-screen help, user's guides, or any other documentation indicates that correct behavior differs from that observed.
- The testers *always* report any event leading to catastrophic behaviors, no matter how intermittent or irreproducible. Such behaviors include any loss of data, a crash, freeze, or hang, or any other reliability, data quality, or severe performance degradation problem involving the system under test, the host system, any cohabiting software, or any interfacing or communicating system.
- Finally, the testers report any circumstance where the system under test does not conform to reasonable expectations of program behavior or quality, or is otherwise confusing, misleading, or ambiguous.

This way of thinking, however, must be balanced against where you are in the project. In the early stages of testing, system quality is often very bad. Testers should focus their efforts at this stage on finding the scary stuff, not worrying about misspellings in the user's guide, for example. Once the system improves, what is often criticized as nitpicky test result interpretation is actually an appropriate attempt by testers to polish the fit and finish of the product. We should not be ashamed to file low-priority bug reports at the appropriate time in the project. This is a form of balanced curiosity.

Focus implies that good testers are alert for discrepancies in interpretations of what it would mean for the system to be *behaving correctly*. Such discrepancies between interpretations can arise not just between a tester and a programmer, but also between two programmers writing communicating components, which is the source of most bugs found during a well-executed integration test phase. A classic example of this kind of bug occurred on a NASA Mars mission where confusion arose about the use of metric or English units for data, particularly in the measurement of velocity and braking force. The use of different units by different programmers resulted in the total loss of the mission—and any valuable information the mission might have generated—when the lander hit the Martian surface at high speed and presumably disintegrated.

In such cases, the bug exists not in one component or the other, but in the interaction between components. Before a single line of buggy code existed, though, the bug simultaneously existed in the heads of two different human beings. Had the right person—a tester, perhaps—at the right time—during requirements specification—thought to ask both of those people the right question—"About the units: English or metric?"—the entire unfortunate scenario could have been avoided.

So, testers must learn to be vigilant for the signs of disagreement or different understandings within the programming organizations. Sometimes asking "dumb questions" such as "I'm sorry, but I'm confused; are we using metric units or English units on this project?" can stimulate discussions that surface these misunderstandings before they result in dangerous, expensive, hard-to-diagnose bugs during system test— or, worse yet, later. This is a major source of value for test organizations. As Fred Brooks wrote in the first edition of *The Mythical Man-Month* over 25 years ago— about projects that had happened in the 1960s—"Long before any code exists, the specification must be handed to an outside testing group to be scrutinized for completeness and clarity. As [V. A.] Vyssotsky [of Bell Lab's Safeguard Project] says, the developers themselves cannot do this: 'They won't tell you they don't understand it; they will happily invent their way through the gaps and obscurities.' "[10]

A bug is a bug is a bug, whether it lives in a component, lives in the intersection of all the components, lives in the whole system, lives in the design, or lives in the requirements. The most effective test teams I've worked on have had implicit or explicit per-

---

10. See *The Mythical Man-Month*, page 142.

mission to report any of these kinds of bug and have been involved early enough to do some good in each area.

PROCEED EFFICIENTLY

To some extent, an efficient test process relies on an efficient test system. This brings us back to the test system development issues discuss in Chapter 11. For example, minimizing test case dependencies and sharing of test data sets prevents unnecessary rework, delays, and possible misinterpretation of test results.

However, efficiency considerations also arise during test execution, even with the most efficient test system. As a test manager, I want the minimal amount of overlapping work and avoidable delays in testing. Part of this involves making clear to each tester which tests they should run and when. In the case study, Jamal used the Assigned To column in the test case summary worksheet to identify an owner for each test. He used the Plan Date column to order the tests for maximum efficiency and to generate information in the right order. Both assignments and planned dates changed for some test cases as the cycle proceeded—e.g., when Jamal took over the security and privacy tests. In such situations, the test lead or manager also needs to communicate changes in assignment and planned dates to the test team.

This may sound like a trivial matter, but it's easy for confusion to creep in here, with two serious consequences. The mismanagement of two precious resources (tester effort and schedule time) entrusted to the test manager is bad enough. Frequently, test managers will require yet more overtime from their team to rescue the schedule because of such errors, which constitutes a failure of leadership that detracts from the managers' ability to get the best work from the team.[11]

This points out the need for the test team to allow the process and the planned tests to adapt to evolving circumstances. Part of testing is encountering unexpected behaviors and researching those anomalies to create a detailed, actionable bug report (see Chapter 14). Since the behaviors *are* unexpected, and since we can't predict with 100% confidence how many bugs we'll find, the test process generates its own fluid state of affairs. In addition, external events such as delayed builds, adjustments in build content, and shifts in management priorities bring change to bear. Testers can't prevent these changes, so the test process must accommodate them. In the case study,

---

11. Disrespecting the team's time is a management deadly sin. Once I witnessed the resignation—in a profane, abrupt, and emotional outburst in the middle of a meeting—of the lead system architect on a project after such an incident. For more insights on this and other management failures, see Tom DeMarco and Tim Lister's book *Peopleware*.

Jamal adapted to changes from within—a miscommunication on bug findings—as well as changes from without—a high level of bugginess in SpeedyWriter and a system administrator's negligent shutdown of a test server. Jamal adjusted the test case assignments, added extra resources, changed the planned execution dates, and pushed lower-priority test cases out to the following test cycle.

As an aside, consider the waste and delay that arose in the case study when the system administrator outside the testing team brought down the server Luis was using for a test. Test environment configuration management is a topic I dealt with at length in my first book, *Managing the Testing Process*, but let me point out in the context of test execution that the test team simply must have complete control of the test environment during this period.

There's a major breakdown in the process somewhere when the kind of error described in the case study happens more than once or maybe twice during a test project. In situations like the Sumatra test team's, where outside people must have administrator permissions on the test environment because they support it, it can be difficult to ensure that no one modifies the test environment without clearance from the test manager or test lead.

On rare occasions in situations like this, people entrusted to support the test environment prove to be more of a hindrance than a help. I've had instances where system administrators took hardware out of the test lab even though it was clearly and exclusively earmarked for the test effort. In such cases, it's better to try to move the test environment support function into the test team, even if you must reduce the scope of your testing to do it, and simply deny logical (i.e., electronic) and physical access to the test equipment to anyone outside the test team. This can entail secret passwords, firewalls, locks, separate test labs, card keys, and so forth. Otherwise, the test project may end up suffering the death of 10,000 cuts as little incidents like "borrowed" hardware and debugging in the test environment gradually reduce testing efficiency to zero.

Finally, an efficient test process should have the lowest possible overhead. In other words, we should devote the most time possible to testing and other activities that generate value for the organization, and the least time possible on everything else. Notice that the daily debriefing meetings, reading each other's bug reports, and other informal test activities that foster communication and sharing of knowledge are not overheads, they are ways to promote efficiency. However, following an inappropriately complex or onerous process, using documentation-heavy processes where the information will not be used later, having standing meetings where one person reports status to the supervisor while everyone else just waits their turn to talk—all these are examples of overhead.

HANDLE CHALLENGES

Since the test execution process is subject to all sorts of unforeseeable and external pressures, there will be challenges. Let's look at a few of these in the following subsections.

DEALING WITH EXTENDED SHIFTS AND OUTSOURCED TESTING

Back in Chapter 6, Jamal made a decision to use an evening shift. He made that decision because of constraints on the test environment. This is not an uncommon reason for choosing to run an evening—or even a graveyard or weekend—testing shift. I chose to run evening and weekend shifts once when I had a shortage of rare engineering prototype Internet appliances and a lot of tests to run in a short period. When testing must be done on production mainframe systems that simply can't be dedicated to testing during normal business hours, sometimes most testing has to happen during off-hours. On another occasion, the need to keep a temperamental stress test running 24 hours a day meant that we needed to baby-sit the tests much of that time. When I was a project manager for a testing lab, we commonly used both evening and weekend shifts.

Extended shifts are not terribly difficult to manage, as long as you keep a few realities in mind. The primary issue is communication. It's harder for people who aren't in the same place at the same time to communicate, and test execution (along with bug reporting) is definitely part of the testing process where communication between the test team members is critical. In the case study, Luis and Emma had a communication breakdown on the same shift, which shows how easily miscommunications happen. Evening shifts limit communication options, and graveyard and weekend shifts limit them even further. The test team will need to make every effort to promote communication—and the test manager will need to put processes in place to ensure it. On an Internet appliance project, we had a two-hour overlap period from 3:00 PM to 5:00 PM every day. During this period the evening shift was expected to read e-mail from that day and ask follow-up questions before the day shift left.

Extended Shifts

Any off-hours work done by people other than those working during normal business hours (approximately 8:00 AM to 5:00 PM). Typical extended shifts include *evening shift* (approximately 4:00 PM to 1:00 AM), *graveyard shift* (approximately midnight to 9:00 AM), and *weekend* or *holiday shift* (any of the previous shifts, but on nonworkdays). Contrast *overtime*, which is work beyond 40 hours per week, but which can involve any shift.

Part of that communication is status gathering. Daily debriefings or status meetings that happen during a structured shift handoff period help. On the Internet appliance project, we held the handoff meeting at around 4:00 PM. During that period, we talked about the testing that had gone on that day and the evening before, and we updated the test case tracking worksheets.

Another issue is scheduling. Everyone will need to know what shift they're on and on which days. The simplest case is that people work the same shift for the whole project. However, this is not always possible. Some testers may see extended shift work as very onerous, and some kind of shift rotation might be necessary. My experience has been that bonuses paid to evening and weekend shift crews tended to make the extended shifts desirable for certain people, ameliorating this problem.

Another issue is support. Assuming that the test team does not administer the test network, you'll need to line up system administration or network operations support during off-hours. This means support staff must give the test team pager numbers, home phone numbers, cell phone numbers, and the like. They must carry those pagers and cell phones at all times, answer their home phone day and night, and in general agree that their evenings or even early mornings can be interrupted by an urgent test team request. I've found this to be more challenging on my projects than lining up testers willing to work extended shifts. In the case study, Jamal was careful to deal with this issue during the test planning process. If you wait until test execution to iron this out, you can expect to encounter resentment, destructive literal compliance, and other forms of active or passive rebellion, including outright refusal.

Finally, consider logistics. People working extended shifts will need badges with off-hours access. Air conditioning units must be left running during the shift. Alarm codes must be provided. Security guards must be notified. Phone switches and PBXes may need to be configured to allow off-hours usage. Facilities people must be willing to help resolve logistical issues that arise.

Outsourcing some or all of a test effort generally creates the same issues as extended test shifts, only more so. Communication is often entirely via phone and e-mail in these cases except for the occasional on-site visit. Even during on-site visits, it is rare that everyone at the test lab comes to the client's site—or vice versa. In addition, on-site visits can be more about management presentations and sales pitches than nuts-and-bolts tactical interaction between the individual contributors. E-mail and phone communications are often complicated by time zones, which limit the periods of over-lapping work and thus the possibility of dialogue on a real-time, interactive, as-needed basis. Test support personnel, such as system administrators, generally do not have a responsibility to provide support for outsource test facilities.

Because of the broad client base of most outsource testing organizations, the specific expertise required to support the system will not be present in their facility. During testing, both minor and serious glitches in installation, maintenance, or operations arise, but the right expert—often wandering the halls not far from the in-house test team—can resolve these in minutes. However, such glitches can render the system unavailable for testing for hours or even days in an outsource test lab. I've seen this happen on more than one testing project.

This section is not a dig against independent testing labs and consultancies—after all, I run one. Nor am I denigrating the value of extended shifts—I use them. However, it's important to plan tests knowing that we will find and run into problems. A test plan that assumes all the tests will pass and the system will work just fine is bound to break down. If you plan your use of extended shifts and outsource testing recognizing the need to handle communication, support, and logistics problems that arise from complex or buggy products, these options will serve you well. In addition, the test team that amplifies its efficiency and effectiveness by leveraging extended shifts and outsource test teams will reap valuable political benefits from being able to achieve better testing in a quicker way, thus building credibility.

ACCOMMODATING HOLIDAYS, CULTURES, AND VACATIONS

Test execution periods—the time of greatest pressure on many projects—often span holidays. Indeed, in the diverse cultural mix present in many companies around the world these days, you might be hard pressed to find a test execution period that didn't span a holiday for one or more of the people on the project.

As Jamal showed in the case study, though, a culturally diverse team is actually a strength, not a weakness, in this regard. On homogeneous projects, everyone will want to take the same holidays off. On diverse projects, many people might be happy to trade holidays like Christmas for their own cultural or religious holidays more attuned to their needs.

Vacations, while not occurring synchronously, do present a challenge in terms of downtime, especially with key players. This can be a problem with tight or high-risk projects, and executive management sometimes cancels all vacation during these times. However, the general case is that someone or another will take a vacation during a long project. Realistically, the other option is that people will burn out and quit.

Whatever the cause of reduced staffing, the watchword is advance notice. I've found that as long as I knew far enough in advance about holidays, cultural requirements, and vacations, I could plan around them. During test execution, it's important to remember which weeks will be short-staffed. The test manager can then shift testing work around those weeks.

CAPTURING THE HISTORY ON THE GROUND

Capturing historical information is especially critical when you have outside dependencies. If you can't get through your planned testing because the test environment is down, that may not be your fault. Perhaps the operations team—charged with supporting the test environment—isn't responding to pages and calls for help. Perhaps competing priorities prevent them from responding as agreed in the test plan. In that case, management needs to understand what these competing priorities are doing to the test effort.

Of course, it is possible that outside teams upon whom you depend are actually opposed to the success of the testing effort or the project as a whole. For obvious political reasons, keeping accurate logs in such situations is a survival issue. While the black arts of corporate politics are beyond the scope of this book, in addition to keeping detailed logs of how external dependencies affected test execution, certainly you'll want to deal with this situation with care and adequate documentation.

IMPLEMENT IMPROVEMENTS

While test execution is tightly bound to the context of the testing effort and the rest of the project, there are some things you can do to fine-tune test execution itself in many cases.

1. Assess where you are and what portions of the test execution process are not under control, including other processes discussed in this book. Maybe some of the sources of chaos are external. Can you figure out a way to reduce the leakage of external chaos into your testing effort?

2. Ensure that you have some idea of what you intend to test and how long it will take to perform those tests, broken down into bite-sized pieces. Two- to four-hour test tasks are sizes that I find very manageable. This need not take the form of detailed, scripted test cases where you count the number of minutes required on average to execute each detailed, unambiguous step. Simply bounding a test charter (e.g., test file manipulation capabilities) with a planned duration (e.g., spend two hours testing file manipulation capabilities) can suffice.

3. Put in place some way of tracking test cases—either using the test case summary and test suite summary worksheets I showed earlier or some other mechanism—both in terms of duration and schedule and in terms of findings. Again, you can start with something very simple, and you may find that this simple technique suffices.

4. Use the effort data you gather in tracking test cases, along with your predictions about the bugs found at various points in a test phase, to predict the amount of time you should allocate for dealing with bugs. A classic pitfall of testing is to fail to anticipate the presence of bugs in the system under test. This results in scheduling tests as if they will pass, which underestimates the effort and duration, often severely.[12]

5. Deal with the need for internal communication and information gathering. A lot of testing problems arise when the testers don't know what one another is doing.

All these steps can be important way stations on the road to getting your test execution processes under control.

Competent testers execute tests with discipline and imagination, and the competent test manager manages the test execution process crisply. The test team adapts and responds to unexpected events and findings, and adds value consistently for the organization. The spotlight is on the test team during test execution.

With the end of this chapter, we wind down our discussion of the Perform step in the test process. Deft performance of the tests generates crisp, complete, and accurate information about the quality of the system. This is the service and product we can deliver to developers, to peer-level managers, to project managers, and even to senior executives.

The delivery of this product and service provides the project team with an opportunity to perfect the system. It also provides us with an opportunity to perfect the test system. In the final chapters of this book, we'll look at reporting results, managing changes to the system, and, ultimately, improving the testing itself.

---

12. The habit of planning tests assuming those tests will fail, not pass, has become so ingrained in my thinking that I forgot to mention it initially. I thank Tim Koomen for pointing out this omission.

Step #	Step	Done?
3.A	Perform: Do the testing and gather the results.	☑
3.D	Acquire and install a test release consisting of some or all of the components in the system under test.	☑
3.F	Assign, track, and manage the set of test cases to be run against each test release.	☑

Part IV

Perfect

I've named this part Perfect. I mean that word as a verb, not an adjective. I will never look back on a project and say, "We did a perfect job of testing." But on each project, I can always work to perfect my testing, to do a better job of testing than on all the previous projects. Perfection is a fine standard against which to gauge our improvements, because we want to be moving toward perfection, continually getting better.

In this last part of the book, we'll examine the processes by which we guide the adaptation and improvement of the system we're developing as well as the test process itself. This happens in part through the effective communication of information, specifically bug reporting and results reporting. We can use this information, as well as other information about our test process, to make intelligent changes.

In the final chapter, we'll look back at the whole test process. We'll return to the big picture we examined in Chapter 1. This will allow us to look for common practices in good testing processes. It will also allow us to examine ways to handle key challenges. Finally, since my goal when writing this book—and presumably your goal in reading it—was to find ways to make test processes better, we'll end by discussing that topic.

Step #	Step	Done?
4.	Perfect: Guide adaptation and improvement.	☐
4.A	Document the bugs found during test execution.	☐
4.C	Communicate test results to key stakeholders.	☐
4.D	Adjust to changes and refine the testing process.	☐

14

WHERE QUALITY FALLS
SHORT: REPORT BUGS

In this chapter, let's look at a test process that, while primarily internal to the test team, produces results that are highly visible: the bug reporting process. In a sense, bug reports are the primary tangible product of the testing process itself, solid technical documentation that describes a failure mode in the system under test that could affect the customer's experience of quality.[1] Each bug report should provide management with the information they need to decide the priority of the bug. For those bugs deemed worth fixing, each bug report should provide the programmer with the information she needs to fix the underlying bug.

Bug reporting is a testing process that meets all four criteria for criticality that I spelled out in the Introduction. It's a process we engage in every day—sometimes many times a day—during test execution. Bug reports are often highly visible, being read by programmers and senior managers alike. Done right, the bug reporting process and the bug reports themselves build teamwork within the test team, as well as the credibility of the test team within the project team. Good bug reports, prioritized by management for repair and fixed by programmers, are the vehicle by which the test team influences an increase in the quality of the system, while bad bug reports can result in dangerous defects escaping to the field. Each tester in the test team must

---

1. However, as Rick Craig reminded me after he read this chapter, in some cases "the test cases themselves can become part of the documentation of the software. As systems age and the requirements and/or design [specifications] get out of date, it is possible that the only documentation of what the system is supposed to do is contained within the test cases."

> **Bug Report**
>
> A technical document written to describe the symptoms of a bug to 1) communicate the impact and circumstances of a quality problem, 2) prioritize the bug for repair, and 3) help the programmer locate the underlying defect and fix it.

master this process to fully realize the team's potential contribution to the development effort.[2]

A BUG REPORTING PROCESS

How can we write the best possible bug reports? Process 10 outlines the bug reporting process I use on many of my projects.[3]

Step #	Step	Done?
1.	Run each test using structured, careful testing techniques.	☐
2.	Reproduce any deviations from expected behavior.	☐
3.	Isolate the bug by checking the effect of key variations, looking for workarounds as well.	☐
4.	Look for the general case, especially one more severe or objectionable.	☐
5.	Compare the abnormal behavior observed with the behavior of the system under similar conditions on this or previous test releases.	☐
6.	Summarize the failure, including the effect on customers or users.	☐
7.	Condense the report, removing unnecessary information.	☐
8.	Disambiguate, removing confusing, misleading, or imprecise words.	☐
9.	Neutralize the bug report, expressing ideas impartially and fairly.	☐
10.	Submit the bug report to a peer review, resolve any problems found, and then enter the bug report into the bug tracking system	☐

PROCESS 10   A BUG REPORTING PROCESS

---

2. Portions of this chapter were previously serialized in *Professional Tester*. I thank Caroline Quentin for her fine editorial work on that article. Portions of this chapter also appear in Erik van Veenendaal's *The Testing Practitioner*. I thank him for including this critical process as part of an industry-recognized approach to dealing with bugs.
3. I benefited from an online discussion I had about this checklist with Bret Pettichord in 1999. I thank him for his contributions to my thinking on this topic.

Because of the criticality of this process, let me spend a couple of pages expanding on the big-picture implications of each of these steps in one place before I branch out into the case study and a closer examination of some of the details of bug reporting.

1. *Structure*—Good bug reporting begins with solid, organized testing. Testing may be manual or automated, scripted or exploratory, but it must be something other than just hacking on the product in an aimless attempt to break it. Sloppy testing yields sloppy bug reports.

2. *Reproduce*—Bugs often take me by surprise—of course! If I could predict in advance when I would find a bug, I wouldn't need to test the system. Reproducing the problem sharpens my understanding of the issue and allows me to document a crisp set of steps that will re-create the failure. I like to use three tries as a rule of thumb. Some uncooperative bugs are intermittent. I report intermittent bugs with a note about the intermittence; e.g., "This failure occurred in two out of three tries."[4]

3. *Isolate*—Many factors can affect the behavior of software, and some of those factors will affect the symptoms of bugs. The way in which a change in the test environment manifests itself in terms of bug behavior is often significant. By changing some key variables, one at a time, in an attempt to change the behavior of the bug, I find that I write more insightful bug reports. Isolating a bug is not easy. I have to understand to some extent how the system under test works. I have to think through my tests before I run them. I also avoid getting into debugging or expending inappropriate amounts of time on trivial issues. However, good bug isolation builds tester credibility and gives the programmer a head start on debugging. In addition, as mentioned in Chapter 3, I can find handy, valuable workarounds as part of isolation.

4. *Generalize*—Often, the symptom I see when I first find a bug is not the most general case. For example, I recently found a problem where a program wouldn't import a specific worksheet from an Excel file. When I dug a bit deeper, though, I realized that it wouldn't import *any* worksheet from any Excel file if the name of the worksheet contained parentheses. It's important, when looking for the general case, not to generalize to the point of absurdity. Not all program crashes, for example, come from the same bug. Nevertheless, trying to find the general rule for how the bug occurs deepens my understanding and helps convince programmers and managers that the problem is not an isolated case.

---

4. Steve Splaine, one of the reviewers of this book, told me that upon finding an intermittent bug, he "tends to include additional information about the [system] configuration...because chances are [the bug is] related to an incompatibility...."

5. *Compare*—Testing often covers the same ground, both when a tester runs the same tests against a later version of software and when a tester runs tests that cover similar conditions. These results can provide important clues to a programmer when I connect the dots. Is the failure a regression? Does the same feature work in other parts of the product? While this kind of research is not always possible—e.g., when a test was blocked against a previous version—it can save the programmers a lot of time if I can find this information.

6. *Summarize*—At this point in the process, I probably understand the failure well enough to see how the problem will affect the customers or users. As part of the change control or bug triage processes (see Chapter 16), it's important to consider the business risks related to each bug as part of deciding whether to fix it. A good bug report includes a summary that communicates to the change control board or bug triage committee in a single sentence the essence and significance of the problem. (The summary field may actually be called the title, synopsis, failure, impact statement, or some other name, but the idea is that it is a short, one-sentence distillation of the overall report.) This summary is invaluable when it becomes time to prioritize the bugs. It also gives the bug report a name for programmers. "Hey, have you fixed that font-change bug yet?" is a question you might ask a programmer that is far more meaningful than "How's work on bug 1716 coming?" Writing a good summary is harder than it looks. Mathematician Blaise Pascal once concluded a long letter with the sentence, "I would have written a shorter letter but I didn't have time." I spend the time to write good summaries because it's the most important sentence in the bug report.

7. *Condense*—Speaking of writing a shorter letter, how about trimming some unnecessary words from my bug reports? I once read a bug report that spent the first page describing how the tester set the high score in Tetris, a video game, which had nothing to do with the failure. Did I care about this tester's achievement? No. Did I need to spend time reading about that? No. Did the tester who wrote that report make me want to pay close attention to his subsequent reports? No. The best bug reports are neither cryptic commentary nor droning, endless, pointless documents. I try to use just the words I need and describe only the steps and information that actually pertain to the bug being reported.

8. *Disambiguate*—To disambiguate is to remove confusing or misleading words that might make a reader wonder what I mean. For example, I could disambiguate this step by using the alternative phrase "be clear" instead of disambiguate. All kidding aside, an ideal bug report leads the programmer by the hand to the bug. For example, what does it mean if I write, "Program died." Did it stop responding but remain on the screen? Did it exit normally? Did it exit abnormally? Did it exit and take down one or more other programs? Did it exit and

cause the computer's operating system to encounter a fatal error? The wording "Program died" is ambiguous, and a good bug report eschews such ambiguity. Clarity is key.[5]

9. *Neutralize*—As the bearer of bad news, I need to express myself calmly and impartially in bug reports. Attacking the programmer, criticizing the underlying error in the code, or using humor or sarcasm to make a point generally backfires. I try to be gentle and fair-minded in my words and implications, and confine my bug reports to statements of fact, not conjecture or hyperbole. Bug reports, once in a bug tracking system, often live forever and can be read by people not on the project team.[6]

10. *Review*—As I mentioned earlier, a bug report is a technical document. Peer reviews, inspections, walkthroughs, and the like are powerful tools for early detection of defects in documents of all kinds, including bug reports. Before you dismiss this step as too time-consuming or a needless roadblock to getting bug reports filed as quickly as possible, consider the delays and frustration that can result when a programmer wastes time trying to reproduce a bug that was actually a test problem, or when a programmer can't figure out what a bug report is about and so returns it as "irreproducible" or "works as designed". The review need not be formal. I've had success where the review requirement was that one tester read another's bug report before any bug report was submitted.

Let me make two more general observations about this process before we go on. First, it's important to remember that writing is creative: two good bug reports on one problem can differ in style and content. The purpose of my bug reporting process is not to standardize bug reports, but rather to ensure quality. Second, this process works best when thought of as a checklist rather than a strict sequential process. The first and last steps—structured testing and a peer review—are logical bookends, but if you feel more comfortable reviewing your wording for neutrality throughout, then go right ahead.

---

5. I benefited from some comments from Johanna Rothman in disambiguating this section, and I thank her for her thoughtful input.
6. This is something Cem Kaner has pointed out in *Testing Computer Software, Second Edition*. You never know who's going to read your bug reports—plaintiff's counsel, perhaps?—so to avoid unnecessary appearances as a witness for the prosecution of your employer, you should write only exactly what you mean. While this may seem melodramatic and unlikely, I worked with an attorney once as part of an attempt to impeach the overall credibility of a development team, which included analyzing the bug reports.

A BIG BUG IN THE BIG BUILD

On Monday, December 16, Luis was running the managed file functionality test against the Big Build. He created a new file and inserted some text. He then tried to change the font of the text by highlighting the text, pulling down the font menu, and selecting the Symbol font. Suddenly, the screen displayed a bunch of symbols, questions marks, and other meaningless noise where nice normal English sentences once were. "Hmm," Luis thought, "that's certainly not in the 'reasonably expected behavior' category." He started his bug report by jotting the following in his notebook.

> Nasty bug trashed contents of new file that I created by formatting some text in Symbol font, wasting my time.

Step #	Step	Done?
1.	Run each test using structured, careful testing techniques.	✔

This might be the way Luis would describe this problem in a test lab conversation with Jamal Brown, the test manager, but he certainly wouldn't put it that way to a programmer—or a development or project manager. Keeping this audience in mind, Luis went back and reproduced the problem two more times. Subsequently, he started entering a bug report in the bug tracking database.

Steps to Reproduce

1. I started the SpeedyWriter editor, then I created a new file.
2. I then typed in four lines of text, repeating "The quick fox jumps over the lazy brown dog" each time, using different effects each time, bold, italic, strikethrough, and underline.
3. I highlighted the text, then pulled down the font menu, and selected Symbol.
4. This nasty bug trashed all the text into meaningless garbage, wasting the user's time.
5. I was able to reproduce this problem three out of three tries.

Step #	Step	Done?
2.	Reproduce any deviations from expected behavior.	✔

This was better. A programmer could read this and get a head start on debugging the problem. However, Luis knew that the SpeedyWriter product, as with any other application, supported a wide range of features and configurations that could affect the behavior of this bug. So, Luis tried a few experiments, identifying a simple workaround in the process. He then added the following section to the bottom of his bug report.

Isolation

On the vague suspicion that this was just a formatting problem, I saved the file, closed SpeedyWriter and reopened the file. The garbage remained.

If you save the file before Symbolizing the contents, the bug does not occur.

The bug does not occur with existing files.

This only happens under Windows 98 OSR2.

Step #	Step	Done?
3.	Isolate the bug by checking the effect of key variations, looking for workarounds as well.	☑

This was a very specific failure mode, so Luis decided to try a few other fonts, as well as checking to see if the font effects, the font styles, and the particular text had anything to do with the bug. He found that both Wingdings and Arial fonts suffered from the same problem. The latter was significant, because Arial fonts were widely used by SpeedyWriter users. However, the experiments with bold, italic, and underlining showed no effect on the bug's manifestation. He also found—as he had expected— that the particular text string or the amount of text had nothing to do with the bug. He deleted the potentially misleading reference to font styles and the text string from step 2 of the report and changed the report (see the italicized portions in the text box below) to emphasize the Arial-related bug (and to fix a minor grammatical error).

Steps to Reproduce

1. I started the SpeedyWriter editor, then I created a new file.
2. I then typed in some text; e.g., try four lines of text, repeating, "The quick fox jumps over the lazy brown dog" each time.
3. I highlighted the text, then pulled down the font menu, and selected *Arial*.
4. This nasty bug trashed all the text into meaningless garbage, wasting the user's time.
5. I was able to reproduce this problem three out of three tries.

Isolation

Also happens with Wingdings and Symbol fonts.

On the vague suspicion that this was just a formatting problem, I saved the file, closed SpeedyWriter and reopened the file. The garbage remained.

If you save the file before *changing the font of* the contents, the bug does not occur.

The bug does not occur with existing files.

This only happens under Windows 98 OSR2.

Step #	Step	Done?
4.	Look for the general case, especially one more severe or objectionable.	☑

Next, Luis reviewed the test logs from the previous cycles of integration and system test and looked at some test reports from the programmer's component test phase. He found that this particular feature had been tested quite a bit, which told him that this problem was a regression in system quality. He added the following line to the Isolation section.

New to the Big Build (3.1.018.TR); same test case passed against builds 3.1.007.TR through 3.1.017.TR.

Step #	Step	Done?
5.	Compare the abnormal behavior observed with the behavior of the system under similar conditions on this or previous test releases.	☑

Now that Luis had a solid understanding of the bug, how it would manifest itself, and how it would affect the user, he wrote the summary line below for the bug report.

Summary

Arial, Wingdings, and Symbol fonts corrupt new files.

Step #	Step	Done?
6.	Summarize the failure, including the effect on customers or users.	☑

Here, Luis captured the impact to the user and the basic nature of the problem in eight words. He felt confident that no one reading this summary would fail to understand what the problem was and why it mattered.

At this point, the bug report was written. All that remained was to spend some time polishing it. First, Luis condensed the report a bit by eliminating extra verbiage, for example rephrasing the following sentence:

If you save the file before changing the font of the contents, the bug does not occur.

as

Saving file before changing font prevents bug.

and dropping the word "I" from the Steps to Reproduce section.

Step #	Step	Done?
7.	Condense the report, removing unnecessary information.	✔

Next, Luis checked the report for ambiguous or confusing wording that might confuse the reader. He changed step 3 from

3. Highlighted the text, then pulled down the font menu, and selected Arial.

to

3. Highlighted *all four lines of* text, then pulled down the font menu, and selected Arial.

Step 4 went from

4. This nasty bug trashed all the text into meaningless garbage, wasting the user's time.

to

> 4. This nasty bug trashed all the text into meaningless garbage, *including control charac-*
> *ters, numbers, and other binary junk,* wasting the user's time.

In the Isolation section, he changed

> Also happens with Wingdings and Symbol fonts.

to

> *Reproduced with same steps using* Wingdings and Symbol fonts.

Finally, he added the some detail to the Isolation line that read

> This only happens under Windows 98 OSR2.

expanding it to say that the bug

> Only happens under Windows 98 OSR2, *not Solaris, Mac, or other Windows flavors.*

Step #	Step	Done?
8.	Disambiguate, removing confusing, misleading, or imprecise words.	✔

To wrap up, Luis scoured the report for any extreme statements or biased comments
that might alarm or distract readers. He decided step 4 was a bit harsh, so he rephrased
that as follows.

> 4. All text converted to control characters, numbers, and other apparently random binary
> data.

Step #	Step	Done?
9.	Neutralize the bug report, expressing ideas impartially and fairly.	☑

Finally, Luis asked Lin-Tsu to review the report.

"Looks pretty good, Luis," Lin-Tsu said. "One question, though: Is this related to that file-creation problem you found in the last test cycle?"

"I don't think so," he replied, "since it seems to be specific to these fonts. The other bug was with specific file types."

"Okay," she responded, "The only other suggestion I'd have would be to remove the word 'garbage' from the isolation section. That's an inflammatory word."

"Oh, I guess I missed that," Luis grinned. "I had started out talking about 'garbage' all over in the report, but trimmed it out everywhere but there. Sorry I missed it."

"No problem, that's what these reviews are for," Lin-Tsu reassured him.

Step #	Step	Done?
10.	Submit the bug report to a peer review, resolve any problems found, and then enter the bug report into the bug tracking system.	☑

The final bug report Luis submitted looked like this.

Summary

Arial, Wingdings, and Symbol fonts corrupt new files.

Steps to Reproduce

1. Started SpeedyWriter editor, then created new file.
2. Typed in some text; e.g., try four lines of text, repeating, "The quick fox jumps over the lazy brown dog" each time.
3. Highlighted all four lines of text, then pulled down the font menu, and selected Arial.
4. All text converted to control characters, numbers, and other apparently random binary data.
5. Reproduced three out of three tries.

Isolation

New to build 3.1.018.TR; same test case passed against builds 3.1.007.TR (System Test entry) through 3.1.017.TR.

Reproduced with same steps using Wingdings and Symbol fonts.

On vague suspicion this was a formatting problem, saved file, closed SpeedyWriter and reopened file, but data corruption remained.

Saving file before changing font prevents bug.

Bug does not occur with existing files.

Only happens under Windows 98, not Solaris, Mac, or other Windows flavors.

This was a good, solid failure description for the bug that Luis observed. It communicated the problem, it could help management decide whether to fix the problem based on the impact to the customer, and it gave the development team some solid leads for their debugging activities.

BEYOND THE FAILURE DESCRIPTION

In addition to the failure description, a good bug tracking systems needs to capture some additional pieces of information to make the overall bug management process work. Two of these are severity and priority.

By "severity" I mean the technical impact on the system under test, the serious of the effects of the bugs. I often use the following scale for severity.

1. *Loss of data*—Bug causes loss of user (end-user, operator, and so on) or system data.
2. *Loss of functionality*—Bug blocks use of a major functional area (can include nonfunctional problems like performance that impose unacceptable delays in functionality).
3. *Loss of functionality with a workaround*—Bug blocks use of a major functional area, but a reasonable affected-user workaround exists.
4. *Partial loss of functionality*—Bug blocks some unessential portion of a functional area.
5. *Cosmetic*—Bug allows normal functionality but with significant blemishes (especially in the user interface or system responsiveness).[7]

---

7. This scale derives from Department of Defense 2167A standard for testing. Plenty of other ways of classifying severity are used. See Tim Dyes's article "Tracking Severity" in *Software Testing and Quality Engineering*, Volume 1, Issue 2 (Mar/Apr 1999), and now at www.stickyminds.com.

By "priority" I mean the importance of fixing the problem, which is a complex business decision in some cases. Factors can include the impact of the bug on the project and the likely success of the product in the marketplace, dependencies between bugs and/or tests, regulatory, standards, or contractual requirements, and, as well, the severity of the bug. I often use the following scale for priority.

1. *Urgent*—Bug requires immediate resolution.
2. *Essential*—Bug is must-fix for release.
3. *Valuable*—Bug would significantly reduce the value of the system to one or more customers or users.
4. *Desirable*—Bug should be resolved in this release if possible within feature, budget, and schedule constraints; otherwise, in next scheduled release.
5. *Discretionary*—Bug could be fixed whenever possible in some future release, allowing for other priorities.

Severity and priority are distinct concepts, with priority the more important of the two. I'll discuss the process of bug prioritization in Chapter 16, but in the meantime let me briefly explain the distinction.

Cursory consideration leads some software, hardware, and systems engineers—including testers—to conclude that high severity implies high priority, and vice versa. That's not always the case. Imagine a bug that involves display of an inappropriate message. That's a severity 5 bug on my scale. What if the inappropriate message includes a profane, lewd, or racist word? Less dramatically, suppose that the product name is displayed incorrectly in the splash screen? These kinds of problems are must-fix for release, severity notwithstanding.

Conversely, a data loss bug that only occurs under certain obscure circumstances on unlikely and obsolete configurations may be severity 1 but priority 5 under my definition. What if our SpeedyWriter editor loses data when we save to a 360KB 5.25-inch floppy diskette? Perhaps, instead of fixing such a bug in the software, we should just document that our product doesn't support such drives.[8]

Another key piece of information for a bug report is the tested version of the software. In the case study, Luis reported a bug against build 3.1.018.TR and noted that builds 3.1.007.TR through 3.1.017.TR did not suffer the same failure mode. In order to capture this kind of information, you'll need to have an under-control test release process, as discussed in Chapter 12.

---

8. Boris Beizer provides a good discussion of bugs and what he calls "bug importance" in *Software Testing Techniques*.

In integrated test management systems, where the bug and test repositories are in the same database, these two repositories can often be linked. Test case results can link to specific bug reports, and bug reports can link to test cases. Such traceability is helpful for both testers and programmers. If the bug tracking database doesn't support this, I'll add to my process, entering a test identifier into the failure description.

Speaking of traceability, some bugs can be tied to specific requirements, business rules, use cases, or quality risks. I'll show you in Chapter 15 how, by tracing the SpeedyWriter test results and bug reports back to the underlying quality risk, the testers can talk in terms of the quality of the system and the risks assessed and those not assessed. Again, good bug tracking systems have allowed me to build in support for such tracing. If not, I'll add a step in the process, where the tester notes this information in the failure description.

Since bugs can be quite dependent on the specific configuration tested, testers should make a habit of noting this as well. This is once again either built into the bug tracking system (via a lookup table for configurations) or captured as part of the failure description.

Another piece of information I have found useful to capture is the affected subsystem, component, or function. For example, for a word processor, I might have the following categories:

- User interface
- Edit engine
- Tools and utilities
- File operations
- Installation and configuration options
- Documentation and packaging
- Other
- Unknown
- N/A

Capturing this information is useful for various metrics, including tuning ongoing and future testing to focus on those areas of the product that exhibit the most problems.

In a typical bug tracking system, the programmer who fixes the bug and possibly the release engineer who integrates the fixed code into the code repository will fill in some fields. These fields don't typically have a lot of impact on the test team, except for information about which build contains the code fix associated with a given bug. Testers may find it useful to run reports on this information when preparing to confirmation test the bug fixes in a given test release.

Finally, let me mention defect removal models and the data a bug tracking database can collect to support those models. Defect removal models allow you to keep track of when each defect entered the system, when it was found, and when it was fixed. (These are called *defect injection*, *defect detection*, and *defect removal*, respectively.) As testers, we know when we found defects and when they're removed, but we'll need the help of the programmers to track when each defect was injected.

I use the word *when* here, but often these defect removal models are not so much interested in specific dates or times as project phases. So, gathering data for a typical defect removal model might mean that each bug report has an associated phase-injected, phase-detected, and phase-removed field, each of which is filled in at the appropriate point. The field would be completed from a pick list, perhaps consisting of typical phases like requirements, design, implementation, component test, integration test, system test, acceptance test, and post-release. In an Incremental or Iterative life-cycle model, you might want to track the increment or iteration number, too.

This data is helpful both as a repository of project data and, ultimately, as a way to improve the process. With a repository of project data, we can gradually build a defect removal model that allows us to estimate how many bugs will be in each system we build and when we'll find them. This is the purpose mentioned in Chapter 3.

Once we have enough of this data to make accurate predictions about bugs and the phases in which we introduce, find, and fix them, we can then try to improve the process. We can set targets for defect detection and removal prior to the conclusion of each phase on the assumption that we can predict the number of bugs we'll introduce. Bugs are less dangerous and costly to the project when they are detected and removed in the same phase as they are injected, since they can't create other bugs. In defect removal terminology, detecting and removing all the bugs injected during each phase would be a 0% defect escape rate.[9]

---

9. For more details, see *Metrics and Models in Software Quality Engineering, Second Edition*, by Stephen Kan, or *CMM in Practice*, by Pankoj Jalote. For a simple approach to this topic, see *Managing the Testing Process, Second Edition*.

RECOGNIZE A GOOD BUG REPORTING PROCESS

So, based on what I've discussed so far, what do test teams do and what do project teams achieve by using a good bug reporting process?

EFFECTIVELY COMMUNICATE USEFUL INFORMATION

As I discussed in Chapter 13, testing generates information that is useful both internally (within the test team) and externally (to the entire project team or even the organization). Bug reports are a major form of this information. Externally, bug reports are part of the information about quality that testers provide to the project, including the change management process (see Chapter 16). To be effective, bug reports should provide the programmers with what they need to know to fix important bugs. Collectively, bug reports feed into the overall project metrics, as I'll discuss in detail in Chapter 15.

Internally, each bug report provides every tester on the test team with an increased understanding of the nature and quality of the system he's testing. (Recall the examples—both positive and negative—from Chapter 13's case study.) Again, bugs found in the previous tests have meaning for the testing performed and the bugs found in subsequent tests.

Beyond well-written failure descriptions, other narrative text, and classification information, what should testers provide to help programmers find fixes for bugs? That can vary quite a bit, depending on the project. However, here are some ideas.

- Testing history—Unless you reboot the entire network on which you're running tests between test cases, there's always a chance that previously run tests can influence the behavior of the current bug. For example, on an Internet appliance project, we had to keep track of what kind of connection failures had occurred on each appliance we were testing and note that in each bug report. The logic here is that a computer is basically a state machine. Each set of actions, unless followed by a reboot, leaves the memory, CPU, storage, and other components in a particular state, which can influence the behavior of subsequent actions. A network of computers is also a state machine, and residual state information on one computer can influence the behavior of other computers. There's almost no end to the information you can capture in this regard. So, as a practical matter, most test teams that capture testing history in bug reports document the test cases run on the system under test before the bug was observed and any other bugs observed on that system prior to this bug.

- Screen captures (*screen shots*) or even video clips—Some operating systems and most GUI-based test tools allow testers to capture the view of a workstation's screen. These pictures can indeed be worth 10,000 words in helping a programmer understand a bug.

- Digital pictures—Having a digital camera in the test lab will allow you to take pictures of the screen or the system following a bug. Screen captures are great, but they don't work if the system has crashed. In addition, if you are testing hardware components, the failures may be physical. It's hard to describe what happens when a screw shears or a computer case cracks, but a picture will make it clear.

- Memory contents (*core dumps*)—Some systems can be configured so that should the system detect an error internally, it will save the entire contents of memory, including registers, to a special file. In UNIX and mainframe parlance, these are called core dumps. Many integrated development environments will allow programmers to browse these core dumps, looking for clues about what was happening when the system failed.

- Internal tracing information—During early testing, if many bugs are detected, especially intermittent ones, you might ask the programmers and the release engineers to deliver what is sometimes called a *debug build*. Alternatively, the build can be instrumented to capture coverage information, which can tell you which statements the system was executing when a bug occurred. Either way, these builds contain special output statements that log internal information. One caveat, though: When I use debug builds in testing, I stop accepting such builds early in the system test phase. I want to have time to run at least most of my tests once against a non–debug build. Instrumentation, debugging logging statements, and other code that will not be deployed with the system can mask or change the behavior of bugs.

- Working files (*scratch files*)—Some systems produce working files during operation. These files often reside in special directories and have a particular format of file names. (For example, Microsoft Office applications often create files with the extension *tmp* in the current working directory.) If testers know where these files live and what they're called, they can attach these files to the bug report or store them in a special location.

- Error logs—Some programs produce error logs when they crash. If the system under test crashes or any cohabiting applications crash before, during, or after the system under test exhibits buggy behavior, you should consider sending these files along.

Many of these items are files. A good commercial bug tracking tool will allow testers to attach one or more files to a bug report. If not, then the test team can set up a directory structure somewhere on a mutually accessible network drive where testers can save such files and programmers can retrieve them. Caution dictates configuring the bug tracking system or network drive permissions to ensure that people cannot purposely or inadvertently delete these files, because they can often be difficult to re-create.

Defect metrics are another major kind of external information. As I mentioned in Chapter 13, the test execution process needs to support gathering key metrics for managing testing and the project as a whole. The bug reporting process should gather all the important information needed for these metrics. The process must work crisply so that metrics that are driven by dates have accurate date information. Testers must take care to categorize bugs appropriately—e.g., in terms of the affected subsystem—so that metrics that analyze bugs by categories are meaningful.

A final kind of useful external information is workaround information. Not every bug can—or even should—be fixed. For such bugs, knowing about workarounds is helpful. Testers can document those workarounds for the customers. Testers can make sure those get handed off to the technical support or help desk staff. On one project, we had a handoff period at the end of system test where two senior test technicians went through the entire backlog of known bugs with two senior customer support technicians to make sure they understood every known bug and every possible workaround for each known bug, if any.

The need to communicate effectively means that the usual rules for good technical writing apply. The writing should be clear, and it should get to the point. It should be appropriate to the audience and speak to them on their terms. Where bug reports do contain jargon and acronyms, those should be well-understood project terms.

One sign of ineffective communication is what I call *bug report ping-pong*. Bug report ping-pong is a game played between tester and programmer where bug reports are kicked unproductively back and forth. These are some typical reasons for these ping-pong games.

- The programmer asserts that the bug is inappropriately assigned to her component or piece of code.
- The programmer responds that a reported bug is irreproducible or is proper behavior.
- Personal issues have arisen between the programmer and the tester who filed the bug report, so the programmer refuses to allow that tester to score points against her with the bug report.

I'll talk more about dealing with personal issues that cloud the process later in this chapter. The irreproducible/works-as-designed problems can be resolved through careful bug reporting, particularly in documenting the steps to reproduce, the expected-versus-actual results, and whether the problem is intermittent.

Bug assignment is a vexing matter. It helps to distinguish between where you see the symptoms of bugs, where the underlying bugs live, and where those bugs can best be killed. On one project, we found a bug that caused loss of data in files saved by applications on the system under test. The root cause was a hardware incompatibility related to the hard drive's connection (the IDE bus) to the system under test and its hard drive. The problem was fixed by making a change in the computer's BIOS (basic input/output system, software that controls the operating system's interaction with the host hardware) that affected the timing of the operating system's read and write operations to the hard drive. So, what was the bug? In the application losing the data? In the way the hard drive communicated with the system? Or perhaps in the way the system communicated with the hard drive? In the read and write code in the BIOS?

From a quality perspective, perhaps we don't care where the bug lives or how it's resolved, as long as the unacceptable behavior goes away. However, from the point of view of the project, these questions sometimes take on larger-than-life political dimension. Management needs to define a workflow that supports proper assignment, and the selection of the right bug reporting tool will help by supporting that workflow. Ultimately, the development manager—not the test team—should be responsible for assigning who will fix particular problems.

DESCRIBE ONE SYMPTOM PER REPORT AND FILE ONE REPORT PER SYMPTOM

Bug reports are about symptoms—observed anomalous behavior—while bug fixes address defects in systems. Certainly, some dissimilar bug reports lead to the same underlying bug. However, experience tells me this is atypical. Duplication of bug reports typically arises when two testers report the identical misbehavior in two separate bug reports. Such duplication of reports means duplication of effort by testers, programmers, and managers.

The converse is also possible. Testers sometimes lump two or three symptoms that are clustered together in a workflow or functional area of the system. I have often seen this lead to not all of the documented problems being fixed. Testers must then either open one or more new bug reports describing the remaining problems or reopen the existing bug report. In such a case, project time has been wasted, both in terms of programmer and tester hours and in terms of the inefficiencies imposed by a bug tracking system. In addition, the resulting bug reporting activity doesn't really reflect reality, so underlying metrics are skewed.

As with the entire process, balance is required, though. I'd rather have two bug reports than no bug report, so I tell my testers not to spend more than five minutes searching the bug tracking system for an existing bug report. In addition, I like to have testers circulate their bug reports via e-mail to the entire team, either as part of the review process or just for general information. I have found this level of effort keeps the duplication rate down to around 5% to 10%, which I think is tolerable.

Likewise, I don't want testers agonizing too much over whether a broken workflow is broken because of the consequences of a single bug rippling through the system or because of multiple bugs. I find that the review process often catches enough of these kinds of bug reports that I don't worry too much about it.

DRAW A CLEAR BOUNDARY BETWEEN TESTING AND DEBUGGING

As Boris Beizer has pointed out, in the earliest stages of establishing test roles, testing is seen as an adjunct to the debugging process. As the testing effort takes root, though, testing is seen as a distinct set of tasks devoted to locating bugs and managing quality risks.[10] In companies with independent test teams, testers focus on testing, and programmers handle the debugging tasks.

While I'll discuss this in more detail in Chapter 16, let's take a quick look at the process associated with finding a failure, fixing the underlying bug, and confirming resolution, as shown in Figure 14-1. The first three steps of this process are test activities, which belong to the test team and occur as part of or in parallel with the bug reporting process. The next three steps are debugging activities, which belong to the development team and happen as part of fixing the problem described in the bug report from the test team. The final step is confirmation and regression testing of the fix, which is again a testing activity. Therefore, this is a seven-step collaborative process that improves the quality of the system under test through closed-loop corrective action driven by bug reports. While the process is collaborative, each individual task belongs clearly to either the test team or the development team.

---

10. See Boris Beizer's *Software Testing Techniques*.

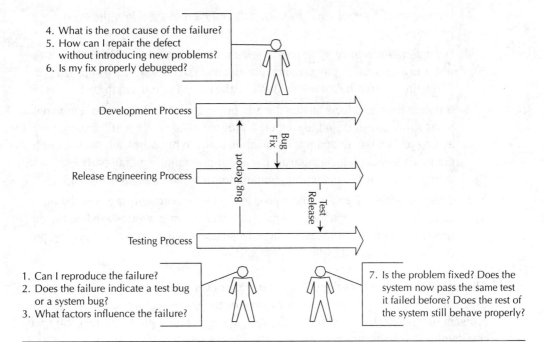

4. What is the root cause of the failure?
5. How can I repair the defect without introducing new problems?
6. Is my fix properly debugged?

Development Process

Bug Fix

Bug Report

Release Engineering Process

Test Release

Testing Process

1. Can I reproduce the failure?
2. Does the failure indicate a test bug or a system bug?
3. What factors influence the failure?

7. Is the problem fixed? Does the system now pass the same test it failed before? Does the rest of the system still behave properly?

FIGURE 14-1 THE FIND/DEBUG/CONFIRM PROCESS

A good bug reporting process supports this separation of duties. As I pointed out earlier, a good bug report gives the programmer all the information he needs to reproduce the problem and start tracking down the bug. The bug reporting and bug management processes are the only vehicles required for communication between the two teams. The handoff in the figure signifies this. The bug reporting process should protect the programmer from having to ask the tester questions about what her bug report means, and it protects the tester from having to spend time duplicating effort in reproducing the problem for the programmer.

Some of my testers have objected to my discouraging their involvement in debugging. Let me explain why this is so important to me when I'm working as a test manager.

1. I have a lot of testing work for my testers to do. I'm held accountable for that work getting done. When testers help programmers fix problems, they're not carrying out critical testing processes.

2. I can't manage my test operation when people lend themselves to the development organization at their discretion. Part of managing is allocating human resources to meet corporate objectives. I can't have reallocation happening on

the say-so of a tester who, frankly, may not have insight into the evolving priorities.

3. Debugging assistance by testers is seldom a wise use of resources. Even if the tester is a competent programmer, presumably the reason he's testing, not programming, is that he's more valuable to the company in a testing role.

4. It boosts egos and feels like teamwork, but it doesn't build careers. I'm happy to structure a tester's job to support a programming career path, usually by adding test toolsmith and test automation tasks to his workload. Such activities are much more conducive to learning about programming than participation in debugging, which is more programming tourism than a resume highlight.

5. These activities often indicate a poor job of bug reporting being done by the tester. If the programmer can't figure out what's going wrong based on the bug report and must ask the tester, then the solution is a crisper bug reporting process, not tester participation in debugging.

All that said, on some occasions testers should or even must participate in debugging, especially when unique test configurations or tools are required to reproduce the problem. It's really the exception to the rule, though, and a good bug reporting process minimizes the occurrence.

HANDLE CHALLENGES

Bug reporting presents the test team with a number of challenges, even when you have the perfect process in place for writing these reports. These challenges are both technical (related to how hard it is intrinsically to report about the unknown) and political (related to the need to manage the interpersonal and team dynamics of criticizing the work of others).

SEPARATING BUGS, FEATURES, AND "SO WHAT"

Ambiguity in—or a complete lack of—requirements or design specifications can complicate the bug reporting process. When programmers respond to bug reports with comments like, "Well, that's the way the system is supposed to work," testers often have no clear way to refute that claim. Rather than let ego get involved in the issue, my usual course of action is to try to resolve the ambiguity through discussions with the various concerned parties. People like the technical support or help desk manager, the sales and marketing team, business analysts, the development manager, and others on the management team will probably have opinions about how the product ought to behave. In addition, the change control board or bug triage committee (see Chapter 16) should be able to help separate real bugs from undocumented features.

One possible response from programmers and managers to a bug report is, "So what?" or "No real user would ever do that," or some variation on those lines. This could be a sign that the manager or programmer making the comment doesn't care about the quality of the system, is confused about the requirements (written or unwritten), or some similar problem. Or it could be a sign that the tester who wrote the bug report didn't communicate effectively. Since we, as testers, can do something about the latter, let's focus on that.

Especially when running tests that don't seem related to realistic customer usage scenarios, testers should look for a way to connect any bugs found to real usage. Testers who don't do so shouldn't be surprised to hear "So what?" Effective communication about test findings is the responsibility of the testers, since we are the ones providing the service. It is incumbent on us, as testers, to make our point. It is not the development or management team's obligation to take our word for it that some obscure failure indicates a pervasive problem in the system.

Programmers are key internal customers for our bug reports, so what they say about the quality of those reports matters. If they want to hear about a "Hey, check out this weird behavior I saw" kind of observation from testers, great. Not many in my experience have, but I have seen these sorts of curious programmers on well-managed projects where quality was seen as just as important as schedule, budget, and features. In general, though, it's important for testers to work with programmers to understand their informational needs when we send them bug reports.

Project managers are another key set of internal customers for our bug reports. I find they typically want to know why they should invest project resources—programmer effort and schedule time—in fixing bugs. My most compelling answers describe how the bugs will hurt the customers or users, resulting in (potentially many) technical support calls and other less tangible costs of (poor) quality. When programmers are under intense schedule and/or budget pressure, I find they tend to exhibit similar bug triage behaviors. On any project where time and budget constraints limit the number of quality problems that can be resolved, looking for the customer impact is a best practice in bug reporting.[11]

This is why, in the bug reporting process I outlined, I stressed connecting the failure to the customer, especially in the summary. The summary is key because it's often the

---

11. This section arose from an online discussion with Bret Pettichord, James Bach, Cem Kaner, Ross Collard, Kathy Iberle, and Alan Jorgensen. I thank them for their insights, though the opinions expressed here are mine.

only part of the bug report read during change control board or bug triage committee meetings, because of the volume of bugs.

I also recommend that testers clearly explain in the Steps to Reproduce and Isolation sections the behavior they expected to see, the behavior they actually saw, and the importance (from a user perspective) of the difference between the two. In the case study example, it was implicit that corruption of data is unexpected behavior, but, for many bugs, behavior can appear reasonable but be buggy in some way. Testers have to point that out in our bug reports.

I encourage testers to take an active role in separating the bugs, features, and "so whats," rather than just packing the bug tracking database with bug reports while ignoring complaints from programmers or others in the project team about the presence of so much noise in the signal. Again, as the people providing an information service to the project team, we are the ones responsible for effectively communicating that information. If people perceive our information as noise, something's seriously broken. One outcome I've heard of from colleagues where they ignored this breakdown was situations where testers had to get permission from development or other project team members before opening a bug report.

Please note that I'm not advocating ignoring problems on the grounds that someone will consider them nitpicky or insignificant. Testers—like programmers—often don't have enough information to make decisions about exactly what quality means for the system under test. If we, as testers, decide to ignore a particular problem in the belief that no user would care, that creates situations where sales, marketing, or business analysis staff can come back later and ask us how such an obvious bug escaped from the testing process. However, as I mentioned in Chapter 13, there's a time to focus on the scary stuff and a time to focus on polishing the product.

HANDLING BUGS THAT GOT FIXED BY ACCIDENT AND IRREPRODUCIBLE SYMPTOMS

I once worked on a project where the development manager released new software daily—or hourly, if urgent bugs were found. We chose not to accept builds into the test lab that often, because it disturbed our execution process to have to do confirmation testing all the time. (Imagine driving and looking only in your rear-view mirror.) Every time we had a bug review meeting with the development manager, in response to any serious bug regardless of whether his team had spent any time trying to fix that bug, he would say, "Well, you need to retest that bug with the latest release. I think we fixed that problem." Finally, I became so exasperated with this response that I told him, "You know, I'm sure you're convinced that you fixed all these bugs by accident, but in my experience a lot fewer bugs get fixed by accident than development managers would like. Until you actually expend some time trying to reproduce the problem and repair the bug, I am not going to ask my team to spend their time retesting bugs."

I'll admit my delivery was a bit raw, but I stand by my comment in terms of course of action. Bugs don't typically get fixed by accident. Frankly, the development manager in this anecdote was using requests to retest every bug against every release on the off chance that somehow many of them magically would go away as a form of squid ink to obfuscate the fact that the system's quality was abysmally bad, and as a mechanism to slow down the onslaught of bugs reported by the test team.

Being a team player is good, but squandering tester time on retesting bugs that no one has spent a millisecond trying to fix is not efficient use of the test team's time. In such circumstances, I would work with the project team to negotiate a process whereby before a bug report is sent back to the test team for confirmation testing, a programmer has specifically tested the system to see if the problem remains.

An added wrinkle is that as difficult as it makes our lives, some bugs just won't produce the same symptom again and again on command like a trained seal. For example, memory leaks depend on specific conditions arising repeatedly over an extended period of time before the system crashes or the application locks up. I once worked on a project where modem connections were dropping sporadically, but we couldn't make the problem occur deliberately. Ultimately, the programmers had to put special probes in the software to track down the problem.

Some people confuse *intermittent* with *unimportant*. Many times, intermittent bugs are also serious bugs. Crashes, losses of modem or network connections, or sudden confusion on the system's part as to how to respond to an input can totally disrupt a user's work and even destroy her data. Features that work sometimes but not at others are features that users will avoid using.

So, I'm always skeptical of claims that a serious intermittent bug "just went away" when neither programmers nor testers can reproduce the bug. I usually keep such bugs open for a few releases (generally two or three weeks) to make sure we don't see them again. (Some organizations have a special "watch" or "monitor" state in which to park these.) I ask programmers what they want the test team to do if we do observe the problem. For example, rebooting a hung system usually destroys the state data that might help a programmer track down the bug. Perhaps the programmer will want to try to burrow into the system through the network to capture this information. And I make sure to keep a record of every time the bug *does* rear its ugly head again. Some sense of the kind of system unreliability that the bug will cause is crucial to intelligent prioritization of the fix effort, and that means that I'll need to be able to report on its frequency.

KEEPING NOISE OUT OF THE SIGNAL

While a bug reporting system is a useful tool for communicating about problems, it is not the only way to do so, and it should not be used to communicate about all problems. Since we're writing bug reports to communicate about a problem in the system under test in order to prioritize and possibly fix that problem, we need to be sure that we use the communication channel that the bug reporting and bug management processes create exclusively for that purpose.

One problem occurs when people use this tool to escalate problems to management. I avoid submitting bug reports that report failures of the *system development process* rather than the *system under test*. For example, if the release engineer didn't deliver the Monday morning build at 9:00 AM, I wouldn't write a bug report with the summary, "Build not delivered on time." I'd go talk to the release engineer and explain the importance of timely receipt of builds. If the issue were an ongoing situation, I'd also escalate to her manager. Of course, if the build was delivered on time but then wouldn't work, I might write a bug report titled "Build 781 fails to install."

Another problem occurs when people make notes to themselves in the bug tracking database. I worked on one project where one programmer—who was otherwise absolutely one of the best, most responsive development partners a test team would ever want to work with—had this habit of writing notes to himself in the bug tracking database. Since he was the only one, it didn't create a huge problem. However, if every programmer had written a note to herself every day on that project, we would have had 25 bug reports in the system that had nothing to do with bugs.

Finally, a noise problem exists when testers report bugs that aren't bugs. In Chapter 13, I mentioned the importance of distinguishing between bugs in the system under test, bugs in the test system, and plain old misunderstandings about how the system ought to behave. In the bug reporting process, reproducing the problem and isolating the causes of the failure aids in making this distinction, as does the peer review at the end.

In any of these cases, the end result is the introduction of noise into a valuable information channel. This can confuse testers and programmers; gum up the bug reporting, status reporting (Chapter 15), and change management (Chapter 16) processes;

and skew the metrics for the project, throwing off any defect removal model you are working with.

BUILDING TRUST AND CREDIBILITY WITH PROGRAMMERS

I once had a tester tell me that he enjoyed testing because he got a chance to catch programmers. He kept track of whose components he had found problems in, and he wasn't satisfied until he'd found a bug in each programmer's code. This kind of "gotcha" attitude can create real problems with bug reporting. If programmers see testing as a game of tag—and having a bug report assigned against their components as the act of being tagged—then the "ping-pong" issue I discussed earlier is sure to arise.

Another pitfall here is when testers or test managers fall into the trap of haranguing individual programmers to see when a particular bug will be fixed. This can create a number of problems. First, if programmers don't report to testers, the testers won't have a lot of insight into what other tasks they might have assigned to them. Interfering with their priorities won't endear you to them or to their manager. Second, if testers have little if any authority over programmers, one very likely outcome is that the testers will only irritate people, without achieving any useful result. Testers can sometimes entice programmers to work on their favorite bug through bribery (lunch) or intellectual challenge (writing a particularly engrossing bug report), but taking the liberty of managing another's team generally won't work.

Another source of trouble arises when testers use the bug report data to create charts or circulate reports that make individuals look bad. For example, many bug tracking tools have an "estimated fix date" field that programmers fill in for their own manager to report when they expect a bug will be fixed. Running a report that shows, for each programmer, which bugs they haven't yet fixed or that are past due would be humiliating. Likewise, running a report of bugs sorted and totaled by component or affected subsystems and including the owner name—i.e., implying that the owner introduced the bug—would be both misleading and harmful to the targeted programmers.

Another issue is credibility. If we file too many bug reports that are nonissues, or make too many mistakes in test result interpretation, sooner or later the impression will be that the testers are not providing credible information. In my experience, it doesn't take too much noise coming out of the test team to damage the team's credibility.

I discussed the topic of correct result interpretation at length in Chapter 13. Just as structured testing is the foundation of the bug reporting process I described, so is the foundation of trust and credibility between programmers and testers. I've found that five specific attitudes or actions when reporting bugs can help.

1. Maintain a project-wide, service-oriented mind-set. What information services can you, as a tester, provide to help the project succeed? In most situations, testers do not succeed if the project fails.

2. Keep your cool during discussion about bug reports with programmers, managers, or other project team members. A passion for quality is good, but anger, frustration, and lost tempers are not.

3. Discuss bug reports with an open mind, accepting the possibility that you might be mistaken, but also defending the reasonable expectations of customers.

4. Submit only quality bug reports and be open to suggestions for improving the quality of your bug reports. Remember that the project team, as the customers for your information products, gets to decide what quality means.

5. Be flexible on delivery and reporting of bugs. If a programmer wants a particular file or screen shot attached to a bug report—assuming that the bug tracking system supports such attachments—be cooperative.

Once the perception arises that we are serious about delivering good bug reports in a way that helps everyone on the project team, word will get around.

SELECTING THE RIGHT BUG TRACKING TOOL

A good bug tracking tool should enable the gathering and management of the information mentioned so far in this chapter. But more is required than that. If information gathering and management were all we wanted, we could use any database as a bug tracking tool. However, the real value of a good bug tracking tool lies in its ability to gather and manage information during each bug report's lifecycle or workflow, from initial discovery to final resolution or deferral.

Figure 14-2 shows one possible example of a bug lifecycle. In this figure, you can see that bug reports move through a series of states (the lifecycle or workflow) to final resolution of some sort, either rejection of the report, confirmed closure of the underlying problem, or deferral of the symptom (and any associated bug reports) as not important to fix for this release. In each nonterminal state, a manager or the change control board (see Chapter 16) specifies an owner who is to move the bug to the next state. A good bug tracking system will implement and automate such a workflow, though project team and management support is required to make the workflow work. Often, as participants move a bug report to the next state, they make some log, status, or history entry in the bug reporting database.

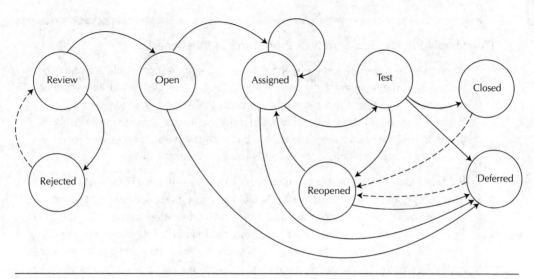

FIGURE 14-2 A BUG LIFECYCLE

The extent to which a bug tracking systems workflow can be customized to match your actual workflows is a key measure of the bug tracking tool's quality. (In situations where management doesn't have a lot of experience with defining these workflows, it's probably a good idea to start with the default in the tool and then fine-tune that as needed.) States in bug report lifecycles or workflows should represent key players in the bug find, fix, and confirm-fixed process. The transitions between states represent handoffs between those key players.

Note that support for the workflows in the bug tracking system can—and perhaps should—be tightly integrated with release management, too. A good bug tracking system will allow the development team, while preparing a test release, to mark as "ready for testing" the bug reports and enhancement requests associated with the changes in the release. The test team, upon receiving the release, can run a report listing all those items in a "ready for testing" state. Often, bug tracking systems can communicate with configuration management tools, automating much of this process.[12]

---

12. I discussed the topic of bug tracking tools at length in *Managing the Testing Process, Second Edition*. I can also recommend Mark Fewster and Dorothy Graham's discussion about the test tool selection process in *Software Test Automation*.

Should We Use Test Scripts or Procedures in Bug Reports?

Some testers—and some test tools—promote cutting-and-pasting whole test scripts or procedures, whether manual or automated, into bug reports as the steps to reproduce or as the whole report. I'm a fan of efficiency, but I've found that testers who use test scripts as the core of their bug reports often display a stunted sense of curiosity about the underlying bug and write ill-conceived bug reports. I have found this approach less of an aid to improve efficiency than an impediment to effectiveness.

Imagine a tester looking out over a field full of rocks, knowing that some nasty bugs live under some of the rocks. Test cases are useful tools for turning over the right set of rocks. However, once we find the bugs, simply saying to a programmer, "Go turn over rock X," does not suffice. First of all, many programmers will not go turn over rock X merely on a tester's say-so. Second of all, how do we know the same bug lives under rock X all the time? Third and perhaps most importantly of all, it is our job as testers to explain the meaning and importance of what we found under rock X, rather than the developer's job to tease that out of us. We testers are selling information services, and it's hardly information to say, "Turned over rock X, saw scurrying things, I think they were bugs." We need to break out the shovel and dig. Explore the area around where we saw the bug. Isolate. Generalize. Compare with other test results. Above all, think.

Now, I *am* in favor of identifying in a bug report the test case(s) that revealed the problem. However, that information is primarily for my test team. When it comes time to perform confirmation and regression testing—i.e., once the developer has used our insightful bug report to repair the underlying problem—then it helps us to know which tests to repeat.

IMPLEMENT IMPROVEMENTS

Bug reporting as a process and as an activity in any given project seldom goes perfectly, so it can usually be improved. How you get your bug reporting process under control depends a lot on where you are now, but let me offer some suggestions.

1. Fix any broken tester attitudes first. The best process in the world won't help if testers and programmers are using the bug reporting process as a weapon against each other.

2. As I said at the beginning of this chapter, the bug report is the most tangible of the information products testers provide. Any kind of process improvement effort that aims to make a better product starts with talking to the customers.

Who are the people who read your bug reports? What about the current process do they like and dislike? How would they like to see the bug reports improved? Just starting to ask these questions sends a powerful signal to the project team, especially when they see you acting on their ideas.

3. If you don't have a bug tracking tool in place, get one. Bug tracking tools are not necessarily expensive, and there are even freeware tools available.[13] You can use a spreadsheet, if absolutely necessary, but text files, word processing documents, or collection of e-mails won't work. Since part of the bug reporting process is gathering metrics, we can't use tools that don't support collective analysis of bug data.

4. Examine the workflow that actually occurs in finding, fixing, and confirming that bugs are fixed, and compare that with what your current bug tracking tool allows you to do. What does the workflow tell you about your key players and handoffs? Can you improve your bug tracking tool's lifecycle to do a better job of capturing the real underlying processes, agreements, handoffs, and key players?

5. If you have an existing tool in place, you should try to adapt it to support a good bug reporting process before deciding that you must replace the tool. Changing your bug tracking system is a big decision, especially if you are in the middle of a project. The technical issues associated with moving data from one tool to another are not trivial—one of my associates and I once spent weeks doing just that—and there are political issues, too. Bug tracking systems are often shared with other groups, such as release management, development, and technical support, and managers of these groups often develop personal dashboards that use bug tracking data. At the right time, changing bug tracking systems can make sense, but I have been able to make do with what I consider one of the worst bug tracking tools on the market.

6. Apply a good bug reporting process, but be flexible and sensitive to priority. On my teams, my only ironclad rule on this process is that every bug report undergo a peer review.

7. Try the peer review step before you dismiss it as a roadblock to efficient testing. Bad bug reports can waste a lot of time. A peer review can be as simple as one

---

13. For example, I have a Microsoft Access database, described in my book *Managing the Testing Process, Second Edition*, that is available for download from my Web site, www.rexblackconsulting.com. (Even if you don't want to use my database, you might want to look at it for a collection of fields I find useful in bug tracking and management.) Steve Splaine, in his book *Testing Web Security*, lists a number of bug tracking tools as well. You can also check out Bugzilla at www.mozilla.org.

tester reading another tester's bug report on a screen before the tester hits the Submit button.

8. Consider introducing a metric to help you measure the quality of your bug reports. For example, what is the reopen rate on bug reports? In other words, how many come back to test marked as fixed, works-as-designed, or irreproducible when they are not fixed properly, are real bugs, or are easy to reproduce? Another metric might be how long, on average, bug reports stay open. A good bug reporting process should help drive both these numbers down.

Whatever changes you implement, patience and perseverance are important. People develop habits of working, especially when it comes to tasks they do over and over again. You'll need to keep this in mind as you work to improve your bug reporting processes.

15

ILLUMINATE THE FOURTH ELEMENT: REPORT THE TEST RESULTS

Years ago, philosophers believed that the world was made of four elements: earth, wind, fire, and water. While modern chemistry has taught us that over a hundred elements exist, the projects I've worked on often consisted of four main elements.

- *Features*—Are we building the right set of functions and behaviors that will solve the users' and customers' real-world problems?
- *Schedule*—Can we deliver this problem solving system in a timely fashion?
- *Budget*—Can we deliver this system in a way that is financially attractive for the users, the customers, the project sponsors, and the people building the system?
- *Quality*—Can we deliver the features such that they are fit for the uses to which users and customers will put them?

Project managers know where projects stand on the budget because CFOs or project accountants can tell them. Project managers know where projects stand on the schedule by tracking progress against milestones and earned value. Project managers know where projects stand on features because programmers, configuration management, and release engineering groups can tell them which features are done. Best practices in software engineering and project management, applied by competent professionals, provide project managers with clear illumination on three of the four elements. But how do project managers shine a light on the quality element?[1]

---

1. Portions of this chapter appeared originally in *Software Testing and Quality Engineering* magazine, Volume 2, Issue 2 (Mar/Apr 2000). I thank Brian Lawrence, Brian Marick, and Alyn Wambeke, who edited that article, for their help.

Part of answering this question was addressed in the previous chapter. In bug reporting, we inform the project team about situations where the answer to the quality question is, No, the system is not fit for use in this specific way. But specific problems are not the whole answer. All too often, project managers operate largely in the dark about the broader quality question, especially in comparison with the other project elements. I believe that this imbalance is one of the reasons that quality often suffers.

In Chapter 1 I mentioned that a well-run test operation should provide information that helps the organization manage the risks to the quality of the system. This information—when delivered in an accurate, timely, credible fashion—shines a light for the project management team, illuminating the fourth element of the project, quality. In this chapter, let's look at how that illumination occurs and how we can best be beacons of light and bearers of knowledge for the project.[2]

A TEST RESULTS REPORTING PROCESS

A generic test results reporting process, shown in Process 11, is simple to describe. This same process applies for both routine project status reporting and emergency or special event analysis, though you will likely be addressing different audiences and answering different questions.

For example, on an Internet appliance project, I presented a set of test status charts at the weekly test project meeting. However, we also had a twice-weekly bug triage meeting where we made tough fix/defer decisions for bugs using a report that showed the summary, severity, priority, and date reported for all bugs opened since the last meeting.

On one occasion, we had a special meeting to analyze the results of some performance tests we had run and to compare those results with earlier predictions of performance based on static models and dynamic simulations. This meeting involved lots of de-

---

2. The metaphor of testing as lighting occurs in Cem Kaner, James Bach, and Bret Pettichord's book *Lessons Learned in Software Testing*, where they wrote that "[Testers] are the headlights of the project." Quardev's manager for corporate intellect and technical solutions, Jonathan Bach, has a personalized license plate that reads "TESTER." The plate is part of Virginia's commemorative lighthouse series that displays a picture of three lighthouses with the caption "Keep the lights shining." I especially like the lighthouse metaphor for testing, because lighthouses shine a light that prevents boats from crashing on the rocks, just as good testing helps keep projects from running aground.

Step #	Step	Done?
1.	Understand the audience, which usually includes all of the stakeholders in the testing process and in system quality, and the goals of the project.	☐
2.	Define the results to be presented, typically the information that would answer the questions your audience would have about testing, especially what the test results mean in terms of project goals.	☐
3.	Select metrics and build reports and charts that answer these questions.	☐
4.	Present the test results to the audience as required.	☐
5.	As needed, tune the report and charts along with the reporting activities for the audience, for each stakeholder, and for the project by repeating steps 1–4.	☐

PROCESS 11   A TEST RESULTS REPORTING PROCESS[A]

tailed charts showing system performance under various conditions, presented head-to-head with the expected performance based on the models and simulation.

Each meeting had a slightly different audience, with different information needs, different questions to be answered. I'm going to use weekly status reporting as the topic of the case study, but please keep in mind that this process also applies to other kinds of results reporting.

Despite the straightforward set of tasks, reporting results is often the most difficult process the test professional faces on any given project. To be effective reporters of test results, test professionals must possess three personal traits. First, they must have the ability to gain profound knowledge in the areas of testing in general, the trends and implications in findings of the test team so far, and the particular test results as of the current moment. Second, they must have effective written and verbal communication skills, even when communicating a complicated and unpopular message. Third, they must have the political abilities to maintain a collective team perception of the test team's credibility and of the accuracy of the information they deliver, especially when those messages indicate that the project is in danger. Let's look at how Jamal Brown, test manager for the Sumatra project, fares with the process and with these three traits.

A. Some readers will recognize this as a variation of Victor Basili's goal-question-metric paradigm. A good source of online information about this technique can be found in Rosenberg and Hyatt's paper "Developing a Successful Metrics Program," found at satc.gsfc.nasa.gov/support/index.html.

Dashboard, Balanced Scorecard

A dashboard, or balanced scorecard, is a collection of metrics, usually displayed as a small set of charts or graphs, that give a high-level view of the status of some activity. The analogy is the dashboard of a car, where a cluster of as few as two or three gauges, together with some warning lights, give the driver the essential information about the state of the vehicle without distracting the driver from the unfolding road and traffic situation outside the windows. The "balanced scorecard" phrase refers to the fact that a good selection of such charts or gauges will balance each other out. In other words, while any one metric might mislead us, the cumulative effect of all the metrics is to provide context for the other metrics that clarifies the meaning of the scorecard as a whole.

JAMAL DEFINES A DASHBOARD—AND REPORTS ON THE BIG BUILD'S TEST RESULTS

Let's start by going back in time in our hypothetical case study, back to when Jamal was writing his test plan. On September 17, Jamal had sent a draft version of his test plan out via e-mail. He also had sent a proposed set of status reporting charts, which he called the test dashboard.

He sent this e-mail out to the key stakeholders in testing and in the Sumatra project. Those stakeholders included John Albertson, vice president of Engineering Services; Harold Jones, vice president of System Engineering; Cicely Rice, vice president of Sales; Jenny Kaufman, manager of New Release Development; Kate Hernandez, manager of SpeedyWriter Product Marketing; Keith Lee, manager of System Operation and Administration; and Yasuhiro Kanagawa, manager of Release Engineering. Collectively, these seven people, together with Jamal Brown, manager of Integration and System Test, and Sundari Copeland, vice president of Finance (in her role as project accountant), made up the Sumatra Project Management team, as defined in the Key Participants section of the Sumatra Project Plan. With the exception of Cicely and Sundari, who participated as needed, the Sumatra Project Management team met weekly to review the project status.

The goals of the project were defined in the Executive Summary section of the Sumatra Project Plan.

Based on the Sumatra Project Plan, Jamal knew the audience and the project goals.

Step #	Step	Done?
1.	Understand the audience, which usually includes all of the stakeholders in the testing process and in system quality, and the goals of the project.	✔

The Sumatra Project Team shall deliver a major upgrade to SpeedyWriter 3.0, with a tentative released version number of SpeedyWriter 3.1. The Sumatra features include fixes to all known customer-critical bugs as of project inception, along with support for an optional document management subsystem. The Sumatra Project Team shall identify and prioritize the specific features in the Sumatra System Requirements Specification. Changes to the project scope, including new, changed, and deleted features, may occur during project execution. The Sumatra Change Control Board shall prioritize such changes.

The Sumatra Project Team shall deliver the final feature set in time for release and revenue realization by the beginning of the second quarter of next year. In addition, the Sumatra Project Team shall complete the project within 10% of budget. To ensure delivery within these schedule and budget goals, Sumatra Project Management may direct changes to the project scope, including, if necessary, simplifying or deleting features.

The Sumatra Project Team shall release a set of features and an overall deliverable that Sumatra Project Management and Software Cafeteria Executive Management believe will meet the customers' and users' reasonable expectations of quality. Furthermore, the Sumatra Project Team shall ensure that all critical risks to system quality—in both new and existing SpeedyWriter features—are reduced to an acceptably low level. To ensure a quality deliverable, Sumatra Project Management may direct changes to the project scope, including, if necessary, simplifying or deleting features.

The project plan spelled out the goals of the project, including goals for testing. In order to help the audience understand whether those goals were being met, Jamal wanted to be able to answer four broad questions.

1. What is the quality of the Sumatra system, as measured by test results so far?
2. How are we doing in terms of covering the critical risks to system quality, and what do our test results tell us about the risks remaining?
3. Is the testing project progressing smoothly and efficiently?
4. How are we doing in terms of fulfilling the planned tests in a timely fashion?

The first two questions focus primarily on the system—specifically the quality of it over time—while the latter two focus more on the process—especially schedule and budget issues. However, Jamal knew from experience that the quality of the system given to a test team has a lot to do with the test team's ability to get through planned tests on schedule and within budget. So, Jamal's goal for status reporting was to be able to answer these four questions in four easy-to-create and easy-to-understand charts.

Step #	Step	Done?
2.	Define the results to be presented, typically the information that would answer the questions your audience would have about testing, especially what the test results mean in terms of project goals.	✔

To do that, Jamal worked closely with the project management team to define the status reporting charts and reports during the test planning stage. They selected a set of charts based on the ones Jamal had used for the previous project, SpeedyWriter 3.0. Now, let's jump back to the testing of the Big Build.

When we last checked in with Jamal in Chapter 13, it was Saturday, December 21. The test team had just wound down the first full cycle of testing. He had just finished updating his test results status report. He had e-mailed the collection of charts—the test dashboard—to the project management team, as well as checking them into the project repository.

On Monday morning, December 23, Jamal presented this status report at the weekly status meeting. When he walked into the conference room, Jamal noticed that Rajesh Gupta, the CEO of Software Cafeteria; Rachel Woods, manager of Technical Publications; and Cosimo Negraev, manager of Customer Support; along with Cicely Rice and Sundari Copeland, had joined the meeting. That makes sense, he thought, since this is the first status meeting where we'll have a good idea of where the Big Build stands. None of the five additional attendees had been closely involved in defining the test dashboard, though. Jamal made a mental note to explain the dashboard itself as he explained the test status.

Test status was third on the agenda, after Jenny Kaufman's report on the development status and Yasuhiro Kanagawa's report on release engineering. When they had finished, Kate Hernandez, who chaired the status meeting, turned to Jamal and said with a smile, "Okay, Jamal, now's the moment we've all been waiting for. How's the Big Build looking, quality-wise?"

Jamal, who had just connected his laptop to the conference room projector, brought up his title slide, which read, "Integration and System Test Status, Increment 3 (Big Build), Cycle 1."

"Well," he began, "before I get into the test results for this cycle, I'd like to acknowledge someone in Keith's team who went above and beyond in making the cycle happen. Petra graciously agreed to come in and support our weekend testing on Saturday and then helped me install the new release when the test cycle was over. While we're talking, the test team is running tests in the test lab, thanks to Petra's extra efforts. Keith, please thank Petra for me?"

"Will do," Keith replied.

Jamal began his status report by saying, "So, how's the Big Build? To answer that, I'm going to show my usual four graphs, which—in honor of our guests—I'll explain thoroughly as we go through them. There's detailed information underlying each of these charts that I'm happy to discuss with people after the meeting, too.

"The executive summary is that testing is going well, with some significant concerns. I'll identify those concerns as we go through the test results dashboard.

"During initial discussions about how testing could best provide useful information, we agreed that the weekly test status should address four questions," Jamal said, changing to the next slide (see Figure 15-1). "First, how is the quality of the Sumatra system, as measured by the test results so far? This question is addressed at a summary level in this chart.

"The chart shows the average number of daily bug reports opened and closed for each test cycle, along with the average daily backlog of bug reports—"

"Backlog?" Rajesh interrupted.

"The difference between the total number of opened and closed bug reports," Jamal explained. Rajesh nodded.

"This chart would look like a swarm of little symbols—most of them just dancing around because of natural process variations—so I'm showing the averages of the daily numbers instead of the daily numbers themselves. Since we take weekly releases, these also represent the averages of the daily opened, closed, and backlog numbers for each test cycle, a cycle being all the tests run against each release.

"In addition, the report shows the total number of bug reports opened and closed, and these two curves are daily totals. The daily calculation makes them bounce a bit because of the testing process. The jumps in the total number of opened bug reports on Fridays are due to exploratory testing, which finds more bugs than scripted testing. The Monday and sometimes Tuesday jumps in the total number of closed bug reports are due to successful confirmation testing of fixes. I show the totals and the weekly averages on different scales. Does the chart make sense?" Everyone nodded.

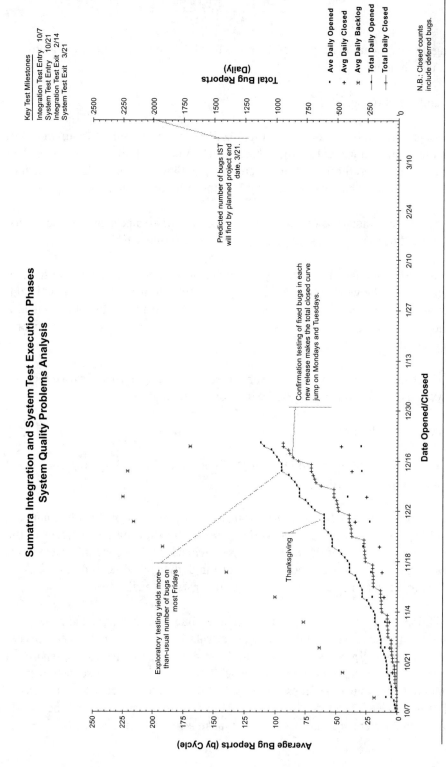

Sumatra Integration and System Test Execution Phases
System Quality Problems Analysis

Key Test Milestones
Integration Test Entry 10/7
System Test Entry 10/21
Integration Test Exit 2/14
System Test Exit 3/21

Total Bug Reports
(Daily)

- Ave Daily Opened
+ Avg Daily Closed
* Avg Daily Backlog
— Total Daily Opened
+ Total Daily Closed

N.B.: Closed counts include deferred bugs.

Predicted number of bugs IST will find by planned project end date, 3/21.

Confirmation testing of fixed bugs in each new release makes the total closed curve jump on Mondays and Tuesdays.

Exploratory testing yields more-than-usual number of bugs on most Fridays

Thanksgiving

Date Opened/Closed

Average Bug Reports (by Cycle)

FIGURE 15-1 QUALITY ASSESSMENT SHOWN IN AN OPENED/CLOSED CHART

"Good." Jamal paused, then continued, "So, this is showing us a few things about quality. First, the bug find rate remains a significant but managed source of risk to the project. A high bug find rate *is* to be expected at this point in the project, since major new functionality is dropping in. Further, the find rate has stabilized over the last four weeks, fluctuating between the mid-20s and high 30s per day. To continue to manage the influx of new bugs, I suggest that we not shift developers who have completed work on new Sumatra features to new development projects, which has happened on a couple of recent projects. I suggest all currently assigned Sumatra developers work on fixing Sumatra bugs for the foreseeable future.

"Second, the bug fix and defer rates are looking good. The total number of closed bug reports is tracking the total number of opened reports closely. The backlog is well under control now, with the average number of daily closed bugs exceeding the average number of daily opened bugs for three out of the last four weeks. That's taken a big bite out of the backlog, which was looking a bit alarming over the last four weeks.

"Third, to be entirely fair, some of that backlog is temporary. The backlog count—and the gap between the opened and closed curves—will paint an overly pessimistic picture. Both tend to go up during the week because many fixed bugs are in the next test release, waiting to be tested and confirmed closed. I did some analysis, and, on average, a given bug is closed or deferred within 12 days of being reported. That means that most must-fix bugs are fixed in the release after they're found or the release afterward. And the bugs really are fixed. Only about one bug fix in 20 fails confirmation testing, and no bug report has failed confirmation testing more than twice."

"Hmm," Cicely said, running her hand thoughtfully through her hair, "you can keep track of bug reopened counts, huh?"

"Yes, our bug tracking tool gathers that information, which is useful."

"We called that the 'recidivism rate' at my previous job," she said with a smile.

"No offense to your former colleagues, Cicely, but I'm trying to avoid potentially loaded words like that wherever I can," Jamal replied.

"We appreciate that, by the way," Jenny put in.

Jamal smiled at Jenny, then continued his report. "Finally, you can see that we're a little over halfway to the predicted total number of bugs to find, which is 2,000. We've run almost all the tests at least once, so we might come in a little low on that number. In other words, the system is better than anticipated."

"Nice to hear," Kate murmured.

"Yes, nice," Jamal agreed, "but not surprising. Remember, my projections were made on historical data—past projects here at Software Cafeteria. What I didn't factor in was that on each project we do, we make some process improvements based on the last project, and we get a little better."

"I should hope so," Harold murmured.

Jamal nodded assent and moved on to the next slide, shown in Figure 15-2. "The next question testing can answer is, Have we run tests that address the 'must-test' risks to system quality, and what have those test results told us about the risks remaining? This chart summarizes where we stand in these risk areas.

"At the start of the project, I facilitated a cross-functional analysis of the risks to Sumatra system quality that included many of the people in this room. We identified and prioritized various potential quality problems. We assigned the appropriate levels of testing based on levels of technical and business risk."

"Can you refresh my memory on the two kinds of risks, Jamal?" Cicely asked.

"Sure," Jamal responded. "Technical risk is the likelihood of a bug existing in the system itself and the impact of that bug on the system. Business risk is the likelihood of a user or customer being affected by that bug and the impact of that bug on the users and customers. Does that make sense?"

"That's great," Cicely smiled. "Thanks, Jamal."

"You're welcome." Jamal continued, "During test design and development, we quantified the relationship between each test case and each specific quality risk. The relationship between a test case and a quality risk can be strong, medium, weak, or nonexistent, which we represented as 9, 3, 1, and 0, respectively. Once we had finished our initial test design and development, we could calculate coverage totals across each specific quality risk and summarize those totals for quality risk categories. Using those totals for each quality risk category, we can say what coverage number would represent having run 100% of the planned tests against that quality risk category. The gray bars on the chart represent the current percentage of the tests run against each quality risk category. Ultimately, each gray bar on the chart should hit right around 100%, though skipped tests and exploratory testing could make us come in a little over or under."

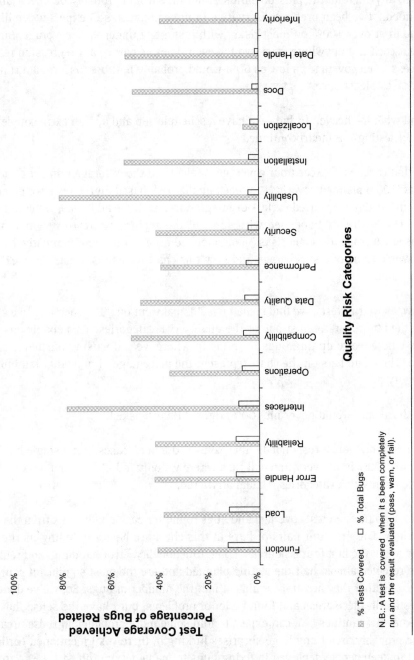

Sumatra Integration and System Test Execution Phases
Quality Risks Bugs and Test Coverage

Test Coverage Achieved
Percentage of Bugs Related

Quality Risk Categories

■ % Tests Covered   □ % Total Bugs

N.B.: A test is covered when it s been completely
run and the result evaluated (pass, warn, or fail).

FIGURE 15-2 TEST COVERAGE AND RESULTS SHOWN BY QUALITY RISKS

"What does 'a little over or under' mean, mathematically?" Sundari asked.

"Well, anywhere in the plus-or-minus 10% range would probably be fine," Jamal responded. "I've been pretty conservative in my estimates, so I expect we're likely to come in at over 100% on most risks, with just a few under 95% coverage. Since we repeat each test anywhere from two to seven times as part of our regression retesting process, even coverage as low as 50% would probably indicate that we had run every test case at least once."

"And what if—heaven forbid—we have a schedule slip and add an extra couple of cycles of testing?" Sundari continued.

"In that case, we'll exceed our coverage. I calculated the coverage number that represents '100% planned coverage' for each quality risk based on the tests we planned to run on the day we started cycle 1 of integration test. If we add tests, we'll add coverage. That's already happened with some of the exploratory testing, which has increased coverage for some risks." Jamal looked around the room inquisitively. "Does the whole issue of test coverage and how this chart measures it make sense?" Nods all around.

"Now, as we run tests, we find some bugs," Jamal went on. "For each bug, we categorize the bug report against one of the quality risk categories. This enables us to assess where we're finding bugs in terms of where we're focusing our testing, risk-wise. The white bars on the chart represent the percentage of bugs that fall into each category."

"So those bars would never hit 100%, right?" Rajesh asked.

"That's right," Jamal responded, "they total 100% in all cases, but a single bar would only hit 100% in the very unusual case where we only found bugs that related to one of the quality risk categories," Jamal answered.

"Let me go through test coverage and bugs found for each quality risk from the left to the right. The first four pairs of bars in this chart are basically telling us the same thing about the first four risk areas. Load, functionality, error handling, and reliability have received almost half the testing planned and are the most significant sources of bugs. Together they account for almost half the number of bugs. So, we've done a lot of testing in these areas and found a lot of problems, but I have the sense that these are known quantities. We can expect to find some more problems in these areas, but there probably aren't any huge surprises lurking in there. As I mentioned earlier, we need to keep people deployed in fixing bugs to manage the problems we've found—

and will continue to find—in these areas, but I feel that we have our head around these risks at this point."

"'Will continue to find?'" Rajesh asked.

"Yes," Jamal explained, "typically, where you've found a large number of bugs, you will find more bugs. The pattern across many, many projects is that bugs tend to congregate in certain ways. One of those ways bugs congregate is in terms of quality risk categories. So, I expect that our testing will find about half the remaining bugs in these four areas."

"Interesting," Rajesh commented. "I would have thought that you would tend to 'reach the bottom,' as it were, in each category at some point."

"That seems logical, yes," Jamal admitted. "However, this counterintuitive pattern of bug clustering is a long-standing observation of software testing."[3]

"To move on to the next risk area, interface testing is mostly complete now. While we found some bugs, most of them are closed at this point."

"So the integration testing was a success?" Kate asked.

"Integration testing does continue for another couple of months, until we get the last increment. However, at this point, it's been a success in the sense that it gave us a lot of opportunities to fix bugs, and we took those opportunities. The system test phase would not be going well right now were it not for the good integration testing—and the good integration bug fixing—we all did," Jamal concluded.

"Operations and maintenance have been tested about as thoroughly as the first four risk categories, with a slightly lower yield of bugs. I feel comfortable with the situation in this risk area, again provided that we deploy sufficient bug fixing resources to stay on top of the remaining bugs we're sure to find in these areas.

---

3. This pattern, though hinted at by Fred Brooks in *The Mythical Man-Month*, was first stated explicitly as far as I know by Glenford Myers in *The Art of Software Testing*. Lately, Robert Sabourin and Kim Davis have done some interesting work in the area of bug clusters and how to apply that knowledge to testing. See their paper "Exploring, Discovering and Exterminating Bug Clusters in Web Applications," available at www.amibug.com.

"Compatibility and data quality have both been pretty thoroughly tested. I don't antic-ipate any nasty surprises in these areas, though we have found—and continue to find—significant bugs in the area of data quality."

Jenny nodded and added, "Yes, the testing your team has done in terms of data qual-ity has absolutely saved our bacon. We could never have found some of those bugs in unit testing."

"Agreed, the complexity of the test environment and some of the more intricate use cases in the area of data quality were essential," Jamal replied; then he continued with his report.

"Performance and security have been tested to the same extent as the first four items, but with about a quarter of the number of bugs being found. I think we're looking good in these risk areas, though I intend to complete all planned testing to be sure. From a business risk perspective, these are both hot items. Even if we hadn't found a single bug to date, I'd suggest we continue testing in these areas."

"You're absolutely right, Jamal, we can't be too careful about performance and secu-rity," Cosimo agreed. "Those two areas probably result in the most painful of our tech support calls."

"Really?" Rajesh asked with a cocked eyebrow.

"Yep," Cosimo replied. "I don't have any quantitative breakdown, but I'd say that at least every week I have a crisis in one or both of those areas."

"I know this is off-topic for this meeting," Rajesh said apologetically to Kate and Ja-mal, "but," he continued, turning to Cosimo, "would you mind running a breakdown of tech support calls corresponding to Jamal's list of quality risks here and let me know how it comes out?"

"Sure," Cosimo replied. "We'd planned on doing that analysis after the Sumatra re-lease to see how we did in terms of risk analysis, but we can do it right now, too."

"Sorry for the interruption, Jamal," Rajesh said with a smile as he closed down his parenthetical conversation with Cosimo.

"I thought it was very germane," Jamal replied, and then he continued. "The usability studies are almost done. We think there's nothing scary hiding there. Good work on the part of your user interface team, Jenny."

Jenny smiled and nodded.

"Localization testing is just now getting going," Jamal continued. "We haven't found anything scary there yet, but we haven't done enough testing to know. Ask me in two weeks and I'll have a much better idea. At this point, this is one of those worrisome 'don't know what we don't know' kinds of risks."

"Two weeks?" Sundari asked.

"Yep," Jamal replied, "we didn't want to spend a lot of money on repeated localization testing, so we only scheduled a couple of passes on it toward the end. These people don't work cheap."

"Couldn't we have done it in-house?" Sundari persisted.

"We could, but I'd need a much larger budget to have a dedicated staff of polyglots and standards experts to handle this in-house. Languages, standards compliance, time and date displays, currencies, and so on, and so on—it's simply harder to do than it might seem."

Sundari shrugged and conceded the point by saying, "I guess there's no free lunch."

"Certainly not an international smorgasbord free lunch, that's for sure," Jamal said with a smile. He continued, "Documentation testing is over half done, nothing big hiding there, right Rachel?"

"Right," the documentation manager agreed.

"Date handling and competitive inferiority also appear to be low risks that we've taken major steps to mitigate," Jamal concluded. "So that's where we stand on risks. Questions?"

Seeing no questions, Jamal went on to the next chart (see Figure 15-3). "The next question for testing is one that measures both the quality of the product and the progress of the testing project: Is the testing project progressing smoothly and efficiently?"

"I don't see what that tells us about the quality of the system." Rajesh commented.

"If the testers can't get through behavioral test cases—which are generally userlike operations—in an effective and efficient fashion, then what will the users' and customers' experience be?" Jamal responded.

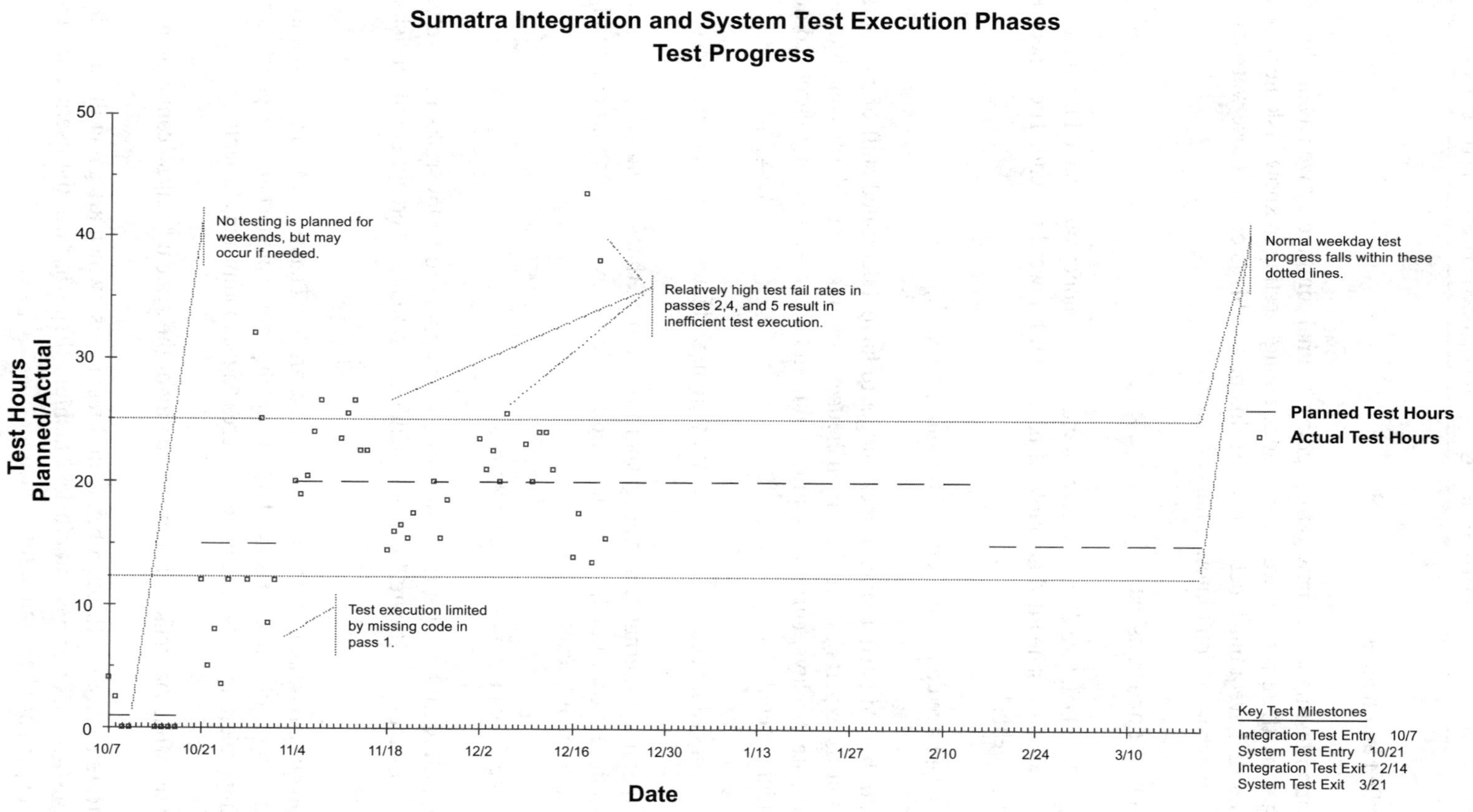

Sumatra Integration and System Test Execution Phases
Test Progress

Normal weekday test progress falls within these dotted lines.

Relatively high test fail rates in passes 2, 4, and 5 result in inefficient test execution.

No testing is planned for weekends, but may occur if needed.

Test execution limited by missing code in pass 1.

—— Planned Test Hours
□ Actual Test Hours

Key Test Milestones
Integration Test Entry 10/7
System Test Entry 10/21
Integration Test Exit 2/14
System Test Exit 3/21

Test Hours
Planned/Actual

50
40
30
20
10
0

Date

10/7 10/21 11/4 11/18 12/2 12/16 12/30 1/13 1/27 2/10 2/24 3/10

FIGURE 15-3 THE EFFICIENCY OF PRODUCT USAGE AND TESTING AS SHOWN BY TEST PROGRESS

"Ohhhhh," Rajesh replied, rubbing an ear and studying the chart anew.

"I show a certain number of planned test execution hours per week, based on the total planned hours for each test cycle. Those are the solid lines. Notice that we have no hours planned on weekends, which gives us the gap between the lines. The boxes show the actual hours achieved each day. Hours are achieved only when a test is completed—pass, fail, or warn—and no further hours will be spent on that test until the next time it's scheduled for execution," Jamal said.

"Which means testing hours can be extended across two or more days but will only count on the last day?" Rajesh asked.

"Right," Jamal said. "It's not as accurate, perhaps, but it keeps the accounting simple. Since the average test effort is less than a day, it's close enough."

"Got it," Rajesh agreed.

"As you can see from this chart, passes 2 and 4, in general, were not very efficient, and pass 5 is shaping up the same way. A relatively high number of tests have failed in these passes, which makes testing take longer. We expect it also reflects a general clunkiness of the product associated with the bug backlog. As the bug backlog goes away, we should see the boxes converge and stay within the dotted lines that represent 'normal' efficiency," Jamal concluded.

"So it's a control chart; is that what you're saying?" Harold asked.

"Oh no, it's not a control chart in the statistical process control sense of the word," Jamal replied quickly. "I don't have that kind of data at this point. The dotted lines represent the kind of day-to-day variation I would expect from test cases spanning days."

"So," Rajesh asked, "how many tests are failing?"

"Glad you asked," Jamal said with a smile, "because that leads me to..." (he advanced his slide, shown in Figure 15-4) "my next chart. This chart answers the fourth and last question: How are we doing in terms of fulfilling the planned tests in a timely fashion? It also tells us something about the quality of the system, though not directly."

"As with the previous chart, the line shows the planned test fulfillment, and the boxes show the actual test fulfillment. This is a cumulative chart, showing the planned and actual figures on a daily total basis for each test pass. At the end of each

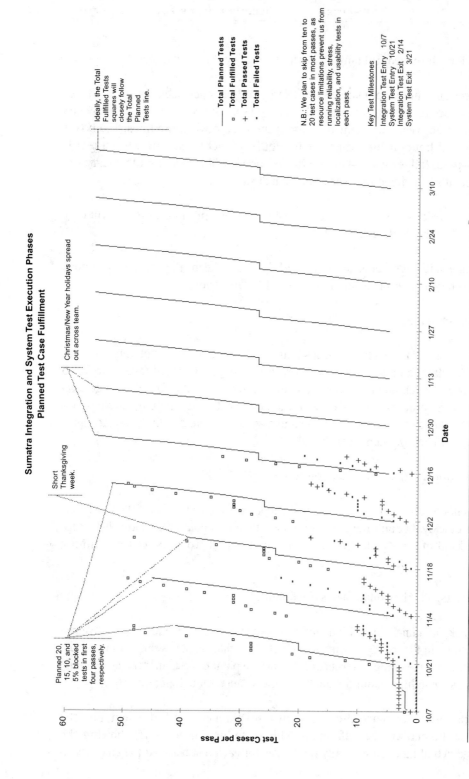

FIGURE 15-4 GETTING THROUGH THE TESTS AS SHOWN BY TEST FULFILLMENT

pass, we start over again at zero. As you can see, the boxes track the lines closely, so we're doing a good job of getting through all the planned tests, albeit a bit inefficiently as shown in the previous chart.

"Now, the little minuses show failed test counts, and the little pluses show passed test counts, again cumulative numbers for each pass. For the first four passes, I expected a certain number of tests to be blocked by missing functionality. That's why the first four Total Planned Tests lines are shorter than the rest. The Thanksgiving holiday makes the third Total Planned Tests line particularly short."

"Where's Christmas on this chart?" Yasuhiro asked.

"Ah, the joys of a multicultural test team," Jamal said, smiling. "A number of my testers who don't observe Christmas agreed to take the days off at other times. So we'll be testing this week. I've already warned the key participants in other teams who might get paged for support. Jenny, I don't know how many of your programmers are working this week, but if the number is low, we may see a little jump in the bug backlog over the next two cycles or so as the programmers catch up on the bugs we find this week."

"I didn't have nearly the luck with holiday horse-trading that Jamal did," Jenny admitted. "We probably will see a little blip in the backlog."

"Jamal, I'm not sure why you say the chart doesn't speak directly to quality." Cicely noted. "You show the number of test cases passed and failed there."

"Test case counts are a tricky thing," Jamal responded. "It's easy to make a case that the counts are meaningless in terms of quality. I can combine two failing test cases and have just one failing test case, or I can split one passing test case and have two passing test cases. I can add tests as I go along. We rarely get to '100% passed' by the end of the project, because we usually decide that some bugs won't get fixed, which means that some tests don't pass. Since we testers are in the bug finding business, we want to run tests that fail. However, that means that the test case failure rates often give an overly pessimistic picture of the quality of the system. So some number of failed tests is to be expected."

"What's the usual number of failed tests as of system test exit?" Rajesh asked.

"I don't know off the top of my head, exactly," Jamal replied, "but for the last couple of releases I'd guess around 15% or 20%. I can get you a more precise number, if you'd like."

"That's close enough," Rajesh said, "since we're clearly not even close yet."

"Yes, we're running about twice that," Jamal replied, "which brings us to the counter-point. I can just as easily make the case that test case counts have some meaning in terms of quality, too. Since we design our tests behaviorally, the tests have some relationship to actions a user might perform and behaviors a user might observe. So a large number of failed tests does tell us something about system quality. It's like a painting in the pointillist style. If you look too closely, all you see are dots, each of which has very little meaning. As you stand back, you see a distinct picture emerge."

Step #	Step	Done?
3.	Select metrics and build reports and charts that answer these questions.	☑

"So, you mentioned concerns, Jamal," Rajesh said. "Care to list some of them?"

"First is that we still have some areas of significant risk that we don't know enough about or in which we know we have some significant problems. Now, I suspect that over the next two or three weeks, those risk areas will get tested and the known bugs will be resolved. Nevertheless, it bears watching. Bug triage will be essential over the next few weeks because I expect we'll continue to find important problems. We are not at the point of finding only 'fit and finish' bugs yet."

Rajesh nodded.

"Second, I briefly alluded to past problems here at Software Cafeteria where we removed developers from bug fixing tasks during system testing and assigned them to new projects. Those removed were typically the most senior developers, who were needed to work on design issues in the new projects. However, what that does—especially when we're still struggling with significant and dangerous bugs—is concentrate the bug fixing responsibility in the hands of people who are most likely to destabilize the design and the system," Jamal said. "Now, I hasten to add that I intend no offense to Jenny's team. There isn't a single bozo working on Sumatra, and I'm not implying that there is. But there are levels of skill. In the past, we have more than once assumed that all we were dealing with were trivial 'fit and finish' bugs. We reduced staff and overall staff skills accordingly. But we actually were dealing with significant bugs that had far-reaching consequences. This resulted in big problems in hitting our schedule, revealed right at the end of the project."

"Point taken," Rajesh said. "Please continue."

"Third, as I mentioned, both the number of test cases failing and the average time to run any given test case are above where I'd like to see those numbers at the end of the project. I have no doubt that these numbers will improve over the next couple of months, but again they are indicators that we need to monitor closely. Should they not trend down by the beginning of February, we have a problem. Once more, this is attached to the need to keep the right staffing level and skills mix in Jenny's team as we wind this project down.

"Finally, remember that the cumulative closed figure in the first chart includes those bugs deferred to the next release—the one after Sumatra. This rate has gone up—and the backlog has gone down—since we made priority 2 bugs eligible for deferral in the change control board meetings."

Rajesh cast a questioning look at Kate and Jenny, who were sitting next to each other.

Kate took up the challenge and said, "Rajesh, an aggressive policy of deferring bugs that we think customers will accept is part of making our delivery with all of the high- and medium-priority functionality in tact. Realistically, the other option is not to complete the final iteration, because we'll have too many programmers focused on fixing bugs."

"I understand the trade-off," Rajesh replied, "but let's not compromise quality excessively in order to ship features that are full of bugs. That doesn't make sense." Before Jenny or Kate could protest, Rajesh swiveled in his chair and raised an eyebrow toward Jamal. "So, Mr. Test Manager, how do you feel about that 'aggressive policy of deferring bugs?'"

Jamal looked Rajesh in the eye and replied, "Not to dodge the question, Mr. CEO, but I see my role as primarily assessing quality and reporting on it. I'm not in the quality cop business. So, as Mr. Test Manager, I'm neutral on the policy."

Rajesh rubbed his goatee, continued to direct his piercing glance at Jamal, and asked, "And as Mr. Jamal Brown, thoughtful human being and vested holder of stock in this company?"

"Personally, I would prefer to see us set the quality bar a bit higher. However," Jamal admitted, "that's always going to be true. What I see day in and day out are problems in quality. We're finding a hundred to a hundred fifty bugs a week or so. I read a lot of bug reports. I talk to my team about a lot of failed tests. That colors my perception. It makes me sensitive to the risks to system quality. Because I'm focusing on those risks, I'm perhaps not seeing others. The schedule and budget risks that Jenny, Kate, and Sundari see are not nearly as visible to me.

"Frankly, Rajesh," Jamal concluded, "I think the best way for you to determine if we've lowered the quality bar too low would be for you to look at all—or at least a sizeable sample—of the bugs we've deferred. If you don't have time to do so, perhaps Cosimo could serve as your proxy. If you or he sees deferred bugs that scare you, then we might need to do a 'reverse bug-scrub' on the deferred bugs to raise the bar a bit. I just don't know enough about how the customers and users see our product to make bet-the-company pronouncements about appropriate bug priorities and triage decisions."

"And is that exactly what you would say to me in my office with the door closed, Jamal?"

"Yes," Jamal replied firmly.

"Okay, when's the next change control board meeting?" Rajesh said.

"Monday the 30th," Kate responded. "We canceled the three meetings this week since we can't get the cross-functional attendance we need to make them work."

"I'll review the deferred bugs between now and then, and I'll be at that meeting with my list of bugs to be revived, if any," Rajesh said. "Are we done with the test status?"

"Yes," Jamal said.

"Good. Nicely presented, Jamal. Very clear," Rajesh concluded. "What's next on the agenda, Kate?"

Step #	Step	Done?
4.	Present the test results to the audience as required.	✔

Recognize a Good Test Results Reporting Process

In the case study, Jamal has a good process for weekly summary test status reporting. What can we say more generally about test team—and project team—behaviors and benefits from a good results reporting process?

DELIVER USEFUL, CREDIBLE, AND TIMELY INFORMATION

As an analogy for the testing process and the reporting of test results, consider a newspaper. A paper that covers local news in other cities but not the one you live in is useless. A paper that doesn't cover financial and business issues when you need information to manage your stock portfolio is useless. A paper in a language you don't understand is useless. A newspaper you don't trust is useless. Yesterday's newspaper is close to useless, and one that is a month old is of historical interest only. I find that test professionals who think of themselves as reporters on the topic of quality, and test leaders and managers who think of themselves as publishers of a newspaper about quality, can use this metaphor to guide the way they report results.

One way to think about your results reporting is to ask yourself, Are we, the test team, providing the right reports, at the right time, with the right frequency, through the right channels? Better yet, ask that question of your peers and managers, of all the stakeholders in the testing process and in the quality of the system.

I find it's important to work iteratively with my peers and senior managers to define the information we all need from the test process. In the case study earlier, Jamal has a set of four charts that make up his test project dashboard. Those charts came about by following the process outlined earlier, starting with the goals of the project and the key stakeholders and proceeding from there to specific metrics that he displays graphically.

One complication is that senior managers and peers might have trouble articulating what they want the test team to measure, and you might have some trouble coming up with ideas on your own if you're new to the test results reporting process. Fortunately, there are lots of good sources for ideas. This chapter is one of those sources, as are Chapters 4 and 5 of my previous book, *Managing the Testing Process, Second Edition*. Stephen Kan in *Metrics and Models in Software Quality Engineering, Second Edition*, Boris Beizer in *Software System Testing and Quality Assurance*, and Pankoj Jalote in *CMM in Practice* discuss various testing and quality-related metrics. Anna Allison wrote a helpful article called "Meaningful Metrics" that can be found at www.stickyminds.com. Space precludes an exhaustive listing of books and articles that you can use as inspiration, but many are listed in the bibliography and occur as footnotes in this chapter.

What Jamal presented in the case study is commonly called a *test dashboard* or *balanced scorecard*, a summary of the status of the test effort. While this kind of collection of reports is appropriate for a status meeting, peer-level managers may want detailed reports in addition to the dashboard. For example, a technical support manager or development manager might want to review detailed bug report information as part of a regular meeting or informal discussion. One size does not fit all. The receiver of information, not the creator of it, defines the usefulness of that information.

Accuracy is another important element of usefulness. Pivotal project decisions are often made based on test results. Should we delay the release? Where should we expend scarce resources late in the project? When presenting at a summary level (e.g., a dashboard) not only must the underlying data (the bug reports, the test results, the coverage tracing, and so on) be accurate, but the analysis you do with that data must be accurate as well. Finally, effective communication means that everyone in the audience received an accurate impression of the test status report from the presentation.

When you are speaking in a public forum like a project status or bug triage meeting, effective communication requires effective public speaking skills. I used to suffer from stage fright. I would sometimes make defensive or terse comments when presenting test results publicly, which made my presentations less effective. When I became nervous, I found I might forget to cover key details, react defensively to honest questions, display nervous mannerisms that distracted the audience, drop my voice when explaining important but controversial details, and otherwise behave in a way that detracted from my message. What I know about public speaking I've learned through trial and error. I've not only presented test results as a test manager for years now, but I've also spoken publicly at conferences, at clients' sites, and at training seminars However, I don't recommend sink-or-swim as a technique for becoming a better public speaker. A variety of books, training courses, and organizations exist to help you calm the quaking nerves when facing a crowd. I recommend exploring those avenues should you suffer from this problem. I wish I had.

I usually find that at least some of the information coming out of a test project is best displayed graphically, as Jamal did in the case study, or in tables. The ubiquity and ease of use of tools like Word, Excel, Visio, and Access—to name just some examples I'm personally familiar with—have, on the one hand, enabled sophisticated analyses and presentations of information.

On the other hand, these same tools can lead to an explosion of truly awful charts, graphs, reports, and other documents. This explosion of pseudo-information can choke a project with inscrutable and jarring displays of page upon page of insignificance, within which might hide a nugget or two of project-critical information. The number of person-years of productivity we have lost and the number of projects that have foundered while managers doodled out pointless graphics and tables is unknown but surely large.

How to Waste Time and Money on Useless Status Reports

I worked on one project where three highly paid consultants from a large firm worked full-time preparing a daily test status report package. Assume an hourly rate of $200 per hour each—which is probably conservative—and do the math. About $5,000 per day.

This project had been going in circles for a couple of months, and the project's business sponsor decided to bring in a new team of test consultants—mine. As one of my early tasks, I asked the project manager which of the charts and reports in the daily status package she used as key indicators to tell her where the project stood. Even though I suspected only a portion of the reports were actually useful, her reply stunned me.

"I don't read any of them, I just throw the damned thing in the trash."

I asked others on the project. Same basic answer.

I would estimate that at least $200,000 went up in smoke on that project, producing a report no one read. Worse yet, the project was operating without many of the benefits available from a test program, even though they were paying for one. They had reduced the return on the testing investment to be only that available from finding and fixing bugs, which was happening at the tactical level between testers and developers. The only good news is that the three consultants were 100% dedicated to the daily status report. Therefore, the work they did on the useless daily status report package wasn't distracting them from anything else they should have been doing.

I started to become aware of this problem as I studied the topic of design, in particular for Web sites. Most useful, though, were Edward Tufte's masterful trilogy of books on information design and display. *The Visual Display of Quantitative Information*, *Envisioning Information*, and *Visual Explanations* have inspired me to do a better job in creating test charts and reports. I highly recommend them. Tufte's comments about the proper use of color, shading, and labels, along with his criticism *chartjunk*, have been especially useful to me.

Accuracy of data and information, effective verbal communication, and well-designed charts, reports, and other documents help to maintain the credibility of the results. I have also found that the higher I go up the management chain, the more presentation matters. I'm not talking about being flashy. Bombastic multimedia sounds and videos and spinning clip art are usually not informative but are distracting. Spending more time trying to understand the audience's information needs up front and designing truly effective and concise presentations that meet those needs produces good presentation.

Timeliness and frequency are also elements of the usefulness and credibility of the results. Peers will probably expect information that is more instantaneous, more frequent, and less processed, while senior managers and executives will expect to receive test status reports less frequently. When senior managers and executives do receive test status reports, they will probably expect those reports to be concise and informative. I like to think of senior and executive management attention to test status like a gas tank: I only have a limited amount of fuel, and I don't want to empty it before the project is over.

Finally, picking the right channels for transmitting the information to the audience influences the information's usefulness, timeliness, and credibility. Consider the following channels for sharing information:

- Project status meetings
- Bug triage meetings (*bug crawls*)
- Emergency meetings to discuss a critical, showstopping bug
- Change control board meetings (see Chapter 16)
- Test phase entry (a.k.a. test readiness review) meetings
- Test phase exit meetings
- Release, ship, deploy, or go/no-go meetings
- Conference calls
- E-mail
- Company intranet
- One-on-one

The manner, kind, detail, and presentation of information can differ considerably across these channels. What would be perfectly appropriate—useful, timely, and credible—in one channel could be entirely inappropriate in other channels, sometimes in a way that could cause serious credibility problems for the test professional misusing the channel. Conversely, being careful about providing useful and timely information to the right people through the right channels sets up a positive feedback loop for your credibility.

RELATE TEST STATUS TO PROJECT PROGRESS— AND INFLUENCE FUTURE PROGRESS

Another positive feedback loop for credibility arises when we relate test status to project progress and lay out a road map to move forward. If we have credibility, people will follow our road map—perhaps not exactly, but we will have influence over the project. If we have no credibility, people will not only disregard our road map, they won't believe our assessment of test status and project progress.

Effective test results reporting is about more than having accurate data and accurate information. It is about more than a well-designed collection of graphics, reports, and charts. It is about more than clever and insightful data analysis. It is about more than a confident and convincing delivery. It is about more than picking the right channel. It is about all these things, it's true, but all these things are tactics. The objective is *effective communication* of test status to test stakeholders. In other words, the test professional's message is *listened to*, the test professional's message is *heard*, the test professional's message is *understood*, and, if the message requires it, the test professional's message is *acted upon*.

In my experience, to communicate effectively about test results, I find I must deliver my message in a way that relates to the overall project and the project goals. For example, what would I say if the project goals were delivering an entertaining video game with some cool features on a shrink-wrapped DVD within a profitable budget and schedule? What would I say if the project goals were delivering a zero-defect system to provide nuclear medicine treatment to cancer patients? Clearly, an identical presentation of test results—even of quantitatively identical results—would be not merely a bad idea, but would be ethically deplorable.

In addition, I must ask myself what the organization wants the testing project to accomplish—and what I want to accomplish. Results reporting is where those accomplishments are articulated, whether in writing, in speaking, in pictures, or in some combination. If one of the accomplishments I'm looking for is having the project team act on my information—i.e., being influential—then results reporting is a key step in the process of influence.

That being the case, I must consider how the project team will respond to the results I report. I don't want to allow the lack of known problems earlier in the project meet with the response that, therefore, no problems will be found. Conversely, if I find a lot of problems and the project is in trouble, then I want to define possible paths to success where I can see them. Now, by "relating to project progress" and "paths to success" I don't necessarily mean "hitting the release date by whatever means necessary." Rather, I mean setting up an intelligent set of trade-offs and decisions about the balance between schedule, budget, features, and quality, within the broader context of the technology, the project, and the organization.

This is especially true for nonroutine discussions, such as an emergency meeting to discuss a critical bug. Consider the explosion of the Challenger space shuttle. The

tragedy of that disaster goes beyond the public incineration of seven people on a frig-
idly cold, clear Florida morning. The deeper tragedy lies in the fact that the day before
it happened, Morton Thiokol engineers presented information about the causal relationship between decreasing temperature and the likelihood of O-ring failure to their
managers and NASA launch officials—information that, had it been effectively communicated, would almost certainly have led to the launch being scrubbed. That is not
to say the engineers were at fault. The engineers understood the information, but the
managers and launch officials didn't understand it. Sadly, neither side figured out
how to bridge that communication gap.

In *Visual Explanations*, Edward Tufte, drawing upon extensive source information,
including a presentation by Richard Feynman to the US congressional investigation,
reworks the presentation. Even though I have only a passing knowledge of materials
science, Tufte's charts showed exactly what could happen to the O-rings in cold
weather.

In a public lecture about his books, including a discussion of the Challenger disaster,
Tufte presented three key lessons for data display design.

1. Show causality.
2. Show all the relevant data.
3. Show managers what they really need to see to make an informed decision.

As shorthand for these three steps, Tufte asked, "What is the thinking task that we
want the person [hearing our report] to engage in?"[4]

Certainly, the Challenger disaster is an incident where engineers could have done a
more effective job of telling a negative story. However, there are also cases where
testers are too effective at telling a story that is overly negative. Consider the following two potential verbal summaries of test status.

Both of these summaries could describe exactly the same point in time for exactly the
same project. Yet the first is a status report that relates to the project objectives and suggests a way to resolve the challenges. The second status report is unremittingly and

---

4. For Tufte's analysis of the Challenger disaster, with extensive sources for further reading, see
   Visual Explanations, pages 38 to 53. The three lessons mentioned earlier summarize the
   opening page of Chapter 1, Graphical Excellence, in *The Visual Display of Quantitative Information*. The public lecture was one I attended in Austin, Texas, on January 28, 2002. At the
   time of writing, the investigation into the Columbia shuttle disintegration was ongoing.

Summary 1: We have run all 517 planned test cases as of last Saturday. Currently, the bug tracking system shows a backlog of 247 bug reports either open or assigned to a developer but not yet resolved. The good news is that we only found ten new bugs this week, down from about 40 per week over the last three weeks of system test. However, because the fix rate since the start of system test is approximately 30 bugs per week, I believe our target date for system test exit—three weeks from today—is at significant risk. Perhaps we should consider a detailed bug review meeting to defer issues we feel are not critical for this release. After that discussion, we might have to address the current schedule.

Summary 2: We've completed our test suites, and what a mess. The test team has found endless bugs, and most of these no one has even *looked* at yet, for gosh sake! We're finding more new bugs every week than Development can fix. There's no way we'll exit system test in three weeks!

perhaps excessively negative. This makes the report—and the reporter—likely to be dismissed as alarmist or greeted with despair. Again, both could describe the same test project status, but the first is related to project progress and likely to be influential.[5]

SHOW TRENDS AND DESTINATIONS IN QUALITY OVER TIME

The combined issues of test status and project progress bring us to the next sign of a good test results reporting process in most situations: Where appropriate, show trends and destinations.

Early test results during development, maintenance, configuration, and integration projects will probably show one snapshot of quality. As the development, maintenance, configuration, or integration efforts proceed, quality will hopefully improve. The snapshot of quality will change over time. As these changes occur, trends will develop. Those trends, when shown appropriately, will tell you not only where the project has been, but where it is headed. Therefore, that trend information will allow astute managers to make predictions of where quality will be in the future. How are we doing in terms of getting the bugs out? When will the system be good enough to ship or deploy?

---

5. On the wider topic of being an influential test professional, see Johanna Rothman's article "The Influential Test Manager," originally published in *Software Testing and Quality Engineering* magazine, Volume 2, Issue 2 (Mar/Apr 2000), and now found at www.stickyminds.com and www.jrothman.com.

In the case study, Jamal's dashboard shows trends as well as estimations of where the project is going. A flattening cumulative open curve indicates stability, or at least the inability of the test team to find many more bugs with the current test system. A cumulative closed curve that converges with the open curve indicates quality, a resolution of the problems found by testing. The test fulfillment chart shows test cases completed—including passed and failed cases as well as those not yet completed. This chart gives managers some insight into how many test cases remain to be run, what proportion of test cases can't be run, and the relative pass and fail situation.

The same source data shown without the time-series information and the predictions or road maps of what needs to happen next would strip out this predictive element. Remember, one of the ways that testing adds value is by guiding the project to success through timely, accurate, credible information for project tracking. This trend and destination information is essential to providing that guidance.

Certainly, there are audiences for whom reports should show snapshots. Detailed, tactical reports for development, operations, business analysis, technical support, and help desk staff should probably focus on those issues needing immediate action. To provide such details, you can use test case, test suite, and bug summaries or even complete bug reports. The test case summary report can list each test case, line by line, with its current status, associated bug reports, tested configurations, and so forth. A bug summary report can show bugs, one per line, with the bug ID, summary or abstract, date opened, severity, and other such information.

One exception to the need to show trends arises when you are acceptance testing a single release from a vendor where configuration and integration are not issues. Test results are probably most appropriately reported as a snapshot. Either the system is fit for use, ready for deployment, or the vendor's offering is not ready. Evaluating a number of competing alternative packages from vendors to determine which one to select is probably most appropriate as a snapshot, too.

USE APPROPRIATE MECHANISMS AND DOCUMENTS

In the earlier case study, Jamal used a slide-show-style presentation consisting of charts created with a spreadsheet program, along with a verbal narrative to explain each chart and what it meant, as the mechanism for reporting results. He also used e-mail as a mechanism, sending the charts out to the meeting attendees beforehand so they could prepare, if desired. This is one way to handle the mechanics of reporting results, and certainly not an unusual one.

The way I manage test projects, reporting summary test results begins with the state of tests executed, the risks mitigated, the bugs found and fixed, and the relationship of all these items to the planned or estimated completion metrics. I organize my own test projects around structured, organized, and measurable test systems with carefully designed and implemented tests, clear traceability between quality risks and tests, and formal bug tracking databases. From this test system I extract meaningful metrics and aggregate data. Some test managers use test systems with more documentation than I do, some are more comfortable with less. Part of linking test results reporting to context, as discussed in Chapter 1, is to use whatever test system works most effectively for you and your test organization.

I also prefer to measure my test results in terms of numbers. I get a deeper understanding than using a purely qualitative approach, and the quantification of key indicators lays the foundation for my understanding of test status. I find that my clients, colleagues, and test teams are usually more comfortable with quantified results. To quote Lord Kelvin, "If...you cannot express [what you are speaking about] in numbers, your knowledge is of a meager and unsatisfactory kind."[6]

When dealing with quantified test results, I find it's important for me to distinguish data from information. I will generally have a blizzard of test data swirling around, changing day by day. Simply dumping a truckload of test data in front of people is not informing; it is confusing. That's why the process I outlined earlier in this chapter links test metrics to the appropriate context, to the project goals, and to the questions people have about those project goals.

Considerations of efficiency of creation and communication also come into play. Ideally, you can summarize detailed test status automatically and effortlessly in the dashboard and other test status reports. Certain recipients of the reports should be able to drill down into easily accessible source data in the areas of bugs, test status, and risk coverage. (For various legitimate reasons, you might want to restrict access to certain details of the test execution process, especially if you feel they would result in misinterpretation, confusion, or even deliberate misdirection.)

---

6. For more about the benefits of various bug and test-related metrics, see Chapters 4 and 5 of my book *Managing the Testing Process, Second Edition*. Another perspective is found in Mike Cohn's article "A Measured Response," originally published in *Software Testing and Quality Engineering* magazine, Volume 4, Issue 5 (Sep/Oct 2002), and now available on www.stickyminds.com.

One approach I saw a large client of mine take was to post the test dashboard on the company intranet. All of the charts were updated automatically at the same time and on a regular schedule, drawing from a standard repository of source data files. This was a very efficient process once they had it set up, though they did invest about three person-months of effort in developing the tools and the process.

Finally, let me point out that the charts and graphs illustrated in the case study are the kind of information you can put together with a certain amount of effort using tools like Excel. Alternatively, you can invest your own resources to build a comprehensive tool, as my client did. However, if you have purchased or are considering purchasing a commercial test management tool, then that tool should generate all the necessary test status reports for you. You might need to configure the tool and set the reports up. Once you have done that, it should require no more effort from you than printing a canned report from a database or a predefined chart in a spreadsheet. If the tool does not generate such reports, or does so in an overly clunky and unfriendly way, then, frankly, that tool does not meet a test professional's reasonable expectations of quality and functionality. If you can, you should reject such a tool in favor of one that does.

TUNE THE COMMUNICATION TO EACH LISTENER

To some extent, I've been generalizing about the audience: Managers tend to need this kind of information, executives this kind, developers this kind, and so on. Such generalizations are helpful for establishing a starting point for metrics and reports, but I encourage you to look for opportunities to tailor your reports to individual stakeholders. You might be surprised to find the new and helpful ways you can provide useful, timely information to the project team if you do.

To take an example outside the software world, consider the information sources you value. Do your interests fit neatly into the stereotypes about you in terms of your gender, age, ethnicity, political beliefs, and so forth? Since I am a man living in the southern United States (Texas), the stereotypes would say that I would read the sports section of the paper. Yet I haven't in years. I never watch professional sports on television. Show me an article about how to cook an Indian or Chinese dinner, though, and I'll read it avidly.

I have worked with marketing managers who were willing to spend time in the test lab, observing test case failures. Some development managers liked to review test cases to make sure their team's unit testing was complementary. Some project managers have wanted up-to-the-minute test status from me, even for situations that were still evolving. Other project managers wanted thoroughly analyzed results.

Again, the point is to communicate information, which is in the eye, ear, and, ultimately, the mind of the receiver. So, I look for ways to tune the delivery of the message to the listeners. I'll prepare special status e-mails, have informal face-to-face discussions, and even attend other manager's status meetings with selected reports.

When I'm tuning the message to the listener, it helps if I can relate to their perspective. What does the listener value? In what way does testing serve her interests? What can I tell her that she needs to know to decide what to do next? What message do I need to deliver—and how—for her to have a clear picture in her mind, from her point of view, of the test status?

Finally, let me point out that since testing is often in a service organization role, it's important that every interaction between the test team and its stakeholders be one that reinforces a positive perception of the test team's contributions. This is especially true when reporting test results, which are often not good news.

Tuning the communication for the listener shows respect for that person, which will promote our contribution. Those of us who come from a technical background also need to think about how to communicate with nontechies. For example, can we report test status, even specific failures, in terms of the project goals rather than core dumps, dereferenced uninitialized pointers, unsupported widgets, and the like? It's helpful—and fun—for testers to have insight into the technology of the system. However, keep in mind that many technological phrases, acronyms, concepts, and jargon might be incomprehensible to some nontechnical individual contributors and managers. Using incomprehensible words does not impress an audience; it confuses them.

That is not to say that the presentation of results should patronize. If people need to understand a thorny technical topic to understand some part of the test status, saying, "It's a geek thing; you wouldn't understand," is insulting to the audience and dangerous to the project. Maybe the audience *needs* to understand. And such a message is also insulting to yourself as a professional, because you're underestimating your own communication skills. Since you're reading this chapter, you probably agree with me that effective communication is an important skill for a test professional. Right now, you're investing time to learn more about how to do it well.

HANDLE CHALLENGES

No matter how good you get at reporting test results, it's always hard. Communication is naturally hard. Communicating about test status is especially challenging, for a number of reasons.

HANDLING THE PRESENTATION

Formal meetings and presentations, as opposed to e-mail, posted, or other noninteractive test status reports, are perhaps the most stressful forums in which to report results. However, such forums are also most likely to be effective. Just because you posted a report on the company intranet doesn't mean anyone will read it. Just because you e-mailed a 2MB Excel file full of charts and graphs doesn't mean anyone will bother to open the attachment. In any noninteractive status reporting, you really have very little way of knowing—short of polling your audience by phone or in person—whether they looked at your report and understood it. So, on many projects, an interactive presentation of test results, whether over a conference call or in person, is a good idea from time to time.

If you're new to the rituals of management, including meetings and presentations, you might consider reading Patricia Ensworth's *The Accidental Project Manager.* For both newbies and old hands, I highly recommend Edward Tufte's *Visual Explanations*, which includes a discussion of presentations. In addition to their ideas on basic presentation skills, consider the following specific points for test managers.

- Arrive ready for status meetings with slides and supporting documentation. The more senior the audience, the fewer slides I bring, but the more carefully I prepare each one. The worse the news, the more underlying data I have on hand and the more carefully I prepare. However, I strive to show the bad news in a small set of clear charts that focuses the audience on the most important messages. In the case study, Jamal was constantly focusing his presentation on what the charts told people about the quality of the system under test, not distracting and counterproductive issues that could have come up, like whether the testing was being done well.

- Walk your audience through your slides, charts, and reports, pointing out the good news and the bad. What's self-evident to test professionals used to reading such charts often has no meaning to management peers and superiors. Worse yet, they might think they understand what the test status means, but be mistaken. In the case study, Jamal carefully interpreted the meaning of the charts, both in general—i.e., the questions each chart could answer—and in particular—i.e., what the information on each chart meant for the project.

- Take suggestions and questions with a smile but avoid reacting. People are problem solving animals, so testers get a lot of suggestions during test status discussions. (This happens to developers, release engineers, and other individual contributors, too.) I try to listen, consider, and be willing to discuss, but I'm never in a hurry to change my carefully crafted test plan, test system, or test processes in response to an off-the-cuff proposal or reaction in a project status meeting.

While these ideas can get you started, I try to keep my eyes and ears, my heart and mind open as I practice presenting test status. I work to emphasize and adopt styles that work—and drop those that don't—with my colleagues. This is especially true for the next challenge.

THE BEARER OF BAD NEWS

It's easy enough to tell people good news that reflects well on their accomplishments and requires no action on their part. For example, "We've run all the tests and found no bugs, so today we're ending system test on schedule." It's harder to communicate bad news, especially when it implies that people in the audience made mistakes and must take action to rectify the consequences of those mistakes.

The response to the bearer of bad news is a natural psychological one, not something new to software engineering. On the title page of his chapter titled "Hatching a Catastrophe," Fred Brooks in *The Mythical Man-Month* includes a picture of a sculpture that depicts Hercules hurling the messenger Lycas to his death for innocently bringing Hercules bad news. Poor Lycas. From time to time, many test professionals have had a similar experience.

In addition to the irrational reasons for the reaction to bad news—and the bearer of it—there are often perfectly rational reasons as well. To return to the earlier example, while it's easy to cast the Morton Thiokol managers and NASA launch officials as the villains of the Challenger disaster, think about it. These managers and officials were being asked to scrub a high-visibility mission, a mission in which the US president himself, Ronald Reagan, had a political interest. The mission carried the first teacher in space, and a woman, too. On both the Cold War level and the gender-equality level, this mission had important symbolism in the mid-1980s. Not only would scrubbing the mission be politically unpopular, it would also be expensive. Finally, consider the position of the Morton Thiokol managers and executives, who were being asked by their engineers to confront and rebuff a powerful and lucrative client. It's only fair that the managers and officials asked the engineers for proof of their concerns. Similarly, when we suggest that a release date be slipped or that more money be spent on testing, it's hardly unreasonable for management to react by asking that we make a strong case.

So, while I can't claim to have mastered this art entirely, test engineers and test managers can see it as a sign of professional achievement when, more often than not, they communicate bad news effectively to reasonable people. Being effective in such situations requires mastery of the details mentioned earlier, but it also requires an appropriate style, manner, and demeanor in presentation. The keys to success will vary for each manager and each management team, but I find the following dos and don'ts helpful.

- Do be calm and patient. A rational presentation communicates facts better than an emotional one. Sometimes I have to explain some details in more than one way before everyone understands. I consider it part of my job to communicate effectively, even with a challenging audience under difficult circumstances.
- Do be considerate. I have access to potentially embarrassing information that could humiliate my management peers if presented incautiously. I'm careful in my use of data relating to failed test cases and specific bug reports, since it can be seen as an attack or an assignment of blame. A carelessly produced report can be used as a weapon by others even if I don't intend to do so.
- Don't be Don Quixote, the Lone Champion of Quality.[7] Don't assume or accept responsibility for the quality of the system unless it's in your job description. My job is typically to serve as an expert in the management of risks to the quality of the system. In the context of test results reporting, that implies competence to report on specific risks, specific tests, specific bugs, and the trends and implications of those findings. I strive to let my facts speak for themselves, to let management pick what gets fixed, and to let development do the fixing.
- Don't be happy about failure. As a talented test manager, Reynolds MacNary, once told me, "Be optimistic on the outside, pessimistic on the inside." As a test manager, I want my test team to run tests, find bugs, and mitigate risks, all in priority order. I am satisfied with my team's professionalism when they do so. Nevertheless, failed tests, high-priority bugs, and dangerous hazards associated with risks *are* bad news for the project. I find I have to resist any temptation to present anything other than an appropriately somber demeanor when presenting failure data, especially when I'd just love to tell someone, "I told you so."

The key theme here is that I'm striving to depersonalize my presentations of bad news, to help distinguish between the message—bad news, a setback to the project—and the messenger—a caring professional who wants to help by giving a timely warning.

---

7. In Miguel Cervantes' book, *Don Quixote*, the title character suffers a brain injury that results in his imagining himself to be a knight-errant. In his delusion, he defends the honor of a maiden who turns out to be a prostitute, and jousts with a windmill he imagines to be a dangerous giant. Test professionals who see themselves as the lone champions of quality are often quixotic figures.

As a metaphor, imagine a doctor who must tell a patient they are suffering from a dangerous, potentially fatal disease. The doctor is certainly helping the patient by telling him about the disease, because the patient can seek treatment quickly. Perhaps the doctor is even intellectually interested in treating the patient and trying her curative skills against the illness. Perhaps, further, the doctor had been warning the patient for years to curtail some behavior that has brought on this illness. Whatever the circumstances, though, it would be beyond unconscionable for a doctor in such a situation to say, "I told you five years ago to quit smoking," to offer a magic cure, to exaggerate her skills in treating the disease or the likelihood of recovery, to dehumanize her patient in his moment of anguish, or to hustle the stricken person out the door quickly to attend to the next patient.

An especially challenging situation for the bearer of bad news is presenting test status in a meeting where a release or deployment decision is being made. The stakes are high, and the need for good information is particularly acute. However, if the news is bad, the test professional is often the lone voice proclaiming the risks related to the quality of the system while everyone else is expressing the feature, schedule, and budget pressures that make releasing or deploying the system *right now* absolutely critical.

Some test managers long for the authority to stop a release. Perhaps these folks feel that a zero-sum game is being played in this discussion, one where quality should prevail over other considerations. But can any one member or portion of a project team succeed if the project fails? To me, it seems that the game being played—if we must see it as a game—is actually one where the sum can easily be much greater than or much less than zero, depending on whether the project team, especially the project management team, makes a smart decision about releasing or deploying the system.

So, I don't play the quality cop role. Indeed, I have on more than one occasion talked clients out of giving me that role. Rather, what I want is a place at the table. I want to be a trusted and influential counselor on the issue of quality. I'm perfectly happy to sit at a release meeting and focus on giving the clearest, most effectively communicated assessment of quality and release readiness I can. (As I mentioned in Chapter 7, I often use the final test phase exit criteria—e.g., the exit criteria from the system test plan—as a measuring stick.) I might even venture an opinion on how I think the current level of quality risk compares to the level of budget, schedule, and feature risks. However, as was the case with Jamal in the case study, it's often not possible for the test manager or any test professional to have all the information needed to make an intelligent, fully informed decision on whether to release the product. However, by the credible and timely delivery of useful information about quality, the test manager can be an irreplaceable purveyor of a key part of the information that the project management team needs to make such an intelligent, fully informed decision. And that is the role I strive to play.[8]

If these are tips for communicating about bad news with reasonable people, what do we do with unreasonable people? Some people are just plain unreasonable with no justification, often to their own detriment as well as to the detriment of those who work with them. Some people have adopted unreasonableness as a management style, especially as a pressure-exerting tactic.[9]

Some people who find the test situation unpleasant respond by trying to bully, drown out, discredit, or obfuscate the meaning of the bad news and, by extension, the bearer. In an environment where people resort to this tactic, while most other managers are receptive to my results report, I focus on maintaining my position, staying reasonable and on message, calm and consistent. (If no one is listening or being reasonable, I've learned it's better simply to shut up.) In meetings where these tactics are used, I focus on communicating clearly to those who are listening. I build relationships with receptive colleagues in an attempt to route information around those who obstruct, obfuscate, or engage in personal attacks.

In *The Art of War*, Sun Tzu cautions the reader that the wise man does not confront the tiger in its den, so likewise the wise general does not engage in battles from a position of weakness. I offer this metaphor not to recommend warlike behavior toward your fellow managers, but to encourage you to get the test organization's natural allies aware of and involved with test case status and bug resolution.

Finally, it bears mentioning that some people are unreasonable about test results reports for perfectly reasonable reasons. Perhaps they are unreasonable because of unrealistic expectations that calcified early in the project. Being an effective communicator of bad news starts right at the beginning, when we are establishing context, assessing quality risks, estimating the project, and planning. Perhaps people are being unreasonable because they don't find the test team to be a credible source of useful and timely information. It's hard to fix credibility problems after the fact, but we can be careful

---

8. For more thoughts on this topic, see "Release Criteria" by Johanna Rothman, originally published in *Software Testing and Quality Engineering*, Volume 4, Issue 2 (Mar/Apr 2002), and now available at www.stickyminds.com and www.jrothman.com.
9. For thoughts on dealing with the pathologically unreasonable and the tactically unreasonable, see Ed Yourdon's book *Death March*. For a good discussion on the effects of extended pressure on teamwork and personnel performance, see Tom DeMarco and Tim Lister's *Peopleware*.

throughout the project to manage both test team effectiveness and the perceptions of test team effectiveness.[10]

AN EVER-CHANGING COMPLEX STORY

Sometimes we might describe the news from testing as "good." Sometimes we might describe it as "bad." Often, it's a mixture of both. But one adjective we can almost always hang on the news from testing is "changing."

Test findings during test execution evolve constantly. If I spend two hours preparing slides for a two-hour project status meeting, I know that by the end of the meeting, my report is stale. On the other hand, if I slap my presentation together quickly, I'll probably walk into the meeting with a less-than-perfect snapshot of test status. So, there's a trade-off between accuracy and timeliness, between being up-to-the-minute and having my story straight. As with the test results interpretation issue discussed in Chapter 13, the correct balance in this trade-off is one that depends on context. In this case, the context revolves around the information needs of the audience.

Does the audience worry about the exact count of test cases, the number of passes and fails, and the like? If so, I must work extra hard to make sure all my reports are consistent, but this means that my results are somewhat out-of-date by the time people get them. Does the audience want the latest story, the breaking news, even if all the details aren't clear? If so, I must work to make the results reporting process fast, albeit at the cost of accuracy from time to time.

To get the balance right, I find I have to involve my managers and other stakeholders in the discussion. Once I explain the time required to achieve particular levels of accuracy and consistency in particular reporting formats, and the trade-offs involved in my being disengaged from the testing process proper while working on such reports, I can usually get the guidance I need to make the right decision.

Perhaps the proper word is "decisions." Each member of the audience may have slightly different desires here. Again, being an effective communicator requires that I target my communication to the listener. While settings in which I report test status to a

---

10. In addition to the management angle, there are also the one-on-one discussions that occur between test professionals and programmers and other individual contributors. Karen Johnson's article "Delivering Unwelcome News to Developers," originally published in *Software Testing and Quality Engineering*, Volume 4, Issue 5 (Sep/Oct 2002), and now available on www.stickyminds.com, has some helpful thoughts about communicating at this level.

group require that I aim for a happy medium across all the listeners, I can also, as I noted earlier, produce tailored information for various stakeholders. These tailored reports can satisfy the listener's specific preferences in balancing timeliness and accuracy.

Even with all the time in the world, no matter how carefully I prepare myself, I can't know everything. For example, I can't speak from memory in detail about every one of 300 or 400 active bug reports. Likewise, I can't answer specific questions about a single condition buried in one of 200 or 300 test cases. When confronted with such questions, I smile and say something like, "Well, you win the game of 'Stump the Dummy!' I don't know the answer to that, but I'll research the issue right away if you'd like."

As long as I am usually well prepared, a forthright admission of ignorance coupled with an unstinting offer to get the information immediately wins out every time over winging it or dodging the question. However, I must be ready to discuss in detail the serious bugs, the most serious test case failures, and the most dangerous risks. Astute managers often ask me fine-grained questions about situations involving data loss, complete functional incapacitation, nasty performance bottlenecks, or impairment of a crown-jewel feature.

MAINTAINING A PASSION FOR QUALITY WHILE GIVING A DISPASSIONATE PRESENTATION

As test professionals, we tend to focus on the problems, the risks, and the downside. That's appropriate, since that's often the role of the test team: to help manage risks to system quality. It makes sense that, as professionals, we would bring a passion to our work. However, that passion can spill over into the Don Quixote type of behavior I mentioned earlier, getting in the way of effective communication. How do we maintain an admirable passion for quality while avoiding becoming a project obstacle?

First, let's recognize that just as it's understandable that programmers and other engineers be challenged by bug reports and information about failed test cases, we testers have a natural human tendency to become ego-involved in how the project management team responds to test status. After all, we want our work to be valued.

However, it's important for us to understand that testing does not happen for its own sake. As I've mentioned before, organizations don't have test groups to satisfy idle intellectual curiosity, but rather to deliver specific quality risk management services to the organization in the context of a specific project. These services help the project management team balance the four elements—quality, features, budget, and schedule—to make a fully informed decision.

IMPLEMENT IMPROVEMENTS

Given that all testers should tailor the specific results reporting work they do, how can we implement improvements? Broadly speaking, I can suggest the following starting points.

1. Start by asking stakeholders what they think of the current information products and services coming out of the test organization. This step by itself—provided that people see appropriate follow-through later—will boost the credibility of the test team, because it shows that you care about the usefulness and timeliness of your results.

2. Be ready to show examples. You can give airy, vague descriptions of what kind of information will come out of some proposed chart or report, but an example—especially one that models realistic situations—will allow people to get a feel for the information they'll actually receive, along with giving you an idea of how they'll react.

3. Take steps of an appropriate size. Implementing a fully automated, integrated dashboard can be a big step. Why take such a big step if you're not completely sure of the information you need? Maybe doing manual analysis for a while, using a spreadsheet, a database, some charting software, and the like, will help nail down what you need.

4. Keep the overhead low. Time that the test team spends analyzing test data, creating charts, updating intranet sites, and the like is time that the test team doesn't spend assessing the quality of the system under test or doing other things that would allow them to do a better job of doing so. Get people exactly the information they need, and not one drop more.

5. As you work to improve the process and as you follow the process, continually monitor the effectiveness of your reporting processes and the perceived effectiveness. People's information needs and their perceptions of the test team can change quickly, so test professionals need to be ready to respond to these changes.

With test results reporting out of the way, haven't we reached the end of the road, the last step of the testing process? After all, we've gone all the way from establishing a testing context to generating the assessment of quality to delivering that information—both at a detailed and a summary level—to the team. That's everything we're paid to do, right?

On some projects, that might be true, but on most of the projects I've worked on, there's one more factor to deal with: change. The definition of the project includes the feature, schedule, budget, and quality targets for the system, and this definition will often change as the project proceeds. This sometimes indicates a failure to do good requirements, design, and planning work up front, but it can also arise from the fact that we learn as a project proceeds. In the next chapter, we'll see how imperfect preparation and desirable learning play a role in changing the project and how those changes affect testing.

16

LEVERAGE OPPORTUNITIES TO LEARN: MANAGE CHANGE AND ITS EFFECTS ON TESTING

In the last two chapters, we looked at the way in which much of the value of testing is delivered to the project team. Bug reports give the project team a tangible opportunity to improve system quality, or to at least take appropriate steps to deal with known bugs when they hit the field. Results reporting lets management know that some risks are perhaps lower than expected—i.e., some tests were run that passed— and gives managers useful overall information to guide the project to success.

This chapter is about how we testers keep adding value to the project as the project evolves and changes.[1] After all, on most projects, we're not going to ship or deploy the same system that showed up for the first test cycle. We hope that the quality will improve as a result of the tests we run. Schedule and budget pressures could change the target feature set or the target amount of testing. Features could prove harder to implement than originally thought, leading to their deletion. Of course, we're going to learn a lot about the system as we run our tests, information that will affect what the right thing is to do next. And, yes, overly optimistic project schedules and budgets, unrealistic expectations about testing, and mistaken faith in unproven technologies often come crashing down during the test execution period, resulting in project reassessments—sometimes dramatic ones.

---

1. Portions of this chapter were previously published as "Test Release Processes" in the *Journal of Software Testing Professionals*, Volume 1, Issue 2. A number of quotes from fellow test professionals appeared in that article. While I have removed the quotes to fit the overall style of this book, the ideas remain. In alphabetical order, I'd like to thank the following people for their insightful contributions: Randall Becker, Ross Collard, Gary Dawson, Harvey Deutsch, Tim Dyes, Danny Faught, Peggy Fouts, Darcy Martin, and Barbara Ruf.

At least some amount of evolution and change has affected almost every project I've worked on. Perhaps that's true for you, too. Such being the case, our test projects must evolve and change in response to such information. This can include everything from risk assessment to budgets, schedules, and plans, to staffing, to the test system, to test releases, to test execution, to bug and results reporting. In short, test professionals must be ready to adapt the whole test process—and every constituent critical process we've discussed so far—in response to project change. By being ready, willing, and able to change, testers remain relevant to the overall project.[2]

A CHANGE MANAGEMENT PROCESS

Process 12 is a simple, generic change management process. You might notice that I have included the bug triage process as part of the change management process. Sometimes these are separated, so let me explain my reasoning.

In many cases, a change is a change. The source of the change request—a bug report from the test team or an enhancement request from marketing—doesn't affect whether the system would need to change in response to the request. The source of the change request might affect the priority of the change request, but it might not. In contract-development situations, a change request might trigger a cost increase to the client, whereas a bug fix might not. However, for mass-market software, we either satisfy customers or we do not. In the mass-market world, certainly there are times when it makes sense to defer to the next release the repair of bugs that are clearly related to violations of established, approved requirements. There are times when it makes sense not to defer an enhancement request that is clearly outside the scope of those same requirements.[3]

Whether you combine bug triage and change control in a single process or you use two processes, the stakes of making both kinds of changes tend to go up as the project goes along. The less time remains, the fewer options we have. So, the closer

---

2. This chapter is aimed primarily at test teams performing testing as part of a development, maintenance, or integration project where the definition of a successful system delivery could change over time. If testing is being done to a make a binary decision—accept or reject this system—then change is less likely, perhaps only in the context of a changed contract. Likewise, if the testing is part of an evaluation of competing systems or components to select the best one for deployment into an organization, then the selection criteria are generally defined up front.

3. As Cem Kaner, James Bach, and Bret Pettichord wrote in *Lessons Learned in Software Testing*, "Think of a project as an ongoing structured conversation about what makes sense to do next," and "There are always late changes."

Step #	Step	Done?
1.	Gather requested changes and bug fixes proposed for inclusion in the current, a future, or an emergency system release.	☐
2.	Review proposed requests during a regular or emergency change control board meeting, via e-mail, or by conference call.	☐
2.A	Assess associated feature, budget, schedule, and quality benefits, costs, issues, and risks for implementation, testing, and release. Defer consideration to a subsequent meeting, and obtain clarifying information if necessary.	☐
2.B	Prioritize or reject each request.	☐
2.C	Identify implementation, testing, and release integration deliverables, and estimated completion dates for each request.	☐
3.	Plan, implement, test, and integrate the change or fix, noting new costs, benefits, issues, or risks.	☐
4.	Present implementation, testing, and release integration results and deliverables for final approval.	☐
4.A	Assess outstanding feature, budget, schedule, and quality costs, benefits, issues, and risks.	☐
4.B	Weigh the benefits of including the change against the costs, issues, and risks.	☐
4.C	Approve or reject inclusion of the change in the appropriate release.	☐
5.	If inclusion is approved, check new or changed system components, project documents, and other deliverables into configuration management.	☐

PROCESS 12   A CHANGE MANAGEMENT PROCESS

we find ourselves to the planned end of the project, the fewer changes we can get away with making without putting at risk existing features, the budget and schedule, and perhaps quality. Therefore, at the end of the project, this process becomes more critical.

Conversely, the earlier in the project we are, the less is at stake for each change. Or, to put it another way, the earlier we are in the project, the more one or more of the four elements of the project—features, budget, schedule, and quality—are up for debate. On the one hand, if the requirements aren't locked down, is a requirement that comes up today that we hadn't heard about yesterday a *change* in any real sense? On the other hand, if most of the features have been implemented using a particular system architecture, a proposal to change to a new design is certainly likely to have far-ranging implications for at least the schedule and budget, and quite possibly for features and quality, too.

So, the right change management process depends on project timing. If the change management process starts at day one, it might be unnecessary overhead. If the process doesn't start until the project has already spun out of control, it might be too late to help. The project management team should decide when to institute change management and how formal—and cautious—to make it over time. Exercising the right degree of change management at the right time in the project is key.

In the case study, we'll focus on that period of time in the project when a formal, cautious change management process is the most critical. Once a change in any element of the project is likely to have significant effects on the other elements, the entire project team must consider each proposed change very carefully.

JAMAL MAKES A CASE—AND ACCOMMODATES

Jamal Brown, test manager at Software Cafeteria, took most of the Christmas holiday week off. However, he did log in from time to time to read bug reports, occasionally adjusting the suggested priority up or down after conferring with the submitter. He also updated his test tracking information as part of a daily conference call with the testers who were working over the holiday.

In addition, he spent time going through the latest set of change requests for Sumatra. These were stored in the same database used to track bugs but were marked as change requests. Of course, sometimes a change request became a bug—and vice versa—but from a change management point of view, the change control board didn't distinguish much between them. All new change requests and bug reports—at least those lodged against Sumatra—came before the Sumatra change control board three times a week for consideration.

Step #	Step	Done?
1.	Gather requested changes and bug fixes proposed for inclusion in the current, a future, or an emergency system release.	✔

Most changes seemed pretty minor, like a new help screen. Some were significant, like a wizard to walk a user through creating an account in a document management system from within SpeedyWriter. Hmm, Jamal thought, sounds as if there might be some hefty compatibility testing implication in that, given the different document management systems we support.

One proposed change was simultaneously seductively cool, intellectually challenging, and downright scary. Muhammad Ajami, in the Fortune 1000 and Government Sales group, had proposed that Software Cafeteria begin acting as an Application Service Provider (ASP). He said that some of his clients, fed up with the high cost of ownership and the low reliability of PC-based systems, were looking to go beyond just thin clients like browsers and information appliances to drive down the costs and drive up reliability. These clients were asking that they be able to outsource the ongoing server-side requirements, too. Rather than operating the large server farm that the OfficeArrow suite required in their environments, they wanted to purchase the service from an Application Service Provider. Muhammad proposed that Software Cafeteria grab the opportunity, starting with Sumatra.

Can't say Muhammad doesn't know the meaning of the cliche "Think outside the box," Jamal thought. It could be a fascinating opportunity, as well as a unique one. Jamal didn't know of any Application Service Providers who offered office suites as the application. That could be because no one had thought of it, Jamal mused, or it could be because it's a terrible idea. Or maybe it's not a terrible idea, just a terribly hard thing to pull off.

Jamal decided to prepare an informal risk analysis to bring to the change control board meeting. As he created it, he focused on the quality risks but also included other risks he could see. As he built this analysis, he became more concerned and decided to distribute the risk analysis document both before and in the change control board meeting. Since that would possibly be seen as sandbagging Muhammad, he decided to e-mail it to him first.

Hi, Muhammad—

I hope you're enjoying the week off. I've done a little work this week, nothing serious, but some of it included looking at the new change requests.

I have to say, I was quite impressed and intrigued by your proposal that we get into the ASP business, starting with Sumatra. However, as I did some risk analysis, I came up with a number of concerns in the area of testing. Since I intend to make these concerns public during the change control board meeting on Monday, I wanted to let you see them first so you don't feel blindsided. Please refer to the attached document for the details.

I will also be sending this document via e-mail Monday morning
prior to the meeting. Should you find any inaccuracies or want to
discuss this document between now and then, please feel free to
give me a call at home, (830) 438-4830, or send me an e-mail.

Regards,

Jamal

On Monday morning, Muhammad hadn't responded, so Jamal e-mailed the document
out to the Change Control Board (CCB) members. The board included John Albertson,
vice president of Engineering Services; Harold Jones, vice president of System Engineering; Jenny Kaufman, manager of New Release Development; Kate Hernandez,
manager of SpeedyWriter Product Marketing; Keith Lee, manager of System Operation
and Administration; Cosimo Negraev, manager of Customer Support; and Yasuhiro
Kanagawa, manager of Release Engineering, along with any interested representa-
tives from the sales team. He also included Rajesh Gupta, the Software Cafeteria's
CEO, who would be at the meeting to address the question of whether too many bugs
were being deferred.

The meeting started on time at 2:00 PM. Kate, as the sponsor of the Sumatra project,
chaired the meeting. The usual agenda was to review new bug reports, then new change
requests, and finally any updates on implementation of fixes or change requests.

Quite a backlog of new bug reports had built up over the last week. Since it was the
first Monday that people were back from the holiday, not everyone had reviewed every bug report. In addition to the "What is that bug report about I haven't read it yet"
questions, there was also a fair amount of circular debate about whether to fix or defer certain issues. Seeing the meeting starting to chase its own tail, Kate intervened.

"Look," she said, "I understand that everyone is busy, but we only get busier if we
have to hash over the same bugs and change requests two or three times because no
one did their homework. Let me go over the three ground rules of the CCB again,
okay? First, everyone comes to the meeting prepared. These meetings take too long if
extensive question-and-answer sessions are required for each bug and change request. If they take too long, people will stop attending, and then we ship a buggy
product. Remember SpeedyWriter 2.7? Second, we spend at most five minutes of discussion per bug or change request. I'm trying to keep these meetings to an hour or
less—we're going to go over that today already because of all the bugs and change requests—but that can only happen if we don't rat-hole on any one topic. If a few people want to talk longer than five minutes about any given bug or change to make a
decision, then we'll defer considering that bug or change to a separate meeting. Fi-

nally, remember that we try to make an implement or reject decision once, not two or three times, and we try to make that decision in the first meeting after the bug or change request is submitted. We don't have time or energy on this project for analysis paralysis, long delays in considering requests, or Hamlet-like debates. Time is stripping away options from us as we sit here, so let's make decisions while we still have choices."

Rajesh, who had been sitting back and letting Kate take control of the rowdy crowd, asked, with a smile on his face, "Hamlet?"

"To fix or not to fix, that is the question, whether 'tis nobler to suffer the slings and arrows of angry customers or to..." Kate let her voice trail off.

"Gotcha," Rajesh said.

"So," Kate concluded, "when we meet next it'll be a New Year, right? I'd like everyone's New Year's resolutions to include getting back to the crisp, tight CCB meetings we were having before the holiday season set in. For the rest of this meeting, I'll ask for a show of hands of everyone who's read a bug report or change request before we discuss it, and if the show of hands isn't unanimous, we'll table that item until Friday."

And thus scolded, the Change Control Board settled into a more efficient pace. Finally, they reach change request 72, the ASP change request. "Has everyone read the change request?" Kate asked.

All hands went up. That was not a coincidence, because Jamal had sent a voice mail message, return receipt requested, asking everyone to read their e-mail. When he hadn't gotten a return receipt from Muhammad, he called Muhammad, who admitted that he had read Jamal's e-mail. While Muhammad wasn't too happy about it, he did agree that the points needed to be presented and considered.

"Okay," Kate said, "I understand there was a little, uh, attention given to this matter up front by our intrepid test manager. I talked to Jenny, and while she doesn't think the implementation effort is too bad, she tends to agree with Jamal's points about the risks."

Keith Lee jumped in and added, "Yasuhiro, Cosimo, and I talked about Jamal's analysis over lunch, and we agree, too."

"All right, all right, let's slow down a bit," Kate said. "Muhammad, per the agenda, you, the submitter, get to present the request and speak in favor first. Usually, we'd go around the room asking for input, but I get the feeling that Jamal is the honorary spokesman for the opposition."

"Well," Jamal fidgeted, "I'm not exactly *opposed*, I'm just *concerned* . . ."

"Of course you're concerned, you're a test manager; don't we pay you to worry?" Kate asked sardonically.

"More than usual on this," Jamal said with a laugh.

"I thought I got to go first," Muhammad asked, somewhat peeved.

"Sorry, you're right, please do so."

"Okay, so I have been talking to a number of current Fortune 1000 and government clients about Sumatra. They really like the concept, but they're worried about total costs of ownership. One of the reasons they like the OfficeArrow suite is that it gets them out of the business of installing applications on everyone's desktop, which is a nightmare in a huge company. And they like the idea of a document management system. That's been a major impediment—especially with big law firms—for a while now. But what they don't like is the thought of having to pay for, support, and maintain a complex server configuration. It's rough enough on some of our clients to actually get the three-tier server configuration set up. Now we're talking about yet more stuff. I think we're going to lose out on some sales.

"That's when it occurred to me that we could provide this as an ASP. Instead of their maintaining and supporting the servers, we create a centralized server farm and leverage that across a bunch of clients. We'll have the technical expertise in-house, which means they won't need to. It'll be a unique selling point. I've tapped some of my potential clients, and my estimate is that we're looking at easily $1 million in additional revenue in the first year just based on people who are already interested. If it's not technically difficult to do—which it sounds from Jenny as if it's not—I say we give it a shot," he concluded.

Kate nodded, then turned to Jamal. "Jamal?"

"All right," Jamal said, "let me start out by saying I really do like Muhammad's idea. I have absolutely no desire to be 'Doctor No' in these meetings, and I think I have a track record of approaching change requests with an open mind. However, I think this is a good idea whose time has not yet come.

"I sent this document to each of you this morning," Jamal said, starting to pass out paper copies, "so I suspect you're familiar with the contents. It's a risk and impact analysis I did after reading and thinking about Muhammad's proposal. I classified various issues into quality risk categories—the same categories we used on the initial quality risk analysis using Failure Mode and Effect Analysis—and then I ranked each one using gut feel and other precise scientific instruments." He smiled. "The rankings are 'very high,' 'high,' 'medium,' 'low,' and 'very low.' I won't bother you with the mediums and below—you can read my analysis if you want to get the details—but let me briefly outline my top five concerns.

"First, in the area of operations and maintenance, the kinds of problems that could endanger continuing operations, I consider the risks very high. We would have to build, test, and support a sophisticated network operations and data center. I've worked at an Internet Service Provider before, and I can tell you this is no cakewalk technically." Keith nodded emphatically as Jamal continued. "So, in terms of testing implications, we would need a testing environment that mimicked—at least closely—the operational environment, which would be expensive and logistically challenging for the test team and for operations. In terms of business implications, we would have high initial and ongoing operation costs, including hardware, software, networking connectivity, and staff. You could easily spend a million dollars a year just keeping this data center up and running.

"Second, in the area of compatibility, the kind of failures that would involve particular hardware, operating system, browser, and server problems, I consider the risks and impacts in this area very high. For Fortune 1000 companies or government agencies, we're talking about storing huge amounts of data for all those documents. Network Attached Storage can run from $25,000 to $250,000 per configuration, and Storage Appliance Networks start at $1 million. So, we're looking at a very expensive test environment and a very experience operational environment.

"Third, in the area of security and privacy, I think we face very high risks. Customers will reasonably expect that their documents never be accessible by other customers. For testing, this means significant increases in these test scenarios. Business-wise, we have serious legal exposure in the event of any incidents in these areas.

"Fourth, an unknown degree of risk exists in the area of competitive inferiority. I can only assume that customers would measure us against other ASPs in different market spaces, but the implications of that are unclear at this point.

"Fifth, in the area of data quality—problems with processing, storing, or retrieving data—I think we face potentially high risks and impacts. Our ASP customers would reasonably expect that we be able to store their data securely, including handling disaster recovery and restoring files after accidental loss. From a testing perspective, this isn't too bad; we just expand the current test scenarios to address various ASP situations. However, the business implications—especially the legal exposure if customer data is lost—are scary.

"Now, I know I said I'd pick the top five, but let me just mention performance, reliability, availability, and stability. Our customers would have understandably high expectations in these areas, wouldn't they? Well, doing a performance test for a large data-center environment would require not just a large data-center-like test environment, but also a lot more tool licenses than I have right now. Also, I'm not sure I can do an MTBF test by March."

"'MTBF?'" Muhammad asked.

"Sorry, 'mean time between failure,'" Jamal replied. "It's a statistically accurate measure, to some level of confidence, of how often the system will go down. Kind of like the 'five nines' ad campaign not too long ago."

There was a silence for a moment. People looked around the room.

"That was a masterful presentation," Rajesh acknowledged. "You seem to be implying, though, that we'd have to build two data centers, basically, one for operations, one for testing."

"Yes, we would," Jamal replied.

"Why is that?" Rajesh asked.

"Because at some point we'd need to upgrade the software in the operations data center, either with new versions of OfficeArrow software or with other components. We'd need to test that new configuration carefully before we went live with it, since availability would be such an important issue."

"I agree, but," Rajesh persisted, "why not use a smaller model configuration?"

"That works fine for testing most functionality," Jamal admitted. "However, bugs in reliability, performance, data quality, and compatibility don't tend to show up the same way—if at all—in stripped-down environments. Let me give you an example. Suppose I run a performance test against a stripped-down server configuration and find that performance degrades unacceptably at 100 users. Now, if the operational environment has five times the CPU power, five times the disk throughput, and five times the memory space, will performance of the operational environment degrade at 500 users, 2,500 users, or 12,500 users?"

Rajesh laughed and replied, "Why, it's been years since I could even pretend to answer such a question, but I know I have smart technical people on my staff who can, right?" He looked around.

"Well," Jenny put in reluctantly, "we can build dynamic statistical simulation models for system performance. We have done that, in fact, for previous releases. When we cross-checked the models against testing in identically configured environments, we could get them pretty close to reality. Those models scaled up to a point, but we never really pushed it. The trick with these simulations is that you have to know where all the choke points and bottlenecks are, be able to anticipate knees in the performance curve, be able to pick the right statistical distributions—the probability density formulas—for each resource . . ." Her voice trailed off as her mind got wrapped up in the complexity of the problem for a moment. "Anyway, there are a lot of details, and if you lose track of any of them, forget about any of them, or get any of them significantly wrong in your model, you get garbage. The only way to check the model is with testing in the real environment."

"But you could," Rajesh insisted, "if you were really, really careful, and really, really smart, build a model that checked out against a stripped-down version and allowed you to predict performance and the like in the data center, right?"

Jamal jumped back in, "Yes, Rajesh, that is of course possible. Aerospace and defense companies do this all the time. There's a lot of modeling and simulation, testing of stripped-down or mocked-up configurations, that goes on when you're talking about a weapons system or an airplane. But keep in mind the missile defense system tests that we read about from time to time or see on the news. Each of those tests is very, very expensive, about a hundred million dollars. I'd bet that a lot of careful simulation and modeling happens before a single missile test occurs. But still some fail. When you're talking about a complex system in a dynamic and unpredictable environment, unforeseen outcomes happen."

Jenny nodded. "Jamal is right. There's no way, short of extensive testing, to know for sure what's going to happen in a complex data center."

"Well, if you can't get it right in a simulation, what makes you think you can get the tests right? Aren't tests just a model for how users will use the system?" Rajesh retorted.

"You're absolutely right, Rajesh, but the choice is not either/or, it's both or just one. We would use the simulation—along with static models like spreadsheets—in both cases," Jamal replied. "However, without testing, we'd have no way of checking our simulation until we went live. With high-availability requirements such as those facing an ASP, we'd be taking a 'bet the company' risk that we had those models right with no confirmation beforehand. We're good, Rajesh," Jamal concluded, "but we're not that good. It's a bet you'd lose, sooner or later. It's quality roulette."

Rajesh looked around the room. "Jenny, I guess you concur? Kate? Keith? Yasuhiro? Everyone?"

Nods all around.

"Okay," Rajesh said, leaning back and wrapping his hands behind his head as he dropped his bombshell, "the reason I pushed this so hard was that I sat in on some of those calls with Muhammad, and I've talked to some of those clients. This is hot. I've also talked to the board of directors and some of the venture capitalists. They are really hot about this, though the VCs—no surprise—aren't hot to spend a lot of money up front. They see Software Cafeteria becoming an office suite Application Service Provider as the next logical step." Rajesh looked around the room slowly, meeting each person's gaze. "So do I."

Jamal leaned back in his chair. Uh-oh, he thought, I came out foursquare against the big guy's pet project. I guess now I find out whether he really meant that bit he said about "wanting our unvarnished opinions" back at the project kick-off meeting.

"But I know I have smart technical people on my staff, and my smart technical people are worried—including you, Jamal," Rajesh said, giving Jamal a look of support and respect. "I rely on the kind of frank and diligent analysis you prepared on this matter, and I think your work sets a standard for everyone on the management team. I'm not dismissing anyone's concerns, or the complexity of the job. Nevertheless, I am laying out a strategic direction for the company. Maybe this isn't the right venue, and I'm probably in for a scolding about the agenda and ground rules from Kate."

Kate, who had been watching the whole exchange in rapt attention, started slightly as she heard her name. "Oh, no, not at all, I'm riveted. I think we can allow the time for this discussion."

"Well, I'm almost done," Rajesh said. "Here's what I propose. Muhammad and I have identified two very hot prospects for this service. Two months after we release Sumatra, I'd like to go live with a beta version of a SpeedyWriter ASP in a small but functional data center. We'll be up front with our customers that we're learning about how to do this well, so there might be hiccups, but we won't lose any data. Harold and John, I'd like you to get the appropriate people in your organizations to work on a plan for how we make this happen." Harold and John both nodded. "We can do that, right?"

"If we're careful," Jenny said, "I think we can make that happen."

"Jamal?"

"Yes," Jamal replied, "I'd need to talk to my team to make sure, but that sounds within the realm of possibility."

"Then we have a plan," Rajesh concluded grandly. "Back to you, Kate."

Step #	Step	Done?
2.	Review proposed requests during a regular or emergency change control board meeting, via e-mail, or by conference call.	☑
2.A	Assess associated feature, budget, schedule, and quality benefits, costs, issues, and risks for implementation, testing, and release. Defer consideration to a subsequent meeting, and obtain clarifying information if necessary.	☑
2.B	Prioritize or reject each request.	☑
2.C	Identify implementation, testing, and release integration deliverables, and estimated completion dates.	☑

The meeting continued, moving on to finalize the implementation, testing, and integration of changes and bug fixes approved previously. In reference to one change, Jamal said with a smile, "I want to remind everyone, after my obstructionist speech a little while ago, that I was all in favor of this change, and am happy to report that it passed the functionality and data quality tests with flying colors."

Step #	Step	Done?
3.	Plan, implement, test, and integrate the change or fix, noting new costs, benefits, issues, or risks.	☑
4.	Present implementation, testing, and release integration results and deliverables for final approval.	☑

Step #	Step	Done?
4.A	Assess outstanding feature, budget, schedule, and quality costs, benefits, issues, and risks.	☑
4.B	Weigh the benefits of including the change against the costs, issues, and risks.	☑
4.C	Approve or reject inclusion of the change in the appropriate release.	☑
5.	If inclusion is approved, check new or changed system components, project documents, and other deliverables into configuration management.	☑

Finally, Rajesh and Cosimo reviewed the bugs they had identified as inappropriately deferred during their review. About a dozen bugs were reopened.

"Jamal," Rajesh said when he had finished the review, "thanks for encouraging me to take a look at these bugs. A dozen isn't a big number, but some of these were certainly concerning bugs."

"Glad to help, Rajesh," Jamal replied.

"On the whole," Rajesh concluded, "out of the thousand or so bugs identified to date, I think we're doing a stellar job of dealing with the dynamics of this project. I can see how this meeting and this change management process is a big part of that. I encourage you all to keep it up."

AN INTERCONNECTED PROCESS

Okay, you might be thinking, I understand that the change management process is critical, but is it a *testing process*? It's true that unlike the other 11 processes in this book, the change management process is primarily a project management team process. In other words, in the change management process, the test team is just one participant in the process. The test team is not the primary, or the most active, participant.

However, the change management process strongly affects the test team, together with the development team and the release engineering team. The change management process influences all the other processes during test execution. The test release process delivers builds with new and fixed content. The test execution process tests the new and fixed content. The bug reporting process identifies specific problems in the changes or fixes. Finally, the results reporting process delivers information to the change control board so the members can decide whether to approve or reject the change or fix. Without effective change management, all these processes work less effectively and less efficiently.

Indeed, in some circumstances, the change management process can push the test team back into earlier processes associated with test preparation. In the case study, Jamal performs a quality risk analysis as part of preparing for the meeting. As a result of the change being approved for a near-term release, Jamal will now revisit the estimation and planning processes for the Application Service Provider offering of SpeedyWriter. In order to test this offering, the test team will probably have to design and implement new tests. Should special skills or more people be required to run these tests, Jamal may need to retain full-time employees or contractors. In fact, a wholesale testing process is probably required for this Application Service Provider effort. In other words, the Application Service Provider release of Sumatra will be its own project, and the testing of that release a subproject within the project.

So, the test team's participation in the change management process is highly visible, especially when a test manager like Jamal brings credible, specific information to bear on the topic of quality risks associated with a change. This process has an important effect on the test team's ability to add value to the project, and that effect becomes more pronounced the more changes there are to manage. Finally, the consequences of failure in this process have a profound effect on test team success. If we don't know what the project is about at a late stage in the project, then we will certainly do the wrong things in testing. Conversely, when a test manager like Jamal takes the reins, the test team's participation in the process enables project success.[4]

RECOGNIZE A GOOD CHANGE MANAGEMENT PROCESS

The change management process is hard to execute. However, a good change management process will help the project team make the right choices.

---

4. This point made, it's fair to say that this chapter represents a test-centric view of change management. The broader project-management perspective is something enlightened test professionals should also consider, since that is part of understanding the project context. A good source for that perspective is Steve McConnell's book *Software Project Survival Guide*, especially Chapter 6.

SELECT THE RIGHT CHANGES IN THE RIGHT ORDER

Time goes by—in life and on projects. Each day that we work on a project, we see the inexorable progress of the calendar toward the scheduled project end date. Each day that we work on a project, we unavoidably deplete the project budget. With less time and money, we face increased risks of project failure if the project team focuses on the wrong things. So, the most critical question is, Are we doing the right things right now to guide the project toward the most successful possible conclusion? In the context of change management, are we making the right changes, are we course correcting in the right direction, are we expending our precious, irreplaceable project resources in the right order?

On many projects I've worked on, there's an ongoing cycle during test execution periods. We make changes to the definition of the project in response to new information about features, budget, schedule, or quality. We test those changes, which generates more information, particularly about quality. That cycle continues until the project management team decides that the test phase exit criteria are met. In the final test phase, often system or acceptance test, this decision also includes a decision about releasing or deploying the system. This is an exquisite balancing act. Do the risks associated with delaying release or deployment for another fix, enhance, and test cycle exceed the risks associated with shipping with the known bugs and without any pending enhancements or uncompleted features?[5]

Because the flow of time will take options away from us, decisiveness is of the essence. During an early revision of this chapter, Harvey Deutsch, a test management colleague of mine, put it this way: "Don't develop what you are not going to test. Don't test what you are not going to release. [Cut] early and often." In other words, across the entire context of the project, is what the project team is working on *right now* the most important set of tasks to enable ultimate project success? A cross-functional change control board, guided by the test results, is able to advise the organization's executives and senior managers effectively on this question.

---

5. In *I Am a Bug!* Robert Sabourin wrote, regarding the issue of remaining bugs considered by a change control board, "We know we are finished when the bugs that are left are the bugs we can live with at least for now!"

BALANCE CONSIDERATIONS OF FEATURES, SCHEDULE, BUDGET, AND QUALITY

A cross-functional team is ideal for dealing with this question because the question, ultimately, spans multiple areas of responsibility and must consider multiple pertinent factors. These include

- The logistics, dependencies, and tasks associated with implementation, testing, and release integration
- The opportunities and risks, costs and benefits, of the proposed change or bug fix
- The capabilities and limitations of the team, in terms of both available effort and skills
- Last but not least, critical business and technical considerations, including system architecture, future requirements, and the long-term direction of the system, the project team, and the organization

All too often in change control board meetings, one question dominates the discussion of bug fixes. Heated arguments break out over whether a particular bug is properly classified as severity 1 or severity 2. The usual subtext of the discussion was that only severity 1 bugs mattered. But compared with the other factors, especially strategic business considerations, such discussions are beside the point. The same applies to discussions about whether to implement a proposed change.

When deciding whether or not to fix a bug or to implement a change, project teams should consider how the associated failure modes or the lack of the change would affect the customers and users, because they are the ultimate arbiters of quality. Conversely, project teams must also consider how risks associated with making the change or fix play out not just in terms of quality, but in terms of the overall project context. In the case study, Jamal's presentation of risk was primarily one of technical and logistical issues related to the risk of implementing the change. Ultimately, though, the strategic direction of the company, the highest level of business consideration, made it the right business decision to proceed. However, Rajesh's plan for moving forward in this strategic direction was tempered, and the risk inherent in it mitigated, by taking into account Jamal's concerns.

This gets to a key lesson implicit in the case study: The process must give all stakeholders and participants a voice. Some unfortunate projects have a change-management-by-temper-tantrum process. One or two project management figures make emotional pronouncements about how important the proposed change or bug fix is, and ignore as obstructionist—or worse—the legitimate concerns and risks described by everyone else.

Certainly senior and executive management have the right—in some cases the duty—to overrule the change control board. Senior managers and executives see the bigger picture, which is their role. However, they are well advised to work for ways to move forward that mitigate, rather than ignore, realistic concerns and risks. To do otherwise is to deny the organization the benefit of the talented individual contributors and line managers in the project team. This is tantamount to driving at night with the headlights of the car turned off.

While senior and executive managers see the big picture, it's important that all participants, even the individual contributors, have some sense of that bigger picture, the organizational and strategic context in which the current project fits. If we have no common agenda across the change control board, the board is nothing more than a political body for hashing out the conflicting desires and preferences of various contending constituencies. People are more likely to hold similar perceptions of the overall level of risk—the assessment of the importance of each risk—and the overall benefits—the reasons for implementing the change or bug fix—when they share a vision of where the system and the organization are going. In other words, a good change management process, and the participants in that process, operate and ground their decisions and advice in the context of a shared vision of the future.

HANDLE CHALLENGES

A number of challenges exist in the change management process, many of which are generic to the testing process as a whole. For the moment, let's look at those that are specific to change management.

THE COMPLEX NATURE OF CHANGE EFFECTS

As not all changes and bug fixes are equal in the level of risk they impose on each of the four project elements, so are not all changes and bug fixes equal in terms of their impact on the various teams. A change that involves only one line of code might require the diligent programmer to spend hours or even days researching the change to make sure nothing will break. A change that requires significant effort by the programmer might be trivial to test and to support in the operational environment, but difficult and time-consuming for the release engineering team to integrate into the build and for the technical writers to document. Or any permutation of those. Even with a coarse change-estimation granularity, say, only classifying efforts as small, medium, or large in each team and then across these five teams—development, testing, operations, release engineering, and technical publications—there are 243 different possible effort combinations.

As an example, on the Internet appliance project I've referred to a number of times, we developed a set of manual test cases that, among other things, tested the workflows through the screens. The screens, in turn, were implemented via HTML in a browser, which was a smart architecture for the client. Some of the issues we identified through these tests, along with field-based usability tests, concerned clunkiness and inelegance in the interface. So, one weekend, the user interface engineers came in and totally reworked the user interface. On Monday morning, we received a new test release—and it had a totally different user interface. When I explained to the user interface engineers that their changes—while certainly good—would cause us to have to reengineer many of our tests, they were incredulous. "Why?" one engineer asked. "They're just links."

In general, the fallacious assumption underlying some change management regimes is that changes that have a small effect on one of the involved teams will likewise have a small effect on all others. In my experience, the effect on the development organization is usually used as the benchmark. If a change requires a significant effort by the programmer or engineer to implement, then management will tend to support a correspondingly large effort to test that change. If the implementation effort was small, though, management may react with skepticism when the test team reports a large schedule or budgetary increase as the testing effect of the change.

However, isn't this assumption of a linear relationship between the effort required by programmers and the effort required by the rest of the team just our old false friend the tester-to-developer ratio, mentioned in Chapter 3? If we assume that y person-hours of testing effort is implied by an effort of x person-hours of programming effort, and we calculate y as follows:

$$y = Rx$$

where R is a fixed constant like the following:

$$\frac{2 testers}{5 developers}$$

then we are right back into using tester-to-developer ratios as an estimation technique. As I mentioned in the section Using Rules of Thumb for Rough Estimation, in

Chapter 3, such ratios can be useful to cross-check our work-breakdown-structure estimates, but not as a primary technique.

Actually, in this situation such ratios are even less useful. Why? Well, in a large project the law of averages will balance out the extremes. When we are talking about a small change or bug fix, the difference in scale between the test effort and the programming effort is often significant.

This problem reemphasizes the need for cross-functional involvement and participation in the change management process as well as the steps of the process that provide for realistic estimation of change impact across all the teams. A good change management process should provide for careful consideration of the effects on each team before a decision is made.

THE RIPPLE EFFECTS OF CHANGE

Beyond the test case reengineering example given earlier, another significant source of this nonlinear relationship between testing and programming effort arises from the rippling of change effects across the system. In some cases, the change involves a component of the system that is central to everything else in the system.

Data and metadata in a central database often fall into this category. I mentioned in an earlier chapter a project where one development team claimed their component of the system was feature complete. However, they kept changing the schema of the master table that held the user information from one test release to the next. This affected testing as much as adding or removing features, since each field was associated with user interface changes and modifications to the workflows and transactions that affected the call-center agents. Also, since four of the other seven or so subsystems in the system used data from this database, the change rippled through to them.

This is a particular problem when, as in the previous example, the system under test is a *system of systems*. Now, changes and their nonlinear effects can ripple across organizational boundaries. In other words, one team of programmers may find the change easy to make in their subsystem, but other teams of programmers, the test team, and other participants find that their whole world is turned upside down by the change.

Again, this brings us back to the need for cross-functional involvement, though in this case the change management team may have a scope beyond the project and representation beyond the project team. For strategic, mission-critical, interlinked systems of systems, changes and bug fixes that could ripple across the entire system may need executive-level consideration.

BECOMING A ROADBLOCK—OR BECOMING PERCEIVED AS A ROADBLOCK

Holy crow, you might be thinking by now, what incredible overhead. Won't this change management process become a huge roadblock to any kind of progress? How can we fix bugs and make changes if we have to get approval from two or three levels of change control boards consisting of dozens of stakeholders all of whom may well have an interest in preserving the status quo and minimizing the level of work imposed on their already overtasked teams?

This is a legitimate concern and one for which there is no easy answer. Change management is not about preventing change, but rather about making sure that due consideration is given to each proposed change before we move forward with it. Any change has associated potential costs and risks, along with opportunities and benefits. So, how risk-averse and how cost-conscious is the organization?

An organization that is fundamentally risk-averse and cost-conscious will probably need and choose a more deliberate change management process. An organization that thinks more about opportunities than risks, and sees the costs associated with changes as bringing even larger benefits in capturing more market share, will be more likely to see a deliberate change management process as a roadblock. So, organizational context matters in determining the right level of formalism and tendency to reject or defer changes.

In the case study, Jamal focused on costs and risks. Rajesh Gupta focused on benefits and opportunities. However, Jamal brought Rajesh's attention to a change control board policy that resulted in over a dozen bugs being inappropriately deferred. In this case, Rajesh accepted Jamal's argument that the costs and risks were, in some cases, too high.

Change control board participants will, to some extent, disagree on the balance to be struck. From time to time, change control board participants will err to one side or the other of the organization's risk-aversion and cost-conscious comfort zones. Indeed, these situations are unavoidable in a cross-functional team. Trying to eliminate disagreements and deviations from perfect balance will probably result in analysis paralysis on the part of the change control board.

However, consistent errors or bias in one direction or the other—approving changes that are too risky or denying changes that are aligned with corporate goals—indicates a problem in the change control board. As mentioned earlier, a shared vision of the future is a key indicator of a good change control process. If change control board members don't have this shared vision or don't share the same vision as the executives, the change control board will become a roadblock.

It's possible that the change control board, all the executives, and all the individual contributors do indeed have a shared vision, yet the change control board is perceived as a roadblock. If the process is overly bureaucratic and formalized for the organizational culture—even if the prioritization, rejection, and acceptance criteria are perfectly aligned with the organization's needs—then people will probably perceive the board as overly likely to reject or defer a change or bug fix. After all, bureaucracies and formal processes have a reputation for being control rods that slow down the motion of an organization, whether for good or ill. We'll revisit this issue of formalization of processes in Chapter 17.

IMPLEMENT IMPROVEMENTS

I know that as a tester and a test manager, I have often felt that change was out of control. However, as I noted earlier, striking the right balance is important. How can we move the change control process toward better balance, yet preserve proper flexibility?

1. As objectively as possible, from the organizational standpoint, analyze the costs and benefits, the risks and opportunities inherent in the current change management process. There is a natural tendency from a test perspective to see primarily risks.[6] Indeed, from the perspective of the individual contributors, any given project is usually made easier by allowing as little change as possible—certainly from the outside of the project—once the project is underway. However, that is seldom, if ever, the right course of action.

2. If the costs and risks outweigh the benefits and opportunities, then consider ways in which the process can change to reduce the costs and risks while treading as lightly as possible on the benefits and opportunities. Again, the usual tendency is to react strongly against unmanaged or undermanaged changes in a project, but introducing a win-lose dynamic between those whose interests are aligned with looser change management and those whose interests are aligned with tighter change management has nothing to do with serving the greater good.

3. If a positive, proactive business case exists to improve the process, ask yourself, as a test manager or test professional, are you the right person to cham-

---

6. For a technique to gather cost and risk data related to changes in the project, see Chapter 6 of *Managing the Testing Process, Second Edition*.

pion that change? Further, is now the right time to make the change? If the answer to the first question is no, then finding the right person—the one most likely to succeed at effecting valuable change—and convincing her to take up the cause is much more likely to work than doing so yourself. If now is not the right time—e.g., it's two weeks from the project end date and everything should be locked down now—then it's better to wait than to initiate a potentially divisive and emotional debate that is extraneous to the business priorities at hand.

4. Consider the politics. All process change is political. There are constituencies for change and constituencies for the status quo. In the case of change management, the differences can be stark, and the more dysfunctional the current change management process, the more strongly it serves one constituency over another. How will you overcome the objections of the status quo constituencies?

This last point brings us back to the general situation, the bigger picture. Process improvement in general must be attached to this bigger picture, and that becomes more important the more contextual and collaborative the process is. The testing process and many of its constituent processes are quite contextual and collaborative. In the next chapter, let's return to the big picture to look at how we can recognize a good testing process, the challenges to achieving such a process, and smart ways to implement improvements in the testing process.

17

RETURN TO THE BIG PICTURE: PERFECT THE TESTING PROCESS

In the first chapter, we looked at the overall testing process, the big picture. In subsequent chapters, we examined each constituent critical process. In this final chapter, let's turn our attention back to the overall testing process. Since we haven't looked at it for a while, let me reproduce that process from Chapter 1, as shown in Process 1.

How can we recognize a good testing process? How can we handle the challenges? How can we move from where our process currently operates to a better way of doing things?

RECOGNIZE A GOOD TEST PROCESS

Throughout this book, we've looked at how test teams and project teams work when they follow good test processes, as well as what they achieve and how they benefit. What can we say about teams that follow a good overall test process?

PROVIDE VALUABLE, ECONOMICAL SERVICES

Many stakeholders, including the senior and executive management team, are uninterested in the test process itself—except as it affects the costs and benefits associated with testing. From an outside perspective, the testing team receives resources, uses those resources to generate valuable information, and then transmits that information in timely, accurate, and credible ways, tailored to the various audiences' needs. From

Step #	Step	Done?
1.	Plan: Understand the testing effort.	☐
1.A	Understand the operational (system, project, and process) context and the organizational context in which the testing will be performed.	☐
1.B	Define and prioritize the risks to system quality, and obtain stakeholder consensus on the extent of testing to mitigate these risks.	☐
1.C	Estimate and obtain management support for the time, resources, and budget required to perform the testing agreed upon in step 1.B.	☐
1.D	Develop a plan for the tasks, dependencies, and participants required to mitigate the risks to system quality, and obtain stakeholder support for this plan.	☐
2.	Prepare: Assemble the people and tests.	☐
2.A	Through staffing and training, build a team of test professionals with the appropriate skills, attitudes, and motivation.	☐
2.B	Design, develop, acquire, and verify the test system that the test team uses to assess the quality of the system under test.	☐
3.	Perform: Do the testing and gather the results.	☐
3.A	Acquire and install a test release consisting of some or all of the components in the system under test.	☐
3.B	Assign, track, and manage the set of test cases to be run against each test release.	☐
4.	Perfect: Guide adaptation and improvement.	☐
4.A	Document the bugs found during test execution.	☐
4.B	Communicate test results to key stakeholders.	☐
4.C	Adjust to changes and refine the testing process.	☐

PROCESS 1   A TESTING PROCESS

the test team perspective, we provide these valuable, economical services through effective and efficient testing that meets the testing stakeholders' requirements.[1]

---

1. Robert Sabourin wrote an insightful article titled "At Your Service," originally published in *Software Testing and Quality Engineering* magazine, Volume 3, Issue 3 (May/June 2001), now found at www.stickyminds.com. In this article, Sabourin discusses the idea of testing and other software engineering teams as service organizations.

Effectiveness means producing a desirable and valuable result. Throughout the book, I've stressed four ways testers produce desirable and valuable results.

1. We find bugs that get fixed—or even prevent bugs.
2. We find bugs that don't get fixed—but are known.
3. We run tests that mitigate (potentially expensive) risks.
4. We help guide the project with timely, accurate, and credible information.

Effectiveness also means that the stakeholders in testing and quality are satisfied with the way in which we deliver these results. This follows from Juran's definition of quality: the presence of the satisfying and the absence of the dissatisfying.

Sometimes the change we need to make to be truly effective doesn't really affect what the testing process does, but rather how the testing process is perceived. Increasing stakeholder satisfaction with the testing process often involves making sure stakeholders have realistic expectations. Using persuasion and political skills to mold expectations is another valuable service testers can provide.

Efficiency means not only producing a desired result, but doing so with the least possible expenditure of resources. Resources include not only money—such as salaries, tools, and host systems—but also time. Delays in the project incur what economists call *opportunity costs*. In mass-market systems, we lose out on the opportunity of selling the system to paying customers. For contract development, we lose out on the opportunity of working on the next profitable project. For internal IT projects, we lose out on the opportunity to benefit from the system.

PERVADE THE PROJECT

Successful testing processes don't involve a small number of people sequestered in a test lab at the end of the project. The test process consists of a complex, interconnected set of activities. Done well, the test process involves and interacts with a wide range of people throughout the entire course of the project. Successful test processes *pervade* the overall development or maintenance project, with the following implications.

- *Pervasive testing is concurrent.* The earlier in the project the test process starts, the more value the project gets from the test process. We prevent bugs by finding defects in requirements and design documents. We give a realistic assessment of the project plan, especially in terms of the time and resources allocated for testing. We focus and define our test efforts through careful planning and analysis. We develop solid, reusable test systems. We use these test systems to perform our testing carefully and deliberately.

- *Pervasive testing is collaborative.* The test team, following the test process, evaluates and assesses deliverables from other teams. Salespeople, marketing staff, business analysts, and users define product requirements. The development team designs and creates the system to be tested. The project and executive management team approves schedules, budgets, and staffing plans. Often, some group outside the test team builds the components into a testable system. For complex test environments, a network operations or system administration team might support the test group in installation, configuration, and support. The test process proceeds smoothly when these teams deliver on their commitments on schedule and as promised to the test team.

- *Pervasive testing is cross-functional.* People across the whole development or maintenance organization have a stake in the test process, and each team must participate in test tasks. Key stakeholders participate in the quality risk analysis effort. Customer support and operations staff help testers understand actual usage profiles. Developers perform adequate unit and component testing. The independent test team performs integration and system testing against the entire system, including all the hardware and software components. These components might come from various teams across the organization or even from other organizations. In some cases, marketing or business analysts manage beta, acceptance, or pilot testing.

- *Pervasive testing cross-pollinates testing and development activities.* Testers apply application domain skills to help sales, marketing, business analysts, and users define a better system. Testers apply technical skills to help developers produce a better design. Testers can suggest enhancements. Testers and developers share test system components such as stubs, harnesses, load generators, and automated GUI scripts. The test tools also make their way to the production and operations teams. Bug reports—with workarounds—get loaded into the knowledge database for customer support agents.

- *Pervasive testing communicates.* The results of the testing process are analyzed, summarized, and reported effectively by the test team to the various test stakeholders. Management uses test results as part of the management dashboard.

A number of factors enable pervasive testing. The stakeholders must have realistic expectations about what services the test team can provide, and must value those services. Because a pervasive test process is connected to a lot of other processes in the project, these connections must involve clearly defined roles, responsibilities, and handoffs. Finally, the overall organizational context must support and reinforce the testing process.

On one project with a small start-up company, I was brought in one month after the company was founded to set up a test group and process. I worked closely with marketing, engineering, and senior management to define the right process, targeted on specific quality risks within the budget and schedule framework they could support. Test toolsmiths worked with the developers to create load generation tools that allowed us to do effective stress testing. Test engineers worked with the performance engineering team to analyze, simulate, and test the server farm, helping to tune the performance for the right user load, based on sales projections we had from the marketing team. The lead test engineers and I participated in project management meetings, bringing a test dashboard that was a key measure of progress. In turn, management supported our efforts. Other individual contributors like programmers and release engineers worked closely with us to ensure smooth handoffs of deliverables. The test process was efficient and effective.

How did this happen? The credit goes to the entire project team, not just testers, but also every developer, manager, marketing analyst, and customer support agent. Everyone endeavored honestly to make testing a pervasive contributor to the project's success.

USE A MATURE PROCESS

A testing process that is pervasive often is—or is becoming—mature. By a mature process, I mean one that has these attributes.

1. *Effective*—The test team, equipped with skilled people and a good test system, consistently produces useful information.
2. *Efficient*—The test team carries out each task properly the first time, thus avoiding rework, and doesn't waste time on tasks that don't relate to what the team is there to do.
3. *Understood*—The testers understand what they're doing and what they're there to do, and likewise the testing and quality stakeholders understand what the test team is doing.
4. *Accepted*—The understandings of the testers and the stakeholders are mutually agreed to.
5. *Organized*—Each tester individually, the test team collectively, and the test team when working with other teams, work in an orderly fashion, with smooth handoffs.
6. *Optimizing*—Testers and others in the organization gather information that is used to improve the testing process.

These attributes are related and reinforce each other. We've spent a lot of time talking about these attributes in this book, especially the first five.

But optimizing is also important, especially in the long term. Even a mature process will lose maturity over time, because of progress. In software, hardware, and systems engineering, as in medicine, science, and other technologies, progress moves at an ever-increasing pace. We either keep up or fall behind.

To use a noncomputer example, the processes of making steel and aluminum enabled leaps in aerospace technology. The Wright brothers tested the first successful airplane by dragging it out to the hills of Kitty Hawk, starting the engine, and seeing what happened next. Would that test process have worked for the Concorde or the Boeing 777? Likewise, as the technologies we work with evolve, our tools, our techniques, and our processes as system testers must adapt and grow.

APPLY THE APPROPRIATE LEVEL OF FORMALITY AND STANDARDIZATION

To achieve process maturity, some organizations use formal process models and standards. Formality can entail creating a formal model of how the process works.

Standardization can entail following established industry standards for processes and documents. Examples include the Institute of Electrical and Electronics Engineers guidelines for test documents (IEEE Standard 829) and the Software Engineering Institute's Capability Maturity Model or the International Standards Organization's requirements for development process documentation.[2]

Standardization can also involve following industry-standard models to assess test process maturity, such as the following:

- Koomen and Pol's Test Process Improvement
- Gelperin and Hiyashi's Testability Maturity Model
- Burgess and Drabick's Testing Capability Maturity Model
- Burnstein, Carlson, and Suwannasart's Testing Maturity Model[3]

---

2. To learn more about these standards, see the *IEEE Software Engineering Standards Collection, 1997 Edition*, Paulk et al.'s *The Capability Maturity Model*, and Schmauch's *ISO 9000 for Software Developers*.
3. For more information on the Test Process Improvement technique, see Koomen and Pol's book *Test Process Improvement*. For a synopsis and comparison of these maturity models, see Drabick's article "Growth of Maturity in the Testing Process" at www.softtest.org/articles/rdrabick3.htm.

A Case Study in the Effects of Inconsistent Process Maturity on a Medical Software Team Merger, by Robert Sabourin, Principal Consultant, AmiBug, Inc.

At a Montreal-based medical software company, I built an effective, service-oriented Software Engineering Team (SET). The SET team offered integration testing, system testing, test analysis, trend analysis, configuration management, code metrics analysis, and formal inspection services. Our clients for these services were the software development projects. Members of the SET team spent time on many different projects; a team of about 10 professionals was working on as many as 20 different projects in a one-month period.

Our company acquired a smaller medical administrative software company. Management wanted to merge product lines and increase local market share. The business integration strategy was simple: The new development team would become a new project team sharing common services—including our SET team, among others.

The new team was proud of their software, which had been written by two key developers working directly with clients. Little documentation existed, the development process was not systematic, the method of testing was ad hoc at best, but they were successful. They used a tight, customer-oriented, code-fix-update process.

Even though the service-oriented SET team wanted happy internal clients from all client project teams using the service, it was difficult to introduce even the concept of test releases from this new team to an independent test team. Bug reporting was a political exercise.

I spent a lot of time trying to smooth the interface between the different functional teams—with limited success. In fact, the key developers on the new team would arbitrarily make changes and then act threatened by any semblance of change control management or systematic bug prioritization.

Meanwhile, other established projects, although far from perfect, had a rhythm and operated with similar levels of process maturity. Basic steps were understood. Code was designed. Code was implemented. Requirement specifications existed. Prioritization was organized. The basic interaction between teams was on friendly terms.

The SET team members did not want to be assigned to the new medical administrative software projects. They would be wasting too much time on phantom bugs, process problems, chaotic interactions with developers, and other bad experiences. Similarly, medical administrative software team members did not want to work with the service-oriented teams, saying they were only slowed down by processes that were neither necessary nor beneficial.

I decided not to use the SET team for the first major medical administrative project, but rather hired an external contractor to run a parallel testing effort. We didn't keep metrics. My only process rule was that we must be able to rebuild anything we ever shipped to a client. Other than that, we didn't even have source control in place.

The project ended and the product worked well enough to get started. However, it required a high degree of maintenance. Many bug fixes and patches had to be released over the first six months. By my normal standards, this project was a failure. The newly merged development team, however, saw this approach as being responsive to their clients. They were heroes who had saved the day every time they succeeded in creating a new fix or patch!

It took three years to fully integrate the product families and development approaches. Use of a shared service-oriented team had to be phased in progressively, one service at a time, and with special care that process maturity related to that service be consistent with other projects.

The moral of this case study? When using a service model, try to make sure all projects being served are operating with similar process maturity!

In some cases, formal process models, standard test strategies, and document templates make good building blocks for successful test projects. Rodger Drabick has created a highly formal model for the entire testing process, from the initial moment of involvement right through to post-project analysis and improvement. This model, the highest level of which is illustrated in Figure 17-1, uses Input-Process-Output diagrams to specify all "the essential elements of a formal test program on a medium-sized (greater than 20,000 source lines of code) or large (greater than 100,000 source lines of code) project." Drabick does not specify any particular documentation standard but does mention that the IEEE 829 standards are suitable.[4]

You can find another formal process for testing described in Rick Craig and Stephan Jaskiel's book *Systematic Software Testing*. Figure 17-2 shows a high-level diagram

---

4. You can find more information about Drabick's complete model in his book *Best Practices for Software Testing* and at www.softtest.org/sigs/material/rdrabick1.htm.

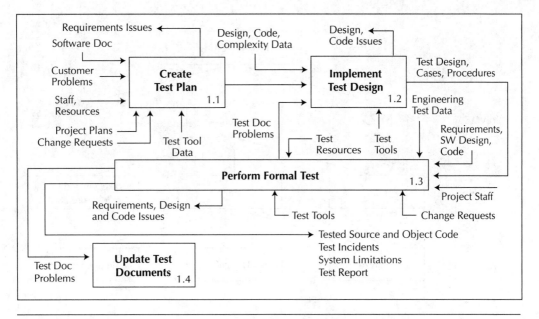

FIGURE 17-1 DRABICK'S LEVEL 1 INPUT-PROCESS-OUTPUT MODEL OF THE TESTING PROCESS (COPYRIGHT © 1995 BY RODGER DRABICK. USED WITH PERMISSION.)

of that process. Like Drabick's model, it starts from initial involvement and ends with postrelease analysis. Along the way, it decomposes testing into the following:

- Levels, typically unit test, integration test, system test, and acceptance Test (each represented as "Level j" in Figure 17-2)
- Phases within each level (e.g., plan, acquire, and measure)
- Activities performed in the phases (e.g., analyze, design, and implement)
- Tasks carried out by individuals to perform the activities

The process uses IEEE Standard 829 for test documentation.[5]

The use of formal process models in testing influences not only the way the testing is done and the way the testing is documented, but also the way the test results are communicated. Sometimes, we communicate our test results casually, discussing the

---

5. For more details, see Craig and Jaskiel's book *Systematic Software Testing*. Michael Schmidt's book *Implementing the IEEE Software Engineering Standards* outlines a complete software development and maintenance process following a large subset of the IEEE Standards.

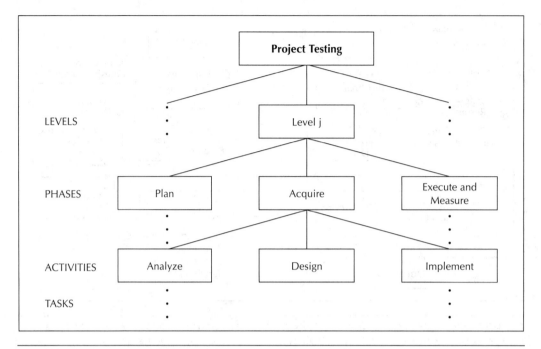

results with stakeholders and internal customers in e-mails and voice mails, on telephone or conference calls, during hallway conversations, and in project-related meetings. Other times, we communicate our results in a more structured fashion, using written accounts, quantitative analyses, graphs, tables, metrics, formal models, and structured documents. Instituting formality might cause the test team to communicate test results more frequently in a structured fashion.

Deciding to institute formality and standardization involves considering trade-offs. On the one hand, there are significant potential benefits. Formalizing and standardizing the testing process can help testers and test managers

- Reduce chaos and unpredictability in the test effort.
- Enable rapid, systematic training of new test team members, in some cases allowing the use of testing neophytes to perform work that would otherwise require a skilled engineer.
- Create and optimize reusable templates and test system components.
- Provide a clear basis for ongoing process improvement.

- Clarify the prerequisites, inputs, dependencies, and outputs for effective and efficient testing.
- Document legal evidence that testing has been done according to generally accepted practices.

In terms of capturing and communicating information, adoption of standards and formalization can

- Build a consistent repository of data across projects for estimating purposes.
- Create generally accepted formats for test results reporting that provide a common language across the entire project team and indeed across the organization.
- Reduce the risk that critical testing information will not be gathered.

Another benefit for some test groups is compliance. For some system development endeavors, an internal, customer, or government regulatory or other authoritative body decrees some style of documentation or process model that is nonnegotiable. The project team must comply to gain permission to release or deploy the system. For example, companies that sell medical systems in the United States must comply with the US federal government's Food and Drug Administration regulations. In some cases businesses that are purchasing systems or system components impose certain requirements on their suppliers that result in formalizing or standardizing the testing process. To give two examples, to bid on defense contracts for the US military, companies must achieve a level of maturity measured through the Capability Maturity Model (CMM), and many large companies purchasing Intel-based PCs insist on certification to Microsoft's standards. Finally, some of these situations are less a matter of compliance than of marketing advantage, such as offshore software companies that achieved ISO 9000 or CMM certification in order to give potential customers confidence in the quality of their work.

On the other hand, there are significant potential pitfalls associated with adopting standards and formal processes. For one thing, it can cost a lot of money to formalize or standardize extensively. Time spent discussing templates, producing formal models of test processes, researching and applying standards, haggling about the pace and approach to process change, and the like is time not spent testing. In some cases these investments can pay off over time, but in many organizations such overheads are simply intolerable within a single project. Lightweight techniques like checklists can help keep costs down.

In addition to the initial costs, overly rigid formalization or standards can reduce efficiency. People sometimes blindly follow processes and end up working in unproductive or even counterproductive ways. Testers can spend a lot of time filling in the blanks on a document template without asking themselves, How does documenting this information help us do better testing? There is the oft-repeated management fable where a son asks his mother why she always cuts off the end of a pork roast before cooking it. The mother says, "I don't know; that's the way Grandma taught me to do it." The son then asks his grandmother, who tells him, "Oh, when your mom was growing up, we didn't have a big enough roasting pan for a whole roast, so I had to cut one end off to make it fit." Flexibility and ways to recognize and handle exceptions to the norm are necessary.

Flexibility and intelligent tailoring are especially important when you're adopting other people's process models, standards, and templates. Different people have different styles of working, and these work styles interact with processes and standards in subtle ways. In the right companies—for example, those already applying mature processes throughout the system lifecycle—you can expect to drop in a standard test process compatible with the existing development process with minimal effort. However, I have worked with a number of companies where trying to introduce formal methods and standard documentation in one stroke would have completely destroyed the test team's ability to add value. Think carefully about assumptions and prerequisites as you study other people's techniques.

When you do so, you'll also be girding yourself against the most corrosive challenge to effective introduction of formal process models, standards, or indeed any process improvement effort: the silver bullet effect. Some people come to believe that templates and flowcharts resolve all testing problems. For example, I received some marketing literature while writing this chapter from a consulting and training company describing their test process. This process appeared to be a proprietary blend of the Software Engineering Institute's Capability Maturity Model and the Institute of Electrical and Electronics Engineers' processes and templates. They claimed that if testers followed their formal approach, the testing effort would meet or exceed the needs of any software project.

Such claims—and such thinking—are dangerous.

You can improve your test process by studying your critical testing processes and the context in which you operate. You can adopt ideas from this and other books, articles, and papers. Formalization and standardization can provide solid benefits, often with a reasonable level of effort and documentation.

However, there's no one right process. You needn't necessarily follow extensive Input-Process-Output diagrams or produce IEEE 829–compliant reports. Perhaps writing down a simple checklist for each critical process and homogenizing your metrics, charts, and reports across the testers in your company will suffice. Do what makes sense in your situation.

EMPLOY APPROPRIATE STRATEGIES

In this book, I have advocated a risk-based testing strategy and described how I apply that strategy. Some test professionals say that system tests should be based strictly on requirements and design specifications, and further that these specifications should unambiguously answer any questions about correct behavior. Requirements, design documents, and indeed test cases are useful models of how the system should work. However, ultimately they all are only models—useful but simplified. Let's not constrain ourselves or our tests to fit strictly within these models.

I mentioned in Chapter 15 that a successful development, maintenance, or acquisition project is one where four elements converge.

- *Features*—Are we building the right set of functions and behaviors that will solve the users' and customers' real-world problems?
- *Schedule*—Can we deliver this problem solving system in a timely fashion?
- *Budget*—Can we deliver this system in a way that makes financial sense to all involved?
- *Quality*—Can we deliver the features such that they are fit for the uses to which users and customers will put them?

If you can answer yes to all four questions, your project will succeed.

Realistically, we know the answers to these questions only after the project has been finished for some period of time. Prior to and during the project, we can only express levels of confidence in or likelihood of success. In other words, the success of the project is at risk during the entire life of the project. So, wise project managers exercise risk management.

Testing is part of a smart risk management strategy for the project. Throughout this book, I've stressed ways to connect testing to risk and risk mitigation. I've demonstrated various tools and techniques for providing services and information to help the project team manage risks related to system quality.

Not everyone uses a risk-based strategy. Here's a brief list of some other test strategies.

- *Exhaustive*—Test everything as completely as you can.
- *Shotgun*—Test wherever and whatever; distribute the test effort across the product.
- *Bug hunting*—Use bug profiles, taxonomies, and hunches to focus testing on where the bugs live.
- *Checklist*—Use checklists developed over time to guide testing.
- *Programmer-guided*—Test according to the programmers' direction and use the programmers as the final authority on correct behavior.
- *Client- or user-guided*—Test according to what the people paying for the system or the domain experts who will use the system say needs testing.
- *Implementation-guided*—Study the system's design, code, architecture, schemas, and so forth to determine where testing should focus.
- *Analytical*—Gather all the information available, study the system's structure, settings, and purposes, and test based on this broad and deep knowledge.
- *Intuitive*—Test according to what the collective experience, wisdom, and gut instincts of the test team say needs testing.
- *Exploratory*—Simultaneously learn about the system, test, find bugs, and refine the test approach and focus.
- *Agile*—Test following lightweight processes, looking for likely bugs, and focus on being able to respond to late changes.
- *Function*—Test every function of the system, one at a time.
- *Requirements- or claims-based*—Test every requirement or product claim.
- *Automated regression*—Test using exclusively automated tests that you can repeat as needed to check for regression.
- *State-based*—Test the various states and state-transitions that can occur.
- *Scenario-based*—Test according to various potential real-world scenarios across the breadth of the system's functionality.
- *Domain-based*—Analyze different domains of inputs, outputs, and data processing that occur in the system, and test the best representative of each domain.
- *High-volume stochastic*—Test with enormous random data sets using an automated tool.
- *Quality-based*—Test according to the important "-ilities" for your system, such as functionality, usability, reliability, performance, scalability, and so forth.[6]

---

6. This list came from an online discussion with Ross Collard, Cem Kaner, Kathy Iberle, and Kamesh Pemmaraju. I acknowledge their contribution.

You might have noticed that lots of these strategies have shown up in my processes. Though the primary driver of my test approach is risk-based, all these other strategies are useful tools that I employ as needed. In addition, while the risk-based approach works in many situations, you should ask yourself whether another strategy wouldn't fit better in your context.

SUCCESSFULLY INTRODUCE TOOLS

Test tools are a thriving business, but many attempts to introduce test tools fail. Why? To quote Fewster and Graham's apt saying, "Automating chaos just gives you faster chaos."[7] Having a solid, repeatable, well-understood process in place lays the groundwork for success in using automated test tools.

This becomes more important as the complexity of the project increases. Figure 17-3 shows how, on low-complexity projects, skilled system professionals, (including test engineers) together with the right technology, can bridge the challenges of the project alone and create a path for the project to deliver the system to users and customers. Figure 17-4 shows that as complexity increases, process begins to support this bridge to prevent it from collapsing under project pressures in the middle. Finally, Figure 17-5 shows that we can augment the development, maintenance, or acquisition process—including the testing process—with tools to bridge even great challenges on very complex projects. The right combination of skilled and dedicated professionals, advanced but stable technology, repeatable and well-understood process, and appropriately applied tools allows us to bring even difficult projects to successful completion.

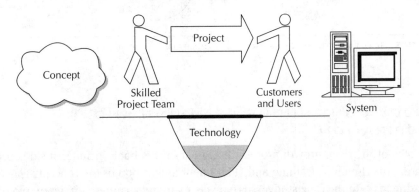

FIGURE 17-3 SKILLS AND TECHNOLOGY BUILD A BRIDGE FOR SIMPLE PROJECTS.

---

7. See Mark Fewster and Dorothy Graham's *Software Test Automation*.

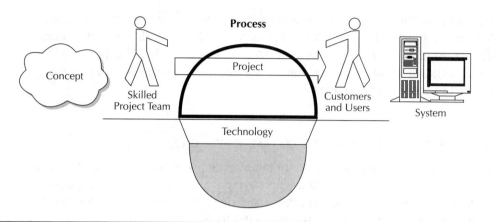

FIGURE 17-4 PROCESS MUST AUGMENT SKILLS AND TECHNOLOGY AS COMPLEXITY INCREASES.

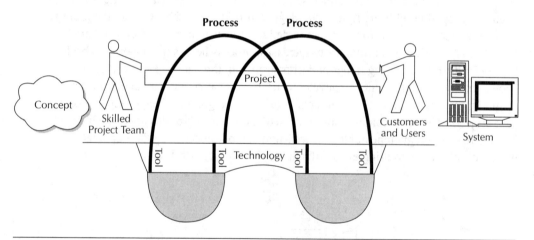

FIGURE 17-5 GOOD PROCESS SUPPORTS SUCCESSFUL TOOL IMPLEMENTATION.

ENJOY CONTINUOUS LEARNING AND INSPIRATION

One step of the team growth process discussed in this book included a skills growth program that involved training and subsequent application of the concepts learned to a testing task. In the case study, Lin-Tsu was to attend a conference, learn about document management, and then create some tests based on what she'd learned. This is one form of learning: Go off, acquire some new skills, and then cement those skills into your mind by applying them.

We can also learn by studying what others have done. Inspections, document reviews, code reviews, and test reviews, besides being quality assurance techniques, are excellent learning opportunities for the participants. Pair programming and pair testing, although still in the experimental stage, show similar promise in terms of learning from our fellow professionals by watching them work.

Another form of learning occurs when we learn by doing something ourselves. My father taught me to play chess by playing chess with me. I learned to ride a bicycle the same way. I didn't study the concepts of chess or bicycle riding. I didn't study other people playing chess or riding bicycles. I simply started playing chess and riding a bicycle, and then learned from successes and failures.

Sometimes, good ideas appear in our heads. Once, when trying to decide the right syntax for test suite and test case definitions in an automated test system I was building, I just happened to be preparing a document in HTML format. This document had nothing to do with the project I was working on, but it was a short item on my to-do list that I could work on while waiting for a good solution to occur to me. Sure enough, as I looked at the tags (e.g., <b> and </b> for begin and end boldface type) in the HTML file, I realized I could use similar tags. For example, I picked <Action> and </Action> to indicate the beginning and end of a stanza telling the test tool about the action portion of a test case. These "aha" moments sometimes come when we stop looking for a solution to our problem, like Archimedes getting into his bathtub.

Learning can be messy. Learning can be hard to manage. But learning is also fun. More importantly, learning is motivational. So many times I've heard in interviews some variation of the statement "What I want out of this job most of all is a chance to keep learning." People who are motivated and learning work harder. Even better, they work smarter and smarter every single day. So, as a manager, I encourage learning. I encourage creativity. I encourage inspiration. I work to make learning, creativity, and inspiration—and the inevitable mistakes that come with them—safe. I find this promotes a fun work environment, a motivating work environment, and a productive work environment.

HANDLE CHALLENGES

We've looked at a number of challenges that arise in specific test processes. For the overall test process, a number of challenges exist as well.[8]

---

8. Another good discussion about high-level test process challenges can be found in Bill Perry and Randy Rice's book *Surviving the Top Ten Challenges of Software Testing*.

HOW CAN WE MEASURE WHAT WE CAN'T DEFINE?

Think back on the definition of quality I've borrowed from J. M. Juran: the presence of satisfying behaviors and the absence of dissatisfying behaviors. Using this definition, perhaps we should measure the number of useful features and the number of bugs observed by users. Perhaps those two numbers measure quality. I'm skeptical, for two reasons.

First, the quality of the system is influenced by *which* bugs remain as much as by *how many* bugs remain. Do we know everything we need to know about quality if all we know is that we removed 90% of the bugs before delivery? Do we know the system will satisfy 90% of our users and customers? Maybe so if all the remaining defects affect the same 10% of the users and customers, but suppose we have one defect that affects 20% of our customers. A similar criticism makes measuring the number of useful features an imperfect and incomplete quality metric. So, while these numbers could be parameters in some quality equation—obviously, more useful features and fewer bugs are desirable—those aren't the only parameters and might not be even the two most important parameters.

My second reason is that not everyone agrees with Juran's definition. *Quality Progress*, the journal of the American Society for Quality, published an article by Robert Hoyer and Brooke Hoyer titled "What Is Quality?" In this article they looked at eight different definitions from eight quality gurus. In addition to Juran's definition, here's a sample of some others they mentioned.

- Phil Crosby: "Conformance to requirements."
- W. Edwards Deming: "Quality [exists] in teams of the agent [the stakeholder]. . . ."
- Genichi Taguchi: Quality is "the loss. . . [caused] to society" by the product or system.

Hoyer and Hoyer claim these varying definitions fall into two categories. What they call *level 1* definitions say that quality is the delivery of products and services "whose measurable characteristics satisfy a fixed set of [numerically] defined specifications." The *level 2* definitions define quality as "independent of...measurable characteristics" and arising from "[satisfying] customer expectations."[9]

---

9. R.W Hoyer and Brooke Hoyer, "What Is Quality?" *Quality Progress*, July 2001.

If we take the level 1 approach, we can measure characteristics and then develop a quality number, graph, or model based on those measures. That number, graph, or model will be inaccurate and imprecise, but it might be useful as a guide.

If we take the level 2 approach, we can accept that such metrics simply *reflect on* the ultimate quality goal—satisfied users and customers—and then focus primarily on that. Selection of this approach doesn't mean that we should give up measuring quality. It does mean that we have to test those measures against the standard of customer and user satisfaction.

IMMATURE DEVELOPMENT OR MAINTENANCE PROCESSES

Earlier, I discussed pervasiveness and process maturity as interlinked attributes of a good test process. While a good test process will pervade the project, note that the project *always* pervades the test process. When the overall project is conducted with a lack of process maturity, we get a chaotic and unpredictable test process, with decreased effectiveness and efficiency.

I like to self-assess the project against the Capability Maturity Model guidelines. Scanning the key process areas, you can probably determine in an hour or so whether the project is operating at the Initial, Repeatable, Defined, Managed, or Optimizing level. (Be tactful and discrete in your use of the knowledge you gain by doing this.) The low project maturity often indicates trouble ahead for the test process.

One special risk to testers working on low-maturity projects arises from the perception that quality—and efforts expended to measure and ensure it—are luxuries. Organizations can't have software without programmers, running networks without network operators, product releases with release engineers, or help lines without technical support staff, but organizations *can*—and some *do*—sell and deploy systems without testing them. Luxuries are the first things cut when times are tough. To quote the authors of *The Capability Maturity Model*, in immature organizations "there is little understanding of how the steps of the software process affect quality, and product quality is difficult to predict. Moreover, activities intended to increase quality, such as reviews and testing, are often curtailed or eliminated when projects fall behind schedule."[10]

---

10. Mark Paulk et al., writing in *The Capability Maturity Model*, page 7.

The inefficiencies imposed on the test team by low project maturity, combined with a management perception of superfluity, make low-maturity projects a dangerous place for testers. Talk a lot to your managers and their managers about their commitment to testing and their expectations of testing if you feel this is the case, and watch for signs of wavering when the going gets tough.

Given the effect immature development processes can have on the test team, test professionals are sometimes tempted to try to drive development process improvement from the testing group. This is dangerous. The quickest, most effective way I've seen to become unpopular and to burn political capital is to become a busybody tester who runs around the organization telling other people how they should do their jobs. If the test organization is not seen as a stellar performer, you'll be seen as a hypocrite who should stick to your own knitting. If the test organization is seen as working well, then you are likely to be considered a meddlesome know-it-all. If you feel that process change is needed across the entire organization, perhaps you can find an executive-level champion who will lead the charge.

UNREALISTIC EXPECTATIONS

Even in high-maturity organizations, testing is often a misunderstood discipline. When you talk to your managers about their expectations, you might find it to be misunderstood in your organization, too. In extreme cases, managers seem to expect the very act of testing to sprinkle some kind of magic quality pixie dust on the system, driving out bugs the way garden pesticides drive out aphids.

I know of one test manager who got a bad yearly performance review and was denied a bonus because his company deployed a product full of bugs. He had previously reported most of these bugs in the bug tracking database and been told by development that those bugs weren't important. Shortly afterward, he found a better job where people were willing to let go of their unrealistic expectations about testing. On one project I worked on, the project manager expected that we would find all the bugs in one pass through the tests, the programmer would then fix them in a day or two, and then our subsequent pass would confirm closure of all the bugs and identify no new ones.

Unrealistic expectations can take many forms. One common form arises from a perception that testing is somehow a trivial task. I had a prospect ask me, while I was writing this book, to implement an entire test process, including completely automated regression testing. I told them that my associates and I could definitely do that. Then they added that they wanted this task done by one mid-level test engineer in six weeks. When I responded that we could probably have a good risk analysis, a realistic estimate, and a solid plan in place in half that time, but that implementation would take months, they decided to look elsewhere.

A whole family of unrealistic expectations lives clustered around the concept that testing should be able to achieve complete coverage with minimal resources. For example, I don't know how to find performance problems unless I can test in userlike environments, which are sometimes expensive. If it's not worth it to the organization to know about performance bugs ahead of time, then they shouldn't spend the money on testing for them. But managers who make that decision should understand that they have accepted increased quality risk to reduce budget risk, and sometimes that's a risk trade-off they may rue.

Another unrealistic expectation I have seen laid on test groups is encapsulated in the hoary management exhortation "Don't tell me about a problem unless you can also suggest a solution." This may be a reasonable tactic to take with some managers and groups, to prevent endless cycles of attempts to avoid accountability. However, the test team is special: We exist only to provide unbiased, accurate information about the current quality of the system. Sometimes the systems we're testing are really buggy. There's a right way and a wrong way to communicate that message, but it's unrealistic for managers to expect testers to have a handy solution for every bug they find. That's just another way of justifying the magic-quality-pixie-dust expectation under the guise of trying to encourage teamwork. Unless testers can talk about problems without known solutions, the project can't enjoy all the benefits of an independent test team.

Part of the expectation problem arises from confusion between testing and quality assurance. A real quality assurance team has cross-functional responsibility and authority for making sure the development and maintenance processes result in a quality system. A test group assesses quality. These are distinct roles and activities, but I have heard many test groups referred to as *quality assurance*.

(If you *are* a real, bona fide quality assurance manager, you have responsibilities for processes outside those described in this book. Also, your hiring needs will differ from those outlined in Chapters 8 and 9. Finally, your own personal competency must be different from that of the typical testing manager. Quality assurance requires an understanding of the entire software development process, advanced programming and other technical knowledge, quality management training, and knowledge of formal process improvement techniques like ISO 9000, Capability Maturity Model, and Total Quality Management.)

Some agreement must exist between the test team and the organization as to what services the test team provides. If your organization clarifies such agreements through mission statements, then use that. If it uses management-by-objectives at the test manager's level, then use that. The goal is to avoid misunderstandings about your role, especially among senior and executive management.

I have worked with many project managers over the years who needed some help in understanding what testing could actually achieve and how it could add value. Most of them were willing to listen, once I figured out how to communicate to them effectively. Some weren't. If you find yourself facing unrealistic expectations, try to understand what motivates the people who hold those expectations. What do they value? What do they worry about? What off-hours recreational activities do they engage in, and can you use metaphors to frame your points within their pastimes? Communicate in those terms.

If that doesn't work—if someone stubbornly clings to unrealistic expectations—then you'll need to have realistic expectations about your options. You can continue your working relationship with that person, knowing that you'll be blamed unfairly from time to time. Or you can find someplace else to work.[11]

RELATIONSHIPS

All too often, I hear about—and encounter—situations where the test team's role is viewed as fundamentally adversarial. However, test teams are often service organizations. Service organizations either have satisfied customers or they go out of business. Clearly, adversarial relationships indicate a lack of satisfaction. Although the topic of how to work well with others in general is beyond the scope of this book, I can offer a few brief suggestions for those challenges unique to the test professional.

First, make sure that you handle any unrealistic expectations that might exist. Many of the relationship problems at the management level come down to unrealistic expectations. Second, work in a cooperative fashion with peers and managers to make clear all roles, relationships, and handoffs that affect the test process. Third, think about who your internal customers and stakeholders are. Some examples include the following:

- Developers who need help with testing and debugging
- Marketing and sales people who want to promote and sell quality systems

---

11. See my article "Stop Destroying My Team with Bad MBOs: A Manager's New Year's Resolution," available on the Internet at www.stickyminds.com, for some thoughts on how unrealistic expectations become quantified performance objectives—and why they shouldn't.

- Business analysts and customers who want quality systems deployed
- Technical support people who don't want angry customers
- Network operations people who want to run server farms that are secure and scalable

You can build solid relationships with these people based on the particular services you can offer them.

Finally, work on building these solid relationships early in the project, before the panic and stress that so often come at the project's end. These relationships will pay off throughout the testing process, not only in making your job less stressful, but also in making the test process more effective and efficient, both in reality and in the perceptions of your colleagues.

"ADDICTED TO TEST"

Some companies institute independent test teams in reaction to a particularly bad— and expensive—project, or as part of a software process improvement effort aimed at improving quality. One common approach is to have the new test team focus on behavioral testing, often during the integration, system, and acceptance testing phases, while the programmers remain responsible for structural testing, for the most part during unit or component test phases.

However, sometimes only the first half of the approach takes root, while the programmer testing withers and dies. Programmers who before considered themselves responsible for thoroughly testing their software become lackadaisical, thinking, "Hey, I don't have to test anymore, that's the test team's job."

A colleague of mine, Ren MacNary, said of this situation that the programmers were "addicted to test." As the programmer testing drops off, the quality of the system coming into the test process is less than what it used to be before independent testing was instituted, when the system went directly from the development team to the users or customers. This creates a cascade of three extremely dangerous situations, one after another, hammering the project and, ultimately, the test team.

First, the integration of the various components after they are completed becomes difficult. Because the components themselves are problematic, attempts to make them work together take a long time and reveal a lot of problems. These problems are difficult to isolate, resulting in arguments where the various programmers of the uncooperative components accuse each other over bugs. Only with tremendous management effort does the integration proceed. Since integration is often underestimated in project schedules anyway, this can introduce large and unforeseen delays at the midpoint of the project schedule.

Second, as the system is integrated, it is handed off to the independent test team barely functional and crawling with major bugs. Because of the schedule delays, the integration and system testing start late, but often the test team receives no corresponding relief in terms of the test completion, since project management declares the project deployment or system release dates sacrosanct. However, in spite of wishful thinking about "finally catching a break during testing," the reality is that the testing takes much longer than originally planned. Not only is testing another activity, like integration, that is often underscoped, but because the product is worse than expected, testing goes much slower than it otherwise would. Major blocking bugs make progress through the planned tests impossible. New test releases show up missing major functions, in some cases even uninstallable. Often, this is the point at which projects collapse completely, with management patience, budgets, or even the viability of the entire company exhausted.

Third, should the project hold together and manage to deploy or release a system, the results are often not good. The test team spends most of their time and energy chasing down bugs using behavioral techniques, when these same bugs could have been found earlier and cheaper in programmer testing with structural techniques. So, they find fewer bugs, which means more bugs escape to the field. When these three situations are combined with unrealistic expectations about the test team, management sometimes blames the test team for them.[12]

To prevent this, start by resolving any unrealistic expectations that exist in people's minds about what the test team can actually accomplish. Next, make sure that the development team acknowledges the need for continued structural testing. Proceed to obtain project management buy-in for such testing during unit or component phases (scheduled, planned, and with adequate resources) that are clearly identified and actively tracked activities on project schedules. Finally, use smoke testing and entry criteria to measure and establish levels of system quality required to enter integration and system testing.

---

12. There's a metric you as a tester can use to quantify the effect of overreliance on late testing, called the *defect detection percentage*. You can find more information on this metric in my book *Managing the Testing Process, Second Edition*, Chapter 4. For a case study on "test addiction," see Elisabeth Hendrickson's article "More Testing, Worse Quality," on her Web site, www.qualitytree.com. Finally, see also Lee Copeland's article "When Helping Doesn't Help," on www.stickyminds.com.

INCREMENTAL PROCESS IMPROVEMENT

Perhaps you've gotten to this point in the book and you're thinking, "Well, you know, our processes are pretty good. I don't want to make any major changes. I wish we could just do everything we do a little bit better." To that end, let me throw out a couple of general-purpose approaches I've used to optimize my testing processes. These fall into two categories. First, fine-tune the big processes. Second, identify and attempt to remove the big process obstacles.

FINE-TUNE THE BIG PROCESSES

First, to fine-tune processes, start by looking at those processes that consume the most time, effort, or resources. Here's a simple technique I learned for process optimization from my days of studying Total Quality Management. I've applied this in organizations where the testing process was working but needed to work better.[13]

Start out by looking at the 12 critical test processes. Select two or three of them that together account for two-thirds or more of your test team's time, effort, or resources. For example, it wouldn't be unusual to find that the bug reporting and test execution processes combined consume two-thirds of the team's effort.

For those critical processes, modify the checklists presented in this book both to fit your current processes and to gather information about the duration, effort, and, if appropriate, cost associated with each step. (You might already have some of this data on test case execution, depending on whether you implemented the test tracking worksheet I discussed in Chapter 13.) As you and your team execute each process, gather the time, effort, and cost for each step. For fine-grained processes, time and effort should be gathered in minutes.

Throughout this data gathering, all the usual caveats of metrics apply. If people think management will use this data against them, they'll bend the data to reflect well on themselves. If people think managers will use this data as a metric of effectiveness in the yearly performance reviews, people will fix the data. If people think managers will use this data to compare people against each other for ranking effectiveness, people

---

13. The training I received was part of the University of California at Los Angeles' Total Quality Management Certification program. In terms of incremental process improvement, the most helpful texts were the Xerox Corporate Education and Training series, *Leadership Through Quality*, especially "Concepts of Quality," "Quality Improvement Process," and "Problem-Solving Process."

might even sabotage each other, leading to a breakdown of team cohesion. You wouldn't want to screw up your team in the effort for improvement.

Once you have data on a dozen or so executions of the process for each of the members of the test team, analyze the data. What are the averages for each step and for the process as a whole? What is the variation for each step and for the process as a whole? Classic quality improvement theory says that to improve process performance, reduce the variation around the average, and then move the average in the desired direction. Be careful in applying this maxim for your test processes, though, because faster isn't necessarily better, and there can be valid reasons for pretty wide variation.

When analyzing your data, separate your data by significant important factors. Look at data for each tester as well as for the whole team. What is the level of individual variation? In the case of bug reporting, look at data for bugs of particular levels of priority and severity, since we expect people to spend more time reporting the more important problems. For test execution, control for variation related to the number of bugs found by a test, as well as setup and teardown time. How does automated versus manual testing affect the data? It's very easy to make mistakes in your statistical analysis of the process data if you mix up data from processes that, for valid reasons, will behave differently.

With this analysis in hand, look for root causes. Is one person having trouble with isolation? Perhaps training is needed for that person. Is everyone having trouble with isolation? Perhaps you don't have sufficient alternative system configurations available and should collect a library of drive images to speed up changing configurations. Is bug reporting slower every Monday after a new build has been installed? Perhaps excessively high bug density in each incoming build leads to confusion about who's tracking what bug.

You might have to gather additional data to test your hypotheses on the root causes of delay, but avoid analysis paralysis. If you have a good hunch on a simple change that is low-risk—i.e., the chances of its backfiring and making the situation worse are very low—then you can make such changes with no additional data. Higher-risk or expensive changes, on the other hand, require more analysis. If you want to buy $100,000 in additional hardware to help isolate bugs more quickly, then you'll need to gather data that support the lack of hardware as the root cause for long isolation, and build a solid business case to justify the investment based on its eventual return.

As you institute process change, look for the duration, effort, and resources to go down slowly over time. Process improvement won't happen right away. Gather data and watch the process improvement occur. If no improvements occur, then figure out why your changes had no impact before you move on to further optimization. If improvement does occur, wait to see that new process stabilize before you move on to the next optimization. Once it does, repeat this optimization process over and over again.

Not all processes that take longer, involve more effort, or cost more are necessarily worse. In the case of bug reporting, you may have one person who always spends the longest time writing bug reports, but who consistently writes the best bug reports. You don't want to optimize time, effort, and resource use but defeat the primary purpose of the process in doing so. Only institute improvements that lead to increased efficiency without reducing the effectiveness of the team. As a matter of fact, improvements should be instituted in such a way that effectiveness is also optimized whenever possible. When you're instituting process improvements, make sure to continue to check the process for good results, using the sections on recognizing good processes for each process in this book.

IDENTIFY AND REMOVE THE BIG PROCESS OBSTACLES

A common source of inefficiency in process is waste and rework. A technique for process optimization that I've used to deal with waste and rework is to track common causes of wasted time, effort, or resources. Have your team, each week, report to you any avoidable incident that wasted more than one hour of schedule time, one hour of effort (person time), or $100 of resources. (If you don't like these thresholds, pick others more appropriate to your context.) Examples are a server taken offline for routine maintenance during a scheduled test execution period, a test run against an old test release, or a weekend lunch for a test team that couldn't get any work done because of logistical problems, respectively.

As you collect this data, start to categorize it and build a data sheet for collecting further information. Here, the objective is to identify obstacles to the test process, not to gather statistics on the test processes themselves. (We just did that in the fine-tuning work earlier.) Events you classify as time-wasting should not be tasks that appear on the process checklists. These events are unexpected roadblocks that prevent your team from working effectively and efficiently.

Once again, keep firmly in mind the usual caveats of metrics. As stated earlier, if testers think you'll use this data against them, they'll bend the data to their benefit. If people outside the organization think you're gathering this data as a weapon against them, it'll create huge problems. Management hates waste and rework, so the data you have is potential dynamite in the wrong hands. In many organizations, you'll need to be very careful about who knows that you're gathering this data.

A Martial Arts Process for Process Improvement, by Philippe Kruchten, Director of Process Development, Rational Software

Shu Ha Ri. These three Japanese kanji characters mean, in some translations, hold, break, leave and, in others, imitate, diverge, separate, respectively. It is also a pattern from budo, aikido, and other Japanese martial arts that applies to stages of learning. And it seems appropriate to apply this pattern to transferring process knowledge.

Shu. First, imitate or simply follow the basic rules until they are completely internalized.

Ha. Second, learn when and how to make exceptions to the rules.

Ri. Third, transcend the basic rules and invent your own rules.

If you skip *Shu* and go too quickly to *Ha*, you have a mess, because the basic rules and principles are not well understood. A similar mess occurs if you try to go too fast from *Ha* to *Ri*, because you might end up reinventing the wheel. You can waste a lot of time improvising your own way if existing best practices are perfectly suitable.

Let's apply this pattern to transferring process knowledge. *Shu*, follow a simple process. Try to understand and internalize the principles, and find your way in the process. *Ha*, customize processes as needed to handle special cases. *Ri*, invent your own process to handle cases for which you find existing processes, even ones you've customized, insufficient.

As you gather data over time, you'll see the 80/20 rule, or Pareto Principle, playing out. Two or three sources of waste will be significant, accounting for two-thirds or more of the waste. The rest will be less important. For each significant source of waste, institute process improvement plans to eliminate the waste. For example, if bad test releases are a continual source of trouble, revisit Chapter 12, and then institute changes to resolve that problem, such as a smoke test.[14]

As you institute the process improvement plan, continue to collect data. You may actually see problems get worse before they get better—process change involves overheads and can create confusion—so don't react right away. However, over time—as long as a few months or a few projects—you should see the new process become second nature to your team. Once this happens, the waste associated with the target

---

14. The change management database described in Chapter 6 of *Managing the Testing Process, Second Edition*, and included in the templates that accompany that book, can be an excellent way to gather this data.

source (or sources) should abate. As soon as the sources of waste stabilize, again start gathering data for process improvement. Which are the two or three sources of two-thirds of the waste now? Time for another process improvement plan.

IMPLEMENT IMPROVEMENTS

OK, so perhaps you want to implement major changes in your testing process. What are some ideas for implementing large-scale changes in a testing process?

1. Identify gaps in your current test processes. This book and books like Koomen and Pol's *Test Process Improvement* and van Veenendaal et. al.'s *The Testing Practitioner* should give you ideas. Remain focused on testing processes that are within your purview, since you can actually change these. Use data sources like bug tracking systems, help desk or field failure data, and past test results, but also feel free to address more subjective but well-substantiated gut feelings.

2. For each gap, understand the advantages and disadvantages of changing the process. Is the need immediate and urgent or long-term and important? What are the risks and costs associated with the current way of working? What are the opportunities and benefits presented by changing the process? Are there personal, political, and practical reasons for change?

3. Select the ideal process change to introduce. Remember that personal, political, and practical forces must play a role in your selection. You'll need to complement these forces with a strong business case.

4. Plan the change. Identify the affected stakeholders. Some of the stakeholders might favor retaining the current process, so you'll need some way of convincing them. Introducing a limited process change as part of a single project is generally lower risk both politically and business-wise, and thus an easier sell. Changing internal processes is easier than changing collaborative processes. Changing less context-sensitive processes is easier than changing more context-sensitive processes.

5. Sell people on your plan for change. Understand and explain the risks of your planned change, along with the benefits.

6. Implement the change, being careful to measure the benefits as they accrue. If you're a manager, adopt appropriate changes in behavior to support these changes in process.[15] For significant changes, the situation might get worse

---

15. For more information on the challenges and obstacles management can create in implementing process change, see Johanna Rothman's insightful article "Manager Heal Thyself," found at www.jrothman.com.

before it gets better. As with testing, the costs of process change accrue before the benefits, so reinforcing the reasons that the change was made and the ultimate benefits is important.

7. Institutionalize the change. Sometimes improvements happen, things get better, and then the organization backslides into old, dysfunctional behavior. The important thing is to stick with it. Make sure the overall culture in the test team or in the development organization changes so that the new process becomes second nature.

8. Go back to step 1 and do it all over again. Organizations that succeed at process improvement make a habit of it. You can always do better. There's always something that can be perfected. This habit of continuous process improvement is what distinguishes the truly excellent software development organizations, the most mature organizations, the industry leaders.

Often, the bigger the change, the slower the change process progresses. A test manager can institute a new way of reporting bugs in a ten-person test team in the space of a quarter. Benefits will often begin to accrue the moment the change is instituted. A vice president of software development instituting a formal test process from scratch can look forward to well over a year of working at that change. Since many test organizations are dissolved within two years of their establishment, it's important that the changes that happen in that year be deliberate, carefully chosen, and targeted toward adding the maximum value.

Jamal Brown Looks Back—and Looks Forward

On the afternoon of March 31, Jamal was sitting in his office, with the door closed, reflecting on the Sumatra project's successes and failures. They had held the exit meeting on March 28, just one week late. The delay was due to the need to finish one final complete pass of testing, after taking a somewhat risky test release with a major bug fix on March 14. But the Golden Candidate had passed the tests—at least, no important bugs had been found—so they had decided to ship the system on Friday afternoon. Jamal had presented a final test report at that meeting, with the overall conclusion that the risks to quality, both known and unknown, were low and no longer justified delaying release. With his manager's permission, Jamal had treated himself by leaving immediately after the meeting, going out of town for the weekend, and showing up at 11:00 on the following Monday morning.

The next push would be working on the Application Service Provider capabilities for SpeedyWriter 3.1—as Sumatra was now officially called—but first, Jamal was to prepare for and attend a Sumatra Project Retrospective. This meeting was scheduled for lunchtime the next day.

Jamal was creating a handout as his contribution for the project. He would think for a minute, call someone on the project team and talk with them, type for a minute, open a book, peruse project e-mails, look at test status, and then repeat the process. After a few hours, he was done. He printed enough copies of the document for all the attendees, and then left for the day with a neat pile of handouts on his desk. Looking back at his desk as he turned out the light, Jamal smiled and thought, We pretty much got it right this time.

Step #	Step	Done?
4.	Perfect: Guide adaptation and improvement.	☑
4.A	Document the bugs found during test execution.	☑
4.B	Communicate test results to key stakeholders.	☑
4.C	Adjust to changes and refine the testing process.	☑

Sumatra Project Retrospective
Test Team Report

What Went Right

So many things went well on this project that it's hard to choose, but I guess the greatest enablers of success were these.

Teamwork—The test team specifically and the project team in general all worked well. Individual contributions ranged from good to excellent. Team cohesion was very high. Team conflict was minimal. A shared vision and a passion for project success were notable throughout, even toward the end. Foundations of success:

- Good management team leadership, including minimizing overtime, excessive pressure, and unproductive meetings
- Realistic and aligned executive, management, and team expectations
- Constancy of management purpose

Risk-based test strategy—The quality risk analysis technique, Failure Mode and Effect Analysis, focused our test effort where the most value was to be had. Foundations of success:

- Cross-functional participation by all stakeholders
- Realistic expectations by all stakeholders
- Constancy of purpose in following through on priorities set in quality risk analysis

Test results reporting—The test team's results were seen as valuable and credible information, delivered in a timely fashion. A significant reduction in post-release costs of external failure was demonstrably achieved through a high proportion of fixed bugs. Foundations of success:

- Gaining early consensus around and understanding of the test dashboard
- Sense of teamwork between testers and programmers such that bug reports were never seen as adversarial
- Test team focus on producing high-quality information

What Went Wrong

The problems were limited and, from what I could tell, more a matter of things that almost went wrong. However, notable opportunities for improvement are these.

Bug triage—At one point, the change control board deferred too many bugs, and these bugs later had to be reactivated by executive intervention. While a preferable outcome to shipping with the bugs, the reactivation represented rework (and thus inefficiency) and increased the risk associated with a decreased amount of time to work on the problems. Opportunities for improvement:

- Possible insufficient executive oversight in the change control board. Increase executive involvement.
- Current process not able to effectively escalate "gray area" defects that might be must-fix for release to an executive level. Define escalation path.

Staffing—We got very lucky in finding an appropriate test automation resource at the last minute. Had this not happened, our testing would have been noticeably less effective, especially against the first few increments. Opportunities for improvement:

- Current contractor company relationships are based primarily on price and include companies focused only on programmer expertise. Identify possible providers of expert outsourcing and contract testing help; build strategic relationship with them to fill urgent gaps as needed.
- Skills in test team are too specialized for testers if needed to fill each other's shoes. Increase focus on training and building a well-rounded test team, including increased training budget.

Plans for the Future

In addition to working on the items identified above as opportunities for improvement, I plan on the following:

Optimize processes—I'll analyze Sumatra test process metrics and look for opportunities to tighten up process in order to increase efficiency and effectiveness. I'll also enhance process metric gathering for future projects to answer efficiency and effectiveness questions that current metrics cannot answer.

Eliminate obstacles—For subsequent projects, I'll introduce data gathering techniques that allow us to track and categorize rework, blockages, downtime, and other obstacles to effective and efficient process execution.

Reduce costs per must-fix defect found—Our cost per must-fix defect found is $500, a stable figure across the last three projects. However, much of our testing budget goes into manually repeating tests to manage regression, which is not very efficient. If we refocus manual testing on running new tests and doing exploratory testing, our cost per must-fix defect will come down, since such tests tend to be more effective at finding must-fix bugs than regression tests are. Since managing regression risk is key, we should work to automate a much larger percentage of our regression testing and also automate it earlier in the lifecycle. I propose a cross-functional task force involving Integration and System Test, Release Engineering, New Release Development, Sustaining Engineering, and Systems Architecture to attack this opportunity. I propose that this task force's mission be to plan and implement a fully automated and integrated regression test harness, working at both the user interface and the business logic layers of the architecture.

Success in these three action areas could, I believe, increase the return on the test investment by as much as 50%, along with reducing test cycle times and increasing the percentage of bugs we find prior to customer release.

CONCLUSION

This book provides ideas on improving your testing processes. These processes are my own personal approach to testing and test management. The case study served as a dynamic example of those techniques in action. By studying the case study documents, you'll have examples and templates at hand to ease the adoption of my methods if so desired. Finally, the sections on recognizing good processes, handling challenges, and implementing improvements should give you hints on how to move forward. Diligent, thoughtful improvement of these 12 critical testing processes will help you provide effective and efficient quality risk management information and services in the course of your testing processes.

Nevertheless, let me end on a note of caution, acknowledging that there is no magic in process by itself. Before the lingo of quality management led us to talk about *processes*, we referred to ways of doing things as *systems*. To have a systematic approach to doing something meant that you had a defined, repeatable process. The Russian author Ivan Turgenev once wrote, "The people who bind themselves to systems are those who are unable to encompass the whole truth and try to catch it by the tail; a system is like the tail of truth, but truth is like a lizard; it leaves its tail in your fingers and runs away knowing full well that it will grow a new one in a twinkling."

Turgenev is right, because process can be binding—and, if misused, blinding. However, if you focus on what is essential to effective and efficient testing in your context, process can be a useful guide. A good process will serve you by freeing you from having to reinvent success each time. Instead, you can let the process serve as your checklist, and focus your creative energies on topics more fulfilling than simply ensuring that you don't forget anything. Best of luck to you with your critical testing processes and all the other essential components of testing success!

GLOSSARY

Acceptance Testing, User Acceptance Testing	A testing phase designed to demonstrate that the system under test meets requirements. The name "user acceptance testing" can imply that users run the testing.
Activity	A logically distinct subset of a phase consisting of a collection of tasks that together produce a single major deliverable.
Alpha Testing, Beta Testing	Testing phases where the system is delivered to internal (alpha) or external (beta) customers and users for exposure to real-world workflows, data, and environments.
Amortize	To distribute the costs and benefits of an investment across a series of time periods (e.g., monthly) or across a set of projects. This distribution represents the fair costs and benefits of the investment in each time period or to each project.
Application Domain Skills, Subject Matter Expertise	Skill or understanding pertaining to whatever field or tasks we're dealing with in our software or hardware; in other words, understanding how our customers and users will employ our creation.
Audition Interview	A portion of the interview process that involves demonstrating the skills required to fill the position; e.g., writing a test case or reporting a bug.
Balanced Scorecard	See *Dashboard*.

Behavioral Tests, Black-Box Tests	Tests based on what externally observable things a system should do, often spelled out in requirements and high-level design specifications.
Beta Testing	See *Alpha Testing*.
Black-Box Tests	See *Behavioral Tests*.
Bug, Defect	A problem that causes or would cause the system to fail to meet one or more user's or customer's reasonable expectations of quality.
Bug Report	A technical document written to describe the symptoms of a bug to 1) communicate the impact and circumstances of a quality problem, 2) prioritize the bug for repair, and 3) help the programmer locate the underlying defect and fix it.
Build, Release, Test Release	An installable software, hardware, or system item—or even a whole system—transmitted to the test group for testing.
Build ID, Release Name, Revision, Revision Number, Version, Version Number	Some sequence of numbers and/or characters that uniquely identifies the release.
Build Manager	See *Release Engineer*.
Build Plan, Release, Engineering Plan	The plan that specifies how the various releases will be built for testing, ultimately, in the field.
Candidate	Someone who has applied to fill an open position and is somewhere along the hiring process but not yet officially hired.
Code and Fix	A development approach that eschews most planning, requirements gathering, and design activities, jumping directly into coding of the system and then fixing bugs that are found. Bugs may be found through formal testing by an independent test team, via ad hoc, informal testing, or by debugging alone. While sometimes suitable for small, low-risk, and low-complexity development or maintenance efforts, this model does not scale up well to large, complex, or high-risk projects.

Component Testing, Subsystem Testing	A testing phase focused on each component or subsystem of the system.
Critical Network	See *Critical Path*.
Critical Path, Critical Network	The set of tasks (in terms of task or activity duration) in the project work-breakdown-structure (honoring all the intertask dependencies) that must be completed on time for the project to complete on time. In other words, the set of tasks that, when laid end-to-end based on their dependencies, determine the earliest possible project completion date consists of those tasks on the project's critical path.
Customers Sponsors	People who have paid, will pay, or might pay money to obtain the system. This payment can occur by funding the system directly, by supporting the funding of the system, by paying a vendor for the system, by purchasing a product or service that includes or uses the system, by paying taxes, or by some other direct or indirect means. A customer can be an organization procuring and/or deploying a system to employee-users or an individual buying a system for their own use.
Dashboard, Balanced Scorecard	A dashboard, or balanced scorecard, is a collection of metrics, usually displayed as a small set of charts or graphs, that give a high-level view of the status of some activity. The analogy is the dashboard of a car, where a cluster of as few as two or three gauges, together with some warning lights, give the driver the essential information about the state of the vehicle without distracting the driver from the unfolding road and traffic situation outside the windows. The "balanced scorecard" phrase refers to the fact that a good selection of such charts or gauges will balance each other out. In other words, while any one metric might mislead us, the cumulative effect of all the metrics is to provide context for the other metrics that clarifies the meaning of the scorecard as a whole.
Defect	See *Bug*.
Development Plan	The plan that specifies how the components that make up the system will be created, including sequencing of those components.

Estimation	A prediction of the schedule and cost associated with a project. In the case of test estimation, it's a prediction of the schedule and cost associated with a test subproject.
Expectation of Quality	The beliefs held by the customers and users about what level of quality the system should provide. Ideally, customers and users will hold reasonable expectations of quality.
	When user or customer expectations are unreasonable, this often indicates a breakdown in the requirements gathering, business analysis, or change control activities. It is often not possible—and usually not desirable—to address unreasonable expectations of quality in the testing process.
Experience of Quality	The opinions about system quality, combined with the general levels of satisfaction or dissatisfaction, held by users and customers as they gain experience with a system. When the experience of quality matches the expectation of quality, the user or customer is usually satisfied; if the experience exceeds expectations, the user or customer is usually delighted; if the experience falls below expectations, the user or customer is usually dissatisfied.
Extended Shifts	Any off-hours work done by people other than those working during normal business hours (approximately 8:00 AM to 5:00 PM). Typical extended shifts include *evening shift* (approximately 4:00 PM to 1:00 AM), *graveyard shift* (approximately 12:00 midnight to 9:00 AM), and *weekend* or *holiday shift* (any of the previous shifts, but on nonworkdays). Contrast *overtime*, which is work beyond 40 hours per week, but which can involve any shift.
Failure Mode	A particular manner or type of failure in the system; i.e., a category of bugs or failures with some distinctive similarity or similarities. Zero, one, or more specific bugs or failures can fall into a single failure mode. In any quality risk analysis where failure modes are considered, the granularity of the failure mode categories—i.e., broad categories that could include many bugs or narrow categories that could include only a few bugs—must be tailored appropriately.

Fully Burdened Staff Rate	The cost for a single staff member, taking into account that person's salary, benefits, proportion of the infrastructure costs, and other associated costs of having employees.
GA Build	See *Golden Build*.
Gold Master	See *Golden Build*.
Golden Build, Gold Master, GA Build	The build or release that is delivered to customers or installed for users. The test release into the test organization that precedes the Golden Build is often called the *Golden Candidate*. If the Golden Candidate is deemed to be sufficiently good, it becomes the Golden Build. (*GA* stands for *General Availability*, usually to all possible customers and users, as opposed to *Limited Availability*, such as a beta or early release to special customers.)
Golden Candidate	The planned final test release, which, if no must-fix bugs are found in it, will also be the version of the system released to the customers; i.e., the *Golden Build*.
Human Resources Department, Personnel Department	A group that facilitates 1) the hiring of employees, contractors, and consultants; 2) defining personnel policies and procedures; and 3) planning and managing salaries and career tracks.
Incremental System Development Lifecycle	A development model where a larger project is broken into a series of increments, each of which delivers a portion of the functionality in the overall project requirements. The requirements are prioritized and delivered in priority order in the appropriate increment. In some (but not all) versions of this model, each subproject follows a "mini-V" Model with its own design, coding, and testing phases. Whatever the process for each increment, test execution tends to start earlier, with the delivery of the first incremental test release, and continue at full strength right up to the moment of deployment or first customer delivery.
Independent Test Team	A group of people, distinct from those charged with building the system under test, whose responsibility is to effectively and efficiently assess and report on the quality of the system under test. I have most often seen this team acting as a service organization to the project team.

Integration Plan	The plan that specifies how the various components will be assembled, hopefully in some logical, multistep sequence, until the entire system is ready to be built.
Integration Testing, Product Testing	A testing phase focused on the relationships and interfaces between pairs and groups of components or subsystems in the system.
Key Quality and Testing Stakeholders, Key Stakeholders	Those staff members who have immediate contact with customers, users, or the testing process, as well as those who have insight into the technical details of the system.
Key Stakeholders	See *Key Quality and Testing Stakeholders*.
Library	See *Repository*.
New Hire	Someone who has received an offer letter and responded, either verbally or in writing, agreeing to fill the offered position.
Offer Letter	A letter from the hiring company to the successful candidate asking the candidate to accept the job for which they interviewed, usually including a detailed job description and quoting a specific salary and start date.
Personnel Department	See *Human Resources Department*.
Phase	A logically distinct stage of a project or subproject consisting of a collection of activities that all produce similar deliverables.
Pilot Testing	A testing phase where the system is put into limited production under close supervision. Hardware pilot tests demonstrate the ability of the assembly line to mass-produce the system. Software pilot tests demonstrate the ability of the system to handle typical operations from live customers on live hardware.
Product Testing	See *Integration Testing*.
Project	A temporary endeavor undertaken to create or provide some unique product, system, or service. The endeavor consists of some sequence of tasks, undertaken by a team of people under some set of resource and time constraints,

Project (*Continued*)	to deliver the product, system, or service to some set of customers and users. The degree of change over the life of the project in the team, budget, schedule, requirements, and target customers and users can vary considerably.
Quality	1. Fitness for use. The presence of features, attributes, and behaviors that satisfy customers and users, and the absence of features, attributes, and behaviors that dissatisfy customers and users. (This definition is appropriate for many contexts, especially market-driven systems.)
	2. Conformance to requirements. The presence of features, attributes, and behaviors that satisfy all the stated requirements, and the absence of features, attributes, and behaviors that deviate from requirements. (This definition is appropriate in some contexts, especially contract-development projects.)
Quality Assurance contrasted with Testing	According to IEEE Standard 610.12-1990, "IEEE Standard Glossary of Software Engineering Terminology," quality assurance (QA) involves "all actions necessary to provide adequate confidence" in system quality and evaluating "the process by which [the system was] developed," whereas testing consists of activities "to detect differences between existing and required conditions (bugs) and to evaluate...features." In other words, QA is focused on end-to-end process correctness, while testing is an assessment of quality.
Quality Risk	A potential failure mode, a way in which the system might not meet reasonable user and customer expectations of quality. Note that a quality risk is a potential, not guaranteed, undesirable outcome with a probability greater than zero and less than one.
	Categories of quality risks exist. Because failure modes are also categories, categories of quality risks are thus categories of categories of potential bugs.
Reference System	A special type of *test oracle* where a system already in existence mimics or models some or all of the desired behaviors of the system under test.

Regression	A system exhibits regression (or has regressed) when, as a result of a change, a new revision of the system, S_{n+1}, contains a bug not present in revisions S_1 though S_n that causes some previously correct operation to misbehave.
Regression Test Gap	For any given change or revision, the difference between the areas of test coverage provided by the entire test set and the test coverage provided by the tests that are actually rerun. For a customer release, the regression test gap can also be considered the extent to which the release was not exposed at some point during testing of that release to the entire test set.
Regression Testing	Testing performed to catch bugs that cause regression.
Release	See *Build*.
Release Engineer, Build Manager, Source Code Control Engineer, Release Manager	The person responsible for creating the test release from source code, data, metadata, help files, Web screens, and any other items needed to build the system.
Release Engineering Plan	See *Build Plan*.
Release Manager	See *Release Engineer*.
Release Name	See *Build ID*.
Repository, Library, Source Code Control System	A software application, usually running on a widely accessible server, that stores the source code, online help, HTML documents, audio files, and other files that, upon compilation and assembly, make up the installable software item, along with storing associated documents like test plans, risk analyses, and requirements specifications.
Return on Investment (ROI)	A measure of the value received from investing in some particular opportunity. The return on investment is the financial benefit of an investment less the initial cost of

Return on Investment (ROI) (*Continued*)	making the investment, all divided by the initial cost, as shown in the following equation: $$ROI = \frac{(Benefit - Cost)}{Cost}$$ ROI is often multiplied by 100% to give a percentage.
Revision	See *Build ID*.
Revision Number	See *Build ID*.
Sanity Test	See *Smoke Test*.
Smoke Test, Sanity Test	A test run against a proposed test release to ensure that it is stable enough to enter testing in the currently active test phase. It is usually a subset of the overall set of tests, preferably automated, that touches every part of the system in at least a cursory way. A good smoke test also keeps the system running long enough that gross problems with reliability and availability will show up. The term derives from electrical engineering, where you power up a circuit and watch for smoking components as an initial test.
Source Code Control Engineer	See *Release Engineer*.
Source Code Control System	See *Repository*.
Sponsors	See *Customers*.
Stakeholders (in the system)	People inside or outside the organizations who are, will be, or might be affected by the project, the system, or the system's quality.
Structural Tests, White-Box Tests	Tests based on the internal details of how a system should work, often spelled out in detailed design, logic, and data.
Stub	A (usually small) piece of software that fills in for or replaces a component of the system under test or the test system to approximate some of the functions being "stubbed out" to the extent necessary to perform certain desired tests.

Subject Matter Expertise	See *Application Domain Skills*.
Subproject	A project within a host project that provides products or services to the host project. By this definition, the test efforts discussed in this book generally are subprojects. The accounting team's issuance of paychecks to project employees is not a subproject, since it's outside the project context. A quality assurance auditor ensuring documented process compliance is not a subproject either, since it serves the organization, not the project.
Subsystem Testing	See *Component Testing*.
System, System under Test, System under Development, System Being Maintained	The entirety of the system (software, hardware, software and hardware, and so on) within the scope of the test effort. This often consists of more than the immediately obvious pieces. For office software, for example, in addition to the executable running on a user's desktop, there can be back-end (e.g., server) components that might have various third-party interfaces, documentation, the delivery and upgrade process, online databases or support facilities, hardware and firmware components, and even infrastructure like LANs, WANs, and the Internet. The word "product" is somewhat more generic, but could incorrectly imply that I'm discussing only mass-market, shrink-wrapped software.
	A system can also be a *system of systems*, where each system interoperates with and depends on one or more other systems, and where each system is essential to the operation of the system of systems. For example, a browser-based application, with the clients, the Web server, the application server, and the database server, is a system of systems.
	Finally, a system can also be a *family of systems*, where each system interoperates with one or more other systems, but where dependencies are limited and systems can be used in a standalone or integrated way. For example, Microsoft Office is a family of software systems.
System Being Maintained	See *System*.

System Development Lifecycle	The subset of the system lifecycle associated with the initial development of a system; i.e., from specification and design through implementation, testing, and initial deployment.
System Lifecycle	The entire set of activities that occur in development, deployment, use, and obsolescence of the system, from initial specification and design through implementation and testing, to support and maintenance, and ultimately to cut-over and retirement of the system.
System Testing	A testing phase focused on the overall and particular behaviors, functions, and responses of the system as a whole.
System under Development	See *System*.
System under Test	See *System*.
Task	The component work elements of an activity, being a coherent set of actions involving a related set of skills.
Technical Skills	Aptitudes addressing the particular techniques and tools we intend to use to create our system, such as programming languages and server and network architecture.
Test Artifacts	Behaviors arising from the artificiality of the test environment or from a test process that diverges from the way the system will behave in the field; misleading behaviors or incorrect results reported by the test system.
Test Case	A sequence of steps consisting of actions to be performed on the system under test. (These steps are sometimes called the *test procedure* or *test script*.) These actions are often associated with some set of data (preloaded or input during the test). The combination of actions taken and data provided to the system under test leads to the test condition. This condition tends to produce results that the test can compare with the expected results; i.e., assess quality under the given test condition. The actions can be performed serially, in parallel, or in some other combination of consecution.

Test Condition	A system state, output, result, or circumstance created by executing a test case, especially one that is interesting from the perspective of assessing system quality.
Test Coverage	1. Structural: the extent to which the test system covers, or exercises, the structure—the code, subsystems, or components—in the system under test. 2. Behavioral: the extent to which the test system covers, or exercises, the behavior—risks to quality, operations, activities, functions, and other uses—of the system under test.
Test Cycle	Execution of some subset of a test pass against a single, identifiable test release.
Test Data	The set of inputs, whether from the user interface, from a stored file, or from another communicating system, that is used in a test case.
Test Engineer	A test team member skilled, educated, and experienced in all areas of testing (planning, design, implementation, and execution) as well as possessing appropriate technical expertise and application domain knowledge. (In some states and countries, people with a title containing the word "engineer" must hold a professional license.) See also *Tester*.
Test Environment	The hardware, software, infrastructure, materiel, and locations required to perform the test effort.
Test Escape	Any field-reported bug that could reasonably have been caught during testing but was not. The term can also refer to a bug that makes its way into a subsequent phase of testing, although it should have been caught in a previous phase.
Test Execution Process	The methods by which the testers and other key test participants will use the testware in the test environment.
Test Granularity	The fineness or coarseness of test focus. A fine-grained test allows the tester to check low-level details, especially of implementation; static and structural tests are finer-grained. A coarse-grained test provides the tester with information on general system operation and requirements; behavioral and live tests are coarser-grained.

Test Level	See *Test Phase*.
Test Management Tools	Tools that manage the objects associated with and the results produced by test systems. Bug and test tracking systems are common examples, but more sophisticated systems provide end-to-end facilities for the test design, implementation, and execution processes. Such systems are often integrated with testing tools, though this sometimes limits the usefulness of the tool to those tests supported by the testing tool.
Test Oracle	A system, method, or technique for predicting or assessing the correctness of behavior of the system under test under specific conditions.
Test Pass	Execution of the tests defined for a given test execution phase (i.e., the entire test set).
Test Phase **Test Level**	A distinct set of testing activities that address a particular group of quality risks, such as component test, integration test, system test, and acceptance test. (I tend to use the word "phase," while others use the word "level.")
Test Professional	See *Tester*.
Test Release	See *Build*.
Test Script	In manual testing, the instructions on how to perform one or more test cases, also often called a *test procedure*. In automated testing, refers to the corresponding machine-executable instructions.
Test Set	All the test suites that the test team plans to run during the current test phase (or level).
Test Specialist	See *Test Technician*.
Test Strategy	The chosen approaches and decisions made that follow from the test project's and test team's goal or mission. The mission is typically effective and efficient testing, and the strategies are the general policies, rules, and principles that support this mission. Test tactics are the specific policies, techniques, processes, and the way testing is done.
Test Subproject	The set of tasks required to provide test services and information to the quality and testing stakeholders on the project team to support the team's ability to manage quality risks.

Test Suite	A collection of logically related test cases, possibly with reuse of cases across multiple suites.
Test System	The test environment, the testware, and the test execution processes that the test team will use to assess the quality of the system under test.
Test Technician, Test Specialist	A test staff member less skilled, educated, and/or experienced than a test engineer in one, two, or all three of the critical skills areas (testing, application domain, and technology). Test technicians are usually qualified for scripted manual test execution and other straightforward technician-level tasks. See also *Tester*.
Tester, Test Professional	Anyone working on test-related tasks such as those described in this book. More specifically, in this book, someone working in a test team, whether permanently or temporarily, as an employee, contractor, or consultant. I'm using this word or phrase as the analog to "developer" or "programmer" in the development team.
Testing	Operationally, a process that assesses the quality of a system, providing services and information products that help the organization manage the risks to system quality. Organizationally, a team that provides these services and products for the projects they serve.
Testing Skills	Abilities relating to accomplishing test-specific tasks, like developing effective test cases and writing thorough bug reports.
Testing Tools	Any system that helps someone perform a testing task, such as designing, implementing, verifying, executing, measuring, or interpreting test cases, test data, or test results. Tools can be spreadsheets, templates, databases, complex custom-developed in-house utilities, or commercially available systems. Tools can be composed and integrated. Some test tools, like capture/playback systems and code coverage utilities, were designed as test tools, while others, like debuggers and scripting languages, play the role accidentally.
Testware	The test cases, test data, test scripts, test tools, test logs, test reports, and associated user's guides or documentation.

Unit Testing	Testing of a small element or unit of the system.
User Acceptance Testing	See *Acceptance Testing*.
Users	People who have operated, will operate, or might operate the system, or those who use the outputs or products of the system. Users are sometimes customers, but not always.
V Model	A variation of the Waterfall model that shows the implementation tasks down the left side of the V and the testing tasks up the right side of the V. Across the V are lines showing how the outputs of each implementation phase drive the development of the test system needed for each testing phase. This is based on the observation that acceptance testing is driven primarily by requirements; system testing by requirements and design; integration testing by requirements, design, and code interfaces; and component testing by requirements, design, code interfaces, and code logic.
Version	See *Build ID*.
Version Number	See *Build ID*.
Waterfall System Development Lifecycle	A development model where the development team performs a series of sequential phases to deliver a system. First the team defines the requirements, next they design the system, and then they implement it. Once the system is implemented, it goes through a sequence of test phases, starting with unit or component testing, followed by integration testing, and finally system testing. (In the case of contract or in-house system development, there is often an acceptance testing phase after system testing.) Some variations of this approach allow for overlap between the phases, rather than requiring completion of all of each phase's tasks before beginning the next phase.
White-Box Tests	See *Structural Tests*.

BIBLIOGRAPHY

Adams, Douglas. *The Hitchhiker's Guide to the Galaxy*. New York: Balantine, 1995.

Allison, Anna. "Meaningful Metrics." *Software Testing and Quality Engineering*, Volume 3, Issue 3 (May/June 2001): pages 38–45.

Bach, James. "Exploratory Testing and the Planning Myth." www.stickyminds.com.

———. "Test Automation Snake-oil." www.satisfice.com.

Bartlett, Robert. "Power Testing." *Proceedings of the Fifth International Quality Week Europe*.

Beizer, Boris. *Black-Box Testing*. New York: Wiley, 1995.

———. "Software Is Different." Software Research's Quality Techniques Newsletter archives. www.soft.com/News/QTN-Online/qtnapr01.html, www.soft.com/News/QTN-Online/qtnmay01.html, www.soft.com/News/QTN-Online/qtnjun01.html.

———. *Software System Testing and Quality Assurance*. New York: International Thomson Computer Press, 1996.

———. *Software Testing Techniques, Second Edition*. New York: Van Nostrand Reinhold, 1990.

Bernstein, Peter. *Against the Gods*. New York: Wiley, 1996.

Binder, Robert. *Testing Object-Oriented Software.* Boston: Addison-Wesley, 1999.

Black, Rex. "Critical Software Testing Processes." *Journal of Software Testing Professionals*, Volume 1, Issue 1 (Mar 2000).

————. "Effective Test Status Reporting." *Software Testing and Quality Engineering*, Volume 2, Issue 2 (Mar/Apr 2000).

————. "Factors That Influence Test Estimation." www.stickyminds.com.

————. "Four Ways Testing Adds Value." *Proceedings of the EuroSTAR 2002 Conference.*

————. *Managing the Testing Process, Second Edition.* New York: Wiley, 2002.

————. "Stop Destroying My Team with Bad MBOs: A Manager's New Year's Resolution." www.stickyminds.com.

————. "Test Estimation." *Software Testing and Quality Engineering*, Volume 4, Issue 6 (Nov/Dec 2002).

————. "The Test Execution Process." *Journal of Software Testing Professionals*, Volume 1, Issue 3 (Sep 2000).

————. "Test Release Processes." *Journal of Software Testing Professionals*, Volume 1, Issue 2 (June 2000).

Black, Rex, and Greg Kubaczkowski. "Mission Made Possible." *Software Testing and Quality Engineering*, Volume 4, Issue 4 (July/Aug 2002).

Boehm, Barry. *Software Engineering Economics.* Prentice-Hall PTR, 1982.

Brooks, Frederick P., Jr. *The Mythical Man-Month.* Reading, Mass.: Addison-Wesley, 1975.

————. *The Mythical Man-Month, Second Edition.* Reading, Mass.: Addison-Wesley, 1995.

Bullock, James. "Calculating the Value of Testing," *Software Testing and Quality Engineering*, Volume 2, Issue 3 (May/June 2000): pages 56–62.

Buwalda, Hans. "Soap Opera Testing." *Proceedings of the STAR East 2000 Conference.*

Campanella, Jack, ed. *Principles of Quality Costs.* Milwaukee, Wisc.: ASQ Quality Press, 1999.

Cervantes, Miguel. *Don Quixote.* New York: Penguin, 2003.

Cohn, Mike. "A Measured Response." *Software Testing and Quality Engineering*, Volume 4, Issue 5 (Sep/Oct 2002).

Collard, Ross. "Test Design: Developing Test Cases from Use Cases." *Software Testing and Quality Engineering*, Volume 1, Issue 4 (July/Aug 1999).

Copeland, Lee. "Exploratory Planning." www.stickyminds.com.

————. *A Practitioner's Guide to Software Test Design.* Norwood, Mass: Artech House, 2004.

————. "When Helping Doesn't Help." www.stickyminds.com.

Craig, Rick, and Stefan Jaskiel. *Systematic Software Testing.* New York: Artech House, 2002.

Crosby, Philip. *Quality Is Free: The Art of Making Quality Certain.* New York: McGraw-Hill, 1979.

De Jaeger, Peter. "The Risk in Risk Management." *Software Testing and Quality Engineering*, Volume 3, Issue 4 (July/Aug 2001): pages 63–64.

DeMarco, Tom. *The Deadline.* New York: Dorset House, 1998.

DeMarco, Tom, and Tim Lister. *Peopleware, Second Edition.* New York: Dorset House, 1999.

DeNardis, Chris. "Perspectives from a Test Manager." *Software Testing and Quality Engineering*, Volume 2, Issue 5 (Sep/Oct 2000).

Deming, W. E. *Out of the Crisis.* Boston: MIT Press, 2000.

Dobbins, James. *Software Quality Assurance and Evaluation.* Milwaukee, Wisc: ASQ Quality Press, 1990.

Drabick, Rodger. *Best Practices for Software Testing*. New York: Dorset House, 2003.

———. "Growth of Maturity in the Testing Process." www.softtest.org/articles/rdrabick3.htm.

———. "Modeling the Formal Testing Process." *Software QA Magazine*, Volume 2, Number 2: pages 20–38.

———. "On-Track Requirements." *Software Testing and Quality Engineering*, Volume 1, Issue 3. Available at www.stickyminds.com.

———. "A Process Model of Software Quality Assurance/Software Quality Engineering." *Software Quality Professional*, Volume 2, Issue 4 (Sep 2000): pages 20–38.

Dustin, Elfriede. "Orthogonally Speaking." *Software Testing and Quality Engineering*, Volume 3, Issue 5 (Sep/Oct 2001).

Dustin, Elfriede, Jeff Rashka, and John Paul. *Automated Software Testing*. Boston: Addison-Wesley, 1999.

Dyes, Tim. "Tracking Severity." *Software Testing and Quality Engineering*, Volume 1, Issue 2 (Mar/Apr 1999).

Ensworth, Patricia. *The Accidental Project Manager*. New York: Wiley, 2001.

Fewster, Mark, and Dorothy Graham. *Software Test Automation*. Harlow, UK: Addison-Wesley, 1999.

Gardner, Robert. "Resolving the Process Paradox." *Quality Progress*, Volume 34, Issue 3 (Mar 2001): pages 51–59.

Gilbreath, Robert. *Winning at Project Management*. New York: Wiley, 1986.

The Guide to the Project Management Body of Knowledge, 2000 Edition. Newtown Square, Penn.: Project Management Institute, 2000.

Hadden, Rita. "Credible Estimation for Small Projects." *Software Quality Professional*, Volume 3, Issue 2 (Mar 2001): pages 7–11.

Hendrickson, Elisabeth. "More Testing, Worse Quality." www.qualitytree.com.

Hetzel, Bill. *The Complete Guide to Software Testing.* New York: Wiley-QED, 1988.

Hoffman, Douglas. "Using Oracles in Testing Automation." www.softwarequality-methods.com.

Hoyer, Robert, and Brooke Hoyer. "What Is Quality?" *Quality Progress*, Volume 34, Issue 7 (July 2001): pages 52–62.

Humphrey, Watts. *Introduction to the Personal Software Process.* Reading, Mass.: Addison-Wesley, 1997.

Iberle, Kathleen, and Susan Bartlett. "Estimating Tester to Developer Ratios (or Not)." *Proceedings of the STAR West Conference 2001.* Orange Park, Fla: Software Quality Engineering, 2001.

International Standards Organization. *ISO/IEC 9126:1991 (E).* Geneva, Switzerland: ISO/IEC Copyright Office, 1991.

Ishikawa, Kaoru. *Guide to Quality Control.* Tokyo: Asian Productivity Organization, 1982.

Jalote, Pankoj. *CMM in Practice.* Boston: Addison-Wesley, 1999.

Johnson, Karen. "Delivering Unwelcome News to Developers." *Software Testing and Quality Engineering*, Volume 4, Issue 5 (Sep/Oct 2002).

Johnson, Paul. *Intellectuals.* New York: Harper and Row, 1988.

Jones, T. Capers. *Estimating Software Costs.* New York: McGraw-Hill, 1995.

Juran, J. M. *Juran on Planning for Quality.* New York: Free Press, 1988.

Juran, J. M., and Frank Gryna, eds. *Quality Control Handbook, Fourth Edition.* New York: McGraw-Hill, 1988.

Kan, Stephen. *Metrics and Models in Software Quality Engineering, Second Edition.* Boston: Addison-Wesley, 2003.

Kaner, Cem. "Architectures of Test Automation." www.kaner.com.

———. "Quality Cost Analysis: Benefits and Risks." www.kaner.com.

Kaner, Cem, James Bach, and Bret Pettichord. *Lessons Learned in Software Testing*. New York: Wiley, 2001.

Kaner, Cem, Jack Falk, and Hung Quoc Nguyen. *Testing Computer Software, Second Edition*. New York: International Thomson Computer Press, 1993.

Kaner, Cem, and David Pels. *Bad Software*. New York: Wiley, 1998.

Kasse, Tim, and Patricia McQuaid. "Software Configuration Management for Project Leaders." *Software Quality Professional*, Volume 2, Issue 4 (Sep 2000): pages 8–19.

Kit, Ed. *Software Testing in the Real World*. Harlow, UK: Addison-Wesley, 1995.

Koomen, Tim, and Martin Pol. *Test Process Improvement*. Harlow, UK: Addison-Wesley, 1999.

Marciniak, John, ed. *Encyclopedia of Software Engineering, Second Edition*. New York: Wiley, 2001.

Marick, Brian. "Classic Testing Mistakes." www.testing.com.

———. *Craft of Software Testing*. Upper Saddle River, NJ: Prentice Hall, 1995.

———. "New Models for Test Development." www.testing.com.

McClintic, Ron. "Load Performance and Scalability Testing Challenges in E-Commerce." *Software Quality*, Number 2 (Winter 2001): pages 1 and 3–5.

McConnell, Steve. *After the Gold Rush*. Redmond, Wash.: Microsoft Press, 1999.

———. *Software Project Survival Guide*. Redmond, Wash.: Microsoft Press, 1998.

McDermott, Robin, Raymond Mikulak, and Michael Beauregard. *The Basics of FMEA*. Portland, Ore: Productivity, 1996.

Mendonca, John, and Robert Lineberger. "Methodology as Road Kill: The Decade-Long Assault on Quality Assurance." *Software Quality*, Number 3 (Spring 2001): pages 1, 3, and 4.

Moore, Geoffrey. *Crossing the Chasm, Second Edition*. New York: Harper Collins, 1999.

Myers, Glenford. *The Art of Software Testing*. New York: Wiley, 1979.

Neumann, Peter. *Computer-Related Risks*. Reading, MA: Addison-Wesley, 1995.

Nguyen, Hung. *Testing Applications on the Web*. New York: Wiley, 2000.

Nielsen, Jakob. *Usability Engineering*. San Francisco: Morgan Kaufmann Publishers, 1993.

Nishi, Yasuharu. "Resource Path Testing: A Framework for Design of System Testing." *Software Quality Professional*, Volume 3, Issue 3 (June 2001).

Nyman, Noel. "Using Monkey Test Tools." *Software Testing and Quality Engineering*, Volume 2, Issue 1 (Jan/Feb 2000).

Paulk, Mark C., Charles V. Weber, Bill Curtis, and Mary Beth Chrissis. *The Capability Maturity Model*. Reading, Mass.: Addison-Wesley, 1995.

Payne, Jeff. "Quality Meets the CEO." *Software Testing and Quality Engineering*, Volume 1, Issue 3 (May/June 1999).

Perry, Dewayne, and Gail Kaiser. "Object-Oriented Programs and Testing." citeseer.nj.nec.com/perry90objectoriented.html.

Perry, William, and Randall Rice. *Surviving the Top Ten Challenges of Software Testing*. New York: Dorset House, 1997.

Petersen, Erik. "Smarter Testing Using the 80/20 Rule." *Proceedings of the STAR West 2002 Conference*.

Plato. *The Trial and Death of Socrates, Third Edition*. New York: Hackett Publishing, 2001.

Pol, Martin, et al. *Software Testing: A Guide to the T-MAP Approach*. Boston: Addison-Wesley, 2001.

Pressman, Roger. *Software Engineering: A Practitioner's Approach, Fourth Edition*. New York: McGraw-Hill, 1997.

Quentin, Geoff. "People Skills, Including the Review as a Test Technique." *Professional Tester*, Volume 2, Issue 2 (June 2001): pages 42–43.

Rosenberg, Linda, and Lawrence Hyatt. "Developing a Successful Metrics Program." satc.gsfc.nasa.gov/support/index.html.

Rothman, Johanna. *Hiring the Best Knowledge Workers, Techies, & Nerds: The Secrets & Science of Hiring Technical People.* New York: Dorset House Publishing, 2004.

———. "The Influential Test Manager." *Software Testing and Quality Engineering*, Volume 2, Issue 2 (Mar/Apr 2000).

———. "It Depends: Deciding on the Correct Ratio of Developers to Testers." www.jrothman.com.

———. "Manager Heal Thyself." www.jrothman.com.

———. "Release Criteria." *Software Testing and Quality Engineering*, Volume 4, Issue 2 (Mar/Apr 2002).

———. "Testing in the Dark." *Software Testing and Quality Engineering*, Volume 1, Issue 2 (Mar/Apr 1999).

Ruhl, Janet. *The Computer Consultant's Guide.* New York: Wiley, 1997.

Sabourin, Robert. "At Your Service." *Software Testing and Quality Engineering*, Volume 3, Issue 3 (May/June 2001): pages 46–52.

———. *I Am a Bug.* Self-published, 1999.

Sabourin, Robert, and Kim Davis. "Exploring, Discovering and Exterminating Bug Clusters in Web Applications." www.amibug.com.

Schmauch, Charles. *ISO 9000 for Software Developers.* Milwaukee, Wisc.: ASQ Quality Press, 1994.

Schmidt, Michael E. C. *Implementing the IEEE Software Engineering Standards.* Indianapolis, Ind.: SAMS Publishing, 2000.

Simmons, Erik. "The Human Side of Risk." *Proceedings of the Fifteenth International Internet and Software Quality Week 2002.*

Slaughter, Sandra, David Harter, and Mayuram Krishnan. "Evaluating the Cost of Software Quality." *Communications of the ACM*, Volume 41, Number 8 (Aug 1998): pages 67–73.

Splaine, Steven. *Testing Web Security*. New York: Wiley, 2002.

Splaine, Steven, et al. *The Web Testing Handbook*. Orange Park, Fla: Software Quality Engineering Publishing, 2001.

Stamatis, D. H. *Failure Mode and Effect Analysis*. Milwaukee, Wisc.: ASQ Quality Press, 1995.

Taguchi, Genichi, and Rajesh Jugulum. "Principles of Taguchi Methods for Software Testing." *Proceedings of the Second World Congress for Software Quality*. Tokyo: Union of Japanese Scientists and Engineers, 2000.

Taylor, Frederick Winslow. *The Principles of Scientific Management*. 1911.

Tolstoy, Leo. *Anna Karenina*. New York: Modern Library, 2000.

Tripp, Leonard, ed. *IEEE Software Engineering Standards Collection, 1997 Edition*. New York: IEEE, 1997.

Tufte, Edward. *Envisioning Information*. Cheshire, Conn.: Graphics Press, 1990.

———. *The Visual Display of Quantitative Information, Second Edition*. Cheshire, Conn.: Graphics Press, 2001.

———. *Visual Explanations*. Cheshire, Conn.: Graphics Press, 1997.

Tzu, Sun. *The Art of War*. New York: Delacorte Press, 1983.

VanDoren, Edmond. "Cyclomatic Complexity." Software Engineering Institute's Software Technology Review. www.sei.cmu.edu/str/descriptions/cyclomatic_body.html.

Van Veenendaal, Erik. *The Testing Practitioner*. Den Bosch, Netherlands: UTN Publishers, 2002.

Van Veenendaal, Erik, Rob Hendriks, and Robert van Vonderen. "Measuring Software Product Quality during Testing." *Professional Tester*, Volume 2, Issue 1 (Mar 2001): pages 26–30.

Walsh, James. *True Odds*. Santa Monica, Calif.: Merritt Publishing, 1996.

Walton, Mary. *The Deming Management Method*. New York: Putnam Publishing Group, 1986.

Weinberg, Gerald M. *The Psychology of Computer Programming*. New York: Van Nostrand Reinhold, 1971.

———. *The Secrets of Consulting*. New York: Dorset House, 1985.

Wert, Jeffrey. *Custer*. New York: Simon & Schuster, 1996.

Wiegers, Karl. *Software Requirements*. Redmond, Wash.: Microsoft Press, 1999.

Wysocki, Robert, Robert Beck, Jr., and David Crane. *Effective Project Management*. New York: Wiley, 1995.

Xerox Corporate Education and Training. "Benchmarking for Quality Improvement." *Leadership Through Quality*. Stamford, Conn: Xerox, 1989.

———. "Concepts of Quality." *Leadership Through Quality*. Stamford, Conn: Xerox, 1988.

———. "Problem-Solving Process." *Leadership Through Quality*. Stamford, Conn: Xerox, 1986.

———. "Quality Improvement Process." *Leadership Through Quality*. Stamford, Conn: Xerox, 1988.

Yourdon, Ed. *Death March*. Upper Saddle River, NJ: Prentice Hall, 1999.

INDEX

Bartlett, Bob, 101

Basics of FMEA, The (McDermott et al.), 38

Basis tests, 300

Becker, Randall, 326, 461

Behavioral coverage, 298

Behavioral coverage assessments, 299

Behavioral test coverage, 300

Behavioral testing, 24–26, 173

Behavioral tests, 25, 313, 520

Beizer, Boris, 268

Berger, Bernie, 232

Best Practices for Software Testing
  (Drabick), 492

Beta test sites, 282

Beta testing, 10, 17–18, 24, 180, 519–520

Big Build
  attack on, 360–368
  big bug, 392–398
  test results, 422–440

Black-box coverage, 298, 304

Black-box testing, 173

Black-Box Testing (Beizer), 173, 280, 296,
  298

Black-box tests, 25, 520

Bolton, Michael, 293

Bottom-up estimation, 81

Box, George, 20

Brainstorming
  quality risk analysis, 38
  quantifying risk, 38–42
  ranking failure, 38

Brooks, Fred, 145

Brook's Law, 146

Budgets, 97, 419
  alliances for selling approach, 124
  amortizing test development work and
    configuration of test equipment, 115
  analyzing ROI (Return on Investment) for
    testing, 98–113
  benefits from testing plan, 118–119
  compromising on, 128–129
  contingency, 128
  cost-of-quality equation, 117
  cutting, 126–127

external failure, 116–117

Failure Mode and Effect Analysis
  worksheet, 127

found and not fixed bugs, 117

fully burdened staff rate, 115–116

hardware, 113

internal failure for test team, 116

minimum investment in testing, 123

mitigating risks, 127

must-fix bugs, 116–117

project tracking information, 118

project-based team assignment strategy,
  113

providing services and products
  customers need, 124

quality risk analysis process, 117

resources, 113–114

ROI (return on investment), 115

saving money in, 128–129

software, 113

Sumatra Project, 113–119

test coverage analysis, 127

testing tools, 113

usability testing, 113

value of risk mitigation, 117–118

work-breakdown-structure, 127

working with other departments, 127

Bug crawls, 444

Bug fixes, 351

Bug report ping-pong, 404

Bug reports, 346, 387–388, 520
  anger discussing, 414
  bias, 375
  bug assignment, 405
  bug workflow, 417
  bugs fixed by accident, 410–412
  bugs that aren't bugs, 412
  building trust and credibility with
    programmers, 413–414
  challenges, 408–415
  clear boundary between testing and
    debugging, 406–408
  commercial bug tracking tool,
    403–404

sharing knowledge, 291
skill levels of testers, 292
test and project stakeholder expectation
  and requirements, 292
test cases, 402
test managers, 449
test plan, 202–204
test releases, 344–347
tight time windows for test execution,
  291
time and resources available to design
  and implement test cases, 292
unambiguous, 291
written test cases, 291
Domain analysis, 295–296
Don Quixote (Cervantes), 453
Drabick, Roger, 492
Draft/feedback/update/finalize cycle, 84
Dumb monkeys, 280, 281
Dyes, Tim, 326, 461
Dynamic tests, 313
Dyson, Esther, 66

E
Edit engine for document management
  system, 279–280
Education, 241–242
Effective Project Management (Wysocki et
  al.), 67, 90
Efficient, 307
Emergency patches, 340
Empirical approach, 180
Employee skills assessment, 252
*Encyclopedia of Software Engineering,
  Second Edition,* 299
Engineering plan, 520
Engineering Services group, 14
Entertainment systems risks, 306
Envisioning Information (Tufte), 443
Equivalence partitioning, 295–296
Error logs, 403
"Estimated Bug Find-Fix Time.xls"
  template, 94
Estimated schedule, developing, 80

Estimates
  accepting context and constraints of
    project, 136
  assigning responsibility for action,
    134–135
  bogus, 149
  challenges, 137–150
  completeness, 133
  compromises, 151–152
  excessive external constraints, 133
  factors affecting, 129–132
  failure, 148–149
  funding problems, 133
  imprecision of, 144–145
  initial, 156
  lack of agreement, 133
  lack of knowledge, 133
  mythical man-month, 145–146
  new technologies and, 132
  nine-month rule, 145–146
  nonstakeholders, 147–148
  obstacles, 151
  overly optimistic, 136
  people outside scope of project, 147
  practicing, 151
  project level, 146
  quick, 137
  rational task durations, 134
  realistic picture of project's future,
    132–134
  realistic schedule, 133–134
  reopening debate about project schedule
    and budget, 123
  reviewing other, 151
  revising, 145
  selling, 121–126
  selling based on risks, 124
  stretching goals, 133
  studying topic, 150–151
  team performance, 132
  tester-to-programmer ratio-based, 82
  unrealistic scheduling, 146
  worked backward from arbitrary ship
    date, 146

Job descriptions, 224, 256–257, 259–260, 263
Jones, Capers, 81
Jorgensen, Alan, 409
Journal of Software Testing Professionals, xix
Juran, J. M., 337, 502
Juran on Planning for Quality (Juran), 4

K
K. Iberle Web site, 82
Kaner, Cem, 409
Kaner Web site, 5, 144, 313, 449
Kelvin, Lord, 60
Key players
  compromising with, 210
  leveraging relationships with other managers, 212
  not stakeholders in project, 212
  not supporting test plans, 209–213
  perception of reasonableness of position, 212–213
  role to play, 210
Key quality and testing stakeholders, 36, 524
Key stakeholders, 36, 133, 524
King Hieron, 273
Koomen, Tim, 81, 355, 383
Kruchten, Philippe, 512

L
Lawrence, Brian, 419
Leadership Through Quality, 509
Lessons Learned in Software Testing (Kaner, Bach, and Pettichord), 172, 313, 369, 420, 462
Library, 327, 524
Lifecycles
  processes, 16
  testing within, 18–23
Lifecycles models
  accuracy, 20–21
  adaptations, 21

code-and-fix frenzy, 23
dependencies, 23
design and implementation of test system, 23
flexibility fitting testing within, 23
object-oriented development, 19–20
selecting best, 19
sequencing, 23
testers involvement, 23
Limited Availability, 72
Lind, Bill, 207
Lint, 24
Live testing, 24, 174, 180
Load testing, 280
LogiGear Corporation Web site, 232
Long-term career path, 257–262
Low-level employees, 222
Lumsoft Web site, 295

M
MacNary, Reynolds, 453, 507
Madame Bovary (Flaubert), 204
Maintenance teams and junior programmer roles, 28
Management
  bogus estimates, 149
  dimensions, 31–33
  inward, 31
  outward, 32–33
  support for estimate, 121–126
  upward, 32–33
"Manager Heal Thyself," 513
Managers, 123
  aware of value testing, 123
  failure to communicate with, 122
  importance of testing, 122
  insight into quality, 110
  interacting directly with, 31
  limited time to convince, 123
  little experience with well-run testing project, 123
  outsourcing, 208
  pay scale for testers, 263